'*Testament* deserves to become an indispensable resource to encourage biblical literacy, both within and without the Church. The reader-friendly format, presenting a sort of canon within the canon, will help many rediscover the greatest book ever written.'

Dale C. Allison Jr
Professor of New Testament and Early Christianity,
Pittsburgh Theological Seminary

'Important as the Bible is, it is also quite unapproachable for many people. *Testament* opens it up to everyone who would like to discover its essential heart. Anyone who reads novels will enjoy this book. It presents the essentials of the Bible in the Bible's own words.'

John Barton
Professor of the Interpretation of Holy Scripture, University of Oxford

'*Testament* is a valuable condensation of the Revised English Bible. The narratives stand together clearly, and everything of the highest literary interest has been preserved. There are readers, not all of them secular, who will benefit greatly by reading Philip Law's responsible and careful abridgement.'

Harold Bloom

'A reader-friendly version which makes me want to read on.'

Rabbi Lionel Blue

'The Bible is, without doubt, one of the greatest literary masterpieces of all time, yet its chapter divisions, frequent duplications and legal material can produce difficulties for all but the most committed reader. *Testament* allows the reader to appreciate the Bible's magnificent literary sweep – from the pioneering days of the patriarchs, through the heady reigns of David and Solomon, the depths of exile, and on to the life of Jesus Christ and apocalyptic hopes for the future. *Testament* will appeal to anyone wanting to acquaint themselves with the narrative basis of Western art and culture.'

Helen K. Bond
Senior Lecturer in New Testament, University of Edinburgh

'This excellent book traces the basic narrative story of the Bible from its first to its last pages. I commend it very warmly indeed. It is a book which led me to say, "I wish I had had that book when I was a student!" Getting to know the Bible can appear to the beginner a daunting task. Yet here help is at hand, for the reader will find that the central story that it has to tell is a connected and meaningful whole. It is made accessible by presenting it in its own terms, not just for beginners, but for the general reader who wants to discover how it all fits together. I am confident that even the expert will find fresh insight in the great sweep of its message. Read it, and you will rediscover the grandeur of its understanding of human life and human history. Learn its story and you will have a treasure for a lifetime!'

Ronald E. Clements
Emeritus Professor of Old Testament, King's College, London

'This sensitively edited version of the Bible is an excellent addition to the bookshelf and will be particularly useful to those unaccustomed to reading the scriptures. It communicates the essence, without diminishing the power.'

Wendy Craig

'For those interested in reading the Bible as literature, which it is of course, *Testament* should prove a most welcome addition to other translations of, and commentary upon, this great book. We all need to know these very human stories that can provide comfort and guidance as we navigate our own troubled times.'

Clyde Edgerton

'This splendid book skilfully presents the great narratives and teachings of the Bible for general readers. I recommend it to all who have always wondered what makes the Bible the world's bestseller.'

Michael Green
Senior Research Fellow, Wycliffe Hall, Oxford

'The Bible is the greatest book ever written, for it narrates the greatest story ever told. For many people today, however, the Bible is a closed, even a dead book – closed and dead because the prospect of actually reading the Bible seems simply too daunting. *Testament* removes that obstacle. This helpful abridgement presents the central storyline of the Bible in a straightforward, story-like manner. And it augments the story with some of the inspiring poetry and prose written by people closely associated with that story. Read *Testament* and catch a glimpse of the power of the Bible. Then read the Bible itself.'

Stanley J. Grenz
Professor of Theology, Carey Theological College, Vancouver BC, and
Professor of Theological Studies, Mars Hill Graduate School, Seattle WA

'This is a timely book that recognizes the continuing place of the Bible and its great narratives within our culture. It makes available at first hand to the general reader those stories which have shaped so much of our art and literature, and which still have a profound importance for modern film, music and art. In this book we are reminded that reading the Bible can be an exhilarating experience. *Testament* deserves to be widely read.'

David Jasper
Professor of Literature and Theology, University of Glasgow

'Here is a rich selection drawn from the actual wording of the Revised English Bible and printed continuously without the distractions of verse divisions so that the reader may savour the main story-line and some of the fundamental teaching.'

I. Howard Marshall
Honorary Research Professor of New Testament, University of Aberdeen

'In an era when many are not walked through the early stages of life with the Bible in hand, the Bible has become sometimes the exclusive domain of a few dedicated professionals. But in *Testament* the groundbreaking story that has shaped the Western world becomes easily accessible and winsomely presented. *Testament* will lead readers from our world back to the Bible.'

Scot McKnight
Assistant Professor of New Testament,
Trinity Evangelical Divinity School, Deerfield, Illinois

'This new initiative, presenting the most important themes, stories and narratives within the Bible, is highly commendable. While this is neither proposed as a book of strict scholarship nor as a new approach to academic biblical exegesis, it is clearly based on research and indebted to informed exegesis of Sacred Scripture. It achieves what it sets out to do: presenting the essence of the message of the Word of God, supporting faith that seeks greater understanding. As a distillation of the whole biblical corpus, *Testament* presents the story of the history of salvation in an attractive and accessible manner.'

Cormac Murphy O'Connor
Archbishop of Westminster

'Reading the Bible from cover to cover is such a daunting prospect that few undertake it. Now, with judicious abridgement, the sources of Jewish tradition and Christian faith are made accessible to the general reader. *Testament* is a brilliant concept that will reveal the excitement and profundity of scripture to a new generation.'

Piers Paul Read

'In *Testament*, Philip Law exercises the kind of applied scholarship that even the angels themselves must applaud. For power, clarity and sheer beauty, it would, I suspect, be impossible to exceed either Law's aesthetic reach or his gift for presenting the Christian Bible as Odyssey as well as primal source of sacred doctrine.

The concept of a narrative Bible is hardly a new one, many scholars and armchair scholars having made their own attempts over the years. What sets this volume apart and elevates it to the state of masterful accomplishment is, in part, Law's keening reverence for the consistency which informs the original, and his skilled employment of familiar conventions to smooth the mind's way as it reads. For example, Christians and Jews alike will find much to praise in Law's graceful melding of portions of Exodus, Leviticus and Numbers to create the *Testament* section, "Israel in the Wilderness." Similarly, in the New Testament, St Paul's defence of his beloved gospel vision has never been more coherent – or, therefore, more potent – than it is in Law's deft and subtle abridgement of the Acts of the Apostles.

In sum, *Testament* is a book that both the world and the Church have long needed. I commend it to all of us.'

Phyllis Tickle

'For those who've been putting aside two years in later life to read the Bible from cover to cover, the good news is: the most important bits are here.'

Jeremy Vine

Philip Law's previous publications include *The Wisdom of Jesus* (Lion/Eerdmans 1996), *A Time to Pray* (Lion/Abingdon 1997) and *Teachings of the Master* (Lion/WJK 1999). He has worked as an editor in religious publishing for over twenty years and is currently the UK Editorial Director of T&T Clark International.

To R.J.M.

TESTAMENT

Compiled and edited by

Philip Law

from the text of the Revised English Bible

Consultant Editors:

Dale C. Allison, Jr
Professor of New Testament and Early Christianity,
Pittsburgh Theological Seminary

John Barton
Professor of the Interpretation of Holy Scripture, University of Oxford

Helen K. Bond
Senior Lecturer in New Testament, University of Edinburgh

Ronald E. Clements
Emeritus Professor of Old Testament, King's College London

Stanley J. Grenz
Professor of Theology, Carey Theological College, Vancouver

David Jasper
Professor of Literature and Theology, University of Glasgow

continuum

Continuum

The Tower Building, 11 York Road, London SE1 7NX

15 East 26th Street, Suite 1703, New York, NY 10010

www.continuumbooks.com

ISBN 0-8264-7991-X (hardback)
      0-8264-7734-8 (paperback)

British Library Cataloguing-in-Publication Data

A catalogue record for this book is available from the British Library

Typeset by Kenneth Burnley, Wirral, Cheshire

Printed on acid-free paper in Great Britain by CPI, Bath, Great Britain

CONTENTS

List of Illustrations and Maps   xi
Introduction   xiii

Part One: From Adam to Moses

1 Creation and Fall   3
2 The Age of the Patriarchs   13
3 The Story of Joseph   42
4 The Exodus   61
5 Israel in the Wilderness   78
6 The Last Words of Moses   109

Part Two: Warriors, Prophets and Kings

7 Joshua and the Conquest of Canaan   119
8 The Age of the Judges   133
9 The Story of Samson   155
10 The Story of Ruth   162
11 Samuel and Saul   168
12 The Story of David   186
13 The Golden Age of Solomon   248
14 The Two Kingdoms   260
15 Elijah and Elisha   266
16 The Decline and Fall of Israel   282
17 The Story of Jonah   288
18 The Decline and Fall of Judah   291
19 The Story of Daniel   303
20 The Story of Esther   317
21 The Return of the Exiles   329

Part Three: Poems, Proverbs and Prophecies

22 The Trials of Job   345
23 Selections from the Psalms   368
24 Sayings of the Wise   381
25 The World According to Ecclesiastes   395
26 The Love Song of Solomon   401
27 Words and Visions of the Prophets   408

Part Four: The Story of the Christ

Prologue   442
28 Birth and Early Years   443
29 Baptism and Early Ministry   451
30 The Sermon on the Mount   468
31 Healings and Teachings   475
32 The Road to Jerusalem   494
33 The Way to the Cross   519
34 Passion and Resurrection   528

Part Five: From Acts to Apocalypse

35 Acts of the Apostles   549
36 Selections from the Letters of St Paul   588
37 Selections from Other Early Christian Letters   609
38 Apocalypse   623

Further Reading   633
Biblical Timeline and Index of Sources   635
Maps   653

LIST OF ILLUSTRATIONS AND MAPS

Adam and Eve expelled from Eden   Inside front cover
Moses breaks the tablets of the Testimony   1
Samson and Delilah   117
Job curses the day he was born   343
The descent from the cross   441
Saul's vision on the road to Damascus   547
The New Jerusalem descending from heaven   Inside back cover

Map 1. The Ancient Near East in Old Testament Times   654–5
Map 2. Palestine in Old Testament Times   656
Map 3. Palestine in New Testament Times   657
Map 4. The Mediterranean in New Testament Times   658–9

Illustrations by Gustave Doré (1832–1883), courtesy Dover Publications, Inc., New York.

Maps by Chartwell Illustrators, London.

INTRODUCTION

Adam and Eve eating the forbidden fruit, Jacob wrestling with the angel, God talking to Moses from the burning bush, Jonah talking to God from the belly of the whale, Jesus walking on water . . . the Bible is full of memorable stories that most people first come across as children, and that many of us only encounter again when we come to read them to our own children, perhaps twenty or thirty years later. We enjoy them as 'children's' stories, but relatively few people revisit or reflect on them as adults.

One reason for this is that the Bible is simply too vast a book to sit down and read from cover to cover. Besides which, anyone who tries to do so soon finds that the Bible is not simply a collection of the great stories they remember from childhood: it includes all sorts of other literature as well: laws, poems, proverbs, prophecies, letters, to name a few.

If you are a practising Jew or Christian you will already have read a fair amount of the Bible, or heard it read aloud during public worship. Some readers may even have studied or discussed parts of the Bible in detail. But few people ever get around to reading long stretches of the Bible as they would other great books, and as a result their understanding of it is fragmented, disjointed, lacking a sense of how different stories and characters fit together into the bigger picture. (I wonder how many quiz-show contestants could place the following biblical figures in the right order: Jonah, Jezebel, Jacob, Jesus?![1])

Even if you have never read a word of the Bible, the chances are that you have, perhaps unknowingly, used biblical words and phrases in your everyday speech. Words such as 'bloodthirsty', 'brokenhearted', 'busybody', 'ecstasy', 'female', 'puberty' and 'scapegoat' are all first used in the Bible; and phrases such as 'a drop in the ocean', 'feet of clay', 'a fly in the ointment', 'a labour of love', 'the powers that be', 'salt of the earth' and 'the skin of my teeth' are also biblical in origin.[2]

Of course, you do not need to have read the Bible in order to understand and appreciate such expressions. However, if you have read any of the classics of Western literature, you will know that some familiarity with the Bible can make a big difference. The works of some of the greatest authors in the English language – Shakespeare, Milton, Melville, Dickinson, Joyce, Eliot, Faulkner among many others – contain countless references to biblical themes and characters, some of them extensive and explicit, others more subtle and covert.

The same is true of other art forms. In the history of music there are works directly based on parts of the Bible – from Handel's 'Messiah' to Lloyd-Weber's 'Jesus Christ Superstar' – while many other musical works allude to or depend on the Bible in some less obvious way, whether it is a scene from a classical opera such as Mozart's 'Don Giovanni' or a contemporary rock song such as U2's 'Pride (In the Name of Love)'.

As with books and music, the Bible has also had a profound influence on film. Again, sometimes this influence is direct and unmistakable – as in cinematic retellings of the life of Jesus, such as *The Greatest Story Ever Told* or *The Last Temptation of Christ* – whereas at other times the influence may only be detected if you are already aware of the biblical resonances that may be implicit in the plot or dialogue. There is a fascinating and growing literature on the interpretation of the Bible in film, while at the same time more and more books are being written on the use of biblical motifs in movies as diverse as *Star Wars*, *The Shawshank Redemption* and *Dead Man Walking*.[3]

When it comes to painting and sculpture, the influence of the Bible, again, is all-pervasive. Up until the eighteenth century virtually every great artist painted scenes from the Old and New Testaments, and it is no exaggeration to say that you cannot truly appreciate the riches of Western art without at least some awareness of the Bible. Think of the works of the Renaissance masters, such as Leonardo's 'The Last Supper' or Michelangelo's 'David', then think of Bruegel's 'The Tower of Babel', Rembrandt's 'Return of the Prodigal Son', Blake's 'The Ancient of Days', Spencer's 'The Resurrection, Cookham' and Dali's 'Christ of St John of the Cross'. (Why *did* he portray a crucified Christ whose hands do not bleed?)

These and countless other works of art can be interpreted and enjoyed so much more readily once you have read the original stories that inspired them.

The Power of Story

The essential purpose of *Testament* is to enable general readers of all ages and backgrounds – agnostics and atheists as well as believers – to read and enjoy the stories of the Bible, and to appreciate them as they would other great literature. For in the end, whatever other claims are made about it, that is what the Bible is: one of the greatest books ever written, containing some of the most powerful stories, memorable poetry, and timeless wisdom the world has known.

With that in mind, my aim has been to arrange the biblical text in a way that will help you to grasp the grand narrative sweep of the stories and events that make up most of the Bible – from the opening account of the Creation in the book of Genesis to the visions of the End in the book of Revelation.

In doing this, I hope that even those readers who have already read the Bible will discover fresh insights and connections – not only between the people and events in the Bible itself, but also between the biblical stories and their own personal stories. For, as with all great stories, those in the Bible are not simply entertaining and informative. They have the power to inspire and move us. They prompt us to think more deeply about how we relate to the personalities and situations we encounter in our own day, about the motives and influences that shape the ways we behave, and about how we respond to the ultimate questions of existence.

Great stories, in other words, have the power to expand our hearts as well as our minds. They can take us into human worlds far removed from our own time and place; they can enhance our perception, stimulate our imagination and touch our emotions, as we identify with the characters depicted in them, and as we experience through those characters something of what it would have been like to be part of their world, their story, their way of life and death.

At times, the world of the Bible can seem very strange, with the miraculous and the mundane, the divine and the human, interconnecting on nearly every page. To what extent the miraculous or supernatural elements in the Bible are intended as descriptions of 'real' historical events continues to be debated – and probably always will be. There are some who regard all such events as having literally happened as the biblical writers describe them; whereas others see in these descriptions the signs of artistic imagination, and view the stories more as parables than as history in the modern sense.

Whatever your own view, one thing is clear: in virtually all the stories in the Bible, God is the main character. (There is just one exception to this. If you want to know what it is you can either start reading *Testament* until you find out for yourself, or turn to the answer below.[4])

Throughout the Bible, God is everywhere present. And God is not only present as the One to whom the human characters direct their prayers; God is also there, taking part in the action and very often answering those prayers in direct and dramatic ways – in dreams, visions, miracles, and through the mouths of angels and prophets.

How you respond to the divine or supernatural element in the Bible is likely to depend very much on your background and upbringing. If you already believe in a God who created the world and who continues to interact with it, then you will probably view the miraculous elements of the Bible rather differently from readers who have no such belief. For these readers, it is still perfectly possible to appreciate the stories in which the supernatural looms large, provided that they exercise 'a willing suspension of disbelief' (to use Coleridge's words) and imagine how the world would have looked to the stories' original writers and readers. For the biblical writers, God and his angels (not to mention Satan and his demons) were an ever-present reality, affecting not only momentous events in the world at large but also the twists and turns of people's everyday lives.

Whatever your own religious or spiritual outlook, the important point is to allow yourself to be engaged by what you read, to be caught up in it, excited, provoked, stimulated, perhaps even amused or disturbed by it.

Then, who knows what might happen? As the poet W. H. Auden said, 'A real book is not one that we read, but one that reads us.'

A Very Brief History of the Bible

The book we call the Bible was not originally a book in the modern sense, but an anthology, or library of different writings, composed by various authors – priests, prophets, poets, sages, apostles – over many hundreds of years. The earliest parts of the Bible were probably written over 3,000 years ago, while the latest part – probably the letter known as 2 Peter – is thought to date from the late first or perhaps the early second century CE. As well as being full of great stories, the Bible includes all sorts of other literature: genealogies, laws, speeches, practical instructions, hymns, prayers, poems, proverbs, theological reflections, prophetic oracles, gospels, parables, sermons, letters and a strange form of prophetic literature known as apocalyptic.

The Bible as we now know it is divided into two parts. The first, much longer part is commonly known as the 'Old' Testament, though for Jews it constitutes their scriptures – the sacred literature of Judaism. In most modern translations of the Bible the Old Testament consists of 39 books (mostly originally written in ancient Hebrew), and these books are normally arranged in four groups: the Law, the historical books, the poetical books and the Prophets.

The books of the Law, from the Hebrew word 'Torah' (meaning 'guidance' or 'instruction') comprise the first five books of the Bible (Genesis, Exodus, Leviticus, Numbers and Deuteronomy), which is why they are also known as the Pentateuch. It is in this section of the Bible that you find not only the Ten Commandments but all the other civil, criminal and religious laws that continue to inform the Jewish faith today (including, for example, the laws concerning the different kinds of meat that may be eaten). However, by no means all of these books are made up of 'law' in the modern sense: they also contain many of the greatest narratives in the entire Bible, including the epic story of Moses and the liberation of the Israelites from Egypt.

The second group, the historical books, takes up the story of ancient Israel after the death of Moses, beginning with the conquest of Canaan under the leadership of Joshua. Then comes the turbulent period of the Judges, followed by the stories of King Saul and King David, the golden age of Solomon, the division of the kingdom, and the succession of good and bad kings who ruled Israel and Judah until the 'regime change' that was imposed on them, first by the Assyrians and then by Babylonians in the sixth century BCE. This is the crisis point in biblical history known as the Exile, when many of the people of Israel and Judah were deported and dispersed throughout the ancient Near East.

After the Exile, the biblical story continues with the books of Ezra and Nehemiah, who led some of the Jews back to their homeland in Judah in the mid fifth century BCE. Finally, the book of Esther tells the story of how the exiled Jews escaped extermination during the period of Persian rule which followed on from that of the Babylonians.

The third group of books, the poetical books, contains some of the most profound and enduring poetry the world has known – from the powerful discourses on the problem of suffering in the book of Job, to the exquisite love poetry of the Song of Solomon.

The fourth group, the Prophets, consists of oracles, visions, poems and other pronouncements brought together under the names of particular prophets, such as Isaiah, Jeremiah and Ezekiel. The earliest of these prophets lived in the sixth century BCE, before the time of the Exile, and the latest were active about a century later, during the time of the restoration when some of the Jews returned to Jerusalem and began to rebuild the Temple.

After the Persian Empire fell to the Greeks (in the fourth century BCE), the world of the ancient Near East changed rapidly. By the time of Jesus (born c. 4 BCE), Palestine was firmly under Roman control. However, Greek remained the common language of the age and it was the Greek translation of the Hebrew Bible, the Septuagint, which the early Christians used as their scripture. They read it and treasured it because they had come to believe that what Jesus had said and done represented the fulfilment of all that these ancient writings stood for. It was not long, however, before the early Christians began composing and collecting a literature of their own, mostly written in a variant of ancient Greek, and this eventually became known as the 'New' Testament.

As with the Old Testament, the 27 books that make up the New Testament include different kinds of writings – gospels, ancient history, letters, and a form of literature known as 'apocalyptic', which depicts in symbolic and coded language the unfolding of God's purpose up to and including the End of the world as we know it.

In contrast to the Old Testament, which took shape over centuries, the books of the New Testament were written in little more than 50 years, beginning from around the middle of the first century CE; and although not all of them were universally acknowledged as scripture until early in the fifth century, most had been in regular circulation and used throughout the Church from at least the middle of the second century CE.

Most scholars think that these New Testament writings were first used during the gatherings of the early Christians, as they met in each other's houses for prayer and worship. These gatherings probably followed the practice of Jewish worship and would have included regular readings from the Old Testament. No doubt they also included readings from the letters and later the gospel accounts of the acts and teachings of Jesus, written by the apostles to encourage and support their fellow believers in their new faith and way of life.

A Note on the Compilation of Testament

For those readers who may be interested, what follows is a brief explanation as to how I have gone about compiling and editing the text of *Testament*. (Readers with little or no prior knowledge of the Bible may well find it more interesting to read this last section of the Introduction *after* they have read *Testament* itself.)

There is no getting away from it: the Bible is a very long book – roughly 600,000 words in the Old Testament and 170,000 in the New. The number of words in *Testament* amounts to a little under 250,000 – which is considerably shorter than, for example, *War and Peace* or *The Lord of the Rings*.

This reduction has largely been achieved by condensing or omitting text that closely resembles or directly repeats information that can be found in different parts of the Bible (for example, portions of the books of Kings and Chronicles), or that interrupts the flow of the narrative (for example, the genealogies in Genesis, the legal codes and instructions for priests that form much of Exodus, Leviticus and Numbers, the lists of tribal territories in Joshua and the detailed descriptions of the Temple in the second book of Chronicles).

At the same time, I have included just a few, often very brief, extracts from the non-narrative books of the Bible (that is, from Psalms, Proverbs, Ecclesiastes, the Song of Solomon, the Old Testament Prophets and the New Testament letters). The aim here is to provide glimpses into the longer writings from which these extracts are taken – enough, at least, to give some insight into their distinctive character and message. Most of these non-narrative writings appear in Part Three of *Testament*: 'Poems, Proverbs and Prophecies', and some readers may prefer to leave these aside and come back to them after reading the narratives that appear in Parts Four and Five: 'The Story of the Christ' and 'From Acts to Apocalypse'.

The order of the contents of *Testament* largely reflects the composition and arrangement of the biblical books to be found in most modern Bibles – with just a few exceptions: instead of appearing among the books of the Prophets, the story of Jonah is positioned so that it acts as an interlude between the stories of the kingdoms of Israel and of Judah in Part Two; the story of Esther is positioned before the writings of Ezra and Nehemiah, set as it is during the time of the Jewish exile under the Persians; and, for similar reasons, the first (narrative) part of Daniel appears just before Esther, whereas the second part (comprising Daniel's visions) is situated alongside the selections from other prophetic and apocalyptic writings at the end of Part Three.

With the New Testament, the four gospel narratives of Matthew, Mark, Luke and John have been combined to form one continuous account of the acts and teachings of Jesus. As a result, I have been able to retain all the parables and sayings of Jesus within a narrative framework that broadly follows that of the four original gospels, while also including almost all of the scenes relating to Jesus's birth, ministry, death and resurrection.

In doing this, I know there are many scholars who argue that the four gospels may only properly be read independently, so that readers can see how the writers selected and edited *their* original sources, resulting in four complementary but distinct views of Jesus, each of which was appropriate to the particular communities for whom they were writing. The aim here, however, is to provide a single, all-inclusive account of the biblical Jesus for people who may or may not decide to go on to read each gospel in its own right. There is also a long tradition that treats the gospels themselves as sources that may be edited and woven together to form a larger composite narrative. This tradition begins in the second century CE with Tatian's *Diatessaron* – an amalgamation of the gospels which, when translated from Greek into Syriac, became the standard gospel used by the Syrian church until the fifth century. This tradition took on a new form with the English Miracle

Plays of the Middle Ages and finds its modern manifestation in various literary and cinematic retellings of the Jesus story – the most recent being Mel Gibson's immensely successful and controversial *The Passion of the Christ*.

As you will probably have gathered by now, *Testament* is not a paraphrase or retelling of the scriptures; rather, I have worked entirely with the words of the Revised English Bible. These days there is a vast and bewildering range of Bible translations to choose from. I have chosen to use the REB because of its smooth and elegant rendering of the long narrative sections that form the greater part of this book.

The REB was first published in 1989 and is now recognized throughout the English-speaking world as one of the best modern English versions of the Bible available. To quote from an online reviewer in Australia:

> As a person who is well-read but has never really read the Bible, I am so glad I found the Revised English Bible . . . Upon reading it, I was struck by how lucidly the Bible's ideas were presented to me . . . The REB, with its beautiful sentences, shows why the Bible is one of the world's great books.[5]

I hope you will find the experience of reading *Testament* as enjoyable and rewarding!

Philip Law
December 2004

Notes
1 Answer: Jacob, Jezebel, Jonah, Jesus.
2 See Malles, Stanley, and McQuain, Jeffrey, *Coined by God: Words and Phrases that First Appear in the English Translations of the Bible* (Norton 2003).
3 For example, Johnson, Robert K., *Reel Spirituality* (Baker 2000).
4 Answer: The Story of Esther (page 317).
5 On Amazon.com, 14 September 2004.

Part One

FROM ADAM TO MOSES

1 | CREATION AND FALL

The Creation

In the beginning God created the heavens and the earth. The earth was a vast waste, darkness covered the deep, and the spirit of God hovered over the surface of the water. God said, 'Let there be light,' and there was light; and God saw the light was good, and he separated light from darkness. He called the light day, and the darkness night. So evening came, and morning came; it was the first day.

God said, 'Let there be a vault between the waters, to separate water from water.' So God made the vault, and separated the water under the vault from the water above it, and so it was; and God called the vault the heavens. Evening came, and morning came, the second day.

God said, 'Let the water under the heavens be gathered into one place, so that dry land may appear'; and so it was. God called the dry land earth, and the gathering of the water he called sea; and God saw that it was good.

Then God said, 'Let the earth produce growing things; let there be on the earth plants that bear seed, and trees bearing fruit each with its own kind of seed.' So it was; the earth produced growing things: plants bearing their own kind of seed and trees bearing fruit, each with its own kind of seed; and God saw that it was good. Evening came, and morning came, the third day.

God said, 'Let there be lights in the vault of the heavens to separate day from night, and let them serve as signs both for festivals and for seasons and years. Let them also shine in the heavens to give light on earth.' So it was; God made two great lights, the greater to govern the day and the lesser to govern the night; he also made the stars. God put these lights in the vault of the heavens to give light on earth, to govern day and night, and to separate light from darkness; and God saw that it was good. Evening came, and morning came, the fourth day.

3

God said, 'Let the water teem with living creatures, and let birds fly above the earth across the vault of the heavens.' God then created the great sea-beasts and all living creatures that move and swarm in the water, according to their various kinds, and every kind of bird; and God saw that it was good. He blessed them and said, 'Be fruitful and increase; fill the water of the sea, and let the birds increase on the land.' Evening came, and morning came, the fifth day.

God said, 'Let the earth bring forth living creatures, according to their various kinds: cattle, creeping things, and wild animals, all according to their various kinds.' So it was; God made wild animals, cattle, and every creeping thing, all according to their various kinds; and he saw that it was good. Then God said, 'Let us make human beings in our image, after our likeness, to have dominion over the fish in the sea, the birds of the air, the cattle, all wild animals on land, and everything that creeps on the earth.'

God created human beings in his own image;
in the image of God he created them;
male and female he created them.

God blessed them and said to them, 'Be fruitful and increase, fill the earth and subdue it, have dominion over the fish in the sea, the birds of the air, and every living thing that moves on the earth.'

God also said, 'Throughout the earth I give you all plants that bear seed, and every tree that bears fruit with seed: they shall be yours for food. All green plants I give for food to the wild animals, to all the birds of the air, and to everything that creeps on the earth, every living creature.' So it was; and God saw all that he had made, and it was very good. Evening came, and morning came, the sixth day.

Thus the heavens and the earth and everything in them were completed. On the sixth day God brought to an end all the work he had been doing; on the seventh day, having finished all his work, God blessed the day and made it holy, because it was the day he finished all his work of creation.

Adam and Eve

This is the story of the heavens and the earth after their creation.

When the Lord God made the earth and the heavens, there was neither shrub nor plant growing on the earth, because the Lord God had sent no rain; nor was there anyone to till the ground. Moisture used to well up out of the earth and water all the surface of the ground.

The Lord God formed a human being from the dust of the ground and breathed into his nostrils the breath of life, so that he became a living creature. The Lord God planted a garden in Eden away to the east, and in it he put the man he had formed. The Lord God made trees grow up from the ground, every kind of tree pleasing to the eye and good for food; and in the middle of the garden he set the tree of life and the tree of the knowledge of good and evil.

The Lord God took the man and put him in the garden of Eden to till it and look after it. 'You may eat from any tree in the garden', he told the man, 'except from the tree of the knowledge of good and evil; the day you eat from that, you are surely doomed to die.' Then the Lord God said, 'It is not good for the man to be alone; I shall make a partner suited to him.' So from the earth he formed all the wild animals and all the birds of the air, and brought them to the man to see what he would call them; whatever the man called each living creature, that would be its name. The man gave names to all cattle, to the birds of the air, and to every wild animal; but for the man himself no suitable partner was found. The Lord God then put the man into a deep sleep and, while he slept, he took one of the man's ribs and closed up the flesh over the place. The rib he had taken out of the man the Lord God built up into a woman, and he brought her to the man. The man said:

> 'This one at last
> is bone from my bones,
> flesh from my flesh!
> She shall be called woman,
> for from man was she taken.'

That is why a man leaves his father and mother and attaches himself to his wife, and the two become one. Both were naked, the man and his wife, but they had no feeling of shame.

The serpent, which was the most cunning of all the creatures the Lord God had made, asked the woman, 'Is it true that God has forbidden you to eat from any tree in the garden?' She replied, 'We may eat the fruit of any tree in the garden, except for the tree in the middle of the garden. God has forbidden us to eat the fruit of that tree or even to touch it; if we do, we shall die.'

'Of course you will not die,' said the serpent; 'for God knows that, as soon as you eat it, your eyes will be opened and you will be like God himself, knowing both good and evil.'

The woman looked at the tree: the fruit would be good to eat; it was pleasing to the eye and desirable for the knowledge it could give. So she took some and ate it; she also gave some to her husband, and he ate it. Then the eyes of both of them were opened, and they knew that they were naked; so they stitched fig-leaves together and made themselves loincloths.

The man and his wife heard the sound of the Lord God walking about in the garden at the time of the evening breeze, and they hid from him among the trees. The Lord God called to the man, 'Where are you?' He replied, 'I heard the sound of you in the garden and I was afraid because I was naked, so I hid.' God said, 'Who told you that you were naked? Have you eaten from the tree which I forbade you to eat from?'

The man replied, 'It was the woman you gave to be with me who gave me fruit from the tree, and I ate it.' The Lord God said to the woman, 'What have you done?' The woman answered, 'It was the serpent who deceived me into eating it.' Then the Lord God said to the serpent:

'Because you have done this you are cursed alone of all cattle and the creatures of the wild.

'On your belly you will crawl,
and dust you will eat
all the days of your life.
I shall put enmity between you and the woman,
between your brood and hers.
They will strike at your head,
and you will strike at their heel.'

To the woman he said:

'I shall give you great labour in childbearing;
with labour you will bear children.
You will desire your husband,
but he will be your master.'

And to the man he said: 'Because you have listened to your wife
and have eaten from the tree which I forbade you,

on your account the earth will be cursed.
You will get your food from it only by labour
all the days of your life;
it will yield thorns and thistles for you.
You will eat of the produce of the field,
and only by the sweat of your brow will you win your bread
until you return to the earth;
for from it you were taken.
Dust you are, to dust you will return.'

The man named his wife Eve because she was the mother of all
living beings. The Lord God made coverings from skins for the
man and his wife and clothed them. But he said, 'The man has
become like one of us, knowing good and evil; what if he now
reaches out and takes fruit from the tree of life also, and eats it
and lives for ever?'

So the Lord God banished him from the garden of Eden to till
the ground from which he had been taken. When he drove him
out, God settled him to the east of the garden of Eden, and he
stationed the cherubim and a sword whirling and flashing to
guard the way to the tree of life.

Cain and Abel

The man lay with his wife Eve, and she conceived and gave birth
to Cain. She said, 'With the help of the Lord I have brought into
being a male child.' Afterwards she had another child, Abel. He
tended the flock, and Cain worked the land. In due season Cain
brought some of the fruits of the earth as an offering to the Lord,
while Abel brought the choicest of the firstborn of his flock. The
Lord regarded Abel and his offering with favour, but not Cain
and his offering. Cain was furious and he glowered. The Lord
said to Cain,

'Why are you angry? Why are you scowling?
If you do well, you hold your head up;
if not, sin is a demon crouching at the door;
it will desire you, and you will be mastered by it.'

Cain said to his brother Abel, 'Let us go out into the country.'
Once there, Cain attacked and murdered his brother. The Lord
asked Cain, 'Where is your brother Abel?' 'I do not know,' Cain
answered. 'Am I my brother's keeper?' The Lord said, 'What
have you done? Your brother's blood is crying out to me from
the ground. Now you are accursed and will be banished from
the very ground which has opened its mouth to receive the
blood you have shed. When you till the ground, it will no longer
yield you its produce. You shall be a wanderer, a fugitive on the
earth.' Cain said to the Lord, 'My punishment is heavier than I
can bear; now you are driving me off the land, and I must hide
myself from your presence. I shall be a wanderer, a fugitive on
the earth, and I can be killed at sight by anyone.' The Lord
answered him, 'No: if anyone kills Cain, sevenfold vengeance
will be exacted from him.' The Lord put a mark on Cain, so that
anyone happening to meet him should not kill him. Cain went
out from the Lord's presence and settled in the land of Nod to
the east of Eden.

Adam lay with his wife again. She gave birth to a son, and
named him Seth, 'for', she said, 'God has granted me another son
in place of Abel, because Cain killed him'. Seth too had a son,
whom he named Enosh. At that time people began to invoke the
Lord by name.

Noah and the Great Flood

The human race began to increase and to spread over the earth
and daughters were born to them. The sons of the gods saw how
beautiful these daughters were, so they took for themselves such
women as they chose. But the Lord said, 'My spirit will not
remain in a human being for ever; because he is mortal flesh, he
will live only for a hundred and twenty years.'

In those days as well as later, when the sons of the gods had
intercourse with the daughters of mortals and children were born
to them, the Nephilim were on the earth; they were the heroes of
old, people of renown.

When the Lord saw how great was the wickedness of human beings on earth, and how their every thought and inclination were always wicked, he bitterly regretted that he had made mankind on earth. He said, 'I shall wipe off the face of the earth this human race which I have created – yes, man and beast, creeping things and birds. I regret that I ever made them.' Noah, however, had won the Lord's favour.

Noah was a righteous man, the one blameless man of his time, and he walked with God. He had three sons: Shem, Ham, and Japheth. God saw that the world was corrupt and full of violence; and seeing this corruption, for the life of everyone on earth was corrupt, God said to Noah, 'I am going to bring the whole human race to an end, for because of them the earth is full of violence. I am about to destroy them, and the earth along with them. Make yourself an ark with ribs of cypress; cover it with reeds and coat it inside and out with pitch. This is to be its design: the length of the ark is to be three hundred cubits, its breadth fifty cubits, and its height thirty cubits. You are to make a roof for the ark, giving it a fall of one cubit when complete; put a door in the side of the ark, and build three decks, lower, middle, and upper.

'I am about to bring the waters of the flood over the earth to destroy from under heaven every human being that has the spirit of life; everything on earth shall perish. But with you I shall make my covenant, and you will go into the ark, you with your sons, your wife, and your sons' wives. You are to bring living creatures of every kind into the ark to keep them alive with you, two of each kind, a male and a female; two of every kind of bird, beast, and creeping thing are to come to you to be kept alive. See that you take and store by you every kind of food that can be eaten; this will be food for you and for them.' Noah carried out exactly all God had commanded him.

In the year when Noah was six hundred years old, on the seventeenth day of the second month, that very day all the springs of the great deep burst out, the windows of the heavens were opened, and rain fell on the earth for forty days and forty nights. That was the day Noah went into the ark with his sons, Shem, Ham, and Japheth, his own wife, and his three sons' wives. Wild animals of every kind, cattle of every kind, every kind of thing that creeps on the ground, and winged birds of every kind – all living creatures came two by two to Noah in the ark. Those which came were one male and one female of all living things; they came in as God had commanded Noah, and the Lord closed the door on him.

The flood continued on the earth for forty days, and the swelling waters lifted up the ark so that it rose high above the ground. The ark floated on the surface of the swollen waters as they increased over the earth. They increased more and more until they covered all the high mountains everywhere under heaven. God wiped out every living creature that existed on earth, man and beast, creeping thing and bird; they were all wiped out over the whole earth, and only Noah and those who were with him in the ark survived.

When the water had increased over the earth for a hundred and fifty days, God took thought for Noah and all the beasts and cattle with him in the ark, and he caused a wind to blow over the earth, so that the water began to subside. The springs of the deep and the windows of the heavens were stopped up, the downpour from the skies was checked. Gradually the water receded from the earth, and by the end of a hundred and fifty days it had abated. On the seventeenth day of the seventh month the ark grounded on the mountains of Ararat. The water continued to abate until the tenth month, and on the first day of the tenth month the tops of the mountains could be seen.

At the end of forty days Noah opened the hatch that he had made in the ark, and sent out a raven; it continued flying to and fro until the water on the earth had dried up. Then Noah sent out a dove to see whether the water on the earth had subsided. But the dove found no place where she could settle because all the earth was under water, and so she came back to him in the ark. Noah reached out and caught her, and brought her into the ark. He waited seven days more and again sent out the dove from the ark. She came back to him towards evening with a freshly plucked olive leaf in her beak. Noah knew then that the water had subsided from the earth's surface. He waited yet another seven days and, when he sent out the dove, she did not come back to him. So it came about that, on the first day of the first month of his six hundred and first year, the water had dried up on the earth, and when Noah removed the hatch and looked out, he saw that the ground was dry.

By the twenty-seventh day of the second month the earth was dry, and God spoke to Noah. 'Come out of the ark together with your wife, your sons, and their wives,' he said. 'Bring out every living creature that is with you, live things of every kind, birds, beasts, and creeping things, and let them spread over the earth and be fruitful and increase on it.' So Noah came out with his sons, his wife, and his sons' wives, and all the animals, creeping things, and birds; everything that moves on the ground came out of the ark, one kind after another.

God said to Noah and his sons: 'I am now establishing my covenant with you and with your descendants after you, and with every living creature that is with you, all birds and cattle, all the animals with you on earth, all that have come out of the ark. I shall sustain my covenant with you: never again will all living creatures be destroyed by the waters of a flood, never again will there be a flood to lay waste the earth.'

God said, 'For all generations to come, this is the sign which I am giving of the covenant between myself and you and all living creatures with you:

> My bow I set in the clouds
> to be a sign of the covenant
> between myself and the earth.
> When I bring clouds over the earth,
> the rainbow will appear in the clouds.

'Then I shall remember the covenant which I have made with you and with all living creatures, and never again will the waters become a flood to destroy all creation.'

The sons of Noah who came out of the ark were Shem, Ham, and Japheth; Ham was the father of Canaan. These three were the sons of Noah, and their descendants spread over the whole earth.

Noah, who was the first tiller of the soil, planted a vineyard. He drank so much of the wine that he became drunk and lay naked inside his tent. Ham, father of Canaan, saw his father naked, and went out and told his two brothers. Shem and Japheth took a cloak, put it on their shoulders, and, walking backwards, covered their father's naked body. They kept their faces averted, so that they did not see his nakedness. When Noah woke from his drunkenness and learnt what his youngest son had done to him, he said:

'Cursed be Canaan!
Most servile of slaves
shall he be to his brothers.'

And he went on:

'Bless, O Lord,
the tents of Shem;
may Canaan be his slave.
May God extend Japheth's boundaries,
let him dwell in the tents of Shem,
may Canaan be his slave.'

After the flood Noah lived for three hundred and fifty years; he
was nine hundred and fifty years old when he died.

The Tower of Babel

There was a time when all the world spoke a single language and
used the same words. As people journeyed in the east, they came
upon a plain in the land of Shinar and settled there. They said to
one another, 'Come, let us make bricks and bake them hard'; they
used bricks for stone and bitumen for mortar. Then they said,
'Let us build ourselves a city and a tower with its top in the heavens and make a name for ourselves, or we shall be dispersed over
the face of the earth.' The Lord came down to see the city and
tower which they had built, and he said, 'Here they are, one
people with a single language, and now they have started to do
this; from now on nothing they have a mind to do will be beyond
their reach. Come, let us go down there and confuse their language, so that they will not understand what they say to one
another.' So the Lord dispersed them from there all over the
earth, and they left off building the city. That is why it is called
Babel, because there the Lord made a babble of the language of
the whole world. It was from that place the Lord scattered people
over the face of the earth.

2 | THE AGE OF THE PATRIARCHS

The Promised Land

These are the descendants of Terah. Terah was the father of
Abram, Nahor, and Haran. Haran was Lot's father. Haran died in
the land of his birth, Ur of the Chaldees, during his father's lifetime. Abram and Nahor married wives; Abram's wife was called
Sarai, and Nahor's Milcah. She was the daughter of Haran, father
of Milcah and Iscah. Sarai was barren; she had no child. Terah
took his son Abram, his grandson Lot the son of Haran, and his
daughter-in-law Sarai, Abram's wife, and they set out from Ur of
the Chaldees for Canaan. But when they reached Harran, they
settled there. Terah was two hundred and five years old when he
died in Harran.

The Lord said to Abram, 'Leave your own country, your kin,
and your father's house, and go to a country that I will show you.
I shall make you into a great nation; I shall bless you and make
your name so great that it will be used in blessings:

> those who bless you, I shall bless;
> those who curse you, I shall curse.
> All the peoples on earth
> will wish to be blessed as you are blessed.'

Abram, who was seventy-five years old when he left Harran, set
out as the Lord had bidden him, and Lot went with him. He took
his wife Sarai, his brother's son Lot, and all the possessions they
had gathered and the dependants they had acquired in Harran,
and they departed for Canaan. When they arrived there, Abram
went on as far as the sanctuary at Shechem, the terebinth tree of
Moreh. (At that time the Canaanites lived in the land.) When the
Lord appeared to him and said, 'I am giving this land to your
descendants,' Abram built an altar there to the Lord who had
appeared to him. From there he moved on to the hill-country east

13

of Bethel and pitched his tent between Bethel on the west and Ai on the east. He built there an altar to the Lord whom he invoked by name. Thus Abram journeyed by stages towards the Negeb.

The land was stricken by a famine so severe that Abram went down to Egypt to live there for a time. As he was about to enter Egypt, he said to his wife Sarai, 'I am well aware that you are a beautiful woman, and I know that when the Egyptians see you and think, "She is his wife," they will let you live but they will kill me. Tell them you are my sister, so that all may go well with me because of you, and my life be spared on your account.'

When Abram arrived in Egypt, the Egyptians saw that Sarai was indeed very beautiful, and Pharaoh's courtiers, when they saw her, sang her praises to Pharaoh. She was taken into Pharaoh's household, and he treated Abram well because of her, and Abram acquired sheep and cattle and donkeys, male and female slaves, she-donkeys, and camels.

But when the Lord inflicted plagues on Pharaoh and his household on account of Abram's wife Sarai, Pharaoh summoned Abram. 'Why have you treated me like this?' he said. 'Why did you not tell me she was your wife? Why did you say she was your sister, so that I took her as a wife? Here she is: take her and go.' Pharaoh gave his men orders, and they sent Abram on his way with his wife and all that belonged to him.

Abram and Lot
From Egypt Abram went up into the Negeb, he and his wife and all that he possessed, and Lot went with him. Abram had become very rich in cattle and in silver and gold. From the Negeb he journeyed by stages towards Bethel, to the place between Bethel and Ai where he had earlier pitched his tent, and where he had previously set up an altar and invoked the Lord by name.

Since Lot, who was travelling with Abram, also possessed sheep and cattle and tents, the land could not support them while they were together. They had so much livestock that they could not settle in the same district, and quarrels arose between Abram's herdsmen and Lot's. (The Canaanites and the Perizzites were then living in the land.) Abram said to Lot, 'There must be no quarrelling between us, or between my herdsmen and yours; for we are close kinsmen. The whole country is there in front of you. Let us part company: if you go north, I shall go south; if you go south, I shall go north.' Lot looked around and saw how well watered the whole plain of Jordan was; all the way to Zoar it was like the Garden of the Lord, like the land of Egypt. This was before the Lord had destroyed Sodom and Gomorrah. So Lot chose all the Jordan plain and took the road to the east. They parted company: Abram settled in Canaan, while Lot settled among the cities of the plain and pitched his tent near Sodom. Now the men of Sodom in their wickedness had committed monstrous sins against the Lord.

After Lot and Abram had parted, the Lord said to Abram, 'Look around from where you are towards north, south, east, and west: all the land you see I shall give to you and to your descendants for ever. I shall make your descendants countless as the dust of the earth; only if the specks of dust on the ground could be counted could your descendants be counted. Now go through the length and breadth of the land, for I am giving it to you.' Abram moved his tent and settled by the terebinths of Mamre at Hebron, where he built an altar to the Lord.

In those days King Amraphel of Shinar, King Arioch of Ellasar, King Kedorlaomer of Elam, and King Tidal of Goyim went to war against King Bera of Sodom, King Birsha of Gomorrah, King Shinab of Admah, King Shemeber of Zeboyim, and the king of Bela, which is Zoar. These kings joined forces in the valley of Siddim, which is now the Dead Sea. Now the valley of Siddim was full of bitumen pits, and when the kings of Sodom and Gomorrah fled, some of their men fell into them, but the rest made their escape to the hills. The four kings captured all the flocks and herds of Sodom and Gomorrah and all their provisions, and withdrew, carrying off Abram's nephew, Lot, who was living in Sodom, and his flocks and herds.

A fugitive brought the news to Abram the Hebrew, who at that time had his camp by the terebinths of Mamre the Amorite. This Mamre was the brother of Eshcol and Aner, allies of Abram. When Abram heard that his kinsman had been taken prisoner, he mustered his three hundred and eighteen retainers, men born in his household, and went in pursuit as far as Dan. Abram and his followers surrounded the enemy by night, routed them, and pursued them as far as Hobah, north of Damascus. He recovered all the flocks and herds and also his kinsman Lot with his flocks and herds, together with the women and all his company. On Abram's return from defeating Kedorlaomer and the allied kings, the king of Sodom came out to meet him in the valley of Shaveh, which is now the King's Valley.

Then the king of Salem, Melchizedek, brought food and wine. He was priest of God Most High, and he pronounced this blessing on Abram:

'Blessed be Abram by God Most High,
Creator of the heavens and the earth.
And blessed be God Most High,
who has delivered your enemies into your hand.'

Then Abram gave him a tithe of all the booty.

The king of Sodom said to Abram, 'Give me the people, and you can take the livestock.' But Abram replied, 'I lift my hand and swear by the Lord, God Most High, Creator of the heavens and the earth: not a thread or a sandal-thong shall I accept of anything that is yours. You will never say, "I made Abram rich."'

Abram's Vision
After this the word of the Lord came to Abram in a vision. He said, 'Do not be afraid, Abram; I am your shield. Your reward will be very great.' Abram replied, 'Lord God, what can you give me, seeing that I am childless? The heir to my household is Eliezer of Damascus. You have given me no children, and so my heir must be a slave born in my house.' The word of the Lord came to him: 'This man will not be your heir; your heir will be a child of your own body.' He brought Abram outside and said, 'Look up at the sky, and count the stars, if you can. So many will your descendants be.'

Abram put his faith in the Lord, who reckoned it to him as righteousness, and said, 'I am the Lord who brought you out from Ur of the Chaldees to give you this land as your possession.' Abram asked, 'Lord God, how can I be sure that I shall occupy it?'

The Lord answered, 'Bring me a heifer three years old, a she-goat three years old, a ram three years old, a turtle-dove, and a young pigeon.' Abram brought him all these, cut the animals in two, and set the pieces opposite each other, but he did not cut the birds in half. Birds of prey swooped down on the carcasses, but he scared them away.

As the sun was going down, Abram fell into a trance and great and fearful darkness came over him. The Lord said to Abram, 'Know this for certain: your descendants will be aliens living in a land that is not their own; they will be enslaved and held in oppression for four hundred years. But I shall punish the nation whose slaves they are, and afterwards they will depart with great possessions. You yourself will join your forefathers in peace and be buried at a ripe old age. But it will be the fourth generation who will return here, for till then the Amorites will not be ripe for punishment.'

Hagar and Ishmael

Abram's wife Sarai had borne him no children. She had, however, an Egyptian slave-girl named Hagar, and Sarai said to Abram, 'The Lord has not let me have a child. Take my slave-girl; perhaps through her I shall have a son.' Abram heeded what his wife said; so Sarai brought her slave-girl, Hagar the Egyptian, to her husband and gave her to Abram as a wife. When this happened Abram had been in Canaan for ten years. He lay with Hagar and she conceived; and when she knew that she was pregnant, she looked down on her mistress. Sarai complained to Abram, 'I am being wronged; you must do something about it. It was I who gave my slave-girl into your arms, but since she has known that she is pregnant, she has despised me. May the Lord see justice done between you and me.' Abram replied, 'Your slave-girl is in your hands; deal with her as you please.' So Sarai ill-treated her and she ran away from her mistress.

The angel of the Lord came upon Hagar by a spring in the wilderness, the spring on the road to Shur, and he said, 'Hagar, Sarai's slave-girl, where have you come from and where are you going?' She answered, 'I am running away from Sarai my mistress.' The angel of the Lord said to her, 'Go back to your mistress and submit to ill-treatment at her hands.' He also said, 'I shall make your descendants too many to be counted.'

Hagar bore Abram a son, and he named the child she bore him Ishmael. Abram was eighty-six years old when she bore Ishmael.

God's Covenant with Abraham

When Abram was ninety-nine years old, the Lord appeared to him and said, 'I am God Almighty. Live always in my presence and be blameless, so that I may make my covenant with you and give you many descendants.' Abram bowed low, and God went on, 'This is my covenant with you: you are to be the father of many nations. Your name will no longer be Abram, but Abraham; for I shall make you father of many nations. I shall make you exceedingly fruitful; I shall make nations out of you, and kings shall spring from you. I shall maintain my covenant with you and your descendants after you, generation after generation, an everlasting covenant: I shall be your God, yours and your descendants'. As a possession for all time I shall give you and your descendants after you the land in which you now are aliens, the whole of Canaan, and I shall be their God.'

God said to Abraham, 'For your part, you must keep my covenant, you and your descendants after you, generation by generation. This is how you are to keep this covenant between myself and you and your descendants after you: circumcise yourselves, every male among you.'

God said to Abraham, 'As for Sarai your wife, you are to call her not Sarai, but Sarah. I shall bless her and give you a son by her. I shall bless her and she will be the mother of nations; from her kings of peoples will spring.' Abraham bowed low, and laughing said to himself, 'Can a son be born to a man who is a hundred years old? Can Sarah bear a child at ninety?' He said to God, 'If only Ishmael might enjoy your special favour!' But God replied, 'No; your wife Sarah will bear you a son, and you are to call him Isaac. With him I shall maintain my covenant as an everlasting covenant for his descendants after him. But I have heard your request about Ishmael; I have blessed him and I shall make him fruitful. I shall give him many descendants; he will be father of twelve princes, and I shall raise a great nation from him. But my covenant I shall fulfil with Isaac, whom Sarah will bear to you at this time next year.' When he had finished talking with Abraham, God left him.

Then Abraham took Ishmael his son, everyone who had been born in his household and everyone he had bought, every male in his household, and that same day he circumcised the flesh of their foreskins as God had commanded him. Abraham was ninety-nine years old when he was circumcised. Ishmael was thirteen years old when he was circumcised. Both Abraham and Ishmael were circumcised on the same day. All the men of

Abraham's household, born in the house or bought from foreigners, were circumcised with him.

The Visit of the Angels

The Lord appeared to Abraham by the terebinths of Mamre, as he was sitting at the opening of his tent in the heat of the day. He looked up and saw three men standing over against him. On seeing them, he hurried from his tent door to meet them. Bowing low he said, 'Sirs, if I have deserved your favour, do not go past your servant without a visit. Let me send for some water so that you may bathe your feet; and rest under this tree, while I fetch a little food so that you may refresh yourselves. Afterwards you may continue the journey which has brought you my way.' They said, 'Very well, do as you say.' So Abraham hurried into the tent to Sarah and said, 'Quick, take three measures of flour, knead it, and make cakes.' He then hastened to the herd, chose a fine, tender calf, and gave it to a servant, who prepared it at once. He took curds and milk and the calf which was now ready, set it all before them, and there under the tree waited on them himself while they ate.

They asked him where Sarah his wife was, and he replied, 'She is in the tent.' One of them said, 'About this time next year I shall come back to you, and your wife Sarah will have a son.' Now Sarah was listening at the opening of the tent close by him. Both Abraham and Sarah were very old, Sarah being well past the age of childbearing. So she laughed to herself and said, 'At my time of life I am past bearing children, and my husband is old.' The Lord said to Abraham, 'Why did Sarah laugh and say, "Can I really bear a child now that I am so old?" Is anything impossible for the Lord? In due season, at this time next year, I shall come back to you, and Sarah will have a son.' Because she was frightened, Sarah lied and denied that she had laughed; but he said, 'Yes, you did laugh.'

The men set out and looked down towards Sodom, and Abraham went with them to see them on their way. The Lord said, 'How great is the outcry over Sodom and Gomorrah! How grave their sin must be! I shall go down and see whether their deeds warrant the outcry reaching me. I must know the truth.' When the men turned and went off towards Sodom, Abraham remained standing before the Lord. Abraham drew near him and asked,

'Will you really sweep away innocent and wicked together? Suppose there are fifty innocent in the city; will you really sweep it away, and not pardon the place because of the fifty innocent there? Far be it from you to do such a thing – to kill innocent and wicked together; for then the innocent would suffer with the wicked. Far be it from you! Should not the judge of all the earth do what is just?' The Lord replied, 'If I find in Sodom fifty innocent, I shall pardon the whole place for their sake.' Abraham said, 'May I make so bold as to speak to the Lord, I who am nothing but dust and ashes: suppose there are five short of fifty innocent? Will you destroy the whole city for the lack of five men?' 'If I find forty-five there,' he replied, 'I shall not destroy it.' Abraham spoke again, 'Suppose forty can be found there?' 'For the sake of the forty I shall not do it,' he replied. Then Abraham said, 'Let not my Lord become angry if I speak again: suppose thirty can be found there?' He answered, 'If I find thirty there, I shall not do it.' Abraham continued, 'May I make so bold as to speak to the Lord: suppose twenty can be found there?' He replied, 'For the sake of the twenty I shall not destroy it.' Abraham said, 'Let not my Lord become angry if I speak just once more: suppose ten can be found there?' 'For the sake of the ten I shall not destroy it,' said the Lord. When the Lord had finished talking to Abraham, he went away, and Abraham returned home.

The Destruction of Sodom

The two angels came to Sodom in the evening while Lot was sitting by the city gate. When he saw them, he rose to meet them and bowing low he said, 'I pray you, sirs, turn aside to your servant's house to spend the night there and bathe your feet. You can continue your journey in the morning.' 'No,' they answered, 'we shall spend the night in the street.' But Lot was so insistent that they accompanied him into his house. He prepared a meal for them, baking unleavened bread for them to eat.

Before they had lain down to sleep, the men of Sodom, both young and old, everyone without exception, surrounded the house. They called to Lot: 'Where are the men who came to you tonight? Bring them out to us so that we may have intercourse with them.' Lot went out into the doorway to them, and, closing the door behind him, said, 'No, my friends, do not do anything so wicked. Look, I have two daughters, virgins both of them; let me bring them out to you, and you can do what you like with them. But do nothing to these men, because they have come under the shelter of my roof.' They said, 'Out of our way! This fellow has come and settled here as an alien, and does he now take it upon himself to judge us? We will treat you worse than them.' They crowded in on Lot and pressed close to break down the door. But the two men inside reached out, pulled Lot into the house, and shut the door. Then they struck those in the doorway, both young and old, with blindness so that they could not find the entrance.

The two men said to Lot, 'Have you anyone here, sons-in-law, sons, or daughters, or anyone else belonging to you in the city? Get them out of this place, because we are going to destroy it. The Lord is aware of the great outcry against its citizens and has sent us to destroy it.' So Lot went out and urged his sons-in-law to get out of the place at once. 'The Lord is about to destroy the city,' he said. But they did not take him seriously.

As soon as it was dawn, the angels urged Lot: 'Quick, take your wife and your two daughters who are here, or you will be destroyed when the city is punished.' When he delayed, they grabbed his hand and the hands of his wife and two daughters, because the Lord had spared him, and they led him to safety outside the city. After they had brought them out, one said, 'Flee for your lives! Do not look back or stop anywhere in the plain. Flee to the hills or you will be destroyed.' Lot replied, 'No, sirs! You have shown your servant favour, and even more by your unfailing care you have saved my life, but I cannot escape to the hills; I shall be overtaken by the disaster, and die. Look, here is a town, only a small place, near enough for me to get to quickly. Let me escape to this small place and save my life.' He said to him, 'I grant your request: I shall not overthrow the town you speak of. But flee there quickly, because I can do nothing until you are there.' That is why the place was called Zoar. The sun had risen over the land as Lot entered Zoar, and the Lord rained down fire and brimstone from the skies on Sodom and Gomorrah. He overthrew those cities and destroyed all the plain, with everyone living there and everything growing in the ground. But Lot's wife looked back, and she turned into a pillar of salt.

Early next morning Abraham went to the place where he had stood in the presence of the Lord. As he looked over Sodom and

Gomorrah and all the wide extent of the plain, he saw thick smoke rising from the earth like smoke from a kiln. Thus it was, when God destroyed the cities of the plain, he took thought for Abraham by rescuing Lot from the total destruction of the cities where he had been living.

Because Lot was afraid to stay in Zoar, he went up from there and settled with his two daughters in the hill-country, where he lived with them in a cave. The elder daughter said to the younger, 'Our father is old and there is not a man in the country to come to us in the usual way. Come now, let us ply our father with wine and then lie with him and in this way preserve the family through our father.' That night they gave him wine to drink, and the elder daughter came and lay with him, and he did not know when she lay down and when she got up. Next day the elder said to the younger, 'Last night I lay with my father. Let us ply him with wine again tonight; then you go in and lie with him. So we shall preserve the family through our father.' They gave their father wine to drink that night also; and the younger daughter went and lay with him, and he did not know when she lay down and when she got up.

In this way both of Lot's daughters came to be pregnant by their father. The elder daughter bore a son and called him Moab; he was the ancestor of the present-day Moabites. The younger also bore a son, whom she called Ben-ammi; he was the ancestor of the present-day Ammonites.

Sarah and Hagar

The Lord showed favour to Sarah as he had promised, and made good what he had said about her. She conceived and at the time foretold by God she bore a son to Abraham in his old age. The son whom Sarah bore to him Abraham named Isaac, and when Isaac was eight days old Abraham circumcised him, as decreed by God. Abraham was a hundred years old when his son Isaac was born. Sarah said, 'God has given me good reason to laugh, and everyone who hears will laugh with me.' She added, 'Whoever would have told Abraham that Sarah would suckle children? Yet I have borne him a son in his old age.' The boy grew and was weaned, and on the day of his weaning Abraham gave a great feast.

Sarah saw the son whom Hagar the Egyptian had borne to Abraham playing with Isaac, and she said to Abraham, 'Drive out this slave-girl and her son! I will not have this slave's son sharing the inheritance with my son Isaac.' Abraham was very upset at this because of Ishmael, but God said to him, 'Do not be upset for the boy and your slave-girl. Do as Sarah says, because it is through Isaac's line that your name will be perpetuated. I shall make a nation of the slave-girl's son, because he also is your child.'

Early next morning Abraham took some food and a full water-skin and gave them to Hagar. He set the child on her shoulder and sent her away, and she wandered about in the wilderness of Beersheba. When the water in the skin was finished, she thrust the child under a bush, then went and sat down some way off, about a bowshot distant. 'How can I watch the child die?' she said, and sat there, weeping bitterly. God heard the child crying, and the angel of God called from heaven to Hagar, 'What is the matter, Hagar? Do not be afraid: God has heard the child crying where you laid him. Go, lift the child and hold him in your arms, because I shall make of him a great nation.' Then God opened her eyes and she saw a well full of water; she went to it, filled the water-skin, and gave the child a drink. God was with the child as he grew up. He lived in the wilderness of Paran and became an archer; and his mother got him a wife from Egypt.

The Binding of Isaac

Some time later God put Abraham to the test. 'Abraham!' he called to him, and Abraham replied, 'Here I am!' God said, 'Take your son, your one and only son Isaac whom you love, and go to the land of Moriah. There you shall offer him as a sacrifice on one of the heights which I shall show you.' Early in the morning Abraham saddled his donkey, and took with him two of his men and his son Isaac; and having split firewood for the sacrifice, he set out for the place of which God had spoken. On the third day Abraham looked up and saw the shrine in the distance. He said to his men, 'Stay here with the donkey while I and the boy go on ahead. We shall worship there, and then come back to you.'

Abraham took the wood for the sacrifice and put it on his son Isaac's shoulder, while he himself carried the fire and the knife. As the two of them went on together, Isaac spoke. 'Father!' he said. Abraham answered, 'What is it, my son?' Isaac said, 'Here are the fire and the wood, but where is the sheep for a sacrifice?'

Abraham answered, 'God will provide himself with a sheep for a sacrifice, my son.' The two of them went on together until they came to the place of which God had spoken. There Abraham built an altar and arranged the wood. He bound his son Isaac and laid him on the altar on top of the wood. He reached out for the knife to slay his son, but the angel of the Lord called to him from heaven, 'Abraham! Abraham!' He answered, 'Here I am!' The angel said, 'Do not raise your hand against the boy; do not touch him. Now I know that you are a godfearing man. You have not withheld from me your son, your only son.' Abraham looked round, and there in a thicket he saw a ram caught by its horns. He went, seized the ram, and offered it as a sacrifice instead of his son. Abraham named that shrine 'The Lord will provide'; and to this day the saying is: 'In the mountain of the Lord it was provided.'

Then the angel of the Lord called from heaven a second time to Abraham and said, 'This is the word of the Lord: By my own self I swear that because you have done this and have not withheld your son, your only son, I shall bless you abundantly and make your descendants as numerous as the stars in the sky or the grains of sand on the seashore. Your descendants will possess the cities of their enemies. All nations on earth will wish to be blessed as your descendants are blessed, because you have been obedient to me.'

Abraham then went back to his men, and together they returned to Beersheba; and there Abraham remained.

Isaac and Rebecca

Abraham was by now a very old man, and the Lord had blessed him in all that he did. Abraham said to the servant who had been longest in his service and was in charge of all he owned, 'Give me your solemn oath: I want you to swear by the Lord, the God of heaven and earth, that you will not take a wife for my son from the women of the Canaanites among whom I am living. You must go to my own country and to my own kindred to find a wife for my son Isaac.' 'What if the woman is unwilling to come with me to this country?' the servant asked. 'Must I take your son back to the land you came from?' Abraham said to him, 'On no account are you to take my son back there. The Lord the God of heaven who took me from my father's house and the land of my birth, the Lord who swore to me that he would give this land to my descendants – he will send his angel before you, and you will take a wife from there for my son. If the woman is unwilling to come with you, then you will be released from your oath to me; only you must not take my son back there.' The servant then put his hand under his master Abraham's thigh and swore that oath.

The servant chose ten camels from his master's herds and, with all kinds of gifts from his master, he went to Aram-naharaim, to the town where Nahor lived. Towards evening, the time when the women go out to draw water, he made the camels kneel down by the well outside the town. 'Lord God of my master Abraham,' he said, 'give me good fortune this day; keep faith with my master Abraham. Here I am by the spring, as the women of the town come out to draw water. I shall say to a girl, "Please lower your jar so that I may drink"; and if she answers, "Drink, and I shall water your camels also," let that be the girl whom you intend for your servant Isaac. In this way I shall know that you have kept faith with my master.'

Before he had finished praying, he saw Rebecca coming out with her water-jar on her shoulder. She was the daughter of Bethuel son of Milcah, the wife of Abraham's brother Nahor. The girl was very beautiful and a virgin guiltless of intercourse with any man. She went down to the spring, filled her jar, and came up again. Abraham's servant hurried to meet her and said, 'Will you give me a little water from your jar?' 'Please drink, sir,' she answered, and at once lowered her jar on to her hand to let him drink. When she had finished giving him a drink, she said, 'I shall draw water for your camels also until they have had enough.' She quickly emptied her jar into the water trough, and then hurrying again to the well she drew water and watered all the camels.

The man was watching quietly to see whether or not the Lord had made his journey successful, and when the camels had finished drinking, he took a gold nose-ring weighing half a shekel, and two bracelets for her wrists weighing ten shekels, also of gold. 'Tell me, please, whose daughter you are,' he said. 'Is there room in your father's house for us to spend the night?' She answered, 'I am the daughter of Bethuel son of Nahor and Milcah; we have plenty of straw and fodder and also room for you to spend the night.' So the man bowed down and prostrated himself before the

Lord and said, 'Blessed be the Lord the God of my master Abraham. His faithfulness to my master has been constant and unfailing, for he has guided me to the house of my master's kinsman.'

The girl ran to her mother's house and told them what had happened. Rebecca had a brother named Laban, and, when he saw the nose-ring, and also the bracelets on his sister's wrists, and heard his sister Rebecca's account of what the man had said to her, he hurried out to the spring. When he got there he found the man still standing by the camels. 'Come in,' he said, 'you whom the Lord has blessed. Why are you staying out here? I have prepared the house and there is a place for the camels.' The man went into the house, while the camels were unloaded and provided with straw and fodder, and water was brought for him and his men to bathe their feet. But when food was set before him, he protested, 'I will not eat until I have delivered my message.' Laban said, 'Let us hear it.'

'I am Abraham's servant,' he answered. 'The Lord has greatly blessed my master, and he has become a wealthy man: the Lord has given him flocks and herds, silver and gold, male and female slaves, camels and donkeys. My master's wife Sarah in her old age bore him a son, to whom he has assigned all that he has. My master made me swear an oath, saying, "You must not take a wife for my son from the women of the Canaanites in whose land I am living; but go to my father's home, to my family, to get a wife for him." I asked, "What if the woman will not come with me?" He answered, "The Lord, in whose presence I have lived, will send his angel with you and make your journey successful."'

Laban and Bethuel replied, 'Since this is from the Lord, we can say nothing for or against it. Here is Rebecca; take her and go. She shall be the wife of your master's son, as the Lord has decreed.' When Abraham's servant heard what they said, he prostrated himself on the ground before the Lord. Then he brought out silver and gold ornaments, and articles of clothing, and gave them to Rebecca, and he gave costly gifts to her brother and her mother. He and his men then ate and drank and spent the night there.

When they rose in the morning, Abraham's servant said, 'Give me leave to go back to my master.' Rebecca's brother and her mother replied, 'Let the girl stay with us for a few days, say ten days, and then she can go.' But he said to them, 'Do not detain me, for it is the Lord who has granted me success. Give me leave to go back to my master.' They said, 'Let us call the girl and see what she says.' They called Rebecca and asked her if she would go with the man, and she answered, 'Yes, I will go.' So they let their sister Rebecca and her maid go with Abraham's servant and his men. They blessed Rebecca and said to her:

'You are our sister, may you be the mother of many children;
may your sons possess the cities of their enemies.'

Rebecca and her companions mounted their camels to follow the man. So the servant took Rebecca and set out.

Isaac meanwhile had moved on as far as Beer-lahai-roi and was living in the Negeb. One evening when he had gone out into the open country hoping to meet them, he looked and saw camels approaching. When Rebecca saw Isaac, she dismounted from her camel, saying to the servant, 'Who is that man walking across the open country towards us?' When the servant answered, 'It is my master,' she took her veil and covered herself. The servant related to Isaac all that had happened. Isaac conducted her into the tent and took her as his wife. So she became his wife, and he loved her and was consoled for the death of his mother.

The Death of Abraham
Abraham had assigned all that he possessed to Isaac; and he had already in his lifetime made gifts to his sons by his concubines and had sent them away eastwards, to a land of the east, out of his son Isaac's way. Abraham had lived for a hundred and seventy-five years when he breathed his last. He died at a great age, a full span of years, and was gathered to his forefathers.

Jacob and Esau
Isaac appealed to the Lord on behalf of his wife because she was childless; the Lord gave heed to his entreaty, and Rebecca conceived. The children pressed on each other in her womb, and she said, 'If all is well, why am I like this?' She went to seek guidance of the Lord, who said to her:

'Two nations are in your womb,
two peoples going their own ways from birth.
One will be stronger than the other;
the elder will be servant to the younger.'

When her time had come, there were indeed twins in her womb.
The first to come out was reddish and covered with hairs like a
cloak, and they named him Esau. Immediately afterwards his
brother was born with his hand grasping Esau's heel, and he was
given the name Jacob. Isaac was sixty years old when they were
born.

As the boys grew up, Esau became a skilful hunter, an outdoor
man, while Jacob lived quietly among the tents. Isaac favoured
Esau because he kept him supplied with game, but Rebecca
favoured Jacob. One day Jacob was preparing broth when Esau
came in from the country, exhausted. He said to Jacob, 'I am
exhausted; give me a helping of that red broth.' This is why he
was called Edom. Jacob retorted, 'Not till you sell me your rights
as the firstborn.' Esau replied, 'Here I am at death's door; what
use is a birthright to me?' Jacob said, 'First give me your oath!' So
he gave him his oath and sold his birthright to Jacob. Then Jacob
gave Esau bread and some lentil broth, and he ate and drank and
went his way.

Jacob Tricks Isaac

When Isaac grew old and his eyes had become so dim that he
could not see, he called for his elder son Esau. 'My son!' he said.
Esau answered, 'Here I am.' Isaac said, 'Listen now: I am old and
I do not know when I may die. Take your hunting gear, your
quiver and bow, and go out into the country and get me some
game. Then make me a savoury dish, the kind I like, and bring it
for me to eat so that I may give you my blessing before I die.'

Now Rebecca had been listening as Isaac talked to his son Esau.
When Esau went off into the country to hunt game for his father,
she said to her son Jacob, 'I have just overheard your father say to
your brother Esau, "Bring me some game and make a savoury
dish for me to eat so that I may bless you in the presence of the
Lord before I die." Listen now to me, my son, and do what I tell
you. Go to the flock and pick me out two fine young kids, and I
shall make them into a savoury dish for your father, the kind he

likes. Then take it in to your father to eat so that he may bless you before he dies.' 'But my brother Esau is a hairy man,' Jacob said to his mother Rebecca, 'and my skin is smooth. Suppose my father touches me; he will know that I am playing a trick on him and I shall bring a curse instead of a blessing on myself.' His mother answered, 'Let any curse for you fall on me, my son. Do as I say; go and fetch me the kids.'

So Jacob went and got them and brought them to his mother, who made them into a savoury dish such as his father liked. Rebecca then took her elder son's clothes, Esau's best clothes which she had by her in the house, and put them on Jacob her younger son. She put the goatskins on his hands and on the smooth nape of his neck. Then she handed to her son Jacob the savoury dish and the bread she had made.

He went in to his father and said, 'Father!' Isaac answered, 'Yes, my son; which are you?' Jacob answered, 'I am Esau, your elder son. I have done as you told me. Come, sit up and eat some of the game I have for you and then give me your blessing.' Isaac said, 'How did you find it so quickly, my son?' Jacob answered, 'Because the Lord your God put it in my way.' Isaac then said to Jacob, 'Come close and let me touch you, my son, to make sure that you are my son Esau.' When Jacob came close to his father, Isaac felt him and said, 'The voice is Jacob's voice, but the hands are the hands of Esau.' He did not recognize him, because his hands were hairy like Esau's, and so he blessed him.

He asked, 'Are you really my son Esau?' and when he answered, 'Yes, I am,' Isaac said, 'Bring me some of the game to eat, my son, so that I may give you my blessing.' Jacob brought it to him, and he ate; he brought him wine also, and he drank it. Then his father said to him, 'Come near, my son, and kiss me.' So he went near and kissed him, and when Isaac smelt the smell of his clothes, he blessed him and said, 'The smell of my son is like the smell of open country blessed by the Lord.

'God give you dew from heaven
and the richness of the earth,
corn and new wine in plenty!
May peoples serve you
and nations bow down to you.
May you be lord over your brothers,

and may your mother's sons bow down to you.
A curse on those who curse you,
but a blessing on those who bless you!'

Isaac finished blessing Jacob, who had scarcely left his father's presence when his brother Esau came in from hunting. He too prepared a savoury dish and brought it to his father. He said, 'Come, father, eat some of the game I have for you, and then give me your blessing.' 'Who are you?' his father Isaac asked him. 'I am Esau, your elder son,' he replied. Then Isaac, greatly agitated, said, 'Then who was it that hunted game and brought it to me? I ate it just before you came in, and I blessed him, and the blessing will stand.' When Esau heard this, he lamented loudly and bitterly. 'Father, bless me too,' he begged. But Isaac said, 'Your brother came full of deceit and took your blessing.' 'He is not called Jacob for nothing,' said Esau. 'This is the second time he has supplanted me. He took away my right as the firstborn, and now he has taken away my blessing. Have you kept back any blessing for me?' Isaac answered, 'I have made him lord over you and set all his brothers under him. I have bestowed upon him grain and new wine for his sustenance. What is there left that I can do for you, my son?' Esau asked, 'Had you then only one blessing, father? Bless me, too, my father.' Esau wept bitterly, and his father Isaac answered:

'Your dwelling will be far from the richness of the earth,
far from the dew of heaven above.
By your sword you will live,
and you will serve your brother.
But the time will come when you grow restive
and break his yoke from your neck.'

Esau harboured a grudge against Jacob because of the blessing which his father had given him, and he said to himself, 'The time of mourning for my father will soon be here; then I am going to kill my brother Jacob.' When Rebecca was told what her elder son Esau was planning, she called Jacob, her younger son, and said to him, 'Your brother Esau is threatening to kill you. Now, my son, listen to me. Be off at once to my brother Laban in Harran, and stay with him for a while until your brother's anger cools. When it has died down and he has forgotten what you did to him, I will send and fetch you back. Why should I lose you both in one day?'

Rebecca said to Isaac, 'I am weary to death of Hittite women! If Jacob marries a Hittite woman like those who live here, my life will not be worth living.' So Isaac called Jacob, and after blessing him, gave him these instructions: 'You are not to marry a Canaanite woman. Go now to the home of Bethuel, your mother's father, in Paddan-aram, and there find a wife, one of the daughters of Laban, your mother's brother. May God Almighty bless you; may he make you fruitful and increase your descendants until they become a community of nations. May he bestow on you and your offspring the blessing given to Abraham, that you may possess the land where you are now living, and which God assigned to Abraham!'

Jacob's Ladder

Jacob set out from Beersheba and journeyed towards Harran. He came to a certain shrine and, because the sun had gone down, he stopped for the night. He took one of the stones there and, using it as a pillow under his head, he lay down to sleep. In a dream he saw a ladder, which rested on the ground with its top reaching to heaven, and angels of God were going up and down on it. The Lord was standing beside him saying, 'I am the Lord, the God of your father Abraham and the God of Isaac. This land on which you are lying I shall give to you and your descendants. They will be countless as the specks of dust on the ground, and you will spread far and wide, to west and east, to north and south. All the families of the earth will wish to be blessed as you and your descendants are blessed. I shall be with you to protect you wherever you go, and I shall bring you back to this land. I shall not leave you until I have done what I have promised you.'

When Jacob woke from his sleep he said, 'Truly the Lord is in this place, and I did not know it.' He was awestruck and said, 'How awesome is this place! This is none other than the house of God; it is the gateway to heaven.' Early in the morning, when Jacob awoke, he took the stone on which his head had rested, and set it up as a sacred pillar, pouring oil over it. He named that place Beth-el; but the earlier name of the town was Luz.

Jacob and Rachel

Jacob, continuing his journey, came to the land of the eastern tribes. There he saw a well in the open country with three flocks of sheep lying beside it, because flocks were watered from that well. Over its mouth was a huge stone, and all the herdsmen used to gather there and roll it off the mouth of the well and water the flocks; then they would replace the stone over the well.

Jacob said to them, 'Where are you from, my friends?' 'We are from Harran,' they replied. He asked them if they knew Laban the grandson of Nahor. They answered, 'Yes, we do.' 'Is he well?' Jacob asked; and they answered, 'Yes, he is well, and there is his daughter Rachel coming with the flock.' Jacob said, 'It is still broad daylight, and not yet time for penning the sheep. Water the flocks and then go and let them graze.' But they replied, 'We cannot, until all the herdsmen have assembled and the stone has been rolled away from the mouth of the well; then we can water our flocks.' While he was talking to them, Rachel arrived with her father's flock, for she was a shepherdess. Immediately Jacob saw Rachel, the daughter of Laban his mother's brother, with Laban's flock, he went forward, rolled the stone off the mouth of the well and watered Laban's sheep. He kissed Rachel, and was moved to tears. When he told her that he was her father's kinsman, Rebecca's son, she ran and told her father. No sooner had Laban heard the news of his sister's son Jacob, than he hurried to meet him, embraced and kissed him, and welcomed him to his home. Jacob told Laban all that had happened, and Laban said, 'Yes, you are my own flesh and blood.'

After Jacob had stayed with him for a whole month, Laban said to him, 'Why should you work for me for nothing simply because you are my kinsman? Tell me what wage you would settle for.' Now Laban had two daughters: the elder was called Leah, and the younger Rachel. Leah was dull-eyed, but Rachel was beautiful in both face and figure, and Jacob had fallen in love with her. He said, 'For your younger daughter Rachel I would work seven years.' Laban replied, 'It is better that I should give her to you than to anyone else; stay with me.'

When Jacob had worked seven years for Rachel, and they seemed like a few days because he loved her, he said to Laban, 'I have served my time. Give me my wife that I may lie with her.' Laban brought all the people of the place together and held a wedding feast. In the evening he took his daughter Leah and brought her to Jacob, and he lay with her. At the same time Laban gave his slave-girl Zilpah to his daughter Leah. But when morning came, there was Leah! Jacob said to Laban, 'What is this you have done to me? It was for Rachel I worked. Why have you played this trick on me?' Laban answered, 'It is against the custom of our country to marry off the younger sister before the elder. Go through with the seven days' feast for the elder, and the younger shall be given you in return for a further seven years' work.' Jacob agreed, and completed the seven days for Leah.

Then Laban gave Jacob his daughter Rachel to be his wife; and to serve Rachel he gave his slave-girl Bilhah. Jacob lay with Rachel also; he loved her rather than Leah, and he worked for Laban for a further seven years. When the Lord saw that Leah was unloved, he granted her a child, but Rachel remained childless. Leah conceived and gave birth to a son; and she called him Reuben, for she said, 'The Lord has seen my humiliation, but now my husband will love me.' Again she conceived and had a son and said, 'The Lord, hearing that I am unloved, has given me this child also'; and she called him Simeon. She conceived again and had a son and said, 'Now that I have borne him three sons my husband will surely be attached to me.' So she called him Levi. Once more she conceived and had a son, and said, 'Now I shall praise the Lord'; therefore she named him Judah. Then for a while she bore no more children.

When Rachel found that she bore Jacob no children, she became jealous of her sister and complained to Jacob, 'Give me sons, or I shall die!' Jacob said angrily to Rachel, 'Can I take the place of God, who has denied you children?' 'Here is my slave-girl Bilhah,' she replied. 'Lie with her, so that she may bear sons to be laid upon my knees, and through her I too may build up a family.' When she gave him her slave-girl Bilhah as a wife, Jacob lay with her, and she conceived and bore him a son.

Then God took thought for Rachel; he heard her prayer and gave her a child. After she conceived and bore a son, she said, 'God has taken away my humiliation.' She named him Joseph, saying, 'May the Lord add another son to me!'

Jacob Escapes from Laban

After Rachel had given birth to Joseph, Jacob said to Laban, 'Send me on my way, for I want to return to my own home and country. Give me my wives and children for whom I have served you, and I shall go; you know what service I have rendered you.'

Laban answered, 'I should like to say this – I have become prosperous and the Lord has blessed me through you. So now tell me what wages I owe you, and I shall give you them.'

'You know how I have served you,' replied Jacob, 'and how your herds have prospered under my care. The few you had when I came have increased beyond measure, and wherever I went the Lord brought you blessings. But is it not time for me to make provision for my family?'

Laban said, 'Then what shall I give you?'

'Nothing at all,' answered Jacob; 'I will tend your flocks and be in charge of them as before, if you will do what I suggest. I shall go through your flocks today and pick out from them every black lamb, and all the brindled and the spotted goats, and they will be my wages. This is a fair offer, and it will be to my own disadvantage later on, when we come to settling my wages: any goat amongst mine that is not spotted or brindled and any lamb that is not black will have been stolen.'

Laban agreed: 'Let it be as you say.' But that same day Laban removed the he-goats that were striped and brindled and all the spotted and brindled she-goats, all that had any white on them, and every ram that was black, and he handed them over to his sons. Then he put a distance of three days' journey between himself and Jacob, while Jacob was tending the rest of Laban's flocks.

So Jacob took fresh rods of poplar, almond, and plane trees, and peeled off strips of bark, exposing the white of the rods. He fixed the peeled rods upright in the troughs at the watering-places where the flocks came to drink, so that they were facing the she-goats that were in heat when they came to drink. They mated beside the rods and gave birth to young that were striped and spotted and brindled. The rams Jacob separated, and let the ewes run only with such of the rams in Laban's flocks as were striped and black; and thus he built up flocks for himself, which he did not add to Laban's sheep. As for the goats, whenever the more vigorous were in heat, he set the rods in front of them at the troughs so that they mated beside the rods. He did not put them there for the weaker goats, and in this way the weaker came to be Laban's and the stronger Jacob's. So Jacob's wealth increased more and more until he possessed great flocks, as well as male and female slaves, camels, and donkeys.

Jacob learnt that Laban's sons were saying, 'Jacob has taken everything that our father had, and all his wealth has come from our father's property.' He noticed also that Laban was not so well disposed to him as he had once been. The Lord said to Jacob, 'Go back to the land of your fathers and to your kindred; I shall be with you.' At once Jacob put his sons and his wives on camels, and he drove off all the cattle and other livestock which he had acquired in Paddan-aram, to go to his father Isaac in Canaan.

When Laban had gone to shear his sheep, Rachel stole the household gods belonging to her father. Jacob hoodwinked Laban the Aramaean and kept his departure secret; he fled with all that he possessed, and soon was over the Euphrates and on the way to the hill-country of Gilead.

Three days later, when Laban heard that Jacob had fled, he took his kinsmen with him and pursued Jacob for seven days until he caught up with him in the hill-country of Gilead. But God came to Laban the Aramaean in a dream by night and said to him, 'Be careful to say nothing to Jacob, not a word.'

When Laban caught up with him, Jacob had pitched his tent in the hill-country of Gilead, and Laban encamped with his kinsmen in the same hill-country. Laban said to Jacob, 'What have you done? You have deceived me and carried off my daughters as though they were captives taken in war. Why did you slip away secretly without telling me? I would have set you on your way with songs and the music of tambourines and harps. You did not even let me kiss my daughters and their children. In this you behaved foolishly. I have it in my power to harm all of you, but last night the God of your father spoke to me; he told me to be careful to say nothing to you, not one word. I expect that really you went away because you were homesick and pining for your father's house; but why did you steal my gods?'

Jacob answered, 'I was afraid; I thought you would take your daughters from me by force. Whoever is found in possession of your gods shall die for it. In the presence of our kinsmen as witnesses, identify anything I have that is yours, and take it back.' Jacob did not know that Rachel had stolen the gods. Laban went into Jacob's tent and Leah's tent and that of the two slave-girls, but he found nothing. After coming from Leah's tent he went into Rachel's. In the meantime Rachel had taken the household gods and put them in the camel-bag and was sitting on them. Laban went through the whole tent but found nothing. Rachel said, 'Do not take it amiss, father, that I cannot rise in your presence: the common lot of woman is upon me.' So for all his searching, Laban did not find the household gods.

Jacob heatedly took Laban to task. 'What have I done wrong?' he exclaimed. 'What is my offence, that you have come after me in hot pursuit and have gone through all my belongings? Have you found a single article belonging to your household? If so, set it here in front of my kinsmen and yours, and let them decide between the two of us. In all the twenty years I have been with you, your ewes and she-goats have never miscarried. I have never eaten rams from your flocks. I have never brought to you the carcass of any animal mangled by wild beasts, but I bore the loss myself. You demanded that I should pay compensation for anything stolen by day or by night. This was the way of it: the heat wore me down by day and the frost by night; I got no sleep. For twenty years I have been in your household. I worked fourteen years for you to win your two daughters and six years for your flocks, and you changed my wages ten times over. If the God of my father, the God of Abraham and the Fear of Isaac, had not been with me, you would now have sent me away empty-handed. But God saw my labour and my hardships, and last night he delivered his verdict.'

Laban answered Jacob, 'The daughters are my daughters, the children are my children, the flocks are my flocks; all you see is mine. But what am I to do now about my daughters and the children they have borne? Come, let us make a pact, you and I, and let there be a witness between us.' So Jacob chose a great stone and set it up as a sacred pillar. Then he told his kinsmen to gather stones, and they took them and built a cairn, and there beside the cairn they ate together.

Laban said to Jacob, 'Here is this cairn, and here the pillar which I have set up between us. Both cairn and pillar are witnesses that I am not to pass beyond this cairn to your side with evil intent, and you must not pass beyond this cairn and this pillar to my side with evil intent. May the God of Abraham and the God of Nahor judge between us.' Jacob swore this oath in the name of the Fear of Isaac, the God of his father. He slaughtered an animal for sacrifice there in the hill-country, and summoned his kinsmen to the feast. They ate together and spent the night there.

Laban rose early in the morning, kissed his daughters and their children, gave them his blessing, and then returned to his home.

As Jacob continued his journey he sent messengers ahead of him to his brother Esau to the district of Seir in Edomite territory, instructing them to say to Esau, 'My lord, your servant Jacob sends this message: I have been living with Laban and have stayed there till now. I have acquired oxen, donkeys, and sheep, as well as male and female slaves, and I am sending to tell you this, my lord, so that I may win your favour.' The messengers returned to Jacob and said, 'We went to your brother Esau and he is already on the way to meet you with four hundred men.'

Jacob Wrestles with God

During the night Jacob rose, and taking his two wives, his two slave-girls, and his eleven sons, he crossed the ford of Jabbok. After he had sent them across the wadi with all that he had, Jacob was left alone, and a man wrestled with him there till daybreak. When the man saw that he could not get the better of Jacob, he struck him in the hollow of his thigh, so that Jacob's hip was dislocated as they wrestled. The man said, 'Let me go, for day is breaking,' but Jacob replied, 'I will not let you go unless you bless me.' The man asked, 'What is your name?' 'Jacob,' he answered. The man said, 'Your name shall no longer be Jacob but Israel, because you have striven with God and with mortals, and have prevailed.' Jacob said, 'Tell me your name, I pray.' He replied, 'Why do you ask my name?' but he gave him his blessing there. Jacob called the place Peniel, 'Because', he said, 'I have seen God face to face yet my life is spared'.

The sun rose as Jacob passed through Penuel, limping because of his hip. That is why to this day the Israelites do not eat the sinew that is on the hollow of the thigh, because the man had struck Jacob on that sinew.

Jacob and Esau Meet Again

Jacob looked up and there was Esau coming with four hundred men. He divided the children between Leah and Rachel and the two slave-girls. He put the slave-girls and their children in front, Leah with her children next, and Rachel and Joseph in the rear. He himself went on ahead of them, bowing low to the ground seven times as he approached his brother. Esau ran to meet him and embraced him; he threw his arms round him and kissed him, and they both wept.

When Esau caught sight of the women and children, he asked, 'Who are these with you?' Jacob replied, 'The children whom God has graciously given to your servant.' The slave-girls came near, each with her children, and they bowed low; then Leah with her children came near and bowed low, and lastly Joseph and Rachel came and bowed low also. Esau said, 'Let us set out, and I shall go at your pace.' But Jacob answered him, 'You must know, my lord, that the children are small; the flocks and herds are suckling their young and I am concerned for them, and if they are overdriven for a single day, my beasts will all die. I beg you, my lord, to go on ahead, and I shall move by easy stages at the pace of the livestock I am driving and the pace of the children, until I come to my lord in Seir.' Esau said, 'Let me detail some of my men to escort you,' but he replied, 'There is no reason why my lord should be so kind.' That day Esau turned back towards Seir, while Jacob set out for Succoth; there he built himself a house and made shelters for his cattle. Therefore he named that place Succoth.

So having journeyed from Paddan-aram, Jacob arrived safely at the town of Shechem in Canaan and pitched his tent to the east of it. The piece of land where he had pitched his tent he bought from the sons of Hamor, Shechem's father, for a hundred sheep. He erected an altar there and called it El-elohey-israel.

The Rape of Dinah

Dinah, the daughter whom Leah had borne to Jacob, went out to visit women of the district, and Shechem, son of Hamor the Hivite, the local prince, saw her. He took her, lay with her, and violated her. But Shechem was deeply attached to Jacob's daughter Dinah; he loved the girl and sought to win her affection. Shechem said to Hamor his father, 'You must get me this girl as my wife.' When Jacob learnt that his daughter Dinah had been dishonoured, his sons were with the herds in the open country, so he held his peace until they came home. Meanwhile Shechem's father Hamor came out to Jacob to talk the matter over with him. When they heard the news Jacob's sons came home from the country; they were distressed and very angry, because in lying with Jacob's daughter Shechem had done what the Israelites hold to be an intolerable outrage. Hamor appealed to them: 'My son Shechem is in love with this girl; I beg you to let him have her as his wife. Let us ally ourselves in marriage; you give us your daughters, and you take ours. If you settle among us, the country is open before you; make your home in it, move about freely, and acquire land of your own.' Shechem said to the girl's father and brothers, 'I am eager to win your favour and I shall give whatever you ask. Fix the bride-price and the gift as high as you like, and I shall give whatever you ask; only, give me the girl in marriage.'

Jacob's sons replied to Shechem and his father Hamor deceitfully, because Shechem had violated their sister Dinah: 'We cannot do this,' they said; 'we cannot give our sister to a man who is uncircumcised, for we look on that as a disgrace. Only on one condition can we give our consent: if you follow our example and have every male among you circumcised, we shall give you our daughters and take yours for ourselves. We will then live among you, and become one people with you. But if you refuse to listen to us and be circumcised, we shall take the girl and go.' Their proposal appeared satisfactory to Hamor and his son Shechem; and the young man, who was held in respect above anyone in his father's house, did not hesitate to do what they had said, because his heart had been captured by Jacob's daughter.

Hamor and Shechem went to the gate of their town and addressed their fellow-townsmen: 'These men are friendly towards us,' they said; 'let them live in our country and move freely in it. The land has room enough for them. Let us marry their daughters and give them ours. But on this condition only will these men agree to live with us as one people: every male among us must be circumcised as they are. Their herds, their livestock, and all their chattels will then be ours. We need only agree to their condition, and then they are free to live with us.' All the able-bodied men agreed with Hamor and his son Shechem, and every able-bodied male among them was circumcised. Then two days later, while they were still in pain, two of Jacob's sons, Simeon and Levi, full brothers to Dinah, after arming themselves with swords, boldly entered the town and killed every male. They cut down Hamor and his son Shechem and took Dinah from Shechem's house and went off. Jacob's other sons came in over the dead bodies and plundered the town which had brought dishonour on their sister. They seized flocks, cattle, donkeys, whatever was inside the town and outside in the open country; they carried off all the wealth, the women, and the children, and looted everything in the houses.

Jacob said to Simeon and Levi, 'You have brought trouble on me; you have brought my name into bad odour among the people of the country, the Canaanites and the Perizzites. My numbers are few; if they combine against me and attack, I shall be destroyed, I and my household with me.' They answered, 'Is our sister to be treated as a common whore?'

God Renews his Covenant

God said to Jacob, 'Go up now to Bethel and, when you have settled there, erect an altar to the God who appeared to you when you fled from your brother Esau.' Jacob said to his household and to all who were with him, 'Get rid of the foreign gods which you have; then purify yourselves, and put on fresh clothes. We are to set off for Bethel, so that I can erect an altar there to the God who answered me when I was in distress; he has been with me wherever I have gone.' They handed over to Jacob all the foreign gods in their possession and the ear-rings they were wearing, and he buried them under the terebinth tree near Shechem.

God appeared again to Jacob after his return from Paddan-aram and blessed him. God said: 'Jacob is now your name, but it is going to be Jacob no longer: your name is to be Israel.'

So Jacob was called Israel. God said to him:

'I am God Almighty.
Be fruitful and increase:
a nation, a host of nations will come from you;
kings also will descend from you.
The land I gave to Abraham and Isaac I give to you;
and to your descendants also I shall give this land.'

When God left him, Jacob raised a sacred pillar of stone in the place where God had spoken with him, and he offered a drink-offering on it and poured oil over it. Jacob called the place where God had spoken with him Bethel.

They moved from Bethel, and when there was still some distance to go to Ephrathah, Rachel went into labour and her pains were severe. While they were on her, the midwife said, 'Do not be afraid, for this is another son for you.' Then with her last breath, as she was dying, she named him Ben-oni, but his father called him Benjamin. So Rachel died and was buried by the side of the road to Ephrathah, that is Bethlehem. Over her grave Jacob set up a sacred pillar; and to this day it is known as the Pillar of Rachel's Grave. Then continuing his journey Israel pitched his tent on the other side of Migdal-eder.

Jacob came to his father Isaac at Mamre near Kiriath-arba, that is Hebron, where Abraham and Isaac had stayed. Isaac was a hundred and eighty years old when he breathed his last. He died and was gathered to his father's kin at this very great age, and his sons Esau and Jacob buried him.

3 | THE STORY OF JOSEPH

Joseph's Dreams

Jacob settled in Canaan, the country in which his father had made his home, and this is an account of Jacob's descendants.

When Joseph was a youth of seventeen, he used to accompany his brothers, the sons of Bilhah and Zilpah, his father's wives, when they were in charge of the flock, and he told tales about them to their father. Because Joseph was a child of his old age, Israel loved him best of all his sons, and he made him a long robe with sleeves. When his brothers saw that their father loved him best, it aroused their hatred and they had nothing but harsh words for him.

Joseph had a dream, and when he told it to his brothers, their hatred of him became still greater. He said to them, 'Listen to this dream I had. We were out in the field binding sheaves, when all at once my sheaf rose and stood upright, and your sheaves gathered round and bowed in homage before my sheaf.' His brothers retorted, 'Do you think that you will indeed be king over us and rule us?' and they hated him still more because of his dreams and what he had said. Then he had another dream, which he related to his father and his brothers. 'Listen!' he said. 'I have had another dream, and in it the sun, the moon, and eleven stars were bowing down to me.' When he told his father and his brothers, his father took him to task: 'What do you mean by this dream of yours?' he asked. 'Are we to come and bow to the ground before you, I and your mother and your brothers?' His brothers were jealous of him, but his father did not forget the incident.

Joseph's brothers had gone to herd their father's flocks at Shechem. Israel said to him, 'Your brothers are herding the flocks at Shechem; I am going to send you to them.' Joseph answered, 'I am ready to go.' Israel told him to go and see if all was well with his brothers and the flocks, and to bring back word to him. So Joseph was sent off from the vale of Hebron and came to

Shechem, where a man met him wandering in the open country and asked him what he was looking for. 'I am looking for my brothers,' he replied. 'Can you tell me where they are herding the flocks?' The man said, 'They have moved from here; I heard them speak of going to Dothan.' Joseph went after his brothers and came up with them at Dothan. They saw him in the distance, and before he reached them, they plotted to kill him. 'Here comes that dreamer,' they said to one another. 'Now is our chance; let us kill him and throw him into one of these cisterns; we can say that a wild beast has devoured him. Then we shall see what becomes of his dreams.' When Reuben heard, he came to his rescue, urging them not to take his life. 'Let us have no bloodshed,' he said. 'Throw him into this cistern in the wilderness, but do him no injury.' Reuben meant to rescue him from their clutches in order to restore him to his father. When Joseph reached his brothers, they stripped him of the long robe with sleeves which he was wearing, picked him up, and threw him into the cistern. It was empty, with no water in it.

They had sat down to eat when, looking up, they saw an Ishmaelite caravan coming from Gilead on the way down to Egypt, with camels carrying gum tragacanth and balm and myrrh. Judah said to his brothers, 'What do we gain by killing our brother and concealing his death? Why not sell him to these Ishmaelites? Let us do him no harm, for after all, he is our brother, our own flesh and blood'; his brothers agreed. Meanwhile some passing Midianite merchants drew Joseph up out of the cistern and sold him for twenty pieces of silver to the Ishmaelites; they brought Joseph to Egypt. When Reuben came back to the cistern, he found Joseph had gone. He tore his clothes and going to his brothers he said, 'The boy is not there. Whatever shall I do?'

Joseph's brothers took the long robe with sleeves, and dipped it in the blood of a goat which they had killed. After tearing the robe, they brought it to their father and said, 'Look what we have found. Do you recognize it? Is this your son's robe or not?' Jacob recognized it. 'It is my son's,' he said. 'A wild beast has devoured him. Joseph has been torn to pieces.' Jacob tore his clothes; he put on sackcloth and for many days he mourned his son. Though his sons and daughters all tried to comfort him, he refused to be comforted. He said, 'No, I shall go to Sheol mourning for my son.' Thus Joseph's father wept for him. The

Midianites meanwhile had sold Joseph in Egypt to Potiphar, one of Pharaoh's court officials, the captain of the guard.

Tamar Tricks Judah

About that time Judah parted from his brothers, and heading south he pitched his tent in company with an Adullamite named Hirah. There he saw Bathshua the daughter of a Canaanite and married her. He lay with her, and she conceived and bore a son, whom she called Er. She conceived again and bore a son, whom she called Onan. Once more she conceived and bore a son whom she called Shelah, and she was at Kezib when she bore him. Judah found a wife for his eldest son Er; her name was Tamar. But Judah's eldest son Er was wicked in the Lord's sight, and the Lord took away his life. Then Judah told Onan to sleep with his brother's wife, to do his duty as the husband's brother and raise up offspring for his brother. But Onan knew that the offspring would not count as his; so whenever he lay with his brother's wife, he spilled his seed on the ground so as not to raise up offspring for his brother. What he did was wicked in the Lord's sight, and the Lord took away his life also. Judah said to his daughter-in-law Tamar, 'Remain as a widow in your father's house until my son Shelah grows up'; for he was afraid that Shelah too might die like his brothers. So Tamar went and stayed in her father's house.

Time passed, and Judah's wife Bathshua died. When he had finished mourning, he and his friend Hirah the Adullamite went up to Timnath at sheep-shearing. When Tamar was told that her father-in-law was on his way to shear his sheep at Timnath, she took off her widow's clothes, covered her face with a veil, and then sat where the road forks on the way to Timnath. She did this because she saw that although Shelah was now grown up she had not been given to him as a wife. When Judah saw her he thought she was a prostitute, for she had veiled her face. He turned to her where she sat by the roadside and said, 'Let me lie with you,' not realizing she was his daughter-in-law. She said, 'What will you give to lie with me?' He answered, 'I shall send you a young goat from my flock.' She said, 'I agree, if you will give me a pledge until you send it.' He asked what pledge he should give her, and she replied, 'Your seal and its cord, and the staff which you are holding.' He handed them over to her and lay with her, and she became pregnant. She then rose and went home, where she took off her veil and put on her widow's clothes again.

Judah sent the goat by his friend the Adullamite in order to recover the pledge from the woman, but he could not find her. When he enquired of the people of that place, 'Where is that temple-prostitute, the one who was sitting where the road forks?' they answered, 'There has been no temple-prostitute here.' So he went back to Judah and reported that he had failed to find her and that the men of the place had said there was no such prostitute there. Judah said, 'Let her keep the pledge, or we shall be a laughing-stock. After all, I did send the kid, even though you could not find her.'

About three months later Judah was told that his daughter-in-law Tamar had played the prostitute and got herself pregnant. 'Bring her out,' ordered Judah, 'so that she may be burnt.' But as she was being brought out, she sent word to her father-in-law. 'The father of my child is the man to whom these things belong,' she said. 'See if you recognize whose they are, this seal, the pattern of the cord, and the staff.' Judah identified them and said, 'She is more in the right than I am, because I did not give her to my son Shelah.' He did not have intercourse with her again.

When her time was come, she was found to have twins in her womb, and while she was in labour one of them put out a hand. The midwife took a scarlet thread and fastened it round the wrist, saying, 'This one appeared first.' No sooner had he drawn back his hand, than his brother came out and the midwife said, 'What! You have broken out first!' So he was named Perez. Soon afterwards his brother was born with the scarlet thread on his wrist, and he was named Zerah.

Potiphar's Wife

When Joseph was taken down to Egypt by the Ishmaelites, he was bought from them by an Egyptian, Potiphar, one of Pharaoh's court officials, the captain of the guard. Joseph prospered, for the Lord was with him. He lived in the house of his Egyptian master, who saw that the Lord was with him and was giving him success in all that he undertook. Thus Joseph won his master's favour, and became his attendant. Indeed, his master put him in charge of his household, and entrusted him with everything he had. From the time that he put Joseph in charge of his household and all his property, the Lord blessed the household through Joseph; the Lord's blessing was on all that was his in house and field. Potiphar left it all in Joseph's care, and concerned himself with nothing but the food he ate.

Now Joseph was handsome in both face and figure, and after a time his master's wife became infatuated with him. 'Come, make love to me,' she said. But Joseph refused. 'Think of my master,' he said; 'he leaves the management of his whole house to me; he has trusted me with all he has. I am as important in this house as he is, and he has withheld nothing from me except you, because you are his wife. How can I do such a wicked thing? It is a sin against God.' Though she kept on at Joseph day after day, he refused to lie with her or be in her company.

One day when he came into the house to see to his duties, and none of the household servants was there indoors, she caught him by his loincloth, saying, 'Come, make love to me,' but he left the loincloth in her hand and ran from the house. When she saw that he had left his loincloth and run out of the house, she called to her servants, 'Look at this! My husband has brought in a Hebrew to bring insult on us. He came in here to rape me, but I gave a loud scream. When he heard me scream and call for help, he ran out, leaving his loincloth behind.' She kept it by her until his master came home, and then she repeated her tale: 'That Hebrew slave you brought in came to my room to make me an object of insult. But when I screamed for help, he ran out of the house, leaving his loincloth behind.'

Joseph's master was furious when he heard his wife's account of what his slave had done to her. He had Joseph seized and thrown into the guardhouse, where the king's prisoners were kept; and there he was confined. But the Lord was with Joseph and kept faith with him, so that he won the favour of the governor of the guardhouse. Joseph was put in charge of the prisoners, and he directed all their work. The governor ceased to concern himself with anything entrusted to Joseph, because the Lord was with him and gave him success in all that he did.

Pharaoh's Dreams

Some time after these events it happened that the king's cup-bearer and the royal baker gave offence to their lord, the king of Egypt. Pharaoh was displeased with his two officials, his chief cupbearer and chief baker, and put them in custody in the house of the captain of the guard, in the guardhouse where Joseph was imprisoned. The captain appointed Joseph as their attendant, and he waited on them.

They had been in prison in the guardhouse for some time, when one night the king's cupbearer and his baker both had dreams, each with a meaning of its own. Coming to them in the morning, Joseph saw that they looked dispirited, and asked these officials in custody with him in his master's house, why they were so downcast that day. They replied, 'We have each had a dream, but there is no one to interpret them.' Joseph said to them, 'All interpretation belongs to God. Why not tell me your dreams?' So the chief cupbearer told Joseph his dream: 'In my dream', he said, 'there was a vine in front of me. On the vine there were three branches, and as soon as it budded, it blossomed and its clusters ripened into grapes. I plucked the grapes and pressed them into Pharaoh's cup which I was holding, and then put the cup into Pharaoh's hand.' Joseph said to him, 'This is the interpretation. The three branches are three days: within three days Pharaoh will raise your head and restore you to your post; then you will put the cup into Pharaoh's hand as you used to do when you were his cupbearer. When things go well with you, remember me and do me the kindness of bringing my case to Pharaoh's notice; help me to get out of this prison. I was carried off by force from the land of the Hebrews, and here I have done nothing to deserve being put into this dungeon.'

When the chief baker saw that the interpretation given by Joseph had been favourable, he said to him, 'I too had a dream, and in my dream there were three baskets of white bread on my head. In the top basket there was every kind of food such as a baker might prepare for Pharaoh, but the birds were eating out of the top basket on my head.' Joseph answered, 'This is the interpretation. The three baskets are three days: within three days Pharaoh will raise your head off your shoulders and hang you on a tree, and the birds of the air will devour the flesh off your bones.'

The third day was Pharaoh's birthday and he gave a banquet for all his officials. He had the chief cupbearer and the chief baker brought up where they were all assembled. The cupbearer was restored to his position, and he put the cup into Pharaoh's hand;

but the baker was hanged. All went as Joseph had said in interpreting the dreams for them. The cupbearer, however, did not bear Joseph in mind; he forgot him.

Two years later Pharaoh had a dream: he was standing by the Nile, when there came up from the river seven cows, sleek and fat, and they grazed among the reeds. Presently seven other cows, gaunt and lean, came up from the river, and stood beside the cows on the river bank. The cows that were gaunt and lean devoured the seven cows that were sleek and fat. Then Pharaoh woke up.

He fell asleep again and had a second dream: he saw seven ears of grain, full and ripe, growing on a single stalk. Springing up after them were seven other ears, thin and shrivelled by the east wind. The thin ears swallowed up the seven ears that were full and plump. Then Pharaoh woke up and found it was a dream.

In the morning Pharaoh's mind was so troubled that he summoned all the dream-interpreters and wise men of Egypt, and told them his dreams; but there was no one who could interpret them for him. Then Pharaoh's chief cupbearer spoke up. 'Now I must mention my offences,' he said: 'Pharaoh was angry with his servants, and imprisoned me and the chief baker in the house of the captain of the guard. One night we both had dreams, each requiring its own interpretation. We had with us there a young Hebrew, a slave of the captain of the guard, and when we told him our dreams he interpreted them for us, giving each dream its own interpretation. Things turned out exactly as the dreams had been interpreted to us: I was restored to my post, the other was hanged.'

Pharaoh thereupon sent for Joseph, and they hurriedly brought him out of the dungeon. After he had shaved and changed his clothes, he came in before Pharaoh, who said to him, 'I have had a dream which no one can interpret. I have heard that you can interpret any dream you hear.' Joseph answered, 'Not I, but God, can give an answer which will reassure Pharaoh.' Then Pharaoh said to him: 'In my dream I was standing on the bank of the Nile, when there came up from the river seven cows, fat and sleek, and they grazed among the reeds. After them seven other cows came up that were in poor condition, very gaunt and lean; in all Egypt I have never seen such gaunt creatures.' These lean, gaunt cows devoured the first cows, the seven fat ones. They

were swallowed up, but no one could have told they were in the
bellies of the others, which looked just as gaunt as before. Then I
woke up. In another dream I saw seven ears of grain, full and
ripe, growing on a single stalk. Springing up after them were
seven other ears, blighted, thin, and shrivelled by the east wind.
The thin ears swallowed up the seven ripe ears. When I spoke to
the dream-interpreters, no one could tell me the meaning.'

Joseph said to Pharaoh, 'Pharaoh's dreams are both the same;
God has told Pharaoh what he is about to do. The seven good
cows are seven years, and the seven good ears of grain are seven
years – it is all one dream. The seven lean and gaunt cows that
came up after them are seven years, and so also are the seven
empty ears of grain blighted by the east wind; there are going to
be seven years of famine. It is as I have told Pharaoh: God has let
Pharaoh see what he is about to do. There are to be seven years of
bumper harvests throughout Egypt. After them will come seven
years of famine; so that the great harvests in Egypt will all be
forgotten, and famine will ruin the country. The good years will
leave no trace in the land because of the famine that follows, for it
will be very severe. That Pharaoh has dreamed this twice means
God is firmly resolved on this plan, and very soon he will put it
into effect.

'Let Pharaoh now look for a man of vision and wisdom and put
him in charge of the country. Pharaoh should take steps to
appoint commissioners over the land to take one fifth of the produce of Egypt during the seven years of plenty. They should
collect all food produced in the good years that are coming and
put the grain under Pharaoh's control as a store of food to be kept
in the towns. This food will be a reserve for the country against
the seven years of famine which will come on Egypt, and so the
country will not be devastated by the famine.'

The plan commended itself both to Pharaoh and to all his
officials, and Pharaoh asked them, 'Could we find another man
like this, one so endowed with the spirit of God?' To Joseph he
said, 'Since God has made all this known to you, no one has your
vision and wisdom. You shall be in charge of my household, and
all my people will respect your every word. Only in regard to the
throne shall I rank higher than you.' Pharaoh went on, 'I hereby
give you authority over the whole land of Egypt.' He took off his
signet ring and put it on Joseph's finger; he had him dressed in

robes of fine linen, and hung a gold chain round his neck. He mounted him in his viceroy's chariot and men cried 'Make way!' before him. Thus Pharaoh made him ruler over all Egypt and said to him, 'I am the Pharaoh, yet without your consent no one will lift hand or foot throughout Egypt.' Pharaoh named him Zaphenath-paneah, and he gave him as his wife Asenath daughter of Potiphera priest of On. Joseph's authority extended over the whole of Egypt.

Joseph was thirty years old at the time he entered the service of Pharaoh king of Egypt. When he left the royal presence, he made a tour of inspection through the land. During the seven years of plenty when there were abundant harvests, Joseph gathered all the food produced in Egypt then and stored it in the towns, putting in each the food from the surrounding country. He stored the grain in huge quantities; it was like the sand of the sea, so much that he stopped measuring: it was beyond all measure.

Before the years of famine came, two sons were born to Joseph by Asenath daughter of Potiphera priest of On. He named the elder Manasseh, 'for', he said, 'God has made me forget all my troubles and my father's family'. He named the second Ephraim, 'for', he said, 'God has made me fruitful in the land of my hardships'. When the seven years of plenty in Egypt came to an end, the seven years of famine began, as Joseph had predicted. There was famine in every country, but there was food throughout Egypt. When the famine came to be felt through all Egypt, the people appealed to Pharaoh for food and he ordered them to go to Joseph and do whatever he told them. When the whole land was in the grip of famine, Joseph opened all the granaries and sold grain to the Egyptians, for the famine was severe. The whole world came to Egypt to buy grain from Joseph, so severe was the famine everywhere.

Joseph's Brothers in Egypt

When Jacob learnt that there was grain in Egypt, he said to his sons, 'Why do you stand staring at each other? I hear there is grain in Egypt. Go down there, and buy some for us to keep us alive and save us from starving to death.' So ten of Joseph's brothers went down to buy grain from Egypt, but Jacob did not let Joseph's brother Benjamin go with them, for fear that he might come to harm.

Thus the sons of Israel went with everyone else to buy grain because of the famine in Canaan. Now Joseph was governor of the land, and it was he who sold the grain to all its people. Joseph's brothers came and bowed to the ground before him, and when he saw his brothers he recognized them but, pretending not to know them, he greeted them harshly. 'Where do you come from?' he demanded. 'From Canaan to buy food,' they answered. Although Joseph had recognized his brothers, they did not recognize him. He remembered the dreams he had had about them and said, 'You are spies; you have come to spy out the weak points in our defences.' 'No, my lord,' they answered; 'your servants have come to buy food. We are all sons of one man. We are honest men; your servants are not spies.' 'No,' he maintained, 'it is to spy out our weaknesses that you have come.' They said, 'There were twelve of us, my lord, all brothers, sons of one man back in Canaan; the youngest is still with our father, and one is lost.' But Joseph insisted, 'As I have already said to you: you are spies. This is how you will be put to the test: unless your youngest brother comes here, I swear by the life of Pharaoh you shall not leave this place. Send one of your number to fetch your brother; the rest of you will remain in prison. Thus your story will be tested to see whether you are telling the truth. If not, then by the life of Pharaoh you must be spies.' With that he kept them in prison for three days.

On the third day Joseph said to them, 'Do what I say and your lives will be spared, for I am a godfearing man: if you are honest men, only one of you brothers shall be kept in prison, while the rest of you may go and take grain for your starving households; but you must bring your youngest brother to me. In this way your words will be proved true, and you will not die.'

They consented, and among themselves they said, 'No doubt we are being punished because of our brother. We saw his distress when he pleaded with us and we refused to listen. That is why this distress has come on us.' Reuben said, 'Did I not warn you not to do wrong to the boy? But you would not listen, and now his blood is on our heads, and we must pay.' They did not know that Joseph understood, since he had used an interpreter. Joseph turned away from them and wept. Then he went back to speak to them, and took Simeon from among them and had him bound before their eyes. He gave orders to fill their bags with grain, to put each man's silver back into his sack again, and to give them provisions for the journey. After this had been done, they loaded their grain on their donkeys and set off. When they stopped for the night, one of them opened his sack to give feed to his donkey, and there at the top was the silver. He said to his brothers, 'My silver has been returned; here it is in my pack.' Bewildered and trembling, they asked one another, 'What is this that God has done to us?'

When they came to their father Jacob in Canaan, they gave him an account of all that had happened to them. They said: 'The man who is lord of the country spoke harshly to us and made out that we were spies. But we said to him, "We are honest men, we are not spies. There were twelve of us, all brothers, sons of the same father. One has disappeared, and the youngest is with our father in Canaan." Then the man, the lord of the country, said to us, "This is how I shall discover if you are honest men: leave one of your brothers with me, take food for your starving households and go; bring your youngest brother to me, and I shall know that you are honest men and not spies. Then I shall restore your brother to you, and you can move around the country freely."' But on emptying their sacks, each of them found his silver inside, and when they and their father saw the bundles of silver, they were afraid. Their father Jacob said to them, 'You have robbed me of my children. Joseph is lost; Simeon is lost; and now you would take Benjamin. Everything is against me.' Reuben said to his father, 'You may put both my sons to death if I do not bring him back to you. Entrust him to me, and I shall bring him back.' But Jacob said, 'My son must not go with you, for his brother is dead and he alone is left. Should he come to any harm on the journey, you will bring down my grey hairs in sorrow to the grave.'

The famine was still severe in the land. When the grain they had brought from Egypt was all used up, their father said to them, 'Go again and buy some more grain for us to eat.' Judah replied, 'But the man warned us that we must not go into his presence unless our brother was with us. If you let our brother go with us, we will go down and buy you food. But if you will not let him, we cannot go, for the man declared, "You shall not come into my presence unless your brother is with you."' Israel said, 'Why have you treated me so badly by telling the man that you had another brother?' They answered, 'The man questioned us closely about ourselves and our family: "Is your father still alive?" he asked, "Have you a brother?" and we answered his questions. How were we to know he would tell us to bring our brother down?' Judah said to Israel his father, 'Send the boy with me; then we can start at once, and save everyone's life, ours, yours, and those of our children. I shall go surety for him, and you may hold me responsible. If I do not bring him back and restore him to you, you can blame me for it all my life. If we had not wasted all this time, we could have made the journey twice by now.'

Their father Israel said to them, 'If it must be so, then do this: in your baggage take, as a gift for the man, some of the produce for which our country is famous: a little balm and honey, with gum tragacanth, myrrh, pistachio nuts, and almonds. Take double the amount of silver with you and give back what was returned to you in your packs; perhaps there was some mistake. Take your brother with you and go straight back to the man. May God Almighty make him kindly disposed to you, and may he send back the one whom you left behind, and Benjamin too. As for me, if I am bereaved, I am bereaved.' So they took the gift and double the amount of silver, and accompanied by Benjamin they started at once for Egypt, where they presented themselves to Joseph.

When Joseph saw Benjamin with them, he said to his steward, 'Bring these men indoors; then kill a beast and prepare a meal, for they are to eat with me at midday.' He brought the men into Joseph's house as he had been ordered. They were afraid because they had been brought there; they thought, 'We have been brought in here because of that affair of the silver which was replaced in our packs the first time. He means to make some charge against us, to inflict punishment on us, seize our donkeys, and make us his slaves.' So they approached Joseph's steward and spoke to him at the door of the house. 'Please listen, my lord,' they said. 'After our first visit to buy food, when we reached the place where we were to spend the night, we opened our packs and each of us found his silver, the full amount of it, at the top of his pack. We have brought it back with us, and we have more silver to buy food. We do not know who put the silver in our packs.' He answered, 'Calm yourselves; do not be afraid. It must have been your God, the God of your father, who hid treasure for you in your packs. I did receive the silver.' Then he brought Simeon out to them.

The steward conducted them into Joseph's house and gave them water to bathe their feet, and provided feed for their donkeys. They had their gifts ready against Joseph's arrival at midday, for they had heard that they were to eat there. When he came into the house, they presented him with the gifts which they had brought, bowing to the ground before him. He asked them how they were and said, 'Is your father well, the old man of whom you spoke? Is he still alive?' 'Yes, my lord, our father is still alive and well,' they answered, bowing low in obeisance. When Joseph looked around he saw his own mother's son, his brother Benjamin, and asked, 'Is this your youngest brother, of whom you told me?' and to Benjamin he said, 'May God be gracious to you, my son!' Joseph, suddenly overcome by his feelings for his brother, was almost in tears, and he went into the inner room and wept. Then, having bathed his face, he came out and, with his feelings now under control, he ordered the meal to be served. He was served by himself, and the brothers by themselves; the Egyptians who were at the meal were also served separately, for to Egyptians it is abhorrent to eat with Hebrews. When at his direction the brothers were seated, the eldest first and so on down to the youngest, they looked at one another in astonishment. Joseph sent them each a portion from what was before him, but Benjamin's portion was five times larger than any of the others. So they feasted and drank with him.

Joseph gave the steward these instructions: 'Fill the men's packs with food, as much as they can carry, and put each man's silver at the top of his pack. And put my goblet, the silver one, at the top of the youngest brother's pack along with the silver for the grain.' He did as Joseph had told him. At first light the brothers were allowed to take their donkeys and set off; but before they had gone very far from the city, Joseph said to his steward, 'Go after those men at once, and when you catch up with them, say, "Why have you repaid good with evil? Why have you stolen the silver goblet? It is the one my lord drinks from, and which he uses for divination. This is a wicked thing you have done."'

When the steward overtook them, he reported his master's words. But they replied, 'My lord, how can you say such things? Heaven forbid that we should do such a thing! Look! The silver we found at the top of our packs we brought back to you from Canaan. Why, then, should we steal silver or gold from your master's house? If any one of us is found with the goblet, he shall die; and, what is more, my lord, the rest of us shall become your slaves.' He said, 'Very well; I accept what you say. Only the one in whose possession it is found will become my slave; the rest will go free.' Each quickly lowered his pack to the ground and opened it, and when the steward searched, beginning with the eldest and finishing with the youngest, the goblet was found in Benjamin's pack.

At this they tore their clothes; then one and all they loaded their donkeys and returned to the city.

Joseph is Reunited with his Brothers

Joseph was still in the house when Judah and his brothers arrived, and they threw themselves on the ground before him. Joseph said, 'What is this you have done? You might have known that a man such as I am uses divination.' Judah said, 'What can we say, my lord? What can we plead, or how can we clear ourselves? God has uncovered our crime. Here we are, my lord, ready to be made your slaves, we ourselves as well as the one who was found with the goblet.' 'Heaven forbid that I should do such a thing!' answered Joseph. 'Only the one who was found with the goblet shall become my slave; the rest of you can go home to your father safe and sound.'

Then Judah went up to him and said, 'Please listen, my lord, and let your servant speak a word, I beg. Do not be angry with me, for you are as great as Pharaoh himself. My lord, you asked us whether we had a father or a brother. We answered, "We have an aged father, and he has a young son born in his old age; this boy's full brother is dead, and since he alone is left of his mother's children, his father loves him." You said to us, your servants, "Bring him down to me so that I may set eyes on him." We told you, my lord, that the boy could not leave his father; his father would die if he left him. But you said, "Unless your youngest brother comes down with you, you shall not enter my presence again." We went back to your servant my father, and reported to him what your lordship had said, so when our father told us to go again and buy food, we answered, "We cannot go down; for without our youngest brother we cannot enter the man's presence; but if our brother is with us, we will go." Then your servant my father said to us, "You know that my wife bore me two sons. One left me, and I said, 'He must have been torn to pieces.' I have not seen him since. If you take this one from me as well, and he comes to any harm, then you will bring down my grey hairs in misery to the grave." Now, my lord, if I return to my father without the boy – and remember, his life is bound up with the boy's – what will happen is this: he will see that the boy is not with us and he will die, and your servants will have brought down our father's grey hairs in sorrow to the grave. Indeed, my lord, it was I who went surety for the boy to my father. I said, "If I do not bring him back to you, then you can blame me for it all my life." Now, my lord, let me remain in place of the boy as my lord's slave, and let him go with his brothers. How can I return to my father without the boy? I could not bear to see the misery which my father would suffer.'

Joseph was no longer able to control his feelings in front of all his attendants, and he called, 'Let everyone leave my presence!' There was nobody present when Joseph made himself known to his brothers, but he wept so loudly that the Egyptians heard him, and news of it got to Pharaoh's household. Joseph said to his brothers, 'I am Joseph! Can my father be still alive?' They were so dumbfounded at finding themselves face to face with Joseph that they could not answer. Joseph said to them, 'Come closer to me,' and when they did so, he said, 'I am your brother Joseph, whom you sold into Egypt. Now do not be distressed or blame yourselves for selling me into slavery here; it was to save lives that God sent me ahead of you. For there have now been two years of famine in the land, and there will be another five years with neither ploughing nor harvest. God sent me on ahead of you to ensure that you will have descendants on earth, and to preserve for you a host of survivors. It is clear that it was not you who sent me here, but God, and he has made me Pharaoh's chief counsellor, lord over his whole household and ruler of all Egypt. Hurry back to my father and give him this message from his son Joseph: "God has made me lord of all Egypt. Come down to me without delay. You will live in the land of Goshen and be near me, you, your children and grandchildren, your flocks and herds, and all that you have. I shall provide for you there and see that you and your household and all that you have are not reduced to want; for there are still five years of famine to come." You can see for yourselves, and so can my brother Benjamin, that it is really Joseph himself who is speaking to you. Tell my father of all the honour which I enjoy in Egypt, tell him all you have seen, and bring him down here with all speed.' He threw his arms round his brother Benjamin and wept, and Benjamin too embraced him weeping. He then kissed each of his brothers and wept over them; after that his brothers were able to talk with him.

When the report reached the royal palace that Joseph's brothers had come, Pharaoh and his officials were pleased. Pharaoh told Joseph to say to his brothers: 'This is what you must do. Load your beasts and go straight back to Canaan. Fetch your father and your households and come to me. I shall give you the best region there is in Egypt, and you will enjoy the fat of the land.' He was also to tell them: 'Take wagons from Egypt for your dependants and your wives and fetch your father back here. Have no regrets at leaving your possessions, for all the best there is in the whole of Egypt is yours.'

Israel's sons followed these instructions, and Joseph supplied them with wagons, as Pharaoh had ordered, and provisions for the journey. To each of them he gave new clothes, but to Benjamin he gave three hundred pieces of silver and five sets of clothes. Moreover he sent his father ten donkeys carrying the finest products of Egypt, and ten she-donkeys laden with grain, bread, and other provisions for the journey. He sent his brothers on their way, warning them not to quarrel among themselves on the road. They set off, and went up from Egypt to their father Jacob in Canaan. When they told him that Joseph was still alive and was ruler of the whole of Egypt, he was stunned at the news and did not believe them. However when they reported to him all that Joseph had said to them, and when he saw the wagons which Joseph had provided to fetch him, his spirit revived. Israel said, 'It is enough! Joseph my son is still alive; I shall go and see him before I die.'

The Israelites Settle in Egypt

Israel set out with all that he had and came to Beersheba, where he offered sacrifices to the God of his father Isaac. God called to Israel in a vision by night, 'Jacob! Jacob!' and he answered, 'I am here.' God said, 'I am God, the God of your father. Do not be afraid to go down to Egypt, for there I shall make you a great nation. I shall go down to Egypt with you, and I myself shall bring you back again without fail; and Joseph's will be the hands that close your eyes.' So Jacob set out from Beersheba. Israel's sons conveyed their father Jacob along with their wives and children in the wagons which Pharaoh had sent to bring him.

Jacob sent Judah ahead to Joseph to advise him that he was on his way to Goshen. They entered Goshen, and Joseph had his chariot yoked to go up there to meet Israel his father. When they met, Joseph threw his arms round him and wept on his shoulder for a long time. Israel said to Joseph, 'I have seen for myself that you are still alive. Now I am ready to die.'

Joseph came and reported to Pharaoh, 'My father and my brothers have arrived from Canaan, with their flocks and herds and everything they possess, and they are now in Goshen.' He had chosen five of his brothers, and he brought them into Pharaoh's presence. When he asked them what their occupation was, they answered, 'We are shepherds like our fathers before us, and we have come to stay in this country, because owing to the severe famine in Canaan there is no pasture there for our flocks. We ask your majesty's leave to settle now in Goshen.' Pharaoh said to Joseph, 'As to your father and your brothers who have come to you, the land of Egypt is at your disposal; settle them in the best part of it. Let them live in Goshen, and if you know of any among them with the skill, make them chief herdsmen in charge of my cattle.'

Then Joseph brought his father in and presented him to Pharaoh. Jacob blessed Pharaoh, who asked him his age, and he answered, 'The years of my life on earth are one hundred and thirty; few and hard have they been – fewer than the years my fathers lived.' Jacob then blessed Pharaoh and withdrew from his presence.

Some time later Joseph was informed that his father was ill, so he took his two sons, Manasseh and Ephraim, with him and came to Jacob. When Jacob heard that his son Joseph had come to him, he gathered his strength and sat up in bed. Jacob said to Joseph, 'Who are these?' 'They are my sons', replied Joseph, 'whom God has given me here.' Israel said, 'Then bring them to me, that I may bless them.' Now Israel's eyes were dim with age, and he could hardly see. Joseph brought the boys close to his father, and he kissed them and embraced them. He said to Joseph, 'I had not expected to see your face again, and now God has let me see your sons as well.' Joseph removed them from his father's knees and bowed to the ground. Then he took the two of them and brought them close to Israel: Ephraim on the right, that is Israel's left; and Manasseh on the left, that is Israel's right. But Israel, crossing his hands, stretched out his right hand and laid it on Ephraim's head, although he was the younger, and laid his left hand on Manasseh's head, even though he was the firstborn. He blessed Joseph and said:

'The God in whose presence my forefathers lived,
my forefathers Abraham and Isaac,
the God who has been my shepherd all my life to this day,
the angel who rescued me from all misfortune,
may he bless these boys;
they will be called by my name,
and by the names of my forefathers, Abraham and Isaac;
may they grow into a great people on earth.'

When Joseph saw his father laying his right hand on Ephraim's head, he was displeased and took hold of his father's hand to move it from Ephraim's head to Manasseh's. He said, 'That is not right, father. This is the firstborn; lay your right hand on his head.' But his father refused; he said, 'I know, my son, I know. He too will become a people, and he too will become great. Yet his younger brother will be greater than he, and his descendants will be a whole nation in themselves.' So he blessed them that day and said:

'When a blessing is pronounced in Israel,
men shall use your names and say,
"May God make you like Ephraim and Manasseh."'

So he set Ephraim before Manasseh. Then Israel drew up his feet on to the bed, breathed his last, and was gathered to his ancestors.

Then Joseph threw himself upon his father, weeping over him and kissing him. He gave orders to the physicians in his service to embalm his father, and they did so, finishing the task in forty days, the usual time required for embalming. The Egyptians mourned Israel for seventy days.

When the period of mourning was over Joseph's brothers were afraid, for they said, 'What if Joseph should bear a grudge against us and pay us back for all the harm we did to him?' They therefore sent a messenger to Joseph to say, 'In his last words to us before he died, your father gave us this message: "Say this to Joseph: I ask you to forgive your brothers' crime and wickedness; I know they did you harm." So now we beg you: forgive our crime, for we are servants of your father's God.' Joseph was moved to tears by their words. His brothers approached and bowed to the ground before him. 'We are your slaves,' they said. But Joseph replied, 'Do not be afraid. Am I in the place of God? You meant to do me harm; but God meant to bring good out of it by preserving the lives of many people, as we see today. Do not be afraid. I shall provide for you and your dependants.' Thus he comforted them and set their minds at rest.

The Death of Joseph

Joseph remained in Egypt, he and his father's household. He lived to be a hundred and ten years old, and saw Ephraim's children to the third generation; he also recognized as his the children of Manasseh's son Machir. He said to his brothers, 'I am about to die; but God will not fail to come to your aid and take you from here to the land which he promised on oath to Abraham, Isaac, and Jacob.' He made the sons of Israel solemnly swear that when God came to their aid, they would carry his bones up with them from there. So Joseph died in Egypt and he was embalmed and laid in a coffin.

4 | THE EXODUS

Slaves in Egypt

These are the names of the sons of Israel who, along with their households, accompanied Jacob to Egypt: Reuben, Simeon, Levi, and Judah; Issachar, Zebulun, and Benjamin; Dan and Naphtali, Gad and Asher. All told there were seventy direct descendants of Jacob. Joseph was already in Egypt.

In course of time Joseph and all his brothers and that entire generation died. The Israelites were prolific and increased greatly, becoming so numerous and strong that the land was full of them. When a new king ascended the throne of Egypt, one who did not know about Joseph, he said to his people, 'These Israelites have become too many and too strong for us. We must take steps to ensure that they increase no further; otherwise we shall find that, if war comes, they will side with the enemy, fight against us, and become masters of the country.' So taskmasters were appointed over them to oppress them with forced labour. This is how Pharaoh's store cities, Pithom and Rameses, were built. But the more oppressive the treatment of the Israelites, the more they increased and spread, until the Egyptians came to loathe them. They ground down their Israelite slaves, and made life bitter for them with their harsh demands, setting them to make mortar and bricks and to do all sorts of tasks in the fields. In every kind of labour they made ruthless use of them.

The king of Egypt issued instructions to the Hebrew midwives, of whom one was called Shiphrah, the other Puah. 'When you are attending the Hebrew women in childbirth,' he told them, 'check as the child is delivered: if it is a boy, kill him; if it is a girl, however, let her live.' But the midwives were godfearing women, and did not heed the king's words; they let the male children live. Pharaoh summoned the midwives and, when he asked them why they had done this and let the male children live, they answered, 'Hebrew women are not like Egyptian women; they go

61

into labour and give birth before the midwife arrives.' God made the midwives prosper, and the people increased in numbers and strength; and because the midwives feared God he gave them families of their own. Pharaoh then issued an order to all the Egyptians that every new-born Hebrew boy was to be thrown into the Nile, but all the girls were to be allowed to live.

A certain man, a descendant of Levi, married a Levite woman. She conceived and bore a son, and when she saw what a fine child he was, she kept him hidden for three months. Unable to conceal him any longer, she got a rush basket for him, made it watertight with pitch and tar, laid him in it, and placed it among the reeds by the bank of the Nile. The child's sister stood some distance away to see what would happen to him.

Pharaoh's daughter came down to bathe in the river, while her ladies-in-waiting walked on the bank. She noticed the basket among the reeds and sent her slave-girl to bring it. When she opened it, there was the baby; it was crying, and she was moved with pity for it. 'This must be one of the Hebrew children,' she said. At this the sister approached Pharaoh's daughter: 'Shall I go and fetch you one of the Hebrew women to act as a wet-nurse for the child?' When Pharaoh's daughter told her to do so, she went and called the baby's mother. Pharaoh's daughter said to her, 'Take the child, nurse him for me, and I shall pay you for it.' She took the child and nursed him at her breast. Then, when he was old enough, she brought him to Pharaoh's daughter, who adopted him and called him Moses, 'because', said she, 'I drew him out of the water'.

One day after Moses was grown up, he went out to his own kinsmen and observed their labours. When he saw an Egyptian strike one of his fellow-Hebrews, he looked this way and that, and, seeing no one about, he struck the Egyptian down and hid his body in the sand. Next day when he went out, he came across two Hebrews fighting. He asked the one who was in the wrong, 'Why are you striking your fellow-countryman?' The man replied, 'Who set you up as an official and judge over us? Do you mean to murder me as you murdered the Egyptian?' Moses was alarmed and said to himself, 'The affair must have become known.' When it came to Pharaoh's ears, he tried to have Moses put to death, but Moses fled from his presence and went and settled in Midian.

As Moses sat by a well one day, the seven daughters of a priest of Midian came to draw water, and when they had filled the troughs to water their father's sheep, some shepherds came and drove them away. But Moses came to the help of the girls and watered the sheep. When they returned to their father, he said, 'How is it that you are back so quickly today?' 'An Egyptian rescued us from the shepherds,' they answered; 'he even drew water for us and watered the sheep.' 'Then where is he?' their father asked. 'Why did you leave him there? Go and invite him to eat with us.' So it came about that Moses agreed to stay with the man, and he gave Moses his daughter Zipporah in marriage. She bore him a son, and Moses called him Gershom, 'because', he said, 'I have become an alien in a foreign land'.

Moses and the Burning Bush

Years passed, during which time the king of Egypt died, but the Israelites still groaned in slavery. They cried out, and their plea for rescue from slavery ascended to God. He heard their groaning and called to mind his covenant with Abraham, Isaac, and Jacob; he observed the plight of Israel and took heed of it. While tending the sheep of his father-in-law Jethro, priest of Midian, Moses led the flock along the west side of the wilderness and came to Horeb, the mountain of God. There an angel of the Lord appeared to him as a fire blazing out from a bush. Although the bush was on fire, it was not being burnt up, and Moses said to himself, 'I must go across and see this remarkable sight. Why ever does the bush not burn away?' When the Lord saw that Moses had turned aside to look, he called to him out of the bush, 'Moses, Moses!' He answered, 'Here I am!' God said, 'Do not come near! Take off your sandals, for the place where you are standing is holy ground.' Then he said, 'I am the God of your father, the God of Abraham, Isaac, and Jacob.' Moses hid his face, for he was afraid to look at God.

The Lord said, 'I have witnessed the misery of my people in Egypt and have heard them crying out because of their oppressors. I know what they are suffering and have come down to rescue them from the power of the Egyptians and to bring them up out of that country into a fine, broad land, a land flowing with milk and honey, the territory of Canaanites, Hittites, Amorites, Perizzites, Hivites, and Jebusites. Come, I shall send you to

Pharaoh, and you are to bring my people Israel out of Egypt.'
'But who am I', Moses said to God, 'that I should approach
Pharaoh and that I should bring the Israelites out of Egypt?' God
answered, 'I am with you. This will be your proof that it is I who
have sent you: when you have brought the people out of Egypt,
you will all worship God here at this mountain.'

Moses said to God, 'If I come to the Israelites and tell them
that the God of their forefathers has sent me to them, and they
ask me his name, what am I to say to them?'

God answered, 'I am that I am. Tell them that I am has sent
you to them.' He continued, 'You are to tell the Israelites that it is
the Lord, the God of their forefathers, the God of Abraham,
Isaac, and Jacob, who has sent you to them. This is my name for
ever; this is my title in every generation.

'The elders will attend to what you say, and then you must go
along with them to the king of Egypt and say to him, "The Lord
the God of the Hebrews has encountered us. Now, we request you
to give us leave to go a three days' journey into the wilderness to
offer sacrifice to the Lord our God." I know well that the king of
Egypt will not allow you to go unless he is compelled. I shall then
stretch out my hand and assail the Egyptians with all the miracles I
shall work among them. After that he will send you away. What is
more, I shall bring this people into such favour with the Egyptians
that, when you go, you will not go empty-handed. Every woman
must ask her neighbour or any woman living in her house for silver
and gold jewellery and for clothing; put them on your sons and
daughters, and plunder the Egyptians.'

'But they will never believe me or listen to what I say,' Moses
protested; 'they will say that it is untrue that the Lord appeared
to me.' The Lord said, 'What is that in your hand?' 'A staff,'
replied Moses. The Lord said, 'Throw it on the ground.' He did
so, and it turned into a snake. Moses drew back hastily, but the
Lord said, 'Put your hand out and seize it by the tail.' When he
took hold of it, it turned back into a staff in his hand. 'This', said
the Lord, 'is to convince the people that the Lord the God of
their forefathers, the God of Abraham, of Isaac, and of Jacob, did
appear to you.'

Then the Lord said to him, 'Put your hand inside the fold of
your cloak.' He did so, and when he drew his hand out the skin
was white as snow with disease. The Lord said, 'Put your hand in

again'; he did so, and when he drew it out this time it was as healthy as the rest of his body. 'Now,' said the Lord, 'if they do not believe you and do not accept the evidence of the first sign, they may be persuaded by the second. But if they are not convinced even by these two signs and will not accept what you say, then fetch some water from the Nile and pour it out on the dry land, and the water from the Nile will turn to blood on the ground.'

'But, Lord,' Moses protested, 'I have never been a man of ready speech, never in my life, not even now that you have spoken to me; I am slow and hesitant.' The Lord said to him, 'Who is it that gives man speech? Who makes him dumb or deaf? Who makes him keen-sighted or blind? Is it not I, the Lord? Go now; I shall help you to speak and show you what to say.' Moses said, 'Lord, send anyone else you like.' At this the Lord became angry with Moses: 'Do you not have a brother, Aaron the Levite? He, I know, will do all the speaking. He is already on his way out to meet you, and he will be overjoyed when he sees you. You are to speak to him and put the words in his mouth; I shall help both of you to speak and tell you both what to do. He will do all the speaking to the people for you; he will be the mouthpiece, and you will be the god he speaks for. And take this staff in your hand; with it you are to work the signs.'

Moses then went back to Jethro his father-in-law and said, 'Let me return to Egypt and see whether my kinsfolk are still alive.' Jethro said, 'Go, and may you have a safe journey.' The Lord spoke to Moses in Midian. 'Go back to Egypt,' he said, 'for all those who wanted to kill you are now dead.' Moses took his wife and children, mounted them on a donkey, and set out for Egypt with the staff of God in his hand. The Lord said to Moses, 'While you are on your way back to Egypt, keep in mind all the portents I have given you power to show. You are to display these before Pharaoh, but I shall make him obstinate and he will not let the people go. Then tell Pharaoh that these are the words of the Lord: Israel is my firstborn son. I tell you, let my son go to worship me. Should you refuse to let him go, I shall kill your firstborn son.'

Meanwhile the Lord had ordered Aaron to go and meet Moses in the wilderness. Aaron did so; he met him at the mountain of God and kissed him. Moses told Aaron everything, the words the

Lord had sent him to say and the signs he had commanded him to perform. Moses and Aaron then went and assembled all the elders of Israel. Aaron repeated to them everything that the Lord had said to Moses; he performed the signs before the people, and they were convinced. When they heard that the Lord had shown his concern for the Israelites and seen their misery, they bowed to the ground in worship.

Let My People Go

After this, Moses and Aaron came to Pharaoh and told him, 'These are the words of the Lord the God of Israel: Let my people go so that they may keep a pilgrim-feast in my honour in the wilderness.' 'Who is the Lord,' said Pharaoh, 'that I should listen to him and let Israel go? I do not acknowledge the Lord: and I tell you I will not let Israel go.' They replied, 'The God of the Hebrews confronted us. Now we request leave to go three days' journey into the wilderness to offer sacrifice to the Lord our God, or else he may attack us with pestilence or sword.' But the Egyptian king answered, 'What do you mean, Moses and Aaron, by distracting the people from their work? Back to your labours! Your people already outnumber the native Egyptians; yet you would have them stop working!'

Pharaoh issued orders that same day to the people's slave-masters and their foremen not to supply the people with the straw used in making bricks, as they had done hitherto. 'Let them go and collect their own straw, but see that they produce the same tally of bricks as before; on no account reduce it. They are lazy, and that is why they are clamouring to go and offer sacrifice to their God. Keep these men hard at work; let them attend to that. Take no notice of their lies.' The slave-masters and foremen went out and said to the people, 'Pharaoh's orders are that no more straw is to be supplied. Go and get it for yourselves wherever you can find it; but there is to be no reduction in your daily task.' So the people scattered all over Egypt to gather stubble for the straw they needed, while the slave-masters kept urging them on, demanding that they should complete, day after day, the same quantity as when straw had been supplied. The Israelite foremen were flogged because they were held responsible by Pharaoh's slave-masters, who demanded, 'Why did you not complete the usual number of bricks yesterday or today?'

The foremen came and appealed to Pharaoh: 'Why does your majesty treat us like this?' they said. 'We are given no straw, yet they keep telling us to make bricks. Here are we being flogged, but the fault lies with your people.' The king replied, 'You are lazy, bone lazy! That is why you keep on about going to offer sacrifice to the Lord. Now get on with your work. You will not be given straw, but you must produce the full tally of bricks.' When they were told that they must not let the daily number of bricks fall short, the Israelite foremen realized the trouble they were in. As they came from Pharaoh's presence they found Moses and Aaron waiting to meet them, and said, 'May this bring the Lord's judgement down on you! You have made us stink in the nostrils of Pharaoh and his subjects; you have put a sword in their hands to slay us.'

Moses went back to the Lord and said, 'Lord, why have you brought trouble on this people? And why did you ever send me? Since I first went to Pharaoh to speak in your name he has treated your people cruelly, and you have done nothing at all to rescue them.' The Lord answered, 'Now you will see what I shall do to Pharaoh: he will be compelled to let them go, he will be forced to drive them from his country.

'Therefore say to the Israelites, "I am the Lord. I shall free you from your labours in Egypt and deliver you from slavery. I shall rescue you with outstretched arm and with mighty acts of judgement. I shall adopt you as my people, and I shall be your God. You will know that I, the Lord, am your God, the God who frees you from your labours in Egypt. I shall lead you to the land which I swore with uplifted hand to give to Abraham, to Isaac, and to Jacob. I shall give it you for your possession. I am the Lord."' But when Moses repeated those words to the Israelites, they would not listen to him; because of their cruel slavery, they had reached the depths of despair.

Then the Lord said to Moses, 'Go and bid Pharaoh king of Egypt let the Israelites leave his country.' Moses protested to the Lord, 'If the Israelites do not listen to me, how will Pharaoh listen to such a halting speaker as me?' The Lord said to Moses and Aaron, 'If Pharaoh demands some portent from you, then you, Moses, must say to Aaron, "Take your staff and throw it down in front of Pharaoh," and it will turn into a serpent.' When Moses and Aaron came to Pharaoh, they did as the Lord had told them; Aaron threw down his staff in front of Pharaoh and his courtiers, and it turned into a serpent. At this, Pharaoh summoned the wise men and the sorcerers, and the Egyptian magicians did the same thing by their spells: every man threw his staff down, and each staff turned into a serpent. But Aaron's staff swallowed up theirs. Pharaoh, however, was obstinate; as the Lord had foretold, he would not listen to Moses and Aaron.

The Ten Plagues

The Lord said to Moses, 'Pharaoh has been obdurate: he has refused to let the people go. In the morning go to him on his way out to the river. Stand on the bank of the Nile to meet him, and take with you the staff that turned into a snake. Say to him: "The Lord the God of the Hebrews sent me with this message for you: Let my people go in order to worship me in the wilderness. So far you have not listened. Now the Lord says: By this you will know that I am the Lord. With this rod I hold in my hand, I shall strike the water of the Nile and it will be changed into blood. The fish will die and the river will stink, and the Egyptians will be unable to drink water from the Nile."'

Moses and Aaron did as the Lord had commanded. In the sight of Pharaoh and his courtiers Aaron lifted his staff and struck the water of the Nile, and all the water was changed to blood. The fish died and the river stank, so that the Egyptians could not drink water from the Nile. There was blood everywhere in Egypt.

But the Egyptian magicians did the same thing by their spells. So Pharaoh still remained obstinate, as the Lord had foretold, and he did not listen to Moses and Aaron. He turned and went into his palace, dismissing the matter from his mind. The Egyptians all dug for drinking water round about the river, because they could not drink from the waters of the Nile itself. This lasted for seven days from the time when the Lord struck the Nile.

The Lord then told Moses to go to Pharaoh and say, 'These are the words of the Lord: Let my people go in order to worship me. If you refuse, I shall bring a plague of frogs over the whole of your territory. The Nile will swarm with them. They will come up from the river into your palace, into your bedroom and onto your bed, into the houses of your courtiers and your people, into your ovens and your kneading troughs. The frogs will clamber over you, your people, and all your courtiers.'

The Lord told Moses to say to Aaron, 'Take your staff in your hand and stretch it out over the rivers, canals, and pools, to bring up frogs on the land of Egypt.' When Aaron stretched his hand over the waters of Egypt, the frogs came up and covered the land. But the magicians did the same thing by their spells: they too brought up frogs on the land of Egypt.

Pharaoh summoned Moses and Aaron. 'Pray to the Lord', he said, 'to remove the frogs from me and my people, and I shall let the people go to sacrifice to the Lord.' Moses and Aaron left Pharaoh's presence, and Moses asked the Lord to remove the frogs which he had brought on Pharaoh. The Lord granted the request, and in house, farmyard, and field all the frogs perished. They were piled into countless heaps and the land stank. But when Pharaoh found that he was given relief he became obdurate; as the Lord had foretold, he would not listen to Moses and Aaron.

The Lord told Moses to say to Aaron, 'Stretch out your staff and strike the dust on the ground, and it will turn into maggots throughout the whole of Egypt.' They obeyed, and when Aaron stretched out his hand with his staff in it and struck the dust, it turned into maggots on man and beast. Throughout Egypt all the dust turned into maggots. The magicians tried to produce maggots in the same way by their spells, but they failed. The maggots were everywhere, on man and beast. 'It is the hand of God,' said the magicians to Pharaoh, but Pharaoh remained obstinate; as the Lord had foretold, he would not listen.

The Lord told Moses to rise early in the morning and stand in Pharaoh's path as he went out to the river, and to say to him, 'These are the words of the Lord: Let my people go in order to worship me. If you refuse, I shall send swarms of flies on you, your courtiers, your people, and your houses; the houses of the Egyptians will be filled with the swarms and so will all the land they live in. But on that day I shall make an exception of Goshen, the land where my people live: there will be no swarms there. Thus you will know that I, the Lord, am here in the land. I shall make a distinction between my people and yours. Tomorrow this sign will appear.' The Lord did this; dense swarms of flies infested Pharaoh's palace and the houses of his courtiers; throughout Egypt the land was threatened with ruin by the swarms. Pharaoh summoned Moses and Aaron. 'I shall let you go,' said Pharaoh, 'and you may sacrifice to your God in the wilderness; only do not go far. Now intercede for me.' Moses answered, 'As soon as I leave you I shall intercede with the Lord. Tomorrow the swarms will depart from Pharaoh, his courtiers, and his people. Only your majesty must not trifle any more with the people by preventing them from going to sacrifice to the Lord.'

Then Moses left Pharaoh and interceded with the Lord. The Lord did as Moses had promised; he removed the swarms from Pharaoh, his courtiers, and his people; not one was left. But once again Pharaoh became obdurate and would not let the people go.

The Lord said to Moses, 'Go in to Pharaoh and tell him, "The Lord the God of the Hebrews says: Let my people go in order to worship me. If you refuse to let them go, if you still keep them in subjection, the Lord will strike your livestock out in the country, the horses and donkeys, camels, cattle, and sheep with a devastating pestilence. But the Lord will make a distinction between Israel's livestock and the livestock of the Egyptians. Of all that belong to Israel not a single one will die."' The Lord fixed a time and said, 'Tomorrow I shall do this throughout the land.' The next day the Lord struck. All the livestock of Egypt died, but from Israel's livestock not one single beast died. Pharaoh made enquiries and was told that from Israel's livestock not an animal had died; and yet he remained obdurate and would not let the people go.

The Lord said to Moses and Aaron, 'Take handfuls of soot from a kiln, and when Moses tosses it into the air in Pharaoh's sight, it will turn into a fine dust over the whole of Egypt. Throughout the land it will produce festering boils on man and beast.' They took the soot from the kiln and when they stood before Pharaoh, Moses tossed it into the air, and it produced festering boils on man and beast. The magicians were no match for Moses because of the boils, which attacked them and all the Egyptians. But the Lord made Pharaoh obstinate; as the Lord had foretold to Moses, he would not listen to Moses and Aaron.

The Lord then told Moses to rise early and confront Pharaoh, saying to him, 'Since you still obstruct my people and will not let them go, tomorrow at this time I shall cause a violent hailstorm to come, such as has never been in Egypt from its first beginnings until now. Send now and bring your herds under cover, and everything you have out in the open field. Anything which happens to be left out in the open, whether man or beast, will die when the hail falls on it.' Those of Pharaoh's subjects who feared the warning of the Lord hurried their slaves and livestock into shelter; but those who did not take it to heart left them in the open.

The Lord said to Moses, 'Stretch your hand towards the sky to bring down hail on the whole land of Egypt, on man and beast and every growing thing throughout the land.' As Moses stretched his staff towards the sky, the Lord sent thunder and hail, with fire flashing to the ground. The Lord rained down hail on the land of Egypt, hail and fiery flashes through the hail, so heavy that there had been nothing like it in all Egypt from the time that Egypt became a nation. Throughout Egypt the hail struck down everything in the fields, both man and beast; it beat down every growing thing and shattered every tree. Only in the land of Goshen, where the Israelites lived, was there no hail.

Pharaoh summoned Moses and Aaron. 'This time I have sinned,' he said; 'the Lord is in the right; I and my people are in the wrong. Intercede with the Lord, for we can bear no more of this thunder and hail. I shall let you go; you need stay no longer.' Moses left Pharaoh's presence and went out of the city, where he lifted up his hands to the Lord in prayer: the thunder and hail ceased, and no more rain fell. When Pharaoh saw that the downpour, the hail, and the thunder had ceased, he went back to his sinful obduracy, he and his courtiers. Pharaoh remained obstinate; as the Lord had foretold through Moses, he would not let the people go.

Pharaoh's courtiers said to him, 'How long must we be caught in this man's toils? Let their menfolk go and worship the Lord their God. Do you not know by now that Egypt is ruined?' So Moses and Aaron were brought back to Pharaoh, and he said to them, 'Go, worship the Lord your God; but who exactly is to go?' 'Everyone,' said Moses, 'young and old, boys and girls, sheep and cattle; for we have to keep the Lord's pilgrim-feast.' Pharaoh replied, 'The Lord be with you if I let you and your dependants go! You have some sinister purpose in mind. No, your menfolk may go and worship the Lord, for that is what you were asking for.' And they were driven from Pharaoh's presence.

The Lord said to Moses, 'Stretch out your hand over Egypt so that locusts may come and invade the land and devour all the vegetation in it, whatever the hail has left.' When Moses stretched out his staff over the land of Egypt, the Lord sent a wind roaring in from the east all that day and all that night; and when morning came the east wind had brought the locusts. They invaded the whole land of Egypt, and settled on all its territory in swarms so dense that the like of them had never been seen before, nor ever will be again. They covered the surface of the whole land till it was black with them; they devoured all the vegetation and all the fruit of the trees that the hail had spared; there was no green left on tree or plant throughout all Egypt.

Pharaoh hastily summoned Moses and Aaron. 'I have sinned against the Lord your God and against you,' he said. 'Forgive my sin, I pray, just this once, and intercede with the Lord your God to remove this deadly plague from me.' When Moses left Pharaoh and interceded with the Lord, the wind was changed by the Lord into a westerly gale, which carried the locusts away and swept them into the Red Sea. Not one locust was left within the borders of Egypt. But the Lord made Pharaoh obstinate, and he would not let the Israelites go.

Then the Lord said to Moses, 'Stretch out your hand towards the sky so that over the land of Egypt there may be a darkness so dense that it can be felt.' Moses stretched out his hand towards the sky, and for three days pitch darkness covered the whole land of Egypt. People could not see one another, and for three days no one stirred from where he was. But where the Israelites were living there was no darkness.

Pharaoh summoned Moses. 'Go, worship the Lord,' he said. 'Your dependants may go with you; but your flocks and herds must remain here.' But Moses said, 'No, you yourself must supply us with animals for sacrifice and whole-offering to the Lord our God; and our own livestock must go with us too – not a hoof must be left behind. We may need animals from our own flocks to worship the Lord our God; we ourselves cannot tell until we are there how we are to worship the Lord.' The Lord made Pharaoh obstinate, and he refused to let them go. 'Be off! Leave me!' he said to Moses. 'Mind you do not see my face again, for on the day you do, you die.' 'You are right,' said Moses; 'I shall not see your face again.'

The Lord said to Moses, 'One last plague I shall bring on Pharaoh and Egypt. When he finally lets you go, he will drive you out forcibly as a man might dismiss a rejected bride.'

Moses said, 'The Lord said: At midnight I shall go out among the Egyptians. All the firstborn in Egypt shall die, from the firstborn of Pharaoh on his throne to the firstborn of the slave-girl at the handmill, besides the firstborn of the cattle. From all over Egypt there will go up a great cry, the like of which has never been heard before, nor ever will be again. But throughout all Israel no sound will be heard from man or beast, not even a dog's bark. Thus you will know that the Lord distinguishes between Egypt and Israel. All these courtiers of yours will come down to me, prostrate themselves, and cry, "Go away, you and all the people who follow at your heels." When that time comes I shall go.' In hot anger, Moses left Pharaoh's presence.

The First Passover

The Lord said to Moses and Aaron in Egypt: 'This month is to be for you the first of the months; you are to make it the first month of the year. Say to the whole community of Israel: On the tenth day of this month let each man procure a lamb or kid for his family, one for each household, but if a household is too small for one lamb or kid, then, taking into account the number of persons, the man and his nearest neighbour may take one between them. They are to share the cost according to the amount each person eats. Your animal, taken either from the sheep or the goats, must be without blemish, a yearling male. Have it in safe keeping until the fourteenth day of this month, and then all the assembled community of Israel must slaughter the victims between dusk and dark. They must take some of the blood and smear it on the two doorposts and on the lintel of the houses in which they eat the victims. On that night they must eat the flesh roasted on the fire; they must eat it with unleavened bread and bitter herbs. You are not to eat any of it raw or even boiled in water, but roasted: head, shins, and entrails. You are not to leave any of it till morning; anything left over until morning must be destroyed by fire.

'This is the way in which you are to eat it: have your belt fastened, sandals on your feet, and your staff in your hand, and you must eat in urgent haste. It is the Lord's Passover. On that night I shall pass through the land of Egypt and kill every firstborn of man and beast. Thus I shall execute judgement, I the Lord, against all the gods of Egypt. As for you, the blood will be a sign on the houses in which you are: when I see the blood I shall pass over you; when I strike Egypt, the mortal blow will not touch you.

'You are to keep this day as a day of remembrance, and make it a pilgrim-feast, a festival of the Lord; generation after generation you are to observe it as a statute for all time. For seven days you are to eat unleavened bread. On the very first day you must rid your houses of leaven; from the first day to the seventh anyone who eats leavened bread is to be expelled from Israel. On the first day there is to be a sacred assembly and on the seventh day a sacred assembly: on these days no work is to be done, except what must be done to provide food for everyone; only that will be allowed. You are to observe the feast of Unleavened Bread because it was on this very day that I brought you out of Egypt in your tribal hosts. Observe this day from generation to generation as a statute for all time. When your children ask you, "What is the meaning of this rite?" you must say, "It is the Lord's Passover, for he passed over the houses of the Israelites in Egypt when he struck the Egyptians and spared our houses."' The people bowed low in worship.

The Israelites went and did exactly as the Lord had commanded Moses and Aaron; and by midnight the Lord had struck down all the firstborn in Egypt, from the firstborn of Pharaoh on his throne to the firstborn of the prisoner in the dungeon, besides the firstborn of cattle. Before night was over Pharaoh rose, he and all his courtiers and all the Egyptians, and there was great wailing, for not a house in Egypt was without its dead.

Pharaoh summoned Moses and Aaron while it was still night and said, 'Up with you! Be off, and leave my people, you and the Israelites. Go and worship the Lord, as you request; take your sheep and cattle, and go; and ask God's blessing on me also.' The Egyptians urged on the people and hurried them out of the country, 'or else', they said, 'we shall all be dead'. The people picked up their dough before it was leavened, wrapped their kneading troughs in their cloaks, and slung them on their shoulders. Meanwhile, as Moses had told them, the Israelites had asked the Egyptians for silver and gold jewellery and for clothing. Because the Lord had made the Egyptians well disposed towards them, they let the Israelites have whatever they asked; in this way the Egyptians were plundered.

The Israelites set out from Rameses on the way to Succoth, about six hundred thousand men on foot, as well as women and children. With them too went a large company of others, and animals in great numbers, both flocks and herds.

The Crossing of the Red Sea

When Pharaoh let the people go, God did not guide them by the road leading towards the Philistines, although that was the shortest way; for he said, 'The people may change their minds when war confronts them, and they may turn back to Egypt.' So God made them go round by way of the wilderness towards the Red Sea. Thus the fifth generation of Israelites departed from Egypt.

Moses took the bones of Joseph with him, because Joseph had exacted an oath from the Israelites: 'Some day', he said, 'God will show his care for you, and then, as you leave, you must take my bones with you.'

They set out from Succoth and encamped at Etham on the edge of the wilderness. And all the time the Lord went before them, by day a pillar of cloud to guide them on their journey, by night a pillar of fire to give them light; so they could travel both by day and by night. The pillar of cloud never left its place in front of the people by day, nor did the pillar of fire by night.

When it was reported to the Egyptian king that the Israelites had gone, he and his courtiers had a change of heart and said, 'What is this we have done? We have let our Israelite slaves go free!' Pharaoh had his chariot yoked, and took his troops with him, six hundred picked chariots and all the other chariots of Egypt, with a commander in each. Then, made obstinate by the Lord, Pharaoh king of Egypt pursued the Israelites as they marched defiantly away. The Egyptians, all Pharaoh's chariots and horses, cavalry and infantry, went in pursuit, and overtook them encamped beside the sea by Pi-hahiroth to the east of Baal-zephon.

Pharaoh was almost upon them when the Israelites looked up and saw the Egyptians close behind, and in terror they clamoured to the Lord for help. They said to Moses, 'Were there no graves in Egypt, that you have brought us here to perish in the wilderness? See what you have done to us by bringing us out of Egypt! Is this not just what we meant when we said in Egypt, "Leave us alone; let us be slaves to the Egyptians"? Better for us to serve as slaves to the Egyptians than to perish in the wilderness.' But Moses answered, 'Have no fear; stand firm and see the deliverance that the Lord will bring you this day; for as sure as you see the Egyptians now, you will never see them again. The Lord will fight for you; so say no more.'

The Lord said to Moses, 'What is the meaning of this clamour? Tell the Israelites to strike camp, and you are to raise high your staff and hold your hand out over the sea to divide it asunder, so that the Israelites can pass through the sea on dry ground.'

The angel of God, who had travelled in front of the Israelites, now moved away to the rear. The pillar of cloud moved from the front and took up its position behind them, thus coming between the Egyptians and the Israelites. The cloud brought on darkness and early nightfall, so that contact was lost throughout the night.

Then Moses held out his hand over the sea, and the Lord drove the sea away with a strong east wind all night long, and turned the seabed into dry land. The waters were divided asunder, and the Israelites went through the sea on the dry ground, while the waters formed a wall to right and left of them. The Egyptians, all Pharaoh's horses, his chariots and cavalry, followed in pursuit into the sea. In the morning watch the Lord looked down on the Egyptian army through the pillar of fire and cloud, and he threw them into a panic. He clogged their chariot wheels and made them drag along heavily, so that the Egyptians said, 'It is the Lord fighting for Israel against Egypt; let us flee.'

Then the Lord said to Moses, 'Hold your hand out over the sea, so that the water may flow back on the Egyptians, their chariots and horsemen.' Moses held his hand out over the sea, and at daybreak the water returned to its usual place and the Egyptians fled before its advance, but the Lord swept them into the sea. As the water came back it covered all Pharaoh's army, the chariots and cavalry, which had pressed the pursuit into the sea. Not one survived. Meanwhile the Israelites had passed along the dry ground through the sea, with the water forming a wall for them to right and to left. That day the Lord saved Israel from the power of Egypt. When the Israelites saw the Egyptians lying dead on the seashore, and saw the great power which the Lord had put forth **against Egypt, the people were in awe of the Lord and put their faith in him and in Moses his servant.**

Then Moses and the Israelites sang this song to the Lord:

'I shall sing to the Lord, for he has risen up in triumph;
horse and rider he has hurled into the sea.
The Lord is a warrior; the Lord is his name.
Your right hand, Lord, is majestic in strength;
your right hand, Lord, shattered the enemy.
At the blast of your anger the sea piled up;
the water stood up like a bank;
out at sea the great deep congealed.

'The enemy boasted, "I shall pursue, I shall overtake;
I shall divide the spoil,
I shall glut my appetite on them;
I shall draw my sword,
I shall rid myself of them."
You blew with your blast; the sea covered them;
they sank like lead in the swelling waves.

'Lord, who is like you among the gods?
Who is like you, majestic in holiness,
worthy of awe and praise, worker of wonders?
You stretched out your right hand;
the earth engulfed them.

'In your constant love you led the people
whom you had redeemed:
You will bring them in and plant them
in the mount that is your possession,
the dwelling-place, Lord, of your own making,
the sanctuary, Lord, which your own hands established.
The Lord will reign for ever and for ever.'

5 | ISRAEL IN THE WILDERNESS

The People Complain

Moses led Israel from the Red Sea out into the wilderness of Shur, where for three days they travelled through the wilderness without finding water. When they came to Marah, they could not drink the water there because it was bitter; that is why the place was called Marah. The people complained to Moses, asking, 'What are we to drink?'

Moses cried to the Lord, who showed him a log which, when thrown into the water, made the water sweet.

They came to Elim, where there were twelve springs and seventy palm trees, and there they encamped beside the water. The whole Israelite community, setting out from Elim, arrived at the wilderness of Sin, which lies between Elim and Sinai. This was on the fifteenth day of the second month after they left Egypt.

The Israelites all complained to Moses and Aaron in the wilderness. They said, 'If only we had died at the Lord's hand in Egypt, where we sat by the fleshpots and had plenty of bread! But you have brought us out into this wilderness to let this whole assembly starve to death.'

The Lord said to Moses, 'I shall rain down bread from heaven for you. Each day the people are to go out and gather a day's supply, so that I can put them to the test and see whether they follow my instructions or not. But on the sixth day, when they prepare what they bring in, it should be twice as much as they gather on other days.'

Moses and Aaron said to all the Israelites, 'In the evening you will know that it was the Lord who brought you out of Egypt, and in the morning you will see the glory of the Lord, because he has listened to your complaints against him. Who are we that you should bring complaints against us?' 'You will know this', Moses said, 'when in answer to your complaints the Lord gives you flesh to eat in the evening, and in the morning bread in plenty. What are we? It is against the Lord that you bring your complaints, not against us.'

Moses told Aaron to say to the whole community of Israel, 'Come into the presence of the Lord, for he has listened to your complaints.' While Aaron was addressing the whole Israelite community, they looked towards the wilderness, and there was the glory of the Lord appearing in the cloud.

The Lord spoke to Moses: 'I have heard the complaints of the Israelites. Say to them: Between dusk and dark you will have flesh to eat and in the morning bread in plenty. You will know that I the Lord am your God.'

That evening a flock of quails flew in and settled over the whole camp; in the morning a fall of dew lay all around it. When the dew was gone, there over the surface of the wilderness fine flakes appeared, fine as hoar-frost on the ground. When the Israelites saw it, they said one to another, 'What is that?' because they did not know what it was. Moses said to them, 'That is the bread which the Lord has given you to eat. Here is the command the Lord has given: Each of you is to gather as much as he can eat: let every man take an omer apiece for every person in his tent.'

Each morning every man gathered as much as he needed; it melted away when the sun grew hot. On the sixth day they gathered twice as much food, two omers each, and when the chiefs of the community all came and told Moses, 'This', he answered, 'is what the Lord has said: Tomorrow is a day of sacred rest, a sabbath holy to the Lord. So bake what you want to bake now, and boil what you want to boil; what remains over put aside to be kept till morning.' So they put it aside till morning as Moses had commanded, and it neither stank nor became infested with maggots. 'Eat it today,' said Moses, 'because today is a sabbath of the Lord. Today you will find none outside. For six days you may gather it, but on the seventh day, the sabbath, there will be none.'

Israel called the food manna; it was like coriander seed, but white, and it tasted like a wafer made with honey. 'This', said Moses, 'is the command which the Lord has given: Take a full omer of it to be kept for future generations, so that they may see the bread with which I fed you in the wilderness when I brought you out of Egypt.'

Moses said to Aaron, 'Take a jar and fill it with an omer of manna, and store it in the presence of the Lord to be kept for future generations.' Aaron did as the Lord had commanded Moses, and stored it before the Testimony for safe keeping. The Israelites ate the manna for forty years until they came to a land where they could settle; they ate it until they came to the border of Canaan.

The whole community of Israel set out from the wilderness of Sin and travelled by stages as the Lord directed. They encamped at Rephidim, but there was no water for the people to drink, and a dispute arose between them and Moses. When they said, 'Give us water to drink,' Moses said, 'Why do you dispute with me? Why do you challenge the Lord?' The people became so thirsty there that they raised an outcry against Moses: 'Why have you brought us out of Egypt with our children and our herds to let us die of thirst?' Moses appealed to the Lord, 'What shall I do with these people? In a moment they will be stoning me.' The Lord answered, 'Go forward ahead of the people; take with you some of the elders of Israel and bring along the staff with which you struck the Nile. Go, you will find me waiting for you there, by a rock in Horeb. Strike the rock; water will pour out of it for the people to drink.' Moses did this in the sight of the elders of Israel. He named the place Massah and Meribah, because the Israelites had disputed with him and put the Lord to the test with their question, 'Is the Lord in our midst or not?'

The Amalekites came and attacked Israel at Rephidim. Moses said to Joshua, 'Pick men for us, and march out tomorrow to fight against Amalek; and I shall stand on the hilltop with the staff of God in my hand.' Joshua did as Moses commanded and fought against Amalek, while Moses, Aaron, and Hur climbed to the top of the hill. Whenever Moses raised his hands Israel had the advantage, and when he lowered his hands the advantage passed to Amalek. When his arms grew heavy they took a stone and put it under him and, as he sat, Aaron and Hur held up his hands, one on each side, so that his hands remained steady till sunset. Thus Joshua defeated Amalek and put its people to the sword.

The Lord said to Moses, 'Record this in writing, and tell it to Joshua in these words: I am resolved to blot out all memory of Amalek from under heaven.' Moses built an altar, and named it 'The Lord is my Banner' and said, 'My oath upon it: the Lord is at war with Amalek generation after generation.'

Moses the Judge

Jethro priest of Midian, father-in-law of Moses, heard all that God had done for Moses and for Israel his people, and how the Lord had brought Israel out of Egypt. When Moses had sent away his wife Zipporah, Jethro his father-in-law had received her and her two sons. The name of the one was Gershom, 'for', said Moses, 'I have become an alien living in a foreign land'; the other's name was Eliezer, 'for', he said, 'the God of my father was my help and saved me from Pharaoh's sword'.

Jethro, Moses' father-in-law, now came to him with his sons and his wife, to the wilderness where he was encamped at the mountain of God. Moses was told, 'Here is Jethro, your father-in-law, coming to you with your wife and her two sons.' Moses went out to meet his father-in-law, bowed low to him, and kissed him. After they had greeted one another and come into the tent, Moses told him all that the Lord had done to Pharaoh and to Egypt for Israel's sake, and about all their hardships on the journey, and how the Lord had saved them. Jethro rejoiced at all the good the Lord had done for Israel in saving them from the power of Egypt.

The next day Moses took his seat to settle disputes among the people, and he was surrounded from morning till evening. At the sight of all that he was doing for the people, Jethro asked, 'What is this you are doing for the people? Why do you sit alone with all of them standing round you from morning till evening?' 'The people come to me to seek God's guidance,' Moses answered. 'Whenever there is a dispute among them, they come to me, and I decide between one party and the other. I make known the statutes and laws of God.' His father-in-law said to him, 'This is not the best way to do it. You will only wear yourself out and wear out the people who are here. The task is too heavy for you; you cannot do it alone. Now listen to me: take my advice, and God be with you. It is for you to be the people's representative before God, and bring their disputes to him, to instruct them in the statutes and laws, and teach them how they must behave and what they must do. But you should search for capable, godfearing men among all the people, honest and incorruptible men, and appoint them over the people as officers over units of a thousand, of a hundred, of fifty, or of ten. They can act as judges for the people at all times; difficult cases they should refer to you, but decide simple cases themselves. In this way your burden will be lightened, as they will be sharing it with you. If you do this, then God will direct you and you will be able to go on. And, moreover, this whole people will arrive at its destination in harmony.'

Moses heeded his father-in-law and did all he had suggested. He chose capable men from all Israel and appointed them leaders of the people, officers over units of a thousand, of a hundred, of fifty, or of ten. They sat as a permanent court, bringing the difficult cases to Moses but deciding simple cases themselves. When his father-in-law went back to his own country, Moses set him on his way.

The Ten Commandments
In the third month after Israel had left Egypt, they came to the wilderness of Sinai.

They set out from Rephidim and, entering the wilderness of Sinai, they encamped there, pitching their tents in front of the mountain. Moses went up to God, and the Lord called to him from the mountain and said, 'This is what you are to say to the house of Jacob and tell the sons of Israel: You yourselves have seen what I did to Egypt, and how I have carried you on eagles' wings and brought you here to me. If only you will now listen to me and keep my covenant, then out of all peoples you will become my special possession; for the whole earth is mine. You will be to me a kingdom of priests, my holy nation. Those are the words you are to speak to the Israelites.'

Moses went down, and summoning the elders of the people he set before them all these commands which the Lord had laid on him. As one the people answered, 'Whatever the Lord has said we shall do.' When Moses brought this answer back to the Lord, the Lord said to him, 'I am coming to you in a thick cloud, so that I may speak to you in the hearing of the people, and so their faith in you may never fail.'

When Moses reported to the Lord the pledge given by the people, the Lord said to him, 'Go to the people and hallow them today and tomorrow and have them wash their clothes. They must be ready by the third day, because on that day the Lord will descend on Mount Sinai in the sight of all the people. You must set bounds for the people, saying, "Take care not to go up the mountain or even to touch its base." Anyone who touches the mountain shall be put to death.'

At dawn on the third day there were peals of thunder and flashes of lightning, dense cloud on the mountain, and a loud trumpet-blast; all the people in the camp trembled.

Moses brought the people out from the camp to meet God, and they took their stand at the foot of the mountain. Mount Sinai was enveloped in smoke because the Lord had come down on it in fire; the smoke rose like the smoke from a kiln; all the people trembled violently, and the sound of the trumpet grew ever louder. Whenever Moses spoke, God answered him in a peal of thunder. The Lord came down on the top of Mount Sinai and summoned Moses up to the mountaintop.

God spoke all these words:

'I am the Lord your God who brought you out of Egypt, out of the land of slavery.

'You must have no other god besides me.

'You must not make a carved image for yourself, nor the likeness of anything in the heavens above, or on the earth below, or in the waters under the earth.

'You must not bow down to them in worship; for I, the Lord your God, am a jealous God, punishing the children for the sins of the parents to the third and fourth generation of those who reject me. But I keep faith with thousands, those who love me and keep my commandments.

'You must not make wrong use of the name of the Lord your God; the Lord will not leave unpunished anyone who misuses his name.

'Remember to keep the sabbath day holy. You have six days to labour and do all your work; but the seventh day is a sabbath of the Lord your God; that day you must not do any work, neither you, nor your son or your daughter, your slave or your slave-girl, your cattle, or the alien residing among you; for in six days the Lord made the heavens and the earth, the sea, and all that is in them, and on the seventh day he rested. Therefore the Lord blessed the sabbath day and declared it holy.

'Honour your father and your mother, so that you may enjoy long life in the land which the Lord your God is giving you.

'Do not commit murder.

'Do not commit adultery.

'Do not steal.

'Do not give false evidence against your neighbour.

'Do not covet your neighbour's household: you must not covet your neighbour's wife, his slave, his slave-girl, his ox, his donkey, or anything that belongs to him.'

When all the people saw how it thundered and the lightning flashed, when they heard the trumpet sound and saw the mountain in smoke, they were afraid and trembled. They stood at a distance and said to Moses, 'Speak to us yourself and we will listen; but do not let God speak to us or we shall die.' Moses answered, 'Do not be afraid. God has come only to test you, so that the fear of him may remain with you and preserve you from sinning.' So the people kept their distance, while Moses approached the dark cloud where God was.

The Lord said to Moses, 'Come up to me on the mountain, stay there, and let me give you the stone tablets with the law and commandment I have written down for their instruction.' Moses with Joshua his assistant set off up the mountain of God; he said to the elders, 'Wait for us here until we come back to you. You have Aaron and Hur; if anyone has a dispute, let him go to them.'

So Moses went up the mountain and a cloud covered it. The glory of the Lord rested on Mount Sinai, and the cloud covered the mountain for six days; on the seventh day he called to Moses out of the cloud. To the Israelites the glory of the Lord looked like a devouring fire on the mountaintop. Moses entered the cloud and went up the mountain; there he stayed forty days and forty nights.

The Golden Calf

When the people saw that Moses was so long in coming down from the mountain, they congregated before Aaron and said, 'Come, make us gods to go before us. As for this Moses, who brought us up from Egypt, we do not know what has become of him.' Aaron answered, 'Take the gold rings from the ears of your wives and daughters, and bring them to me.' So all the people stripped themselves of their gold ear-rings and brought them to Aaron. He received them from their hands, cast the metal in a mould, and made it into the image of a bull-calf; then they said, 'Israel, these are your gods that brought you up from Egypt.' Seeing this, Aaron built an altar in front of it and announced, 'Tomorrow there is to be a feast to the Lord.' Next day the people rose early, offered whole-offerings, and brought shared-offerings. After this they sat down to eat and drink and then gave themselves up to revelry.

The Lord said to Moses, 'Go down at once, for your people, the people you brought up from Egypt, have committed a monstrous act. They have lost no time in turning aside from the way which I commanded them to follow, and cast for themselves a metal image of a bull-calf; they have prostrated themselves before it, sacrificed to it, and said, "Israel, these are your gods that brought you up from Egypt."' The Lord said to Moses, 'I have considered this people, and I see their stubbornness. Now, let me alone to pour out my anger on them, so that I may put an end to them and make a great nation spring from you.'

Moses set himself to placate the Lord his God: 'Lord,' he said, 'why pour out your anger on your people, whom you brought out of Egypt with great power and a strong hand? Why let the Egyptians say, "He meant evil when he took them out, to kill them in the mountains and wipe them off the face of the earth"? Turn from your anger, and think better of the evil you intend against your people. Remember Abraham, Isaac, and Israel, your servants, to whom you swore by your own self: "I shall make your descendants countless as the stars in the heavens, and all this land, of which I have spoken, I shall give to them, and they will possess it for ever."' So the Lord thought better of the evil with which he had threatened his people.

Moses went back down the mountain holding the two tablets of the Testimony, inscribed on both sides, on the front and on the back. The tablets were the handiwork of God, and the writing was God's writing, engraved on the tablets. Joshua, hearing the uproar the people were making, said to Moses, 'Listen! There is fighting in the camp.' Moses replied,

'This is not the sound of warriors,
nor the sound of a defeated people;
it is the sound of singing that I hear.'

As he approached the camp, Moses saw the bull-calf and the dancing, and in a burst of anger he flung down the tablets and shattered them at the foot of the mountain. He took the calf they had made and burnt it; he ground it to powder, sprinkled it on water, and made the Israelites drink it.

He demanded of Aaron, 'What did this people do to you that you should have brought such great guilt upon them?' Aaron replied, 'Please do not be angry, my lord. You know how wicked the people are. They said to me, "Make us gods to go ahead of us, because, as for this Moses, who brought us up from Egypt, we do not know what has become of him." So I said to them, "Those of you who have any gold, take it off." They gave it to me, I threw it in the fire, and out came this bull-calf.'

Moses saw that the people were out of control and that Aaron had laid them open to the secret malice of their enemies. He took his place at the gate of the camp and said, 'Who is on the Lord's side? Come here to me'; and the Levites all rallied to him. He said to them, 'The Lord the God of Israel has said: Arm yourselves, each of you, with his sword. Go through the camp from gate to gate and back again. Each of you kill brother, friend, neighbour.' The Levites obeyed, and about three thousand of the people died that day. Moses said, 'You have been installed as priests to the Lord today, because you have turned each against his own son and his own brother and so have brought a blessing this day upon yourselves.'

The next day Moses said to the people, 'You have committed a great sin. Now I shall go up to the Lord; perhaps I may be able to secure pardon for your sin.' When he went back to the Lord he said, 'Oh, what a great sin this people has committed: they have made themselves gods of gold.

'Now if you will forgive them, forgive; but if not, blot out my name, I pray, from your book which you have written.' The Lord answered Moses, 'Whoever has sinned against me, him I shall blot out from my book. Now go, lead the people to the place of which I have told you. My angel will go ahead of you, but a day will come when I shall punish them for their sin.'

God Reveals His Glory

Moses used to take the Tent and set it up outside the camp some distance away. He called it the Tent of Meeting, and everyone who sought the Lord would go outside the camp to the Tent of Meeting. Whenever Moses went out to the Tent, all the people would rise and stand, each at the door of his tent, and follow Moses with their eyes until he had entered the Tent. When Moses entered it, the pillar of cloud came down, and stayed at the entrance to the Tent while the Lord spoke with Moses. As soon as the people saw the pillar of cloud standing at the entrance to the Tent, they would all prostrate themselves, each at the door of his tent. The Lord used to speak with Moses face to face, as one man speaks to another, and Moses then returned to the camp, but his attendant, Joshua son of Nun, never moved from inside the Tent.

Moses said to the Lord, 'You tell me to lead up this people without letting me know whom you will send with me, even though you have said to me, "I know you by name, and, what is more, you have found favour with me." If I have indeed won your favour, then teach me to know your ways, so that I can know you and continue in favour with you, for this nation is your own people.' The Lord answered, 'I shall go myself and set your mind at rest.' Moses said to him, 'Indeed if you do not go yourself, do not send us up from here; for how can it ever be known that I and your people have found favour with you, except by your going with us? So we shall be distinct, I and your people, from all the peoples on earth.' The Lord said to Moses, 'I shall do what you have asked, because you have found favour with me, and I know you by name.'

But Moses prayed, 'Show me your glory.' The Lord answered, 'I shall make all my goodness pass before you, and I shall pronounce in your hearing the name "Lord". I shall be gracious to whom I shall be gracious, and I shall have compassion on whom I shall have compassion.' But he added, 'My face you cannot see, for no mortal may see me and live.' The Lord said, 'Here is a place beside me. Take your stand on the rock and, when my glory passes by, I shall put you in a crevice of the rock and cover you with my hand until I have passed by. Then I shall take away my hand, and you will see my back, but my face must not be seen.'

The Lord said to Moses, 'Cut for yourself two stone tablets like the former ones, and I shall write on them the words which were on the first tablets which you broke. Be ready by morning, and then go up Mount Sinai, and present yourself to me there on the top. No one is to go up with you, no one must even be seen anywhere on the mountain, nor must flocks or herds graze within sight of that mountain.' So Moses cut two stone tablets like the first, and early in the morning he went up Mount Sinai as the Lord had commanded him, taking the two stone tablets in his hands. The Lord came down in the cloud, and, as Moses stood there in his presence, he pronounced the name 'Lord'. He passed in front of Moses and proclaimed: 'The Lord, the Lord, a God compassionate and gracious, long-suffering, ever faithful and true, remaining faithful to thousands, forgiving iniquity, rebellion, and sin but without acquitting the guilty, one who punishes children and grandchildren to the third and fourth generation for the iniquity of their fathers!'

At once Moses bowed to the ground in worship. He said, 'If I have indeed won your favour, Lord, then please go in our company. However stubborn a people they are, forgive our iniquity and our sin, and take us as your own possession.' The Lord said: 'Here and now I am making a covenant. In full view of all your people I shall do such miracles as have never been performed in all the world or in any nation. All the peoples among whom you live shall see the work of the Lord, for it is an awesome thing that I shall do for you. Observe all I command you this day; and I for my part shall drive out before you the Amorites, Canaanites, Hittites, Perizzites, Hivites, and Jebusites. Beware of making an alliance with the inhabitants of the land against which you are going, or they will prove a snare in your midst. You must demolish their altars, smash their sacred pillars, and cut down their sacred poles. You are not to bow in worship to any other god, for the Lord's name is the Jealous God, and a jealous God he is.'

The Lord said to Moses, 'Write these words down, because the covenant I make with you and with Israel is on those terms.' So Moses remained there with the Lord forty days and forty nights without food or drink. The Lord wrote down the words of the covenant, the Ten Commandments, on the tablets.

At length Moses came down from Mount Sinai with the two stone tablets of the Testimony in his hands, and when he came down, he did not know that the skin of his face shone because he had been talking with the Lord. When Aaron and the Israelites saw how the skin of Moses' face shone, they were afraid to approach him. He called out to them, and Aaron and all the chiefs in the community turned towards him. Moses spoke to them, and after that all the Israelites drew near. He gave them all the commands with which the Lord had charged him on Mount Sinai.

When Moses finished what he had to say, he put a veil over his face. But whenever he went in before the Lord to speak with him, he left the veil off until he came out. Then he would go out and tell the Israelites all the commands he had received. The Israelites would see how the skin of Moses' face shone, and he would put the veil back over his face until he went in again to speak with the Lord.

The Consecration of the Tabernacle

The Lord said to Moses: 'On the first day of the first month you are to set up the Tabernacle of the Tent of Meeting. Put the Ark of the Testimony in it and screen the Ark with the curtain. Bring in the table and lay it; then bring in the lampstand and mount its lamps. Then set the gold altar of incense in front of the Ark of the Testimony and put the screen of the entrance of the Tabernacle in place. Place the altar of whole-offering in front of the entrance of the Tabernacle of the Tent of Meeting, and the basin between the Tent of Meeting and the altar, and put water in it. Set up the court all round, and put in place the screen at the entrance of the court.

'With the anointing oil anoint the Tabernacle and everything in it, thus consecrating it and all its furnishings; it will then be holy. Anoint the altar of whole-offering and all its vessels, thus consecrating it; it will be most holy. Anoint the basin and its stand and consecrate it.

'Bring Aaron and his sons to the entrance of the Tent of Meeting and wash them with the water. Then clothe Aaron with the sacred vestments, anoint him, and consecrate him to be my priest. Then bring forward his sons, clothe them in tunics, and anoint them as you anointed their father; and they will be my priests. Their anointing inaugurates a hereditary priesthood for all time.'

Moses did everything exactly as the Lord had commanded him and the cloud covered the Tent of Meeting, and the glory of the Lord filled the Tabernacle. Moses was unable to enter the Tent of Meeting, because the cloud had settled on it and the glory of the Lord filled the Tabernacle. At every stage of their journey, when the cloud lifted from the Tabernacle, the Israelites used to break camp; but if the cloud did not lift from the Tabernacle, they used not to break camp until such time as it did lift. For the cloud of the Lord was over the Tabernacle by day, and there was fire in the cloud by night, and all the Israelites could see it at every stage of their journey.

Animal Sacrifices

The Lord summoned Moses and spoke to him from the Tent of Meeting. He told him to say to the Israelites: 'When anyone among you presents an animal as an offering to the Lord, it may be chosen either from the herd or from the flock. If his offering is a whole-offering from the herd, he must present a male without blemish; he must present it at the entrance to the Tent of Meeting so as to secure acceptance before the Lord.

'If anyone among the ordinary lay people sins inadvertently and does what is forbidden in any of the Lord's commandments, thereby incurring guilt, and the sin he has committed is made known to him, he must bring as his offering for the sin which he has committed a she-goat without blemish. He must lay his hand on the head of the victim and slaughter it at the place where the whole-offering is slaughtered. The priest must then take some of its blood with his finger and smear it on the horns of the altar of whole-offering; the rest of the blood he is to pour out at the base of the altar. He must remove all its fat as the fat is removed from the shared-offering, and burn it on the altar as a soothing odour to the Lord. Thus the priest is to make expiation for that person's guilt, and it will be forgiven him.'

Clean and Unclean Animals

The Lord told Moses and Aaron to say to the Israelites: 'These are the creatures you may eat: Of all the larger land animals you may eat any hoofed animal which has cloven hoofs and also chews the cud; those which only have cloven hoofs or only chew the cud you must not eat. These are: the camel, because though it chews the cud it does not have cloven hoofs, and is unclean for you; the rock-badger, because though it chews the cud it does not have cloven hoofs, and is unclean for you; the hare, because though it chews the cud it does not have a parted foot; it is unclean for you; the pig, because although it is a hoofed animal with cloven hoofs it does not chew the cud, and is unclean for you. You must not contaminate yourselves through any creatures that swarm; you must not defile yourselves with them and make yourselves unclean by them. For I am the Lord your God; you are to make yourselves holy and keep yourselves holy, because I am holy.'

The Day of Atonement

The Lord spoke to Moses: 'Tell your brother Aaron that on pain of death he must not enter the sanctuary behind the curtain, which is in front of the cover over the Ark, except at the appointed time; for I appear in the cloud above the cover. When Aaron enters the sanctuary, this is what he must do. He must bring a young bull for a purification-offering and a ram for a whole-offering; he is to wear a sacred linen tunic and linen shorts to cover himself, and he is to put a linen sash round his waist and wind a linen turban round his head; all these are sacred vestments, and he must bathe in water before putting them on. He is to receive from the community of the Israelites two he-goats for a purification-offering and a ram for a whole-offering.

'He must offer the bull reserved for his purification-offering and make expiation for himself and his household. Then he must take the two he-goats and set them before the Lord at the entrance to the Tent of Meeting. He must cast lots over the two goats, one to be for the Lord and the other for Azazel. He must present the goat on which the lot for the Lord has fallen and deal with it as a purification-offering.

'When Aaron has finished the purification of the sanctuary, the Tent of Meeting, and the altar, he is to bring forward the live goat. Laying both his hands on its head he must confess over it all the iniquities of the Israelites and all their acts of rebellion, that is all their sins; he is to lay his hands on the head of the goat and send it away into the wilderness in the charge of a man who is waiting ready. The goat will carry all their iniquities upon itself into some barren waste, where the man will release it, there in the wilderness.

'This is to be a rule binding on you for all time: on the tenth day of the seventh month you must fast; you, whether native Israelite or alien settler among you, must do no work, because on this day expiation will be made on your behalf to cleanse you, and so make you clean before the Lord from all your sins.'

Love Your Neighbour as Yourself

The Lord told Moses to say to the whole Israelite community: 'You must be holy, because I, the Lord your God, am holy. Each one of you must revere his mother and father. You must keep my sabbaths. I am the Lord your God. Do not resort to idols or make for yourselves gods of cast metal. I am the Lord your God.

'When you reap the harvest in your land, do not reap right up to the edges of your field, or gather the gleanings of your crop. Do not completely strip your vineyard, or pick up the fallen grapes; leave them for the poor and for the alien. I am the Lord your God.

'You must not steal; you must not cheat or deceive a fellow-countryman. You must not swear in my name with intent to deceive and thus profane the name of your God. I am the Lord.

'You are not to oppress your neighbour or rob him. Do not keep back a hired man's wages till next morning. Do not treat the deaf with contempt, or put an obstacle in the way of the blind; you are to fear your God. I am the Lord.

'You are not to pervert justice, either by favouring the poor or by subservience to the great. You are to administer justice to your fellow-countryman with strict fairness. Do not go about spreading slander among your father's kin; do not take sides against your neighbour on a capital charge. I am the Lord. You are not to nurse hatred towards your brother. Reprove your fellow-countryman frankly, and so you will have no share in his guilt. Never seek revenge or cherish a grudge towards your kinsfolk; you must love your neighbour as yourself. I am the Lord.'

The Priestly Blessing
On the first day of the second month in the second year after the Israelites came out of Egypt, the Lord spoke to Moses in the Tent of Meeting in the wilderness of Sinai.

The Lord said to Moses, 'Say this to Aaron and his sons: These are the words with which you are to bless the Israelites:

> May the Lord bless you and guard you;
> may the Lord make his face shine on you and be gracious
>   to you;
> may the Lord look kindly on you and give you peace.

'So they are to invoke my name on the Israelites, and I shall bless them.'

The Ark of the Covenant

In the second year, on the twentieth day of the second month, the cloud lifted from the Tabernacle of the Testimony.

Then they moved off from the mountain of the Lord and journeyed for three days, and the Ark of the Covenant of the Lord kept three days' journey ahead of them to find them a place to rest. The cloud of the Lord was over them by day when they moved camp. Whenever the Ark set out, Moses said,

'Arise, Lord, and may your enemies be scattered;
may those hostile to you flee at your approach.'

Whenever it halted, he said,

'Rest, Lord of the countless thousands of Israel.'

The People Ask for Meat

A mixed company of strangers had joined the Israelites, and these people began to be greedy for better things. Even the Israelites themselves with renewed weeping cried out, 'If only we had meat! Remember how in Egypt we had fish for the asking, cucumbers and watermelons, leeks and onions and garlic. Now our appetite is gone; wherever we look there is nothing except this manna.' (The manna looked like coriander seed, the colour of bdellium. The people went about collecting it to grind in hand-mills or pound in mortars; they cooked it in a pot and made it into cakes, which tasted like butter-cakes. When dew fell on the camp at night, the manna would fall with it.)

Moses heard all the people lamenting in their families at the opening of their tents. The Lord became very angry, and Moses was troubled, and said to the Lord, 'Why have you brought trouble on your servant? How have I displeased the Lord that I am burdened with all this people? Am I their mother? Have I brought them into the world, and am I called on to carry them in my arms, like a nurse with a baby, to the land promised by you on oath to their fathers? Where am I to find meat to give them all? They pester me with their wailing and their "Give us meat to eat." This whole people is a burden too heavy for me; I cannot carry it alone. If that is your purpose for me, then kill me outright: if I have found favour with you, spare me this trouble afflicting me.'

The Lord answered Moses, 'Assemble for me seventy of Israel's elders, men known to you as elders and officers in the community; bring them to the Tent of Meeting, and there let them take their place with you. I shall come down and speak with you there. I shall withdraw part of the spirit which is conferred on you and bestow it on them, and they will share with you the burden of the people; then you will not have to bear it alone. And say to the people: Sanctify yourselves in readiness for tomorrow; you will have meat to eat. You wailed in the Lord's hearing; you said, "If only we had meat! In Egypt we lived well." The Lord will give you meat and you will eat it. Not for one day only, nor for two days, nor five, nor ten, nor twenty, but for a whole month you will eat it until it comes out at your nostrils and makes you sick; because you have rejected the Lord who is in your midst, wailing in his presence and saying, "Why did we ever come out of Egypt?".'

There sprang up a wind from the Lord, which drove quails in from the west, and they were flying all round the camp for the distance of a day's journey, three feet above the ground. The people were busy gathering quails all that day and night, and all next day, and even those who got least gathered ten homers of them. They spread them out to dry all about the camp. But the meat was scarcely between their teeth, and they had not so much as bitten it, when the Lord's anger flared up against the people and he struck them with a severe plague. That place came to be called Kibroth-hattaavah, because there they buried the people who had been greedy for meat.

Miriam and Aaron Complain

From Kibroth-hattaavah the Israelites went on to Hazeroth, and while they were there, Miriam and Aaron began to find fault with Moses. They criticized him for his Cushite wife (for he had married a Cushite woman), and they complained, 'Is Moses the only one by whom the Lord has spoken? Has he not spoken by us as well?' – though Moses was a man of great humility, the most humble man on earth. But the Lord heard them and at once said to Moses, Aaron, and Miriam, 'Go out all three of you to the Tent of Meeting.' When they went out, the Lord descended in a pillar of cloud and, standing at the entrance to the tent, he summoned Aaron and Miriam. The two of them came forward, and the Lord said,

'Listen to my words.
If he were your prophet and nothing more,
I would make myself known to him in a vision,
I would speak with him in a dream.
But my servant Moses is not such a prophet;
of all my household he alone is faithful.
With him I speak face to face,
openly and not in riddles.
He sees the very form of the Lord.
How dare you speak against my servant Moses?'

With his anger still hot against them, the Lord left them; and as the cloud moved from the tent, there was Miriam, her skin diseased and white as snow. When Aaron, turning towards her, saw her skin diseased, he said to Moses, 'My lord, do not make us pay the penalty of sin, foolish and wicked though we have been. Let her not be like something stillborn, whose flesh is half eaten away when it comes from the womb.' So Moses cried, 'Lord, not this! Heal her, I pray.' The Lord answered, 'Suppose her father had spat in her face, would she not have to remain in disgrace for seven days? Let her be confined outside the camp for seven days and then be brought back.' So Miriam was shut outside for seven days, and the people did not strike camp until she was brought back.

A Land Flowing with Milk and Honey

After that they moved on from Hazeroth and pitched camp in the wilderness of Paran. The Lord said to Moses, 'Send men out to explore Canaan, the land which I am going to give to the Israelites; from each ancestral tribe send one man, a man of high rank.'

When Moses sent them to explore Canaan, he said, 'Make your way up by the Negeb, up into the hill-country, and see what the land is like, and whether the people who live there are strong or weak, few or many. See whether the country in which they live is easy or difficult, and whether their towns are open or fortified. Is the land fertile or barren, and is it wooded or not? Go boldly in and bring some of its fruit.' It was the season when the first grapes were ripe.

After forty days they returned from exploring the country and, coming back to Moses and Aaron and the whole community of

Israelites at Kadesh in the wilderness of Paran, they made their report, and showed them the fruit of the country. They gave Moses this account: 'We made our way into the land to which you sent us. It is flowing with milk and honey, and here is the fruit it grows; but its inhabitants are formidable, and the towns are fortified and very large; indeed, we saw there the descendants of Anak. We also saw the Amalekites who live in the Negeb, Hittites, Jebusites, and Amorites who live in the hill-country, and the Canaanites who live by the sea and along the Jordan.'

Caleb silenced the people for Moses. 'Let us go up at once and occupy the country,' he said; 'we are well able to conquer it.' But the men who had gone with him said, 'No, we cannot attack these people; they are too strong for us.' Their report to the Israelites about the land which they had explored was discouraging: 'The country we explored', they said, 'will swallow up any who go to live in it. All the people we saw there are men of gigantic stature. When we set eyes on the Nephilim (the sons of Anak belong to the Nephilim) we felt no bigger than grasshoppers; and that is how we must have been in their eyes.'

At this the whole Israelite community cried out in dismay and the people wept all night long. Everyone complained against Moses and Aaron: 'If only we had died in Egypt or in the wilderness!' they said. 'Why should the Lord bring us to this land, to die in battle and leave our wives and our dependants to become the spoils of war? It would be better for us to go back to Egypt.' And they spoke of choosing someone to lead them back there.

Then Moses and Aaron flung themselves on the ground before the assembled community of the Israelites, and two of those who had explored the land, Joshua son of Nun and Caleb son of Jephunneh, tore their clothes, and encouraged the whole community: 'The country we travelled through and explored', they said, 'is a very good land indeed. If the Lord is pleased with us, he will bring us into this land, a land flowing with milk and honey, and give it to us. But you must not act in defiance of the Lord. You need not fear the people of the country, for we shall devour them. They have lost the protection that they had: the **Lord is with us. You have nothing to fear from them.' As the whole assembly threatened to stone them, the glory of the Lord appeared in the Tent of Meeting to all the Israelites.**

The Lord said to Moses, 'How much longer will this people set me at naught? How much longer will they refuse to trust me in spite of all the signs I have shown among them? I shall strike them with pestilence. I shall deny them their heritage, and you and your descendants I shall make into a nation greater and more numerous than they.' But Moses answered the Lord, 'You have borne with this people from Egypt all the way here; forgive their iniquity, I beseech you, as befits your great and constant love.'

The Lord said, 'Your prayer is answered, and I pardon them. But as I live, and as the glory of the Lord fills the whole earth, not one of all those who have seen my glory and the signs which I wrought in Egypt and in the wilderness shall see the country which I promised on oath to their fathers. Ten times they have challenged me and not obeyed my voice. None of those who have set me at naught shall see this land. But my servant Caleb showed a different spirit and remained loyal to me. Because of this, I shall bring him into the land in which he has already set foot, the territory of the Amalekites and the Canaanites who dwell in the Vale, and I shall put his descendants in possession of it.

'I, the Lord, have spoken. This I swear to do to all this wicked community who have combined against me. There will be an end of them here in this wilderness; here they will die.'

The Rebellion of Korah, Dathan and Abiram

Korah son of Izhar, son of Kohath, son of Levi, along with the Reubenites Dathan and Abiram sons of Eliab and On son of Peleth, challenged the authority of Moses. Siding with them in their revolt were two hundred and fifty Israelites, all chiefs of the community, conveners of assembly and men of good standing. They confronted Moses and Aaron and said, 'You take too much on yourselves. Each and every member of the community is holy and the Lord is among them. Why do you set yourselves up above the assembly of the Lord?'

Moses sent to fetch Dathan and Abiram sons of Eliab, but they answered, 'We will not come. Is it not enough that you have brought us away from a land flowing with milk and honey to let us die in the wilderness? Must you also set yourself up as prince over us? What is more, you have not brought us into a land flowing with milk and honey, nor have you given us fields and vineyards to inherit. Do you think you can hoodwink men like us? We are not coming.' Moses became very angry, and said to the Lord, 'Take no notice of their murmuring. I have not taken from them so much as a single donkey; I have not wronged any of them.'

Moses said to Korah, 'Present yourselves before the Lord tomorrow, you and all your company, you and they and Aaron. Each man of you is to take his censer and put incense on it. Then you shall present them before the Lord with their two hundred and fifty censers, and you and Aaron shall also bring your censers.' So each man took his censer, put fire in it, and placed incense on it. Moses and Aaron took their stand at the entrance to the Tent of Meeting, and Korah gathered his whole company together and faced them.

Then the glory of the Lord appeared to the whole community, and the Lord said to Moses and Aaron, 'Stand apart from them, so that I may make an end of them in a single moment.' But Moses and Aaron prostrated themselves and said, 'God, you God of the spirits of all mankind, if one man sins, will you be angry with the whole community?' But the Lord said to Moses, 'Tell them all to stand back from the dwellings of Korah, Dathan, and Abiram.'

Moses rose and went to Dathan and Abiram, and the elders of Israel followed him. He said to the whole community, 'Stand well away from the tents of these wicked men; touch nothing of theirs, or you will be swept away because of all their sins.' So they moved away from the dwellings of Korah, Dathan, and Abiram. Dathan and Abiram had come out and were standing at the entrance of their tents with their wives, their children, and their dependants. Moses said, 'By this you shall know that it is the Lord who sent me to do all I have done, and it was not my own heart that prompted me. If these men die a natural death, merely sharing the common fate of man, then the Lord has not sent me; but if the Lord works a miracle, and the ground opens its mouth and swallows them and all that is theirs, and they go down alive to Sheol, then you will know that these men have set the Lord at naught.'

Hardly had Moses spoken when the ground beneath them split apart; the earth opened its mouth and swallowed them and their homes – all the followers of Korah and all their property. They went down alive into Sheol with all that they had; the earth closed over them, and they vanished from the assembly. At their cries all the Israelites around them fled. 'Look out!' they shouted. 'The earth might swallow us.' Fire came out from the Lord and consumed the two hundred and fifty men presenting the incense.

Then the Lord said to Moses, 'Order Eleazar son of Aaron the priest to set aside the censers from the burnt remains, and scatter the fire from them a long way off, because they are holy. The censers of these men who sinned at the cost of their lives you shall make into beaten plates to overlay the altar; they are holy, because they have been presented before the Lord. Let them be a sign to the Israelites.'

Aaron's Staff

The Lord said to Moses, 'Speak to the Israelites and get from them a staff for each tribe, one from every tribal chief, twelve in all, and write each man's name on his staff. On Levi's staff write Aaron's name, for there must be one staff for each head of a tribe. Put them all in the Tent of Meeting before the Testimony, where I meet you, and the staff of the man whom I choose will put forth buds. I shall rid myself of the complaints of these Israelites, who keep on complaining against you.'

Moses gave those instructions to the Israelites, and each of their chiefs handed him a staff for his tribe, twelve in all, and Aaron's staff among them. Moses laid them before the Lord in the Tent of the Testimony, and next day when he entered the tent, he found that Aaron's staff, the staff for the tribe of Levi, had budded. Indeed, it had put forth buds, blossomed, and produced ripe almonds. Moses then brought out the staffs from before the Lord and showed them to all the Israelites; they saw for themselves, and each man took his own staff. The Lord said to Moses, 'Put back Aaron's staff in front of the Testimony to be kept as a warning to rebels, so that you may rid me of their complaints, and then they will not die.' Moses did this, doing exactly as the Lord had commanded him.

Water from the Rock

In the first month the whole community of Israel arrived in the wilderness of Zin and stayed some time at Kadesh. Miriam died and was buried there.

As the community was without water, the people gathered against Moses and Aaron.

They disputed with Moses. 'If only we had perished when our brothers perished before the Lord!' they said. 'Why have you brought the Lord's assembly into this wilderness for us and our livestock to die here? Why did you make us come up from Egypt to land us in this terrible place, where nothing will grow, neither grain nor figs nor vines nor pomegranates? There is not even water to drink.'

Moses and Aaron went from the assembly to the entrance of the Tent of Meeting, where they prostrated themselves, and the glory of the Lord appeared to them. The Lord said to Moses, 'Take your staff, and then with Aaron your brother assemble the community, and in front of them all command the rock to yield its waters. Thus you will produce water for the community out of the rock, for them and their livestock to drink.' Moses took his staff from before the Lord, as he had been ordered. He with Aaron assembled the people in front of the rock, and said to them, 'Listen, you rebels. Must we get water for you out of this rock?' Moses raised his hand and struck the rock twice with his staff. Water gushed out in abundance and they all drank, men and animals. But the Lord said to Moses and Aaron, 'You did not trust me so far as to uphold my holiness in the sight of the Israelites; therefore you will not lead this assembly into the land I am giving them.' Such were the waters of Meribah, where the people disputed with the Lord and through which his holiness was upheld.

The Death of Aaron

The whole community of Israel set out from Kadesh and came to Mount Hor. There, near the frontier of Edom, the Lord said to Moses and Aaron, 'Aaron is now to be gathered to his father's kin. He will not enter the land which I am giving to the Israelites, because over the waters of Meribah you both rebelled against my command. Take Aaron and his son Eleazar, and go up Mount Hor. Strip Aaron of his robes and invest Eleazar his son with them, for Aaron is to be taken from you: he will die there.' Moses did as the Lord had commanded: in full view of the whole community they went up Mount Hor, where Moses stripped Aaron of his robes and invested his son Eleazar with them. Aaron died there on the mountaintop. When Moses and Eleazar came down from the mountain, the whole Israelite community saw that Aaron had died, and all the people mourned for thirty days.

The Bronze Serpent

From Mount Hor they left by way of the Red Sea to march round the flank of Edom. But on the way the people grew impatient and spoke against God and Moses. 'Why have you brought us up from Egypt', they said, 'to die in the desert where there is neither food nor water? We are heartily sick of this miserable fare.' Then the Lord sent venomous snakes among them, and they bit the Israelites so that many of them died. The people came to Moses and said, 'We sinned when we spoke against the Lord and you. Plead with the Lord to rid us of the snakes.' Moses interceded for the people, and the Lord told him to make a serpent and erect it as a standard, so that anyone who had been bitten could look at it and recover.

Balaam and the Donkey

The Israelites moved on and encamped in the lowlands of Moab on the farther side of the Jordan opposite Jericho, and Moab was in terror of the people because there were so many of them. The Moabites were overcome with fear at the sight of them; and they said to the elders of Midian, 'This horde will soon eat up everything round us as an ox eats up the new grass in the field.' Balak son of Zippor, who was at that time king of Moab, sent a deputation to summon Balaam son of Beor, who was at Pethor by the Euphrates in the land of the Amavites, with this message, 'A whole nation has just arrived from Egypt: they cover the face of the country and are settling at my very door. Come at once and lay a curse on them, because they are too many for me. I may then be able to defeat them and drive them out of the country. I know that those whom you bless are blessed, and those whom you curse are cursed.'

The elders of Moab and Midian took the fees for augury with them, and coming to Balaam they gave him Balak's message. 'Spend this night here,' he replied, 'and I shall give you whatever answer the Lord gives me.' So the Moabite chiefs stayed with Balaam. God came to Balaam and asked him, 'Who are these men with you?' Balaam replied, 'Balak son of Zippor king of Moab has sent them to me and he says, "A people which has just come out of Egypt is covering the face of the country. Come at once and put a curse on them for me; then I may be able to give battle and drive them away."' God said to Balaam, 'You are not to go with them or curse the people, because they are to be blessed.' So when Balaam rose in the morning he said to Balak's chiefs, 'Go back to your own country; the Lord has refused to let me go with you.' The Moabite chiefs took their leave and went back to Balak, and reported to him that Balaam had refused to come with them.

Balak sent a second embassy, larger and more high-powered than the first. When they came to Balaam they said, 'This is the message from Balak son of Zippor: "Let nothing stand in the way of your coming to me. I shall confer great honour upon you and do whatever you ask me. But you must come and put a curse on this people for me."' Balaam gave this answer to Balak's messengers: 'Even if Balak were to give me all the silver and gold in his palace, I could not disobey the command of the Lord my God in anything, small or great. But stay here for this night, as the others did, that I may learn what more the Lord may have to say to me.' During the night God came to Balaam and said to him, 'If these men have come to summon you, then rise and go with them, but do only what I tell you.' When morning came Balaam rose, saddled his donkey, and went with the Moabite chiefs.

But God was angry because Balaam was going, and as he came riding on his donkey, accompanied by his two servants, the angel of the Lord took his stand in the road to bar his way. When the donkey saw the angel standing in the road with his sword drawn, she turned off the road into the fields, and Balaam beat her to bring her back on to the road. The angel of the Lord then stood where the road ran through a hollow, with enclosed vineyards on either side. The donkey saw the angel and, squeezing herself against the wall, she crushed Balaam's foot against it, and again he beat her. The angel of the Lord moved on farther and stood in a narrow place where there was no room to turn to either right or left. When the donkey saw the angel, she lay down under Balaam. At that Balaam lost his temper and beat the donkey with his staff.

The Lord then made the donkey speak, and she said to Balaam, 'What have I done? This is the third time you have beaten me.' Balaam answered, 'You have been making a fool of me. If I had had a sword with me, I should have killed you on the spot.' But the donkey answered, 'Am I not still the donkey which you have ridden all your life? Have I ever taken such a liberty with you before?' He said, 'No.' Then the Lord opened Balaam's eyes: he saw the angel of the Lord standing in the road with his sword drawn, and he bowed down and prostrated himself. The angel said to him, 'What do you mean by beating your donkey three times like this? I came out to bar your way, but you made straight for me, and three times your donkey saw me and turned aside. If she had not turned aside, I should by now have killed you, while sparing her.' 'I have done wrong,' Balaam replied to the angel of the Lord. 'I did not know that you stood confronting me in the road. But now, if my journey displeases you, I shall turn back.' The angel of the Lord said to Balaam, 'Go with the men; but say only what I tell you.' So Balaam went on with Balak's chiefs.

When Balak heard that Balaam was coming, he went out to meet him as far as Ar of Moab by the Arnon on his frontier. Balak said to Balaam, 'Did I not send time and again to summon you? Why did you not come? Did you think that I could not do you honour?' Balaam replied, 'I have come, as you see. But now that I am here, what power have I of myself to say anything? It is only whatever word God puts into my mouth that I can speak.' So Balaam went with Balak till they came to Kiriath-huzoth, and Balak slaughtered cattle and sheep and sent portions to Balaam and to the chiefs who were with him.

In the morning Balak took Balaam and led him up to Bamoth-baal, from where he could see the full extent of the Israelite host. Then Balaam said to Balak, 'Build me here seven altars and prepare for me seven bulls and seven rams.' Balak followed Balaam's instructions; after offering a bull and a ram on each altar, he said to him, 'I have prepared the seven altars, and I have offered the bull and the ram on each altar.' Balaam answered, 'You stand here beside your sacrifice, and let me go off by myself. It may be that the Lord will meet me. Whatever he reveals to me, I shall tell you.' He went off to a height, where God met him. The Lord put words into Balaam's mouth and said, 'Go back to Balak, and speak as I tell you.' He went back, and found Balak standing by his sacrifice, and with him all the Moabite chiefs. Then Balaam uttered his oracle:

'From Aram, from the mountains of the east,
Balak king of Moab has brought me:
"Come, lay a curse on Jacob for me," he said.
"Come, denounce Israel."
How can I curse someone God has not cursed,

how denounce someone the Lord has not denounced?
From the rocky heights I see them,
I watch them from the rounded hills.
I see a people that dwells apart,
that has not made itself one with the nations.
Who can count the host of Jacob
or number the myriads of Israel?
Let me die as those who are righteous die;
grant that my end may be as theirs!'

Balak said, 'What is this you have done? I sent for you to put a
curse on my enemies, and what you have done is to bless them.'
Balaam replied, 'I can but keep to the words which the Lord puts
into my mouth.'

Balak then said to him, 'Come with me now to another place
from which you will see them, though not the full extent of them;
you will not see them all. Curse them for me from there.' So he
took him to the Field of the Watchers on the summit of Pisgah,
where he built seven altars and offered a bull and a ram on each
altar. Balaam said to Balak, 'You stand beside your sacrifice; I
shall meet the Lord over there.' The Lord met Balaam and put
words into his mouth, and said, 'Go back to Balak, and speak as I
tell you.' He went, and found him standing beside his sacrifice
with the Moabite chiefs. Balak asked what the Lord had said, and
Balaam uttered his oracle:

'Up, Balak, and listen:
hear what I am charged to say, son of Zippor.
God is not a mortal that he should lie,
not a man that he should change his mind.
Would he speak, and not make it good?
What he proclaims, will he not fulfil?
I have received a command to bless;
I shall bless, and I cannot gainsay it.'

Then Balak said to Balaam, 'You will not put a curse on them;
then at least do not bless them.' He answered, 'Did I not warn
you that I must do whatever the Lord tells me?' Balak said,
'Come, let me take you to another place; perhaps God will be
pleased to let you curse them for me there.' So he took Balaam to

the summit of Peor overlooking Jeshimon, and Balaam told him to build seven altars for him there and prepare seven bulls and seven rams. Balak did as Balaam had said, and he offered a bull and a ram on each altar.

But now that Balaam knew that the Lord wished him to bless Israel, he did not go and resort to divination as before. He turned towards the desert, and before his eyes he saw Israel encamped tribe by tribe; and, the spirit of God coming on him, he uttered his oracle:

'The word of Balaam son of Beor,
who with opened eyes sees in a trance
the vision from the Almighty:
Jacob, how fair are your tents,
Israel, your encampments,
like long palm groves,
like cedars beside the waters!
Blessed be those who bless you,
and let them who curse you be accursed!'

At that Balak's anger was aroused against Balaam; beating his hands together, he cried, 'It was to curse my enemies that I summoned you, and three times you have persisted in blessing them. Off with you at once to your own place! I promised to confer great honour upon you, but now the Lord has kept this honour from you.' Balaam answered, 'But I said to your messengers: "Were Balak to give me all the silver and gold in his palace, I could not disobey the command of the Lord by doing anything of my own will, good or bad. What the Lord says to me, that is what I must say." Now I am going to my own people; but first, let me warn you what this people will do to yours in the days to come.' Then he uttered his oracle:

'The word of Balaam son of Beor,
who shares the knowledge of the Most High:
a star will come forth out of Jacob,
a comet will arise from Israel.
He will smite the warriors of Moab,
and beat down all the sons of Sheth.
Edom will be his by conquest

and Seir, his enemy, will become his.
Israel will do valiant deeds;
Jacob will trample them down,
the last survivor from Ar will he destroy.'

Then Balaam arose and returned home, and Balak also went on
his way.

The Zeal of Phinehas

When the Israelites were in Shittim, the men began to have intercourse with Moabite women, who invited them to the sacrifices
offered to their gods. The Israelites ate the sacrificial food and
prostrated themselves before the gods of Moab; they joined in the
worship of the Baal of Peor. This aroused the anger of the Lord,
who said to Moses, 'Take all the leaders of the people and hurl
them down to their death before the Lord in the full light of day,
that the fury of my anger may turn away from Israel.' Moses gave
this order to the judges of Israel: 'Each of you put to death those
of his tribe who have joined in the worship of the Baal of Peor.'

One of the Israelites brought a Midianite woman into his
family in open defiance of Moses and all the community of Israel,
while they were weeping by the entrance of the Tent of Meeting.
When Phinehas son of Eleazar, son of Aaron the priest, saw him,
he got up from the assembly and took a spear, and went into the
nuptial tent after the Israelite, where he transfixed the two of
them, the Israelite and the woman, pinning them together. Then
the plague which had attacked the Israelites was brought to a
stop; but twenty-four thousand had already died.

The Lord said to Moses, 'Phinehas son of Eleazar, son of
Aaron the priest, has turned my wrath away from the Israelites;
he displayed among them the same jealous anger that moved me,
and therefore I did not exterminate the Israelites in my jealous
anger. Make known that I hereby grant him my covenant pledge
of prosperity: he and his descendants after him shall enjoy the
priesthood under a covenant for all time, because he showed his
zeal for his God and made expiation for the Israelites.' The name
of the Israelite struck down with the Midianite woman was Zimri
son of Salu, a chief in a Simeonite family, and the Midianite
woman's name was Cozbi daughter of Zur, who was the tribal
head of an ancestral house in Midian.

Holy War

The Lord said to Moses, 'You are to exact vengeance for Israel on the Midianites. After that you will be gathered to your father's kin.'

Moses addressed the people: 'Let men among you be drafted for active service; they are to fall on Midian and exact vengeance in the Lord's name. Send out a thousand men from each of the tribes of Israel.' So men were called up from the clans of Israel, a thousand from each tribe, twelve thousand in all, drafted for active service. Moses sent out this force, a thousand from each tribe, with Phinehas son of Eleazar the priest, who was in charge of the sacred equipment and of the trumpets to give the signal for the battle cry. They made war on Midian as the Lord had commanded Moses, and slew every male. In addition to those slain in battle they killed the five kings of Midian – Evi, Rekem, Zur, Hur, and Reba – and they put to death also Balaam son of Beor. The Israelites took the Midianites' women and dependants captive, and carried off all their herds, flocks, and property. They set fire to all the towns in which they lived, and all their encampments. They collected the spoil and plunder, both man and beast, and brought it all – captives, plunder, and spoil – to Moses and Eleazar the priest and to the whole Israelite community at the camp in the lowlands of Moab by the Jordan over against Jericho.

Moses and Eleazar the priest and all the chiefs of the community went to meet them outside the camp. Moses spoke angrily to the officers of the army, the commanders of units of a thousand and of a hundred, who were returning from the campaign: 'Have you spared all the women?' he said. 'Remember, it was they who, on Balaam's departure, set about seducing the Israelites into disloyalty to the Lord in the affair at Peor, so that the plague struck the community of the Lord. Now kill every male child, and kill every woman who has had intercourse with a man, but you may spare for yourselves every woman among them who has not had intercourse. You yourselves, every one of you who has taken life and every one who has touched the dead, must remain outside the camp for seven days. Purify yourselves and your captives on the third day and on the seventh day, and purify also every piece of clothing, every article made of hide, everything woven of goats' hair, and everything made of wood.'

The Lord said to Moses, 'You and Eleazar the priest and the heads of families in the community must count everything that has been captured, whether human beings or animals, and divide them equally between the fighting men who went on the campaign and the rest of the community. Levy a tribute for the Lord: from the combatants it is to be one out of every five hundred, whether human beings, cattle, donkeys, or sheep, to be taken out of their share and given to Eleazar the priest as a contribution for the Lord. Out of the Israelites' share it is to be one out of every fifty taken, whether human beings or cattle, donkeys, or sheep, all the animals, to be given to the Levites who are in charge of the Lord's Tabernacle.' Moses and Eleazar the priest did as the Lord had commanded Moses.

6 | THE LAST WORDS OF MOSES

God's Chosen People

These are the words that Moses addressed to all Israel in the wilderness beyond the Jordan.

I have taught you statutes and laws, as the Lord my God commanded me; see that you keep them when you go into and occupy the land. Observe them carefully, for thereby you will display your wisdom and understanding to other peoples. When they hear about all these statutes, they will say, 'What a wise and understanding people this great nation is!' What great nation has a god close at hand as the Lord our God is close to us whenever we call to him? What great nation is there whose statutes and laws are so just, as is all this code of laws which I am setting before you today?

But take care: keep careful watch on yourselves so that you do not forget the things that you have seen with your own eyes; do not let them pass from your minds as long as you live, but teach them to your children and to your children's children. You must never forget the day when you stood before the Lord your God at Horeb, and the Lord said to me, 'Assemble the people for me; I shall make them hear my words and they will learn to fear me all their lives in the land, and they will teach their children to do so.' Then you came near and stood at the foot of the mountain, which was ablaze with fire to the very skies, and there was dark cloud and thick mist. When the Lord spoke to you from the heart of the fire you heard a voice speaking, but you saw no form; there was only a voice. He announced to you the terms of his covenant, bidding you observe the Ten Commandments, which he wrote on two stone tablets.

Search into days gone by, long before your time, beginning at the day when God created man on earth; search from one end of heaven to the other, and ask if any deed as mighty as this has been seen or heard. Did any people ever hear the voice of a god speaking from the heart of the fire, as you heard it, and remain alive?

Or did a god ever attempt to come and take a nation for himself away from another nation, with a challenge, and with signs, portents, and wars, with a strong hand and an outstretched arm, and with great deeds of terror, like all you saw the Lord your God do for you in Egypt? You have had sure proof that the Lord is God; there is none other. From heaven he let you hear his voice for your instruction, and on earth he let you see his great fire, and from the heart of the fire you heard his words.

The Shema

Hear, Israel: the Lord is our God, the Lord our one God; and you must love the Lord your God with all your heart and with all your soul and with all your strength. These commandments which I give you this day are to be remembered and taken to heart; repeat them to your children, and speak of them both indoors and out of doors, when you lie down and when you get up. Bind them as a sign on your hand and wear them as a pendant on your forehead; write them on the doorposts of your houses and on your gates.

The Lord your God will bring you into the land which he swore to your forefathers Abraham, Isaac, and Jacob that he would give you, a land of large, fine towns which you did not build, houses full of good things which you did not provide, cisterns hewn from the rock but not by you, and vineyards and olive groves which you did not plant.

When he brings you in and you have all you want to eat, see that you do not forget the Lord who brought you out of Egypt, out of that land of slavery. You are to fear the Lord your God; serve him alone, and take your oaths in his name. You must not go after other gods, gods of the nations around you; if you do, the anger of the Lord your God who is among you will be roused against you, and he will sweep you off the face of the earth, for the Lord your God is a jealous God. You must not put the Lord your God to the test as you did at Massah. You must diligently keep the commandments of the Lord your God and the precepts and statutes which he gave you.

When the Lord your God brings you into the land which you are about to enter to occupy it, when he drives out many nations before you – Hittites, Girgashites, Amorites, Canaanites, Perizzites, Hivites, and Jebusites, seven nations more numerous and powerful than you – and when the Lord your God delivers them into your power for you to defeat, you must exterminate them. You must not make an alliance with them or spare them. You must not intermarry with them, giving your daughters to their sons or taking their daughters for your sons, because if you do, they will draw your children away from the Lord to serve other gods. Then the anger of the Lord will be roused against you and he will soon destroy you. But this is what you must do to them: pull down their altars, break their sacred pillars, hack down their sacred poles, and burn their idols, for you are a people holy to the Lord your God, and he has chosen you out of all peoples on earth to be his special possession.

It was not because you were more numerous than any other nation that the Lord cared for you and chose you, for you were the smallest of all nations; it was because the Lord loved you and stood by his oath to your forefathers, that he brought you out with his strong hand and redeemed you from the place of slavery, from the power of Pharaoh king of Egypt. Know then that the Lord your God is God, the faithful God; with those who love him and keep his commandments he keeps covenant and faith for a thousand generations, but those who defy and reject him he repays with destruction: he will not be slow to requite any who reject him.

Justice and Mercy

In every settlement which the Lord your God is giving you, you must appoint for yourselves judges and officers, tribe by tribe, and they will dispense true justice to the people. You must not pervert the course of justice or show favour or accept a bribe; for bribery makes the wise person blind and the just person give a crooked answer. Justice, and justice alone, must be your aim, so that you may live and occupy the land which the Lord your God is giving you.

You must not keep back the wages of a man who is poor and needy, whether a fellow-countryman or an alien living in your country in one of your settlements. Pay him his wages on the same day before sunset, for he is poor and he relies on them: otherwise he may appeal to the Lord against you, and you will be guilty of sin.

Parents are not to be put to death for their children, nor children for their parents; each one may be put to death only for his own sin.

You must not deprive aliens and the fatherless of justice or take a widow's cloak in pledge. Bear in mind that you were slaves in Egypt and the Lord your God redeemed you from there; that is why I command you to do this.

When you reap the harvest in your field and overlook a sheaf, do not go back to pick it up; it is to be left for the alien, the fatherless, and the widow, so that the Lord your God may bless you in all that you undertake.

When you beat your olive trees, do not strip them afterwards; what is left is for the alien, the fatherless, and the widow.

When you gather the grapes from your vineyard, do not glean afterwards; what is left is for the alien, the fatherless, and the widow. Keep in mind that you were slaves in Egypt; that is why I command you to do this.

Final Warnings

Moses, with the elders of Israel, gave the people this charge:

'When you have crossed the Jordan you are to set up these stones on Mount Ebal, as I instruct you this day, and coat them with plaster. Build an altar there to the Lord your God, an altar of stones on which no iron tool is to be used. Build the altar of the Lord your God with blocks of undressed stone, and offer whole-offerings on it to the Lord your God. Slaughter shared-offerings and eat them there, and rejoice before the Lord your God. Inscribe on the stones all the words of this law, engraving them clearly and carefully.

'If you faithfully obey the Lord your God by diligently observing all his commandments which I lay on you this day, then the Lord your God will raise you high above all nations of the earth. All people on earth seeing that the Lord has named you as his very own will go in fear of you. The Lord will make you prosper greatly in the fruit of your body and of your cattle, and in the fruit of the soil in the land which he swore to your forefathers to give you. May the Lord open the heavens for you, his rich storehouse, to give your land rain at the proper time and bless everything to which you turn your hand. You may lend to many nations, but borrow from none; the Lord will make you the head and not the tail: you will always be at the top and never at the bottom, if you listen to the commandments of the Lord your God, which I give you this day to keep and to fulfil. Deviate neither to right nor to left from all the things which I command you this day, and do not go after other gods to serve them.

'But if you will not obey the Lord your God by diligently observing all his commandments and statutes which I lay upon you this day, then you who were countless as the stars in the heavens will be left few in number, because you did not obey the Lord your God. Just as the Lord took delight in you, prospering you and increasing your numbers, so now it will be his delight to ruin and exterminate you, and you will be uprooted from the land which you are entering to occupy.

'The Lord will disperse you among all peoples from one end of the earth to the other, and there you will serve other gods of whom neither you nor your forefathers have had experience, gods of wood and stone. Among those nations you will find no peace, no resting-place for the sole of your foot. Then the Lord will give you an unquiet mind, dim eyes, and failing appetite. Your life will hang continually in suspense, fear will beset you night and day, and you will find no security all your life long. Every morning you will say, "Would God it were evening!" and every evening, "Would God it were morning!" because of the terror that fills your heart and because of the sights you see. The Lord will bring you back sorrowing to Egypt by that very road of which I said to you, "You shall not see that road again"; there you will offer yourselves for sale as slaves to your enemies, but there will be no buyer.'

The Song of Moses

The Lord said to Moses, 'You are about to die and join your fore-fathers, and then this people, when they come into the land and live among foreigners, will wantonly worship their gods; they will abandon me and break the covenant which I have made with them. My anger will be roused against them on that day, and I shall abandon them and hide my face from them. They will be an easy prey, and many terrible disasters will come upon them. On that day they will say, "These disasters have come because our God is not among us." On that day I shall hide my face because of all the evil they have done in turning to other gods.

'Now write down this song and teach it to the Israelites; make them repeat it, so that it may be a witness for me against them.'

That day Moses wrote down this song and taught it to the Israelites.

When I proclaim the name of the Lord,
you will respond: 'Great is our God,
the Creator, whose work is perfect!'

Is he not your father who formed you?
Did he not make you and establish you?
When the Most High gave each nation its heritage,
when he divided all mankind,
he laid down the boundaries for peoples
according to the number of the sons of God;
but the Lord's share was his own people,
Jacob was his allotted portion.

He found his people in a desert land,
in a barren, howling waste.
He protected and trained them,
he guarded them as the apple of his eye.
As an eagle watches over its nest,
hovers above its young,
spreads its pinions and takes them up,
and bears them on its wings,
the Lord alone led his people,
no alien god at his side.

He made them ride over the heights of the earth
and fed them on the harvest of the fields;
he satisfied them with honey from the crags
with the finest flour of wheat;
and you, his people, drank red wine from the juice of the
    grape.

The Death of Moses

That same day the Lord said to Moses, 'Go up the mountain of the Abarim, Mount Nebo in Moab, to the east of Jericho, and view the land of Canaan that I am giving to the Israelites for their possession. On this mountain you will die and be gathered to your father's kin, just as Aaron your brother died on Mount Hor and was gathered to his father's kin. This is because both of you broke faith with me at the waters of Meribah-kadesh in the wilderness of Zin, when you did not uphold my holiness among the Israelites. You may see the land from a distance, but you may not enter the land I am giving to the Israelites.'

Moses went up from the lowlands of Moab to Mount Nebo, to the top of Pisgah eastwards from Jericho, and the Lord showed him the whole land, from Gilead to Dan; the whole of Naphtali; the territory of Ephraim and Manasseh, and all Judah as far as the western sea; the Negeb and the plain; the valley of Jericho, city of palm trees, as far as Zoar. The Lord said to him, 'This is the land which I swore to Abraham, Isaac, and Jacob that I would give to their descendants. I have let you see it with your own eyes, but you will not cross over into it.'

There in the Moabite country Moses the servant of the Lord died, as the Lord had said. He was buried in a valley in Moab opposite Beth-peor; but to this day no one knows his burial-place. Moses was a hundred and twenty years old when he died, his sight undimmed, his vigour unimpaired.

There has never yet risen in Israel a prophet like Moses, whom the Lord knew face to face.

Part Two

WARRIORS, PROPHETS AND KINGS

7 | JOSHUA AND THE CONQUEST OF CANAAN

Rahab and the Spies

After the death of Moses the Lord's servant, the Lord said to Joshua son of Nun, Moses' assistant, 'Now that my servant Moses is dead, get ready to cross the Jordan, you and all this people, to the land which I am giving to the Israelites. Every place where you set foot is yours: I have given it to you, as I promised Moses. From the desert and this Lebanon to the great river, the Euphrates, and across all the Hittite country westwards to the Great Sea, all of it is to be your territory. This is my command: be strong, be resolute; do not be fearful or discouraged, for wherever you go the Lord your God is with you.'

Joshua son of Nun sent out two spies secretly from Shittim with orders to reconnoitre the land and especially Jericho. The two men set off and came to the house of a prostitute named Rahab to spend the night there. When it was reported to the king of Jericho that some Israelites had arrived that night to explore the country, he sent word to Rahab: 'Bring out the men who have come to you and are now in your house, for they have come to spy out the whole country.' The woman, who had taken the two men and hidden them, replied, 'True, the men did come to me, but I did not know where they came from; and at nightfall when it was time to shut the gate, they had gone. I do not know where they were going, but if you hurry after them you may overtake them.' In fact, she had brought them up on to the roof and concealed them among the stalks of flax which she had laid out there in rows. The messengers went in pursuit of them in the direction of the fords of the Jordan, and as soon as they had gone out the gate was closed.

The men had not yet settled down, when Rahab came up to them on the roof, and said, 'I know that the Lord has given the land to you; terror of you has fallen upon us, and the whole country is panic-stricken. We have heard how the Lord dried up the waters of the Red Sea before you when you came out of Egypt, and what you did to Sihon and Og, the two Amorite kings beyond the Jordan, for you destroyed them. When we heard this, our courage failed; your coming has left no spirit in any of us; for the Lord your God is God in heaven above and on earth below. Swear to me by the Lord that you will keep faith with my family, as I have kept faith with you. Give me a token of good faith; promise that you will spare the lives of my father and mother, my brothers and sisters, and all who belong to them, and preserve us from death.' The men replied, 'Our lives for yours, so long as you do not betray our business. When the Lord gives us the country, we shall deal loyally and faithfully by you.'

She then let them down through a window by a rope; for the house where she lived was on an angle of the wall. 'Make for the hills,' she said, 'or the pursuers will come upon you. Hide there for three days until they return; then go on your way.' The men warned her that, unless she did what they told her, they would be free from the oath she had made them take. 'When we invade the land,' they said, 'you must fasten this strand of scarlet cord in the window through which you have lowered us, and get everybody together here inside the house, your father and mother, your brothers, and all your family. Should anybody go out of doors into the street, his blood will be on his own head; we shall be free of the oath. But if a hand is laid on anyone who stays indoors with you, his blood be on our heads! Remember too that, if you betray our business, then we shall be free of the oath you have made us take.' 'It shall be as you say,' she replied, and sent them on their way. When they had gone, she fastened the strand of scarlet cord in the window.

The men made their way into the hills and stayed there for three days until the pursuers returned. They had searched all along the road, but had not found them. The two men then came down from the hills and crossed the river. When they joined up with Joshua son of Nun, they reported all that had happened to them. 'The Lord has delivered the whole country into our hands,' they said; 'the inhabitants are all panic-stricken at our approach.'

The Crossing of the Jordan

Early in the morning Joshua and all the Israelites set out from Shittim and came to the Jordan, where they encamped before crossing. At the end of three days the officers passed through the camp, giving the people these instructions: 'When you see the Ark of the Covenant of the Lord your God being carried forward by the levitical priests, then you too must leave your positions and set out. Follow it, but do not go close to it; keep some distance behind, about two thousand cubits. It will show you the route you are to follow, for you have not travelled this way before.' Joshua said to the people, 'Consecrate yourselves, for tomorrow the Lord will perform a great miracle among you.' To the priests he said, 'Lift the Ark of the Covenant and move ahead of the people.'

The people set out from their encampment to cross the Jordan, with the priests in front carrying the Ark of the Covenant. Now the Jordan is in full flood in all its reaches throughout the time of harvest, but as soon as the priests reached the Jordan and their feet touched the water at the edge, the water flowing down from upstream was brought to a standstill; it piled up like a bank for a long way back, as far as Adam, a town near Zarethan. The water coming down to the sea of the Arabah, the Dead Sea, was completely cut off, and the people crossed over opposite Jericho. The priests carrying the Ark of the Covenant of the Lord stood firmly on the dry bed in the middle of the river, and all Israel passed over on dry ground.

When the whole nation had completed the crossing of the Jordan, the Lord said to Joshua, 'Choose twelve men from the people, one from each tribe, and order them to take up twelve stones from this place in the middle of the Jordan, where the priests have taken their stand. They are to carry the stones across and place them in the camp where you spend the night.' Joshua summoned the twelve Israelites whom he had appointed, one man from each tribe, and said to them, 'Go over in front of the Ark of the Lord your God as far as the middle of the Jordan, and let each of you take up a stone on his shoulder, one for each of the tribes of Israel. These stones are to stand as a memorial among you: in days to come, when your children ask what these stones mean, you will tell them how the waters of the Jordan were cut off before the Ark of the Covenant of the Lord.'

That day the Lord exalted Joshua in the eyes of all Israel, and the people revered him, as they had revered Moses all his life.

The Lord said to Joshua, 'Command the priests carrying the Ark of the Testimony to come up from the Jordan.' Joshua passed the command to the priests; and no sooner had the priests carrying the Ark of the Covenant of the Lord come up from the river bed, and set foot on dry land, than the waters of the Jordan returned to their course and filled up all its reaches as before.

On the tenth day of the first month the people went up from the Jordan and encamped in Gilgal in the district east of Jericho, and there Joshua set up these twelve stones they had taken from the Jordan. While the Israelites were encamped in Gilgal, at sunset on the fourteenth day of the month they kept the Passover in the lowlands of Jericho. On the day after the Passover they ate of the produce of the country, roasted grain and loaves made without leaven. It was from that day, when they first ate the produce of the country, that the manna ceased. The Israelites got no more manna; that year they ate what had grown in the land of Canaan.

When Joshua was near Jericho he looked up and saw a man standing in front of him with a drawn sword in his hand. Joshua approached him and asked, 'Are you for us or for our enemies?' The man replied, 'Neither! I am here as captain of the army of the Lord.' Joshua prostrated himself in homage, and said, 'What have you to say to your servant, my lord?' The captain of the Lord's army answered, 'Remove your sandals, for the place where you are standing is holy'; and Joshua did so.

The Fall of Jericho

Jericho was bolted and barred against the Israelites; no one could go out or in. The Lord said to Joshua, 'See, I am delivering Jericho, its king, and his warriors into your hands. You are to march round the city with all your fighting men, making the circuit of it once a day for six days. Seven priests carrying seven trumpets made from rams' horns are to go ahead of the Ark. On the seventh day you are to march round the city seven times with the priests blowing their trumpets. At the blast of the rams' horns, when you hear the trumpet sound, the whole army must raise a great shout; the city wall will collapse and the army will advance, every man straight ahead.'

Joshua son of Nun summoned the priests and gave them instructions: 'Take up the Ark of the Covenant; let seven priests with seven trumpets of ram's horn go ahead of the Ark of the Lord.' Then he gave orders to the army: 'Move on, march round the city, and let the men who have been drafted go in front of the Ark of the Lord.'

After Joshua had issued this command to the army, the seven priests carrying the seven trumpets of ram's horn before the Lord moved on and blew the trumpets; the Ark of the Covenant of the Lord followed them. The drafted men marched in front of the priests who blew the trumpets, and the rearguard came behind the Ark, the trumpets sounding as they marched. But Joshua commanded the army not to shout, or to raise their voices or even utter a word, till the day when he would tell them to shout; then they were to give a mighty shout. Thus he made the Ark of the Lord go round the city, making the circuit of it once, and then they returned to the camp and spent the night there. Joshua rose early next morning, and the priests took up the Ark of the Lord. The seven priests carrying the seven trumpets of ram's horn marched in front of the Ark of the Lord, blowing the trumpets as they went, with the drafted men in front of them and the rearguard following the Ark, the trumpets sounding as they marched. They marched round the city once on the second day and returned to the camp; this they did for six days.

On the seventh day they rose at dawn and marched seven times round the city in the same way; that was the only day on which they marched round seven times. The seventh time, as the priests blew the trumpets, Joshua said to the army, 'Shout! The Lord has given you the city. The city is to be under solemn ban: everything in it belongs to the Lord. No one is to be spared except the prostitute Rahab and everyone who is with her in the house, because she hid the men we sent. And you must beware of coveting anything that is forbidden under the ban; you must take none of it for yourselves, or else you will put the Israelite camp itself under the ban and bring disaster on it. All silver and gold, all the vessels of copper and iron, are to be holy; they belong to the Lord and must go into his treasury.'

So the trumpets were blown, and when the army heard the trumpets sound, they raised a great shout, and the wall collapsed. The army advanced on the city, every man straight ahead, and they captured it. Under the ban they destroyed everything there; they put everyone to the sword, men and women, young and old, as well as the cattle, the sheep, and the donkeys.

The two men who had been sent out to reconnoitre the land were told by Joshua to go to the prostitute's house and bring out the woman and all who belonged to her, as they had sworn to do. The young men went and brought out Rahab, her father and mother, her brothers, and all who belonged to her; they brought the whole family and placed them outside the Israelite camp. The city and everything in it were then set on fire, except that the silver and gold and the vessels of copper and iron were deposited in the treasury of the Lord's house. Thus Joshua spared the lives of Rahab the prostitute, her household, and all who belonged to her, because she had hidden the men whom Joshua had sent to reconnoitre Jericho; she and her family settled permanently among the Israelites.

At that time Joshua pronounced this curse:

'May the Lord's curse light on anyone who comes forward to
    rebuild this city of Jericho:
the laying of its foundations shall cost him his eldest son,
the setting up of its gates shall cost him his youngest.'

The Lord was with Joshua, and his fame spread throughout the country.

The Sin of Achan
In a perfidious act, however, Israelites violated the ban: Achan son of Carmi, son of Zabdi, son of Zerah, of the tribe of Judah, took some of the forbidden things, and the Lord's anger blazed out against Israel.

Joshua sent men from Jericho with orders to go up to Ai, near Beth-aven, east of Bethel, and reconnoitre the land. The men went and explored Ai, and on their return reported to Joshua that there was no need for the whole army to move: 'Let some two or three thousand men advance to attack Ai. Do not have the whole army toil up there; the population is small.' About three thousand troops went up, but they were routed by the men of Ai, who killed some thirty-six of them; they chased the rest all the way from the gate to the Quarries and killed them on the pass. At this the courage of the people melted and flowed away like water.

Joshua and the elders of Israel tore their clothes and flung themselves face downwards to the ground; throwing dust on their heads, they lay in front of the Ark of the Lord till evening. Joshua cried, 'Alas, Lord God, why did you bring this people across the Jordan just to hand us over to the Amorites to be destroyed? If only we had been content to settle on the other side of the Jordan! I beseech you, Lord; what can I say, now that Israel has been routed by the enemy? When the Canaanites and all the other natives of the country hear of this, they will close in upon us and wipe us off the face of the earth. What will you do then for the honour of your great name?'

The Lord answered, 'Stand up; why lie prostrate on your face? Israel has sinned: they have violated the covenant which I laid upon them; they have taken things forbidden under the ban; they have stolen them; they have concealed them by putting them among their own possessions. That is why the Israelites cannot stand against their enemies: they are defeated because they have brought themselves under the ban. Unless you Israelites destroy every single thing among you that is forbidden under the ban, I shall be with you no longer.

'Get up and consecrate the people; tell them they must consecrate themselves for tomorrow. Say to them that these are the words of the Lord the God of Israel: You have among you forbidden things, Israel, and you will not be able to stand against your enemies until you have rid yourselves of these things. In the morning come forward tribe by tribe, and the tribe which the Lord takes must come forward clan by clan; the clan which the Lord takes must come forward family by family, and the family which the Lord takes must come forward man by man. The man who is taken as the harbourer of forbidden things must be burnt, he and all that is his, because he has violated the covenant of the Lord and committed an outrage in Israel.'

Early next morning Joshua rose and had Israel come forward tribe by tribe, and the tribe of Judah was taken; he brought forward the clans of Judah, and the clan of Zerah was taken; then the clan of Zerah family by family, and the family of Zabdi was taken. He had that family brought forward man by man, and Achan son of Carmi, son of Zabdi, son of Zerah, of the tribe of Judah, was taken.

Then Joshua said to Achan, 'My son, give honour to the Lord the God of Israel and make your confession to him. Tell me what you have done; hide nothing from me.' Achan answered, 'It is true; I have sinned against the Lord the God of Israel. This is what I did: among the booty I saw a fine mantle from Shinar, two hundred shekels of silver, and a bar of gold weighing fifty shekels; I coveted them and I took them. You will find them hidden in the ground inside my tent, with the silver underneath.' Joshua sent messengers, who went straight to the tent, and there it was hidden in the tent with the silver underneath. They took the things from the tent, brought them to Joshua and all the Israelites, and laid them out before the Lord.

Then Joshua and all Israel with him took Achan son of Zerah, with the silver, the mantle, and the bar of gold, together with his sons and daughters, his oxen, his donkeys, and his sheep, his tent, and everything he had, and they brought them up to the vale of Achor. Joshua said, 'What trouble you have brought on us! Now the Lord will bring trouble on you.' Then all the Israelites stoned him to death; and they raised over him a great cairn of stones which is there to this day. So the Lord's anger was abated.

The Fall of Ai

The Lord said to Joshua, 'Do not be afraid or discouraged; take the whole army with you and go and attack Ai. I am delivering the king of Ai into your hands, along with his people, his city, and his territory. Deal with Ai and its king as you dealt with Jericho and its king, except that you may keep for yourselves the cattle and any other spoil you take. Set an ambush for the city to the west of it.'

Early in the morning Joshua mustered the army and, with Joshua himself and the elders of Israel at its head, they marched against Ai. All the armed forces with him marched on until they came within sight of the city, where they encamped north of Ai, with the valley between them and the city. Joshua took some five thousand men and set them in ambush between Bethel and Ai to the west of the city. When the king of Ai saw them, he and the citizens set off hurriedly and marched out to do battle against Israel, being unaware that an ambush had been prepared for him to the west of the city. Joshua and the Israelites made as if they were worsted by them and fled towards the wilderness, while all the people of the city were called out in pursuit. In pursuing Joshua they were drawn away from the city, until not a man was left in Ai; they had all gone out in pursuit of the Israelites and thus had left the place wide open.

The Lord then said to Joshua, 'Point towards Ai with the dagger you are holding, for I will deliver the city into your hands.' Joshua pointed with his dagger towards Ai and, at his signal, the men in ambush rose quickly from their position; dashing into the city, they captured it and at once set it on fire. The men of Ai looked back and saw the smoke from the city already going up to the sky; they were powerless to make their escape in any direction.

The Israelites who had feigned flight towards the wilderness now turned on their pursuers, for when Joshua and all the Israelites with him saw that the men in ambush had seized the city and that smoke from it was already going up, they faced about and attacked the men of Ai. Those who had come out to contend with the Israelites were now hemmed in by Israelites on both sides of them, and the Israelites cut them down until there was not a single survivor; no one escaped. Only the king of Ai was taken alive and brought to Joshua.

When the Israelites had slain all the inhabitants of Ai in the open country and the wilderness where they had pursued them, and the massacre was complete, they all went back to Ai and put it to the sword. The number who fell that day, men and women, was twelve thousand, the whole population of Ai. Joshua held out his dagger and did not draw back his hand until all who lived in Ai had been destroyed; but the Israelites kept for themselves the cattle and any other spoil that they took, following the Lord's instructions given to Joshua.

So Joshua burnt Ai to the ground, and left it the desolate ruined mound it remains to this day. He hanged the king of Ai on a gibbet and left him there till evening. At sunset they cut down the body on Joshua's orders and flung it on the ground at the entrance of the city gate. Over it they raised a great cairn of stones, which is there to this day.

The Treaty with the Gibeonites

News of these happenings reached all the kings west of the Jordan, in the hill-country, in the Shephelah, and in all the coast of the Great Sea running up to the Lebanon, and the kings of the Hittites, Amorites, Canaanites, Perizzites, Hivites, and Jebusites agreed to join forces and fight against Joshua and Israel.

When the inhabitants of Gibeon heard how Joshua had dealt with Jericho and Ai, they resorted to a ruse: they set out after disguising themselves, with old sacks on their donkeys, old wine-skins split and mended, old and patched sandals for their feet, old clothing to wear, and by way of provisions nothing but dry and crumbling bread. They came to Joshua in the camp at Gilgal, where they said to him and the Israelites, 'We have come from a distant country to ask you now to grant us a treaty.' The Israelites said to these Hivites, 'But it may be that you live in our neigh-bourhood: if so, how can we grant you a treaty?' They said to Joshua, 'We are your slaves.'

Joshua asked them who they were and where they came from. 'Sir,' they replied, 'our country is very far away, and we have come because of the renown of the Lord your God. Look at our bread; it was hot from the oven when we packed it at home on the day we came away. Now, as you see, it is dry and crumbling. Here are our wineskins; they were new when we filled them, and now they are all split; look at our clothes and our sandals, worn out by the very long journey.' Without seeking guidance from the Lord, the leaders of the community accepted some of their provi-sions. Joshua received them peaceably and granted them a treaty, promising to spare their lives, and the leaders ratified it on oath.

However, within three days of granting them the treaty the Israelites learnt that these people were in fact neighbours, living nearby. The Israelites then set out and on the third day they reached their towns, Gibeon, Kephirah, Beeroth, and Kiriath-jearim.

Joshua summoned the Gibeonites and said to them, 'Why did you play this trick on us? You told us that you live a long way off, when in fact you are near neighbours. From now there is a curse on you: for all time you shall provide us with slaves, to cut wood and draw water for the house of my God.' They answered Joshua, 'We were told, sir, that the Lord your God had commanded his servant Moses to give you the whole country and to wipe out its inhabitants; so because of you we were in terror of our lives, and that is why we did this. We are in your hands: do with us what-ever you think right and proper.' What he did was this: he saved them from death at the hands of the Israelites, and they did not kill them; but from that day he assigned them to cut wood and draw water for the community and for the altar of the Lord. And to this day they do so at the place which the Lord chose.

The Day the Sun Stood Still

When King Adoni-zedek of Jerusalem heard that Joshua had captured and destroyed Ai, dealing with Ai and its king as he had dealt with Jericho and its king, and also that the inhabitants of Gibeon had come to terms with Israel and were living among them, he was greatly alarmed; for Gibeon was a large place, like a royal city: it was larger than Ai, and its men were all good fighters. So King Adoni-zedek of Jerusalem sent this message to King Hoham of Hebron, King Piram of Jarmuth, King Japhia of Lachish, and King Debir of Eglon: 'Come up and assist me to attack Gibeon, because it has come to terms with Joshua and the Israelites.'

The five Amorite kings, the kings of Jerusalem, Hebron, Jarmuth, Lachish, and Eglon, advanced with their united forces to take up position for the attack on Gibeon. The Gibeonites sent word to Joshua in the camp at Gilgal: 'Do not abandon your slaves; come quickly to our relief. Come and help us, for all the Amorite kings in the hill-country have joined forces against us.' When Joshua went up from Gilgal followed by his whole force, all his warriors, the Lord said to him, 'Do not be afraid; I have delivered these kings into your hands, and not one of them will be able to withstand you.' After a night march from Gilgal, Joshua launched a surprise assault on the five kings, and the Lord threw them into confusion before the Israelites. Joshua utterly defeated them at Gibeon; he pursued them down the pass of Beth-horon and kept up the attack as far as Azekah and Makkedah. As they fled from Israel down the pass, the Lord hurled great hailstones at them out of the sky all the way to Azekah, and they perished: more died from the hailstones than were slain by the swords of the Israelites.

On that day when the Lord delivered up the Amorites into the hands of Israel, Joshua spoke with the Lord, and in the presence of Israel said:

'Stand still, you sun, at Gibeon;
you moon, at the vale of Aijalon.'

The sun stood still and the moon halted until the nation had taken vengeance on its enemies, as indeed is written in the Book of Jashar. The sun stayed in mid-heaven and made no haste to set for almost a whole day. Never before or since has there been such a day as that on which the Lord listened to the voice of a mortal.

The five kings fled and hid in a cave at Makkedah, and Joshua was told that they had been found hiding there. Joshua replied, 'Roll large stones against the mouth of the cave, and post men there to keep watch over the kings. But you yourselves must not stay. Keep up the pursuit, attack your enemies from the rear and do not let them reach their towns; the Lord your God has delivered them into your hands.' When Joshua and the Israelites had completed the work of slaughter and everyone had been put to the sword – all except a few survivors who escaped into the fortified towns – the whole army returned safely to Joshua at Makkedah; not one of the Israelites suffered so much as a scratch.

Joshua gave the order: 'Open up the mouth of the cave, and bring out those five kings to me.' This was done; the five kings, the kings of Jerusalem, Hebron, Jarmuth, Lachish, and Eglon, were taken from the cave and brought to Joshua. When he had summoned all the Israelites he said to the commanders of the troops who had served with him, 'Come forward and put your feet on the necks of these kings.' They did so, and Joshua said to them, 'Do not be afraid or discouraged; be strong and resolute; for the Lord will do this to every enemy whom you fight.' He fell on the kings and slew them; then he hung their bodies on five gibbets, where they remained hanging till evening. At sunset they were taken down on Joshua's orders and thrown into the cave in which they had hidden; large stones were piled against its mouth, where they remain to this very day.

The Last Words of Joshua

Joshua took the whole land, the hill-country, all the Negeb, all the land of Goshen, the Shephelah, the Arabah, and the Israelite hill-country with the adjoining lowlands. His conquests extended from the bare mountain which leads up to Seir as far as Baal-gad in the vale of Lebanon under Mount Hermon. He captured all their kings, struck them down, and put them to death. It was a lengthy campaign he waged against all those kingdoms; except for the Hivites who lived in Gibeon, not one of their towns or cities came to terms with the Israelites; all had to be taken by storm. It was the Lord's purpose that they should offer stubborn resistance to the Israelites, and thus be annihilated and utterly destroyed.

Joshua was now very old. He summoned all Israel, their elders and heads of families, their judges and officers, and said to them, 'I am now an old man, far advanced in years.You have seen for yourselves everything the Lord your God has done to all these peoples for your sake; it was the Lord God himself who fought for you. I have allotted to you tribe by tribe your holdings, the land of all the peoples that I have wiped out and of all these that remain between the Jordan and the Great Sea which lies towards the setting sun. The Lord your God himself drove them out at your approach; he dispossessed them to make way for you, and you occupied their land, as the Lord your God had promised you. Be very resolute therefore to observe and perform everything written in the book of the law of Moses, without swerving either to the right or to the left.'

Joshua said to all the people: 'This is the word of the Lord the God of Israel: Long ago your forefathers, including Terah the father of Abraham and Nahor, lived beyond the Euphrates and served other gods. I took your ancestor Abraham from beside the Euphrates and led him through the length and breadth of Canaan. I gave him many descendants: I gave him Isaac, and to Isaac I gave Jacob and Esau. I assigned the hill-country of Seir to Esau as his possession; Jacob and his sons went down to Egypt. Later I sent Moses and Aaron, and I struck the Egyptians with plagues – you know well what I did among them – and after that I brought you out.

'Now hold the Lord in awe, and serve him in loyalty and truth. Put away the gods your fathers served beyond the Euphrates and in Egypt, and serve the Lord. But if it does not please you to serve the Lord, choose here and now whom you will serve: the gods whom your forefathers served beyond the Euphrates, or the gods of the Amorites in whose land you are living. But I and my family, we shall serve the Lord.'

The people answered, 'God forbid that we should forsake the Lord to serve other gods! We shall serve the Lord our God and his voice we shall obey.'

So Joshua made a covenant for the people that day; he drew up a statute and an ordinance for them in Shechem and recorded its terms in the book of the law of God. He took a great stone and set it up there under the terebinth in the sanctuary of the Lord. He said to all the people, 'You see this stone – it will be a witness against us; for it has heard all the words which the Lord has spoken to us. If you renounce your God, it will be a witness against you.' Then Joshua dismissed the people, each man to his allotted holding.

After these events, Joshua son of Nun, the servant of the Lord, died at the age of a hundred and ten. They buried him within his own holding in Timnath-serah to the north of Mount Gaash in the hill-country of Ephraim. Israel served the Lord throughout the lifetime of Joshua, and of the elders who outlived him and who knew all that the Lord had done for Israel.

8 | THE AGE OF THE JUDGES

The Israelites Turn Away from God
When that whole generation was gathered to its forefathers, and was succeeded by another generation, who did not acknowledge the Lord and did not know what he had done for Israel, then the Israelites did what was wrong in the eyes of the Lord by serving the baalim. They forsook the Lord, their fathers' God who had brought them out of Egypt, and went after other gods, the gods of the peoples among whom they lived; by bowing down before them they provoked the Lord to anger; they forsook the Lord and served the baalim and the ashtaroth. In his anger the Lord made them the prey of bands of raiders and plunderers; he sold them into the power of their enemies around them, so that they could no longer stand against them. Every time they went out to do battle the Lord brought disaster on them, as he had said when he gave them his solemn warning; and they were in dire straits.

Then the Lord raised up judges to rescue them from the marauding bands, yet even to their judges they did not listen. They prostituted themselves by worshipping other gods and bowed down before them; all too soon they abandoned the path of obedience to the Lord's commands which their forefathers had followed. They did not obey the Lord. Whenever the Lord set up a judge over them, he was with that judge, and kept them safe from their enemies so long as the judge lived. The Lord would relent when he heard them groaning under oppression and tyranny. But on the death of the judge they would relapse into corruption deeper than that of their predecessors and go after other gods; serving them and bowing before them, they would give up none of their evil practices and wilful ways.

Ehud Defeats the Moabites
King Eglon of Moab mustered the Ammonites and the Amalekites, attacked Israel, and took possession of the city of

133

palm trees. The Israelites were subject to King Eglon of Moab for eighteen years.

Then they cried to the Lord for help, and to deliver them he raised up Ehud son of Gera the Benjamite; he was left-handed. The Israelites sent him to hand over their tribute to King Eglon. Ehud had made himself a two-edged sword, about eighteen inches long, which he fastened on his right side under his clothes when he brought the tribute to King Eglon. Eglon was a very fat man.

After Ehud had finished presenting the tribute, he sent on the men who had carried it, while he himself turned back from the Carved Stones at Gilgal. 'My lord king,' he said, 'I have a message for you in private.' Eglon called for silence and dismissed all his attendants. Ehud then approached him as he sat in the roof-chamber of his summer palace. He said, 'Your majesty, I have a message from God for you.' As Eglon rose from his seat, Ehud reached with his left hand, drew the sword from his right side, and drove it into Eglon's belly. The hilt went in after the blade and the fat closed over the blade, for he did not draw the sword out but left it protruding behind. Ehud then went out to the porch, where he shut the door on him and fastened it.

After he had gone, Eglon's servants came and, finding the doors fastened, they said, 'He must be relieving himself in the closet of his summer palace.' They waited until they became alarmed and, when he still did not open the door of the roof-chamber, they took the key and opened the door; and there was their master lying dead on the floor.

While they had been waiting, Ehud had made good his escape; he passed the Carved Stones and escaped to Seirah. Once there, he sounded the trumpet in the hill-country of Ephraim, and the Israelites went down from the hills with him at their head. He said to them, 'Follow me, for the Lord has delivered your enemies, the Moabites, into your hands.' They went down after him, and held the fords of the Jordan against the Moabites, allowing no one to cross. They killed at that time some ten thousand Moabites, all of them stalwart and valiant fighters; not one escaped. Moab became subject to Israel on that day, and the land was at peace for eighty years.

Deborah and Barak Defeat the Cannanites

After Ehud's death the Israelites once again did what was wrong in the eyes of the Lord, and he sold them into the power of Jabin, the Canaanite king who ruled in Hazor. The commander of his forces was Sisera, who lived in Harosheth-of-the-Gentiles. The Israelites cried to the Lord for help, because Sisera with his nine hundred iron-clad chariots had oppressed Israel harshly for twenty years.

At that time Deborah wife of Lappidoth, a prophetess, was judge in Israel. It was her custom to sit under the Palm Tree of Deborah between Ramah and Bethel in the hill-country of Ephraim, and Israelites seeking a judgement went up to her. She sent for Barak son of Abinoam from Kedesh in Naphtali and said to him, 'This is the command of the Lord the God of Israel: Go and lead out ten thousand men from Naphtali and Zebulun and bring them with you to Mount Tabor. I shall draw out to you at the wadi Kishon Jabin's commander Sisera, along with his chariots and troops, and deliver him into your power.' Barak answered, 'If you go with me, I shall go, but if you will not go, neither shall I.' 'Certainly I shall go with you,' she said, 'but this venture will bring you no glory, because the Lord will leave Sisera to fall into the hands of a woman.' Deborah set off with Barak and went to Kedesh. Barak mustered Zebulun and Naphtali to Kedesh and marched up with ten thousand followers; Deborah went up with him.

Now Heber the Kenite had parted company with the Kenites, the descendants of Hobab, Moses' brother-in-law, and he had pitched his tent at Elon-bezaanannim near Kedesh. When it was reported to Sisera that Barak son of Abinoam had gone up to Mount Tabor, he mustered all nine hundred of his iron-clad chariots, along with all the troops he had, and marched from Harosheth-of-the-Gentiles to the wadi Kishon. Deborah said to Barak, 'Up! This day the Lord is to give Sisera into your hands. See, the Lord has marched out at your head!' Barak came down from Mount Tabor with ten thousand men at his back, and the Lord threw Sisera and all his chariots and army into panic-stricken rout before Barak's onslaught; Sisera himself dismounted from his chariot and fled on foot. Barak pursued the chariots and the troops as far as Harosheth, and the whole army was put to the sword; not a man was left alive.

Meanwhile Sisera fled on foot to the tent of Jael wife of Heber the Kenite, because King Jabin of Hazor and the household of Heber the Kenite were on friendly terms. Jael came out to greet Sisera and said, 'Come in, my lord, come in here; do not be afraid.' He went into the tent, and she covered him with a rug. He said to her, 'Give me some water to drink, for I am thirsty.' She opened a skin of milk, gave him a drink, and covered him again. He said to her, 'Stand at the tent door, and if anyone comes and asks if there is a man here, say "No."' But as Sisera lay fast asleep through exhaustion Jael took a tent-peg, picked up a mallet, and, creeping up to him, drove the peg into his temple, so that it went down into the ground, and Sisera died. When Barak came by in pursuit of Sisera, Jael went out to meet him. 'Come,' she said, 'I shall show you the man you are looking for.' He went in with her, and there was Sisera lying dead with the tent-peg in his temple. That day God gave victory to the Israelites over King Jabin of Canaan, and they pressed home their attacks upon him until he was destroyed.

On that day Deborah and Barak son of Abinoam sang this song:

'Blest above women be Jael
wife of Heber the Kenite;
blest above all women in the tents.
He asked for water: she gave him milk,
she offered him curds in a bowl fit for a chieftain.
She reached out her hand for the tent-peg,
her right hand for the workman's hammer.
With the hammer she struck Sisera, crushing his head;
with a shattering blow she pierced his temple.
At her feet he sank, he fell, he lay prone;
at her feet he sank down and fell.
Where he sank down, there he fell, done to death.

'The mother of Sisera peered through the lattice,
through the window she peered and cried,
"Why is his chariot so long in coming?
Why is the clatter of his chariots so delayed?"
The wisest of her ladies answered her,
yes, she found her own answer:

"They must be finding spoil, taking their shares,
a damsel for each man, two damsels,
booty of dyed stuffs for Sisera,
booty of dyed stuffs,
dyed stuff and brocade, two lengths of brocade
to grace the victor's neck."

'So perish all your enemies, Lord;
but let those who love you be like the sun rising in strength.'

The land was at peace for forty years.

Gideon Defeats the Midianites
The Israelites did what was wrong in the eyes of the Lord and he delivered them into the hands of Midian for seven years. The Midianites were too strong for the Israelites, who were forced to find themselves hollow places in the mountains, in caves and fastnesses. If the Israelites had sown seed, the Midianites and the Amalekites and other eastern tribes would come up and attack Israel, pitching their camps in the country and destroying the crops as far as the outskirts of Gaza. They left nothing to support life in Israel, neither sheep nor ox nor donkey. They came up with their herds and their tents, swarming like locusts; they and their camels were past counting. They would come into the land and lay it waste. The Israelites, brought to destitution by the Midianites, cried to the Lord for help.

The angel of the Lord came to Ophrah and sat under the terebinth which belonged to Joash the Abiezrite. While Gideon son of Joash was threshing wheat in the winepress, so that he might keep it out of sight of the Midianites, the angel of the Lord appeared to him and said, 'You are a brave man, and the Lord is with you.' 'Pray, my lord,' said Gideon, 'if the Lord really is with us, why has all this happened to us? What has become of all those wonderful deeds of his, of which we have heard from our forefathers, when they told us how the Lord brought us up from Egypt? But now the Lord has cast us off and delivered us into the power of the Midianites.'

The Lord turned to him and said, 'Go and use this strength of yours to free Israel from the Midianites. It is I who send you.' Gideon said, 'Pray, my lord, how can I save Israel? Look at my clan: it is the weakest in Manasseh, and I am the least in my father's family.' The Lord answered, 'I shall be with you, and you will lay low all Midian as one man.'

That night the Lord said to Gideon, 'Take a young bull of your father's, the yearling bull; tear down the altar of Baal belonging to your father, and cut down the sacred pole which stands beside it. Then build an altar of the proper pattern to the Lord your God on the top of this earthwork; take the yearling bull and offer it as a whole-offering with the wood of the sacred pole that you cut down.' Gideon took ten of his servants and did as the Lord had told him; but because he was afraid of his father's family and the people of the town, he did it by night and not by day.

When the people rose early next morning, they found the altar of Baal overturned, the sacred pole which had stood beside it cut down, and the yearling bull offered up as a whole-offering on an altar which had been built. They asked among themselves who had done it, and, after searching enquiries, they declared it was Gideon son of Joash. The townspeople said to Joash, 'Bring out your son. He has overturned the altar of Baal and cut down the sacred pole beside it; he must die.' But as they crowded round him Joash retorted, 'Are you pleading Baal's cause then? Do you think it is for you to save him? Whoever pleads his cause shall be put to death at dawn. If Baal is a god, and someone has torn down his altar, let him take up his own cause.' That day Joash named Gideon Jerubbaal, saying, 'Let Baal plead his own cause against this man, for he has torn down his altar.'

When all the Midianites, the Amalekites, and the eastern tribes joined forces, crossed the river, and encamped in the valley of Jezreel, the spirit of the Lord took possession of Gideon. He sounded the trumpet to call out the Abiezrites to follow him, and sent messengers all through Manasseh; and they too rallied to him. He sent messengers to Asher, Zebulun, and Naphtali, and they advanced to meet the others.

Gideon said to God, 'If indeed you are going to deliver Israel through me as you promised, I shall put a fleece of wool on the threshing-floor, and if there is dew on the fleece while all the ground is dry, then I shall be sure that it is through me you will deliver Israel as you promised.' And that is what happened. When he rose early next day and wrung out the fleece, he squeezed enough dew from it to fill a bowl with water. Gideon then said to God, 'Do not be angry with me, but give me leave to speak once again. Allow me, I pray, to make one more test with the fleece. This time let the fleece be dry, and all the ground be covered with dew.' God let it be so that night: the fleece alone was dry, and all over the ground there was dew.

Early next morning Jerubbaal, that is Gideon, with all his troops pitched camp at En-harod; the Midianite encampment was in the valley to the north of his by the hill at Moreh. The Lord said to Gideon, 'Those with you are more than I need to deliver Midian into their hands: Israel might claim the glory for themselves and say that it is their own strength that has given them the victory. Make a proclamation now to the army to say that anyone who is afraid or anxious is to leave Mount Galud at once and go home.' Twenty-two thousand of them went, and ten thousand remained.

'There are still too many,' said the Lord to Gideon. 'Bring them down to the water, and I shall separate them for you there. If I say to you, "This man shall go with you," he shall go; and if I say, "This man shall not go," he shall not go.' When Gideon brought the men down to the water, the Lord said to him, 'Make every man who laps the water with his tongue like a dog stand on one side, and on the other every man who kneels down and drinks.' The number of those who lapped, putting their hands to their mouths, was three hundred; all the rest had gone down on their knees to drink. The Lord said, 'By means of the three hundred men who lapped I shall save you and give Midian into your power; the rest may go home.' Gideon sent all these Israelites home, but he kept the three hundred, and they took with them the jars and the trumpets which the people had.

The Midianite camp was below him in the valley, and that night the Lord said to Gideon, 'Go down at once and attack the camp, for I have delivered it into your hands. If you are afraid to do so, then go down first with your servant Purah, and when you hear what they are saying, that will give you courage to attack the camp.' So he and his servant Purah went down to the outposts of the camp where the fighting men were stationed. The Midianites, the Amalekites, and all the eastern tribes were so many that they lay there in the valley like a swarm of locusts; there was no counting their camels, which in number were like grains of sand on the seashore. As Gideon came close, there was a man telling his comrades about a dream. He said, 'I dreamt that I saw a barley loaf rolling over and over through the Midianite camp; it came to a tent, struck it, and the tent collapsed and turned upside down.' The other answered, 'This can be none other than the sword of Gideon son of Joash the Israelite. God has delivered Midian and the whole army into his hands.'

When Gideon heard the account of the dream and its interpretation, he bowed down in worship. Then going back to the Israelite camp he said, 'Let us go! The Lord has delivered the camp of the Midianites into our hands.' He divided the three hundred men into three companies, and furnished every man with a trumpet and an empty jar, with a torch inside each jar. 'Watch me,' he said to them. 'When I come to the edge of the camp, do exactly as I do. When I and those with me blow our trumpets, you too all round the camp blow your trumpets and shout, "For the Lord and for Gideon!"'

Gideon and the hundred men who were with him reached the outskirts of the camp at the beginning of the middle watch, just after the posting of the sentries. They blew the trumpets and smashed the jars they were holding. All three companies blew their trumpets and smashed their jars; then, grasping the torches in their left hands and the trumpets in their right, they shouted, 'A sword for the Lord and for Gideon!' Every man stood where he was, all round the camp, and the whole camp leapt up in a panic and took flight. When the three hundred blew their trumpets, the Lord set all the men in the camp fighting against each other. They fled as far as Beth-shittah in the direction of Zererah, as far as the ridge of Abel-meholah near Tabbath.

The Israelites from Naphtali and Asher and all Manasseh were called out to pursue the Midianites. Gideon also sent messengers throughout the hill-country of Ephraim to say: 'Come down and cut off the Midianites. Hold the fords of the Jordan against them as far as Beth-barah.'

Gideon came to the Jordan, and he and his three hundred men crossed over to continue the pursuit, exhausted though they were. He said to the people of Succoth, 'Will you give my followers some bread? They are exhausted, and I am pursuing Zebah and Zalmunna, the kings of Midian.' But the chief men of Succoth replied, 'Are Zebah and Zalmunna already in your hands, that we should give bread to your troops?' Gideon said, 'For that, when the Lord delivers Zebah and Zalmunna into my hands, I shall thresh your bodies with desert thorns and briars.' He went on from there to Penuel and made the same request; the people of Penuel gave the same answer as had the people of Succoth.

He said to them, 'When I return victorious, I shall pull down your tower.'

Zebah and Zalmunna were at Karkor with an army of about fifteen thousand men. Those were all that remained of the entire host of the eastern tribes, a hundred and twenty thousand warriors having fallen in battle. Gideon advanced along the track used by the tent-dwellers east of Nobah and Jogbehah, and his attack caught the enemy off guard. Zebah and Zalmunna fled; but he went in pursuit of the Midianite kings and captured them both; and their whole army melted away.

As Gideon son of Joash was returning from battle by the ascent of Heres, he caught a young man from Succoth. When questioned the young man listed for him the names of the rulers of Succoth and its elders, seventy-seven in all. Gideon then came to the people of Succoth and said, 'Here are Zebah and Zalmunna, about whom you taunted me. "Are Zebah and Zalmunna already in your hands," you said, "that we should give your exhausted men bread?"' Then he took the elders of Succoth and inflicted punishment on them with desert thorns and briars. He also pulled down the tower of Penuel and put the men of the town to death.

He said to Zebah and Zalmunna, 'What sort of men did you kill in Tabor?' They answered, 'They were like you; every one had the look of a king's son.' 'They were my brothers,' he said, 'my mother's sons. I swear by the Lord, if you had let them live I would not have killed you.' Then he said to his eldest son Jether, 'Stand up and kill them.' But he was still only a lad, and did not draw his sword, because he was afraid. Zebah and Zalmunna said, 'Rise up yourself and dispatch us, for you have a man's strength.' So Gideon got up and killed them both, and he took the crescents from the necks of their camels.

The Israelites said to Gideon, 'You have saved us from the Midianites; now you be our ruler, you and your son and your grandson.' But Gideon replied, 'I shall not rule over you, nor will my son; the Lord will rule over you.' He went on, 'I have a request to make: will every one of you give me an ear-ring from his booty?' – for the enemy, being Ishmaelites, wore gold ear-rings. They said, 'Of course we shall give them.' So a cloak was spread out and every man threw on to it a gold ear-ring from his booty. The ear-rings he asked for weighed seventeen hundred shekels of gold; this was in addition to the crescents and pendants and the purple robes worn by the Midianite kings, and not counting the chains on the necks of their camels. Gideon made the gold into an ephod which he set up in his own town of Ophrah. All the Israelites went astray by worshipping it, and it became a snare for Gideon and his household.

Thus the Midianites were subdued by the Israelites; they could no longer hold up their heads. For forty years the land was at peace, all the lifetime of Gideon, that is Jerubbaal son of Joash; and he retired to his own home. Gideon had seventy sons, his own offspring, for he had many wives. He had a concubine who lived in Shechem, and she also bore him a son, whom he named Abimelech. Gideon son of Joash died at a ripe old age and was buried in his father's grave at Ophrah-of-the-Abiezrites.

After Gideon's death the Israelites again went astray: they worshipped the baalim and made Baal-berith their god. They were unmindful of the Lord their God who had delivered them from all their enemies around them, nor did they show to the family of Jerubbaal, that is Gideon, the loyalty that was due to them for all the good he had done Israel.

Abimelech the King
Abimelech son of Jerubbaal went to Shechem to his mother's brothers, and spoke with them and with the rest of the clan of his mother's family. 'I beg you,' he said, 'whisper a word in the ears of all the people of Shechem. Ask them which is better for them: that seventy men, all the sons of Jerubbaal, should rule over them, or one man. Tell them to remember that I am their own flesh and blood.' When his mother's kinsfolk repeated all this to every Shechemite on his behalf, they were moved to come over to Abimelech's side, because, as they said, he was their kinsman. They gave him seventy pieces of silver from the temple of Baal-berith, and with these he hired good-for-nothing, reckless fellows as his followers. He went to his father's house in Ophrah and butchered his seventy brothers, the sons of Jerubbaal, on a single stone block, all but Jotham, the youngest, who survived because

he had gone into hiding. Then all the inhabitants of Shechem and all Beth-millo came together and made Abimelech king beside the propped-up terebinth at Shechem.

After Abimelech had been prince over Israel for three years, God sent an evil spirit to create a breach between Abimelech and the inhabitants of Shechem, and they broke faith with him. This was done in order that the violent murder of the seventy sons of Jerubbaal might recoil on their brother Abimelech who did the murder, and on the people of Shechem who encouraged him to do it. The people of Shechem set men to lie in wait for him on the hilltops, and they robbed all who passed that way. But Abimelech had word of it.

Next day the people came out into the open country, and this was reported to Abimelech. He took his supporters, divided them into three companies, and lay in wait in the open country; when he saw the people coming out of the city, he rose and attacked them. Abimelech and the company with him advanced rapidly and took up position at the entrance of the city gate, while the other two companies made a dash against all those who were in the open and struck them down. Abimelech kept up the attack on the city all that day and, when he captured it, he slaughtered the people inside, razed the city to the ground, and sowed it with salt.

When news of this reached the occupants of the tower of Shechem, they took refuge in the crypt of the temple of Elberith. It was reported to Abimelech that all the occupants of the tower of Shechem had flocked together, and he and all his men went up Mount Zalmon, where with an axe he cut brushwood. He took it and, hoisting it on his shoulder, he said to his men, 'You see what I am doing; quick, do the same.' Each man cut brushwood and then following Abimelech they laid the brushwood on the crypt. They burnt it over the heads of the occupants of the tower, and they all died, about a thousand men and women.

Abimelech proceeded to Thebez, which he besieged and captured. There was a strong tower in the middle of the town, and all the townspeople, men and women, took refuge there. They shut themselves in and went up on the roof. Abimelech came up to the tower and attacked it, and as he approached the entrance to set fire to it, a woman threw a millstone down on his head and fractured his skull. He called hurriedly to his armour-bearer and said, 'Draw your sword and dispatch me, or it will be said of me:

A woman killed him.' So the young man ran him through, and he died. When the Israelites saw that Abimelech was dead, they all went back to their homes. In this way God repaid the crime which Abimelech had committed against his father by the murder of his seventy brothers, and brought all the wickedness of the men of Shechem on their own heads.

Jephthah Defeats the Ammonites

Jephthah the Gileadite was an intrepid warrior; he was the son of Gilead by a prostitute. Gilead's wife also bore him sons, and when they grew up they drove Jephthah away, saying to him, 'You have no inheritance in our father's house; you are another woman's son.' To escape his brothers, Jephthah fled and settled in the land of Tob, and a number of good-for-nothing fellows rallied to him and became his followers.

The time came when the Ammonites launched an offensive against Israel and, when the fighting began, the elders of Gilead went to fetch Jephthah from the land of Tob. 'Come and be our commander so that we can fight the Ammonites,' they said to him. But Jephthah answered, 'You drove me from my father's house in hatred. Why come to me now when you are in trouble?' 'It is because of that', they replied, 'that we have turned to you now. Come with us, fight the Ammonites, and become head over all the inhabitants of Gilead.' Jephthah said to them, 'If you ask me back to fight the Ammonites and if the Lord delivers them into my hands, then I must become your head.' The Gilead elders said to him, 'We swear by the Lord, who will be witness between us, that we will do what you say.' Jephthah then went with the elders of Gilead, and the people made him their head and commander. And at Mizpah, in the presence of the Lord, Jephthah repeated the terms he had laid down.

Jephthah sent a mission to the king of Ammon to ask what quarrel he had with them that made him invade their country. The king replied to the messengers: 'When the Israelites came up from Egypt, they seized our land all the way from the Arnon to the Jabbok and the Jordan. Now return these lands peaceably.' Jephthah sent a second mission to the king of Ammon to say, 'This is Jephthah's answer: The Lord the God of Israel drove out the Amorites for the benefit of his people Israel. And do you now propose to take their place? It is for you to possess whatever

Kemosh your god gives you; and all that the Lord our God gave us as we advanced is ours.

'For that matter, are you any better than Balak son of Zippor, king of Moab? Did he ever pick a quarrel with Israel or attack them? For three hundred years Israelites have lived in Heshbon and its dependent villages, in Aroer and its villages, and in all the towns by the Arnon. Why did you not retake them during all that time? We have done you no wrong; it is you who are doing us wrong by attacking us. The Lord who is judge will decide this day between the Israelites and the Ammonites.' But the king of the Ammonites would not listen to the message Jephthah sent him.

Then Jephthah made this vow to the Lord: 'If you will deliver the Ammonites into my hands, then the first creature that comes out of the door of my house to meet me when I return from them safely shall be the Lord's; I shall offer that as a whole-offering.'

So Jephthah crossed over to attack the Ammonites, and the Lord delivered them into his hands. He routed them with very great slaughter all the way from Aroer to near Minnith, taking twenty towns, and as far as Abel-keramim. Thus Ammon was subdued by Israel.

When Jephthah arrived home in Mizpah, it was his daughter who came out to meet him with tambourines and dancing. She was his only child; apart from her he had neither son nor daughter. At the sight of her, he tore his clothes and said, 'Oh, my daughter, you have broken my heart! Such calamity you have brought on me! I have made a vow to the Lord and I cannot go back on it.'

She replied, 'Father, since you have made a vow to the Lord, do to me as your vow demands, now that the Lord has avenged you on the Ammonites, your enemies. But, father, grant me this one favour: spare me for two months, that I may roam the hills with my companions and mourn that I must die a virgin.' 'Go,' he said, and he let her depart for two months. She went with her companions and mourned her virginity on the hills. At the end of two months she came back to her father, and he fulfilled the vow he had made; she died a virgin. It became a tradition that the daughters of Israel should go year by year and commemorate for four days the daughter of Jephthah the Gileadite.

The Ephraimites mustered their forces and, crossing over to Zaphon, said to Jephthah, 'Why did you march against the

Ammonites and not summon us to go with you? We shall burn your house over your head.' Jephthah answered, 'I and my people had a grave feud with the Ammonites, and had I appealed to you for help, you would not have saved us from them. When I saw that we were not to look for help from you, I took my life in my hands and marched against the Ammonites, and the Lord delivered them into my power. So why do you now attack me?' Jephthah then mustered all the men of Gilead and fought Ephraim, and the Gileadites defeated them. The Gileadites seized the fords of the Jordan and held them against Ephraim. When any Ephraimite who had escaped wished to cross, the men of Gilead would ask, 'Are you an Ephraimite?' and if he said, 'No,' they would retort, 'Say "Shibboleth."' He would say 'Sibboleth,' and because he could not pronounce the word properly, they seized him and killed him at the fords. At that time forty-two thousand men of Ephraim lost their lives.

Jephthah was judge over Israel for six years; when he died he was buried in his own town in Gilead.

Micah and the Idol

Once there was a man named Micah from the hill-country of Ephraim who said to his mother, 'You remember the eleven hundred pieces of silver which were stolen from you, and how in my hearing you called down a curse on the thief? I have the money; I took it, and now I give it back to you.' His mother said, 'May the Lord bless you, my son!' He gave back the eleven hundred pieces of silver to his mother, and she said, 'I now solemnly dedicate this silver to the Lord for the benefit of my son, to make a carved image and a cast idol.'

When he returned the money to his mother, she handed two hundred of the pieces of silver to a silversmith, who made them into an image and an idol, which were placed in Micah's house. This man Micah had a shrine, and he made an ephod and teraphim and installed one of his sons to be his priest.

There was a young man from Bethlehem in Judah, from the clan of Judah, a Levite named Ben-gershom. He had left the city of Bethlehem to go and find somewhere to live. On his way he came to Micah's house in the hill-country of Ephraim. Micah asked him, 'Where have you come from?' and he replied, 'I am a Levite from Bethlehem in Judah, and I am looking for somewhere to live.' 'Stay with me and be a father and priest to me,' Micah said. 'I shall give you ten pieces of silver a year, and provide you with food and clothes.' The Levite agreed to stay with the man, who treated him as one of his own family. Micah installed the Levite, and the young man became his priest and a member of his household. Micah said, 'Now I know that the Lord will make me prosper, because I have a Levite as my priest.'

In those days, when Israel had no king, the tribe of Dan was looking for territory to occupy, because they had not so far come into possession of the territory allotted to them among the tribes of Israel. The Danites therefore sent out five of their valiant fighters from Zorah and Eshtaol, instructing them to reconnoitre and explore the land. As they followed their instructions, they came to Micah's house in the hill-country of Ephraim and spent the night there. While at the house, they recognized the speech of the young Levite, and turning they said, 'Who brought you here, and what are you doing? What is your business here?' He explained, 'Micah did such and such: he hired me and I have become his priest.' They said to him, 'Then enquire of God on our behalf whether our mission will be successful.' The priest replied, 'Go and prosper. The Lord looks favourably on the mission you have undertaken.'

The five men went on their way and came to Laish. There they found the inhabitants living free of care in the same way as the Sidonians, quiet and carefree with nothing lacking in the country. They were a long way from the Sidonians, and had no contact with the Aramaeans.

On their return to Zorah and Eshtaol, the five men were asked by their kinsmen for their report, and they replied, 'Go and attack them at once. The land that we saw was very good. Why hang back? Do not hesitate to go there and take possession. When you get there, you will find a people living a carefree life in a wide expanse of open country. It is a place where nothing on earth is lacking, and God has delivered it into your hands.'

Six hundred fully armed men from the Danite clan set out from Zorah and Eshtaol, and went up country, where they encamped in Kiriath-jearim in Judah, which is why that place is called Mahaneh-dan to this day; it lies west of Kiriath-jearim. From there they passed on to the hill-country of Ephraim until they came to Micah's house. The five men who had been sent to reconnoitre the country round Laish addressed their kinsmen. 'Do you know', they said, 'that in one of these houses there are an ephod and teraphim, an image and an idol? Now consider what you had best do.'

They turned aside to Micah's house and greeted him. As the six hundred armed Danites took their stand at the entrance of the gate, the five men who had gone to explore the country went indoors to take the image and the idol, the ephod and the teraphim; the priest meanwhile was standing at the entrance with the six hundred armed men. When the five men entered Micah's house and laid hands on the image and the idol, the ephod and the teraphim, the priest asked them what they were doing. They said to him, 'Be quiet; not a word. Come with us and be to us a father and priest. Which is better, to be priest in the household of one man or to be priest to a tribe and clan in Israel?' This pleased the priest, and carrying off the ephod and the teraphim, the image and the idol, he went with the people. They set out on their way, putting their dependants, herds, and possessions in front.

The Danites had gone some distance from Micah's house, when his neighbours were called out in pursuit. As they caught up with them, they shouted, and the Danites turned round and said to Micah, 'What is the matter with you that you have called out your men?' 'You have taken the gods which I made for myself and have taken the priest,' he answered; 'you have gone off and left me nothing. How can you ask, "What is the matter with you?".' The Danites said to him, 'Not another word from you! We are desperate men and if we set about you it will be the death of you and your family.' With that the Danites went on their way, and Micah, seeing that they were too strong for him, turned and went home.

Carrying off the things which Micah had made for himself along with his priest, the Danites then attacked Laish, whose people were quiet and carefree. They put the people to the sword and set fire to their town. There was no one to save them, for it was a long way from Sidon and they had no contact with the Aramaeans; the town was in the valley near Beth-rehob. They rebuilt the town and settled in it, naming it Dan after their fore-father Dan, a son of Israel; its original name was Laish. The Danites set up the image, and Jonathan son of Gershom, son of Moses, and his sons were priests to the tribe of Dan until the exile.

A Levite and his Concubine

In those days when Israel had no king, a Levite residing in the heart of the hill-country of Ephraim had taken himself a concubine from Bethlehem in Judah. In a fit of anger she had left him and gone to her father's house in Bethlehem in Judah. When she had been there four months, her husband set out after her, with his servant and two donkeys, to appeal to her and bring her back. She brought him into the house of her father, who was delighted to see him and made him welcome. Being pressed by his father-in-law, the girl's father, he stayed there three days, and they were regaled with food and drink during their visit. On the fourth day, they rose early in the morning, and the Levite prepared to leave, but the father said to his son-in-law, 'Have a bite of something to sustain you before you go,' and the two of them sat down and ate and drank together. The girl's father said to the man, 'Why not spend the night and enjoy yourself?' The man, however, rose to go, but his father-in-law urged him to stay, and again he stayed for the night. He rose early in the morning on the fifth day to depart, but the girl's father said, 'Have something to eat first.' So they lingered till late afternoon, eating and drinking together. Then the man stood up to go with his concubine and his servant, but his father-in-law said, 'Look, the day is wearing on towards sunset. Spend the night here and enjoy yourself, and tomorrow rise early and set out for home.' But the man would not stay the night; he set off on his journey.

He reached a point opposite Jebus, that is Jerusalem, with his two laden donkeys and his concubine. Since they were close to Jebus and the day was nearly gone, the servant said to his master, 'Do let us turn into this Jebusite town for the night.' His master replied, 'No, not into a strange town where the people are not Israelites; let us go on to Gibeah. Come, we will go and find some other place, Gibeah or Ramah, to spend the night.' So they went on until sunset overtook them; they were then near Gibeah which belongs to Benjamin. They turned in there to spend the night, and went and sat down in the open square of the town; but nobody took them into his house for the night.

At nightfall an old man was coming home from his work in the fields. He was from the hill-country of Ephraim, though he lived in Gibeah, where the people were Benjamites. When his eye lighted on the traveller in the town square, he asked him where he was going and where he came from. He answered, 'We are travelling from Bethlehem in Judah to the heart of the hill-country of Ephraim. I come from there; I have been to Bethlehem in Judah and I am going home, but nobody has taken me into his house. I have straw and provender for our donkeys, food and wine for myself, the girl, and the young man; we have all we need.' The old man said, 'You are welcome. I shall supply all your wants; you must not spend the night in the open.' He took him inside, where he provided fodder for the donkeys. Then, having bathed their feet, they all ate and drank.

While they were enjoying themselves, some of the most depraved scoundrels in the town surrounded the house, beating the door violently and shouting to the old man whose house it was, 'Bring out the man who has come to your house, for us to have intercourse with him.' The owner of the house went outside to them and said, 'No, my friends, do nothing so wicked. This man is my guest; do not commit this outrage. Here are my daughter, who is a virgin, and the man's concubine; let me bring them out to you. Abuse them and do what you please; but you must not commit such an outrage against this man.' When the men refused to listen to him, the Levite took his concubine and thrust her outside for them. They raped and abused her all night till the morning; only when dawn broke did they let her go. The woman came at day-break and collapsed at the entrance of the man's house where her husband was, and lay there until it was light.

Her husband rose in the morning and opened the door of the house to be on his way, and there was his concubine lying at the door with her hands on the threshold. He said to her, 'Get up and let us be off'; but there was no answer. So he lifted her on to his donkey and set off for home. When he arrived there, he picked up a knife, took hold of his concubine, and cut her limb by limb into twelve pieces, which he then sent through the length and breadth of Israel. He told the men he sent with them to say to every Israelite, 'Has the like of this happened or been seen from the time the Israelites came up from Egypt till today? Consider among yourselves and speak your minds.' Everyone who saw them said, 'Since that time no such thing has ever happened or been seen.'

All the Israelites, the whole community from Dan to Beersheba and also from Gilead, left their homes and as one man assembled before the Lord at Mizpah. The Israelites asked how this wicked crime happened, and the Levite, to whom the murdered woman belonged, answered, 'I and my concubine arrived at Gibeah in Benjamin to spend the night. The townsmen of Gibeah rose against me that night and surrounded the house where I was, intending to kill me; and they raped my concubine so that she died. I took her and cut her in pieces, and sent the pieces through the length and breadth of Israel, because of the abominable out-rage they had committed in Israel. It is for you, the whole of Israel, to come to a decision as to what action should be taken.'

As one man all the people stood up and declared, 'Not one of us will go back to his tent, not one will return home. But this is what we shall do to Gibeah: we shall draw lots for the attack, and in all the tribes of Israel we shall take ten men out of every hun-dred, a hundred out of every thousand, and a thousand out of every ten thousand, and they will collect provisions for the army, for those who have taken the field against Gibeah in Benjamin to avenge the outrage committed in Israel.' Thus all the Israelites, united to a man, were massed against the town.

The tribes of Israel sent messengers throughout the tribe of Benjamin saying, 'What crime is this that has taken place among you? Hand over to us now those scoundrels in Gibeah; we shall put them to death and purge Israel of this wickedness.' The Benjamites, however, refused to listen to their fellow-Israelites. They flocked from their towns to Gibeah to do battle with the Israelites, and that day they mustered out of their towns twenty-six thousand men armed with swords. There were also seven hundred picked men from Gibeah, left-handed men, who could sling a stone and not miss by a hair's breadth. The Israelites, without the Benjamites, numbered four hundred thousand men armed with swords, every one a warrior. The Israelites at once moved on to Bethel and there sought an oracle from God. 'Which of us is to lead the attack on the Benjamites?' they enquired, and the Lord's answer was, 'Judah is to lead the attack.'

The Israelites set out at dawn and encamped opposite Gibeah. They advanced to do battle with the Benjamites and drew up their forces before the town. The Benjamites sallied out from Gibeah and laid low twenty-two thousand of Israel on the field that day. The Israelites went up to Bethel, where they lamented before the Lord until evening, and enquired whether they should again attack their kinsmen the Benjamites. The Lord said, 'Go up to the attack.' The Israelite army took fresh courage and formed up again on the same ground as the first day. So on the second day they advanced against the Benjamites, who sallied out from Gibeah to meet them and laid low on the field another eighteen thousand armed men.

The Israelites, the whole army, went back to Bethel, where they sat before the Lord lamenting and fasting until evening, and they offered whole-offerings and shared-offerings before the Lord. In those days the Ark of the Covenant of God was there, and Phinehas son of Eleazar, son of Aaron, served before the Lord. The Israelites enquired of the Lord, 'Shall we again march out to battle against Benjamin our kin, or shall we desist?' The Lord answered, 'Attack! Tomorrow I shall deliver him into your hands.'

The Israelites posted men in ambush all round Gibeah, and on the third day they advanced against the Benjamites and drew up their forces at Gibeah as before. The Benjamites sallied out to meet them, and were drawn away from the town. They began the attack as before by killing a few Israelites, about thirty, on the highways which led across open country, one to Bethel and the other to Gibeon. They thought that once again they were inflicting a defeat, but the Israelites had planned a retreat to draw them out on the highways away from the town. Meanwhile the main body of Israelites left their positions and re-formed at Baal-tamar, while those in ambush, ten thousand picked men all told, burst out from their position in the neighbourhood of Gibeah and came in on the east of the town. There was soon heavy fighting; yet the Benjamites did not suspect the disaster threatening them. So the Lord put Benjamin to flight before Israel. Twenty-five thousand armed men of Benjamin fell in battle that day, all valiant warriors. The six hundred who survived made off into the wilderness as far as the Rock of Rimmon, and there they remained for four months. The Israelites then turned back to deal with the other Benjamites, and put to the sword the people in the towns and the cattle, every creature that they found; they also set fire to every town within their reach.

The Israelites had taken an oath at Mizpah that none of them would give his daughter in marriage to a Benjamite. The people now came to Bethel and remained there in God's presence till sunset, raising their voices in bitter lamentation. 'Lord God of

Israel,' they cried, 'why has it happened among us that one tribe should this day be lost to Israel?' Early next morning the people built an altar there and offered whole-offerings and shared-offerings. At that the Israelites asked themselves whether among all the tribes of Israel there was any who did not go up to the assembly before the Lord; for under the terms of the weighty oath they had sworn, anyone who had not gone up to the Lord at Mizpah was to be put to death. The Israelites felt remorse over their kinsmen the Benjamites, because, as they said, 'This day one whole tribe has been lopped off Israel.'

They asked, 'What shall we do to provide wives for those who are left, as we ourselves have sworn to the Lord not to give any of our daughters to them in marriage? Is there anyone in all the tribes of Israel who did not go up to the Lord at Mizpah?' Now it happened that no one from Jabesh-gilead had come to the camp for the assembly; so when they held a roll-call of the people, they found that none of the inhabitants of Jabesh-gilead was present. The community therefore sent off twelve thousand valiant fighting men with orders to go and put the inhabitants of Jabesh-gilead to the sword, men, women, and dependants. 'This is what you are to do,' they said: 'put to death every male person, and every woman who has had intercourse with a man, but spare any who are virgins.' This they did. Among the inhabitants of Jabesh-gilead they found four hundred young women who were virgins and had not had intercourse with a man, and they brought them to the camp at Shiloh in Canaan. The whole community sent messengers to the Benjamites at the Rock of Rimmon to parley with them, and peace was proclaimed. The Benjamites came back then, and were given those of the women of Jabesh-gilead who had been spared; but these were not enough.

The people were still full of remorse over Benjamin because the Lord had made this gap in the tribes of Israel. The elders of the community said, 'What can we do for wives for those who are left, as all the women in Benjamin have been wiped out?' They said, 'Heirs there must be for the surviving Benjamites! Then Israel will not see one of its tribes destroyed. Yet we cannot give them our own daughters in marriage, because we have sworn that there shall be a curse on the man who gives a wife to a Benjamite.'

They bethought themselves of the pilgrimage in honour of the Lord, made every year to Shiloh, the place which lies to the north of Bethel, on the east side of the highway from Bethel to Shechem and to the south of Lebonah. They told the Benjamites to go and hide in the vineyards. 'Keep watch,' they said, 'and when the girls of Shiloh come out to take part in the dance, come from the vineyards, and each of you seize one of them for his wife; then be off to the territory of Benjamin. If their fathers or brothers come and complain to us, we shall say to them, "Let them keep them with your approval, for none of us has captured a wife in battle. Had you yourselves given them the women, you would now have incurred guilt."'

The Benjamites did this; they carried off as many wives as they needed, snatching them from the dance; then they went their way back to their own territory, where they rebuilt their towns and settled in them. The Israelites also dispersed by tribes and families, and every man returned to his own holding.

In those days there was no king in Israel; everyone did what was right in his own eyes.

9 | THE STORY OF SAMSON

The Birth of Samson

Once more the Israelites did what was wrong in the eyes of the Lord, and he delivered them into the hands of the Philistines for forty years.

There was a certain man from Zorah of the tribe of Dan whose name was Manoah and whose wife was barren; she had no child. The angel of the Lord appeared to her and said, 'Though you are barren and have no child, you will conceive and give birth to a son. Now be careful to drink no wine or strong drink, and to eat no forbidden food. You will conceive and give birth to a son, and no razor must touch his head, for the boy is to be a Nazirite, consecrated to God from birth. He will strike the first blow for Israel's freedom from the power of the Philistines.'

The woman went and told her husband. 'A man of God came to me,' she said to him; 'his appearance was that of an angel of God, most terrible to see. I did not ask him where he came from, nor did he tell me his name, but he said to me, "You are going to conceive and give birth to a son. From now on drink no wine or strong drink and eat no forbidden food, for the boy is to be a Nazirite, consecrated to God from his birth to the day of his death."'

Manoah prayed to the Lord, 'If it is pleasing to you, Lord, let the man of God whom you sent come again to tell us what we are to do for the boy that is to be born.' God heard Manoah's prayer, and the angel of God came again to the woman, as she was sitting in the field. Her husband not being with her, the woman ran quickly and said to him, 'The man who came to me the other day has appeared to me again.' Manoah went with her at once and approached the man and said, 'Are you the man who talked with my wife?' 'Yes,' he replied, 'I am.' 'Now when your words come true,' Manoah said, 'what kind of boy will he be and what will he do?' The angel of the Lord answered, 'Your wife must be careful to do all that I told her: she must not taste anything that comes from the vine; she must drink no wine or strong drink, and she must eat no forbidden food. She must do whatever I say.'

Manoah said to the angel of the Lord, 'May we urge you to stay? Let us prepare a young goat for you.' The angel replied, 'Though you urge me to stay, I shall not eat your food; but prepare a whole-offering if you will, and offer that to the Lord.' Manoah did not know that he was the angel of the Lord, and said to him, 'What is your name? For we shall want to honour you when your words come true.' The angel of the Lord said to him, 'How can you ask my name? It is a name of wonder.' Manoah took a young goat with the proper grain-offering, and offered it on the rock to the Lord, to him whose works are full of wonder. While Manoah and his wife were watching, the flame went up from the altar towards heaven, and the angel of the Lord ascended in the flame. Seeing this, Manoah and his wife fell face downward to the ground.

The angel of the Lord did not appear again to Manoah and his wife. When Manoah realized that it had been the angel of the Lord, he said to his wife, 'We are doomed to die, for we have seen God.' But she replied, 'If the Lord had wanted to kill us, he would not have accepted a whole-offering and a grain-offering at our hands; he would not now have let us see and hear all this.'

The woman gave birth to a son and named him Samson. The boy grew up in Mahaneh-dan between Zorah and Eshtaol, and the Lord blessed him, and the spirit of the Lord began to move him.

Samson and the Philistines

Samson went down to Timnah, and there a woman, one of the Philistines, caught his notice. On his return he told his father and mother that he had seen this Philistine woman in Timnah and asked them to get her for him as his wife. His parents protested, 'Is there no woman among your cousins or in all our own people? Must you go to the uncircumcised Philistines to find a wife?' But Samson said to his father, 'Get her for me, because she pleases me.' Neither his father nor his mother knew that the Lord was at work in this, seeking an opportunity against the Philistines, who at that time held Israel in subjection.

Samson went down to Timnah and, when he reached the vineyards there, a young lion came at him growling. The spirit of the

Lord suddenly seized him and, without any weapon in his hand, Samson tore the lion to pieces as if it were a kid. He did not tell his parents what he had done. Then he went down and spoke to the woman, and she pleased him.

When, after a time, he went down again to make her his wife, he turned aside to look at the carcass of the lion, and saw there was a swarm of bees in it, and honey. He scraped the honey into his hands and went on, eating as he went. When he came to his father and mother, he gave them some and they ate it; but he did not tell them that he had scraped the honey out of the lion's carcass.

His father went down to see the woman, and Samson gave a feast there as the custom of young men was. When the people saw him, they picked thirty companions to escort him. Samson said to them, 'Let me ask you a riddle. If you can solve it during the seven days of the feast, I shall give you thirty lengths of linen and thirty changes of clothing; but if you cannot guess the answer, then you will give me thirty lengths of linen and thirty changes of clothing.' 'Tell us your riddle,' they said; 'let us hear it.' So he said to them:

'Out of the eater came something to eat;
out of the strong came something sweet.'

At the end of three days they had failed to guess the answer. On the fourth day they said to Samson's wife, 'Coax your husband and make him explain the riddle to you, or we shall burn you and your father's house. Did you invite us here to beggar us?' So Samson's wife wept on his shoulder and said, 'You only hate me, you do not love me. You have asked my kinsfolk a riddle and you have not told it to me.' He said to her, 'I have not told it even to my father and mother; and am I to tell it to you?' But she wept on his shoulder every day until the seven feast days were ended, and on the seventh day, because she pestered him so, he told her, and she told the riddle to her kinsfolk. So on the seventh day the men of the city said to Samson just before he entered the bridal chamber:

'What is sweeter than honey?
What is stronger than a lion?'

He replied, 'If you had not ploughed with my heifer, you would not have solved my riddle.' Then the spirit of the Lord suddenly seized him, and he went down to Ashkelon, where he killed thirty men, took their belts, and gave their clothes to the men who had answered his riddle; then in a furious temper he went off to his father's house. Samson's wife was given in marriage to the one who had been his groomsman.

After a while, during the time of wheat harvest, Samson went to visit his wife, taking a young goat as a present for her. He said, 'I am going to my wife in our bridal chamber,' but her father would not let him in. He said, 'I was sure that you were really hostile to her, so I gave her in marriage to your groomsman. Her young sister is better than she is – take her instead.' Samson said, 'This time I shall settle my score with the Philistines; I shall do them some real harm.' He went and caught three hundred jackals and got some torches; he tied the jackals tail to tail and fastened a torch between each pair of tails. He then lit the torches and turned the jackals loose in the standing grain of the Philistines, setting fire to standing grain and sheaves, as well as to vineyards and olive groves.

'Who has done this?' the Philistines demanded, and when they were told that it was Samson, because the Timnite, his father-in-law, had taken his wife and given her to his groomsman, they came and burnt her and her father to death. Samson said to them, 'If you do things like that, I swear I will be revenged on you before I have done.' He smote them hip and thigh, causing great slaughter; and after that he went down to live in a cave in the Rock of Etam.

The Philistines came up and pitched camp in Judah, and over-ran Lehi. The Judahites said, 'Why have you attacked us?' They answered, 'We have come to take Samson prisoner, and do to him as he did to us.' Then three thousand men from Judah went down to the cave in the Rock of Etam, where they said to Samson, 'Surely you know that the Philistines are our masters? Now look what you have done to us.' He answered, 'I only did to them as they had done to me.' They told him, 'We have come down to bind you and hand you over to the Philistines.' 'Swear to me that you will not set upon me yourselves,' he said. 'No, we shall not kill you,' they answered; 'we shall only bind you and hand you over to them.' They bound him with two new ropes and brought him up from the cave in the Rock.

When Samson came to Lehi, the Philistines met him with shouts of triumph; but the spirit of the Lord suddenly seized him, the ropes on his arms became like burnt tow, and his bonds melted away. He came on the fresh jaw-bone of a donkey, and seizing it he slew a thousand men. He made up this saying:

> 'With the jaw-bone of a donkey
> I have flayed them like donkeys;
> with the jaw-bone of a donkey
> I have slain a thousand men.'

Having said this he threw away the jaw-bone; and he called that place Ramath-lehi.

Samson and Delilah

Samson went to Gaza, and seeing a prostitute there he lay with her. The people of Gaza heard that Samson had come, and they gathered round and lay in wait for him all night at the city gate. During the night, however, they took no action, saying to themselves, 'When dawn comes we shall kill him.' Samson stayed in bed till midnight; but then he rose, took hold of the doors of the city gate and the two gateposts, and pulled them out, bar and all; he hoisted them on his shoulders, and carried them to the top of the hill east of Hebron.

Afterwards Samson fell in love with a woman named Delilah, who lived by the wadi of Sorek. The lords of the Philistines went up to her and said, 'Cajole him and find out what gives him his great strength, and how we can overpower and bind him and render him helpless. We shall each give you eleven hundred pieces of silver.'

Delilah said to Samson, 'Tell me, what gives you your great strength? How could you be bound and made helpless?' 'If I were bound with seven fresh bowstrings not yet dry,' replied Samson, 'then I should become no stronger than any other man.' The lords of the Philistines brought her seven fresh bowstrings not yet dry, and she bound him with them. She had men concealed in the inner room, and she cried, 'Samson, the Philistines are upon you!' Thereupon he snapped the bowstrings as a strand of tow snaps at the touch of fire, and his strength was not impaired.

Delilah said to Samson, 'You have made a fool of me and lied to me. Now tell me this time how you can be bound.' He said to her, 'If I were tightly bound with new ropes that have never been used, then I should become no stronger than any other man.' Delilah took new ropes and bound him with them. Then, with men concealed in the inner room, she cried, 'Samson, the Philistines are upon you!' But he snapped the ropes off his arms like thread.

Delilah said to him, 'You are still making a fool of me, still lying to me. Tell me: how can you be bound?' He said, 'Take the seven loose locks of my hair, weave them into the warp, and drive them tight with the beater; then I shall become no stronger than any other man.' So she lulled him to sleep, wove the seven loose locks of his hair into the warp, drove them tight with the beater, and cried, 'Samson, the Philistines are upon you!' He woke from sleep and pulled away the warp and the loom with it.

She said to him, 'How can you say you love me when you do not confide in me? This is the third time you have made a fool of me and have not told me what gives you your great strength.' She so pestered him with these words day after day, pressing him hard and wearying him to death, that he told her the whole secret. 'No razor has touched my head,' he said, 'because I am a Nazirite, consecrated to God from the day of my birth. If my head were shaved, then my strength would leave me, and I should become no stronger than any other man.'

Delilah realized that he had told her his secret, and she sent word to the lords of the Philistines: 'Come up at once,' she said; 'he has told me his secret.' The lords of the Philistines came, bringing the money with them. She lulled Samson to sleep on her lap, and then summoned a man to shave the seven locks of his hair. She was now making him helpless. When his strength had left him, she cried, 'Samson, the Philistines are upon you!' He woke from his sleep and thought, 'I will go out as usual and shake myself!'; he did not know that the Lord had left him. Then the Philistines seized him, gouged out his eyes, and brought him down to Gaza. There they bound him with bronze fetters, and he was set to grinding grain in the prison. But his hair, after it had been shaved, began to grow again.

The lords of the Philistines assembled to offer a great sacrifice to their god Dagon, and to rejoice and say,

'Our god has delivered into our hands
Samson our enemy.'

The people, when they saw him, praised their god, chanting:

'Our god has delivered our enemy into our hands,
the scourge of our land who piled it with our dead.'

The Death of Samson
When they grew merry, they said, 'Call Samson, and let him entertain us.' When Samson was summoned from prison, he was a source of entertainment to them. They then stood him between the pillars, and Samson said to the boy who led him by the hand, 'Put me where I can feel the pillars which support the temple, so that I may lean against them.' The temple was full of men and women, and all the lords of the Philistines were there, and there were about three thousand men and women on the roof watching the entertainment.

Samson cried to the Lord and said, 'Remember me, Lord God, remember me: for this one occasion, God, give me strength, and let me at one stroke be avenged on the Philistines for my two eyes.' He put his arms round the two central pillars which supported the temple, his right arm round one and his left round the other and, bracing himself, he said, 'Let me die with the Philistines.' Then Samson leaned forward with all his might, and the temple crashed down on the lords and all the people who were in it. So the dead whom he killed at his death were more than those he had killed in his life.

His brothers and all his father's family came down, carried him up to the grave of his father Manoah between Zorah and Eshtaol, and buried him there. He had been judge over Israel for twenty years.

10 | THE STORY OF RUTH

Ruth and Naomi

Once, in the time of the Judges when there was a famine in the land, a man from Bethlehem in Judah went with his wife and two sons to live in Moabite territory. The man's name was Elimelech, his wife was Naomi, and his sons were Mahlon and Chilion; they were Ephrathites from Bethlehem in Judah. They came to Moab and settled there.

Elimelech died, and Naomi was left a widow with her two sons. The sons married Moabite women, one of whom was called Orpah and the other Ruth. They had lived there about ten years when both Mahlon and Chilion died. Then Naomi, bereaved of her two sons as well as of her husband, got ready to return to her own country with her daughters-in-law, because she heard in Moab that the Lord had shown his care for his people by giving them food. Accompanied by her two daughters-in-law she left the place where she had been living, and they took the road leading back to Judah.

Naomi said to her daughters-in-law, 'Go back, both of you, home to your own mothers. May the Lord keep faith with you, as you have kept faith with the dead and with me; and may he grant each of you the security of a home with a new husband.' And she kissed them goodbye. They wept aloud and said, 'No, we shall return with you to your people.' But Naomi insisted, 'Go back, my daughters. Why should you come with me? Am I likely to bear any more sons to be husbands for you? Go back, my daughters, go; for I am too old to marry again. But if I could say that I had hope of a child, even if I were to be married tonight and were to bear sons, would you, then, wait until they grew up? Would you on their account remain unmarried? No, my daughters! For your sakes I feel bitter that the Lord has inflicted such misfortune on me.' At this they wept still more. Then Orpah kissed her mother-in-law and took her leave, but Ruth clung to her.

'Look,' said Naomi, 'your sister-in-law has gone back to her people and her god. Go, follow her.' Ruth answered, 'Do not urge me to go back and desert you. Where you go, I shall go, and where you stay, I shall stay. Your people will be my people, and your God my God. Where you die, I shall die, and there be buried. I solemnly declare before the Lord that nothing but death will part me from you.' When Naomi saw that Ruth was determined to go with her, she said no more.

The two of them went on until they came to Bethlehem, where their arrival set the whole town buzzing with excitement. The women cried, 'Can this be Naomi?' 'Do not call me Naomi,' she said; 'call me Mara, for the Almighty has made my life very bitter. I went away full, and the Lord has brought me back empty. Why call me Naomi? The Lord has pronounced against me, the Almighty has brought me misfortune.'

That was how Naomi's daughter-in-law, Ruth the Moabite, returned with her from Moab; they arrived in Bethlehem just as the barley harvest was beginning.

Ruth and Boaz

Naomi had a relative on her husband's side, a prominent and well-to-do member of Elimelech's family; his name was Boaz. One day Ruth the Moabite asked Naomi, 'May I go to the harvest fields and glean behind anyone who will allow me?' 'Yes, go, my daughter,' she replied. So Ruth went gleaning in the fields behind the reapers. As it happened, she was in that strip of the fields which belonged to Boaz of Elimelech's family, and there was Boaz himself coming out from Bethlehem. He greeted the reapers, 'The Lord be with you!' and they responded, 'The Lord bless you!' 'Whose girl is this?' he asked the servant in charge of the reapers. The servant answered, 'She is a Moabite girl who has come back with Naomi from Moab. She asked if she might glean, gathering among the sheaves behind the reapers. She came and has been on her feet from morning till now; she has hardly had a moment's rest in the shelter.'

Boaz said to Ruth, 'Listen, my daughter: do not go to glean in any other field. Do not look any farther, but stay close to my servant-girls. Watch where the men reap, and follow the gleaners; I have told the men not to molest you. Any time you are thirsty, go and drink from the jars they have filled.' She bowed to the ground and said, 'Why are you so kind as to take notice of me, when I am just a foreigner?' Boaz answered, 'I have been told the whole story of what you have done for your mother-in-law since the death of your husband, how you left father and mother and homeland and came among a people you did not know before. The Lord reward you for what you have done; may you be richly repaid by the Lord the God of Israel, under whose wings you have come for refuge.' She said: 'I hope you will continue to be pleased with me, sir, for you have eased my mind by speaking kindly to me, though I am not one of your slave-girls.'

When mealtime came round, Boaz said to Ruth, 'Come over here and have something to eat. Dip your piece of bread in the vinegar.' She sat down beside the reapers, and he passed her some roasted grain. She ate all she wanted and still had some left. When she got up to glean, Boaz instructed the men to allow her to glean right among the sheaves. 'Do not find fault with her,' he added; 'you may even pull out some ears of grain from the handfuls as you cut, and leave them for her to glean; do not check her.'

Ruth gleaned in the field until sunset, and when she beat out what she had gathered it came to about a bushel of barley. She carried it into the town and showed her mother-in-law how much she had got; she also brought out and handed her what she had left over from the meal. Her mother-in-law asked, 'Where did you glean today? Which way did you go? Blessings on the man who took notice of you!' She told her mother-in-law in whose field she had been working. 'The owner of the field where I worked today', she said, 'is a man called Boaz.' Naomi exclaimed, 'Blessings on him from the Lord, who has kept faith with the living and the dead! This man', she explained, 'is related to us; he is one of our very near kinsmen.' 'And what is more,' Ruth said, 'he told me to stay close to his workers until they had finished all his harvest.' Naomi said, 'My daughter, it would be as well for you to go with his girls; in another field you might come to harm.' So Ruth kept close to them, gleaning with them till the end of both barley and wheat harvests; but she lived with her mother-in-law.

One day Naomi, Ruth's mother-in-law, said to her, 'My daughter, I want to see you settled happily. Now there is our kinsman Boaz, whose girls you have been with. Tonight he will be winnowing barley at the threshing-floor. Bathe and anoint yourself with perfumed oil, then get dressed and go down to the threshing-floor; but do not make yourself known to the man until he has finished eating and drinking. When he lies down make sure you know the place where he is. Then go in, turn back the covering at his feet and lie down. He will tell you what to do.' 'I will do everything you say,' replied Ruth.

She went down to the threshing-floor and did exactly as her mother-in-law had told her. When Boaz had eaten and drunk, he felt at peace with the world and went and lay down to sleep at the far end of the heap of grain. Ruth came quietly, turned back the covering at his feet and lay down. About midnight the man woke with a start; he turned over, and there, lying at his feet, was a woman! 'Who are you?' he said. 'Sir, it is I, Ruth,' she replied. 'Spread the skirt of your cloak over me, for you are my next-of-kin.' Boaz said, 'The Lord bless you, my daughter! You are proving yourself more devoted to the family than ever by not running after any young man, whether rich or poor. Set your mind at rest, my daughter: I shall do all you ask, for the whole town knows what a fine woman you are. Yes, it is true that I am a near kinsman; but there is one even closer than I am. Stay tonight, and then in the morning, if he is willing to act as your next-of-kin, well and good; but if he is not, then as sure as the Lord lives, I shall do so. Now lie down till morning.'

She lay at his feet till next morning, but rose before it was light enough for one man to recognize another; Boaz had it in mind that no one should know that the woman had been to the threshing-floor. He said to her, 'Take the cloak you are wearing, and hold it out.' When she did so, he poured in six measures of barley and lifted it for her to carry, and she went off to the town.

When she came to her mother-in-law, Naomi asked, 'How did things go with you, my daughter?' Ruth related all that the man had done for her, and she added, 'He gave me these six measures of barley; he would not let me come home to my mother-in-law empty-handed.' Naomi said, 'Wait, my daughter, until you see what will come of it; he will not rest till he has settled the matter this very day.'

Boaz meanwhile had gone up to the town gate and was sitting there when the next-of-kin of whom he had spoken came past. Calling him by name, Boaz cried, 'Come over here and sit down.' He went over and sat down. Boaz also stopped ten of the town's elders and asked them to sit there. When they were seated, he addressed the next-of-kin: 'You will remember the strip of field that belonged to our kinsman Elimelech. Naomi is selling it, now that she has returned from Moab. I promised to open the matter with you, to ask you to acquire it in the presence of those sitting here and in the presence of the elders of my people. If you are going to do your duty as next-of-kin, then do so; but if not, some-one must do it. So tell me, and then I shall know, for I come after you as next-of-kin.' He answered, 'I shall act as next-of-kin.' Boaz continued: 'On the day you take over the field from Naomi, I take over the widow, Ruth the Moabite, so as to perpetuate the name of the dead man on his holding.' 'Then I cannot act,' said the next-of-kin, 'lest it should be detrimental to my own holding; and as I cannot act, you yourself must take over my duty as next-of-kin.'

Now it used to be the custom when ratifying any transaction by which property was redeemed or transferred for a man to take off his sandal and give it to the other party; this was the form of attestation in Israel. Accordingly when the next-of-kin said to Boaz, 'You must take it over,' he drew off his sandal and handed it over. Then Boaz addressed the elders and all the other people there: 'You are witnesses this day that I have taken over from Naomi all that belonged to Elimelech and all that belonged to Chilion and Mahlon; and, further, that I have taken over Mahlon's widow, Ruth the Moabite, to be my wife, in order to keep alive the dead man's name on his holding, so that his name may not be missing among his kindred and at the gate of his native town. You are witnesses this day.' All who were at the gate, including the elders, replied, 'We are witnesses. May the Lord make this woman, who is about to come into your home, to be like Rachel and Leah, the two who built up the family of Israel. May you do a worthy deed in Ephrathah by keeping this name alive in Bethlehem. Through the offspring the Lord gives you by this young woman may your family be like the family of Perez, whom Tamar bore to Judah.'

So Boaz took Ruth and she became his wife. When they had come together the Lord caused her to conceive, and she gave birth to a son. The women said to Naomi, 'Blessed be the Lord, who has not left you this day without next-of-kin. May the name of your dead son be kept alive in Israel! The child will give you renewed life and be your support and stay in your old age, for your devoted daughter-in-law, who has proved better to you than seven sons, has borne him.' Naomi took the child and laid him in her own lap, and she became his foster-mother. Her women neighbours gave him a name: 'Naomi has a son; we shall call him Obed,' they said. He became the father of Jesse, David's father.

11 | SAMUEL AND SAUL

Samuel's Birth and Childhood

There was a certain man from Ramathaim, a Zuphite from the hill-country of Ephraim, named Elkanah son of Jeroham, son of Elihu, son of Tohu, son of Zuph an Ephraimite. He had two wives, Hannah and Peninnah; Peninnah had children, but Hannah was childless. Every year this man went up from his town to worship and offer sacrifice to the Lord of Hosts at Shiloh, where Eli's two sons, Hophni and Phinehas, were priests of the Lord.

When Elkanah sacrificed, he gave several shares of the meat to his wife Peninnah with all her sons and daughters; but to Hannah he gave only one share; the Lord had not granted her children, yet it was Hannah whom Elkanah loved. Hannah's rival also used to torment and humiliate her because she had no children. This happened year after year when they went up to the house of the Lord; her rival used to torment her, until she was in tears and would not eat. Her husband Elkanah said to her, 'Hannah, why are you crying and eating nothing? Why are you so miserable? Am I not more to you than ten sons?'

After they had finished eating and drinking at the sacrifice at Shiloh, Hannah rose in deep distress, and weeping bitterly stood before the Lord and prayed to him. Meanwhile Eli the priest was sitting on his seat beside the door of the temple of the Lord. Hannah made this vow: 'Lord of Hosts, if you will only take notice of my trouble and remember me, if you will not forget me but grant me offspring, then I shall give the child to the Lord for the whole of his life, and no razor shall ever touch his head.'

For a long time she went on praying before the Lord, while Eli watched her lips. Hannah was praying silently; her lips were moving although her voice could not be heard, and Eli took her for a drunken woman. 'Enough of this drunken behaviour!' he said to her. 'Leave off until the effect of the wine has gone.' 'Oh, sir!' she answered, 'I am a heart-broken woman; I have drunk neither wine nor strong drink, but I have been pouring out my feelings before the Lord. Do not think me so devoid of shame, sir; all this time I have been speaking out of the depths of my grief and misery.' Eli said, 'Go in peace, and may the God of Israel grant what you have asked of him.' Hannah replied, 'May I be worthy of your kindness.' And no longer downcast she went away and had something to eat.

Next morning they were up early and, after prostrating themselves before the Lord, returned to their home at Ramah. Elkanah had intercourse with his wife Hannah, and the Lord remembered her; she conceived, and in due time bore a son, whom she named Samuel, 'because', she said, 'I asked the Lord for him'.

Elkanah with his whole household went up to make the annual sacrifice to the Lord and to keep his vow. Hannah did not go; she said to her husband, 'After the child is weaned I shall come up with him to present him before the Lord; then he is to stay there always.' Her husband Elkanah said to her, 'Do what you think best; stay at home until you have weaned him. Only, may the Lord indeed see your vow fulfilled.' So the woman stayed behind and nursed her son until she had weaned him.

When she had weaned him, she took him up with her. She took also a bull three years old, an ephah of flour, and a skin of wine, and she brought him, child as he was, into the house of the Lord at Shiloh. When the bull had been slaughtered, Hannah brought the boy to Eli and said, 'Sir, as sure as you live, I am the woman who stood here beside you praying to the Lord. It was this boy that I prayed for and the Lord has granted what I asked. Now I make him over to the Lord; for his whole life he is lent to the Lord.' And they prostrated themselves there before the Lord.

Then Hannah offered this prayer:

'My heart exults in the Lord,
in the Lord I now hold my head high;
I gloat over my enemies;
I rejoice because you have saved me.

Strong men stand in mute dismay,
but those who faltered put on new strength.
Those who had plenty sell themselves for a crust,

and the hungry grow strong again.
The barren woman bears seven children,
and the mother of many sons is left to languish.'

Then Elkanah went home to Ramah, but the boy remained behind in the service of the Lord under Eli the priest.

God's Judgement on the House of Eli

Eli's sons were scoundrels with little regard for the Lord. The custom of the priests in their dealings with the people was this: when anyone offered a sacrifice, the priest's servant would come while the flesh was stewing and would thrust a three-pronged fork into the cauldron or pan or kettle or pot; and the priest would take whatever the fork brought out. This should have been their practice whenever Israelites came to sacrifice at Shiloh; but now, even before the fat was burnt, the priest's servant would come and say to the person who was sacrificing, 'Give me meat to roast for the priest; he will not accept what has been already stewed, only raw meat.'

And if the man protested, 'Let them burn the fat first, and then take what you want,' the servant would say, 'No, hand it over now, or I shall take it by force.' The young men's sin was very great in the Lord's sight, for they caused what was offered to him to be brought into general contempt.

When Eli, now a very old man, heard a detailed account of how his sons were treating all the Israelites, and how they lay with the women who were serving at the entrance to the Tent of Meeting, he said to them, 'Why do you do such things? I hear from every quarter how wickedly you behave. Do stop it, my sons; for this is not a good report that I hear spreading among the Lord's people. If someone sins against another, God will intervene; but if someone sins against the Lord, who can intercede for him?' They would not listen, however, to their father's rebuke, for the Lord meant to bring about their death.

The boy Samuel was in the Lord's service under Eli. In those days the word of the Lord was rarely heard, and there was no outpouring of vision. One night Eli, whose eyes were dim and his sight failing, was lying down in his usual place, while Samuel slept in the temple of the Lord where the Ark of God was. Before the lamp of God had gone out, the Lord called him, and Samuel answered, 'Here I am!' and ran to Eli saying, 'You called me: here I am.' 'No, I did not call you,' said Eli; 'lie down again.' So he went and lay down. The Lord called Samuel again, and he got up and went to Eli. 'Here I am!' he said. 'Surely you called me.' 'I did not call, my son,' he answered; 'lie down again.' Samuel had not yet come to know the Lord, and the word of the Lord had not been disclosed to him. When the Lord called him for the third time, he again went to Eli and said, 'Here I am! You did call me.' Then Eli understood that it was the Lord calling the boy; he told Samuel to go and lie down and said, 'If someone calls once more, say, "Speak, Lord; your servant is listening."' So Samuel went and lay down in his place.

Then the Lord came, and standing there called, 'Samuel, Samuel!' as before. Samuel answered, 'Speak, your servant is listening.' The Lord said, 'Soon I shall do something in Israel which will ring in the ears of all who hear it. When that day comes I shall make good every word from beginning to end that I have spoken against Eli and his family. You are to tell him that my judgement on his house will stand for ever because he knew of his sons' blasphemies against God and did not restrain them. Therefore I have sworn to the family of Eli that their abuse of sacrifices and offerings will never be expiated.'

Samuel lay down till morning, when he opened the doors of the house of the Lord; but he was afraid to tell Eli about the vision. Eli called Samuel: 'Samuel, my son!' he said; and Samuel answered, 'Here I am!' Eli asked, 'What did the Lord say to you? Do not hide it from me. God's curse upon you if you conceal from me one word of all that he said to you.' Then Samuel told him everything, concealing nothing. Eli said, 'The Lord must do what is good in his eyes.'

As Samuel grew up, the Lord was with him, and none of his words went unfulfilled. From Dan to Beersheba, all Israel recognized that Samuel was attested as a prophet of the Lord.

The Philistines and the Ark

The time came when the Philistines mustered for battle against Israel, and the Israelites, marching out to meet them, encamped near Eben-ezer, while the Philistines' camp was at Aphek. The Philistines drew up their lines facing the Israelites, and when battle was joined the Israelites were defeated by the Philistines, who killed about four thousand men on the field. When their army got back to camp, the Israelite elders asked, 'Why did the Lord let us be defeated today by the Philistines? Let us fetch the Ark of the Covenant of the Lord from Shiloh to go with us and deliver us from the power of our enemies.' The army sent to Shiloh and fetched the Ark of the Covenant of the Lord of Hosts, who is enthroned upon the cherubim; Eli's two sons, Hophni and Phinehas, were there with the Ark.

When the Ark came into the camp it was greeted with such a great shout by all the Israelites that the earth rang. The Philistines, hearing the noise, asked, 'What is this great shouting in the camp of the Hebrews?' When they learned that the Ark of the Lord had come into the camp, they were alarmed. 'A god has come into the camp,' they cried. 'We are lost! No such thing has ever happened before. We are utterly lost! Who can deliver us from the power of this mighty god? This is the god who broke the Egyptians and crushed them in the wilderness. Courage, act like men, you Philistines, or you will become slaves to the Hebrews as they were to you. Be men, and fight!' The Philistines then gave battle, and the Israelites were defeated and fled to their homes. It was a great defeat, and thirty thousand Israelite foot-soldiers fell. The Ark of God was captured, and Eli's two sons, Hophni and Phinehas, perished.

A Benjamite ran from the battlefield and reached Shiloh on the same day, his clothes torn and dust on his head. When he arrived Eli was sitting on a seat by the road to Mizpah, for he was deeply troubled about the Ark of God. The man entered the town with his news, and all the people cried out in horror. When Eli heard the uproar, he asked, 'What does it mean?' The man hurried to Eli and told him. Eli was ninety-eight years old and sat staring with sightless eyes. The man said to him, 'I am the one who has just come from the battle. I fled from the field this very day.' Eli asked, 'What is the news, my son?' The runner answered, 'The Israelites have fled before the Philistines; the army has suffered severe losses; your two sons, Hophni and Phinehas, are dead; and the Ark of God is taken.' At the mention of the Ark of God, Eli fell backwards from his seat by the gate and broke his neck, for he was an old man and heavy. So he died; he had been judge over Israel for forty years.

His daughter-in-law, the wife of Phinehas, was pregnant and near her time, and when she heard of the capture of the Ark and the deaths of her father-in-law and her husband, she went into labour and she crouched down and was delivered. As she lay dying, the women who attended her said, 'Do not be afraid; you have a son.' But she did not answer or heed what they said. She named the boy Ichabod, saying, 'Glory has departed from Israel,' referring to the capture of the Ark of God and the deaths of her father-in-law and her husband; 'Glory has departed from Israel,' she said, 'because the Ark of God is taken.'

After the Philistines had captured the Ark of God, they brought it from Eben-ezer to Ashdod, where they carried it into the temple of Dagon and set it beside the god. When the people of Ashdod rose next morning, there was Dagon fallen face downwards on the ground before the Ark of the Lord. They lifted him up and put him back in his place. But next morning when they rose, Dagon had again fallen face downwards on the ground before the Ark of the Lord, with his head and his two hands lying broken off beside his platform; only Dagon's body remained on it. That is why to this day the priests of Dagon and all who enter the temple of Dagon at Ashdod do not set foot on Dagon's platform.

The Lord's hand oppressed the people of Ashdod. He threw them into despair; he plagued them with tumours, and their territory swarmed with rats. There was death and destruction all through the city. Seeing this, the men of Ashdod decided, 'The Ark of the God of Israel must not stay here, for his hand is pressing on us and on Dagon our god.'

When they called together all the Philistine lords to ask what should be done with the Ark, they were told, 'If you send the Ark of the God of Israel back, do not let it go empty, but send it back with an offering by way of compensation; if you are then healed you will know why his hand had not been lifted from you.' When they were asked, 'What should we send to him?' they answered, 'Send five tumours modelled in gold and five gold rats, one for each of the Philistine lords, for the same plague afflicted all of you and your lords. Make models of your tumours and of the rats which are ravaging the land, and give honour to the God of Israel; perhaps he will relax the pressure of his hand on you, your god, and your land. Why be stubborn like Pharaoh and the Egyptians? Remember how this God made sport of them until they let Israel go.

'Now make ready a new wagon with two milch cows which have never been yoked; harness the cows to the wagon, but take their calves away and keep them in their stall. Fetch the Ark of the Lord and put it on the wagon, place beside it in a casket the gold offerings that you are sending to him, and let it go where it will. Watch: if it goes up towards its own territory to Beth-shemesh, then it was the Lord who has inflicted this great injury on us; but if not, then we shall know that it was not his hand that struck us, but that we have been the victims of chance.'

They did this: they took two milch cows and harnessed them to a wagon, meanwhile shutting up their calves in the stall; they placed the Ark of the Lord on the wagon together with the casket containing the gold rats, and the models of their tumours. The cows went straight in the direction of Beth-shemesh; they kept to the road, lowing as they went and turning neither right nor left, while the Philistine lords followed them as far as the territory of Beth-shemesh.

The people of Beth-shemesh, busy harvesting their wheat in the valley, looked up and saw the Ark, and they rejoiced at the sight. The wagon came to the field of Joshua of Beth-shemesh and halted there, close by a great stone. The people chopped up the wood of the wagon and offered the cows as a whole-offering to the Lord. The Levites who lifted down the Ark of the Lord and the casket containing the gold offerings laid them on the great stone; and the men of Beth-shemesh offered whole-offerings and shared-offerings that day to the Lord. The five lords of the Philistines watched all this, and returned to Ekron the same day.

But the sons of Jeconiah did not rejoice with the rest of the men of Beth-shemesh when they welcomed the Ark of the Lord, and he struck down seventy of them. The people mourned because the Lord had struck them so heavy a blow, and the men of Beth-shemesh said, 'No one is safe in the presence of the Lord, this holy God. To whom can we send the Ark, to be rid of him?' So they sent this message to the inhabitants of Kiriath-jearim: 'The Philistines have returned the Ark of the Lord; come down and take charge of it.' The men of Kiriath-jearim came and took the Ark of the Lord away; they brought it into the house of Abinadab on the hill and consecrated his son Eleazar as its custodian.

Samuel the Judge

For a long while, some twenty years in all, the Ark was housed in Kiriath-jearim. Then there was a movement throughout Israel to follow the Lord, and Samuel addressed these words to the whole nation: 'If your return to the Lord is whole-hearted, banish the foreign gods and the ashtaroth from your shrines; turn to the Lord with heart and mind, and worship him alone, and he will deliver you from the Philistines.' So the Israelites banished the baalim and the ashtaroth, and worshipped the Lord alone.

Samuel summoned all Israel to an assembly at Mizpah, so that he might intercede with the Lord for them. When they had assembled, they drew water and poured it out before the Lord and fasted all day, confessing that they had sinned against the Lord. When the Philistines heard that the Israelites had assembled at Mizpah, their lords marched against them. The Israelites heard that the Philistines were advancing, and they were afraid and begged Samuel, 'Do not cease to pray for us to the Lord our God to save us from the power of the Philistines.' Samuel took a sucking-lamb, offered it up complete as a whole-offering, and prayed aloud to the Lord on behalf of Israel, and the Lord answered his prayer. As Samuel was offering the sacrifice and the Philistines were advancing to the attack, the Lord with mighty thunder threw the Philistines into confusion. They fled in panic before the Israelites, who set out from Mizpah in pursuit and kept up the slaughter of the Philistines till they reached a point below Beth-car. The towns they had captured were restored to Israel, and from Ekron to Gath the borderland was freed from Philistine control. Between Israel and the Amorites also peace was maintained.

Samuel acted as judge in Israel as long as he lived, and every year went on circuit to Bethel, Gilgal, and Mizpah; he dispensed justice at all these places. But always he went back to Ramah; that was his home and the place from which he governed Israel, and there he built an altar to the Lord.

The People Demand a King

When Samuel grew old, he appointed his sons to be judges in Israel. The eldest son was called Joel and the second Abiah; they acted as judges in Beersheba. His sons did not follow their father's ways but were intent on their own profit, taking bribes and perverting the course of justice. So all the elders of Israel met, and came to Samuel at Ramah. They said to him, 'You are now old and your sons do not follow your ways; appoint us a king to rule us, like all the other nations.' But their request for a king displeased Samuel. He prayed to the Lord, and the Lord told him, 'Listen to the people and all that they are saying; they have not rejected you, it is I whom they have rejected, I whom they will not have to be their king. They are now doing to you just what they have done to me since I brought them up from Egypt: they have forsaken me and worshipped other gods. Hear what they have to say now, but give them a solemn warning and tell them what sort of king will rule them.'

Samuel reported to the people who were asking him for a king all that the Lord had said to him. 'This will be the sort of king who will bear rule over you,' he said. 'He will take your sons and make them serve in his chariots and with his cavalry, and they will run before his chariot. Some he will appoint officers over units of a thousand and units of fifty. Others will plough his fields and reap his harvest; others again will make weapons of war and equipment for the chariots. He will take your daughters for perfumers, cooks, and bakers. He will seize the best of your fields, vineyards, and olive groves, and give them to his courtiers. He will take a tenth of your grain and your vintage to give to his eunuchs and courtiers. Your slaves, both men and women, and the best of your cattle and your donkeys he will take for his own use. He will take a tenth of your flocks, and you yourselves will become his slaves. There will come a day when you will cry out against the king whom you have chosen; but the Lord will not answer you on that day.'

The people, however, refused to listen to Samuel. 'No,' they said, 'we must have a king over us; then we shall be like other nations, with a king to rule us, to lead us out to war and fight our battles.' When Samuel heard what the people had decided, he told the Lord, who said, 'Take them at their word and appoint them a king.' Samuel then dismissed all the Israelites to their homes.

The Anointing of Saul

There was a man from the territory of Benjamin, whose name was Kish son of Abiel, son of Zeror, son of Bechorath, son of

Aphiah a Benjamite. He was a man of substance, and had a son named Saul, a young man in his prime; there was no better man among the Israelites than he. He stood a head taller than any of the people.

One day some donkeys belonging to Saul's father Kish had strayed, so he said to his son Saul, 'Take one of the servants with you, and go and look for the donkeys.' They crossed the hill-country of Ephraim and went through the district of Shalisha but did not find them; they passed through the district of Shaalim but they were not there; they passed through the district of Benjamin but again did not find them. When they reached the district of Zuph, Saul said to the servant who was with him, 'Come, we ought to turn back, or my father will stop thinking about the donkeys and begin to worry about us.' The servant answered, 'There is a man of God in this town who has a great reputation, because everything he says comes true. Suppose we go there; he may tell us which way to take.' So they went up to the town and, just as they were going in, there was Samuel coming towards them on his way up to the shrine.

The day before Saul's arrival there, the Lord had disclosed his intention to Samuel: 'At this time tomorrow', he said, 'I shall send you a man from the territory of Benjamin, and you are to anoint him prince over my people Israel. He will deliver my people from the Philistines; for I have seen the sufferings of my people, and their cry has reached my ears.' The moment Saul appeared the Lord said to Samuel, 'Here is the man of whom I spoke to you. This man will govern my people.' Saul came up to Samuel in the gateway and said, 'Tell me, please, where the seer lives.' Samuel replied, 'I am the seer. Go on ahead of me to the shrine and eat with me today; in the morning I shall set you on your way, after telling you what you have on your mind. Trouble yourself no more about the donkeys lost three days ago; they have been found. To whom does the tribute of all Israel belong? It belongs to you and to your whole ancestral house.' 'But I am a Benjamite,' said Saul, 'from the smallest of the tribes of Israel, and my family is the least important of all the families of the tribe of Benjamin. Why do you say this to me?'

Saul dined with Samuel that day, and when they came down from the shrine to the town a bed was spread on the roof for Saul, and he stayed there that night. At dawn Samuel called to Saul on the roof, 'Get up, and I shall set you on your way.' When Saul rose, he and Samuel went outside together, and as they came to the edge of the town, Samuel said to Saul, 'Tell the boy to go on ahead.' He did so; then Samuel said, 'Stay here a moment, and I shall tell you what God has said.'

Samuel took a flask of oil and poured it over Saul's head; he kissed him and said, 'The Lord anoints you prince over his people Israel. You are to rule the people of the Lord and deliver them from the enemies round about. You will receive a sign that the Lord has anointed you prince to govern his possession: when you leave me today, you will meet two men by Rachel's tomb at Zelzah in the territory of Benjamin. They will tell you that the donkeys you set out to look for have been found and that your father is concerned for them no longer; he is anxious about you and keeps saying, "What shall I do about my son?" From there go across country as far as the terebinth of Tabor, where three men going up to Bethel to worship God will meet you. One of them will be carrying three young goats, the second three loaves, and the third a skin of wine. They will greet you and offer you two loaves, which you will accept. Then when you reach the hill of God, where the Philistine governor resides, you will meet a company of prophets coming down from the shrine, led by lute, drum, fife, and lyre, and filled with prophetic rapture. The spirit of the Lord will suddenly take possession of you, and you too will be rapt like a prophet and become another man. When these signs happen, do whatever the occasion demands; God will be with you. You are to go down to Gilgal ahead of me, and I shall come to you to sacrifice whole-offerings and shared-offerings. Wait seven days until I join you; then I shall tell you what to do.'

As Saul turned to leave Samuel, God made him a different person. On that same day all these signs happened. When they reached the hill there was a company of prophets coming to meet him, and the spirit of God suddenly took possession of him, so that he too was filled with prophetic rapture. When people who had known him previously saw that he was rapt like the prophets, they said to one another, 'What can have happened to the son of Kish? Is Saul also among the prophets?' One of the men of that place said, 'And whose sons are they?' Hence the proverb, 'Is Saul also among the prophets?' When the prophetic rapture had passed, he went home. Saul's uncle said to him and the boy,

'Where have you been?' Saul answered 'To look for the donkeys, and when we could not find them, we went to Samuel.' His uncle said, 'Tell me what Samuel said.' 'He told us that the donkeys had been found,' replied Saul; but he did not repeat what Samuel had said about his being king.

Saul Defeats the Ammonites

Samuel summoned the Israelites to the Lord at Mizpah and said to them, 'This is the word of the Lord the God of Israel: I brought Israel up from Egypt; I delivered you from the Egyptians and from all the kingdoms that oppressed you. But today you have rejected your God who saved you from all your misery and distress; you have said, "No, set a king over us." Therefore take up your positions now before the Lord tribe by tribe and clan by clan.'

Samuel presented all the tribes of Israel, and Benjamin was picked by lot. Then he presented the tribe of Benjamin, family by family, and the family of Matri was picked. He presented the family of Matri, man by man, and Saul son of Kish was picked; but when search was made he was not to be found. They went on to ask the Lord, 'Will the man be coming?' The Lord answered, 'There he is, hiding among the baggage.' So some ran and fetched him out, and as he took his stand among the people, he was a head taller than anyone else. Samuel said to the people, 'Look at the man whom the Lord has chosen; there is no one like him in this whole nation.' They all acclaimed him, shouting, 'Long live the king!'

Samuel explained to the people the nature of a king, and made a written record of it on a scroll which he deposited before the Lord. He then dismissed them to their homes. Saul too went home to Gibeah, and with him went some fighting men whose hearts God had moved. But there were scoundrels who said, 'How can this fellow deliver us?' They thought nothing of him and brought him no gifts.

About a month later Nahash the Ammonite attacked and besieged Jabesh-gilead. The men of Jabesh said to Nahash, 'Grant us terms and we will be your subjects.' Nahash answered, 'On one condition only shall I grant you terms: that I gouge out the right eye of every one of you and bring disgrace on all Israel.' The elders of Jabesh-gilead said, 'Give us seven days' respite to send messengers throughout Israel and then, if no one relieves us, we shall surrender to you.' The messengers came to Gibeah, where Saul lived, and delivered their message, and all the people broke into lamentation and weeping. Saul was just coming from the field, driving in the oxen, and asked why the people were lamenting; and they told him what the men of Jabesh had said. When Saul heard this, the spirit of God suddenly seized him; in anger he took a pair of oxen, cut them in pieces, and sent messengers with the pieces all through Israel to proclaim that the same would be done to the oxen of any man who did not follow Saul and Samuel to battle. The fear of the Lord fell upon the people and they came out to a man. Saul mustered them in Bezek, three hundred thousand men from Israel and thirty thousand from Judah. He said to the messengers, 'Tell the men of Jabesh-gilead, "Victory will be yours tomorrow by the time the sun is hot."'

When they received this message, the men of Jabesh took heart; but they said to Nahash, 'Tomorrow we shall surrender to you, and then you may deal with us as you think fit.' Next day Saul with his men in three columns forced a way right into the enemy camp during the morning watch and massacred the Ammonites until the day grew hot; those who survived were scattered until no two of them were left together.

The people said to Samuel, 'Who said that Saul should not reign over us? Hand the men over to us to be put to death.' But Saul said, 'No man is to be put to death on a day when the Lord has won such a victory in Israel.' Samuel said to the people, 'Let us now go to Gilgal and there establish the kingship anew.' So they all went to Gilgal and invested Saul there as king in the presence of the Lord. They sacrificed shared-offerings before the Lord, and Saul and all the Israelites celebrated with great joy.

Samuel thus addressed the assembled Israelites: 'I have listened to your request and installed a king to rule over you. If you will revere the Lord and give true and loyal service, if you do not rebel against his commands, and if you and the king who reigns over you are faithful to the Lord your God, well and good; but if you do not obey the Lord, and if you rebel against his commands, then his hand will be against you and against your king.

'As for me, God forbid that I should sin against the Lord by ceasing to pray for you. I shall show you what is right and good: to revere the Lord and worship him faithfully with all your heart;

for consider what great things he has done for you. But if you persist in wickedness, both you and your king will be swept away.'

Jonathan Defeats the Philistines

The Philistines mustered to attack Israel; they had thirty thousand chariots and six thousand horses, with infantry as countless as sand on the seashore. They went up and camped at Michmash, to the east of Beth-aven. The Israelites found themselves in sore straits, for the army was hard pressed, so they hid themselves in caves and holes and among the rocks, in pits and cisterns.

The Philistines had posted a company of troops to hold the pass of Michmash, and one day Saul's son Jonathan said to his armour-bearer, 'Come, let us go over to the Philistine outpost across there.' He did not tell his father, who at the time had his tent under the pomegranate tree at Migron on the outskirts of Gibeah; with him were about six hundred men. Jonathan said, 'We shall cross over and let the men see us. If they say, "Stay there till we come to you," then we shall stay where we are and not go up to them. But if they say, "Come up to us," we shall go up; that will be the proof that the Lord has given them into our power.' The two showed themselves to the Philistine outpost. 'Look!' said the Philistines. 'Hebrews coming out of the holes where they have been hiding!' And they called across to Jonathan and his armour-bearer, 'Come up to us; we shall show you something.' Jonathan said to the armour-bearer, 'Come on, the Lord has put them into Israel's power.' Jonathan climbed up on hands and feet, and the armour-bearer followed him. The Philistines fell before Jonathan, and the armour-bearer, coming behind, dispatched them. In that first attack Jonathan and his armour-bearer killed about twenty of them, like men cutting a furrow across a half-acre field. Terror spread throughout the army in the camp and in the field; the men at the post and the raiding parties were terrified. The very ground quaked, and there was great panic.

Saul's men on the watch in Gibeah of Benjamin saw the mob of Philistines surging to and fro in confusion. Saul ordered his forces to call the roll to find out who was missing and, when it was called, they found that Jonathan and his armour-bearer were absent. Saul said to Ahijah, 'Bring forward the ephod,' for it was he who at that time carried the ephod before Israel. While Saul was speaking, the confusion in the Philistine camp kept increasing, and he said to the priest, 'Hold your hand.' Then Saul and all his men made a concerted rush for the battlefield, where they found the enemy in complete disorder, every man's sword against his fellow. Those Hebrews who up to now had been under the Philistines, and had been with them in camp, changed sides and joined the Israelites under Saul and Jonathan. When all the Israelites in hiding in the hill-country of Ephraim heard that the Philistines were in flight, they also joined in and set off in close pursuit. That day the Lord delivered Israel, and the fighting passed on beyond Beth-aven.

The Israelites had been driven to exhaustion on that day. Saul had issued this warning to the troops: 'A curse on any man who takes food before nightfall and before I have taken vengeance on my enemies.' So no one tasted any food. There was honeycomb in the countryside; but when his men came upon it, dripping with honey though it was, not one of them put his hand to his mouth for fear of the curse. Jonathan, however, had not heard his father's interdict to the army, and he stretched out the stick that was in his hand, dipped the end of it in the honeycomb, put it to his mouth, and was refreshed. One of the people said to him, 'Your father strictly forbade this, saying, "A curse on the man who eats food today!" And the men are faint.' Jonathan said, 'My father has done the people great harm; see how I am refreshed by this mere taste of honey. How much better if the army had eaten today whatever they took from their enemies by way of spoil! Then there would indeed have been a great slaughter of Philistines.'

Israel defeated the Philistines that day, and pursued them from Michmash to Aijalon. But the troops were so faint with hunger that they turned to plunder and seized sheep, cattle, and calves; they slaughtered them on the bare ground, and ate the meat with the blood in it. Someone told Saul that the people were sinning against the Lord by eating meat with the blood in it. 'This is treacherous behaviour!' cried Saul. 'Roll a great stone here at once.' He then said, 'Go about among the troops and tell them to bring their oxen and sheep, and to slaughter and eat them here; and so they will not sin against the Lord by eating meat with the blood in it.' So as night fell each man came, driving his own ox, and slaughtered it there. Thus Saul came to

erect an altar to the Lord, and this was the first altar to the Lord
that he erected.

Saul said, 'Let us go down and make a night attack on the
Philistines and harry them till daylight; we will not spare a single
one of them.' His men answered, 'Do what you think best,' but the
priest said, 'Let us first consult God.' Saul enquired of God, 'Shall
I pursue the Philistines? Will you put them into Israel's power?'
But he received no answer. So he said, 'Let all the leaders of the
people come forward and let us find out where the sin lies this day.
As the Lord, the deliverer of Israel, lives, even if the sin lies in my
son Jonathan, he shall die.' Not a soul answered him. Then he said
to the Israelites, 'All of you stand on one side, and I and my son
Jonathan will stand on the other.' His men answered, 'Do what
you think best.' Saul said to the Lord the God of Israel, 'Why have
you not answered your servant today? Lord God of Israel, if this
guilt lies in me or in my son Jonathan, let the lot be Urim; if it lies
in your people Israel, let it be Thummim.' Jonathan and Saul were
taken, and the people were cleared. Then Saul said, 'Cast lots
between me and my son Jonathan'; and Jonathan was taken.

Saul said to Jonathan, 'Tell me what you have done.' Jonathan
told him, 'True, I did taste a little honey on the tip of my stick.
Here I am; I am ready to die.' Then Saul swore a solemn oath
that Jonathan should die. But his men said to Saul, 'Shall
Jonathan die, Jonathan who has won this great victory in Israel?
God forbid! As the Lord lives, not a hair of his head shall fall to
the ground, for he has been at work with God today.' So the army
delivered Jonathan and he did not die. Saul broke off the pursuit
of the Philistines, who then made their way home.

The Rejection of Saul

Samuel said to Saul, 'The Lord sent me to anoint you king over
his people Israel. Now listen to the voice of the Lord: this is the
very word of the Lord of Hosts: I shall punish the Amalekites for
what they did to Israel, when they opposed them on their way up
from Egypt. Go now, fall upon the Amalekites, destroy them, and
put their property under ban. Spare no one; put them all to
death, men and women, children and babes in arms, herds and
flocks, camels and donkeys.'

Saul called out the levy and reviewed them at Telaim: there
were two hundred thousand foot-soldiers and another ten

thousand from Judah. When he reached the city of Amalek, he halted for a time in the valley. Meanwhile he sent word to the Kenites to leave the Amalekites and come down, 'or', he said, 'I shall destroy you as well as them; but you were friendly to Israel as they came up from Egypt'. So the Kenites left the Amalekites.

Saul inflicted defeat on the Amalekites all the way from Havilah to Shur on the borders of Egypt. Agag king of the Amalekites he took alive, but he destroyed all the people, putting them to the sword. Saul and his army spared Agag and the best of the sheep and cattle, the fat beasts and the lambs, and everything worth keeping; these they were unwilling to destroy, but anything that was useless and of no value they destroyed.

The word of the Lord came to Samuel: 'I repent of having made Saul king, for he has turned away from me and has not obeyed my instructions.' Samuel was angry; all night long he cried aloud to the Lord. Early next morning he went to meet Saul, but was told that he had gone to Carmel, for he had set up a monument to himself there, and then had turned and gone on down to Gilgal. There Samuel found him, and Saul greeted him with the words, 'The Lord's blessing on you! I have carried out the Lord's instructions.' 'What then is this bleating of sheep in my ears?' demanded Samuel. 'How do I come to hear the lowing of cattle?' Saul answered, 'The troops have taken them from the Amalekites. These are what they spared, the best of the sheep and cattle, to sacrifice to the Lord your God; the rest we completely destroyed.' Samuel said to Saul, 'Be quiet! Let me tell you what the Lord said to me last night.' 'Tell me,' said Saul. So Samuel went on, 'Once you thought little of yourself, but now you are head of the tribes of Israel. The Lord, who anointed you king over Israel, charged you with the destruction of that wicked nation, the Amalekites; you were to go and wage war against them until you had wiped them out. Why then did you not obey the Lord? Why did you swoop on the spoil, so doing what was wrong in the eyes of the Lord?' Saul answered, 'But I did obey the Lord; I went where the Lord sent me, and I have brought back Agag king of the Amalekites. The rest of them I destroyed. Out of the spoil the troops took sheep and oxen, the choicest of the animals laid under ban, to sacrifice to the Lord your God at Gilgal.' Samuel then said:

'Does the Lord desire whole-offerings and sacrifices
as he desires obedience?
To obey is better than sacrifice,
and to listen to him better than the fat of rams.
Rebellion is as sinful as witchcraft,
arrogance as evil as idolatry.
Because you have rejected the word of the Lord,
he has rejected you as king.'

Saul said to Samuel, 'I have sinned. I have not complied with the Lord's command or with your instructions: I was afraid of the troops and gave in to them. But now forgive my sin, I implore you, and come back with me, and I shall bow in worship before the Lord.' Samuel answered, 'I shall not come back with you; you have rejected the word of the Lord and therefore the Lord has rejected you as king over Israel.' As he turned to go, Saul caught the corner of his cloak and it tore. And Samuel said to him, 'The Lord has torn the kingdom of Israel from your hand today and will give it to another, a better man than you. God who is the Splendour of Israel does not deceive, nor does he change his mind, as a mortal might do.' Saul pleaded, 'I have sinned; but honour me this once before the elders of my people and before Israel and come back with me, and I will bow in worship before the Lord your God.' Samuel went back with Saul, and Saul worshipped the Lord.

Samuel said, 'Bring Agag king of the Amalekites.' So Agag came to him with faltering step and said, 'Surely the bitterness of death has passed.' Samuel said,

'As your sword has made women childless,
so your mother will be childless among women.'

Then Samuel hewed Agag in pieces before the Lord at Gilgal.

Saul went to his own home at Gibeah, and Samuel went to Ramah; and he never saw Saul again to his dying day, but he grieved for him, because the Lord had repented of having made him king over Israel.

12 | THE STORY OF DAVID

The Anointing of David

The Lord said to Samuel, 'How long will you grieve because I have rejected Saul as king of Israel? Fill your horn with oil and take it with you; I am sending you to Jesse of Bethlehem; for I have chosen myself a king from among his sons.' Samuel answered, 'How can I go? If Saul hears of it, he will kill me.' 'Take a heifer with you,' said the Lord; 'say you have come to offer a sacrifice to the Lord, and invite Jesse to the sacrifice; then I shall show you what you must do. You are to anoint for me the man whom I indicate to you.' Samuel did as the Lord had told him, and went to Bethlehem, where the elders came in haste to meet him, saying, 'Why have you come? Is all well?' 'All is well,' said Samuel; 'I have come to sacrifice to the Lord. Purify yourselves and come with me to the sacrifice.' He himself purified Jesse and his sons and invited them to the sacrifice.

When they came, and Samuel saw Eliab, he thought, 'Surely here, before the Lord, is his anointed king.' But the Lord said to him, 'Pay no attention to his outward appearance and stature, for I have rejected him. The Lord does not see as a mortal sees; mortals see only appearances but the Lord sees into the heart.' Then Jesse called Abinadab and had him pass before Samuel, but he said, 'No, the Lord has not chosen this one.' Next he presented Shammah, of whom Samuel said, 'Nor has the Lord chosen him.' Seven of his sons were presented to Samuel by Jesse, but he said, 'The Lord has not chosen any of these.'

Samuel asked, 'Are these all the sons you have?' 'There is still the youngest,' replied Jesse, 'but he is looking after the sheep.' Samuel said to Jesse, 'Send and fetch him; we will not sit down until he comes.' So he sent and fetched him. He was handsome, with ruddy cheeks and bright eyes. The Lord said, 'Rise and anoint him: this is the man.' Samuel took the horn of oil and anointed him in the presence of his brothers, and the spirit of the

Lord came upon David and was with him from that day onwards. Then Samuel set out on his way to Ramah.

David and Goliath

The spirit of the Lord had forsaken Saul, and at times an evil spirit from the Lord would seize him suddenly. His servants said to him, 'You see how an evil spirit from God seizes you; sir, why do you not command your servants here to go and find someone who can play on the lyre? Then, when an evil spirit from God comes on you, he can play and you will recover.' Saul said to his servants, 'Find me someone who can play well and bring him to me.' One of his attendants said, 'I have seen a son of Jesse of Bethlehem who can play; he is a brave man and a good fighter, wise in speech and handsome, and the Lord is with him.'

Saul therefore dispatched messengers to ask Jesse to send him his son David, who was with the sheep. Jesse took a batch of bread, a skin of wine, and a kid, and sent them to Saul by his son David. David came to Saul and entered his service; Saul loved him dearly, and David became his armour-bearer. Saul sent word to Jesse: 'Allow David to stay in my service, for I am pleased with him.' And whenever an evil spirit from God came upon Saul, David would take his lyre and play it, so that relief would come to Saul; he would recover and the evil spirit would leave him alone.

The Philistines mustered their forces for war; they massed at Socoh in Judah and encamped between Socoh and Azekah at Ephes-dammim. Saul and the Israelites also mustered, and they encamped in the valley of Elah. They drew up their lines of battle facing the Philistines, the Philistines occupying a position on one hill and the Israelites on another, with a valley between them.

A champion came out from the Philistine camp, a man named Goliath, from Gath; he was over nine feet in height. He had a bronze helmet on his head, and he wore plate armour of bronze, weighing five thousand shekels. On his legs were bronze greaves, and one of his weapons was a bronze dagger. The shaft of his spear was like a weaver's beam, and its head, which was of iron, weighed six hundred shekels. His shield-bearer marched ahead of him.

The champion stood and shouted to the ranks of Israel, 'Why do you come out to do battle? I am the Philistine champion and you are Saul's men. Choose your man to meet me. If he defeats and kills me in fair fight, we shall become your slaves; but if I vanquish and kill him, you will be our slaves and serve us. Here and now I challenge the ranks of Israel. Get me a man, and we will fight it out.' When Saul and the Israelites heard what the Philistine said, they were all shaken and deeply afraid.

David was the son of an Ephrathite called Jesse, who had eight sons, and who by Saul's time had become old, well advanced in years. His three eldest sons had followed Saul to the war; the eldest was called Eliab, the next Abinadab, and the third Shammah; David was the youngest. When the three eldest followed Saul, David used to go from attending Saul to minding his father's flocks at Bethlehem.

Morning and evening for forty days the Philistine came forward and took up his stance. Then one day Jesse said to his son David, 'Take your brothers an ephah of this roasted grain and these ten loaves of bread, and go with them as quickly as you can to the camp. These ten cream-cheeses are for you to take to their commanding officer. See if your brothers are well and bring back some token from them.' Saul and the brothers and all the Israelites were in the valley of Elah, fighting the Philistines.

Early next morning David, having left someone in charge of the sheep, set out on his errand and went as Jesse had told him. He reached the lines just as the army was going out to take up position and was raising the war cry. The Israelites and the Philistines drew up their ranks opposite each other. David left his things in the charge of the quartermaster, ran to the line, and went up to his brothers to greet them. While he was talking with them the Philistine champion, Goliath from Gath, came out from the Philistine ranks and issued his challenge in the same words as before; and David heard him. When the Israelites saw the man they fell back before him in fear.

'Look at this man who comes out day after day to defy Israel,' they said. 'The king is to give a rich reward to the man who kills him; he will also give him his daughter in marriage and will exempt his family from service due in Israel.' David asked the men near him, 'What is to be done for the man who kills this Philistine and wipes out this disgrace? And who is he, an uncircumcised Philistine, to defy the armies of the living God?' The soldiers, repeating what had been said, told him what was to be done for the man who killed him.

David's elder brother Eliab overheard him talking with the men and angrily demanded, 'What are you doing here? And whom have you left to look after those few sheep in the wilderness? I know you, you impudent young rascal; you have only come to see the fighting.' David answered, 'Now what have I done? I only asked a question.' He turned away from him to someone else and repeated his question, but everybody gave him the same answer.

David's words were overheard and reported to Saul, who sent for him. David said to him, 'Let no one lose heart! I shall go and fight this Philistine.' Saul answered, 'You are not able to fight this Philistine; you are only a lad, and he has been a fighting man all his life.' David said to Saul, 'Sir, I am my father's shepherd; whenever a lion or bear comes and carries off a sheep from the flock, I go out after it and attack it and rescue the victim from its jaws. Then if it turns on me, I seize it by the beard and batter it to death. I have killed lions and bears, and this uncircumcised Philistine will fare no better than they; he has defied the ranks of the living God. The Lord who saved me from the lion and the bear will save me from this Philistine.' 'Go then,' said Saul; 'and the Lord be with you.'

He put his own tunic on David, placed a bronze helmet on his head, and gave him a coat of mail to wear; he then fastened his sword on David over his tunic. But David held back, because he had not tried them, and said to Saul, 'I cannot go with these, because I am not used to them.' David took them off, then picked up his stick, chose five smooth stones from the wadi, and put them in a shepherd's bag which served as his pouch, and, sling in hand, went to meet the Philistine.

The Philistine, preceded by his shield-bearer, came on towards David. He looked David up and down and had nothing but disdain for this lad with his ruddy cheeks and bright eyes. He said to David, 'Am I a dog that you come out against me with sticks?' He cursed him in the name of his god, and said, 'Come, I shall give your flesh to the birds and the beasts.' David answered, 'You have come against me with sword and spear and dagger, but I come against you in the name of the Lord of Hosts, the God of the ranks of Israel which you have defied. The Lord will put you into my power this day; I shall strike you down and cut your head off and leave your carcass and the carcasses of the Philistines to the birds and the wild beasts; the whole world will know that there is a God in Israel. All those who are gathered here will see that the Lord saves without sword or spear; the battle is the Lord's, and he will put you all into our power.'

When the Philistine began moving closer to attack, David ran quickly to engage him. Reaching into his bag, he took out a stone, which he slung and struck the Philistine on the forehead. The stone sank into his head, and he fell prone on the ground. So with sling and stone David proved the victor; though he had no sword, he struck down the Philistine and gave him a mortal wound. He ran up to the Philistine and stood over him; then, grasping his sword, he drew it out of the scabbard, dispatched him, and cut off his head.

When the Philistines saw the fate of their champion, they turned and fled. The men of Israel and Judah at once raised the war cry and closely pursued them all the way to Gath and up to the gates of Ekron. The road that runs to Shaaraim, Gath, and Ekron was strewn with their dead. On their return from the pursuit of the Philistines, the Israelites plundered their camp. David took Goliath's head and carried it to Jerusalem, but he put Goliath's weapons in his own tent.

As Saul watched David go out to meet the Philistine, he said to Abner his commander-in-chief, 'That youth there, Abner, whose son is he?' 'By your life, your majesty,' replied Abner, 'I do not know.' The king said, 'Go and find out whose son the stripling is.'

When David came back after killing the Philistine, Abner took him and presented him to Saul with the Philistine's head still in his hand. Saul asked him, 'Whose son are you, young man?' and David answered, 'I am the son of your servant Jesse of Bethlehem.'

David Escapes from Saul

That same day, when Saul had finished talking with David, he kept him and would not let him return any more to his father's house, for he saw that Jonathan had given his heart to David and had grown to love him as himself. Jonathan and David made a solemn compact because each loved the other as dearly as himself. Jonathan stripped off the cloak and tunic he was wearing, and gave them to David, together with his sword, his bow, and his belt.

At the homecoming of the army and the return of David from slaying the Philistine, the women from all the cities and towns of Israel came out singing and dancing to meet King Saul, rejoicing with tambourines and three-stringed instruments.

The women as they made merry sang to one another:

'Saul struck down thousands,
but David tens of thousands.'

Saul was furious, and the words rankled. He said, 'They have ascribed to David tens of thousands and to me only thousands. What more can they do but make him king?' From that time forward Saul kept a jealous eye on David.

Next day an evil spirit from God seized on Saul. He fell into a frenzy in the house, and David played the lyre to him as he had done before. Saul had a spear in his hand, and he hurled it at David, meaning to pin him to the wall; but twice David dodged aside. After this Saul was afraid of David, because he saw that the Lord had forsaken him and was with David. He therefore removed David from his household and appointed him to the command of a thousand men. David led his men into action, and succeeded in everything that he undertook, because the Lord was with him. When Saul saw how successful he was, he was more afraid of him than ever. But all Israel and Judah loved David because he took the field at their head.

Saul said to David, 'Here is my elder daughter Merab; I shall give her to you in marriage, but in return you must serve me valiantly and fight the Lord's battles.' For Saul meant David to meet his end not at his hands but at the hands of the Philistines. David answered Saul, 'Who am I and what are my father's people, my kinsfolk, in Israel, that I should become the king's son-in-law?' However, when the time came for Saul's daughter Merab to be married to David, she had already been given to Adriel of Meholah.

But Michal, Saul's other daughter, fell in love with David, and when Saul was told of this, he saw that it suited his plans. He said to himself, 'I will give her to him; let her be the bait that lures him to his death at the hands of the Philistines.' So Saul proposed a second time to make David his son-in-law, and ordered his courtiers to say to David privately, 'The king is well disposed to you and you are dear to us all; now is the time for you to marry into the king's family.' When they spoke in this way to David, he said to them, 'Do you think that marrying the king's daughter is a matter of so little consequence that a poor man of no account, like myself, can do it?'

The courtiers reported what David had said, and Saul replied, 'Tell David this: all the king wants as the bride-price is the foreskins of a hundred Philistines, by way of vengeance on his enemies.' Saul was counting on David's death at the hands of the Philistines. The courtiers told David what Saul had said, and marriage with the king's daughter on these terms pleased him well. Before the appointed time, David went out with his men and slew two hundred Philistines; he brought their foreskins and counted them out to the king in order to be accepted as his son-in-law. Saul then married his daughter Michal to David.

That night Saul sent servants to keep watch on David's house, intending to kill him in the morning. But David's wife Michal warned him to get away that night, 'or tomorrow', she said, 'you will be a dead man'. She let David down through a window and he slipped away and escaped. Michal then took their household god and put it on the bed; at its head she laid a goat's-hair rug and covered it all with a cloak. When the men arrived to arrest David she told them he was ill. Saul, however, sent them back to see David for themselves. 'Bring him to me, bed and all,' he ordered, 'so that I may kill him.' When they came, there was the household god on the bed and the goat's-hair rug at its head. Saul said to Michal, 'Why have you played this trick on me and let my enemy get away?' Michal answered, 'He said to me, "Help me to escape or I shall kill you."'

Meanwhile David made good his escape, and coming to Samuel at Ramah, he described how Saul had treated him. He and Samuel went to Naioth and stayed there. When Saul was told that David was at Naioth, he sent a party of men to seize him. But at the sight of the company of prophets in a frenzy, with Samuel standing at their head, the spirit of God came upon them and they fell into prophetic frenzy. When this was reported to Saul he sent another party; these also fell into a frenzy, and when he sent men a third time, they did the same. Saul himself then set out for Ramah and came to the great cistern in Secu. He asked where Samuel and David were and was told that they were at Naioth in

Ramah. On his way there the spirit of God came upon him too and he went on, in a prophetic frenzy as he went, till he came to Naioth in Ramah. There he too stripped off his clothes and like the rest fell into a frenzy before Samuel and lay down naked all that day and throughout that night. That is the reason for the saying, 'Is Saul also among the prophets?'

David made his escape from Naioth in Ramah and came to Jonathan. 'What have I done?' he asked. 'What is my offence? What wrong does your father think I have done, that he seeks my life?' Jonathan answered, 'God forbid! There is no thought of putting you to death. I am sure my father will not do anything whatever without telling me. Why should my father hide such a thing from me? I cannot believe it!' David said, 'I am ready to swear to it: your father has said to himself, "Jonathan must not know this or he will resent it," because he knows that you have a high regard for me. As the Lord lives, your life upon it, I am only a step away from death.' Jonathan said to David, 'What do you want me to do for you?' David answered, 'It is new moon tomorrow, and I am to dine with the king. But let me go and lie hidden in the fields until the third evening, and if your father misses me, say, "David asked me for leave to hurry off on a visit to his home in Bethlehem, for it is the annual sacrifice there for the whole family." If he says, "Good," it will be well for me; but if he flies into a rage, you will know that he is set on doing me harm. My lord, keep faith with me; for you and I have entered into a solemn compact before the Lord. Kill me yourself if I am guilty, but do not let me fall into your father's hands.' 'God forbid!' cried Jonathan. 'If I find my father set on doing you harm, I shall tell you.' David answered Jonathan, 'How will you let me know if he answers harshly?' Jonathan said, 'Let us go into the fields,' and so they went there together.

Jonathan said, 'I promise you, David, in the sight of the Lord the God of Israel, this time tomorrow I shall sound my father for the third time and, if he is well disposed to you, I shall send and let you know. If my father means mischief, may the Lord do the same to me and more, if I do not let you know and get you safely away. The Lord be with you as he has been with my father! I know that as long as I live you will show me faithful friendship, as the Lord requires; and if I should die, you will continue loyal to my family for ever. When the Lord rids the earth of all David's enemies, may the Lord call him to account if he and his house are no longer my friends.' Jonathan pledged himself afresh to David because of his love for him, for he loved him as himself.

Jonathan said, 'Tomorrow is the new moon, and you will be missed when your place is empty. So the day after tomorrow go down at nightfall to the place where you hid on the day when the affair started; stay by the mound there. I shall shoot three arrows towards it as though aiming at a target. Then I shall send my boy to find the arrows. If I say to him, "Look, the arrows are on this side of you; pick them up," then you can come out of hiding. You will be quite safe, I swear it, for there will be nothing amiss. But if I say to him, "Look, the arrows are on the other side of you, farther on," then the Lord has said that you must go; the Lord stands witness between us for ever to the pledges we have exchanged.'

David hid in the fields, and when the new moon came the king sat down to eat at mealtime. Saul took his customary seat by the wall, and Abner sat beside him; Jonathan too was present, but David's place was empty. That day Saul said nothing, for he thought that David was absent by some chance, perhaps because he was ritually unclean. But on the second day, the day after the new moon, David's place was still empty, and Saul said to his son Jonathan, 'Why has the son of Jesse not come to the feast, either yesterday or today?' Jonathan answered, 'David asked permission to go to Bethlehem. He asked my leave and said, "Our family is holding a sacrifice in the town and my brother himself has told me to be there. Now, if you have any regard for me, let me slip away to see my brothers." That is why he has not come to the king's table.' Saul's anger blazed up against Jonathan and he said, 'You son of a crooked and rebellious mother! I know perfectly well you have made a friend of the son of Jesse only to bring shame on yourself and dishonour on your mother. But as long as Jesse's son remains alive on the earth, neither you nor your kingdom will be established. Send at once and fetch him; he deserves to die.' Jonathan answered his father, 'Deserves to die? Why? What has he done?' At that, Saul picked up his spear and threatened to kill him; and Jonathan knew that his father was bent on David's death. He left the table in a rage and ate nothing on the second day of the festival; for he was indignant on David's behalf and because his father had humiliated him.

Next morning Jonathan, accompanied by a young boy, went out into the fields to keep the appointment with David. He said to the boy, 'Run ahead and find the arrows I shoot.' As the boy ran on, he shot the arrows over his head. When the boy reached the place where the arrows had fallen, Jonathan called out after him, 'Look, the arrows are beyond you. Hurry! Go quickly! Do not delay.' The boy gathered up the arrows and brought them to his master but only Jonathan and David knew what this meant; the boy knew nothing. Jonathan handed his weapons to the boy and told him to take them back to the town.

When the boy had gone, David got up from behind the mound and bowed humbly three times. Then they kissed one another and shed tears together, until David's grief was even greater than Jonathan's. Jonathan said to David, 'Go in safety; we have pledged each other in the name of the Lord who is witness for ever between you and me and between your descendants and mine.'

David went off at once, while Jonathan returned to the town. David made his way to Nob to the priest Ahimelech, who hurried out to meet him and asked, 'Why are you alone and unattended?' David answered Ahimelech, 'I am under orders from the king: I was to let no one know about the mission on which he was sending me or what these orders were. When I took leave of my men I told them to meet me in such and such a place. Now, what have you got by you? Let me have five loaves, or as many as you can find.' The priest answered David, 'I have no ordinary bread available. There is only the sacred bread; but have the young men kept themselves from women?' David answered the priest, 'Women have been denied us as hitherto when I have been on campaign, even an ordinary campaign, and the young men's bodies have remained holy; and how much more will they be holy today!' So, as there was no other bread there, the priest gave him the sacred bread, the Bread of the Presence, which had just been taken from the presence of the Lord to be replaced by freshly baked bread on the day that the old was removed. One of Saul's servants happened to be there that day, detained before the Lord; his name was Doeg the Edomite, and he was the chief of Saul's herdsmen. David said to Ahimelech, 'Have you a spear or sword here at hand? I have no sword or other weapon with me, because the king's business was urgent.' The priest answered, 'There is the sword of Goliath the Philistine whom you slew in the valley of Elah; it is wrapped up in a cloak behind the ephod. If you want to take that, take it; there is no other weapon here.' David said, 'There is no sword like it; give it to me.'

That day David went on his way, fleeing from Saul, and came to King Achish of Gath. The servants of Achish said to him, 'Surely this is David, the king of his country, the man of whom they sang as they danced:

> "Saul struck down thousands,
> but David tens of thousands."'

These comments were not lost on David, and he became very much afraid of King Achish of Gath. So he altered his behaviour in public and acted like a madman in front of them all, scrabbling on the double doors of the city gate and dribbling down his beard. Achish said to his servants, 'The man is insane! Why bring him to me? Am I short of madmen that you bring this one to plague me? Must I have this fellow in my house?'

David the Fugitive
David stole away from there and went to the cave of Adullam, and, when his brothers and all the members of his family heard where he was, they went down and joined him there. Everyone in any kind of distress or in debt or with a grievance gathered round him, about four hundred in number, and he became their chief. From there David went to Mizpeh in Moab and said to the king of Moab, 'Let my father and mother come and take shelter with you until I know what God will do for me.' He left them at the court of the king of Moab, and they stayed there as long as David remained in his stronghold.

The prophet Gad said to David, 'You must not stay in your stronghold; go at once into Judah.' David went as far as the forest of Hareth. News that the whereabouts of David and his men was known reached Saul while he was in Gibeah, sitting under the tamarisk tree on the hilltop with his spear in his hand and all his retainers standing about him. He said to them, 'Listen to me, you Benjamites: do you expect the son of Jesse to give you all fields and vineyards, or make you all officers over units of a thousand and a hundred? Is that why you have all conspired against me?

Not one of you told me when my son made a compact with the son of Jesse; none of you spared a thought for me or told me that my son had set against me my own servant, who is lying in wait for me now.'

Doeg the Edomite, who was standing with Saul's servants, spoke up: 'I saw the son of Jesse coming to Nob, to Ahimelech son of Ahitub. Ahimelech consulted the Lord on his behalf, then gave him food and handed over to him the sword of Goliath the Philistine.' The king sent for Ahimelech the priest and his whole family, who were priests at Nob, and they all came to him. Saul said, 'Now listen, you son of Ahitub,' and the man answered, 'Yes, my lord?' Saul said to him, 'Why have you and the son of Jesse plotted against me? You gave him food and a sword, and consulted God on his behalf; and now he has risen against me and is at this moment lying in wait for me.' 'And who among all your servants', answered Ahimelech, 'is like David, a man to be trusted, the king's son-in-law, appointed to your staff and holding an honourable place in your household? Have I on this occasion done something profane in consulting God on his behalf? God forbid! I trust that my lord the king will not accuse me or my family; for I know nothing whatever about it.' But the king said, 'Ahimelech, you shall die, you and all your family.' He then said to the bodyguard attending him, 'Turn on the priests of the Lord and kill them; for they are in league with David, and, though they knew that he was a fugitive, they did not inform me.' The king's men, however, were unwilling to raise a hand against the priests of the Lord. The king therefore said to Doeg the Edomite, 'You, Doeg, go and fall on the priests'; so Doeg went and fell upon the priests, killing that day with his own hand eighty-five men who wore the linen ephod. He put to the sword every living thing in Nob, the town of the priests: men and women, children and babes in arms, oxen, donkeys, and sheep.

One of Ahimelech's sons named Abiathar made his escape and joined David. He told David how Saul had killed the priests of the Lord, and David said to him, 'When Doeg the Edomite was there that day, I knew that he would certainly tell Saul. I have brought this on all the members of your father's house. Stay here with me, have no fear; he who seeks your life seeks mine, and you will be safe with me.'

The Philistines had launched an assault on Keilah and were plundering the threshing-floors. When this was reported to David, he consulted the Lord and asked whether he should go and attack these Philistines. The Lord answered, 'Go, attack them, and relieve Keilah.' But David's men said to him, 'Here in Judah we are afraid. How much worse if we challenge the Philistine forces at Keilah!' David consulted the Lord once again and got the answer, 'Go down at once to Keilah; I shall give the Philistines into your hands.' David and his men marched to Keilah, fought the Philistines, and carried off their livestock; they inflicted a heavy defeat on them and relieved the inhabitants of Keilah.

When Abiathar son of Ahimelech fled and joined David at Keilah, he brought an ephod with him. It was reported to Saul that David had entered Keilah, and he said, 'God has put him into my hands; for he has walked into a trap by entering a walled town with its barred gates.' He called out all the army to march on Keilah and besiege David and his men.

When David learnt how Saul planned his overthrow, he told Abiathar the priest to bring the ephod, and then he prayed, 'Lord God of Israel, I your servant have heard that Saul intends to come to Keilah and destroy the town because of me. Will the townspeople of Keilah surrender me to him? Will Saul come down as I have heard? Lord God of Israel, I pray you, tell your servant.' The Lord answered, 'He will come.' David asked, 'Will the citizens of Keilah surrender me and my men to Saul?' and the Lord answered, 'They will.' At once David left Keilah with his men, who numbered about six hundred, and moved about from place to place. When it was reported to Saul that David had escaped from Keilah, he called off the operation.

David was living in the fastnesses of the wilderness of Ziph, in the hill-country, and though Saul went daily in search of him, God did not put him into his power. David was at Horesh in the wilderness of Ziph, when he learnt that Saul had come out to seek his life. Saul's son Jonathan came to David at Horesh and gave him fresh courage in God's name: 'Do not be afraid,' he said; 'my father's hand will not touch you. You will become king of Israel and I shall rank after you. This my father knows.' After the two of them had made a solemn compact before the Lord, David remained in Horesh and Jonathan went home.

The Ziphites brought to Saul at Gibeah the news that David was in hiding among them in the fastnesses of Horesh on the hill of Hachilah, south of Jeshimon. 'Let your majesty come down whenever you will,' they said, 'and it will be our business to surrender him to you.' Saul replied, 'The Lord's blessing on you; you have rendered me a service. Go now and make further enquiry, and find out exactly where he is and who saw him there. They tell me that he is crafty enough to outwit me. Find out which of his hiding-places he is using; then come back to me at such and such a place, and I shall go with you. So long as he stays in this country, I shall hunt him down, if I have to go through all the clans of Judah one by one.' They left for Ziph without delay, ahead of Saul.

David and his men were in the wilderness of Maon in the Arabah to the south of Jeshimon. Saul set off with his men to look for him; but David got word of it and went down to a refuge in the rocks, and there he stayed in the wilderness of Maon. On hearing this, Saul went into the wilderness after him; he was on one side of the hill, David and his men on the other. While David and his men were trying desperately to get away, and Saul and his followers were closing in for the capture, a runner brought a message to Saul: 'Come at once! The Philistines are invading the land.' Saul called off the pursuit of David and turned back to face the Philistines. This is why that place is called the Dividing Rock. David went up from there and lived in the fastnesses of En-gedi.

David and Abigail

There was a man in Maon who had property at Carmel and owned three thousand sheep and a thousand goats; and he was shearing his flocks in Carmel. His name was Nabal and his wife's name Abigail; she was a beautiful and intelligent woman, but her husband, a Calebite, was surly and mean. David heard in the wilderness that Nabal was shearing his flocks, and sent ten of his young men, saying to them, 'Go up to Carmel, find Nabal, and give him my greetings. You are to say, "All good wishes for the year ahead! Prosperity to yourself, your household, and all that is yours! I hear that you are shearing. Your shepherds have been with us lately and we did not molest them; nothing of theirs was missing all the time they were in Carmel. Ask your own men and they will tell you. Receive my men kindly, for this is an auspicious day with us, and give what you can to David your son and your servant."'

David's servants came and delivered this message to Nabal in David's name. When they paused, Nabal answered, 'Who is David? Who is this son of Jesse? In these days there are many slaves who break away from their masters. Am I to take my food and my wine and the meat I have provided for my shearers, and give it to men who come from I know not where?' David's servants turned and made their way back to him and told him all this. He said to his followers, 'Buckle on your swords, all of you.' So they buckled on their swords, as did David, and they followed him, four hundred of them, while two hundred stayed behind with the baggage.

One of Nabal's servants said to Abigail, Nabal's wife, 'David sent messengers from the wilderness to ask our master politely for a present, and he flared up at them. The men have been very good to us and have not molested us, nor did we miss anything all the time we were going about with them in the open country. They were as good as a wall round us, night and day, while we were minding the flocks. Consider carefully what you had better do, for it is certain ruin for our master and his whole house; he is such a wretched fellow that it is no good talking to him.'

Abigail hastily collected two hundred loaves and two skins of wine, five sheep ready dressed, five measures of roasted grain, a hundred bunches of raisins, and two hundred cakes of dried figs, and loaded them on donkeys, but told her husband nothing about it. She said to her servants, 'Go on ahead, I shall follow you.' As she made her way on her donkey, hidden by the hill, there were David and his men coming down towards her, and she met them. David had said, 'It was a waste of time to protect this fellow's property in the wilderness so well that nothing of his was missing. He has repaid me evil for good.' David swore a solemn oath: 'God do the same to me and more if I leave him a single mother's son alive by morning!'

When Abigail saw David she dismounted in haste and prostrated herself before him, bowing low to the ground at his feet, and said, 'Let me take the blame, my lord, but allow your humble servant to speak out, and let my lord give me a hearing. How can you take any notice of this wretched fellow? He is just what his name Nabal means: "Churl" is his name, and churlish his behaviour. Sir, I did not myself see the men you sent. And now, sir, the Lord has restrained you from starting a blood feud and from striking a blow for yourself. As the Lord lives, your life upon it, your enemies and all who want to see you ruined will be like Nabal. Here is the present which I, your humble servant, have brought; give it to the young men under your command. Forgive me, my lord, if I am presuming; for the Lord will establish your family for ever, because you have fought his battles. No calamity will overtake you as long as you live. If anyone tries to pursue you and take your life, the Lord your God will wrap your life up and put it with his own treasure, but the lives of your enemies he will hurl away like stones from a sling. When the Lord has made good all his promises to you, and has made you ruler of Israel, there will be no reason why you should stumble or your courage should falter because you have shed innocent blood or struck a blow for yourself. Then when the Lord makes all you do prosper, remember me, your servant.'

David said to Abigail, 'Blessed be the Lord the God of Israel who today has sent you to meet me. A blessing on your good sense, a blessing on you because you have saved me today from the guilt of bloodshed and from striking a blow for myself. For I swear by the life of the Lord the God of Israel who has kept me from doing you wrong: if you had not come at once to meet me, not a man of Nabal's household, not a single mother's son, would have been left alive by morning.' Then David accepted from her what she had brought him and said, 'Go home in peace; I have listened to you and I grant your request.'

On her return she found Nabal holding a right royal banquet in his house. He grew merry and became very drunk, so drunk that his wife said nothing at all to him till daybreak. In the morning, when the wine had worn off, she told him everything, and he had a seizure and lay there like a log. Some ten days later the Lord struck him and he died.

When David heard that Nabal was dead he said, 'Blessed be the Lord, who has himself punished Nabal for his insult, and has kept me his servant from doing wrong. The Lord has made Nabal's wrongdoing recoil on his own head.' David then sent a message to Abigail proposing that she should become his wife. His servants came to her at Carmel and said, 'David has sent us to fetch you to be his wife.' She rose and prostrated herself with her face to the ground, and said, 'I am his slave to command; I would wash the feet of my lord's servants.' Abigail made her preparations with all speed and, with her five maids in attendance and accompanied by David's messengers, she set out on a donkey; and she became David's wife. David had also married Ahinoam of Jezreel; both these women became his wives. Saul meanwhile had given his daughter Michal, David's wife, to Palti son of Laish from Gallim.

David Spares Saul's Life

The Ziphites came to Saul at Gibeah with the news that David was in hiding on the hill of Hachilah overlooking Jeshimon. Saul went down at once to the wilderness of Ziph, taking with him three thousand picked men, to search for David there. He encamped beside the road on the hill of Hachilah overlooking Jeshimon, while David was still in the wilderness. As soon as David learnt that Saul had come to the wilderness in pursuit of him, he sent out scouts and found that Saul had reached such and such a place. He went at once to the place where Saul had pitched his camp, and observed where Saul and Abner son of Ner, the commander-in-chief, were lying. Saul lay within the lines with his troops encamped in a circle round him. David turned to Ahimelech the Hittite and Abishai son of Zeruiah, Joab's brother, and said, 'Who will venture with me into the camp to Saul?' Abishai answered, 'I will.'

David and Abishai entered the camp at night, and there was Saul lying asleep within the lines with his spear thrust into the ground beside his head. Abner and the army were asleep all around him. Abishai said to David, 'God has put your enemy into your power today. Let me strike him and pin him to the ground with one thrust of the spear. I shall not have to strike twice.' David said to him, 'Do him no harm. Who has ever lifted his hand against the Lord's anointed and gone unpunished? As the Lord lives,' David went on, 'the Lord will strike him down; either his time will come and he will die, or he will go down to battle and meet his end. God forbid that I should lift my hand against the Lord's anointed! But now let us take the spear which is by his head, and the water-jar, and go.' So David took the spear and the water-jar from beside Saul's head, and they left. The whole camp was asleep; no one saw him, no one knew anything, no one woke. A deep sleep sent by the Lord had fallen on them.

Then David crossed over to the other side and stood on the top of a hill at some distance; there was a wide stretch between them. David shouted across to the army and hailed Abner son of Ner, 'Answer me, Abner!' He answered, 'Who are you to shout to the king?' David said to Abner, 'Do you call yourself a man? Is there anyone like you in Israel? Why, then, did you not keep watch over your lord the king, when someone came to harm your lord the king? This was not well done. As the Lord lives, you deserve to die, all of you, because you have not kept watch over your master the Lord's anointed. Look! Where are the king's spear and the water-jar that were by his head?'

Saul recognized David's voice and said, 'Is that you, David my son?' 'Yes, your majesty, it is,' said David. 'Why must my lord pursue me? What have I done? What mischief am I plotting? Listen, my lord king, to what I have to say. If it is the Lord who has set you against me, may an offering be acceptable to him; but if it is mortals, a curse on them in the Lord's name! For they have ousted me today from my share in the Lord's possession and have banished me to serve other gods! Do not let my blood be shed on foreign soil, far from the presence of the Lord, just because the king of Israel came out to look for a flea, as one might hunt a partridge over the hills.'

Saul said, 'I have done wrong; come back, David my son. You have held my life precious this day, and I will never harm you again. I have been a fool, I have been sadly in the wrong.' David answered, 'Here is the king's spear; let one of your men come across and fetch it. The Lord who rewards uprightness and loyalty will reward the man into whose power he put you today, for I refused to lift my hand against the Lord's anointed. As I held your life precious today, so may the Lord hold mine precious and deliver me from every distress.' Saul said to David, 'A blessing on you, David my son! You will do great things and be triumphant.' With that David went on his way and Saul returned home.

David the Mercenary

David thought to himself, 'One of these days I shall be killed by Saul. The best thing for me to do will be to escape into Philistine territory; then Saul will give up all further hope of finding me anywhere in Israel, search as he may, and I shall escape his clutches.' So David and his six hundred men set out and crossed the frontier to Achish son of Maoch, king of Gath. David settled in Gath with Achish, taking with him his men and their families and his two wives, Ahinoam of Jezreel and Abigail of Carmel, Nabal's widow. Saul was told that David had escaped to Gath, and he abandoned the search.

David said to Achish, 'If I stand well in your opinion, grant me a place in one of your country towns where I may settle. Why should I remain in the royal city with your majesty?' Achish granted him Ziklag on that day: that is why Ziklag still belongs to the kings of Judah.

David spent a year and four months in Philistine country. He and his men would sally out and raid the Geshurites, the Gizrites, and the Amalekites, for it was they who inhabited the country from Telaim all the way to Shur and Egypt. When David raided any territory he left no one alive, man or woman; he took flocks and herds, donkeys and camels, and clothes too, and then came back again to Achish. Achish would ask, 'Where was your raid today?' and David would answer, 'The Negeb of Judah' or 'The Negeb of the Jerahmeelites' or 'The Negeb of the Kenites'. He let neither man nor woman survive to be brought back to Gath, for fear that they might denounce him and his men for what they had done. This was his practice as long as he remained with the Philistines. Achish trusted him, thinking that David had made himself so obnoxious among his own people the Israelites that he would remain his vassal all his life.

At that time the Philistines mustered their army for an attack on Israel, and Achish said to David, 'You know that you and your men must take the field with me.' David answered, 'Good, you will learn what your servant can do.' Achish said, 'I will make you my bodyguard for life.'

The Witch of En-dor

By this time Samuel was dead, and all Israel had mourned for him and buried him in Ramah, his own town; and Saul had banished from the land all who trafficked with ghosts and spirits. The Philistines mustered and encamped at Shunem, and Saul mustered all the Israelites and encamped at Gilboa. At the sight of the Philistine forces, Saul was afraid, indeed struck to the heart by terror. He enquired of the Lord, but the Lord did not answer him, neither by dreams, nor by Urim, nor by prophets. So he said to his servants, 'Find a woman who has a familiar spirit, and I will go and enquire through her.' They told him that there was such a woman at En-dor.

Saul put on different clothes and went in disguise with two of his men. He came to the woman by night and said, 'Tell me my fortune by consulting the dead, and call up the man I name to you.' The woman answered, 'Surely you know what Saul has done, how he has made away with those who call up ghosts and spirits; why do you press me to do what will lead to my death?' Saul swore her an oath: 'As the Lord lives, no harm shall come to you for this.' The woman asked whom she should call up, and Saul answered, 'Samuel.' When the woman saw Samuel appear, she shrieked and said to Saul, 'Why have you deceived me? You are Saul!' The king said to her, 'Do not be afraid. What do you see?' The woman answered, 'I see a ghostly form coming up from the earth.' 'What is it like?' he asked; she answered, 'Like an old man coming up, wrapped in a cloak.' Then Saul knew it was Samuel, and he bowed low with his face to the ground, and prostrated himself.

Samuel said to Saul, 'Why have you disturbed me and raised me?' Saul answered, 'I am in great trouble; the Philistines are waging war against me, and God has turned away; he no longer answers me through prophets or through dreams, and I have summoned you to tell me what I should do.' Samuel said, 'Why do you ask me, now that the Lord has turned from you and become your adversary? He has done what he foretold through me. He has wrested the kingdom from your hand and given it to another, to David. You have not obeyed the Lord, or executed the judgement of his fierce anger against the Amalekites; that is why he has done this to you today. For the same reason the Lord will let your people Israel fall along with you into the hands of the Philistines. What is more, tomorrow you and your sons will be with me. I tell you again: the Lord will give the Israelite army into the power of the Philistines.' Saul was overcome, and terrified by Samuel's words he fell full length to the ground. He had no strength left, for he had eaten nothing all day and all night.

The woman went to Saul and, seeing how deeply shaken he was, she said, 'I listened to what you said and I risked my life to obey you. Now listen to me: let me set before you a little food to give you strength for your journey.' He refused to eat anything, but when his servants joined the woman in pressing him, he yielded, rose from the ground, and sat on the couch. The woman had a fattened calf at home, which she quickly slaughtered; she also took some meal, kneaded it, and baked unleavened loaves. She set the food before Saul and his servants, and when they had eaten they set off that same night.

David Defeats the Amalekites

The Philistines mustered their entire army at Aphek; the Israelites encamped at En-harod in Jezreel. While the Philistine lords were advancing with their troops in units of a hundred and a thousand, David and his men were in the rear of the column with Achish. The Philistine commanders asked, 'What are those Hebrews doing here?' Achish answered, 'This is David, the servant of King Saul of Israel who has been with me now for a year or more. Ever since he came over to me I have had no fault to find with him.' The commanders were indignant and said, 'Send the man back to the place you allotted to him. He must not fight side by side with us, for he may turn traitor in the battle. What better way to buy his master's favour, than at the price of our lives? This is that David of whom they sang, as they danced:

> "Saul struck down thousands,
> but David tens of thousands."'

Achish summoned David and said to him, 'As the Lord lives, you are an upright man and your service on my campaigns has well satisfied me. I have had no fault to find with you ever since you joined me, but the lords are not willing to accept you. Now go home in peace, and you will then be doing nothing that they can regard as wrong.' David protested, 'What have I done, or what fault have you found in me from the day I first entered your service till now, that I should not come and fight against the enemies of my lord the king?' Achish answered, 'I agree that you have been as true to me as an angel of God, but the Philistine commanders insist that you are not to fight alongside them. Now rise early tomorrow with those of your lord's subjects who have followed you, and go to the town which I allotted to you; harbour no resentment, for I am well satisfied with you. Be up early and start as soon as it is light.' So in the morning David and his men made an early start to go back to the land of the Philistines, while the Philistines went on to Jezreel.

On the third day David and his men reached Ziklag. In the mean time the Amalekites had made a raid into the Negeb, attacked Ziklag, and set it on fire. They had taken captive all the women, young and old. They did not put any to death, but carried them off as they continued their march. When David and his men came to the town, they found it destroyed by fire, and their wives, their sons, and their daughters taken captive. David and the people with him wept aloud until they could weep no more. David's two wives, Ahinoam of Jezreel and Abigail widow of Nabal of Carmel, were among the captives. David was in a desperate position because the troops, embittered by the loss of their sons and daughters, threatened to stone him.

David sought strength in the Lord his God, and told Abiathar the priest, son of Ahimelech, to bring the ephod. When Abiathar had brought the ephod, David enquired of the Lord, 'Shall I pursue these raiders? And shall I overtake them?' The answer came, 'Pursue them: you will overtake them and rescue everyone.' David and his six hundred men set out and reached the wadi of Besor. Two hundred of them who were too exhausted to cross the wadi stayed behind, and David with four hundred pressed on in pursuit.

In the open country they came across an Egyptian and took him to David. They gave him food to eat and water to drink, also a lump of dried figs and two bunches of raisins. When he had eaten he revived; for he had had nothing to eat or drink for three days and nights. David asked him, 'Whose slave are you, and where have you come from?' 'I am an Egyptian,' he answered, 'the slave of an Amalekite, but my master left me behind because three days ago I fell ill. We had raided the Negeb of the Kerethites, part of Judah, and the Negeb of Caleb; we also burned down Ziklag.' David asked, 'Can you guide me to the raiders?' 'Swear to me by God', he answered, 'that you will not put me to death or hand me back to my master, and I shall guide you to them.' He led him down, and there they found the Amalekites scattered everywhere, eating and drinking and celebrating the great mass of spoil taken from the Philistine and Judaean territories.

David attacked from dawn to dusk and continued till next day; only four hundred young men mounted on camels got away. David rescued all those whom the Amalekites had taken captive, including his two wives. No one was missing, young or old, sons or daughters, nor was any of the spoil missing, anything they had seized for themselves: David recovered everything. They took all the flocks and herds, drove the cattle before him and said, 'This is David's spoil.'

When David returned to the two hundred men who had been too exhausted to follow him and whom he had left behind at the wadi of Besor, they came forward to meet him and his men. David greeted them all, enquiring how things were with them. But some of those who had gone with David, rogues and scoundrels, broke in and said, 'These men did not go with us; we will not allot them any of the spoil that we have recaptured, except that each of them may take his wife and children and go.' 'That', said David, 'you must not do, considering what the Lord has given us, and how he has kept us safe and given the raiding party into our hands. Who could agree with what you propose? Those who stayed with the stores are to have the same share as those who went into battle. All must share and share alike.' From that time onwards, this has been the established custom in Israel down to this day.

The Deaths of Saul and Jonathan

The Philistines engaged Israel in battle, and the Israelites were routed, leaving their dead on Mount Gilboa. The Philistines closely pursued Saul and his sons, and Jonathan, Abinadab, and Malchishua, the sons of Saul, were killed. The battle went hard for Saul, and when the archers caught up with him they wounded him severely. He said to his armour-bearer, 'Draw your sword and run me through, so that these uncircumcised brutes may not come and taunt me and make sport of me.' But the armour-bearer refused; he dared not do it. Thereupon Saul took his own sword and fell on it. When the armour-bearer saw that Saul was dead, he too fell on his sword and died with him. So they died together on that day, Saul, his three sons, and his armour-bearer, as well as all his men. When the Israelites in the neighbourhood of the valley and of the Jordan saw that the other Israelites had fled and that Saul and his sons had perished, they fled likewise, abandoning their towns; and the Philistines moved in and occupied them.

Next day, when the Philistines came to strip the slain, they found Saul and his three sons lying dead on Mount Gilboa. They cut off his head and stripped him of his armour; then they sent messengers through the length and breadth of their land to carry the good news to idols and people alike. They deposited his armour in the temple of Ashtoreth and nailed his body on the wall of Beth-shan. When the inhabitants of Jabesh-gilead heard what the Philistines had done to Saul, all the warriors among them set out and journeyed through the night to recover the bodies of Saul and his sons from the wall of Beth-shan. They brought them back to Jabesh and burned them; they took the bones and buried them under the tamarisk tree in Jabesh, and for seven days they fasted.

After Saul's death David returned from his victory over the Amalekites and spent two days in Ziklag. On the third day a man came from Saul's camp; his clothes were torn and there was dust on his head. Coming into David's presence he fell to the ground and did obeisance. David asked him where he had come from, and he replied, 'I have escaped from the Israelite camp.' David said, 'What is the news? Tell me.' 'The army has been driven from the field,' he answered, 'many have fallen in battle, and Saul and Jonathan his son are dead.' David said to the young man who brought the news, 'How do you know that Saul and Jonathan are dead?' He answered, 'It so happened that I was on Mount Gilboa and saw Saul leaning on his spear with the chariots and horsemen closing in on him. He turned and, seeing me, called to me. I said, "What is it, sir?" He asked me who I was, and I said, "An Amalekite." He said to me, "Come and stand over me and dispatch me. I still live, but the throes of death have seized me." So I stood over him and dealt him the death blow, for I knew that, stricken as he was, he could not live. Then I took the crown from his head and the armlet from his arm, and I have brought them here to you, my lord.' At that David and all the men with him took hold of their clothes and tore them. They mourned and wept, and they fasted till evening because Saul and Jonathan his son and the army of the Lord and the house of Israel had fallen in battle.

David said to the young man who brought him the news, 'Where do you come from?' and he answered, 'I am the son of an alien, an Amalekite.' 'How is it', said David, 'that you were not afraid to raise your hand to kill the Lord's anointed?'

Summoning one of his own young men he ordered him to fall upon the Amalekite. The young man struck him down and he died. David said, 'Your blood be on your own head; for out of your own mouth you condemned yourself by saying, "I killed the Lord's anointed."'

David raised this lament over Saul and Jonathan his son; and he ordered that this dirge over them should be taught to the people of Judah. It was written down and may be found in the Book of Jashar:

Israel, upon your heights your beauty lies slain!
How are the warriors fallen!

Do not tell it in Gath
or proclaim it in the streets of Ashkelon,
in case the Philistine maidens rejoice,
and the daughters of the uncircumcised exult.

Hills of Gilboa, let no dew or rain fall on you,
no showers on the uplands!
For there the shields of the warriors lie tarnished,
and the shield of Saul, no longer bright with oil.
The bow of Jonathan never held back
from the breast of the foeman, from the blood of the slain;
the sword of Saul never returned empty to the scabbard.

Beloved and lovely were Saul and Jonathan;
neither in life nor in death were they parted.
They were swifter than eagles, stronger than lions.

Daughters of Israel, weep for Saul,
who clothed you in scarlet and rich embroideries,
who spangled your attire with jewels of gold.

How are the warriors fallen on the field of battle!
Jonathan lies slain on your heights.

I grieve for you, Jonathan my brother;
you were most dear to me;
your love for me was wonderful,
surpassing the love of women.

How are the warriors fallen,
and their armour abandoned on the battlefield!

David, King of Judah

Afterwards David enquired of the Lord, 'Shall I go up into one of the towns of Judah?' The Lord answered, 'Go.' David asked, 'Where shall I go?' and the answer was, 'To Hebron.' So David went up there with his two wives, Ahinoam of Jezreel and Abigail widow of Nabal of Carmel. David also brought the men who had joined him, with their families, and they settled in Hebron and the neighbouring towns. The men of Judah came, and there they anointed David king over the house of Judah.

It was reported to David that the men of Jabesh-gilead had buried Saul, and he sent them this message: 'The Lord bless you because you kept faith with Saul your lord and buried him. For this may the Lord keep faith and truth with you, and I for my part will show you favour too, because you have done this. Be strong, be valiant, now that Saul your lord is dead, and the people of Judah have anointed me to be king over them.'

Meanwhile Saul's commander-in-chief, Abner son of Ner, had taken Saul's son Ishbosheth, brought him across to Mahanaim, and made him king over Gilead, the Asherites, Jezreel, Ephraim, and Benjamin, and all Israel. Ishbosheth was forty years old when he became king over Israel, and he reigned for two years. The tribe of Judah, however, followed David. David's rule over Judah in Hebron lasted seven and a half years.

Abner son of Ner, with the troops of Saul's son Ishbosheth, marched out from Mahanaim to Gibeon, and Joab son of Zeruiah marched out with David's troops from Hebron. They met at the pool of Gibeon and took up their positions, one force on one side of the pool and the other on the opposite side. Abner said to Joab, 'Let the young men come forward and join in single combat before us.' Joab agreed. So they came up, one by one, and took their places, twelve for Benjamin and Ishbosheth and twelve from David's men. Each man seized his opponent by the head and thrust his sword into his opponent's side; and thus they fell together. That is why that place, which lies in Gibeon, was called the Field of Blades.

There ensued a very hard-fought battle that day, and Abner and the men of Israel were defeated by David's troops. All three sons of Zeruiah were there, Joab, Abishai, and Asahel. Asahel, who was swift as a gazelle of the plains, chased after Abner, swerving to neither right nor left in his pursuit. Abner glanced back and said, 'Is it you, Asahel?' Asahel answered, 'It is.' Abner said, 'Turn aside to right or left; tackle one of the young men and win his belt for yourself.' But Asahel would not abandon the pursuit.

Abner again urged him to give it up. 'Why should I kill you?' he said. 'How could I look Joab your brother in the face?' When he still refused to turn away, Abner struck him in the belly with a back-thrust of his spear so that the spear came out through his back, and he fell dead in his tracks. All who came to the place where Asahel lay dead stopped there. But Joab and Abishai kept up the pursuit of Abner, until, at sunset, they reached the hill of Ammah, opposite Giah on the road leading to the pastures of Gibeon.

The Benjamites rallied to Abner and, forming themselves into a single group, took their stand on the top of a hill. Abner called to Joab, 'Must the slaughter go on for ever? Can you not see the bitterness that will result? How long before you recall the troops from the pursuit of their kinsmen?' Joab answered, 'As God lives, if you had not spoken, they would not have given up the pursuit till morning.' Then Joab sounded the trumpet, and the troops all halted; they abandoned the pursuit of the Israelites, and the fighting ceased.

Abner and his men moved along the Arabah all that night, crossed the Jordan, and continued all morning till they reached Mahanaim. After Joab returned from the pursuit of Abner, he mustered his troops and found that, besides Asahel, nineteen of David's men were missing. David's forces had routed the Benjamites and the followers of Abner, killing three hundred and sixty of them. They took up Asahel and buried him in his father's tomb at Bethlehem. Joab and his men marched all night, and as day broke they reached Hebron.

The war between the house of Saul and the house of David was long drawn out, David growing steadily stronger while the house of Saul became weaker.

Sons were born to David at Hebron. His eldest was Amnon, whose mother was Ahinoam from Jezreel; his second Cileab, whose mother was Abigail widow of Nabal from Carmel; the third Absalom, whose mother was Maacah daughter of Talmai king of Geshur; the fourth Adonijah, whose mother was Haggith; the fifth Shephatiah, whose mother was Abital; and the sixth Ithream, whose mother was David's wife Eglah. These were born to David at Hebron.

As the war between the houses of Saul and David went on, Abner gradually strengthened his position in the house of Saul.

Now Saul had had a concubine named Rizpah daughter of Aiah. Ishbosheth challenged Abner, 'Why have you slept with my father's concubine?' Abner, angered by this, exclaimed, 'Do you take me for a Judahite dog? Up to now I have been loyal to the house of your father Saul, to his brothers and friends, and I have not betrayed you into David's hands; yet you choose this moment to charge me with an offence over a woman. But now, so help me God, I shall do all I can to bring about what the Lord swore to do for David: I shall set to work to overthrow the house of Saul and to establish David's throne over Israel and Judah from Dan to Beersheba.' Ishbosheth dared not say another word; he was too much afraid of Abner.

Abner sent envoys on his own behalf to David with the message, 'Who is to control the land? Let us come to terms, and you will have my support in bringing the whole of Israel over to you.' David's answer was: 'Good, I will come to terms with you, but on one condition: that you do not come into my presence without bringing Saul's daughter Michal to me.' David also sent messengers to Saul's son Ishbosheth with the demand: 'Hand over to me my wife Michal for whom I gave a hundred Philistine foreskins as the bride-price.' Thereupon Ishbosheth sent and took her from her husband, Paltiel son of Laish. Her husband followed her as far as Bahurim, weeping all the way, until Abner ordered him back, and he went.

Abner conferred with the elders of Israel: 'For some time past', he said, 'you have wanted David for your king. Now is the time to act, for this is the word of the Lord about David: "By the hand of my servant David I shall deliver my people Israel from the Philistines and from all their enemies."' Abner spoke also to the Benjamites and then went to report to David at Hebron all that the Israelites and the Benjamites had agreed. When Abner, attended by twenty men, arrived, David gave a feast for him and his men. Abner said to David, 'I shall now go and bring the whole of Israel over to your majesty. They will make a covenant with you, and you will be king over a realm after your own heart.' David dismissed Abner, granting him safe conduct.

Just then David's men and Joab returned from a raid, bringing a great quantity of plunder with them. Abner, having been dismissed, was no longer with David in Hebron. Joab and the whole force with him were greeted on their arrival with the news that Abner son of Ner had been with the king and had departed under safe conduct.

Joab went in to the king and said, 'What have you done? You have had Abner here with you. How could you let him go and get clean away? You know Abner son of Ner: his purpose in coming was to deceive you, to learn about your movements, and to find out everything you are doing.'

Leaving David's presence, Joab sent messengers after Abner, and they brought him back from the Pool of Sirah; but David knew nothing of this. On Abner's return to Hebron, Joab drew him aside in the gateway, as though to speak privately with him, and there, in revenge for his brother Asahel, he stabbed him in the belly, and he died.

When David heard the news he said, 'In the sight of the Lord I and my kingdom are for ever innocent of the blood of Abner son of Ner. May it recoil on the head of Joab and on all his family! May the house of Joab never be free from running sore or foul disease, nor lack a son fit only to ply the distaff or doomed to die by the sword or beg his bread!' Joab and Abishai his brother slew Abner because he had killed their brother Asahel in battle at Gibeon. Then David ordered Joab and all the troops with him to tear their clothes, put on sackcloth, and mourn for Abner, and the king himself walked behind the bier. They buried Abner in Hebron and the king wept aloud at the tomb, while all the people wept with him. The king made this lament for Abner:

Must Abner die so base a death?
Your hands were not bound,
    your feet not fettered;
you fell as one who falls at the hands of a criminal.

The people all wept again for him.

They came to urge David to eat something; but it was still day and he took an oath, 'So help me God! I refuse to touch food of any kind before sunset.' The people noted this with approval; indeed, everything the king did pleased them all. It was then known throughout Israel that the king had had no hand in the murder of Abner son of Ner. The king said to his servants, 'You must know that a warrior, a great man, has fallen this day in Israel. Anointed king though I am, I feel weak and powerless in face of these ruthless sons of Zeruiah; they are too much for me. May the Lord requite the wrongdoer as his wrongdoing deserves.'

When Saul's son Ishbosheth heard that Abner had met his death in Hebron, his courage failed him, and all Israel was alarmed. Ishbosheth had two officers, who were captains of raiding parties, and whose names were Baanah and Rechab; they were Benjamites, sons of Rimmon of Beeroth, Beeroth being reckoned part of Benjamin; but the Beerothites had sought refuge in Gittaim, where they have lived as aliens ever since.

Rechab and Baanah, the sons of Rimmon of Beeroth, came to Ishbosheth's house in the heat of the day, while he was taking his midday rest. The door-keeper had been sifting wheat, but she had grown drowsy and fallen asleep, so Rechab and his brother Baanah slipped past, found their way to the room where Ishbosheth was asleep on the bed, and attacked and killed him. They cut off his head and took it with them and, making their way along the Arabah all night, came to Hebron. They brought Ishbosheth's head to David there and said to the king, 'Here is the head of Ishbosheth son of Saul, your enemy, who sought your life. The Lord has avenged your majesty today on Saul and on his family.' David answered Rechab and his brother Baanah: 'As the Lord lives, who has delivered me from all my troubles, I seized the man who brought me word that Saul was dead and thought he was bringing good news; I killed him in Ziklag. That was how I rewarded him for his news! How much more shall I reward wicked men who have killed an innocent man on his bed in his own house! Am I not to take vengeance on you now for the blood you have shed, and rid the earth of you?' David gave the word, and the young men killed them; they cut off their hands and feet and hung them up beside the pool in Hebron; but the head of Ishbosheth they took and buried in Abner's tomb at Hebron.

David, King of All Israel

All the tribes of Israel came to David at Hebron and said to him,
'We are your own flesh and blood. In the past, while Saul was
still king over us, it was you that led the forces of Israel on their
campaigns. To you the Lord said, "You are to be shepherd of
my people Israel; you are to be their prince."' The elders of
Israel all came to the king at Hebron; there David made a
covenant with them before the Lord, and they anointed David
king over Israel.

David came to the throne at the age of thirty and reigned for
forty years. In Hebron he had ruled over Judah for seven and a
half years, and in Jerusalem he reigned over Israel and Judah
combined for thirty-three years.

The king and his men went to Jerusalem to attack the
Jebusites, the inhabitants of that region. The Jebusites said to
David, 'You will never come in here, not till you have disposed of
the blind and the lame,' stressing that David would never come
in. None the less David did capture the stronghold of Zion, and it
is now known as the City of David. On that day David had said,
'Everyone who is eager to attack the Jebusites, let him get up the
water-shaft to reach the lame and the blind, David's bitter enemies.' That is why they say, 'No one who is blind or lame is to
come into the Lord's house.'

David took up his residence in the stronghold and called it the
City of David. He built up the city around it, starting at the Millo
and working inwards. David steadily grew more and more powerful, for the Lord the God of Hosts was with him. King Hiram of
Tyre sent envoys to David with cedar logs, and with them car-
penters and stonemasons, who built David a house. David knew
by now that the Lord had confirmed him as king over Israel and
had enhanced his royal power for the sake of his people Israel.

David again summoned the picked men of Israel, thirty thousand in all, and went with the whole army that was then with him
to Baalath-judah to fetch from there the Ark of God which bore
the name of the Lord of Hosts, who is enthroned upon the cherubim. They mounted the Ark of God on a new cart and conveyed
it from Abinadab's house on the hill, with Uzzah and Ahio, sons
of Abinadab, guiding the cart. They led it with the Ark of God
upon it from Abinadab's house on the hill, with Ahio walking in
front. David and all Israel danced for joy before the Lord with all

their might to the sound of singing, of lyres, lutes, tambourines, castanets, and cymbals.

When they came to a certain threshing-floor, the oxen stumbled, and Uzzah reached out and held the Ark of God. The Lord was angry with Uzzah and struck him down for his imprudent action, and he died there beside the Ark of God. David was vexed because the Lord's anger had broken out on Uzzah, and he called the place Perez-uzzah, the name it still bears.

David was afraid of the Lord that day and said, 'How can the Ark of the Lord come to me?' He felt he could not take the Ark of the Lord with him to the City of David; he turned aside and carried it to the house of Obed-edom the Gittite. The Ark of the Lord remained at Obed-edom's house for three months, and the Lord blessed Obed-edom and his whole household.

When David was informed that the Lord had blessed Obed-edom's family and all that he possessed because of the Ark of God, he went and brought the Ark of God from the house of Obed-edom up to the City of David amid rejoicing. When the bearers of the Ark of the Lord had gone six steps he sacrificed a bull and a buffalo. He was wearing a linen ephod, and he danced with abandon before the Lord, as he and all the Israelites brought up the Ark of the Lord with acclamation and blowing of trumpets. As the Ark of the Lord was entering the City of David, Saul's daughter Michal looked down from a window and saw King David leaping and whirling before the Lord, and she despised him in her heart.

After they had brought the Ark of the Lord, they put it in its place inside the tent that David had set up for it, and David offered whole-offerings and shared-offerings before the Lord. Having completed these sacrifices, David blessed the people in the name of the Lord of Hosts, and distributed food to them all, a flat loaf of bread, a portion of meat, and a cake of raisins, to every man and woman in the whole gathering of the Israelites. Then all the people went home.

David returned to greet his household, and Michal, Saul's daughter, came out to meet him. She said, 'What a glorious day for the king of Israel, when he made an exhibition of himself in the sight of his servants' slave-girls, as any vulgar clown might do!' David answered her, 'But it was done in the presence of the Lord, who chose me instead of your father and his family and appointed me prince over Israel, the people of the Lord. Before the Lord I shall dance for joy, yes, and I shall earn yet more disgrace and demean myself still more in your eyes; but those slave-girls of whom you speak, they will hold me in honour for it.'

To her dying day Michal, Saul's daughter, was childless.

Once the king was established in his palace and the Lord had given him security from his enemies on all sides, he said to Nathan the prophet, 'Here I am living in a house of cedar, while the Ark of God is housed in a tent.' Nathan answered, 'Do whatever you have in mind, for the Lord is with you.' But that same night the word of the Lord came to Nathan: 'Go and say to David my servant, This is the word of the Lord: Are you to build me a house to dwell in? Down to this day I have never dwelt in a house since I brought Israel up from Egypt; I lived in a tent and a tabernacle. Wherever I journeyed with Israel, did I ever ask any of the judges whom I appointed shepherds of my people Israel why they had not built me a cedar house?

'Then say this to my servant David: This is the word of the Lord of Hosts: I took you from the pastures and from following the sheep to be prince over my people Israel. I have been with you wherever you have gone, and have destroyed all the enemies in your path. I shall bring you fame like the fame of the great ones of the earth. I shall assign a place for my people Israel; there I shall plant them to dwell in their own land. They will be disturbed no more; never again will the wicked oppress them as they did in the past, from the day when I appointed judges over my people Israel; and I shall give you peace from all your enemies.

'The Lord has told you that he would build up your royal house. When your life ends and you rest with your forefathers, I shall set up one of your family, one of your own children, to succeed you, and I shall establish his kingdom. It is he who is to build a house in honour of my name, and I shall establish his royal throne for all time. I shall be a father to him, and he will be my son. When he does wrong, I shall punish him as any father might, and not spare the rod. But my love will never be withdrawn from him as I withdrew it from Saul, whom I removed from your path. Your family and your kingdom will be established for ever in my sight; your throne will endure for all time.'

Nathan recounted to David all that had been said to him and all that had been revealed. Then King David went into the presence of the Lord and, taking his place there, said, 'Who am I, Lord God, and what is my family, that you have brought me thus far? There is none like you; there is no God but you, as everything we have heard bears witness. And your people Israel, to whom can they be compared? Is there any other nation on earth whom you, God, have set out to redeem from slavery to be your people? You have won renown for yourself by great and awesome deeds, driving out other nations and their gods to make way for your people whom you redeemed from Egypt. You have established your people Israel as your own for ever, and you, Lord, have become their God.

'Now, Lord God, perform for all time what you have promised for your servant and his house; make good what you have promised. May your fame be great for evermore, and let people say, "The Lord of Hosts is God over Israel"; and may the house of your servant David be established before you.'

David ruled over the whole of Israel and maintained law and justice among all his people. Joab son of Zeruiah was in command of the army; Jehoshaphat son of Ahilud was secretary of state; Zadok and Abiathar son of Ahimelech, son of Ahitub, were priests; Seraiah was adjutant-general; Benaiah son of Jehoiada commanded the Kerethite and Pelethite guards. David's sons were priests.

David enquired, 'Is any member of Saul's family left, to whom I can show kindness for Jonathan's sake?' A servant of Saul's family named Ziba was summoned to David, who asked, 'Are you Ziba?' He answered, 'Your servant, sir.' The king asked, 'Is there any member of Saul's family still alive to whom I may show the kindness that God requires?' 'Yes,' said Ziba, 'there is still a son of Jonathan alive; he is a cripple, lame in both feet.' 'Where is he?' said the king, and Ziba answered, 'He is staying with Machir son of Ammiel in Lo-debar.'

The king had him fetched from Lodebar, from the house of Machir son of Ammiel, and when Mephibosheth, son of Jonathan and grandson of Saul, entered David's presence, he prostrated himself and did obeisance. David said to him, 'Mephibosheth!' and he answered, 'Your servant, sir.' Then David said, 'Do not be afraid; I mean to show you kindness for your father Jonathan's sake; I shall restore to you the whole estate of your grandfather Saul and you will have a regular place at my table.' Mephibosheth prostrated himself again and said, 'Who am I that you should spare a thought for a dead dog like me?'

David summoned Saul's servant Ziba and said, 'I assign to your master's grandson all the property that belonged to Saul and his family. You and your sons and your slaves must cultivate the land and bring in the harvest to provide for your master's household, but Mephibosheth your master's grandson shall have a regular place at my table.' Ziba, who had fifteen sons and twenty slaves, answered: 'I shall do all that your majesty commands.' So Mephibosheth took his place in the royal household like one of the king's sons. He had a young son, named Mica; and the members of Ziba's household were all Mephibosheth's servants, while Mephibosheth lived in Jerusalem and had his regular place at the king's table, crippled as he was in both feet.

David and Bathsheba

At the turn of the year, when kings go out to battle, David sent Joab out with his other officers and all the Israelite forces, and they ravaged Ammon and laid siege to Rabbah. David remained in Jerusalem, and one evening, as he got up from his couch and walked about on the roof of the palace, he saw from there a woman bathing, and she was very beautiful. He made enquiries about the woman and was told, 'It must be Bathsheba daughter of Eliam and wife of Uriah the Hittite.' He sent messengers to fetch her, and when she came to him, he had intercourse with her, though she was still purifying herself after her period, and then she went home. She conceived, and sent word to David that she was pregnant.

David ordered Joab to send Uriah the Hittite to him. Joab did so, and when Uriah arrived, David asked him for news of Joab and the troops and how the campaign was going, and then said to him, 'Go down to your house and wash your feet after your journey.' As he left the palace, a present from the king followed him. Uriah, however, did not return to his house; he lay down by the palace gate with all the king's servants. David, learning that Uriah had not gone home, said to him, 'You have had a long journey; why did you not go home?' Uriah answered, 'Israel and Judah are under canvas, and so is the Ark, and my lord Joab and your majesty's officers are camping in the open; how can I go home to eat and drink and to sleep with my wife? By your life, I cannot do this!' David then said to Uriah, 'Stay here another day, and tomorrow I shall let you go.' So Uriah stayed in Jerusalem that day. On the following day David invited him to eat and drink with him and made him drunk. But in the evening Uriah went out to lie down in his blanket among the king's servants and did not go home.

In the morning David wrote a letter to Joab and sent it with Uriah. In it he wrote, 'Put Uriah opposite the enemy where the fighting is fiercest and then fall back, and leave him to meet his death.' So Joab, during the siege of the city, stationed Uriah at a point where he knew the enemy had expert troops. The men of the city sallied out and engaged Joab, and some of David's guards fell; Uriah the Hittite was also killed. Joab sent David a dispatch with all the news of the battle and gave the messenger these instructions: 'When you have finished your report to the king, he may be angry and ask, "Why did you go so near the city during the fight? You must have known there would be shooting from the wall. Remember who killed Abimelech son of Jerubbesheth. Was it not a woman who threw down an upper millstone on him from the wall of Thebez and killed him? Why did you go near the wall?" – if he asks this, then tell him, "Your servant Uriah the Hittite also is dead."'

The messenger set out and, when he came to David, he made his report as Joab had instructed him. David, angry with Joab, said to the messenger, 'Why did you go so near the city during the fight? You must have known you would be struck down from the wall. Remember who killed Abimelech son of Jerubbesheth. Was it not a woman who threw down an upper millstone on him from the wall of Thebez and killed him? Why did you go near the wall?' He answered, 'The enemy massed against us and sallied out into the open; we drove them back as far as the gateway. There the archers shot down at us from the wall and some of your majesty's men fell; and your servant Uriah the Hittite is dead.' David told the messenger to say this to Joab: 'Do not let the matter distress you – there is no knowing where the sword will strike. Press home your attack on the city, take it, and raze it to the ground'; and to tell him to take heart.

When Uriah's wife heard that her husband was dead, she mourned for him. Once the period of mourning was over, David sent for her and brought her into the palace; she became his wife and bore him a son. But what David had done was wrong in the eyes of the Lord.

The Lord sent Nathan the prophet to David, and when he entered the king's presence, he said, 'In a certain town there lived two men, one rich, the other poor. The rich man had large flocks and herds; the poor man had nothing of his own except one little ewe lamb he had bought. He reared it, and it grew up in his home together with his children. It shared his food, drank from his cup, and nestled in his arms; it was like a daughter to him. One day a traveller came to the rich man's house, and he, too mean to take something from his own flock or herd to serve to his guest, took the poor man's lamb and served that up.'

David was very angry, and burst out, 'As the Lord lives, the man who did this deserves to die! He shall pay for the lamb four times over, because he has done this and shown no pity.'

Nathan said to David, 'You are the man! This is the word of the Lord the God of Israel to you: I anointed you king over Israel, I rescued you from the power of Saul, I gave you your master's daughter and his wives to be your own, I gave you the daughters of Israel and Judah; and, had this not been enough, I would have added other favours as well. Why then have you flouted the Lord's word by doing what is wrong in my eyes? You have struck down Uriah the Hittite with the sword; the man himself you murdered by the sword of the Ammonites, and you have stolen his wife. Now, therefore, since you have despised me and taken the wife of Uriah the Hittite to be your own wife, your family will never again have rest from the sword. This is the word of the Lord: I shall bring trouble on you from within your own family. I shall take your wives and give them to another man before your eyes, and he will lie with them in broad daylight. What you did was done in secret; but I shall do this in broad daylight for all Israel to see.' David said to Nathan, 'I have sinned against the Lord.' Nathan answered, 'The Lord has laid on another the consequences of your sin: you will not die, but, since by this deed you have shown your contempt for the Lord, the child who will be born to you shall die.'

After Nathan had gone home, the Lord struck the boy whom Uriah's wife had borne to David, and he became very ill. David prayed to God for the child; he fasted and went in and spent the nights lying in sackcloth on the ground. The older men of his household tried to get him to rise, but he refused and would eat no food with them. On the seventh day the child died, and David's servants were afraid to tell him. 'While the boy was alive', they said, 'we spoke to him, and he did not listen to us; how can we now tell him that the boy is dead? He may do something desperate.' David saw his servants whispering among themselves and realized that the boy was dead. He asked, 'Is the child dead?' and they answered, 'Yes, he is dead.'

David then rose from the ground, bathed and anointed himself, and put on fresh clothes; he entered the house of the Lord and prostrated himself there. Afterwards he returned home; he ordered food to be brought and, when it was set before him, ate it. His servants asked him, 'What is this? While the boy lived you fasted and wept for him, but now that he is dead you rise and eat.' 'While the boy was still alive', he answered, 'I fasted and wept, thinking, "It may be that the Lord will be gracious to me, and the boy will live." But now that he is dead, why should I fast? Can I bring him back again? I shall go to him; he will not come back to me.' David consoled Bathsheba his wife; he went to her and had intercourse with her, and she gave birth to a son and called him Solomon.

The Rape of Tamar

The following occurred some time later. David's son Absalom had a beautiful sister named Tamar, and David's son Amnon fell in love with her. Amnon was so tormented that he became ill with love for his half-sister; for he thought it an impossible thing to approach her since she was a virgin. But Amnon had a friend, a very shrewd man named Jonadab, son of David's brother Shimeah, and he said to Amnon, 'Why are you, the king's son, so low-spirited morning after morning? Will you not tell me?' Amnon told him that he was in love with Tamar, his brother Absalom's sister. Jonadab said to him, 'Take to your bed and pretend to be ill. When your father comes to visit you, say to him, "Please let my sister Tamar come and give me my food. Let her prepare it in front of me, so that I may watch her and then take it from her own hands."' So Amnon lay down and pretended to be ill. When the king came to visit him, he said, 'Sir, let my sister Tamar come and make a few bread-cakes in front of me, and serve them to me with her own hands.'

David sent a message to Tamar in the palace: 'Go to your brother Amnon's quarters and prepare a meal for him.' Tamar came to her brother and found him lying down. She took some dough, kneaded it, and made cakes in front of him; having baked them, she took the pan and turned them out before him. But Amnon refused to eat and ordered everyone out of the room. When they had all gone, he said to Tamar, 'Bring the food over to the recess so that I may eat from your own hands.' Tamar took the cakes she had made and brought them to Amnon her brother in the recess. When she offered them to him, he caught hold of her and said, 'Sister, come to bed with me.' She answered, 'No, my brother, do not dishonour me. Such things are not done in Israel; do not behave so infamously. Where could I go and hide my disgrace? You would sink as low as the most infamous in Israel. Why not speak to the king for me? He will not refuse you leave to marry me.' But he would not listen; he overpowered and raped her.

Then Amnon was filled with intense revulsion; his revulsion for her was stronger than the love he had felt; he said to her, 'Get up and go.' She answered, 'No, this great wrong, your sending me away, is worse than anything else you have done to me.' He would not listen to her; he summoned the servant who attended him and said, 'Rid me of this woman; put her out and bolt the door after her.' The servant turned her out and bolted the door. She had on a long robe with sleeves, the usual dress of unmarried princesses. Tamar threw ashes over her head, tore the robe that she was wearing, put her hand on her head, and went away, sobbing as she went.

Her brother Absalom asked her, 'Has your brother Amnon been with you? Keep this to yourself; he is your brother. Do not take it to heart.' Forlorn and desolate, Tamar remained in her brother Absalom's house. When King David heard the whole story he was very angry; but he would not hurt Amnon because he was his eldest son and he loved him. Absalom did not speak a single word to Amnon, friendly or unfriendly, but he hated him for having dishonoured his sister Tamar.

Two years later Absalom invited all the king's sons to his sheep-shearing at Baal-hazor, near Ephron. He approached the king and said, 'Sir, I am shearing; will your majesty and your servants come?' The king answered, 'No, my son, we must not all come and be a burden to you.' Absalom pressed him, but David was still unwilling to go and dismissed him with his blessing. Absalom said, 'If you will not come, may my brother Amnon come with us?' 'Why should he go with you?' the king asked; but Absalom pressed him again, so he let Amnon and all the other princes go with him.

Absalom prepared a feast fit for a king, and gave this order to his servants: 'Watch your chance, and when Amnon is merry with wine and I say to you, "Strike Amnon," then kill him. You have nothing to fear; these are my orders. Be bold and resolute.' Absalom's servants did to Amnon as Absalom had ordered, whereupon all the king's sons immediately mounted their mules and fled.

While they were on their way, a rumour reached David that Absalom had murdered all the royal princes and that not one was left alive. The king stood up and tore his clothes and then threw himself on the ground; all his servants were standing round him with their clothes torn. Then Jonadab, son of David's brother Shimeah, said, 'My lord must not think that all the young princes have been murdered; only Amnon is dead. Absalom has gone about with a scowl on his face ever since Amnon ravished his sister Tamar. Your majesty must not pay attention to what is no more than a rumour that all the princes are dead; only Amnon is dead.' Absalom meanwhile had made good his escape.

The sentry on duty saw a crowd of people coming down the hill from the direction of Horonaim. He came and reported to the king, 'I see men coming down the hill from Horonaim.' Jonadab said to the king, 'Here come the royal princes, just as I said they would.' As he finished speaking, the princes came in and broke into loud lamentations; the king and all his servants also wept bitterly.

Absalom went to take refuge with Talmai son of Ammihud king of Geshur; and for a long while the king mourned for Amnon. Absalom, having escaped to Geshur, stayed there for three years; and David's heart went out to him with longing, as he became reconciled to the death of Amnon.

The Rebellion of Absalom

Joab son of Zeruiah saw that the king longed in his heart for Absalom, so he sent for a wise woman from Tekoah and said to her, 'Pretend to be a mourner; put on mourning garb, go without anointing yourself, and behave like a woman who has been bereaved these many days. Then go to the king and repeat what I tell you.' He told her exactly what she was to say.

When the woman from Tekoah came into the king's presence, she bowed to the ground in homage and cried, 'Help, your majesty!' The king asked, 'What is it?' She answered, 'Sir, I am a widow; my husband is dead. I had two sons; they came to blows out in the country where there was no one to part them, and one struck the other and killed him. Now, sir, the kinsmen have confronted me with the demand, "Hand over the one who killed his brother, so that we can put him to death for taking his brother's life, and so cut off the succession." If they do this, they will stamp out my last live ember and leave my husband without name or descendant on the earth.' 'Go home,' said the king to the woman, 'and I shall settle your case.'

But the woman continued, 'The guilt be on me, your majesty, and on my father's house; let the king and his throne be blameless.' The king said, 'If anyone says anything more to you, bring him to me and he will not trouble you again.' Then the woman went on, 'Let your majesty call upon the Lord your God, to prevent the next-of-kin from doing their worst and destroying my son.' The king swore, 'As the Lord lives, not a hair of your son's head shall fall to the ground.'

The woman then said, 'May I add one word more, your majesty?' 'Say on,' said the king. So she continued, 'How then could it enter your head to do this same wrong to God's people? By the decision you have pronounced, your majesty, you condemn yourself in that you have refused to bring back the one you banished. We shall all die; we shall be like water that is spilt on the ground and lost; but God will spare the man who does not set himself to keep the outlaw in banishment.

'I came to say this to your majesty because the people have threatened me: I thought, "If I can only speak to the king, perhaps he will attend to my case; for he will listen, and he will save me from anyone who is seeking to cut off me and my son together from God's own possession." I thought too that the words of my lord the king would be a comfort to me; for your majesty is like the angel of God and can decide between right and wrong. May the Lord your God be with you!'

The king said to the woman, 'Tell me no lies: I shall now ask you a question.' 'Let your majesty speak,' she said. The king asked, 'Is the hand of Joab behind you in all this?' 'Your life upon it, sir!' she answered. 'When your majesty asks a question, there is no way round it, right or left. Yes, your servant Joab did prompt me; it was he who put the whole story into my mouth. He did it to give a new turn to this affair. Your majesty is as wise as the angel of God and knows all that goes on in the land.'

The king said to Joab, 'You have my consent; go and bring back the young man Absalom.' Then Joab humbly prostrated himself, took leave of the king with a blessing, and said, 'Now I know that I have found favour with your majesty, because you have granted my humble petition.' Joab went at once to Geshur and brought Absalom to Jerusalem. But the king said, 'Let him go to his own quarters; he shall not come into my presence.' So Absalom repaired to his own quarters and did not enter the king's presence.

In all Israel no man was so much admired for his beauty as Absalom; from the crown of his head to the sole of his foot he was without flaw. When he cut his hair (as had to be done every year, for he found it heavy), it weighed two hundred shekels by the royal standard. Three sons were born to Absalom, and a daughter named Tamar, who became a very beautiful woman.

Absalom lived in Jerusalem for two whole years without entering the king's presence. Then he summoned Joab, intending to send a message by him to the king, but Joab refused to come; he sent for him a second time, but he still refused. Absalom said to his servants, 'You know that Joab has a field next to mine with barley growing in it; go and set fire to it.' When Absalom's servants set fire to the field, Joab promptly came to Absalom in his own quarters and demanded, 'Why have your servants set fire to my field?' Absalom answered, 'I had sent for you to come here, so that I could ask you to give the king this message from me: "Why did I leave Geshur? It would be better for me if I were still there. Let me now come into your majesty's presence and, if I have done any wrong, put me to death."' When Joab went to the king and told him, he summoned Absalom, who came and prostrated himself humbly, and the king greeted him with a kiss.

After this Absalom provided himself with a chariot and horses and fifty outrunners.

He made it a practice to rise early and stand by the road leading through the city gate, and would hail everyone who had a case to bring before the king for judgement and ask him which town he came from. When he answered, 'I come, sir, from such and such a tribe of Israel,' Absalom would say to him, 'I can see that you have a very good case, but you will get no hearing from the king.' He would add, 'If only I were appointed judge in the land, it would be my business to see that everyone with a lawsuit or a claim got justice from me.' Whenever a man approached to prostrate himself, Absalom would stretch out his hand, take hold of him, and kiss him. By behaving like this to every Israelite who sought justice from the king, Absalom stole the affections of the people.

At the end of four years, Absalom said to the king, 'Give me leave to go to Hebron to fulfil a vow there that I made to the Lord. When I lived at Geshur in Aram, I vowed, "If the Lord brings me back to Jerusalem, I shall worship the Lord in Hebron."' The king answered, 'You may go'; so he set off and went to Hebron.

Absalom sent runners through all the tribes of Israel with this message: 'As soon as you hear the sound of the trumpet, then say, "Absalom has become king in Hebron."' Two hundred men accompanied Absalom from Jerusalem; they were invited as guests and went in all innocence, knowing nothing of the affair. Absalom also sent to summon Ahithophel the Gilonite, David's counsellor, from Giloh his town, where he was offering the customary sacrifices. The conspiracy gathered strength, and Absalom's supporters increased in number.

A messenger brought the news to David that the men of Israel had transferred their allegiance to Absalom. The king said to those who were with him in Jerusalem, 'We must get away at once, or there will be no escape from Absalom for any of us. Make haste, or else he will soon be upon us, bringing disaster and putting the city to the sword.' The king's servants said to him, 'Whatever your majesty thinks best; we are ready.'

The king set out, and all his household followed him except ten concubines whom he left in charge of the palace.

At the Far House the king and all the people who were with him halted. His own servants then stood at his side, while the Kerethite and Pelethite guards and Ittai with the six hundred

Gittites under him marched past the king. The king said to Ittai the Gittite, 'Why should you come with us? Go back and stay with the new king, for you are a foreigner and, what is more, an exile from your own country. You came only yesterday, and must you today be compelled to share my wanderings when I do not know where I am going? Go back home and take your countrymen with you; and may the Lord ever be your steadfast friend.' Ittai answered, 'As the Lord lives, your life upon it, wherever you may be whether for life or death, I, your servant, shall be there.' David said to Ittai, 'It is well, march on!' And Ittai the Gittite marched on with his whole company and all the dependants who were with him. The whole countryside resounded with their weeping. The king remained standing while all the people crossed the wadi of the Kidron before him, by way of the olive tree in the wilderness.

Zadok also was there and all the Levites with him, carrying the Ark of the Covenant of God. They set it down beside Abiathar until all the army had passed out of the city. The king said to Zadok, 'Take the Ark of God back into the city. If I find favour with the Lord, he will bring me back and let me see the Ark and its dwelling-place again. But if he says he does not want me, then here I am; let him do what he pleases with me.' The king went on to say to Zadok the priest, 'Are you not a seer? You may safely go back to the city, you and Abiathar, and take with you the two young men, Ahimaaz your son and Abiathar's son Jonathan. I shall wait at the Fords of the Wilderness until you can send word to me.' Then Zadok and Abiathar took the Ark of God back to Jerusalem and remained there.

David wept as he went up the slope of the mount of Olives; he was bareheaded and went barefoot. The people with him all had their heads uncovered and wept as they went. David had been told that Ahithophel was among the conspirators with Absalom, and he prayed, 'Lord, frustrate the counsel of Ahithophel.'

As David was approaching the top of the ridge where it was the custom to prostrate oneself to God, Hushai the Archite was there to meet him with his tunic torn and dust on his head. David said to him, 'If you come with me you will only be a hindrance; but you can help me to frustrate Ahithophel's plans if you go back to the city and say to Absalom, "I shall be your majesty's servant. In the past I was your father's servant; now I shall be yours." You will have with you, as you know, the priests Zadok and Abiathar; report to them everything that you hear in the royal palace. They have with them Zadok's son Ahimaaz and Abiathar's son Jonathan, and through them you may pass on to me everything you hear.' So Hushai, David's friend, came to the city as Absalom was entering Jerusalem.

When David had moved on a little from the top of the ridge, he was met by Ziba the servant of Mephibosheth, who had with him a pair of donkeys saddled and loaded with two hundred loaves of bread, a hundred clusters of raisins, a hundred bunches of summer fruit, and a skin of wine. The king asked, 'What are you doing with these?' Ziba answered, 'The donkeys are for the king's family to ride on, the bread and the summer fruit are for his servants to eat, and the wine for anyone who becomes exhausted in the wilderness.' The king asked, 'Where is your master's grandson?' 'He is staying in Jerusalem,' said Ziba, 'for he thought that the Israelites might now restore to him his grandfather's kingdom.' The king said to Ziba, 'You shall have everything that belongs to Mephibosheth.' Ziba said, 'I am your humble servant, sir; may I always find favour with your majesty.'

As King David approached Bahurim, a man of Saul's family, whose name was Shimei son of Gera, came out, cursing all the while. He showered stones right and left on David and on all the king's servants and on everyone, soldiers and people alike. With curses Shimei shouted: 'Get out, get out, you murderous scoundrel! The Lord has taken vengeance on you for the blood of the house of Saul whose throne you took, and he has given the kingdom to your son Absalom. You murderer, see how your crimes have overtaken you!'

Abishai son of Zeruiah said to the king, 'Why let this dead dog curse your majesty? I will go across and strike off his head.' But the king said, 'What has this to do with us, you sons of Zeruiah? If he curses because the Lord has told him to curse David, who can question it?' David said to Abishai and to all his servants, 'If my very own son is out to kill me, who can wonder at this Benjamite? Let him be, let him curse; for the Lord has told him to. Perhaps the Lord will mark my sufferings and bestow a blessing on me in place of the curse laid on me this day.' David and his men continued on their way, and Shimei kept abreast along the ridge of the hill parallel to David's path, cursing as he went and hurling stones across the valley at him and covering him with dust. When the king and all the people with him reached the Jordan, they rested there, for they were worn out.

By now Absalom and all his Israelites had reached Jerusalem, and Ahithophel was with him. When Hushai the Archite, David's friend, met Absalom he said, 'Long live the king! Long live the king!' But Absalom retorted, 'Is this your loyalty to your friend? Why did you not go with him?' Hushai answered, 'Because I mean to attach myself to the man chosen by the Lord and by this people and by all the men of Israel, and with him I shall stay. After all, whom ought I to serve? Should I not serve the son? I shall serve you as I have served your father.'

Absalom said to Ahithophel, 'Give us your advice: how shall we act?' Ahithophel answered, 'Lie with your father's concubines whom he left in charge of the palace. Then all Israel will come to hear that you have given great cause of offence to your father, and this will confirm the resolution of your followers.' So they set up a tent for Absalom on the roof, and he lay with his father's concubines in the sight of all Israel.

In those days a man would seek counsel of Ahithophel as if he were making an enquiry of the word of God; that was how Ahithophel's counsel was esteemed by both David and Absalom. Ahithophel said to Absalom, 'Let me pick twelve thousand men to go in pursuit of David tonight. If I overtake him when he is tired and dispirited I shall cut him off from his people and they will all scatter; I shall kill no one but the king. I shall bring all the people over to you as a bride is brought to her husband. It is only one man's life that you are seeking; the rest of the people will be unharmed.' Absalom and all the elders of Israel approved of Ahithophel's advice; but Absalom said, 'Now summon Hushai the Archite and let us also hear what he has to say.' When Hushai came, Absalom told him what Ahithophel had said and asked him, 'Shall we do as he advises? If not, speak up.'

Hushai said to Absalom, 'For once the counsel that Ahithophel has given is not good. You know', he went on, 'that your father and the men with him are hardened warriors and savage as a bear in the wilds robbed of her cubs. Your father is an old campaigner and will not spend the night with the main body; even now he will be lying hidden in a pit or in some such place. Then if any of your men are killed at the outset, whoever hears the news will say, "Disaster has overtaken Absalom's followers." The courage of the most resolute and lion-hearted will melt away, for all Israel knows that your father is a man of war and has seasoned warriors with him.

'Here is my advice. Wait until the whole of Israel, from Dan to Beersheba, is gathered about you, countless as grains of sand on the seashore, and then march to battle with them in person. When we come on him somewhere, wherever he may be, and descend on him like dew falling on the ground, not a man of his family or of his followers will be left alive. If he retreats into a town, all Israel will bring ropes to that town, and we shall drag it into a ravine until not a stone can be found on the site.' Absalom and all the Israelites said, 'Hushai the Archite has given us better advice than Ahithophel.' It was the Lord's purpose to frustrate Ahithophel's good advice and so bring disaster on Absalom.

Hushai told Zadok and Abiathar the priests all the advice that Ahithophel had given to Absalom and the elders of Israel, and also what he himself had advised. 'Now send quickly to David', he said, 'and warn him not to spend the night at the Fords of the Wilderness but to cross the river at once, before an overwhelming blow can be launched at the king and his followers.' Jonathan and Ahimaaz were waiting at En-rogel, and a servant-girl used to go and tell them what happened and they would pass it on to King David; for they dared not risk being seen entering the city. But a lad saw them and told Absalom; so the two of them hurried to Bahurim to the house of a man who had a cistern in his court-yard, and they climbed down into it. The man's wife took a covering, spread it over the mouth of the cistern, and scattered grain over it, so that nothing would be noticed. Absalom's servants came to the house and asked the woman, 'Where are Ahimaaz and Jonathan?' She answered, 'They went past the pool.' The men searched, but not finding them they returned to Jerusalem. As soon as they had gone the two climbed out of the cistern and went off to report to King David. They said to him, 'Get over the water at once, and with all speed!' and they told him Ahithophel's plan against him. So David and all his company began at once to cross the Jordan; by daybreak there was not one who had not reached the other bank.

When Ahithophel saw that his advice had not been taken he saddled his donkey, went straight home to his own town, gave his last instructions to his household, and then hanged himself. So he died and was buried in his father's grave.

By the time that Absalom had crossed the Jordan with the Israelites, David was already at Mahanaim. Absalom had appointed Amasa as commander-in-chief in Joab's place; he was the son of a man named Ithra, an Ishmaelite, by Abigal daughter of Nahash and sister to Joab's mother Zeruiah. The Israelites and Absalom camped in the district of Gilead.

When David came to Mahanaim, he was met by Shobi son of Nahash from the Ammonite town Rabbah, Machir son of Ammiel from Lo-debar, and Barzillai the Gileadite from Rogelim, bringing mattresses and blankets, bowls, and jugs. They brought also wheat and barley, flour and roasted grain, beans and lentils, honey and curds, sheep and fat cattle, and offered them to David and his people to eat, knowing that the people must be hungry and thirsty and weary in the wilderness.

David reviewed the troops who were with him, and appointed officers over units of a thousand and of a hundred. He divided his army in three, one division under the command of Joab, one under Joab's brother Abishai son of Zeruiah, and the third under Ittai the Gittite. The king announced to the troops that he himself was coming out with them. But they said, 'No, you must not; if we take to flight, no one will care, nor will they even if half of us are killed; but you are worth ten thousand of us, and it would be better now for you to remain in the town in support.' The king answered, 'I shall do what you think best.' He stood beside the gate, while all the army marched past by hundreds and by thousands, and he gave this order to Joab, Abishai, and Ittai: 'Deal gently with the young man Absalom for my sake.' The whole army heard the king giving each of the officers the order about Absalom.

The army took the field against the Israelites, and a battle was fought in the forest of Ephron. There the Israelites were routed before the onslaught of David's men, and the loss of life was great, for twenty thousand fell. The fighting spread over the whole countryside, and the forest took toll of more people that day than the sword.

Some of David's men caught sight of Absalom; he was riding his mule and, as it passed beneath a large oak, his head was caught in its boughs; he was left in mid-air, while the mule went on from under him. One of the men who saw this told Joab, 'I saw Absalom hanging from an oak.' While the man was telling him, Joab broke in, 'You saw him? Why did you not strike him to the ground then and there? I would have given you ten pieces of silver and a belt.' The man answered, 'If you were to put into my hands a thousand pieces of silver, I would not lift a finger against the king's son; we all heard the king giving orders to you and Abishai and Ittai to take care of the young man Absalom. If I had dealt him a treacherous blow, the king would soon have known, and you would have kept well out of it.' 'That is a lie!' said Joab. 'I will make a start and show you.' He picked up three javelins and drove them into Absalom's chest while he was held fast in the tree and still alive. Then ten young men who were Joab's armour-bearers closed in on Absalom, struck at him, and killed him. Joab sounded the trumpet, and the army came back from the pursuit of Israel, because he had called on them to halt. They took Absalom's body and flung it into a large pit in the forest, and raised over it a great cairn of stones. The Israelites all fled to their homes.

The pillar in the King's Valley had been set up by Absalom in his lifetime, for he said, 'I have no son to carry on my name.' He had named the pillar after himself, and to this day it is called Absalom's Monument.

Ahimaaz son of Zadok said, 'Let me run and take the news to the king that the Lord has avenged him and delivered him from his enemies.' But Joab replied, 'This is no day for you to be the bearer of news. Another day you may have news to carry, but not today, because the king's son is dead.' Joab told a Cushite to go and report to the king what he had seen. The Cushite bowed to Joab and set off running. Ahimaaz pleaded again with Joab, 'Come what may,' he said, 'let me run after the Cushite.' 'Why should you, my son?' asked Joab. 'You will get no reward for your news.' 'Come what may,' he said, 'let me run.' 'Go, then,' said Joab. So Ahimaaz ran by the road through the plain of the Jordan and outstripped the Cushite.

David was sitting between the inner and outer gates and the watchman had gone up to the roof of the gatehouse by the wall of the town. Looking out and seeing a man running alone, the watchman called to the king and told him. 'If he is alone,' said the king, 'then he is bringing news.' The man continued to approach, and then the watchman saw another man running. He called down into the gate, 'Look, there is another man running alone.' The king said, 'He too brings news.' The watchman said, 'I see by the way he runs that the first runner is Ahimaaz son of Zadok.' The king said, 'He is a good man and shall earn the reward for good news.'

Ahimaaz called out to the king, 'All is well!' He bowed low before him and said, 'Blessed be the Lord your God who has given into your hands the men who rebelled against your majesty.' The king asked, 'Is all well with the young man Absalom?' Ahimaaz answered, 'Sir, when your servant Joab sent me, I saw a great commotion, but I did not know what had happened.' The king told him to stand on one side; so he turned aside and waited there.

Then the Cushite came in and said, 'Good news for my lord the king! The Lord has avenged you this day on all those who rebelled against you.' The king said to the Cushite, 'Is all well with the young man Absalom?' The Cushite answered, 'May all the king's enemies and all rebels intent on harming you be as that young man is.' The king was deeply moved and went up to the roof-chamber over the gate and wept, crying out as he went, 'O, my son! Absalom my son, my son Absalom! Would that I had died instead of you! O Absalom, my son, my son.'

Joab was told that the king was weeping and mourning for Absalom; and that day's victory was turned for the whole army into mourning, because the troops heard how the king grieved for his son; they stole into the city like men ashamed to show their faces after fleeing from a battle. The king covered his face and cried aloud, 'My son Absalom; O Absalom, my son, my son.'

Joab came into the king's quarters and said to him, 'All your servants, who have saved you and your sons and daughters, your wives and your concubines, you have covered with shame this day by showing love for those who hate you and hate for those who love you. Today you have made it clear to officers and men alike that we are nothing to you; I realize that if Absalom were still alive and all of us dead, you would be content. Now go at once and give your servants some encouragement; if you refuse, I swear by the Lord that by nightfall not a man will remain with you, and that would be a worse disaster than any you have suffered since your earliest days.' At that the king rose and took his seat by the gate; and when the army was told that the king was sitting at the gate, they assembled before him there.

Meanwhile the Israelites had scattered to their homes. Throughout all the tribes of Israel people were discussing it among themselves and saying, 'The king has saved us from our enemies and freed us from the power of the Philistines, and now he has fled the country because of Absalom. But Absalom, whom we anointed king, has fallen in battle; so now why have we no plans for bringing the king back?'

What all Israel was saying came to the king's ears, and he sent word to Zadok and Abiathar the priests: 'Ask the elders of Judah why they should be the last to bring the king back to his palace. Tell them, "You are my brothers, my own flesh and blood; why are you last to bring me back?" And say to Amasa, "You are my own flesh and blood. So help me God, you shall be my commander-in-chief for the rest of your life in place of Joab."' Thus David swayed the hearts of all in Judah, and one and all they sent to the king, urging him and his men to return.

When on his way back the king reached the Jordan, the men of Judah came to Gilgal to meet him and escort him across the river. Shimei son of Gera the Benjamite from Bahurim hastened down among the men of Judah to meet King David with a thousand men from Benjamin; Ziba was there too, the servant of Saul's family, with his fifteen sons and twenty servants. They rushed into the Jordan under the king's eyes and crossed to and fro conveying his household in order to win his favour. Shimei son of Gera, when he had crossed the river, threw himself down before the king and said, 'I beg your majesty not to remember how disgracefully your servant behaved when your majesty left Jerusalem; do not hold it against me. I humbly acknowledge that I did wrong, and today I am the first of all the house of Joseph to come down to meet your majesty.' Abishai son of Zeruiah objected. 'Ought not Shimei to be put to death', he said, 'because he cursed the Lord's anointed prince?' David answered, 'What right have you, you sons of Zeruiah, to oppose me today? Should anyone be put to death this day in Israel? I know now that I am king of Israel.' The king said to Shimei, 'You shall not die,' and he confirmed it with an oath.

Saul's grandson Mephibosheth also went down to meet the king. He had not bathed his feet, trimmed his beard, or washed his clothes, from the day the king went away until he returned victorious. When he came from Jerusalem to meet the king, David said to him, 'Why did you not go with me, Mephibosheth?' He answered, 'Sir, my servant deceived me; I did intend to harness my donkey and ride with the king (for I am lame), but his stories set your majesty against me. Your majesty is like the angel of God; you must do what you think right. My father's whole family, one and all, deserved to die at your majesty's hands, but you gave me, your servant, my place at your table. What further favour can I expect of the king?' The king answered, 'You have said enough. My decision is that you and Ziba are to share the estate.' Mephibosheth said, 'Let him have it all, now that your majesty has come home victorious.'

Barzillai the Gileadite too had come down from Rogelim, and he went as far as the Jordan with the king to escort him on his way. Barzillai was very old, eighty years of age; it was he who had provided for the king while he was at Mahanaim, for he was a man of great wealth. The king said to Barzillai, 'Cross over with me and I shall provide for you in my household in Jerusalem.' Barzillai answered, 'Your servant is far too old to go up with your majesty to Jerusalem. I am now eighty years old. I cannot tell what is pleasant and what is not; I cannot taste what I eat or drink; I can no longer listen to the voices of men and women singing. Why should I be a further burden on your majesty? Your servant will attend the king for a short way across the Jordan; and why should the king reward me so handsomely? Let me go back and end my days in my own town near the grave of my father and mother. Here is my son Kimham; let him cross over with your majesty, and do for him what you think best.' The king answered, 'Let Kimham cross with me, and I shall do for him whatever you think best; and I shall do for you whatever you ask.'

All the people crossed the Jordan while the king waited. The king then kissed Barzillai and gave him his blessing. Barzillai returned home; the king crossed to Gilgal, Kimham with him.

The whole army of Judah had escorted the king over the river, as had also half the army of Israel. But the Israelites all kept coming to the king and saying, 'Why should our brothers of Judah have got possession of the king's person by joining King David's own men and then escorting him and his household across the Jordan?' The answer of all the men of Judah to the

Israelites was, 'Because his majesty is our near kinsman. Why should you resent it? Have we eaten at the king's expense? Have we received any gifts?' The men of Israel answered, 'We have ten times your interest in the king and, what is more, we are senior to you; why do you disparage us? Were we not the first to speak of bringing the king back?' The men of Judah used language even fiercer than the men of Israel.

Sheba's Rebellion

A scoundrel named Sheba son of Bichri, a man of Benjamin, happened to be there. He sounded the trumpet and cried out:

> 'We have no share in David,
> no lot in the son of Jesse.
> Every man to his tent, O Israel!'

All the men of Israel deserted David to follow Sheba son of Bichri, but the men of Judah stood by their king and followed him from the Jordan to Jerusalem.

When David went up to his palace in Jerusalem he took the ten concubines whom he had left in charge of the palace and put them in a house under guard; he maintained them but did not have intercourse with them. They were kept in seclusion, living as if they were widows until the day of their death.

The king said to Amasa, 'Call up the men of Judah and appear before me again in three days' time.' Amasa went to call up the men of Judah, but he took longer than the time fixed by the king. David said to Abishai, 'Sheba son of Bichri will give us more trouble than Absalom; take the royal bodyguard and follow him closely in case he occupies some fortified cities and escapes us.' Joab, along with the Kerethite and Pelethite guards and all the fighting men, marched out behind Abishai, and left Jerusalem in pursuit of Sheba son of Bichri.

When they reached the great stone in Gibeon, Amasa came to meet them. Joab was wearing his tunic and over it a belt supporting a sword in its scabbard. He came forward, concealing his treachery, and said to Amasa, 'I hope you are well, my brother,' and with his right hand he grasped Amasa's beard to kiss him. Amasa was not on his guard against the sword in Joab's hand. Joab struck him with it in the belly and his entrails poured out to the ground; he did not have to strike a second blow, for Amasa was dead. Joab with his brother Abishai went on in pursuit of Sheba son of Bichri. One of Joab's men stood over Amasa and called out, 'Follow Joab, all who are for Joab and for David!' Amasa's body lay soaked in blood in the middle of the road, and when the man saw how all the people stopped, he rolled him off the road into the field and threw a cloak over him; for everyone who came by stopped at the sight of the body. When it had been removed from the road, they all went on and followed Joab in pursuit of Sheba son of Bichri.

Sheba passed through all the tribes of Israel until he came to Abel-beth-maacah, and all the clan of Bichri rallied to him and followed him into the city. Joab's forces came up and besieged him in Abel-beth-maacah, raised a siege-ramp against it, and began undermining the wall to bring it down. Then a wise woman stood on the rampart and called from the city, 'Listen, listen! Tell Joab to come here and let me speak with him.' When he came forward the woman said, 'Are you Joab?' He answered, 'I am.' 'Listen to what I have to say, sir,' she said. 'I am listening,' he replied. 'In the old days', she went on, 'there was a saying, "Go to Abel for the answer," and that settled the matter. My town is known to be one of the most peaceable and loyal in Israel; she is like a watchful mother in Israel, and you are seeking to kill her. Would you destroy the Lord's own possession?' Joab answered, 'God forbid, far be it from me to ruin or destroy! That is not our aim; but a man from the hill-country of Ephraim named Sheba son of Bichri has raised a revolt against King David. Surrender this one man, and I shall retire from the city.' The woman said to Joab, 'His head will be thrown over the wall to you.' Then the woman went to the people, who, persuaded by her wisdom, cut off Sheba's head and threw it to Joab. He then sounded the trumpet, and the whole army withdrew from the town; they dispersed to their homes, while Joab went back to the king in Jerusalem.

The Gibeonites' Revenge

In David's reign there was a famine that lasted for three successive years. David consulted the Lord, who answered, 'Blood-guilt rests on Saul and on his family because he put the Gibeonites to death.' (The Gibeonites were not of Israelite descent; they were a remnant of Amorite stock whom the Israelites had sworn that they would spare. Saul, however, in his zeal for Israel and Judah had sought to exterminate them.) King David summoned the Gibeonites, therefore, and said to them, 'What can be done for you? How can I make expiation, so that you may have cause to bless the Lord's own people?' The Gibeonites answered, 'Our feud with Saul and his family cannot be settled in silver or gold, and there is no other man in Israel whose death would content us.' 'Then what do you want me to do for you?' asked David. They answered, 'Let us make an end of the man who caused our undoing and ruined us, so that he will never again have his place within the borders of Israel. Hand over to us seven of that man's descendants, and we shall hurl them down to their death before the Lord in Gibeah of Saul, the Lord's chosen one.' The king agreed to hand them over. He spared Mephibosheth son of Jonathan, son of Saul, because of the oath that had been taken in the Lord's name by David and Saul's son Jonathan, but the king took the two sons whom Rizpah daughter of Aiah had borne to Saul, Armoni and Mephibosheth, and the five sons whom Merab, Saul's daughter, had borne to Adriel son of Barzillai of Meholah. He handed them over to the Gibeonites, and they flung them down from the mountain before the Lord; the seven of them fell together. They were put to death in the first days of harvest at the beginning of the barley harvest.

Rizpah daughter of Aiah took sackcloth and spread it out as a bed for herself on the rock, from the beginning of harvest until the rains came and fell from the heavens on the bodies. She kept the birds away from them by day and the wild beasts by night. When David was told what Rizpah the concubine of Saul had done, he went and got the bones of Saul and his son Jonathan from the citizens of Jabesh-gilead, who had carried them off from the public square at Beth-shan, where the Philistines had hung them on the day they defeated Saul at Gilboa. He removed the bones of Saul and Jonathan from there and gathered up the bones of the men who had been hurled to death. They buried the bones of Saul and his son Jonathan at Zela in Benjamin, in the grave of his father Kish. Everything was done as the king ordered, and thereafter the Lord was willing to accept prayers offered for the country.

David's Census

Once again the Israelites felt the Lord's anger, when he incited David against them and instructed him to take a census of Israel and Judah. The king commanded Joab and the officers of the army with him to go round all the tribes of Israel, from Dan to Beersheba, and make a record of the people and report back the number to him. Joab answered, 'Even if the Lord your God should increase the people a hundredfold and your majesty should live to see it, what pleasure would that give your majesty?' But Joab and the officers, being overruled by the king, left his presence in order to take the census.

They crossed the Jordan and began at Aroer and the town at the wadi, proceeding towards Gad and Jazer. They came to Gilead and to the land of the Hittites, to Kadesh, and then to Dan and Iyyon and so round towards Sidon. They went as far as the walled city of Tyre and all the towns of the Hivites and Canaanites, and then went on to the Negeb of Judah at Beersheba. They covered the whole country and arrived back at Jerusalem after nine months and twenty days. Joab reported to the king the numbers recorded: the number of able-bodied men, capable of bearing arms, was eight hundred thousand in Israel and five hundred thousand in Judah.

After he had taken the census, David was overcome with remorse, and said to the Lord, 'I have acted very wickedly: I pray you, Lord, remove your servant's guilt, for I have been very foolish.' When he rose next morning, the command of the Lord had come to the prophet Gad, David's seer, to go and tell David: 'This is the word of the Lord: I offer you three things; choose one and I shall bring it upon you.' Gad came to David and reported this to him and said, 'Is it to be three years of famine in your land, or three months of flight with the enemy in close pursuit, or three days of pestilence in your land? Consider carefully now what answer I am to take back to him who sent me.' David said to Gad, 'This is a desperate plight I am in; let us fall into the hands of the Lord, for his mercy is great; and let me not fall into the hands of men.'

The Lord sent a pestilence throughout Israel from the morning till the end of the appointed time; from Dan to Beersheba seventy thousand of the people died. The angel stretched out his arm towards Jerusalem to destroy it; but the Lord repented of the evil and said to the angel who was destroying the people, 'Enough! Stay your hand.' At that moment the angel of the Lord was at the threshing-floor of Araunah the Jebusite.

When David saw the angel who was striking down the people, he said to the Lord, 'It is I who have sinned, I who committed the wrong; but these poor sheep, what have they done? Let your hand fall on me and on my family.'

Gad came to David that day and said, 'Go and set up an altar to the Lord on the threshing-floor of Araunah the Jebusite.' David obeyed Gad's instructions, and went up as the Lord had commanded. When Araunah looked down and saw the king and his servants coming towards him, he went out and, prostrating himself before the king, said, 'Why has your majesty come to visit his servant?' David answered, 'To buy the threshing-floor from you so that I may build an altar to the Lord, and the plague which has attacked the people may be stopped.' Araunah answered, 'I beg your majesty to take it and sacrifice what you think fit. See, here are the oxen for the whole-offering, and the threshing-sledges and the ox-yokes for fuel.' Araunah gave it all to the king for his own use and said to him, 'May the Lord your God accept you.' But the king said to Araunah, 'No, I shall buy it from you; I am not going to offer up to the Lord my God whole-offerings that have cost me nothing.' So David bought the threshing-floor and the oxen for fifty shekels of silver. He built an altar to the Lord there and offered whole-offerings and shared-offerings. Then the Lord yielded to his prayer for the land, and the plague in Israel stopped.

Adonijah Claims the Throne

King David was now a very old man, and, though they wrapped clothes round him, he could not keep warm. His attendants said to him, 'Let us find a young virgin for your majesty, to attend you and take care of you; and let her lie in your arms, sir, and make you warm.' After searching throughout Israel for a beautiful maiden, they found Abishag, a Shunammite, and brought her to the king. She was a very beautiful girl. She took care of the king and waited on him, but he did not have intercourse with her.

Adonijah, whose mother was Haggith, was boasting that he was to be king. He provided himself with chariots and horses and fifty outrunners. His father never corrected him or asked why he behaved as he did. He was next in age to Absalom, and was a very handsome man too. He took counsel with Joab son of Zeruiah and with Abiathar the priest, and they assured him of their support; but Zadok the priest, Benaiah son of Jehoiada, Nathan the prophet, Shimei, Rei, and David's bodyguard of heroes did not take his side. Adonijah then held a sacrifice of sheep, oxen, and buffaloes at the stone Zoheleth beside En-rogel; he invited all his royal brothers and all those officers of the household who were of the tribe of Judah, but he did not invite Nathan the prophet, Benaiah and the bodyguard, or Solomon his brother.

Nathan said to Bathsheba, Solomon's mother, 'Have you not heard that Adonijah son of Haggith has become king, without the knowledge of our lord David? Now come, let me advise you what to do for your own safety and for the safety of your son Solomon. Go in at once to the king and say to him, "Did not your majesty swear to me, your servant, that my son Solomon should succeed you as king, and that it was he who should sit on your throne? Why then has Adonijah become king?" While you are still there speaking to the king, I shall come in after you and confirm your words.'

Bathsheba went to the king in his private chamber; he was now very old, and Abishag the Shunammite was waiting on him. Bathsheba bowed before the king and did obeisance. 'What is your request?' asked the king. She answered, 'My lord, you yourself swore to me your servant, by the Lord your God, that my son Solomon should succeed you as king and sit on your throne. But now, here is Adonijah become king, all unknown to your majesty. He has sacrificed great numbers of oxen, buffaloes, and sheep, and has invited to the feast all the king's sons, with Abiathar the priest and Joab the commander-in-chief, but he has not invited your servant Solomon. Your majesty, all Israel is now looking to you to announce your successor on the throne. Otherwise, when you, sir, rest with your forefathers, my son Solomon and I will be treated as criminals.'

Bathsheba was still addressing the king when Nathan the prophet arrived. The king was informed that Nathan was there; he came into the king's presence and prostrated himself. 'My lord,' he said, 'has your majesty declared that Adonijah should succeed you and sit on your throne? He has today gone down and sacrificed great numbers of oxen, buffaloes, and sheep, and has invited to the feast all the king's sons, the commanders of the army, and Abiathar the priest; and at this very moment they are eating and drinking in his presence and shouting, "Long live King Adonijah!" But he has not invited me your servant, Zadok the priest, Benaiah son of Jehoiada, or your servant Solomon. Has this been done by your majesty's authority? You have not told us your servants who should succeed you on the throne.'

King David said, 'Call Bathsheba,' and when she came into his presence and stood before him, the king swore an oath to her: 'As the Lord lives, who has delivered me from all my troubles, I swore by the Lord the God of Israel that Solomon your son should succeed me and that he should sit on my throne; this day I give effect to my oath.' Bathsheba bowed low to the king, did obeisance, and said, 'May my lord King David live for ever!'

King David said, 'Summon Zadok the priest, Nathan the prophet, and Benaiah son of Jehoiada,' and, when they came into the king's presence, he gave them this order: 'Take the officers of the household with you; mount my son Solomon on the king's mule and escort him down to Gihon. There let Zadok the priest and Nathan the prophet anoint him king over Israel. Then sound the trumpet and shout, "Long live King Solomon!" When you escort him home again let him come and sit on my throne and reign in my place; for he is the man that I have designated to be prince over Israel and Judah.' Benaiah son of Jehoiada answered the king, 'It will be done. And may the Lord, the God of my lord the king, confirm it! As the Lord has been with your majesty, so may he be with Solomon; may he make his throne even greater than the throne of my lord King David.'

The Anointing of Solomon

Zadok the priest, Nathan the prophet, and Benaiah son of Jehoiada, together with the Kerethite and Pelethite guards, went down and, mounting Solomon on King David's mule, they escorted him to Gihon. Zadok the priest took the horn of oil from the Tent of the Lord and anointed Solomon; they sounded the trumpet and all the people shouted, 'Long live King Solomon!' Then all the people escorted him home in procession, with great rejoicing and playing of pipes, so that the very earth split with the noise.

Adonijah and his guests had just finished their banquet when the noise reached their ears. On hearing the sound of the trumpet, Joab exclaimed, 'What is the meaning of this uproar in the city?' Even as he was speaking, Jonathan son of Abiathar the priest arrived. 'Come in,' said Adonijah. 'You are an honourable man and must be a bringer of good news.' 'Far from it,' Jonathan replied; 'our lord King David has made Solomon king. He has sent with him Zadok the priest, Nathan the prophet, and Benaiah son of Jehoiada, together with the Kerethite and Pelethite guards, and they have mounted Solomon on the king's mule, and Zadok the priest and Nathan the prophet have anointed him king at Gihon. They have now escorted him home rejoicing, and the city is in an uproar. That was the noise you heard. More than that, Solomon has taken his seat on the royal throne. Yes, and the officers of the household have been to our lord, King David, and greeted him in this fashion: "May your God make the name of Solomon your son more famous than your own and his throne even greater than yours," and the king bowed upon his couch. What is more, he said this: "Blessed be the Lord the God of Israel who has set a successor on my throne this day while I am still alive to see it."'

Adonijah's guests all rose in panic and dispersed. Adonijah himself, in fear of Solomon, went at once to the altar and grasped hold of its horns. A message was sent to Solomon: 'Adonijah, in his fear of King Solomon, is clinging to the horns of the altar; he says, "Let King Solomon swear to me here and now that he will not put his servant to the sword."' Solomon said, 'If he proves himself an honourable man, not a hair of his head will fall to the ground; but if he is found making trouble, he must die.'

Then King Solomon sent and had him brought down from the altar. He came in and prostrated himself before the king, and Solomon said to him, 'Go to your house.'

The Last Words of David

As the time of David's death drew near, he gave this charge to his son Solomon: 'I am about to go the way of all the earth. Be strong and show yourself a man. Fulfil your duty to the Lord your God; conform to his ways, observe his statutes and his commandments, his judgements and his solemn precepts, as they are written in the law of Moses, so that you may prosper in whatever you do and whichever way you turn, and that the Lord may fulfil this promise that he made about me: "If your descendants are careful to walk faithfully in my sight with all their heart and with all their soul, you shall never lack a successor on the throne of Israel."

'You know how Joab son of Zeruiah treated me and what he did to two commanders-in-chief in Israel, Abner son of Ner and Amasa son of Jether. He killed them both, breaking the peace by bloody acts of war; and with that blood he stained the belt about his waist and the sandals on his feet. Act as your wisdom prompts you, and do not let his grey hairs go down to the grave in peace. Show constant friendship to the family of Barzillai of Gilead; let them have their place at your table; they rallied to me when I was a fugitive from your brother Absalom. Do not forget Shimei son of Gera, the Benjamite from Bahurim, who cursed me bitterly the day I went to Mahanaim. True, he came down to meet me at the Jordan, and I swore by the Lord that I would not put him to death. But you do not need to let him go unpunished now; you are a wise man and will know how to deal with him; bring down his grey hairs in blood to the grave.'

David assembled at Jerusalem all the officers of Israel, the officers over the tribes, over the divisions engaged in the king's service, over the units of a thousand and a hundred, and officials in charge of all the property and the cattle of the king and of his sons, as well as the eunuchs, the heroes, and all the men of ability.

King David stood up and addressed them: 'Hear me, my kinsmen and my people. Out of all my sons – for the Lord gave me many sons – he has chosen Solomon to sit on the throne of the Lord's sovereignty over Israel.

'And you, Solomon my son, acknowledge your father's God and serve him with whole heart and willing mind, for the Lord searches all hearts and discerns whatever plan may be devised. If you search for him, he will let you find him, but if you forsake him, he will cast you off for ever.'

David blessed the Lord in the presence of all the assembly, saying:

'Blessed are you, Lord God of our father Israel,
from of old and for ever.

Yours, Lord, is the greatness and the power,
the glory, the splendour, and the majesty;
for everything in heaven and on earth is yours;

yours, Lord, is the sovereignty,
and you are exalted over all as head.

Wealth and honour come from you; you rule over all;
might and power are of your disposing;
yours it is to give power and strength to all.

Now, our God, we give you thanks
and praise your glorious name.'

Turning to the whole assembly, David said, 'Now bless the Lord
your God.' Then all the assembly blessed the Lord the God of
their forefathers, bowing low and prostrating themselves before
the Lord and the king.

13 | THE GOLDEN AGE OF SOLOMON

Solomon Secures the Throne

David son of Jesse had ruled over the whole of Israel, and the length of his reign over Israel was forty years, seven years in Hebron and thirty-three in Jerusalem. He died in ripe old age, full of years, wealth, and honour; and Solomon his son ruled in his stead.

Then Adonijah son of Haggith came to Bathsheba, Solomon's mother. 'Do you come as a friend?' she asked. 'As a friend,' he answered; 'I have something to discuss with you.' 'Tell me,' she said. 'You know', he went on, 'that the throne was mine and that all Israel was looking to me to be king; but I was passed over and the throne has gone to my brother; it was his by the will of the Lord. Now I have one request to make of you; do not refuse me.' 'What is it?' she said. He answered, 'Will you ask King Solomon (he will never refuse you) to give me Abishag the Shunammite in marriage?' 'Very well,' said Bathsheba, 'I shall speak to the king on your behalf.'

When Bathsheba went in to King Solomon to speak for Adonijah, the king rose to meet her and do obeisance to her. Then he seated himself on his throne, and a throne was set for the king's mother at his right hand. She said, 'I have one small request to make of you; do not refuse me.' 'What is it, mother?' he replied. 'I will not refuse you.' 'It is this,' she said, 'that Abishag the Shunammite be given in marriage to your brother Adonijah.' At that King Solomon answered, 'Why do you ask that Abishag the Shunammite be given to Adonijah? You might as well ask the kingdom for him; he is my elder brother and has both Abiathar the priest and Joab son of Zeruiah on his side.' Then he swore by the Lord: 'So help me God, Adonijah must pay for this with his life. As the Lord lives, who has established me and set me on the throne of David my father and has founded a house for me as he promised, this very day Adonijah must be put to death!' King

Solomon sent Benaiah son of Jehoiada with orders to strike him down; so Adonijah died.

Abiathar the priest was told by the king to go to Anathoth to his estate. 'You deserve to die,' he said, 'but in spite of this day's work I shall not put you to death, for you carried the Ark of the Lord God before my father David, and you shared in all the hardships he endured.' Solomon deposed Abiathar from his office as priest of the Lord, so fulfilling the sentence pronounced by the Lord against the house of Eli in Shiloh.

When news of all this reached Joab, he fled to the Tent of the Lord and laid hold of the horns of the altar; for he had sided with Adonijah, though not with Absalom. When King Solomon was told that Joab had fled to the Tent of the Lord and was beside the altar, he sent Benaiah son of Jehoiada with orders to strike him down. Benaiah came to the Tent of the Lord and ordered Joab in the king's name to come away. But he said, 'No, I will die here.' Benaiah reported Joab's answer to the king, and the king said, 'Let him have his way; strike him down and bury him, and so rid me and my father's house of the guilt for the blood that he wantonly shed. The Lord will hold him responsible for his own death, because he struck down two innocent men who were better men than he, Abner son of Ner, commander of the army of Israel, and Amasa son of Jether, commander of the army of Judah, and ran them through with the sword, without my father David's knowledge. Let the guilt of their blood recoil on Joab and his descendants for all time; but may David and his descendants, his house and his throne, enjoy perpetual prosperity from the Lord.' Benaiah son of Jehoiada went up to the altar and struck Joab down and killed him, and he was buried at his house out in the country.

The king appointed Benaiah to command the army in place of Joab, and installed Zadok the priest in the place of Abiathar.

Next the king sent for Shimei and said to him, 'Build yourself a house in Jerusalem and stay there; you are not to leave the city for any other place. If ever you leave and cross the wadi Kidron, know for certain that you will die. Your blood will be on your own head.' Shimei replied, 'I accept your sentence; I shall do as your majesty commands.'

For a long time Shimei remained in Jerusalem. But when three years later two of his slaves ran away to Achish son of Maacah, king of Gath, and this was reported to Shimei, he at once saddled his donkey and went to Achish in search of his slaves; he reached Gath and brought them back. When King Solomon was informed that Shimei had gone from Jerusalem to Gath and back, he sent for him and said, 'Did I not require you to swear by the Lord? Did I not give you this solemn warning: "If ever you leave this city for any other place, know for certain that you will die"? You said, "I accept your sentence; I shall obey." Why then have you not kept the oath which you swore by the Lord, and the order which I gave you? Shimei, you know in your heart what mischief you did to my father David; the Lord is now making that mischief recoil on your own head. But King Solomon is blessed, and the throne of David will be secure before the Lord for all time.' The king then gave orders to Benaiah son of Jehoiada, who went out and struck Shimei down, and he died. Thus Solomon's royal power was securely established.

Solomon's Wisdom

Solomon allied himself to Pharaoh king of Egypt by marrying his daughter. He brought her to the City of David, until he had finished building his palace and the house of the Lord and the wall round Jerusalem. The people however continued to sacrifice at the shrines, for up to that time no house had been built for the name of the Lord. Solomon himself loved the Lord, conforming to the precepts laid down by his father David; but he too slaughtered and burnt sacrifices at the shrines.

The king went to Gibeon to offer a sacrifice, for that was the chief shrine, where he used to offer a thousand whole-offerings on the altar. That night the Lord appeared to Solomon there in a dream. God said, 'What shall I give you? Tell me.' He answered, 'You have shown great and constant love to your servant David my father, because he walked before you in loyalty, righteousness, and integrity of heart; and you have maintained this great and constant love towards him and now you have given him a son to succeed him on the throne.

'Now, Lord my God, you have made your servant king in place of my father David, though I am a mere child, unskilled in leadership. Here I am in the midst of your people, the people of your choice, too many to be numbered or counted. Grant your servant, therefore, a heart with skill to listen, so that he may govern your people justly and distinguish good from evil. Otherwise who is equal to the task of governing this great people of yours?'

The Lord was well pleased that this was what Solomon had asked for, and God said, 'Because you have asked for this, and not for long life, or for wealth, or for the lives of your enemies, but have asked for discernment in administering justice, I grant your request; I give you a heart so wise and so understanding that there has been none like you before your time, nor will there be after you. What is more, I give you those things for which you did not ask, such wealth and glory as no king of your time can match. If you conform to my ways and observe my ordinances and commandments, as your father David did, I will also give you long life.' Then Solomon awoke, and realized it was a dream.

Solomon came to Jerusalem and stood before the Ark of the Covenant of the Lord, where he sacrificed whole-offerings and brought shared-offerings, and gave a banquet for all his household.

Two women who were prostitutes approached the king at that time, and as they stood before him one said, 'My lord, this woman and I share a house, and I gave birth to a child when she was there with me. On the third day after my baby was born she too gave birth to a child. We were alone; no one else was with us in the house; only the two of us were there. During the night this woman's child died because she lay on it, and she got up in the middle of the night, took my baby from my side while I, your servant, was asleep, and laid it on her bosom, putting her dead child on mine. When I got up in the morning to feed my baby, I found him dead; but when I looked at him closely, I found that it was not the child that I had borne.' The other woman broke in, 'No, the living child is mine; yours is the dead one,' while the first insisted, 'No, the dead child is yours; mine is the living one.' So they went on arguing before the king.

The king thought to himself, 'One of them says, "This is my child, the living one; yours is the dead one." The other says, "No, it is your child that is dead and mine that is alive."' Then he said, 'Fetch me a sword.' When a sword was brought, the king gave the order: 'Cut the living child in two and give half to one woman and half to the other.' At this the woman who was the mother of the living child, moved with love for her child, said to the king, 'Oh, sir, let her have the baby! Whatever you do, do not kill it.' The other said, 'Let neither of us have it; cut it in two.' The king then spoke up: 'Give the living baby to the first woman,' he said; 'do not kill it. She is its mother.' When Israel heard the judgement which the king had given, they all stood in awe of him; for they saw that he possessed wisdom from God for administering justice.

The people of Judah and Israel were countless as the sands of the sea; they ate and drank and enjoyed life. Solomon ruled over all the kingdoms from the river Euphrates to Philistia and as far as the frontier of Egypt; they paid tribute and were subject to him all his life. For he was paramount over all the region west of the Euphrates from Tiphsah to Gaza, ruling all the kings west of the river; and he enjoyed peace on all sides. All through his reign the people of Judah and Israel lived in peace, everyone from Dan to Beersheba under his own vine and his own fig tree.

God gave Solomon deep wisdom and insight, and understanding as wide as the sand on the seashore, so that Solomon's wisdom surpassed that of all the men of the east and of all Egypt. For he was wiser than any man, wiser than Ethan the Ezrahite, and Heman, Calcol, and Darda, the sons of Mahol; his fame spread among all the surrounding nations. He propounded three thousand proverbs, and his songs numbered a thousand and five.

Solomon's Temple

Solomon resolved to build a house for the name of the Lord and a royal palace for himself.

He engaged seventy thousand bearers and eighty thousand quarrymen, and three thousand six hundred men to superintend them. He sent this message to King Huram of Tyre: 'You were so good as to send my father David cedar-wood to build his royal residence. Now I am about to build a house for the name of the Lord my God and to consecrate it to him. Send me now a skilled craftsman, one able to work in gold and silver, bronze, and iron, and in purple, crimson, and violet yarn, one who is also an expert engraver and will work in Judah and in Jerusalem with my skilled workmen who were provided by David my father. Send me also cedar, pine, and algum timber from Lebanon, for I know that your men are expert at felling the trees of Lebanon; my men will work with yours to get an ample supply of timber ready for me, for the house which I shall build will be great and wonderful. I shall supply provisions for your servants, the woodmen who fell the trees: twenty thousand kor of wheat and twenty thousand kor of barley, with twenty thousand bath of wine and twenty thousand bath of oil.'

King Huram of Tyre sent this letter in reply: 'It is because of the love which the Lord has for his people that he has made you king over them.' The letter continued, 'Blessed be the Lord the God of Israel, maker of heaven and earth, who has given to King David a wise son, endowed with insight and understanding, to build a house for the Lord and a royal palace for himself.

'I now send you my expert Huram, a skilful and experienced craftsman. He is the son of a Danite woman and a Tyrian father; he is an experienced worker in gold and silver, bronze and iron, stone and wood, as well as in purple, violet, and crimson yarn, and in fine linen; he is also a trained engraver who will be able to work with your own skilled craftsmen and those of my lord David your father, to any design submitted to him. Now let my lord send his servants the wheat and the barley, the oil and the wine, which he promised; we shall fell all the timber in Lebanon that you need and float it as rafts to the roadstead at Joppa; you can convey it up to Jerusalem.'

Solomon took a census of all the aliens resident in Israel, similar to the census which David his father had taken; these were found to be a hundred and fifty-three thousand six hundred. He made seventy thousand of them bearers, and eighty thousand quarrymen, and three thousand six hundred superintendents to make the people work.

Then Solomon began to build the house of the Lord in Jerusalem on Mount Moriah, where the Lord had appeared to his father David; it was the site which David had prepared on the threshing-floor of Ornan the Jebusite. He began to build in the second month of the fourth year of his reign. These are the foundations which Solomon laid for building the house of God: according to the old standard of measurement the length was sixty cubits and the breadth twenty. The vestibule in front of the house was twenty cubits long, spanning the whole breadth of the house, and its height was twenty; on the inside he overlaid it with pure gold. He panelled the large chamber with pine, covered it with fine gold, and carved on it palm trees and chain-work. He adorned the house with precious stones for decoration and with gold from Parvaim. He overlaid the whole house with gold, its rafters and frames, its walls and doors; and he carved cherubim on the walls.

He made the Most Holy Place twenty cubits long, corresponding to the breadth of the house, and twenty cubits broad. He overlaid it all with six hundred talents of fine gold, and the weight of the gold nails was fifty shekels. He also covered the upper chambers with gold.

In the Most Holy Place he carved two images of cherubim and overlaid them with gold. The total span of the wings of the cherubim was twenty cubits. A wing of one cherub extended five cubits to touch the wall of the house, while its other wing reached out five cubits to meet a wing of the other cherub. Similarly, a wing of the second cherub extended five cubits to touch the other wall of the house, while its other wing met a wing of the first cherub. The wings of these cherubim extended twenty cubits; they stood with their feet on the ground, facing the outer chamber. He made the veil of violet, purple, and crimson yarn, and fine linen, and embroidered cherubim on it.

In front of the house he erected two pillars eighteen cubits high, with a capital five cubits high on top of each. He made chain-work like a necklace and set it round the tops of the pillars, and he carved a hundred pomegranates and set them in the chain-work. He erected the pillars in front of the temple, one on the right and one on the left; the one on the right he named Jachin and the one on the left Boaz.

Solomon made also all the furnishings for the house of God: the golden altar, the tables upon which was set the Bread of the Presence, the lampstands of red gold whose lamps burned before the inner shrine in the prescribed manner, the flowers, lamps, and tongs of solid gold, the snuffers, tossing-bowls, saucers, and firepans of red gold, and, at the entrance to the house, the inner doors leading to the Most Holy Place and those leading to the sanctuary, of gold.

When all the work which Solomon did for the house of the Lord was completed, he brought in the treasures dedicated by his father David, the silver, the gold, and the vessels, and deposited them in the treasuries of the house of God.

Then Solomon summoned the elders of Israel, and all the heads of the tribes who were chiefs of families in Israel, to assemble in Jerusalem, in order to bring up the Ark of the Covenant of the Lord from the City of David, which is called Zion. All the men of Israel were assembled in the king's presence at the pilgrim-feast in the seventh month. When the elders of Israel had all arrived, the Levites lifted the Ark and carried it up; the Tent of Meeting and all the sacred furnishings of the Tent were carried by the priests and the Levites. King Solomon and the whole congregation of Israel assembled with him before the Ark sacrificed sheep and oxen in numbers past counting or reckoning.

The priests brought in the Ark of the Covenant of the Lord to its place, in the inner shrine of the house, the Most Holy Place, beneath the wings of the cherubim. The cherubim, whose wings were spread over the place of the Ark, formed a canopy above the Ark and its poles. The poles projected, and their ends were visible from the Holy Place immediately in front of the inner shrine, but from nowhere else outside; they are there to this day. There was nothing inside the Ark but the two tablets which Moses had put there at Horeb, when the Lord made the covenant with the Israelites after they left Egypt.

When the priests came out of the Holy Place (for all the priests who were present had hallowed themselves without keeping to their divisions), all the levitical singers, Asaph, Heman, and Jeduthun, their sons, and their kinsmen, attired in fine linen, stood with cymbals, lutes, and lyres to the east of the altar, together with a hundred and twenty priests who blew trumpets. Now the trumpeters and the singers joined in unison to sound forth praise and thanksgiving to the Lord, and the song was raised with trumpets, cymbals, and musical instruments, in praise of the Lord, because 'it is good, for his love endures for ever'; and the house was filled with the cloud of the glory of the Lord. The priests could not continue to minister because of the cloud, for the glory of the Lord filled the house of God.

Then Solomon said:

'The Lord has caused the sun to shine in the heavens;
but he has said he would dwell in thick darkness.

I have built you a lofty house,
a dwelling-place for you to occupy for ever.'

While the whole assembly of Israelites stood, the king turned and, spreading out his hands towards heaven, he said, 'Lord God of Israel, there is no God like you in heaven or on earth, keeping covenant with your servants and showing them constant love while they continue faithful to you with all their heart. Lord God of Israel, let the promise which you made to your servant David be now confirmed.

'But can God indeed dwell with mortals on earth? Heaven itself, the highest heaven, cannot contain you; how much less this house that I have built! Yet attend, Lord my God, to the prayer and the supplication of your servant; listen to the cry and the prayer which your servant makes before you, that your eyes may ever be on this house day and night, this place where you said you would set your name. Hear your servant when he prays towards this place. Hear the supplications of your servant and of your people Israel when they pray towards this place. Hear from heaven your dwelling and, when you hear, forgive.

'Should anyone wrong a neighbour and be adjured to take an oath, and come to take the oath before your altar in this house, then hear from heaven and take action: be your servants' judge, requiting the guilty person and bringing his deeds on his own head, acquitting the innocent and rewarding him as his innocence may deserve.

'Should they sin against you (and who is free from sin?) and should you in your anger give them over to an enemy who carries them captive to a land far or near; and should they then in the land of their captivity have a change of heart and turn back and make supplication to you there and say, "We have sinned and acted perversely and wickedly," and turn back to you wholeheartedly in the land of their captivity to which they have been taken, and pray, turning towards their land which you gave to their forefathers and towards this city which you chose and this house which I have built for your name; then from heaven your dwelling-place hear their prayer and supplications and maintain their cause. Forgive your people their sins against you. Now, my God, let your eyes be open and your ears attentive to the prayer made in this place.

'Arise now, Lord God, and come to your resting-place,
you and your powerful Ark.
Let your priests, Lord God, be clothed with salvation
and your loyal servants rejoice in prosperity.

Lord God, do not reject your anointed one;
remember the loyal service of David your servant.'

As Solomon finished this prayer, fire came down from heaven
and consumed the whole-offering and the sacrifices, while the
glory of the Lord filled the house. The priests were unable to
enter the house of the Lord because the glory of the Lord had
filled it. All the Israelites witnessed the fire coming down with the
glory of the Lord on the house, and where they were on the
paved court they bowed low to the ground and worshipped and
gave thanks to the Lord, because 'it is good, for his love endures
for ever'.

The king and all the people offered sacrifice before the Lord;
King Solomon offered a sacrifice of twenty-two thousand oxen
and a hundred and twenty thousand sheep. Thus the king and all
the people dedicated the house of God. The priests stood at their
appointed posts; so too the Levites with their musical instruments for the Lord's service, which King David had made for
giving thanks to the Lord – 'for his love endures for ever' –
whenever he rendered praise with their help; opposite them, the
priests sounded their trumpets, while all the Israelites were
standing. Then Solomon consecrated the centre of the court
which lay in front of the house of the Lord; there he offered the
whole-offerings and the fat portions of the shared-offerings,
because the bronze altar which he had made could not accommo-
date the whole-offering, the grain-offering, and the fat portions.

So Solomon and with him all Israel, a very great assembly from
Lebo-hamath to the wadi of Egypt, celebrated the pilgrim-feast at
that time for seven days. On the eighth day they held a closing
ceremony; for they had celebrated the dedication of the altar for
seven days, and the pilgrim-feast lasted seven days. On the
twenty-third day of the seventh month he dismissed the people to
their homes, happy and glad at heart for all the prosperity
granted by the Lord to David, to Solomon, and to his people
Israel.

The Visit of the Queen of Sheba

The queen of Sheba heard of Solomon's fame and came to test him with enigmatic questions. She arrived in Jerusalem with a very large retinue, camels laden with spices, gold in vast quantity, and precious stones. When she came to Solomon, she talked to him about everything she had on her mind. Solomon answered all her questions; not one of them was too hard for the king to answer. When the queen of Sheba observed all the wisdom of Solomon, the palace he had built, the food on his table, the courtiers sitting around him, and his attendants standing behind in their livery, his cupbearers, and the whole-offerings which he used to offer in the house of the Lord, she was overcome with amazement.

She said to the king, 'The account which I heard in my own country about your achievements and your wisdom was true, but I did not believe what they told me until I came and saw for myself. Indeed I was not told half of it; your wisdom and your prosperity far surpass all I had heard of them. Happy are your wives, happy these courtiers of yours who are in attendance on you every day and hear your wisdom! Blessed be the Lord your God who has delighted in you and has set you on the throne of Israel; because he loves Israel unendingly, he has made you king to maintain law and justice.' She presented the king with a hundred and twenty talents of gold, spices in great abundance, and precious stones. Never again did such a quantity of spices come as the queen of Sheba gave to King Solomon.

King Solomon gave the queen of Sheba whatever she desired and asked for, in addition to all that he gave her of his royal bounty. Then she departed with her retinue and went back to her own land.

Thus King Solomon outdid all the kings of the earth in wealth and wisdom, and the whole world courted him to hear the wisdom with which God had endowed his mind. Each one brought his gift with him, vessels of silver and gold, garments, perfumes and spices, horses and mules in annual tribute. Solomon amassed chariots and horses; he had fourteen hundred chariots and twelve thousand horses; he stationed some in the chariot-towns, while others he kept at hand in Jerusalem. He made silver as common in Jerusalem as stone, and cedar as plentiful as the sycomore-fig is in the Shephelah. Horses were imported from Egypt and Kue for Solomon; the merchants of the king obtained them from Kue by purchase. Chariots were imported from Egypt for six hundred silver shekels each, and horses for a hundred and fifty; in the same way the merchants obtained them for export from all the kings of the Hittites and the kings of Aram.

Solomon's Apostasy

King Solomon loved many foreign women; in addition to Pharaoh's daughter there were Moabite, Ammonite, Edomite, Sidonian, and Hittite women, from the nations with whom the Lord had forbidden the Israelites to intermarry, 'because', he said, 'they will entice you to serve their gods'. But Solomon was devoted to them and loved them dearly. He had seven hundred wives, all princesses, and three hundred concubines, and they influenced him, for as he grew old, his wives turned his heart to follow other gods, and he did not remain wholly loyal to the Lord his God as his father David had been. He followed Ashtoreth, goddess of the Sidonians, and Milcom, the loathsome god of the Ammonites. Thus Solomon did what was wrong in the eyes of the Lord, and was not wholehearted in his loyalty to the Lord as his father David had been. He built a shrine for Kemosh, the loathsome god of Moab, on the heights to the east of Jerusalem, and one for Milcom, the loathsome god of the Ammonites. These things he did for the gods to whom all his foreign wives burnt offerings and made sacrifices.

The Lord was angry with Solomon because his heart had turned away from the Lord the God of Israel, who had appeared to him twice and had strictly commanded him not to follow other gods; but he disobeyed the Lord's command. The Lord therefore said to Solomon, 'Because you have done this and have not kept my covenant and my statutes as I commanded you, I will tear the kingdom from you and give it to your servant. Nevertheless, for the sake of your father David I will not do this in your day; I will tear it out of your son's hand. Even so not the whole kingdom; I will leave him one tribe for the sake of my servant David and for the sake of Jerusalem, my chosen city.'

14 | THE TWO KINGDOMS

Jeroboam's Rebellion

Jeroboam son of Nebat, one of Solomon's courtiers, an Ephrathite from Zeredah, whose widowed mother was named Zeruah, rebelled against the king. This is the story of his rebellion. When Solomon built the Millo and closed the breach in the wall of the city of his father David, he saw how the young man worked, for Jeroboam was a man of great ability, and the king put him in charge of all the labour-gangs in the tribal district of Joseph. On one occasion when Jeroboam left Jerusalem, the prophet Ahijah from Shiloh met him on the road. The prophet was wearing a new cloak and, when the two of them were alone out in the open country, Ahijah, taking hold of the new cloak he was wearing, tore it into twelve pieces, and said to Jeroboam, 'Take for yourself ten pieces, for the Lord the God of Israel has declared that he is about to tear the kingdom from the hand of Solomon and give you ten tribes. But, says the Lord, one tribe will remain Solomon's, for the sake of my servant David and for the sake of Jerusalem, the city I have chosen out of all the tribes of Israel. I shall do this because Solomon has forsaken me; he has bowed down before Ashtoreth goddess of the Sidonians, Kemosh god of Moab, and Milcom god of the Ammonites, and has not conformed to my ways. He has not done what is right in my eyes or observed my statutes and judgements as David his father did.

'Nevertheless I shall not take the whole kingdom from him, but shall maintain his rule as long as he lives, for the sake of my chosen servant David, who did observe my commandments and statutes. But I shall take the kingdom, that is the ten tribes, from his son and give it to you. To his son I shall give one tribe, that my servant David may always have a lamp burning before me in Jerusalem, the city which I chose to receive my name. I shall appoint you to rule over all that you can desire, and to be king over Israel. If you pay heed to all my commands, if you conform to my ways and do what is right in my eyes, observing my statutes and commandments as my servant David did, then I shall be with you. I shall establish your family for ever as I did for David; I shall give Israel to you, and punish David's descendants as they have deserved, but not for ever.'

After this Solomon sought to kill Jeroboam, but he fled to King Shishak in Egypt and remained there till Solomon's death.

The other acts and events of Solomon's reign, and all his wisdom, are recorded in the annals of Solomon. The reign of King Solomon in Jerusalem over the whole of Israel lasted forty years. Then he rested with his forefathers and was buried in the city of David his father; he was succeeded by his son Rehoboam.

Rehoboam went to Shechem, for all Israel had gone there to make him king. When Jeroboam son of Nebat, who was still in Egypt, heard of it, he remained there, having taken refuge in Egypt to escape King Solomon. The people now recalled him, and he and all the assembly of Israel came to Rehoboam and said, 'Your father laid a harsh yoke upon us; but if you will now lighten the harsh labour he imposed and the heavy yoke he laid on us, we shall serve you.' 'Give me three days,' he said, 'and then come back.'

When the people had gone, King Rehoboam consulted the elders who had been in attendance during the lifetime of his father Solomon: 'What answer do you advise me to give to this people?' They said, 'If today you are willing to serve this people, show yourself their servant now and speak kindly to them, and they will be your servants ever after.' But he rejected the advice given him by the elders, and consulted the young men who had grown up with him, and were now in attendance; he asked them, 'What answer do you advise me to give to this people's request that I should lighten the yoke which my father laid on them?' The young men replied, 'Give this answer to the people who say that your father made their yoke heavy and ask you to lighten it; tell them: "My little finger is thicker than my father's loins. My father laid a heavy yoke on you, but I shall make it heavier. My father whipped you, but I shall flay you."'

Jeroboam and the people all came to Rehoboam on the third day, as the king had ordered. The king gave them a harsh answer; he rejected the advice which the elders had given him and spoke to the people as the young men had advised: 'My father made your yoke heavy, but I shall make it heavier. My father whipped you, but I shall flay you.' The king would not listen to the people; for the Lord had given this turn to the affair in order that the word he had spoken by Ahijah of Shiloh to Jeroboam son of Nebat might be fulfilled.

When all Israel saw that the king would not listen to them, they answered:

'What share have we in David?
We have no lot in the son of Jesse.
Away to your tents, Israel!
Now see to your own house, David!'

With that Israel went off to their homes. Rehoboam ruled only over those Israelites who lived in the cities and towns of Judah.

Jeroboam, King of Israel

When Rehoboam reached Jerusalem, he mustered the tribes of Judah and Benjamin, a hundred and eighty thousand chosen warriors, to fight against Israel and recover his kingdom. But this word of God came to Shemaiah the man of God: 'Say to Rehoboam son of Solomon, king of Judah, and to all Judah and Benjamin and the rest of the people, This is the word of the Lord: You are not to go up to make war on your kinsmen the Israelites. Return to your homes, for this is my doing.' They listened to the word of the Lord and went back, as the Lord had told them.

Jeroboam rebuilt Shechem in the hill-country of Ephraim and took up residence there; from there he went out and built Penuel. 'As things now stand,' he said to himself, 'the kingdom will revert to the house of David. If these people go up to sacrifice in the house of the Lord in Jerusalem, it will revive their allegiance to their lord King Rehoboam of Judah, and they will kill me and return to King Rehoboam.' After taking counsel about the matter he made two calves of gold and said to the people, 'You have gone up to Jerusalem long enough; here are your gods, Israel, that brought you up from Egypt.' One he set up at Bethel and the other he put at Dan, and this thing became a sin in Israel; the people went to Bethel to worship the one, and all the way to Dan to worship the other.

He also erected temple buildings at shrines and appointed priests who did not belong to the Levites, from every class of the people. He instituted a pilgrim-feast on the fifteenth day of the eighth month like that in Judah, and he offered sacrifices on the altar. This he did at Bethel, sacrificing to the calves that he had made and compelling the priests of the shrines, which he had set up, to serve at Bethel. He went up on the fifteenth day of the eighth month to the altar that he had made at Bethel; there, in a month of his own choosing, he instituted for the Israelites a pilgrim-feast and himself went up to the altar to burn the sacrifice.

As Jeroboam stood by the altar to burn the sacrifice, a man of God from Judah, moved by the word of the Lord, appeared at Bethel. He inveighed against the altar in the Lord's name, crying out, 'O altar, altar! This is the word of the Lord: Listen! To the house of David a child shall be born named Josiah. On you he will sacrifice the priests of the shrines who make offerings on you, and he will burn human bones on you.' He gave a sign the same day: 'This is the sign which the Lord has ordained: This altar will be split asunder and the ashes on it will be scattered.' When King Jeroboam heard the sentence which the man of God pronounced against the altar at Bethel, he pointed to him from the altar and cried, 'Seize him!' Immediately the hand which he had pointed at him became paralysed, so that he could not draw it back. The altar too was split asunder and the ashes were scattered, in fulfil-ment of the sign that the man of God had given at the Lord's command. The king appealed to the man of God to placate the Lord his God and pray for him that his hand might be restored. The man of God did as he asked; the king's hand was restored and became as it had been before.

After this Jeroboam still did not abandon his evil ways, but went on appointing priests for the shrines from all classes of the people; any man who offered himself he would consecrate to be priest of a shrine. By doing this he brought guilt on his own house and doomed it to utter destruction.

Ahijah's Prophecy

At that time Jeroboam's son Abijah fell ill, and Jeroboam said to his wife, 'Go at once to Shiloh, but disguise yourself so that people will not recognize you as my wife. Ahijah the prophet is there, he who said I was to be king over this people. Take with you ten loaves, some raisins, and a jar of honey. Go to him and he will tell you what will happen to the boy.' Jeroboam's wife did so; she set off at once for Shiloh and came to Ahijah's house. Now as Ahijah could not see, for his eyes were fixed in the blindness of old age, the Lord had said to him, 'Jeroboam's wife is on her way to consult you about her son, who is ill; you are to give her such and such an answer.'

When she came in, concealing who she was, and Ahijah heard her footsteps at the door, he said, 'Come in, wife of Jeroboam. Why conceal who you are? I have heavy news for you. Go, tell Jeroboam: "This is the word of the Lord the God of Israel: I raised you out of the people and appointed you prince over my people Israel; I tore the kingdom from the house of David and gave it to you. But you have not been like my servant David, who kept my commands and followed me with his whole heart, doing only what was right in my eyes. You have outdone all your predecessors in wickedness; you have provoked me to anger by making for yourself other gods and images of cast metal; and you have turned your back on me. For this I am going to bring disaster on the house of Jeroboam; I shall destroy them all, every mother's son, whether still under the protection of the family or not, and I shall sweep away the house of Jeroboam in Israel, as one sweeps away dung until none is left. Those of that house who die in the town shall be food for the dogs, and those who die in the country shall be food for the birds. It is the word of the Lord."

'Go home now; the moment you set foot in the town, the child will die. All Israel will mourn for him and bury him; he alone of all Jeroboam's family will have proper burial, because in him alone could the Lord the God of Israel find anything good.

'The Lord will set up a king over Israel who will put an end to the house of Jeroboam. This first; and what next? The Lord will strike Israel, till it trembles like a reed in the water; he will uproot its people from this good land which he gave to their forefathers and scatter them beyond the Euphrates, because they have made their sacred poles, thus provoking the Lord's anger. He will abandon Israel because of the sins that Jeroboam has committed and has led Israel to commit.'

Jeroboam's wife went away back to Tirzah and, as she crossed the threshold of the house, the boy died. They buried him, and all Israel mourned over him; and thus the word of the Lord was fulfilled which he had spoken through his servant Ahijah the prophet.

Rehoboam, King of Judah

Rehoboam son of Solomon was forty-one years old when he came to the throne, and he reigned for seventeen years in Jerusalem, the city where the Lord had chosen, out of all the tribes of Israel, to set his name. Rehoboam's mother was a woman of Ammon called Naamah. Judah did what was wrong in the eyes of the Lord, rousing his jealous indignation by the sins they committed, which were beyond anything that their forefathers had done. They erected shrines, sacred pillars, and sacred poles on every high hill and under every spreading tree. Worse still, all over the country there were male prostitutes attached to the shrines, and the people adopted all the abominable practices of the nations whom the Lord had dispossessed in favour of Israel.

In the fifth year of Rehoboam's reign King Shishak of Egypt attacked Jerusalem, and carried away the treasures of the house of the Lord and of the king's palace; he seized everything, including all the gold shields made for Solomon. King Rehoboam replaced them with bronze shields and entrusted them to the officers of the escort who guarded the entrance of the palace. Whenever the king entered the house of the Lord, the escort carried them; afterwards they returned them to the guardroom.

The other acts and events of Rehoboam's reign are recorded in the annals of the kings of Judah.

There was continual fighting between him and Jeroboam.

15 | ELIJAH AND ELISHA

Elijah and the Drought

In the eighteenth year of the reign of Jeroboam son of Nebat, Abijam became king of Judah. He reigned in Jerusalem for three years; his son Asa succeeded him.

Ahab son of Omri became king of Israel in the thirty-eighth year of King Asa of Judah, and he reigned over Israel in Samaria for twenty-two years. More than any of his predecessors he did what was wrong in the eyes of the Lord. As if it were not enough for him to follow the sinful ways of Jeroboam son of Nebat, he took as his wife Jezebel daughter of King Ethbaal of Sidon, and went and served Baal; he prostrated himself before him and erected an altar to him in the temple of Baal which he built in Samaria. He also set up a sacred pole; indeed he did more to provoke the anger of the Lord the God of Israel than all the kings of Israel before him.

Elijah the Tishbite from Tishbe in Gilead said to Ahab, 'I swear by the life of the Lord the God of Israel, whose servant I am, that there will be neither dew nor rain these coming years unless I give the word.' Then the word of the Lord came to him: 'Leave this place, turn eastwards, and go into hiding in the wadi of Kerith east of the Jordan. You are to drink from the stream, and I have commanded the ravens to feed you there.' Elijah did as the Lord had told him: he went and stayed in the wadi of Kerith east of the Jordan, and the ravens brought him bread and meat morning and evening, and he drank from the stream.

After a while the stream dried up, for there had been no rain in the land. Then the word of the Lord came to him: 'Go now to Zarephath, a village of Sidon, and stay there; I have commanded a widow there to feed you.' He went off to Zarephath, and when he reached the entrance to the village, he saw a widow gathering sticks. He called to her, 'Please bring me a little water in a pitcher to drink.'

As she went to fetch it, he called after her, 'Bring me, please, a piece of bread as well.' But she answered, 'As the Lord your God lives, I have no food baked, only a handful of flour in a jar and a little oil in a flask. I am just gathering two or three sticks to go and cook it for my son and myself before we die.' 'Have no fear,' said Elijah; 'go and do as you have said. But first make me a small cake from what you have and bring it out to me, and after that make something for your son and yourself. For this is the word of the Lord the God of Israel: The jar of flour will not give out, nor the flask of oil fail, until the Lord sends rain on the land.' She went and did as Elijah had said, and there was food for him and for her and her family for a long time. The jar of flour did not give out, nor did the flask of oil fail, as the word of the Lord foretold through Elijah.

Afterwards the son of the woman, the owner of the house, fell ill and was in a very bad way, until at last his breathing stopped. The woman said to Elijah, 'What made you interfere, you man of God? You came here to bring my sins to light and cause my son's death!' 'Give me your son,' he said. He took the boy from her arms and carried him up to the roof-chamber where his lodging was, and laid him on his bed. He called out to the Lord, 'Lord my God, is this your care for the widow with whom I lodge, that you have been so cruel to her son?' Then he breathed deeply on the child three times and called to the Lord, 'I pray, Lord my God, let the breath of life return to the body of this child.' The Lord listened to Elijah's cry, and the breath of life returned to the child's body, and he revived.

Elijah lifted him and took him down from the roof-chamber into the house, and giving him to his mother he said, 'Look, your son is alive.' She said to Elijah, 'Now I know for certain that you are a man of God and that the word of the Lord on your lips is truth.'

Time went by, and in the third year the word of the Lord came to Elijah: 'Go, appear before Ahab, and I shall send rain on the land.' So Elijah went to show himself to Ahab. As soon as Ahab saw Elijah, he said to him, 'Is it you, you troubler of Israel?' 'It is not I who have brought trouble on Israel,' Elijah replied, 'but you and your father's family, by forsaking the commandments of the Lord and following Baal. Now summon all Israel to meet me on Mount Carmel, including the four hundred and fifty prophets of

Baal and the four hundred prophets of the goddess Asherah, who are attached to Jezebel's household.' So Ahab sent throughout the length and breadth of Israel and assembled the prophets on Mount Carmel.

The Slaughter of the Prophets of Baal

Elijah stepped forward towards all the people there and said, 'How long will you sit on the fence? If the Lord is God, follow him; but if Baal, then follow him.' Not a word did they answer. Then Elijah said, 'I am the only prophet of the Lord still left, but there are four hundred and fifty prophets of Baal. Bring two bulls for us. Let them choose one for themselves, cut it up, and lay it on the wood without setting fire to it, and I shall prepare the other and lay it on the wood without setting fire to it. Then invoke your god by name and I shall invoke the Lord by name; the god who answers by fire, he is God.' The people all shouted their approval.

Elijah said to the prophets of Baal, 'Choose one of the bulls and offer it first, for there are more of you; invoke your god by name, but do not set fire to the wood.' They took the bull provided for them and offered it, and they invoked Baal by name from morning until noon, crying, 'Baal, answer us'; but there was no sound, no answer. They danced wildly by the altar they had set up. At midday Elijah mocked them: 'Call louder, for he is a god. It may be he is deep in thought, or engaged, or on a journey; or he may have gone to sleep and must be woken up.' They cried still louder and, as was their custom, gashed themselves with swords and spears until the blood flowed. All afternoon they raved and ranted till the hour of the regular offering, but still there was no sound, no answer, no sign of attention.

Elijah said to the people, 'Come here to me,' and they all came to him. He repaired the altar of the Lord which had been torn down. He took twelve stones, one for each tribe of the sons of Jacob, him who was named Israel by the word of the Lord. With these stones he built an altar in the name of the Lord, and dug a trench round it big enough to hold two measures of seed; he arranged the wood, cut up the bull, and laid it on the wood. Then he said, 'Fill four jars with water and pour it on the whole-offering and on the wood.' They did so; he said, 'Do it again.' They did it again; he said, 'Do it a third time.' They did it a third time, and the water ran all round the altar and even filled the trench.

At the hour of the regular offering the prophet Elijah came forward and prayed, 'Lord God of Abraham, of Isaac, and of Israel, let it be known today that you are God in Israel and that I am your servant and have done all these things at your command. Answer me, Lord, answer me and let this people know that you, Lord, are God and that it is you who have brought them back to their allegiance.' The fire of the Lord fell, consuming the whole-offering, the wood, the stones, and the earth, and licking up the water in the trench. At the sight the people all bowed with their faces to the ground and cried, 'The Lord is God, the Lord is God.' Elijah said to them, 'Seize the prophets of Baal; let not one of them escape.' They were seized, and Elijah took them down to the Kishon and slaughtered them there in the valley.

Elijah said to Ahab, 'Go back now, eat and drink, for I hear the sound of heavy rain.' He did so, while Elijah himself climbed to the crest of Carmel, where he bowed down to the ground and put his face between his knees. He said to his servant, 'Go and look toward the west.' He went and looked; 'There is nothing to see,' he said. Seven times Elijah ordered him back, and seven times he went. The seventh time he said, 'I see a cloud no bigger than a man's hand, coming up from the west.' 'Now go', said Elijah, 'and tell Ahab to harness his chariot and be off, or the rain will stop him.' Meanwhile the sky grew black with clouds, the wind rose, and heavy rain began to fall. Ahab mounted his chariot and set off for Jezreel; and the power of the Lord was on Elijah: he tucked up his robe and ran before Ahab all the way to Jezreel.

Elijah Escapes from Jezebel

When Ahab told Jezebel all that Elijah had done and how he had put all the prophets to the sword, she sent this message to Elijah, 'The gods do the same to me and more, unless by this time tomorrow I have taken your life as you took theirs.' In fear he fled for his life, and when he reached Beersheba in Judah he left his servant there, while he himself went a day's journey into the wilderness. He came to a broom bush, and sitting down under it he prayed for death: 'It is enough,' he said; 'now, Lord, take away my life, for I am no better than my fathers before me.' He lay down under the bush and, while he slept, an angel touched him and said, 'Rise and eat.' He looked, and there at his head was a cake baked on hot stones, and a pitcher of water. He ate and drank and lay down again. The angel of the Lord came again and touched him a second time, saying, 'Rise and eat; the journey is too much for you.' He rose and ate and drank and, sustained by this food, he went on for forty days and forty nights to Horeb, the mount of God. There he entered a cave where he spent the night.

The word of the Lord came to him: 'Why are you here, Elijah?' 'Because of my great zeal for the Lord the God of Hosts,' he replied. 'The people of Israel have forsaken your covenant, torn down your altars, and put your prophets to the sword. I alone am left, and they seek to take my life.' To this the answer came: 'Go and stand on the mount before the Lord.' The Lord was passing by: a great and strong wind came, rending mountains and shattering rocks before him, but the Lord was not in the wind; and after the wind there was an earthquake, but the Lord was not in the earthquake; and after the earthquake fire, but the Lord was not in the fire; and after the fire a faint murmuring sound. When Elijah heard it, he wrapped his face in his cloak and went out and stood at the entrance to the cave. There came a voice: 'Why are you here, Elijah?' 'Because of my great zeal for the Lord the God of Hosts,' he replied. 'The people of Israel have forsaken your covenant, torn down your altars, and put your prophets to the sword. I alone am left, and they seek to take my life.'

The Lord said to him, 'Go back by way of the wilderness of Damascus, enter the city, and anoint Hazael to be king of Aram; anoint also Jehu son of Nimshi to be king of Israel, and Elisha son of Shaphat of Abel-meholah to be prophet in your place. Whoever escapes the sword of Hazael Jehu will slay, and whoever escapes the sword of Jehu Elisha will slay. But I shall leave seven thousand in Israel, all who have not bowed the knee to Baal, all whose lips have not kissed him.'

Elijah departed and found Elisha son of Shaphat ploughing; there were twelve pair of oxen ahead of him, and he himself was with the last of them. As Elijah passed, he threw his cloak over him. Elisha, leaving his oxen, ran after Elijah and said, 'Let me kiss my father and mother goodbye, and then I shall follow you.' 'Go back,' he replied; 'what have I done to prevent you?' He followed him no farther but went home, took his pair of oxen, slaughtered them, and burnt the wooden yokes to cook the flesh, which he gave to the people to eat. He then followed Elijah and became his disciple.

Naboth's Vineyard

Some time later there occurred an incident involving Naboth of Jezreel, who had a vineyard in Jezreel adjoining the palace of King Ahab of Samaria. Ahab made a proposal to Naboth: 'Your vineyard is close to my palace; let me have it for a garden, and I shall give you a better vineyard in exchange for it or, if you prefer, I shall give you its value in silver.' But Naboth answered, 'The Lord forbid that I should surrender to you land which has always been in my family.' Ahab went home sullen and angry because Naboth had refused to let him have his ancestral holding. He took to his bed, covered his face, and refused to eat. When his wife Jezebel came in to him and asked, 'Why this sullenness, and why do you refuse to eat?' he replied, 'I proposed that Naboth of Jezreel should let me have his vineyard at its value or, if he liked, in exchange for another; but he refused to let me have it.' 'Are you or are you not king in Israel?' retorted Jezebel. 'Come, eat and take heart; I shall make you a gift of the vineyard of Naboth of Jezreel.'

She wrote letters in Ahab's name, sealed them with his seal, and sent them to the elders and notables of Naboth's city, who sat in council with him. She wrote: 'Proclaim a fast and give Naboth the seat of honour among the people. Opposite him seat two unprincipled rogues to charge him with cursing God and the king; then take him out and stone him to death.' The elders and notables of Naboth's city carried out the instructions Jezebel had sent them in her letter: they proclaimed a fast and gave Naboth the seat of honour. The two unprincipled rogues came in, sat opposite him, and charged him publicly with cursing God and the king. He was then taken outside the city and stoned, and word was sent to Jezebel that Naboth had been stoned to death.

As soon as Jezebel heard of the death of Naboth, she said to Ahab, 'Get up and take possession of the vineyard which Naboth refused to sell you, for he is no longer alive; Naboth of Jezreel is dead.'

On hearing that Naboth was dead, Ahab got up and went to the vineyard to take possession.

The word of the Lord came to Elijah the Tishbite: 'Go down at once to King Ahab of Israel, who is in Samaria; you will find him in Naboth's vineyard, where he has gone to take possession. Say to him, "This is the word of the Lord: Have you murdered and seized property?" Say to him, "This is the word of the Lord: Where dogs licked the blood of Naboth, there dogs will lick your blood."' Ahab said to Elijah, 'So you have found me, my enemy.' 'Yes,' he said, 'because you have sold yourself to do what is wrong in the eyes of the Lord. I shall bring disaster on you; I shall sweep you away and destroy every mother's son of the house of Ahab in Israel, whether under protection of the family or not. I shall deal with your house as I dealt with the house of Jeroboam son of Nebat and that of Baasha son of Ahijah, because you have provoked my anger and led Israel into sin.' The Lord went on to say of Jezebel, 'Jezebel will be eaten by dogs near the rampart of Jezreel. Of the house of Ahab, those who die in the city will be food for the dogs, and those who die in the country food for the birds.'

When Ahab heard Elijah's words, he tore his clothes, put on sackcloth, and fasted; he lay down in his sackcloth and went about moaning. The word of the Lord came to Elijah the Tishbite: 'Have you seen how Ahab has humbled himself before me? Because he has thus humbled himself, I shall not bring disaster on his house in his own lifetime, but in that of his son.'

The Death of Ahab
For three years there was no war between the Aramaeans and the Israelites. In the third year King Jehoshaphat of Judah went down to visit the king of Israel, who had said to his ministers, 'You know that Ramoth-gilead belongs to us, and yet we do nothing to recover it from the king of Aram'; and to Jehoshaphat he said, 'Will you join me in attacking Ramoth-gilead?' Jehoshaphat replied, 'What is mine is yours: myself, my people, and my horses.'

The king of Israel and King Jehoshaphat of Judah marched on Ramoth-gilead. The king of Israel went into battle in disguise, for he had said to Jehoshaphat, 'I shall disguise myself to go into battle, but you must wear your royal robes.' The king of Aram had ordered the thirty-two captains of his chariots not to engage all and sundry, but the king of Israel alone. When the captains saw Jehoshaphat, they thought he was the king of Israel and turned to attack him, but Jehoshaphat cried out, and when the captains saw that he was not the king of Israel, they broke off the attack on him.

One man, however, drew his bow at random and hit the king of Israel where the breastplate joins the plates of the armour. The king said to his driver, 'Turn about and take me out of the line; I am wounded.' When the day's fighting reached its height, the king was facing the Aramaeans, propped up in his chariot, and the blood from his wound flowed down to the floor of the chariot; and in the evening he died. At sunset the herald went through the ranks, crying, 'Every man to his city, every man to his country.' Thus the king died. He was brought to Samaria and buried there. The chariot was swilled out at the pool of Samaria where the prostitutes washed themselves, and dogs licked up the blood, in fulfilment of the word the Lord had spoken.

The other acts and events of Ahab's reign, the palace he decorated with ivory and all the towns he built, are recorded in the annals of the kings of Israel. Ahab rested with his forefathers and was succeeded by his son Ahaziah.

Elijah and the Chariot of Fire

Elijah and Elisha had set out from Gilgal. Elijah said to Elisha, 'Stay here; for the Lord has sent me to Bethel.' Elisha replied, 'As the Lord lives, your life upon it, I shall not leave you.' They went down country to Bethel, and there a company of prophets came out to Elisha and said to him, 'Do you know that the Lord is going to take your lord and master from you today?' 'I do know,' he replied; 'say nothing.'

Elijah said to him, 'Stay here, Elisha; for the Lord has sent me to Jericho.' He replied, 'As the Lord lives, your life upon it, I shall not leave you.' So they went to Jericho, and there a company of prophets came up to Elisha and said to him, 'Do you know that the Lord is going to take your lord and master from you today?' 'I do know,' he replied; 'say nothing.'

Then Elijah said to him, 'Stay here; for the Lord has sent me to the Jordan.' The other replied, 'As the Lord lives, your life upon it, I shall not leave you.' So the two of them went on. Fifty of the prophets followed, and stood watching from a distance as the two of them stopped by the Jordan.

Elijah took his cloak, rolled it up, and struck the water with it. The water divided to right and left, and both crossed over on dry ground.

While they were crossing, Elijah said to Elisha, 'Tell me what I can do for you before I am taken from you.' Elisha said, 'Let me inherit a double share of your spirit.' 'You have asked a hard thing,' said Elijah. 'If you see me taken from you, your wish will be granted; if you do not, it will not be granted.' They went on, talking as they went, and suddenly there appeared a chariot of fire and horses of fire, which separated them from one another, and Elijah was carried up to heaven in a whirlwind. At the sight Elisha cried out, 'My father, my father, the chariot and the horsemen of Israel!' and he saw him no more.

He clutched hold of his mantle and tore it in two. He picked up the cloak which had fallen from Elijah, and went back and stood on the bank of the Jordan. There he struck the water with Elijah's cloak, saying as he did so, 'Where is the Lord, the God of Elijah?' As he too struck the water, it divided to right and left, and he crossed over.

The people of the city said to Elisha, 'Lord, you can see how pleasantly situated our city is, but the water is polluted and the country is sterile.' He said, 'Fetch me a new, unused bowl and put salt in it.' When they had brought it, he went out to the spring and, throwing the salt into it, he said, 'This is the word of the Lord: I purify this water. It shall no longer cause death or sterility.' The water has remained pure till this day, in fulfilment of Elisha's word.

From there he went up to Bethel and, as he was on his way, some small boys came out of the town and jeered at him, saying, 'Get along with you, bald head, get along.' He turned round, looked at them, and cursed them in the name of the Lord; and two she-bears came out of a wood and mauled forty-two of them. From there he went on to Mount Carmel, and thence back to Samaria.

Elisha and the Shunammite Woman

It happened once that Elisha went over to Shunem. There was a well-to-do woman there who pressed him to accept hospitality, and afterwards whenever he came that way, he stopped there for a meal. One day she said to her husband, 'I know that this man who comes here regularly is a holy man of God. Why not build up the wall to make him a small roof-chamber, and put in it a bed, a table, a seat, and a lamp, and let him stay there whenever he comes to us?'

One time when he arrived there and went to this roof-chamber to lie down, he said to Gehazi, his servant, 'Call this Shunammite woman.' When he called her and she appeared before the prophet, Elisha said to his servant, 'Say to her, "You have taken all this trouble for us. What can I do for you? Shall I speak for you to the king or to the commander-in-chief?"' But she replied, 'I am content where I am, among my own people.' He said, 'Then what can be done for her?' Gehazi said, 'There is only this: she has no child and her husband is old.' 'Call her back,' Elisha said. When she was called and appeared in the doorway, he said, 'In due season, this time next year, you will have a son in your arms.' But she said, 'No, no, my lord, you are a man of God and would not lie to your servant.' Next year in due season the woman conceived and bore a son, as Elisha had foretold.

When the child was old enough, he went out one day to his father among the reapers. All of a sudden he cried out to his father, 'Oh, my head, my head!' His father told a servant to carry the child to his mother, and when he was brought to her, he sat on her lap till midday, and then he died.

She went up, laid him on the bed of the man of God, shut the door, and went out. She called her husband and said, 'Send me one of the servants and a she-donkey; I must go to the man of God as fast as I can, and come straight back.' 'Why go to him today?' he asked. 'It is neither new moon nor sabbath.' 'Never mind that,' she answered. When the donkey was saddled, she said to her servant, 'Lead on and do not slacken pace unless I tell you.' So she set out and came to the man of God on Mount Carmel.

The man of God spied her in the distance and said to Gehazi, his servant, 'That is the Shunammite woman coming. Run and meet her, and ask, "Is all well with you? Is all well with your husband? Is all well with the boy?"' She answered, 'All is well.' When she reached the man of God on the hill, she clutched his feet. Gehazi came forward to push her away, but the man of God said, 'Let her alone; she is in great distress, and the Lord has concealed it from me and not told me.' 'My lord,' she said, 'did I ask for a son? Did I not beg you not to raise my hopes and then dash them?' Elisha turned to Gehazi: 'Hitch up your cloak; take my staff with you and run. If you meet anyone on the way, do not stop to greet him; if anyone greets you, do not answer. Lay my staff on the boy's face.' But the mother cried, 'As the Lord lives, your life upon it, I shall not leave you.' So he got up and followed her.

Gehazi went on ahead and laid the staff on the boy's face, but there was no sound or sign of life, so he went back to meet Elisha and told him that the boy had not stirred. When Elisha entered the house, there was the dead boy, where he had been laid on the bed. He went into the room, shut the door on the two of them, and prayed to the Lord. Then, getting on to the bed, he lay upon the child, put his mouth to the child's mouth, his eyes to his eyes, and his hands to his hands; as he crouched upon him, the child's body grew warm. Elisha got up and walked once up and down the room; getting on to the bed again, he crouched upon him and breathed into him seven times, and the boy opened his eyes. The prophet summoned Gehazi and said, 'Call the Shunammite woman.' She answered his call and the prophet said, 'Take up your child.' She came in and prostrated herself before him. Then she took up her son and went out.

The Healing of Naaman

Naaman, commander of the king of Aram's army, was a great man and highly esteemed by his master, because through him the Lord had given victory to Aram; he was a mighty warrior, but he was a leper. On one of their raids the Aramaeans brought back as a captive from the land of Israel a young girl, who became a servant to Naaman's wife. She said to her mistress, 'If only my master could meet the prophet who lives in Samaria, he would cure him of the leprosy.' Naaman went and reported to his master what the Israelite girl had said. 'Certainly you may go,' said the king of Aram, 'and I shall send a letter to the king of Israel.'

Naaman set off, taking with him ten talents of silver, six thousand shekels of gold, and ten changes of clothing. He delivered the letter to the king of Israel; it read: 'This letter is to inform you that I am sending to you my servant Naaman, and I beg you to cure him of his leprosy.' When the king of Israel read the letter, he tore his clothes and said, 'Am I God to kill and to make alive, that this fellow sends to me to cure a man of his disease? See how he picks a quarrel with me.' When Elisha, the man of God, heard how the king of Israel had torn his clothes, he sent him this message: 'Why did you tear your clothes? Let the man come to me, and he will know that there is a prophet in Israel.' When Naaman came with his horses and chariots and halted at the entrance to Elisha's house, Elisha sent out a messenger to say to him, 'If you go and wash seven times in the Jordan, your flesh will be restored and you will be clean.'

At this Naaman was furious and went away, saying, 'I thought he would at least have come out and stood and invoked the Lord his God by name, waved his hand over the place, and cured me of the leprosy. Are not Abana and Pharpar, rivers of Damascus, better than all the waters of Israel? Can I not wash in them and be clean?' So he turned and went off in a rage.

But his servants came to him and said, 'If the prophet had told you to do something difficult, would you not do it? How much more should you, then, if he says to you, "Wash and be clean"!' So he went down and dipped himself in the Jordan seven times as the man of God had told him, and his flesh was restored so that it was like a little child's, and he was clean.

Accompanied by his retinue he went back to the man of God and standing before him said, 'Now I know that there is no god anywhere in the world except in Israel. Will you accept a token of gratitude from your servant?' 'As the Lord lives, whom I serve,' said the prophet, 'I shall accept nothing.' Though pressed to accept, he refused. 'Then if you will not,' said Naaman, 'let me, sir, have two mules' load of earth, for I shall no longer offer whole-offering or sacrifice to any god but the Lord. In one matter only may the Lord pardon me: when my master goes to the temple of Rimmon to worship, leaning on my arm, and I worship in the temple of Rimmon when he worships there, for this let the Lord pardon me.' Elisha bade him go in peace.

Naaman had gone only a short distance on his way, when Gehazi, the servant of Elisha the man of God, said to himself, 'Has my master let this Aramaean, Naaman, go without accepting what he brought? As the Lord lives, I shall run after him and get something from him.' So Gehazi hurried after Naaman. When Naaman saw him running after him, he alighted from his chariot to meet him saying, 'Is anything wrong?' 'Nothing,' replied Gehazi, 'but my master sent me to say that two young men of the company of prophets from the hill-country of Ephraim have just arrived. Could you provide them with a talent of silver and two changes of clothing?' Naaman said, 'By all means; take two talents.' He pressed him to take them; then he tied up the two talents of silver in two bags, and the two changes of clothing, and gave them to two of his servants, and they walked ahead carrying them. When Gehazi came to the citadel he took them from the two servants, deposited them in the house, and dismissed the men; and they went away.

When he went in and stood before his master, Elisha said, 'Where have you been, Gehazi?' 'Nowhere,' said Gehazi. But he said to him, 'Was I not present in spirit when the man turned and got down from his chariot to meet you? Was it a time to get money and garments, olive trees and vineyards, sheep and oxen, slaves and slave-girls? Naaman's leprosy will fasten on you and on your descendants for ever.' Gehazi left Elisha's presence, his skin diseased, white as snow.

The Plundering of the Arameans

Once, when the king of Aram was at war with Israel, he held a conference with his staff at which he said, 'I mean to attack in such and such a direction.' The man of God warned the king of Israel: 'Take care to avoid this place, for the Aramaeans are going down there.' The king of Israel sent word to the place about which the man of God had given him this warning; and the king took special precautions every time he found himself near that place. The king of Aram was greatly incensed at this and, summoning his staff, he said to them, 'Tell me, which of us is for the king of Israel?' 'There is no one, my lord king,' said one of his staff; 'but Elisha, the prophet in Israel, tells the king of Israel the very words you speak in your bedchamber.' 'Go, find out where he is,' said the king, 'and I shall send and seize him.' It was reported to him that the prophet was at Dothan, and he sent a strong force there with horses and chariots. They came by night and surrounded the town.

When the attendant of the man of God rose and went out early next morning, he saw a force with horses and chariots surrounding the town. 'Oh, master,' he said, 'which way are we to turn?' Elisha answered, 'Do not be afraid, for those on our side are more than those on theirs.' He offered this prayer: 'Lord, open his eyes and let him see.' The Lord opened the young man's eyes, and he saw the hills covered with horses and chariots of fire all around Elisha. As the Aramaeans came down towards him, Elisha prayed to the Lord: 'Strike this host, I pray, with blindness'; and they were struck blind as Elisha had asked. Elisha said to them, 'You are on the wrong road; this is not the town. Follow me and I will lead you to the man you are looking for.' And he led them to Samaria.

As soon as they had entered Samaria, Elisha prayed, 'Lord, open the eyes of these men and let them see again.' He opened their eyes, and they saw that they were inside Samaria. When the king of Israel saw them, he said to Elisha, 'My father, am I to destroy them?' 'No, you must not do that,' he answered. 'Would you destroy those whom you have not taken prisoner with your own sword and bow? As for these men, provide them with food and water, and let them eat and drink and go back to their master.' So he prepared a great feast for them; they ate and drank and then were sent back to their master. From that time Aramaean raids on Israel ceased.

But later, Ben-hadad king of Aram mustered his whole army and marched to the siege of Samaria. The city was near starvation, and they were besieging it so closely that a donkey's head was sold for eighty shekels of silver, and a quarter of a kab of locust-beans for five shekels. One day, as the king of Israel was walking along the city wall, a woman called to him, 'Help, my lord king!' He said, 'If the Lord does not bring you help, where can I find help for you? From threshing-floor or from winepress? What is your trouble?' She replied, 'This woman said to me, "Give up your child for us to eat today, and we will eat mine tomorrow." So we cooked my son and ate him; but when I said to her the next day, "Now give up your child for us to eat," she had hidden him.' When he heard the woman's story, the king tore his clothes. He was walking along the wall at the time, and, when the people looked, they saw that he had sackcloth underneath, next to his skin. He said, 'The Lord do the same to me and more, if the head of Elisha son of Shaphat stays on his shoulders today.'

Elisha was sitting at home, the elders with him. The king had dispatched one of those at court, but, before the messenger arrived, Elisha said to the elders, 'See how this son of a murderer has sent to behead me! When the messenger comes, be sure to close the door and hold it fast against him. Can you not hear his master following on his heels?' While he was still speaking, the king arrived and said, 'Look at our plight! This is the Lord's doing. Why should I wait any longer for him to help us?' Elisha answered, 'Hear this word from the Lord: By this time tomorrow a shekel will buy a measure of flour or two measures of barley at the gate of Samaria.' The officer on whose arm the king leaned said to the man of God, 'Even if the Lord were to open windows in the sky, such a thing could not happen!' He answered, 'You will see it with your own eyes, but you will not eat any of it.'

At the city gate were four lepers. They said to one another, 'Why should we stay here and wait for death? If we say we will go into the city, the famine is there, and we shall die; if we stay here, we shall die. Well then, let us go to the camp of the Aramaeans and give ourselves up: if they spare us, we shall live; if they put us to death, we can but die.'

At dusk they set out for the Aramaean camp, and when they reached the outskirts, they found no one there. The Lord had caused the Aramaean army to hear a sound like that of chariots and horses and a great host, so that the word went round: 'The king of Israel has hired the kings of the Hittites and the kings of Egypt to attack us.' They had taken to flight in the dusk, abandoning their tents, horses, and donkeys. Leaving the camp as it stood, they had fled for their lives. Those lepers came to the outskirts of the camp, where they went into a tent. They ate and drank, looted silver and gold and clothing, and made off and hid them. Then they came back, went into another tent and rifled it, and made off and hid the loot.

But they said to one another, 'What we are doing is not right. This is a day of good news and we are keeping it to ourselves. If we wait till morning, we shall be held to blame. We must go now and give the news to the king's household.' So they went and called to the watch at the city gate and described how they had gone to the Aramaean camp and found not one man in it and had heard no human voice: nothing but horses and donkeys tethered, and the tents left as they were. The watch called out and announced the news to the king's household in the palace.

The king rose in the night and said to his staff, 'I shall tell you what the Aramaeans have done. They know we are starving, so they have left their camp to go and hide in the open country, expecting us to come out, and then they can take us alive and enter the city.' One of his staff said, 'Send out a party of men with some of the horses that are left; if they live, they will be as well off as all the other Israelites who are still left; if they die, they will be no worse off than all those who have already perished. Let them go and see what has happened.' They picked two mounted men, and the king dispatched them in the track of the Aramaean army with the order to go and find out what had happened. Having followed as far as the Jordan and found the whole road littered with clothing and equipment which the Aramaeans had discarded in their haste, the messengers returned and made their report to the king.

The people went out and plundered the Aramaean camp, and a measure of flour was sold for a shekel and two measures of barley for a shekel, so that the word of the Lord came true. The king had appointed the officer on whose arm he leaned to take charge of the gate, and the crowd trampled him to death there, just as the man of God had foretold when the king visited him. For when the man of God said to the king, 'By this time tomorrow a shekel will buy two measures of barley or one measure of flour at the gate of Samaria,' the officer had answered, 'Even if the Lord were to open windows in the sky, such a thing could not happen!' And the man of God had said, 'You will see it with your own eyes, but you will not eat any of it.'

16 | THE DECLINE AND FALL OF ISRAEL

The Destruction of the House of Ahab

In the twelfth year of Jehoram son of Ahab king of Israel, Ahaziah son of King Joram of Judah became king. Ahaziah was twenty-two years old when he came to the throne, and he reigned in Jerusalem for one year; his mother was Athaliah granddaughter of King Omri of Israel. He followed the practices of the house of Ahab and did what was wrong in the eyes of the Lord like the house of Ahab, for he was connected with that house by marriage. He allied himself with Jehoram son of Ahab to fight against King Hazael of Aram at Ramoth-gilead. But King Jehoram was wounded by the Aramaeans, and retired to Jezreel to recover from the wounds inflicted on him at Ramoth in battle with King Hazael. Because of Jehoram's injury Ahaziah son of Joram king of Judah went down to Jezreel to visit him.

Elisha the prophet summoned one of the company of prophets and said to him, 'Get ready for the road; take this flask of oil with you and go to Ramoth-gilead. When you arrive, look there for Jehu son of Jehoshaphat, son of Nimshi; go in and call him aside from his fellow officers, and lead him through to an inner room. Take the flask and pour the oil on his head and say, "This is the word of the Lord: I anoint you king over Israel." After that open the door and flee for your life.'

The young prophet went to Ramoth-gilead, and when he arrived, he found the officers sitting together. He said, 'Sir, I have a word for you.' 'For which of us?' asked Jehu. 'For you, sir,' he said. Jehu rose and went into the house, where the prophet poured the oil on his head, saying, 'This is the word of the Lord the God of Israel: I anoint you king over Israel, the people of the Lord. You are to strike down the house of Ahab your master, and I shall take vengeance on Jezebel for the blood of my servants the prophets and for the blood of all the Lord's servants. The entire house of Ahab will perish. Jezebel will be devoured by dogs in the plot of ground at Jezreel and no one will bury her.' With that he opened the door and fled.

When Jehu rejoined the king's officers, they said to him, 'Is all well? What did this crazy fellow want with you?' 'You know him and his ideas,' he said. 'That is no answer!' they replied. 'Tell us what happened.' 'I shall tell you exactly what he said: "This is the word of the Lord: I anoint you king over Israel."' They snatched up their cloaks and spread them under him at the top of the steps, and they sounded the trumpet and shouted, 'Jehu is king.'

Jehu son of Jehoshaphat, son of Nimshi, organized a conspiracy against Jehoram, while Jehoram and all the Israelites were defending Ramoth-gilead against King Hazael of Aram. King Jehoram had returned to Jezreel to recover from the wounds inflicted on him by the Aramaeans in his battle against Hazael. Jehu said to his colleagues, 'If you are on my side, see that no one escapes from the city to carry the news to Jezreel.' He mounted his chariot and drove to Jezreel, for Jehoram was laid up there and King Ahaziah of Judah had gone down to visit him.

The watchman standing on the watch-tower in Jezreel saw Jehu's troops approaching and called out, 'I see a troop of men.' Jehoram said, 'Fetch a horseman and send to meet them and ask if they come peaceably.' The horseman went to meet him and said, 'The king asks, "Is it peace?"' Jehu said, 'Peace? What is that to do with you? Fall in behind me.' The watchman reported, 'The messenger has met them but is not coming back.' A second horseman was sent; when he met them, he also said, 'The king asks, "Is it peace?"' 'Peace?' said Jehu. 'What is that to do with you? Fall in behind me.' The watchman reported, 'He has met them but is not coming back. The driving is like the driving of Jehu son of Nimshi, for he drives furiously.'

'Harness my chariot,' said Jehoram. When it was ready King Jehoram of Israel and King Ahaziah of Judah went out each in his own chariot to meet Jehu, and they met him by the plot of Naboth of Jezreel.

When Jehoram saw Jehu, he said, 'Is it peace, Jehu?' He replied, 'Do you call it peace while your mother Jezebel keeps up her obscene idol-worship and monstrous sorceries?' Jehoram wheeled about and fled, crying out, 'Treachery, Ahaziah!' Jehu drew his bow and shot Jehoram between the shoulders; the arrow pierced his heart and he slumped down in his chariot. Jehu said to Bidkar, his lieutenant, 'Pick him up and throw him into the plot of land belonging to Naboth of Jezreel; remember how, when you and I were riding side by side behind Ahab his father, the Lord pronounced this sentence against him: "It is the word of the Lord: as surely as I saw yesterday the blood of Naboth and the blood of his sons, I will requite you on this plot of land." Pick him up, therefore, and throw him into the plot and so fulfil the word of the Lord.' When King Ahaziah of Judah saw this he fled by the road to Beth-haggan. Jehu pursued him and said, 'Get him too.' They shot him down in his chariot on the road up the valley near Ibleam, but he escaped to Megiddo and died there. His servants conveyed his body to Jerusalem by chariot and buried him in his tomb with his forefathers in the city of David.

Then Jehu came to Jezreel. When Jezebel heard what had happened she painted her eyes and adorned her hair, and she stood looking down from a window. As Jehu entered the gate, she said, 'Is it peace, you Zimri, you murderer of your master?' He looked up at the window and said, 'Who is on my side? Who?' Two or three eunuchs looked out to him, and he said, 'Throw her down.' They threw her down, and some of her blood splashed on to the wall and the horses, which trampled her underfoot. Jehu went in and ate and drank. 'See to this accursed woman,' he said, 'and bury her; for she is a king's daughter.' But when they went to bury her they found nothing of her but the skull, the feet, and the palms of her hands. When they went back and told him, Jehu said, 'It is the word of the Lord which his servant Elijah the Tishbite spoke, when he said, "In the plot of ground at Jezreel the dogs will devour the flesh of Jezebel, and Jezebel's corpse will lie like dung on the ground in the plot at Jezreel so that no one will be able to say: This is Jezebel."'

There were seventy sons of Ahab left in Samaria. Jehu therefore sent a letter to Samaria, addressed to the rulers of the city, the elders, and the guardians of Ahab's sons, in which he wrote: 'You have in your care your master's family as well as his chariots and horses, fortified cities, and weapons; therefore, whenever this letter reaches you, choose the best and the most suitable of your master's sons, set him on his father's throne, and fight for your master's house.' They were panic-stricken and said, 'If two kings could not stand against him, what hope is there that we can?' Therefore the comptroller of the household and the governor of the city, with the elders and the children's guardians, sent this message to Jehu: 'We are your servants. Whatever you tell us we shall do; but we shall not make anyone king. Do as you think fit.'

So in a second letter to them Jehu wrote: 'If you are on my side and will obey my orders, then bring the heads of your master's sons to me at Jezreel by this time tomorrow.' The royal princes, seventy in all, were with the nobles of the city who had charge of their upbringing. When the letter arrived, they took the royal princes and killed all seventy; they piled their heads in baskets and sent the heads to Jehu in Jezreel. When the messenger came to him and reported that they had brought the heads of the royal princes, he ordered them to be piled in two heaps and left till morning at the entrance to the city gate.

In the morning Jehu went out, and standing there said to all the people, 'You are fair-minded judges. I conspired against my master and killed him, but who put all these to death? Be sure then that every word which the Lord has spoken against the house of Ahab will be fulfilled, and that the Lord has now done what he promised through his servant Elijah.' So Jehu put to death all who were left of the house of Ahab in Jezreel, as well as all Ahab's nobles, his close friends, and priests, until he had left not one survivor.

Then he set out for Samaria, and put to death all of Ahab's house who were left there and so blotted it out, in fulfilment of the word which the Lord had spoken to Elijah.

Jehu called all the people together and said to them, 'Ahab served the Baal a little; Jehu will serve him much. Now summon all the prophets of Baal, all his ministers and priests; not one must be missing. For I am holding a great sacrifice to Baal, and no one who is missing from it shall live.' In this way Jehu outwitted the ministers of Baal in order to destroy them. Jehu gave the order, 'Proclaim a sacred ceremony for Baal.' This was done, and Jehu himself sent word throughout Israel. All the ministers of Baal came; there was not a man left who did not come, and when they went into the temple of Baal, it was filled from end to end. Jehu said to the person who had charge of the wardrobe, 'Bring out robes for all the ministers of Baal'; and he brought them out. Then Jehu and Jehonadab son of Rechab went into the temple of Baal and said to the ministers, 'Look carefully and make sure that there are no servants of the Lord here with you, but only the ministers of Baal.' Then they went in to offer sacrifices and whole-offerings.

Jehu had stationed eighty of his men outside and warned them, 'I shall hold you responsible for these men, and if anyone of you lets one of them escape he will pay for it with his own life.' When he had finished offering the whole-offering, Jehu ordered the guards and officers to go in and cut them all down, and let not one of them escape. They were slain without quarter, and the guard and the officers threw them out. Then going into the keep of the temple of Baal, they brought out the sacred pole from the temple and burnt it; they overthrew the sacred pillar of the Baal and pulled down the temple itself and made a privy of it – as it is today. Thus Jehu stamped out the worship of Baal in Israel. He did not however abandon the sins of Jeroboam son of Nebat who led Israel into sin: he maintained the worship of the golden calves of Bethel and Dan.

The Lord said to Jehu, 'You have done well in carrying out what is right in my eyes, and you have done to the house of Ahab all that it was in my mind to do. Therefore your sons to the fourth generation will occupy the throne of Israel.' Jehu rested with his forefathers and was buried in Samaria. His son Jehoahaz succeeded him. Jehu had reigned over Israel in Samaria for twenty-eight years.

The End of the Kingdom of Israel

Hoshea son of Elah became king over Israel and he reigned in Samaria for nine years. He did what was wrong in the eyes of the Lord, but not as previous kings of Israel had done. King Shalmaneser of Assyria marched up against Hoshea, who had been tributary to him, but when the king of Assyria discovered that Hoshea was being disloyal to him, sending envoys to the king of Egypt at So, and withholding the annual tribute which he had been paying, the king of Assyria seized and imprisoned him. He overran the whole country and, reaching Samaria, besieged it for three years.

In the ninth year of Hoshea he captured Samaria and deported its people to Assyria, and settled them in Halah and on the Habor, the river of Gozan, and in the towns of Media.

All this came about because the Israelites had sinned against the Lord their God who brought them up from Egypt, from the despotic rule of Pharaoh king of Egypt; they paid homage to other gods and observed the laws and customs of the nations whom the Lord had dispossessed before them, and uttered blasphemies against the Lord their God.

Still the Lord solemnly charged Israel and Judah by every prophet and seer, saying, 'Give up your evil ways; keep my commandments and statutes given in all the law which I enjoined on your forefathers and delivered to you through my servants the prophets.' They would not listen, however, but were as stubborn and rebellious as their forefathers had been, for they too refused to put their trust in the Lord their God. They rejected his statutes and the covenant which he had made with their forefathers and the solemn warnings which he had given to them. Following worthless idols they became worthless themselves and imitated the nations round about them, which the Lord had forbidden them to do. Forsaking every commandment of the Lord their God, they made themselves images, two calves of cast metal, and also a sacred pole. They prostrated themselves to all the host of heaven and worshipped Baal; they made their sons and daughters pass through the fire. They practised augury and divination; they sold themselves to do what was wrong in the eyes of the Lord and so provoked his anger.

Thus it was that the Lord was incensed against Israel and banished them from his presence; only the tribe of Judah was left.

17 | THE STORY OF JONAH

Jonah Flees from the Lord

The word of the Lord came to Jonah son of Amittai: 'Go to the great city of Nineveh; go and denounce it, for I am confronted by its wickedness.' But to escape from the Lord Jonah set out for Tarshish. He went down to Joppa, where he found a ship bound for Tarshish. He paid the fare and went on board to travel with it to Tarshish out of the reach of the Lord.

The Lord let loose a hurricane on the sea, which rose so high that the ship threatened to break up in the storm. The sailors were terror-stricken; everyone cried out to his own god for help, and they threw things overboard to lighten the ship. Meanwhile Jonah, who had gone below deck, was lying there fast asleep. When the captain came upon him he said, 'What, fast asleep? Get up and call to your god! Perhaps he will spare a thought for us, and we shall not perish.'

The sailors said among themselves, 'Let us cast lots to find who is to blame for our misfortune.' They cast lots, and when Jonah was singled out they wanted to be told how he was to blame. They questioned him: 'What is your business? Where do you come from? Which is your country? What is your nationality?' 'I am a Hebrew,' he answered, 'and I worship the Lord the God of heaven, who made both sea and dry land.' At this the sailors were even more afraid. 'What is this you have done?' they said, because they knew he was trying to escape from the Lord, for he had told them. 'What must we do with you to make the sea calm for us?' they asked; for it was getting worse. 'Pick me up and throw me overboard,' he replied; 'then the sea will go down. I know it is my fault that this great storm has struck you.' Though the crew rowed hard to put back to land it was no use, for the sea was running higher and higher. At last they called to the Lord, 'Do not let us perish, Lord, for this man's life; do not hold us responsible for the death of an innocent man, for all this, Lord, is what you yourself have brought about.' Then they took Jonah and threw him overboard, and the raging of the sea subsided. Seized by a great fear of the Lord, the men offered a sacrifice and made vows to him.

The Lord ordained that a great fish should swallow Jonah, and he remained in its belly for three days and three nights. From the fish's belly Jonah offered this prayer to the Lord his God:

'In my distress I called to the Lord,
and he answered me;
from deep within Sheol I cried for help,
and you heard my voice.
You cast me into the depths,
into the heart of the ocean,
and the flood closed around me;
all your surging waves swept over me.

'The water about me rose to my neck,
for the deep was closing over me;
seaweed twined about my head
at the roots of the mountains;
I was sinking into a world
whose bars would hold me fast for ever.
But you brought me up, Lord my God, alive from the pit.'

The Lord commanded the fish, and it spewed Jonah out on the dry land.

Jonah and the Ninevites
A second time the word of the Lord came to Jonah: 'Go to the great city of Nineveh; go and denounce it in the words I give you.' Jonah obeyed and went at once to Nineveh. It was a vast city, three days' journey across, and Jonah began by going a day's journey into it. Then he proclaimed: 'In forty days Nineveh will be overthrown!'

The people of Nineveh took to heart this warning from God; they declared a public fast, and high and low alike put on sackcloth. When the news reached the king of Nineveh he rose from his throne, laid aside his robes of state, covered himself with sackcloth, and sat in ashes. He had this proclamation made in

Nineveh: 'By decree of the king and his nobles, neither man nor beast is to touch any food; neither herd nor flock may eat or drink. Every person and every animal is to be covered with sackcloth. Let all pray with fervour to God, and let them abandon their wicked ways and the injustice they practise. It may be that God will relent and turn from his fierce anger: and so we shall not perish.' When God saw what they did and how they gave up their wicked ways, he relented and did not inflict on them the punishment he had threatened.

This greatly displeased Jonah. In anger he prayed to the Lord: 'It is just as I feared, Lord, when I was still in my own country, and it was to forestall this that I tried to escape to Tarshish. I knew that you are a gracious and compassionate God, long-suffering, ever constant, always ready to relent and not inflict punishment. Now take away my life, Lord: I should be better dead than alive.'

'Are you right to be angry?' said the Lord.

Jonah went out and sat down to the east of Nineveh, where he made himself a shelter and sat in its shade, waiting to see what would happen in the city. The Lord God ordained that a climbing gourd should grow up above Jonah's head to throw its shade over him and relieve his discomfort, and he was very glad of it. But at dawn the next day God ordained that a worm should attack the gourd, and it withered; and when the sun came up God ordained that a scorching wind should blow from the east. The sun beat down on Jonah's head till he grew faint, and he prayed for death; 'I should be better dead than alive,' he said. At this God asked, 'Are you right to be angry over the gourd?' 'Yes,' Jonah replied, 'mortally angry!' But the Lord said, 'You are sorry about the gourd, though you did not have the trouble of growing it, a plant which came up one night and died the next. And should not I be sorry about the great city of Nineveh, with its hundred and twenty thousand people who cannot tell their right hand from their left, as well as cattle without number?'

18 | THE DECLINE AND FALL OF JUDAH

Queen Athaliah

The inhabitants of Jerusalem made Ahaziah king of Judah. He was twenty-two years old when he came to the throne, and he reigned in Jerusalem for one year; his mother was Athaliah granddaughter of Omri.

He did what was wrong in the eyes of the Lord in the alliance he made with Jehoram son of Ahab king of Israel, to fight against King Hazael of Aram. Jehoram was wounded by the Aramaeans, and Ahaziah went down to Jezreel to visit him. During the visit he went out with Jehoram to meet Jehu son of Nimshi, who put him to death.

As soon as Athaliah mother of Ahaziah saw that her son was dead, she set out to get rid of the whole royal line of the house of Judah. But Jehosheba the daughter of King Joram took Ahaziah's son Joash and stole him away from among the princes who were being murdered; she put him and his nurse in a bedchamber. Thus Jehosheba daughter of King Joram and wife of Jehoiada the priest, because she was Ahaziah's sister, hid Joash from Athaliah so that she did not put him to death.

He remained concealed with them in the house of God for six years, while Athaliah ruled the country.

In the seventh year Jehoiada felt himself strong enough to make an agreement with Azariah son of Jeroham, Ishmael son of Jehohanan, Azariah son of Obed, Maaseiah son of Adaiah, and Elishaphat son of Zichri, all captains of units of a hundred. They went throughout Judah and gathered to Jerusalem the Levites from all the cities of Judah and the heads of clans in Israel, and they came to Jerusalem. The whole assembly made a compact with the king in the house of God, and Jehoiada said to them, 'Here is the king's son! He will be king, as the Lord promised that David's descendants should be. This is what you must do: one third of you, priests and Levites, as you come on duty on the sabbath, are to be on guard at the threshold gates, another third are to be in the royal palace, and another third are to be at the Foundation Gate, while all the people will be in the courts of the house of the Lord. No one must enter the house of the Lord except the priests and the attendant Levites; they may enter, for they are holy, but all the people must continue to keep the Lord's charge. The Levites must mount guard round the king, each man holding his weapons, and anyone who tries to enter the house is to be put to death. They are to stay with the king wherever he goes.'

The Levites and all Judah carried out the orders of Jehoiada the priest to the letter. He stationed all the troops round the king, each man holding his weapon, from corner to corner of the house to north and south. Then they brought out the king's son, put the crown on his head, handed him the testimony, and proclaimed him king. When Jehoiada and his sons anointed him, a shout went up: 'Long live the king.'

When Athaliah heard the noise made by the people as they ran and cheered the king, she came into the house of the Lord where the people were, and found the king standing by the pillar at the entrance, amidst outbursts of song and fanfares of trumpets in his honour; all the populace were rejoicing and blowing trumpets, and singers with musical instruments were leading the celebrations. Athaliah tore her clothes and cried, 'Treason! Treason!' Jehoiada the priest gave orders to the captains in command of the troops: 'Bring her outside the precincts and put to the sword anyone in attendance on her'; for the priest said, 'Do not kill her in the house of the Lord.'

They took her and brought her to the royal palace and there at the passage to the Horse Gate they put her to death.

Hezekiah

In the third year of Hoshea son of Elah, king of Israel, Hezekiah son of King Ahaz of Judah became king. He was twenty-five years old when he came to the throne, and he reigned in Jerusalem for twenty-nine years; his mother was Abi daughter of Zechariah. He did what was right in the eyes of the Lord, as his ancestor David had done. It was he who suppressed the shrines, smashed the sacred pillars, cut down every sacred pole, and broke up the bronze serpent that Moses had made, for up to that time the Israelites had been in the habit of burning sacrifices to it; they called it Nehush-tan. He put his trust in the Lord the God of Israel; there was nobody like him among all the kings of Judah who succeeded him or among those who had gone before him. He remained loyal to the Lord and did not fail in his allegiance to him, and he kept the commandments which the Lord had given to Moses. The Lord was with him and he prospered in all that he undertook. He rebelled against the king of Assyria and was no longer subject to him; he conquered the Philistine country as far as Gaza and its boundaries, from watch-tower to fortified city.

In the fourteenth year of King Hezekiah's reign, King Sennacherib of Assyria attacked and captured all the fortified towns of Judah. Hezekiah sent a message to the king of Assyria at Lachish: 'I have done wrong; withdraw from me, and I shall pay any penalty you impose upon me.' The king of Assyria laid on Hezekiah king of Judah a penalty of three hundred talents of silver and thirty talents of gold; and Hezekiah gave him all the silver found in the house of the Lord and in the treasuries of the palace. At that time Hezekiah stripped of their gold the doors of the temple of the Lord and the door-frames which he himself had plated, and gave it to the king of Assyria.

From Lachish the king of Assyria sent the commander-in-chief, the chief eunuch, and the chief officer with a strong force to King Hezekiah at Jerusalem. They marched up and when they reached Jerusalem they halted by the conduit of the Upper Pool on the causeway leading to the Fuller's Field. When they called for the king, the comptroller of the household, Eliakim son of Hilkiah, came out to them with Shebna, the adjutant-general, and Joah son of Asaph, the secretary of state.

The chief officer said to them, 'Tell Hezekiah that this is the message of the Great King, the king of Assyria: "What ground have you for this confidence of yours? Do you think words can take the place of skill and military strength? On whom then do you rely for support in your rebellion against me? On Egypt? Egypt is a splintered cane that will run into a man's hand and pierce it if he leans on it. That is what Pharaoh king of Egypt proves to all who rely on him. And if you tell me that you are relying on the Lord your God, is he not the god whose shrines and altars Hezekiah has suppressed, telling Judah and Jerusalem they must worship at this altar in Jerusalem?"

'Now, make a deal with my master the king of Assyria: I shall give you two thousand horses if you can find riders for them. How then can you reject the authority of even the least of my master's servants and rely on Egypt for chariots and horsemen? Do you think that I have come to attack this place and destroy it without the consent of the Lord? No; the Lord himself said to me, "Go up and destroy this land."'

Eliakim son of Hilkiah, Shebna, and Joah said to the chief officer, 'Please speak to us in Aramaic, for we understand it; do not speak Hebrew to us within earshot of the people on the city wall.'

The chief officer answered, 'Is it to your master and to you that my master has sent me to say this? Is it not to the people sitting on the wall who, like you, will have to eat their own dung and drink their own urine?'

Then he stood and shouted in Hebrew, 'Hear the message of the Great King, the king of Assyria! These are the king's words: "Do not be taken in by Hezekiah. He is powerless to save you from me. Do not let him persuade you to rely on the Lord, and tell you that the Lord will surely save you and that this city will never be surrendered to the king of Assyria." Do not listen to Hezekiah, for this is what the king of Assyria says: "Make your peace with me, and surrender. Then every one of you will eat the fruit of his own vine and of his own fig tree, and drink the water of his own cistern, until I come and take you to a land like your own, a land of grain and new wine, of bread and vineyards, of olives, fine oil, and honey – life for you all, instead of death. Do not listen to Hezekiah; he will only mislead you by telling you that the Lord will save you. Did any god of the nations save his land from the king of Assyria's power? Where are the gods of Hamath and Arpad? Where are the gods of Sepharvaim, Hena, and Ivvah? Where are the gods of Samaria? Did they save Samaria from me? Among all the gods of the nations is there one who saved his land from me? So how is the Lord to save Jerusalem?"'

The people remained silent and said not a word in reply, for the king had given orders that no one was to answer him. Eliakim son of Hilkiah, comptroller of the household, Shebna the adjutant-general, and Joah son of Asaph, secretary of state, came to Hezekiah with their clothes torn and reported the words of the chief officer.

When King Hezekiah heard their report, he tore his clothes, put on sackcloth, and went into the house of the Lord. He sent Eliakim comptroller of the household, Shebna the adjutant-general, and the senior priests, all wearing sackcloth, to the prophet Isaiah son of Amoz, to give him this message from the king: 'Today is a day of trouble for us, a day of reproof and contumely. We are like a woman who has no strength to bring to birth the child she is carrying. It may be that the Lord your God will give heed to all the words of the chief officer whom his master the king of Assyria sent to taunt the living God, and will confute the words which the Lord your God heard. Offer a prayer for those who still survive.'

When King Hezekiah's servants came to Isaiah, they were given this answer for their master: 'Here is the word of the Lord: Do not be alarmed at what you heard when the Assyrian king's minions blasphemed me. I shall sap his morale till at a mere rumour he will withdraw to his own country; and there I shall make him fall by the sword.'

Meanwhile the chief officer went back, and having heard that the king of Assyria had moved camp from Lachish, he found him attacking Libnah. But when the king learnt that King Tirhakah of Cush was on the way to engage him in battle, he sent messengers again to King Hezekiah of Judah to say to him, 'How can you be deluded by your God on whom you rely when he promises that Jerusalem will not fall into the hands of the king of Assyria? You yourself must have heard what the kings of Assyria have done to all countries: they utterly destroyed them. Can you then hope to escape? Did their gods save the nations which my predecessors wiped out: Gozan, Harran, Rezeph, and the people of Eden living in Telassar? Where are the kings of Hamath, of Arpad, and of Lahir, Sepharvaim, Hena, and Ivvah?'

Hezekiah received the letter from the messengers and, having read it, he went up to the house of the Lord and spread it out before the Lord with this prayer: 'Lord God of Israel, enthroned on the cherubim, you alone are God of all the kingdoms of the world; you made heaven and earth. Incline your ear, Lord, and listen; open your eyes, Lord, and see; hear the words that Sennacherib has sent to taunt the living God. Lord, it is true that the kings of Assyria have laid waste the nations and their lands and have consigned their gods to the flames. They destroyed them, because they were no gods but the work of men's hands, mere wood and stone. Now, Lord our God, save us from his power, so that all the kingdoms of the earth may know that you alone, Lord, are God.'

Isaiah son of Amoz sent Hezekiah the following message: 'This is the word of the Lord the God of Israel: I have heard your prayer to me concerning King Sennacherib of Assyria. This will be the sign for you: this year you will eat the leavings of the grain and in the second year what is self-sown; but in the third year you will sow and reap, plant vineyards and eat their fruit. The survivors left in Judah will strike fresh root below ground and yield fruit above ground, for a remnant will come out of Jerusalem and survivors from Mount Zion. The zeal of the Lord will perform this.

'Therefore, this is the word of the Lord about the king of Assyria:

He will not enter this city
or shoot an arrow there,
he will not advance against it with shield
or cast up a siege-ramp against it.

By the way he came he will go back;
he will not enter this city.
This is the word of the Lord.

I shall shield this city to deliver it
for my own sake and for the sake of my servant David.'

That night the angel of the Lord went out and struck down a hundred and eighty-five thousand in the Assyrian camp; when morning dawned, there they all lay dead. King Sennacherib of Assyria broke camp and marched away; he went back to Nineveh and remained there. One day, while he was worshipping in the temple of his god Nisroch, Adrammelech and Sharezer his sons assassinated him and made their escape to the land of Ararat. His son Esarhaddon succeeded him.

At this time Hezekiah became mortally ill, and the prophet Isaiah son of Amoz came to him with this message from the Lord: 'Give your last instructions to your household, for you are dying;

you will not recover.' Hezekiah turned his face to the wall and offered this prayer to the Lord: 'Lord, remember how I have lived before you, faithful and loyal in your service, doing always what was pleasing to you.' And he wept bitterly. But before Isaiah had left the citadel, the word of the Lord came to him: 'Go back and say to Hezekiah, the prince of my people: This is the word of the Lord the God of your father David: I have heard your prayer and seen your tears; I shall heal you, and on the third day you will go up to the house of the Lord. I shall add fifteen years to your life and deliver you and this city from the king of Assyria. I shall protect this city for my own sake and for the sake of my servant David.'

Isaiah told them to prepare a fig-plaster; when it was made and applied to the inflammation, Hezekiah recovered. He asked Isaiah what proof there was that the Lord would cure him and that he would go up to the house of the Lord on the third day. Isaiah replied, 'This will be your proof from the Lord that he will do what he has promised; will the shadow go forward ten steps or back ten steps?' Hezekiah answered, 'It is an easy thing for the shadow to move forward ten steps; rather let it go back ten steps.' Isaiah the prophet called to the Lord, and he made the shadow go back ten steps where it had advanced down the stairway of Ahaz.

At that time the king of Babylon, Merodach-baladan son of Baladan, sent envoys with a gift to Hezekiah, for he heard that he had been ill. Hezekiah welcomed them and showed them all his treasury, the silver and gold, the spices and fragrant oil, his armoury, and everything to be found among his treasures; there was nothing in his palace or in his whole realm that Hezekiah did not show them.

The prophet Isaiah came to King Hezekiah and asked, 'What did these men say? Where did they come from?' 'They came from a distant country,' Hezekiah answered, 'from Babylon.' 'What did they see in your palace?' Isaiah demanded. 'They saw everything,' was the reply; 'there was nothing among my treasures that I did not show them.' Isaiah said to Hezekiah, 'Hear the word of the Lord: The time is coming, says the Lord, when everything in your palace, and all that your forefathers have amassed till the present day, will be carried away to Babylon; not a thing will be left. And some of your sons, your own offspring, will be taken from you to serve as eunuchs in the palace of the king of

Babylon.' Hezekiah answered, 'The word of the Lord which you have spoken is good,' for he was thinking to himself that peace and security would last out his lifetime.

The other events of Hezekiah's reign, his exploits, and how he made the pool and the conduit and brought water into the city, are recorded in the annals of the kings of Judah.

Josiah

Hezekiah rested with his forefathers, and his son Manasseh succeeded him. Manasseh was twelve years old when he came to the throne, and he reigned in Jerusalem for fifty-five years; his son Amon succeeded him. Amon was twenty-two years old when he came to the throne, and he reigned in Jerusalem for two years; his son Josiah succeeded him.

Josiah was eight years old when he came to the throne, and he reigned in Jerusalem for thirty-one years. He did what was right in the eyes of the Lord, following in the footsteps of his forefather David, and deviating neither to the right nor to the left.

In the eighth year of his reign, when he was still a youth, he began to seek guidance of the God of his forefather David; and in the twelfth year he began to purge Judah and Jerusalem of the shrines and the sacred poles, and the carved idols and the metal images. He saw to it that the altars for the baalim were destroyed and he hacked down the incense-altars which stood above them; he broke in pieces the sacred poles and the carved and metal images, grinding them to powder and scattering it on the graves of those who had sacrificed to them. He burnt the bones of the priests on their altars and purged Judah and Jerusalem. In the towns of Manasseh, Ephraim, and Simeon, and as far as Naphtali, he burnt down their houses wherever he found them; he destroyed the altars and the sacred poles, ground the idols to powder, and hacked down the incense-altars throughout the land of Israel. Then he returned to Jerusalem.

In the eighteenth year of his reign, after he had purified the land and the house of the Lord, Josiah sent Shaphan son of Azaliah and Maaseiah the governor of the city and Joah son of Joahaz the secretary of state to repair the house of the Lord his God. They came to Hilkiah the high priest and delivered to him the silver that had been brought to the house of God. When they were fetching out the silver, the priest Hilkiah discovered the scroll of the law of the Lord which had been given through Moses. Hilkiah told Shaphan the adjutant-general that he had discovered the scroll of the law in the house of the Lord; he gave the scroll to Shaphan, who brought it to the king and reported to him: 'Your servants are doing all that was entrusted to them. They have melted down the silver in the house of the Lord and have handed it over to the supervisors of the work and the workmen.'

Shaphan the adjutant-general also told the king of the scroll that the priest Hilkiah had given him; and he read from it in the king's presence. When the king heard what was written in the scroll of the law, he tore his clothes. He ordered Hilkiah, Ahikam son of Shaphan, Abdon son of Micah, Shaphan the adjutant-general, and Asaiah the king's attendant to go and seek guidance of the Lord for himself and for all who still remained in Israel and Judah, about the contents of the scroll that had been discovered. 'Great must be the wrath of the Lord,' he said, 'and it has been poured out on us, because our forefathers did not observe the Lord's command and do all that is written in this scroll.'

Hilkiah and those whom the king had instructed went to Huldah the prophetess, wife of Shallum son of Tikvah, son of Hasrah, the keeper of the wardrobe, and consulted her at her home in the Second Quarter of Jerusalem. 'This is the word of the Lord the God of Israel,' she answered: 'Tell the man who sent you to me that this is what the Lord says: I am about to bring disaster on this place and its inhabitants, fulfilling all the imprecations recorded in the scroll which was read in the presence of the king of Judah, because they have forsaken me and burnt sacrifices to other gods, provoking my anger with all the idols they have made with their own hands; for this my wrath will be poured out on this place and will not be quenched. Tell the king of Judah who sent you to seek guidance of the Lord that this is what the Lord the God of Israel says: You have listened to my words and shown a willing heart and humbled yourself before God when you heard what I said about this place and its inhabitants; you humbled yourself and tore your clothes and wept before me. Because of this, I for my part have listened to you. This is the word of the Lord. Therefore I shall gather you to your forefathers, and you will be gathered to your grave in peace; you will not live to see all the disaster which I am bringing on this place and its inhabitants.' They brought back this answer to the king.

At the king's summons all the elders of Judah and Jerusalem were assembled, and he went up to the house of the Lord, taking with him all the men of Judah, the inhabitants of Jerusalem, the priests, and the Levites, the entire population, high and low. There he read out to them the whole scroll of the covenant which had been discovered in the house of the Lord. Then, standing by the pillar, the king entered into a covenant before the Lord to obey him and keep his commandments, his testimonies, and his statutes with all his heart and soul, and so carry out the terms of the covenant written in the scroll.

Josiah kept a Passover to the Lord in Jerusalem, the Passover lamb being killed on the fourteenth day of the first month. He appointed the priests to their offices and encouraged them in the service of the house of the Lord. He said to the Levites, who instructed Israel and were dedicated to the Lord, 'Put the sacred Ark in the house which Solomon son of David king of Israel built. As it is not to be carried about on your shoulders, you are now to serve the Lord your God and his people Israel: prepare yourselves by families according to your divisions, following the written instructions of David king of Israel and those of Solomon his son.'

The people of Israel who were present kept the Passover at that time and the pilgrim-feast of Unleavened Bread for seven days. No Passover like it had been kept in Israel since the days of the prophet Samuel; none of the kings of Israel had ever kept such a Passover as Josiah kept, with the priests and Levites and all Judah and Israel who were present and the inhabitants of Jerusalem. This Passover was kept in the eighteenth year of Josiah's reign.

Some time after Josiah had thus organized the entire service of the house of the Lord, King Necho marched up from Egypt to attack Carchemish on the Euphrates; Josiah went out to confront him.

Necho sent envoys, saying, 'King of Judah, what do you want with me? I have no quarrel with you today, only with those with whom I am at war. God has purposed, to speed me on my way, and God is on my side. Do not stand in his way, or he will destroy you.' Josiah would not be deflected from his purpose but determined to fight; he refused to listen to Necho's words spoken at God's command, and he sallied out to join battle in the vale of Megiddo. The archers shot at him; he was severely wounded and told his bodyguard to take him away. They lifted him out of his chariot and conveyed him in his viceroy's chariot to Jerusalem. There he died and was buried among the tombs of his ancestors, and all Judah and Jerusalem mourned for him.

The End of the Kingdom of Judah

The people of the land took Josiah's son Jehoahaz and made him king at Jerusalem in place of his father. He was twenty-three years old when he came to the throne, and he reigned in Jerusalem for three months. Then Necho king of Egypt removed him from the throne in Jerusalem and imposed on the land an indemnity of a hundred talents of silver and one talent of gold. He made Jehoahaz's brother Eliakim king over Judah and Jerusalem in his place, and changed his name to Jehoiakim. He carried away his brother Jehoahaz to Egypt.

Jehoiakim was twenty-five years old when he came to the throne, and he reigned in Jerusalem for eleven years. He did what was wrong in the eyes of the Lord his God. King Nebuchadnezzar of Babylon launched an attack against him, put him in bronze fetters, and took him to Babylon. His son Jehoiachin succeeded him.

Jehoiachin was eight years old when he came to the throne, and he reigned in Jerusalem for three months and ten days. He did what was wrong in the eyes of the Lord. At the turn of the year King Nebuchadnezzar sent and brought him to Babylon, together with the choicest vessels of the house of the Lord, and made his father's brother Zedekiah king over Judah and Jerusalem.

Zedekiah was twenty-one years old when he came to the throne, and he reigned in Jerusalem for eleven years. He did what was wrong in the eyes of the Lord his God; he did not defer to the guidance of the prophet Jeremiah, the spokesman of the Lord. He also rebelled against King Nebuchadnezzar, who had laid on him a solemn oath of allegiance. He was stubborn and obstinate and refused to return to the Lord the God of Israel. All the chiefs of Judah and the priests and the people became more and more unfaithful, following all the abominable practices of the other nations; and they defiled the house of the Lord which he had hallowed in Jerusalem.

The Lord God of their forefathers had warned them time and again through his messengers, for he took pity on his people and on his dwelling-place; but they never ceased to deride his messengers, scorn his words, and scoff at his prophets, until the anger of the Lord burst out against his people and could not be appeased. He brought against them the king of the Chaldaeans, who put their young men to the sword in the sanctuary and spared neither young man nor maiden, neither the old nor the weak; God gave them all into his power.

Nebuchadnezzar took all the vessels of the house of God, great and small, and the treasures of the house of the Lord and of the king and his officers – all these he took to Babylon. They set fire to the house of God, razed to the ground the city wall of Jerusalem, and burnt down all its stately mansions and all the cherished possessions in them until everything was destroyed. Those who escaped the sword he carried captive to Babylon, and they became slaves to him and his sons until the sovereignty passed to the Persians, while the land of Israel ran the full term of its sabbaths. All the time that it lay desolate it kept the sabbath rest, to complete seventy years in fulfilment of the word of the Lord by the prophet Jeremiah.

19 | THE STORY OF DANIEL

Daniel in Babylon

In the third year of the reign of King Jehoiakim of Judah, Nebuchadnezzar, the Babylonian king, came and laid siege to Jerusalem. The Lord handed King Jehoiakim over to him, together with all that was left of the vessels from the house of God; and he carried them off to the land of Shinar, to the temple of his god, where he placed the vessels in the temple treasury.

The king ordered Ashpenaz, his chief eunuch, to bring into the palace some of the Israelite exiles, members of their royal house and of the nobility. They were to be young men free from physical defect, handsome in appearance, at home in all branches of knowledge, well-informed, intelligent, and so fitted for service in the royal court; and he was to instruct them in the writings and language of the Chaldaeans. The king assigned them a daily allowance of fine food and wine from the royal table, and their training was to last for three years; at the end of that time they would enter his service. Among them were certain Jews: Daniel, Hananiah, Mishael, and Azariah. To them the master of the eunuchs gave new names: Daniel he called Belteshazzar, Hananiah Shadrach, Mishael Meshach, and Azariah Abed-nego.

Daniel determined not to become contaminated with the food and wine from the royal table, and begged the master of the eunuchs to excuse him from touching it. God caused the master to look on Daniel with kindness and goodwill, and to Daniel's request he replied, 'I am afraid of my lord the king: he has assigned you food and drink, and if he were to see you and your companions looking miserable compared with the other young men of your own age, my head would be forfeit.' Then Daniel said to the attendant whom the master of the eunuchs had put in charge of Hananiah, Mishael, Azariah, and himself, 'Submit us to this test for ten days: give us only vegetables to eat and water to drink; then compare our appearance with that of the young men who have lived on the king's food, and be guided in your treatment of us by what you see for yourself.' He agreed to the proposal and submitted them to this test. At the end of the ten days they looked healthier and better nourished than any of the young men who had lived on the food from the king. So the attendant took away the food assigned to them and the wine they were to drink, and gave them vegetables only.

To all four of these young men God gave knowledge, understanding of books, and learning of every kind, and Daniel had a gift for interpreting visions and dreams of every kind. At the time appointed by the king for introducing the young men to court, the master of the eunuchs brought them into the presence of Nebuchadnezzar. The king talked with them all, but found none of them to compare with Daniel, Hananiah, Mishael, and Azariah; so they entered the royal service.

Whenever the king consulted them on any matter calling for insight and judgement, he found them ten times superior to all the magicians and exorcists in his whole kingdom.

Daniel remained there until the accession of King Cyrus.

Nebuchadnezzar's Dream
In the second year of his reign Nebuchadnezzar was troubled by dreams he had, so much so that he could not sleep. He gave orders for the magicians, exorcists, sorcerers, and Chaldaeans to be summoned to expound to him what he had been dreaming. When they presented themselves before the king, he said to them, 'I have had a dream, and my mind has been troubled to know what the dream was.' The Chaldaeans, speaking in Aramaic, said, 'Long live the king! Relate the dream to us, your servants, and we shall give you the interpretation.' The king answered, 'This is my firm decision: if you do not make both dream and interpretation known to me, you will be hacked limb from limb and your houses will be reduced to rubble. But if you tell me the dream and its interpretation, you will be richly rewarded by me and loaded with honours. Tell me, then, the dream and its interpretation.' They said again, 'Let the king relate the dream to his servants, and we shall tell him the interpretation.' The king rejoined, 'It is clear to me that you are trying to gain time, because you see that I have come to this firm decision: if you do not make the dream known to me, there is but one verdict for you, and one only. What is

more, you have conspired to tell me mischievous lies to my face in the hope that with time things may alter. Relate the dream to me, therefore, and then I shall know that you can give me its interpretation.' The Chaldaeans answered, 'No one on earth can tell your majesty what you wish to know. No king, however great and powerful, has ever made such a demand of a magician, exorcist, or Chaldaean. What your majesty asks is too hard; none but the gods can tell you, and they dwell remote from mortals.' At this the king became furious, and in great rage he ordered all the wise men of Babylon to be put to death.

A decree was issued for the execution of the wise men, and search was made for Daniel and his companions.

As Arioch, captain of the royal bodyguard, set out to execute the wise men of Babylon, Daniel made a discreet and tactful approach to him. He said, 'May I ask you, sir, as the king's representative, why his majesty has issued so peremptory a decree?' Arioch explained the matter, and Daniel went to the king and begged to be allowed a certain time by which he would give the king the interpretation. He then went home and made the matter known to Hananiah, Mishael, and Azariah, his companions, saying they should implore the God of heaven to disclose this secret in his mercy, so that they should not be put to death along with the rest of the wise men of Babylon.

The secret was then revealed to Daniel in a vision by night, and he blessed the God of heaven in these words: 'Blessed be God's name from age to age, for to him belong wisdom and power.'

Daniel therefore went to Arioch, whom the king had charged with the execution of the wise men of Babylon. He approached him and said, 'Do not put the wise men to death; bring me before the king and I shall tell him the interpretation of his dream.' Greatly agitated, Arioch brought Daniel before the king. 'I have found among the Jewish exiles', he said, 'a man who will make known to your majesty the interpretation of your dream.' The king asked Daniel (who was also called Belteshazzar), 'Are you able to make known to me what I saw in my dream and to interpret it?'

Daniel answered: 'No wise man, exorcist, magician, or diviner can tell your majesty the secret about which you ask. But there is in heaven a God who reveals secrets, and he has made known to King Nebuchadnezzar what is to be at the end of this age. This is the dream and these are the visions that came into your head: the thoughts that came to you, your majesty, as you lay on your bed, concerned the future, and he who reveals secrets has made known to you what is to be. This secret has been revealed to me, not because I am wiser than anyone alive, but in order that your majesty may know the interpretation and understand the thoughts which have entered your mind.

'As you watched, there appeared to your majesty a great image. Huge and dazzling, it stood before you, fearsome to behold. The head of the image was of fine gold, its chest and arms of silver, its belly and thighs of bronze, its legs of iron, its feet part iron and part clay. While you watched, you saw a stone hewn from a mountain by no human hand; it struck the image on its feet of iron and clay and shattered them. Then the iron, the clay, the bronze, the silver, and the gold were all shattered into fragments, and as if they were chaff from a summer threshing-floor the wind swept them away until no trace of them remained. But the stone which struck the image grew and became a huge mountain and filled the whole earth.

'That was the dream; now we shall relate to your majesty its interpretation. Your majesty, the king of kings, to whom the God of heaven has given the kingdom with its power, its might, and its honour, in whose hands he has placed mankind wherever they live, the wild animals, and the birds of the air, granting you sovereignty over them all: you yourself are that head of gold. After you there will arise another kingdom, inferior to yours, then a third kingdom, of bronze, which will have sovereignty over the whole world. There will be a fourth kingdom, strong as iron; just as iron shatters and breaks all things, it will shatter and crush all the others. As in your vision the feet and toes were part potter's clay and part iron, so it will be a divided kingdom, and just as you saw iron mixed with clay from the ground, so it will have in it something of the strength of iron. The toes being part iron and part clay means that the kingdom will be partly strong and partly brittle. As in your vision the iron was mixed with the clay, so there will be a mixing of families by intermarriage, but such alliances will not be stable: iron does not mix with clay. In the times of those kings the God of heaven will establish a kingdom which will never be destroyed, nor will it ever pass to another people; it will shatter all these kingdoms and make an end of them, while it will itself endure for ever. This is the meaning of your vision of the stone being hewn from a mountain by no human hand, and then shattering the iron, the bronze, the clay, the silver, and the gold. A mighty God has made known to your majesty what is to be hereafter. The dream and its interpretation are true and trustworthy.'

At this King Nebuchadnezzar prostrated himself and did homage to Daniel, and he gave orders that there should be presented to him a tribute of grain and soothing offerings. 'Truly,' he said, 'your God is indeed God of gods and Lord over kings, and a revealer of secrets, since you have been able to reveal this secret.' The king then promoted Daniel to high position and bestowed on him many rich gifts. He gave him authority over the whole province of Babylon and put him in charge of all Babylon's wise men. At Daniel's request the king appointed Shadrach, Meshach, and Abed-nego to administer the province of Babylon, while Daniel himself remained at court.

The Blazing Furnace
King Nebuchadnezzar made a gold image, ninety feet high and nine feet broad, and had it set up on the plain of Dura in the province of Babylon. The king then summoned the satraps, prefects, governors, counsellors, treasurers, judges, magistrates, and all the provincial officials to assemble and attend the dedication of the image he had set up. The satraps, prefects, governors, counsellors, treasurers, judges, magistrates, and all governors of provinces assembled for the dedication of the image King Nebuchadnezzar had set up, and they took their places in front of the image. A herald proclaimed in a loud voice, 'Peoples and nations of every language, you are commanded, when you hear the sound of horn, pipe, zither, triangle, dulcimer, a full consort of music, to prostrate yourselves and worship the gold image which King Nebuchadnezzar has set up. Whosoever does not prostrate himself and worship will be thrown forthwith into a blazing furnace.' Accordingly, no sooner did the sound of horn, pipe, zither, triangle, dulcimer, a full consort of music, reach them than all the peoples and nations of every language prostrated themselves and worshipped the gold image set up by King Nebuchadnezzar.

Some Chaldaeans seized the opportunity to approach the king with a malicious accusation against the Jews. They said, 'Long live the king! Your majesty has issued a decree that everyone who hears the sound of horn, pipe, zither, triangle, dulcimer, a full consort of music, must fall down and worship the gold image; and whoever does not do so will be thrown into a blazing furnace. There are certain Jews whom you have put in charge of the administration of the province of Babylon. These men, Shadrach, Meshach, and Abed-nego, have disregarded your royal command; they do not serve your gods, nor do they worship the gold image you set up.' In furious rage Nebuchadnezzar ordered Shadrach, Meshach, and Abed-nego to be fetched, and when they were brought into his presence, he asked them, 'Is it true, Shadrach, Meshach, and Abed-nego, that you do not serve my gods or worship the gold image which I have set up? Now if you are ready to prostrate yourselves as soon as you hear the sound of horn, pipe, zither, triangle, dulcimer, a full consort of music, and to worship the image that I have made, well and good. But if you do not worship it, you will be thrown forthwith into the blazing furnace; and what god is there that can deliver you from my power?' Their reply to the king was: 'Your majesty, we have no need to answer you on this matter. If there is a god who is able to save us from the blazing furnace, it is our God whom we serve; he will deliver us from your majesty's power. But if not, be it known to your majesty that we shall neither serve your gods nor worship the gold image you have set up.'

At this Nebuchadnezzar was furious with them, and his face became distorted with anger. He ordered that the furnace should be heated to seven times its usual heat, and commanded some of the strongest men in his army to bind Shadrach, Meshach, and Abed-nego and throw them into the blazing furnace. Then, just as they were, in trousers, shirts, headdresses, and their other clothes, they were bound and thrown into the furnace. Because the king's order was peremptory and the furnace exceedingly hot, those who were carrying the three men were killed by the flames; and Shadrach, Meshach, and Abed-nego fell bound into the blazing furnace.

Then King Nebuchadnezzar, greatly agitated, sprang to his feet, saying to his courtiers, 'Was it not three men whom we threw bound into the fire?' They answered, 'Yes, certainly, your majesty.' 'Yet', he insisted, 'I can see four men walking about in the fire, free and unharmed; and the fourth looks like a god.'

Nebuchadnezzar approached the furnace door and called, 'Shadrach, Meshach, and Abed-nego, servants of the Most High God, come out!' When Shadrach, Meshach, and Abed-nego emerged from the fire, the satraps, prefects, governors, and the king's courtiers gathered round them and saw how the fire had had no power to harm their bodies. The hair of their heads had not been singed, their trousers were untouched, and no smell of fire lingered about them.

Nebuchadnezzar declared: 'Blessed be the God of Shadrach, Meshach, and Abed-nego! He has sent his angel to save his servants who, trusting in him, disobeyed the royal command; they were willing to submit themselves to the fire rather than to serve or worship any god other than their own God. I therefore issue this decree: anyone, whatever his people, nation, or language, if he speaks blasphemy against the God of Shadrach, Meshach, and Abed-nego, is to be hacked limb from limb and his house is to be reduced to rubble; for there is no other god who can save in such a manner.'

Then the king advanced the fortunes of Shadrach, Meshach, and Abed-nego in the province of Babylon.

Nebuchadnezzar's Madness

King Nebuchadnezzar to all peoples and nations of every language throughout the whole world: May your prosperity increase! It is my pleasure to recount the signs and wonders which the Most High God has worked for me:

How great are his signs,
how mighty his wonders!
His kingdom is an everlasting kingdom,
his sovereignty endures through all generations.

I, Nebuchadnezzar, was living contentedly at home in the luxury of my palace, but as I lay on my bed, I had a dream which filled me with fear, and the fantasies and visions which came into my head caused me dismay. I issued an order summoning to my presence all the wise men of Babylon to make known to me the interpretation of the dream. When the magicians, exorcists, Chaldaeans, and diviners came in, I related my dream to them, but they were unable to interpret it for me. Finally there came before me Daniel, who is called Belteshazzar after the name of my god, a man in whom resides the spirit of the holy gods. To him also I related the dream: 'Belteshazzar, chief of the magicians, you have in you, as I know, the spirit of the holy gods, and no secret baffles you; listen to what I saw in my dream, and tell me its interpretation.

'This is the vision which came to me while I lay on my bed:

'As I was looking,
there appeared a very lofty tree at the centre of the earth;
the tree grew great and became strong;
its top reached to the sky,
and it was visible to earth's farthest bounds.
Its foliage was beautiful
and its fruit abundant,
and it yielded food for all.
Beneath it the wild beasts found shelter,
the birds lodged in the branches,
and from it all living creatures fed.

'This is what I saw in the vision which came to me while I lay on my bed:

'There appeared a watcher,
a holy one coming down from heaven.
In a mighty voice he cried,
"Hew down the tree, lop off the branches,
strip away its foliage and scatter the fruit;
let the wild beasts flee from beneath it
and the birds from its branches;
but leave the stump with its roots in the ground.

'"So, bound with iron and bronze among the lush grass,
let him be drenched with the dew of heaven
and share the lot of the beasts in their pasture –
his mind will cease to be human,
and he will be given the mind of a beast.
Seven times will pass over him.
The issue has been determined by the watchers
and the sentence pronounced by the holy ones.

'"Thereby the living will know that the Most High is sovereign in the kingdom of men: he gives the kingdom to whom he wills, and may appoint over it the lowliest of mankind."

'This is the dream which I, King Nebuchadnezzar, dreamt; now, Belteshazzar, tell me its interpretation, for, though not one of the wise men in all my kingdom is able to make its meaning known to me, you can do it, because in you is the spirit of the holy gods.'

Daniel, who was called Belteshazzar, was dumbfounded for a moment, dismayed by his thoughts; but the king said, 'Do not let the dream and its interpretation dismay you.' Belteshazzar answered, 'My lord, if only the dream applied to those who hate you and its interpretation to your enemies! The tree which you saw grow great and become strong, reaching with its top to the sky and visible to earth's farthest bounds, its foliage beautiful and its fruit abundant, a tree which yielded food for all, beneath which the wild beasts dwelt and in whose branches the birds lodged: that tree, your majesty, is you. You have become great and strong; your power has grown and reaches the sky; your sovereignty extends to the ends of the earth. Also, your majesty, you saw a watcher, a holy one, coming down from heaven and saying, "Hew down the tree and destroy it, but leave the stump with its roots in the ground. So, bound with iron and bronze among the lush grass, let him be drenched with the dew of heaven and share the lot of the beasts until seven times pass over him."

'This is the interpretation, your majesty: it is a decree of the Most High which affects my lord the king. You will be banished from human society; you will be made to live with the wild beasts; like oxen you will feed on grass, and you will be drenched with the dew of heaven. Seven times will pass over you until you have acknowledged that the Most High is sovereign over the realm of humanity and gives it to whom he wills. As the command was given to leave the stump of the tree with its roots, by this you may know that from the time you acknowledge the sovereignty of Heaven your rule will endure. Your majesty, be advised by me: let charitable deeds replace your sins, generosity to the poor your wrongdoing. It may be that you will long enjoy contentment.'

All this befell King Nebuchadnezzar. At the end of twelve months the king was walking on the roof of the royal palace at

Babylon, and he exclaimed, 'Is not this Babylon the great which I have built as a royal residence by my mighty power and for the honour of my own majesty?' The words were still on his lips, when there came a voice from heaven: 'To you, King Nebuchadnezzar, the word is spoken: the kingdom has passed from you. You are banished from human society; you are to live with the wild beasts and feed on grass like oxen. Seven times will pass over you until you have acknowledged that the Most High is sovereign over the realm of humanity and gives it to whom he will.' At that very moment this judgement came upon Nebuchadnezzar: he was banished from human society to eat grass like oxen, and his body was drenched with the dew of heaven, until his hair became shaggy like an eagle and his nails grew like birds' claws.

At the end of the appointed time, I, Nebuchadnezzar, looked up towards heaven and I was restored to my right mind. I blessed the Most High, praising and glorifying the Ever-living One:

> His sovereignty is everlasting
> and his kingdom endures through all generations.
> All who dwell on earth count for nothing;
> he does as he pleases with the host of heaven
> and with those who dwell on earth.
> No one can oppose his power
> or question what he does.

At that very time I was restored to my right mind and, for the glory of my kingdom, my majesty and royal splendour returned to me. My courtiers and my nobles sought audience of me, and I was re-established in my kingdom and my power was greatly increased. Now I, Nebuchadnezzar, praise and exalt and glorify the King of heaven; for all his acts are right and his ways are just, and he can bring low those whose conduct is arrogant.

The Writing on the Wall

King Belshazzar gave a grand banquet for a thousand of his nobles and he was drinking wine in their presence. Under the influence of the wine, Belshazzar gave orders for the vessels of gold and silver which his father Nebuchadnezzar had taken from the temple at Jerusalem to be fetched, so that he and his nobles, along with his concubines and courtesans, might drink from them. So those vessels belonging to the house of God, the temple at Jerusalem, were brought, and the king, the nobles, and the concubines and courtesans drank from them. They drank their wine and they praised their gods of gold, silver, bronze, iron, wood, and stone.

Suddenly there appeared the fingers of a human hand writing on the plaster of the palace wall opposite the lamp, and the king saw the palm of the hand as it wrote. At this the king turned pale; dismay filled his mind, the strength went from his legs, and his knees knocked together. He called in a loud voice for the exorcists, Chaldaeans, and diviners to be brought in; then, addressing Babylon's wise men, he said, 'Whoever reads this writing and tells me its interpretation shall be robed in purple and have a gold chain hung round his neck, and he shall rank third in the kingdom.'

All the king's wise men came, but they could neither read the writing nor make known to the king its interpretation. Then his deep dismay drove all colour from King Belshazzar's cheeks, and his nobles were in a state of confusion.

Drawn by what the king and his nobles were saying, the queen entered the banqueting hall: 'Long live the king!' she said. 'Why this dismay, and why do you look so pale? There is a man in your kingdom who has the spirit of the holy gods in him; he was known in your father's time to possess clear insight and godlike wisdom, so that King Nebuchadnezzar, your father, appointed him chief of the magicians, exorcists, Chaldaeans, and diviners. This Daniel, whom the king named Belteshazzar, is known to have exceptional ability, with knowledge and insight, and the gift of interpreting dreams, explaining riddles, and unravelling problems; let him be summoned now and he will give the interpretation.'

Daniel was then brought into the royal presence, and the king addressed him: 'So you are Daniel, one of the Jewish exiles whom my royal father brought from Judah. I am informed that the spirit of the gods resides in you and that you are known as a man of clear insight and exceptional wisdom. The wise men, the exorcists, have just been brought before me to read this writing and make known its interpretation to me, but they have been unable to give its meaning. I am told that you are able to furnish interpretations and unravel problems. Now, if you can read the writing and make known the interpretation, you shall be robed in purple and have a gold chain hung round your neck, and you shall rank third in the kingdom.' Daniel replied, 'Your majesty, I do not look for gifts from you; give your rewards to another. Nevertheless I shall read your majesty the writing and make known to you its interpretation.

'My lord king, the Most High God gave a kingdom with power, glory, and majesty to your father Nebuchadnezzar; and, because of the power he bestowed on him, all peoples and nations of every language trembled with fear before him. He put to death whom he would and spared whom he would, he promoted them at will and at will abased them. But, when he became haughty and stubborn and presumptuous, he was deposed from his royal throne and stripped of his glory. He was banished from human society, and his mind became like that of an animal; he had to live with the wild asses and to feed on grass like oxen, and his body was drenched with the dew of heaven, until he came to acknowledge that the Most High God is sovereign over the realm of humanity and appoints over it whom he will. But although you knew all this, you, his son Belshazzar, did not humble your heart. You have set yourself up against the Lord of heaven; his temple vessels have been fetched for you and your nobles, your concubines and courtesans to drink from them. You have praised gods fashioned from silver, gold, bronze, iron, wood, and stone, which cannot see or hear or know, and you have not given glory to God, from whom comes your every breath, and in whose charge are all your ways. That is why he sent the hand and why it wrote this inscription.

'The words inscribed were: "*Mene mene tekel u-pharsin.*" Their interpretation is this: mene, God has numbered the days of your kingdom and brought it to an end; tekel, you have been weighed in the balance and found wanting; u-pharsin, your kingdom has been divided and given to the Medes and Persians.' Then at Belshazzar's command Daniel was robed in purple and a gold chain was hung round his neck, and proclamation was made that he should rank third in the kingdom.

That very night Belshazzar king of the Chaldaeans was slain, and Darius the Mede took the kingdom, being then about sixty-two years old.

Daniel in the Lion Pit

It pleased Darius to appoint a hundred and twenty satraps to be in charge throughout his kingdom, and over them three chief ministers, to whom the satraps were to submit their reports so that the king's interests might not suffer; of these three ministers, Daniel was one. Daniel outshone the other ministers and the satraps because of his exceptional ability, and it was the king's intention to appoint him over the whole kingdom. Then the ministers and satraps began to look round for some pretext to attack Daniel's administration of the kingdom, but they failed to find any malpractice on his part, for he was faithful to his trust. Since they could discover neither negligence nor malpractice, they said, 'We shall not find any ground for bringing a charge against this Daniel unless it is connected with his religion.' These ministers and satraps, having watched for an opportunity to approach the king, said to him, 'Long live King Darius! We, the ministers of the kingdom, prefects, satraps, courtiers, and governors, have taken counsel and all are agreed that the king should issue a decree and bring into force a binding edict to the effect that whoever presents a petition to any god or human being other than the king during the next thirty days is to be thrown into the lion-pit. Now let your majesty issue the edict and have it put in writing so that it becomes unalterable, for the law of the Medes and Persians may never be revoked.' Accordingly the edict was signed by King Darius.

When Daniel learnt that this decree had been issued, he went into his house. It had in the roof-chamber windows open towards Jerusalem; and there he knelt down three times a day and offered prayers and praises to his God as was his custom. His enemies, on the watch for an opportunity to catch him, found Daniel at his prayers making supplication to his God. They then went into the king's presence and reminded him of the edict. 'Your majesty,' they said, 'have you not issued an edict that any person who, within the next thirty days, presents a petition to any god or human being other than your majesty is to be thrown into the lion-pit?' The king answered, 'The matter has been determined in accordance with the law of the Medes and Persians, which may not be revoked.' So they said to the king, 'Daniel, one of the Jewish exiles, has disregarded both your majesty and the edict, and is making petition to his God three times a day.' When the king heard this, he was greatly distressed; he tried to think of a way to save Daniel, and continued his efforts till sunset.

The men watched for an opportunity to approach the king, and said to him, 'Your majesty must know that by the law of the Medes and Persians no edict or decree issued by the king may be altered.' Then the king gave the order for Daniel to be brought and thrown into the lion-pit; but he said to Daniel, 'Your God whom you serve at all times, may he save you.' A stone was brought and put over the mouth of the pit, and the king sealed it with his signet and with the signets of his nobles, so that no attempt could be made to rescue Daniel.

The king went to his palace and spent the night fasting; no woman was brought to him, and sleep eluded him. He was greatly agitated and, at the first light of dawn, he rose and went to the lion-pit. When he came near he called anxiously, 'Daniel, servant of the living God, has your God whom you serve continually been able to save you from the lions?' Daniel answered, 'Long live the king! My God sent his angel to shut the lions' mouths and they have not injured me; he judged me innocent, and moreover I had done your majesty no injury.' The king was overjoyed and gave orders that Daniel should be taken up out of the pit. When this was done no trace of injury was found on him, because he had put his faith in his God. By order of the king those who out of malice had accused Daniel were brought and flung into the lion-pit along with their children and their wives, and before they reached the bottom the lions were upon them and devoured them, bones and all.

King Darius wrote to all peoples and nations of every language throughout the whole world: 'May your prosperity increase! I have issue a decree that in all my royal domains everyone is to fear and reverence the God of Daniel,

> 'for he is the living God, the everlasting,
> whose kingly power will never be destroyed;
> whose sovereignty will have no end –
> a saviour, a deliverer, a worker of signs and wonders
> in heaven and on earth,
> who has delivered Daniel from the power of the lions.'

Prosperity attended Daniel during the reigns of Darius and Cyrus the Persian.

20 | THE STORY OF ESTHER

The Orphan Queen
The events here related happened in the days of Ahasuerus, that
Ahasuerus who ruled from India to Ethiopia, a hundred and
twenty-seven provinces, at the time when he was settled on the
royal throne in Susa, the capital city. In the third year of his reign
he gave a banquet for all his officers and his courtiers; the
Persians and Medes in full force, along with his nobles and
provincial rulers, were in attendance. He put on display for many
days, a hundred and eighty in all, the dazzling wealth of his kingdom and the pomp and splendour of his realm. At the end of that
time the king gave a banquet for all the people present in Susa the
capital city, both high and low; it lasted for seven days and was
held in the garden court of the royal pavilion. There were white
curtains and violet hangings fastened to silver rings by cords of
fine linen with purple thread; the pillars were of marble, and gold
and silver couches were placed on a mosaic pavement of mala-
chite, marble, mother-of-pearl, and turquoise. Wine was served
in golden goblets, each of a different design: the king's wine
flowed in royal style, and the drinking was according to no fixed
rule, for the king had laid down that all the palace stewards
should respect the wishes of each guest. Queen Vashti too gave
a banquet for the women inside the royal palace of King
Ahasuerus.

On the seventh day, when he was merry with wine, the king
ordered Mehuman, Biztha, Harbona, Bigtha, Abagtha, Zethar, and
Carcas, the seven eunuchs who were in attendance on the king's
person, to bring Queen Vashti into his presence wearing her royal
diadem, in order to display her beauty to the people and to the
officers; for she was indeed a beautiful woman. But when the royal
command was conveyed to her by the eunuchs, Queen Vashti
refused to come. This greatly incensed the king, and his wrath
flared up. He conferred with wise men versed in precedents, for it

was his custom to consult all who were expert in law and usage. Those closest to the king were Carshena, Shethar, Admatha, Tarshish, Meres, Marsena, and Memucan, the seven vicegerents of Persia and Media; they had access to the king and occupied the premier positions in the kingdom.

'What', he asked, 'does the law require to be done with Queen Vashti for disobeying my royal command conveyed to her by the eunuchs?'

In the presence of the king and the vicegerents, Memucan declared: 'Queen Vashti has done wrong, not to the king alone, but also to all the officers and to all the peoples in every province of King Ahasuerus. The queen's conduct will come to the ears of all women and embolden them to treat their husbands with disrespect; they will say, "King Ahasuerus ordered Queen Vashti to be brought before him, but she would not come!" The great ladies of Persia and Media, who have heard what the queen has said, will quote this day to all the king's officers, and there will be no end to the disrespect and discord!

'If it please your majesty, let a royal decree be issued by you, and let it be inscribed among the laws of the Persians and Medes, never to be revoked, that Vashti shall not again appear before King Ahasuerus; and let your majesty give her place as queen to another who is more worthy of it than she. When the edict made by the king is proclaimed throughout the length and breadth of the kingdom, all women, high and low alike, will give honour to their husbands.'

The advice pleased the king and the vicegerents, and the king did as Memucan had proposed. Dispatches were sent to all the king's provinces, to every province in its own script and to every people in their own language, in order that each man, whatever language he spoke, should be master in his own house.

Some time later, when the anger of King Ahasuerus had died down, he called Vashti to mind, remembering what she had done and what had been decreed against her. The king's attendants said: 'Let there be sought out for your majesty beautiful young virgins; let your majesty appoint commissioners in every province of your kingdom to assemble all these beautiful young virgins and bring them to the women's quarters in the capital Susa. Have them placed under the care of Hegai, the king's eunuch who has charge of the women, and let him provide the cosmetics they need. The girl who is most acceptable to the king shall become queen in place of Vashti.' The advice pleased the king, and he acted on it.

In Susa the capital there lived a Jew named Mordecai son of Jair, son of Shimei, son of Kish, a Benjamite; he had been taken into exile from Jerusalem among those whom King Nebuchadnezzar of Babylon had carried away with King Jeconiah of Judah. He had a foster-child Hadassah, that is, Esther, his uncle's daughter, who had neither father nor mother. She was a beautiful and charming girl, and after the death of her parents, Mordecai had adopted her as his own daughter.

When the king's order and decree were proclaimed and many girls were brought to Susa the capital to be committed to the care of Hegai, who had charge of the women, Esther too was taken to the palace to be entrusted to him. He found her pleasing, and she received his special favour: he promptly supplied her with her cosmetics and her allowance of food, and also with seven specially chosen maids from the king's palace. She and her maids were marked out for favourable treatment in the women's quarters.

Esther had not disclosed her race or family, because Mordecai had forbidden her to do so. Every day Mordecai would walk past the forecourt of the women's quarters to learn how Esther fared and what was happening to her.

The full period of preparation before a girl went to King Ahasuerus was twelve months: six months' treatment with oil of myrrh, and six months' with perfumes and cosmetics. At the end of this each girl's turn came, and, when she went from the women's quarters to the king's palace, she was allowed to take with her whatever she asked. She would enter the palace in the evening and return in the morning to another part of the women's quarters, to be under the care of Shaashgaz, the king's eunuch in charge of the concubines. She would not go again to the king unless he expressed a wish for her and she was summoned by name.

When the turn came for Esther, the girl Mordecai had adopted, the daughter of his uncle Abihail, to go in to the king, she asked for nothing to take with her except what was advised by Hegai, the king's eunuch in charge of the women. Esther charmed all who saw her, and when she was brought to King Ahasuerus in the royal palace, in the tenth month, the month of

Tebeth, in the seventh year of his reign, the king loved her more than any of his other women. He treated her with greater favour and kindness than all the rest of the virgins, and placed a royal diadem on her head, making her queen in place of Vashti. Then in Esther's honour the king gave a great banquet, to which were invited all his officers and courtiers. He also proclaimed a holiday throughout his provinces and distributed gifts worthy of a king.

Mordecai was in attendance in the court. On his instructions Esther had not disclosed her family or her race, obeying Mordecai in this as she used to do when she was his ward. One day when Mordecai was at court, two of the king's eunuchs, Bigthan and Teresh, keepers of the threshold who were disaffected, were plotting to assassinate King Ahasuerus. This became known to Mordecai, who told Queen Esther; and she, on behalf of Mordecai, informed the king. The matter was investigated and, the report being confirmed, the two men were hanged on the gallows. All this was recorded in the court chronicle in the king's presence.

Haman Plots against the Jews

It was after those events that King Ahasuerus promoted Haman son of Hammedatha the Agagite, advancing him and giving him precedence above all his fellow officers. Everyone in attendance on the king at court bowed down and did obeisance to Haman, for so the king had commanded; but Mordecai would not bow or do obeisance. The courtiers said to him, 'Why do you flout his majesty's command?' They challenged him day after day, and when he refused to listen they informed Haman, in order to discover if Mordecai's conduct would be tolerated, for he had told them that he was a Jew. Haman was furious when he saw that Mordecai was not bowing down or doing obeisance to him; but having learnt who Mordecai's people were, he scorned to lay hands on him alone; he looked for a way to exterminate not only Mordecai but all the Jews throughout the whole kingdom.

In the twelfth year of King Ahasuerus, in the first month, Nisan, they cast lots – Pur as it is called – in the presence of Haman, taking the days and months one by one, and the lot fell on the thirteenth day of the twelfth month, the month of Adar.

Haman said to King Ahasuerus: 'Dispersed in scattered groups among the peoples throughout the provinces of your realm, there is a certain people whose laws are different from those of every other people. They do not observe the king's laws, and it does not befit your majesty to tolerate them. If it please your majesty, let an order be drawn up for their destruction; and I shall hand over to your majesty's officials the sum of ten thousand talents of silver, to be deposited in the royal treasury.' The king drew off the signet ring from his finger and gave it to Haman son of Hammedatha the Agagite, the enemy of the Jews. 'Keep the money,' he said, 'and deal with the people as you think best.'

On the thirteenth day of the first month the king's secretaries were summoned and, in accordance with Haman's instructions, a writ was issued to the king's satraps and the governors of every province, and to the rulers over each separate people. It was drawn up in the name of King Ahasuerus and sealed with the king's signet, and transcribed for each province in its own script and for each people in their own language. Dispatches were sent by courier to all the king's provinces with orders to destroy, slay, and exterminate all Jews, young and old, women and children, in one day, the thirteenth day of the twelfth month, the month of Adar; their goods were to be treated as spoil. A copy of the writ was to be issued as a decree in every province and to be publicly displayed to all the peoples, so that they might be ready for that day. At the king's command the couriers set off post-haste, and the decree was issued in Susa the capital city. The king and Haman sat down to carouse, but in the city of Susa confusion reigned.

Esther Saves her People

When Mordecai learnt of all that had been done, he tore his clothes and put on sackcloth and ashes. He went out through the city, lamenting loudly and bitterly, until he came right in front of the palace gate; no one wearing sackcloth was allowed to pass through that gate. In every province reached by the royal command and decree there was great mourning among the Jews, with fasting and weeping and beating of the breast; most of them lay down on beds of sackcloth and ashes. When Queen Esther's maids and eunuchs came in and told her, she was greatly distraught. She sent clothes for Mordecai to wear instead of his sackcloth; but he would not accept them.

Esther then summoned Hathach, one of the king's eunuchs appointed to wait on her, and ordered him to find out from Mordecai what was the trouble and the reason for it. Hathach went out to Mordecai in the city square opposite the palace, and Mordecai told him all that had happened to him and how much money Haman had offered to pay into the royal treasury for the destruction of the Jews. He also gave him a copy of the writ for their extermination, which had been issued in Susa, so that he might show it to Esther and tell her about it, directing her to go to the king to implore his favour and intercede for her people. When Hathach came in and informed Esther of what Mordecai had said, she told him to take back this message: 'All the courtiers and the people in the king's provinces know that if any person, man or woman, enters the royal presence in the inner court without being summoned, there is but one law: that person shall be put to death, unless the king extends to him the gold sceptre; only then may he live. What is more, I have not been summoned to the king for the last thirty days.'

When Mordecai was told what Esther had said, he sent this reply, 'Do not imagine, Esther, that, because you are in the royal palace, you alone of all the Jews will escape. If you remain silent at such a time as this, relief and deliverance for the Jews will appear from another quarter; but you and your father's family will perish. And who knows whether it is not for a time like this that you have become queen?' Esther sent this answer back to Mordecai: 'Go and assemble all the Jews that are in Susa, and fast on my behalf; for three days, night and day, take neither food nor drink, and I also will fast with my maids. After that, in defiance of the law, I shall go to the king; if I perish, I perish.' Mordecai then went away and did exactly as Esther had bidden him.

On the third day Esther arrayed herself in her royal robes and stood in the inner court, facing the palace itself; the king was seated on his royal throne in the palace, opposite the entrance. When he caught sight of Queen Esther standing in the court, he extended to her the gold sceptre he held, for she had obtained his favour. Esther approached and touched the tip of the sceptre. The king said to her, 'What is it, Queen Esther? Whatever you request, up to half my kingdom, it shall be granted you.' 'If it please your majesty,' she answered, 'will you come today, my lord, and Haman with you, to a banquet I have prepared for you?'

The king gave orders for Haman to be brought with all speed to meet Esther's wishes; and the king and Haman went to the banquet she had prepared.

Over the wine the king said to Esther, 'Whatever you ask will be given you; whatever you request, up to half my kingdom, will be granted.' Esther replied, 'What I ask and request is this: If I have found favour with your majesty, and if it please you, my lord, to give me what I ask and to grant my request, will your majesty and Haman come again tomorrow to the banquet that I shall prepare for you both? Tomorrow I shall do as your majesty says.'

Haman left the royal presence that day overjoyed and in the best of spirits, but as soon as he saw Mordecai in the king's court and observed that he did not rise or defer to him, he was furious; yet he kept control of himself. When he arrived home, he sent for his friends and for Zeresh his wife and held forth to them about the splendour of his wealth and his many sons, and how the king had promoted him and advanced him above the other officers and courtiers. 'Nor is that all,' Haman went on; 'Queen Esther had no one but myself come with the king to the banquet which she had prepared; and I am invited by her again tomorrow with the king. Yet all this gives me no satisfaction so long as I see that Jew Mordecai in attendance at the king's court.' His wife Zeresh and all his friends said to him, 'Have a gallows set up, seventy-five feet high, and in the morning propose to the king that Mordecai be hanged on it. Then you can go with the king to the banquet and enjoy yourself.' This advice seemed good to Haman, and he set up the gallows.

That night sleep eluded the king, so he ordered the chronicle of memorable events to be brought, and it was read to him. There it was found recorded how Mordecai had furnished information about Bigthana and Teresh, the two royal eunuchs among the keepers of the threshold who had plotted to assassinate King Ahasuerus. When the king asked what honour or dignity had been conferred on Mordecai for this, his attendants said, 'Nothing has been done for him.' 'Who is in the court?' said the king. As Haman had just then entered the outer court of the palace to propose to the king that Mordecai should be hanged on the gallows he had prepared for him, the king's attendants replied, 'Haman is standing there in the court.' 'Let him enter!'

commanded the king. When he came in, the king asked him, 'What should be done for the man whom the king wishes to honour?' Haman thought to himself, 'Whom, other than myself, would the king wish to honour?' So he answered, 'For the man whom the king wishes to honour, let there be brought a royal robe which the king himself has worn, and a horse on which the king rides, with a royal diadem on its head. Let the robe and the horse be handed over to one of the king's noble officers, and let him invest the man whom the king wishes to honour and lead him mounted on the horse through the city square, proclaiming as he goes: "This is what is done for the man whom the king wishes to honour."' The king said to Haman, 'Take the robe and the horse at once, as you have said, and do this for Mordecai the Jew who is present at court. Let nothing be omitted of all you have proposed.'

Haman took the robe and the horse, invested Mordecai, and led him on horseback through the city square, proclaiming before him: 'This is what is done for the man whom the king wishes to honour.'

Mordecai then returned to court, while Haman in grief hurried off home with his head veiled. When he told his wife Zeresh and all his friends everything that had happened to him, the response he got from his advisers and Zeresh was: 'If you have begun to fall before Mordecai, and he is a Jew, you cannot get the better of him; your downfall before him is certain.' While they were still talking with him, the king's eunuchs arrived and Haman was hurried off to the banquet Esther had prepared.

So the king and Haman went to Queen Esther's banquet, and again on that second day over the wine the king said, 'Whatever you ask will be given you, Queen Esther. Whatever you request, up to half my kingdom, it will be granted.' She answered, 'If I have found favour with your majesty, and if it please you, my lord, what I ask is that my own life and the lives of my people be spared. For we have been sold, I and my people, to be destroyed, slain, and exterminated. If it had been a matter of selling us, men and women alike, into slavery, I should have kept silence; for then our plight would not have been such as to injure the king's interests.' King Ahasuerus demanded, 'Who is he, and where is he, who has dared to do such a thing?' 'A ruthless enemy,' she answered, 'this wicked Haman!' Haman stood aghast before the king and queen. In a rage the king rose from the banquet and went into the garden of the pavilion, while Haman remained where he was to plead for his life with Queen Esther; for he saw that in the king's mind his fate was determined. When the king returned from the pavilion garden to the banqueting hall, Haman had flung himself on the couch where Esther was reclining. The king exclaimed, 'Will he even assault the queen in the palace before my very eyes?' The words had no sooner left the king's lips than Haman's face was covered. Harbona, one of the eunuchs in attendance on the king, said, 'There is a gallows seventy-five feet high standing at Haman's house; he had it erected for Mordecai, whose evidence once saved your majesty.' 'Let Haman be hanged on it!' said the king. So they hanged Haman on the gallows he had prepared for Mordecai. Then the king's anger subsided.

That same day King Ahasuerus gave Queen Esther the property of Haman, the enemy of the Jews, and Mordecai came into the king's presence, for Esther had revealed his relationship to her. The king drew off his signet ring, which he had taken back from Haman, and gave it to Mordecai. Esther put Mordecai in charge of Haman's property.

Once again Esther addressed the king, falling at his feet and imploring him with tears to thwart the wickedness of Haman the Agagite and frustrate his plot against the Jews. The king extended his gold sceptre towards her, and she rose and stood before him. 'May it please your majesty,' Esther said; 'if I have found favour with you, and if what I propose seems right to your majesty and I have won your approval, let a writ be issued to recall the dispatches which Haman son of Hammedatha the Agagite wrote in pursuance of his plan to destroy the Jews in all the royal provinces. For how can I bear to witness the disaster which threatens my people? How can I bear to witness the destruction of my kindred?' King Ahasuerus said to Queen Esther and to Mordecai the Jew, 'I have given Haman's property to Esther, and he has been hanged on the gallows because he threatened the lives of the Jews. Now you may issue a writ in my name concerning the Jews, in whatever terms you think fit, and seal it with the royal signet; no order written in the name of the king and sealed with the royal signet can be rescinded.'

On the twenty-third day of the third month, the month of Sivan, the king's secretaries were summoned, and a writ exactly as Mordecai directed was issued to the Jews, and to the satraps, the governors, and the rulers of the hundred and twenty-seven provinces from India to Ethiopia; it was issued for each province in its own script and for each people in their own language, and also for the Jews in their script and language. The writ was drawn up in the name of King Ahasuerus and sealed with the royal signet, and dispatches were sent by couriers mounted on horses from the royal stables. By these dispatches the king granted permission to the Jews in each and every city to assemble in self-defence, and to destroy, slay, and exterminate every man, woman, and child, of any people or province which might attack them, and to treat their goods as spoil, throughout all the provinces of King Ahasuerus, in one day, the thirteenth day of Adar, the twelfth month. A copy of the writ was to be issued as a decree in every province and published to all peoples, and the Jews were to be ready for that day, the day of vengeance on their enemies. Couriers, mounted on horses from the royal stables, set off post-haste at the king's urgent command; and the decree was proclaimed also in Susa the capital.

When Mordecai left the king's presence in a royal robe of violet and white, wearing an imposing gold crown and a cloak of fine linen with purple thread, the city of Susa shouted for joy. All was light and joy, gladness and honour for the Jews; in every province and city reached by the royal command and decree there was joy and gladness for the Jews, feasting and holiday. And many of the peoples of the world professed Judaism, because fear of the Jews had fallen on them.

On the thirteenth day of Adar, the twelfth month, the time came for the king's command and decree to be carried out. That very day on which the enemies of the Jews had hoped to triumph over them was to become the day when the Jews should triumph over those who hated them. Throughout all the provinces of King Ahasuerus, the Jews assembled in their cities to attack those who had sought to bring disaster on them. None could offer resistance, because fear of them had fallen on all the peoples. The rulers of the provinces, the satraps and the governors, and the royal officials all aided the Jews, out of fear of Mordecai, for he had become a person of great power in the royal palace, and as the power of the man increased, his fame spread throughout every province. The Jews put all their enemies to the sword. There was great slaughter and destruction, and they worked their will on those who hated them.

In Susa the capital the Jews slaughtered five hundred men; and they also put to death Parshandatha, Dalphon, Aspatha, Poratha, Adalia, Aridatha, Parmashta, Arisai, Aridai, and Vaizatha, the ten sons of Haman son of Hammedatha, the persecutor of the Jews; but they took no plunder.

That day when the number of those killed in Susa was reported to the king, he said to Queen Esther, 'In Susa the capital the Jews have slaughtered five hundred men; they have killed the ten sons of Haman; what will they have done in the rest of the provinces of the kingdom? Whatever you ask will be given you; whatever further request you have, it will be granted.' Esther replied, 'If it please your majesty, let the Jews in Susa be permitted tomorrow also to take action according to this day's decree; and let the bodies of Haman's ten sons be hung up on the gallows.' The king gave orders for this to be done; the decree was issued in Susa, and Haman's ten sons were hung up on the gallows. The Jews in Susa assembled again on the fourteenth day of the month of Adar and killed there three hundred men; but they took no plunder.

The rest of the Jews throughout the king's provinces rallied in self-defence and so had respite from their enemies; they slaughtered seventy-five thousand of those who hated them, but they took no plunder. That was on the thirteenth day of the month of Adar; on the fourteenth day they rested and made it a day of feasting and joy. The Jews in Susa had assembled on both the thirteenth and fourteenth days of the month; they rested on the fifteenth day and made that a day of feasting and joy. This explains why Jews in the countryside who live in remote villages observe the fourteenth day of Adar with joy and feasting as a holiday, sending presents of food to one another.

Mordecai put these things on record, and he sent letters to all the Jews throughout the provinces of King Ahasuerus, both near and far, requiring them to observe annually the fourteenth and fifteenth days of the month of Adar as the days on which the Jews had respite from their enemies; that was the month which was changed for them from sorrow into joy, from a time of mourning to a holiday. They were to observe them as days of feasting and joy, days for sending presents of food to one another and gifts to the poor.

The Jews undertook to continue the practice that they had begun in accordance with Mordecai's letter. This they did because Haman son of Hammedatha the Agagite, the enemy of all the Jews, had plotted to destroy them and had cast lots – Pur as it is called – with intent to crush and destroy them. But when the matter came before the king, he issued written orders that the wicked plot which Haman had devised against the Jews should recoil on his own head, and that he and his sons should be hanged on the gallows. This is why these days were named Purim, from the word Pur. Accordingly, because of all that was written in this letter, because of all they had seen and experienced in this affair, the Jews resolved and undertook, on behalf of themselves, their descendants, and all who might join them, to observe without fail these two days as a yearly festival in the prescribed manner and at the appointed time; further, that these days were to be remembered and celebrated throughout all generations, in every family, province, and city, so that the observance of the days of Purim should never lapse among the Jews, and the commemoration of them should never cease among their descendants.

By the command of Esther these regulations for Purim were confirmed and put in writing.

21 | THE RETURN OF THE EXILES

The Rebuilding of the Temple
In the first year of King Cyrus of Persia the Lord, to fulfil his word spoken through Jeremiah, inspired the king to issue throughout his kingdom the following proclamation, which he also put in writing:

The decree of King Cyrus of Persia.

The Lord the God of the heavens has given me all the king-doms of the earth, and he himself has charged me to build him a house at Jerusalem in Judah. Whoever among you belongs to his people, may his God be with him; and let him go up to Jerusalem in Judah, and build the house of the Lord the God of Israel.

Thereupon the heads of families of Judah and Benjamin came forward, along with the priests and the Levites, all whom God had moved to go up and rebuild the house of the Lord.

On their arrival in Jerusalem, certain of the heads of families offered to rebuild the house of God on its original site. According to their ability they gave to the treasury for the fabric a total of sixty-one thousand drachmas of gold, five thousand minas of silver, and one hundred priestly vestments. The priests, the Levites, and some of the people stayed in Jerusalem and the neigh-bourhood; the singers, the door-keepers and the temple servitors, and all the rest of the Israelites, lived in their own towns.

When the seventh month came, the Israelites now being settled in their towns, the people came together with one accord to Jerusalem, and Jeshua son of Jozadak along with his fellow priests, and Zerubbabel son of Shealtiel, with his colleagues, set to work.

When the builders had laid the foundation of the temple of the Lord, the priests in their robes took their places with their trumpets, and the Levites, the sons of Asaph, with cymbals, to praise the Lord in the manner prescribed by King David of Israel. They chanted praises and thanksgiving to the Lord, singing, 'It is good to give thanks to the Lord, for his love towards Israel endures for ever.' The whole people raised a great shout of praise to the Lord because the foundation of the Lord's house had been laid. Many of the priests and Levites and heads of families, who were old enough to have seen the former house, wept and wailed aloud when they saw the foundation of this house laid, while many others shouted for joy at the tops of their voices.

When those who were hostile to Judah and Benjamin heard that the returned exiles were building a temple to the Lord the God of Israel, they approached Zerubbabel and Jeshua and the heads of families. 'Let us build with you,' they said, 'for like you we seek your God, and have sacrificed to him ever since the days of King Esarhaddon of Assyria who brought us here.' But Zerub-babel and Jeshua and the rest of the heads of the Israelite families replied, 'It is not for you to share in building the house for our God; we alone are to build it for the Lord the God of Israel, as his majesty King Cyrus of Persia commanded us.'

Then the people of the land caused the Jews to lose heart and made them afraid to continue building; and, in order to thwart the purpose of the Jews, those people bribed officials at court to act against them. This continued throughout the lifetime of King Cyrus of Persia and into the reign of King Darius. From then onwards the work on the house of God in Jerusalem ceased; it remained at a standstill till the second year of the reign of King Darius of Persia.

The prophets Haggai and Zechariah son of Iddo prophesied to the Jews in Judah and Jerusalem, rebuking them in the name of the God of Israel. Then Zerubbabel son of Shealtiel and Jeshua son of Jozadak, with the prophets of God at their side to help them, began at once to rebuild the house of God in Jerusalem.

The house was completed on the third day of the month of Adar, in the sixth year of the reign of King Darius.

Then the Israelites, priests, Levites, and all the other exiles who had returned, celebrated the rededication of this house of God with great rejoicing. At its rededication they offered one hundred bulls, two hundred rams, and four hundred lambs, and as a purification-offering for all Israel twelve he-goats, corresponding to the number of the tribes of Israel. They re-established the priests in their groups and the Levites in their divisions for the service of God in Jerusalem, as prescribed in the book of Moses.

On the fourteenth day of the first month the returned exiles observed the Passover. The priests and the Levites, one and all, had purified themselves; all of them were ritually clean, and they killed the Passover lamb for all the exiles who had returned, for their fellow priests, and for themselves. It was eaten by the Israelites who had returned from exile and by all who had held aloof from the peoples of the land and their uncleanness, and had sought the Lord the God of Israel. They observed the pilgrim-feast of Unleavened Bread for seven days with rejoicing.

Ezra the Scribe

It was after these events, in the reign of King Artaxerxes of Persia, that Ezra had come up from Babylon; he was a scribe, expert in the law of Moses which the Lord the God of Israel had given them. The king granted him everything he requested, for the favour of the Lord his God was with him. He was accompanied to Jerusalem by some Israelites, priests, Levites, temple singers, door-keepers, and temple servitors in the seventh year of King Artaxerxes. They reached Jerusalem in the fifth month, in the seventh year of the king.

This is a copy of the letter which King Artaxerxes had given to Ezra the priest and scribe.

Artaxerxes, King of Kings, to Ezra the priest and scribe learned in the law of the God of heaven.

This is my decision. I hereby issue a decree that any of the people of Israel or of its priests or Levites in my kingdom who volunteer to go to Jerusalem may go with you. You are sent by the king and his seven counsellors to consider the situation in Judah and Jerusalem with regard to the law of your God with which you are entrusted. You are also to convey the silver and gold which the king and his counsellors have freely offered to the God of Israel whose dwelling is in Jerusalem, together with any silver and gold that you may find throughout the province of Babylon.

Then Ezra the scribe said, 'Blessed is the Lord the God of our fathers who has put such a thing as this into the king's mind, to glorify the house of the Lord in Jerusalem, and has made the king and his counsellors and all his high officers well disposed towards me!'

Encouraged by the help of the Lord my God, I gathered leading men out of Israel to go up with me. Then I set apart twelve of the chiefs of the priests, together with Sherebiah and Hashabiah and ten of their kinsmen. I weighed out for them the silver and gold and the vessels, the contribution for the house of our God presented by the king, his counsellors and officers, and by all the Israelites there present, as their contribution to the house of our God.

After weighing it, I handed over to them six hundred and fifty talents of silver, a hundred silver vessels weighing two talents, a hundred talents of gold, twenty gold dishes worth a thousand darics, and two vessels of a fine red copper, precious as gold. I said, 'Just as you are consecrated to the Lord, so too are the sacred vessels; the silver and gold are a voluntary offering to the Lord the God of your fathers. Guard them with all vigilance until you weigh them at Jerusalem in the rooms of the Lord's house in the presence of the chiefs of the priests, the Levites, and the heads of the families of Israel.' So the priests and the Levites received the consignment of silver and gold and vessels, to be taken to the house of God in Jerusalem.

On the twelfth day of the first month we struck camp at the river Ahava and set out for Jerusalem. Under the protection of our God, who saved us from enemy attack and ambush on the way, we reached Jerusalem and rested there for three days. On the fourth day the silver and gold and vessels were weighed and handed over in the house of our God into the charge of Meremoth son of Uriah the priest, with whom was Eleazar son of Phinehas; present with them were the Levites Jozabad son of Jeshua and Noadiah son of Binnui. Everything was counted and weighed and every weight recorded then and there.

Once this business had been concluded, the leaders came to me and said, 'The people of Israel, including even priests and Levites, have not kept themselves apart from the alien population and from the abominable practices of the Canaanites, Hittites, Perizzites, Jebusites, Ammonites, Moabites, Egyptians, and

Amorites. They have taken women of these nations as wives for themselves and their sons, so that the holy race has become mixed with the alien population; and the leaders and magistrates have been the chief offenders.'

At this news I tore my robe and mantle; I plucked tufts from my beard and the hair of my head and sat appalled. All who went in fear of the words of the God of Israel gathered round me because of the offence of these exiles; and I sat appalled until the evening sacrifice. Then, at the evening sacrifice, with my robe and mantle torn, I rose from my self-abasement and, kneeling down, held out my hands in prayer to the Lord my God.

'I am humiliated, my God,' I said, 'I am ashamed, my God, to lift my face to you. Our sins tower above us, and our guilt is so great that it reaches high heaven. For we have neglected your commandments, given us through your servants the prophets. You said: "The land which you are going to occupy is a land defiled with the pollution of its heathen population and their abominable practices; they have filled it with their impure ways from end to end. Now therefore do not marry your daughters to their sons or take their daughters for your sons; nor must you ever seek their welfare or prosperity. Only thus will you be strong and enjoy the good things of the land, and hand it on as an ever-lasting possession to your descendants." After all that has come upon us through our evil deeds and great guilt – although you, our God, have punished us less than our iniquities deserved and have allowed us to survive as now we do – shall we once again dis-obey your commands and intermarry with peoples who indulge in such abominable practices? Would you not be so angry with us as to destroy us till no remnant, no survivor was left? Lord God of Israel, you are just; for we today are a remnant that has survived. In all our guilt we are here before you; because of it we can no longer stand in your presence.'

While Ezra was praying and making confession, prostrate in tears before the house of God, there gathered round him a vast throng of Israelites, men, women, and children, and there was widespread lamentation among the crowd. Shecaniah son of Jehiel, one of the family of Elam, spoke up and said to Ezra, 'We have broken faith with our God in taking foreign wives from the peoples of the land. But in spite of this, there is still hope for Israel. Let us now pledge ourselves to our God to get rid of all such wives with their children, according to your counsel, my lord, and the counsel of those who go in fear of the command of our God; and let the law take its course. Rise up, the matter is in your hands; and we are with you. Take strong action!' Ezra got up and put the chiefs of the priests, the Levites, and all the Israelites on oath to act in this way, and they took the oath. Ezra then left the forecourt of the house of God and went to the room of Jehohanan grandson of Eliashib. He stayed there, eating no bread and drinking no water, for he was still mourning for the unfaithfulness of the returned exiles.

A proclamation was issued throughout Judah and Jerusalem directing all the returned exiles to assemble at Jerusalem. If any failed to arrive within three days, as decided by the chief officers and the elders, they were to have all their property confiscated and would themselves be excluded from the community that had come from exile. Three days later, on the twentieth day of the ninth month, all the men of Judah and Benjamin had assembled in Jerusalem, where they all sat in the open space before the house of God, full of apprehension and shivering in the heavy rain. Ezra the priest stood up and addressed them: 'You have broken faith in marrying foreign women,' he said 'and have added to Israel's guilt. Now, make confession to the Lord the God of your fathers; do his will, cut yourselves off from the peoples of the land and from your foreign wives.'

The whole company assented loudly, saying, 'We shall do as you say! But', they added, 'our numbers are great; it is the rainy season and we cannot stay out in the open. Besides, this is not the work of one or two days only, for the offence is rife amongst us. Let our leading men act for the whole assembly, and let all those who have married foreign wives present themselves at stated times, accompanied by the elders and judges for each town, until our God's fierce anger at what has been done is averted from us.' Only Jonathan son of Asahel and Jahzeiah son of Tikvah, supported by Meshullam and Shabbethai the Levite, opposed this.

The returned exiles duly put this into effect, and Ezra the priest selected, each by name, certain men, heads of households representing their families. They met in session to investigate the matter on the first day of the tenth month, and by the first day of the first month the enquiry into all the marriages with foreign women was brought to a conclusion.

The Memoirs of Nehemiah

The narrative of Nehemiah son of Hacaliah.

In the month of Kislev in the twentieth year, when I was in Susa the capital city, it happened that one of my brothers, Hanani, arrived with some other Judaeans. I asked them about Jerusalem and about the Jews, the families still remaining of those who survived the captivity. They told me that those who had survived the captivity and still lived in the province were facing dire trouble and derision; the wall of Jerusalem was broken down and its gates had been destroyed by fire.

When I heard this news, I sat and wept, mourning for several days, fasting and praying before the God of heaven. I was then cupbearer to the king.

One day, in the month of Nisan, in the twentieth year of King Artaxerxes, when his wine was ready, I took it and handed it to the king, and as I stood before him my face revealed my unhappiness. The king asked, 'Why do you look so unhappy? You are not ill; it can be nothing but a feeling of unhappiness.' I was very much afraid, but I answered, 'May the king live for ever! But how can I help looking unhappy when the city where my forefathers are buried lies in ruins with its gates burnt down?' 'What then do you want?' asked the king. With a prayer to the God of heaven, I answered, 'If it please your majesty, and if I enjoy your favour, I beg you to send me to Judah, to the city where my forefathers are buried, so that I may rebuild it.' The king, with the queen consort sitting beside him, asked me, 'How long will the journey last, and when will you return?' When I told him how long I should be, the king approved the request and let me go.

I then said to him, 'If it please your majesty, let letters be given me for the governors in the province of Beyond-Euphrates, with orders to grant me safe passage until I reach Judah. Let me have also a letter for Asaph, the keeper of your royal forests, instructing him to supply me with timber to make beams for the gates of the citadel, which adjoins the temple, and for the city wall, and for the temple which is the object of my journey.' The king granted my requests, for the gracious hand of my God was upon me.

I came in due course to the governors in the province of Beyond-Euphrates and presented the king's letters to them; the king had given me an escort of army officers with cavalry. But when Sanballat the Horonite and the slave Tobiah, an Ammonite, heard this, they were greatly displeased that someone should have come to promote the interests of the Israelites.

When I arrived in Jerusalem, I waited three days. Then I set out by night, taking a few men with me, but without telling anyone what my God was prompting me to do for Jerusalem. Taking no beast with me except the one on which I myself rode, I went out by night through the Valley Gate towards the Dragon Spring and the Dung Gate; and I inspected the places where the walls of Jerusalem had been broken down, and its gates, which had been destroyed by fire. Then I passed on to the Fountain Gate and the King's Pool; but there was no room for me to ride through. I went up the valley by night and inspected the city wall; then I re-entered the city through the Valley Gate. So I arrived back without the magistrates knowing where I had been or what I was doing, for I had not yet told the Jews, neither the priests, the nobles, the magistrates, nor any of those who would be responsible for the work.

Then I said to them, 'You see what trouble we are in: Jerusalem lies in ruins, its gates destroyed by fire. Come, let us rebuild the wall of Jerusalem and suffer derision no more.' I told them also how the gracious hand of my God had been upon me and also what the king had said to me. They replied, 'Let us start the rebuilding,' and they set about the work vigorously and to good purpose.

The news that we were rebuilding the wall roused the indignation of Sanballat, and angrily he jeered at the Jews, saying in front of his companions and of the garrison in Samaria, 'What do these feeble Jews think they are doing? Do they mean to reconstruct the place? Do they hope to offer sacrifice and finish the work in a day?'

We built up the wall until it was continuous all round up to half its height; and the people worked with a will. But when Sanballat and Tobiah, and the Arabs and Ammonites and Ashdodites, heard that the new work on the walls of Jerusalem had made progress and that the closing up of the breaches had gone ahead, they were furious, and all banded together to launch an attack on Jerusalem and create confusion. So we prayed to our God, and posted a guard against them day and night.

Our adversaries said, 'Before they know it or see anything, we shall be upon them, killing them and putting an end to the work.'

When the Jews living nearby came into the city, they warned us a dozen times that our adversaries would gather from every place where they lived to attack us, and that they would station themselves on the lowest levels below the wall, on patches of open ground. Accordingly I posted my people by families, armed with swords, spears, and bows. Then, having surveyed the position, I addressed the nobles, the magistrates, and the rest of the people. 'Do not be afraid of them,' I said. 'Remember the Lord, great and terrible, and fight for your brothers, your sons and daughters, your wives and your homes.' When our enemies heard that everything was known to us, and that God had frustrated their plans, we all returned to the wall, each to his task.

From that day forward half the men under me were engaged in the actual building, while the other half stood by holding their spears, shields, and bows, and wearing coats of mail; and officers supervised all the people of Judah who were engaged on the wall. The porters carrying the loads held their load with one hand and a weapon with the other. The builders had their swords attached to their belts as they built. The trumpeter stayed beside me, and I said to the nobles, the magistrates, and all the people: 'The work is great and extends over much ground, and we are widely separated on the wall, each man at some distance from his neighbour. Wherever you hear the trumpet sound, rally to us there, and our God will fight for us.' So with half the men holding spears we continued the work from daybreak until the stars came out. At the same time I had said to the people, 'Let every man and his servant remain all night inside Jerusalem, to act as a guard for us by night and a working party by day.' Neither I nor my kinsmen nor the men under me nor my bodyguard ever took off our clothes; each one kept his right hand on his spear.

There came a time when the common people, both men and women, raised a great outcry against their fellow Jews. Some complained that they had to give their sons and daughters as pledges for food to eat to keep themselves alive; others that they were mortgaging their fields, vineyards, and homes to buy grain during the famine; still others that they were borrowing money on their fields and vineyards to pay the king's tax. 'But', they said, 'our bodily needs are the same as other people's, our children are as good as theirs; yet here we are, forcing our sons and daughters into slavery. Some of our daughters are already enslaved, and there is nothing we can do, because our fields and vineyards now belong to others.'

When I heard their outcry and the story they told, I was greatly incensed, but I controlled my feelings and reasoned with the nobles and the magistrates. I said to them, 'You are holding your fellow Jews as pledges for debt.' I rebuked them severely and said, 'As far as we have been able, we have bought back our fellow Jews who had been sold to foreigners; but you are now selling your own fellow countrymen, and they will have to be bought back by us!' They were silent and had not a word to say.

I went on, 'What you are doing is wrong. You ought to live so much in the fear of our God that you are above reproach in the eyes of the nations who are our enemies. Speaking for myself, I and my kinsmen and the men under me are advancing them money and grain. Let us give up this taking of pledges for debt. This very day give them back their fields and vineyards, their olive groves and houses, as well as the income in money, in grain, new wine, and oil.' 'We shall give them back', they promised, 'and exact nothing more. We shall do as you say.' Then after summoning the priests I put the offenders on oath to do as they had promised. Also I shook out the fold of my robe and said, 'So may God shake out from house and property every man who fails to keep this promise. May he be shaken out like this and emptied!' All the assembled people said 'Amen' and praised the Lord; and they did as they had promised.

God, remember me favourably for all that I have done for this people!

When it was reported to Sanballat, Tobiah, Geshem the Arab, and the rest of our enemies that I had rebuilt the wall and not a single gap remained in it – although I had not yet set up the gates in the gateways – Sanballat and Geshem sent me an invitation to come and confer with them at Hakkephirim in the plain of Ono; their intention was to do me some harm. So I sent messengers to them with this reply: 'I have important work on my hands at the moment and am unable to come down. Why should the work be brought to a standstill while I leave it and come down to you?'

Four times they sent me a similar invitation, and each time I gave them the same answer. On a fifth occasion Sanballat made a similar approach, but this time his servant came with an open letter. It ran as follows: 'It is reported among the nations, and

Gashmu confirms it, that you and the Jews are plotting rebellion, and that is why you are building the wall; it is further reported that you yourself want to be king, and have even appointed prophets to make this proclamation concerning you in Jerusalem: "Judah has a king!" Such matters will certainly get to the king's notice; so come at once and let us talk them over.' I sent this reply: 'No such thing as you allege has taken place; your imagination has invented the whole story.' They were all trying to intimidate us, in the hope that we should then relax our efforts and that the work would never be completed. Strengthen me for the work, was my prayer.

On the twenty-fifth day of the month of Elul the wall was finished; it had taken fifty-two days. When all our enemies heard of it, and all the surrounding nations saw it, they thought it a very wonderful achievement, and recognized it was by the help of our God that this work had been accomplished.

When the seventh month came, and the Israelites were now settled in their towns, all the people assembled with one accord in the broad space in front of the Water Gate, and requested Ezra the scribe to bring the book of the law of Moses, which the Lord had enjoined upon Israel. On the first day of the seventh month, Ezra the priest brought the law before the whole assembly, both men and women, and all who were capable of understanding what they heard. From early morning till noon he read aloud from it, facing the square in front of the Water Gate.

On the second day the heads of families of the whole people, with the priests and the Levites, assembled before Ezra the scribe to study the law. They found written in the law that the Lord had given commandment through Moses that the Israelites were to live in booths during the feast of the seventh month; they should issue this proclamation throughout all their towns and in Jerusalem: 'Go out to the hills and fetch branches of olive and wild olive, myrtle and palm, and other leafy boughs, to make booths as prescribed.' So the people went and fetched branches and made booths for themselves, each on his own roof, and in their courtyards and in the precincts of the house of God, and in the square at the Water Gate and the square at the Ephraim Gate. The whole community of those who had returned from the captivity made booths and lived in them, a thing that the Israelites had not done from the days of Joshua son of Nun until that day;

and there was very great rejoicing. The book of the law of God was read day by day, from the first day to the last. They kept the feast for seven days, and on the eighth day there was a closing ceremony, according to the rule.

Then I assembled the leading men of Judah on the city wall, and appointed two large choirs to give thanks. One went in procession to the right, going along the wall to the Dung Gate. They went past the Fountain Gate and thence straight forward by the steps up to the City of David, by the ascent to the city wall, past the house of David, and on to the Water Gate on the east. The other thanksgiving choir went to the left, and I followed it with half the leading men of the people, continuing along the wall, past the Tower of the Ovens to the Broad Wall, and past the Ephraim Gate, and over the Jeshanah Gate, and over the Fish Gate, taking in the Tower of Hananel and the Tower of the Hundred, as far as the Sheep Gate; and they halted at the Guardhouse Gate.

Then the two thanksgiving choirs took their place in the house of God, and I and half the magistrates with me. The singers, led by Izrahiah, raised their voices. A great sacrifice was celebrated that day, and they all rejoiced because God had given them great cause for rejoicing; the women and children rejoiced with them. And the rejoicing in Jerusalem was heard a long way off.

Part Three

POEMS, PROVERBS AND PROPHECIES

22 | THE TRIALS OF JOB

Prologue: Satan's Challenge

There lived in the land of Uz a man of blameless and upright life named Job, who feared God and set his face against wrongdoing. He had seven sons and three daughters; and he owned seven thousand sheep, three thousand camels, five hundred yoke of oxen, and five hundred she-donkeys, together with a large number of slaves. Thus Job was the greatest man in all the East.

The day came when the members of the court of heaven took their places in the presence of the Lord, and the Adversary, Satan, was there among them. The Lord asked him where he had been. 'Ranging over the earth', said the Adversary, 'from end to end.' The Lord asked him, 'Have you considered my servant Job? You will find no one like him on earth, a man of blameless and upright life, who fears God and sets his face against wrongdoing.' 'Has not Job good reason to be godfearing?' answered the Adversary. 'Have you not hedged him round on every side with your protection, him and his family and all his possessions? Whatever he does you bless, and everywhere his herds have increased beyond measure. But just stretch out your hand and touch all that he has, and see if he will not curse you to your face.' 'Very well,' said the Lord. 'All that he has is in your power; only the man himself you must not touch.' With that the Adversary left the Lord's presence.

On the day when Job's sons and daughters were eating and drinking in the eldest brother's house, a messenger came to Job and said, 'The oxen were ploughing and the donkeys were grazing near them, when the Sabaeans swooped down and carried them off, after putting the herdsmen to the sword; only I have escaped to bring you the news.' While he was still speaking, another messenger arrived and said, 'God's fire flashed from heaven, striking the sheep and the shepherds and burning them up; only I have escaped to bring you the news.' While he was still

345

speaking, another arrived and said, 'The Chaldaeans, three bands of them, have made a raid on the camels and carried them off, after putting those tending them to the sword; only I have escaped to bring you the news.' While this man was speaking, yet another arrived and said, 'Your sons and daughters were eating and drinking in their eldest brother's house, when suddenly a whirlwind swept across from the desert and struck the four corners of the house, which fell on the young people. They are dead, and only I have escaped to bring you the news.'

At this Job stood up, tore his cloak, shaved his head, and threw himself prostrate on the ground, saying:

'Naked I came from the womb,
naked I shall return whence I came.
The Lord gives and the Lord takes away;
blessed be the name of the Lord.'

Throughout all this Job did not sin, nor did he ascribe any fault to God.

Once again the day came when the members of the court of heaven took their places in the presence of the Lord, and the Adversary was there among them. The Lord enquired where he had been. 'Ranging over the earth', said the Adversary, 'from end to end.' The Lord asked, 'Have you considered my servant Job? You will find no one like him on earth, a man of blameless and upright life, who fears God and sets his face against wrongdoing. You incited me to ruin him without cause, but he still holds fast to his integrity.' The Adversary replied, 'Skin for skin! To save himself there is nothing a man will withhold. But just reach out your hand and touch his bones and his flesh, and see if he will not curse you to your face.' The Lord said to the Adversary, 'So be it. He is in your power; only spare his life.'

When the Adversary left the Lord's presence, he afflicted Job with running sores from the soles of his feet to the crown of his head, and Job took a piece of a broken pot to scratch himself as he sat among the ashes. His wife said to him, 'Why do you still hold fast to your integrity? Curse God, and die!' He answered, 'You talk as any impious woman might talk. If we accept good from God, shall we not accept evil?' Throughout all this, Job did not utter one sinful word.

When Job's three friends, Eliphaz of Teman, Bildad of Shuah, and Zophar of Naamah, heard of all these calamities which had overtaken him, they set out from their homes, arranging to go and condole with him and comfort him. But when they first saw him from a distance, they did not recognize him; they wept aloud, tore their cloaks, and tossed dust into the air over their heads.

For seven days and seven nights they sat beside him on the ground, and none of them spoke a word to him, for they saw that his suffering was very great.

After this Job broke his silence and cursed the day of his birth.

Job

Perish the day when I was born,
and the night which said, 'A boy is conceived'!
May that day turn to darkness;
may God above not look for it,
nor light of dawn shine on it.
May gloom and deep darkness claim it again;
may cloud smother that day, blackness eclipse its sun.
May no star shine out in its twilight;
may it wait for a dawn that never breaks,
and never see the eyelids of the morning,
because it did not shut the doors of the womb that bore me
and keep trouble away from my sight.

Why was I not stillborn,
why did I not perish when I came from the womb?
Why was I ever laid on my mother's knees
or put to suck at her breasts?
Or why was I not concealed like an untimely birth,
like an infant who never saw the light?
For now I should be lying in the quiet grave,
asleep in death, at rest
with kings and their earthly counsellors
who built for themselves cities now laid waste.

Why should the sufferer be born to see the light?
Why is life given to those who find it so bitter?

First Cycle of Speeches

Eliphaz

If one should venture a word with you, would you lose patience?
Yet who could curb his tongue any longer?
Think how you once encouraged many,
how you braced feeble arms,
how a word from you upheld those who stumbled
and put strength into failing knees.
But now adversity comes on you, and you are impatient;
it touches you, and you are dismayed.
Does your piety give you no assurance?
Does your blameless life afford you no hope?
For consider, has any innocent person ever perished?
Where have the upright ever been destroyed?

Mischief does not grow out of the ground,
nor does trouble spring from the soil;
yet man is born to trouble,
as surely as birds fly upwards.

For my part, I would make my appeal to God;
I would lay my plea before him
who does great and unsearchable things,
marvels beyond all reckoning.

Job

Have I the strength to go on waiting?
What end have I to expect, that I should be patient?
Is my strength the strength of stone,
or is my flesh made of bronze?
Do I ever give voice to injustice?
Have I not the sense to discern when my words are wild?

Does not every mortal have hard service on earth,
and are not his days like those of a hired labourer,
like those of a slave longing for the shade
or a servant kept waiting for his wages?
So months of futility are my portion,
troubled nights are my lot.

My days pass more swiftly than a weaver's shuttle
and come to an end as the thread of life runs out.

Remember that my life is but a breath of wind;
I shall never again see good times.

Bildad
How long will you go on saying such things,
those long-winded ramblings of an old man?
Does God pervert justice?
Does the Almighty pervert what is right?
If your sons sinned against him,
he has left them to be victims of their own iniquity.
If only you yourself will seek God
and plead for the favour of the Almighty,
if you are pure and upright,
then indeed he will watch over you
and see your just intent fulfilled.

Job
Though I am in the right, I get no answer,
even if I plead with my accuser for mercy.
If I summoned him to court and he responded,
I do not believe that he would listen to my plea;
for he strikes at me for a trifle
and rains blows on me without cause.

If I am to be accounted guilty,
why do I waste my labour?
Though I were to wash myself with soap
and cleanse my hands with lye,
you would thrust me into the miry pit
and my clothes would render me loathsome.

God is not as I am, not someone I can challenge,
and say, 'Let us confront one another in court.'
If only there were one to arbitrate between us
and impose his authority on us both,
so that God might take his rod from my back,
and terror of him might not come on me suddenly.

I should then speak out without fear of him,
for I know I am not what I am thought to be.

I am sickened of life;
I shall give free rein to my complaints,
speaking out in the bitterness of my soul.
I shall say to God, Do not condemn me,
but let me know the charge against me.

Zophar
Is this spate of words to go unanswered?
Must the glib of tongue always be right?
Is your endless talk to reduce others to silence?
When you speak irreverently, is no one to take you to task?
You claim that your opinions are sound;
you say to God, 'I am spotless in your sight.'
But if only God would speak
and open his lips to reply,
to expound to you the secrets of wisdom,
for wonderful are its achievements!
Know then that God exacts from you
less than your sin deserves.

Job
No doubt you are intelligent people,
and when you die, wisdom will perish!
But I have sense, as well as you;
in no way do I fall short of you.
Your moralizing talk is so much dross,
your arguments crumble like clay.
Be silent, leave me to speak my mind,
and let what may come upon me!

Every being born of woman is short-lived and full of trouble.
He blossoms like a flower and withers away;
fleeting as a shadow, he does not endure;
he is like a wineskin that perishes
or a garment that moths have eaten.
If a tree is cut down,
there is hope that it will sprout again

and fresh shoots will not fail.
Though its root becomes old in the earth,
its stump dying in the ground,
yet when it scents water it may break into bud
and make new growth like a young plant.
But when a human being dies all his power vanishes;
he expires, and where is he then?
As the waters of a lake dwindle,
or as a river shrinks and runs dry,
so mortal man lies down, never to rise
until the very sky splits open.

Second Cycle of Speeches

Eliphaz

Would a sensible person give vent to such hot-air arguments
or puff himself up with an east wind?
Would he bandy useless words
and speeches so unprofitable?
Why! You even banish the fear of God from your mind,
cutting off all communication with him.
Your iniquity dictates what you say,
and deceit is your chosen language.
You are condemned out of your own mouth, not by me;
your own lips testify against you.
What do you know that we do not know?
What insight have you that we do not share?
We have age and white hairs in our company,
men older than your father.

I shall tell you, if only you will listen;
I shall recount what I have seen –
the wicked through all their days are racked with anxiety;
so it is with the tyrant through all the years allotted to him.
The noise of the hunter's scare rings in his ears;
even in time of peace the marauder swoops down on him;
he cannot hope to escape from dark death;
he is marked down for the sword;
he is flung out as food for vultures;

he knows that his destruction is certain.
Scorching heat will shrivel his shoots,
and his blossom will be shaken off by the wind.
He deceives himself, trusting in his high rank,
for all his dealings will come to nothing.

Job

I have heard such things so often before!
You are trouble-makers one and all!
You say, 'Will this windbag never have done?'
or 'What makes him so stubborn in argument?'
If you and I were to change places, I could talk as you do;
how I could harangue you and wag my head at you!
But no, I would speak words of encouragement,
and my condolences would be unrestrained.

Let not the earth cover my blood,
and let my cry for justice find no rest!
For now my witness is in heaven;
there is One on high ready to answer for me.
My appeal will come before God,
while my eyes turn anxiously to him.
If only there were one to arbitrate between man and God,
as between a man and his neighbour!
For there are but few years to come
before I take the road from which there is no return.

My mind is distraught, my days are numbered,
and the grave awaits me.
Wherever I turn, I am taunted,
and my eye meets nothing but sneers.
I am held up as a byword in every land,
a marvel for all to see;
my eyes are dimmed by grief,
my limbs wasted to a shadow.
But come on, one and all, try again!
I shall not find one who is wise among you.

Bildad
How soon will you bridle your tongue?
Show some sense, and then we can talk.
What do you mean by treating us as no more than cattle?
Are we nothing but brute beasts to you?
Is the earth to be deserted to prove you right,
or the rocks to be moved from their place?

No, it is the evildoer whose light is extinguished,
from whose fire no flame will rekindle;
the light in his tent fades,
his lamp beside him dies down.
A noose lies hidden for him in the ground
and a trap in his path.
He is plucked from the safety of his home,
and death's terrors escort him to their king.
All memory of him vanishes from the earth
and he leaves no name in the inhabited world.
He is thrust out from light into darkness
and banished from the land of the living.
Such is the fate of the dwellings of evildoers,
of the homes of those who care nothing for God.

Job
How long will you grieve me
and crush me with words?
You have insulted me now a dozen times
and shamelessly wronged me.
I tell you, God himself has put me in the wrong
and drawn his net about me.
If I shout 'Violence!' no one answers;
if I appeal for help, I get no justice.
He has blocked my path so that I cannot go forward,
he has planted a hedge across my way.

My kinsfolk hold aloof,
my acquaintances are wholly estranged from me;
my relatives and friends fall away.
My retainers have forgotten me;

my slave-girls treat me as a stranger;
I have become an alien in their eyes.

Pity me, have pity on me, you that are my friends,
for the hand of God has touched me.
Must you pursue me as God pursues me?
Have you not had your teeth in me long enough?
Would that my words might be written down,
that they might be engraved in an inscription,
incised with an iron tool and filled with lead,
carved in rock as a witness!
But I know that my vindicator lives
and that he will rise last to speak in court;
I shall discern my witness standing at my side
and see my defending counsel, even God himself,
whom I shall see with my own eyes,
I myself and no other.

Zophar

I have heard arguments that are an outrage to me,
but a spirit beyond my understanding gives me the answers.
Surely you know that since time began,
since mortals were first set on the earth, this has been true:
the triumph of a wicked person is short-lived,
the glee of one who is godless lasts but a moment!
Though in his pride he stands high as the heavens,
and his head touches the clouds,
he will be swept utterly away like his own dung,
and those used to seeing him will say, 'Where is he?'
The youthful vigour which filled his bones
will lie with him in the earth.
His sons will curry favour with the poor;
his children will give back his wealth.

Though evil tastes sweet in his mouth,
and he savours it, rolling it round his tongue,
though he lingers over it and will not let it go,
and holds it back on his palate,
yet his food turns in his stomach,
changing to asps' venom within him.

Because his appetite gave him no rest,
he let nothing he craved escape him;
because nothing survived his greed,
therefore his wellbeing does not last.

Job

Give careful heed to my words,
and let that be the comfort you offer me.
Bear with me while I have my say;
after I have spoken, you may mock.
When I stop to think, I am filled with horror,
and my whole body shudders.

Why do the wicked live on,
hale in old age, and great and powerful?
They see their children settled around them,
their descendants flourishing,
their households secure and safe;
the rod of God's justice does not reach them.
They say to God, 'Leave us alone;
we do not want to know your ways!
What is the Almighty that we should worship him,
or what should we gain by entreating his favour?'
You say, 'The trouble a man earns, God reserves for his sons';
no, let him be paid for it in full and be punished.
Let his own eyes witness the condemnation come on him;
may the wrath of the Almighty be the cup he drinks.
What joy will he have in his children after him,
if his months are numbered?
Can any human being teach God,
when it is he who judges even those in heaven above?

I tell you this: one man dies crowned with success,
lapped in security and comfort,
his loins full of vigour
and the marrow juicy in his bones;
another dies in bitterness of soul,
never having tasted prosperity.
Side by side they are laid in the earth,
and worms are the shroud of both.

How futile, then, is the comfort you offer me!
How false your answers ring!

Third Cycle of Speeches

Eliphaz
Can anyone be any benefit to God?
Can he benefit even from the wise?
Is it an advantage to the Almighty if you are righteous?
What gain to him if your conduct is perfect?
Does he arraign you for your piety –
is it on this count he brings you to trial?
No: it is because your wickedness is so great,
and your depravity passes all bounds.
Without cause you exact pledges from your brothers,
leaving them stripped of their clothes and naked.
You have sent widows away empty-handed,
the fatherless you have left without support.

Surely God is at the zenith of the heavens
and looks down on the topmost stars, high as they are.
Yet you say, 'What can God know?
Can he see through thick darkness to judge?
His eyes cannot pierce the curtain of the clouds
as he moves to and fro on the vault of heaven.'

Come to terms with God and you will prosper;
that is the way to mend your fortune.

Job
Even today my thoughts are embittered,
for God's hand is heavy on me in my trouble.
If only I knew how to reach him,
how to enter his court,
I should state my case before him
and set out my arguments in full.
My feet have kept to the path he has set me;
without deviating I have kept to his way.

I do not neglect the commands he issues,
I have treasured in my heart all he says.

When he decides, who can turn him from his purpose?
What he desires, he does.
Whatever he determines for me, that he carries out;
his mind is full of plans like these.
That is why I am fearful of meeting him;
when I think about it, I am afraid;
it is God who makes me faint-hearted,
the Almighty who fills me with fear,
yet I am not reduced to silence by the darkness
or by the mystery which hides him.

Bildad

Authority and awe are with him
who has established peace in his realm on high.
His squadrons are without number;
at whom will they not spring from ambush?
How then can a mere mortal be justified in God's sight,
or one born of woman be regarded as virtuous?
If the circling moon is found wanting,
and the stars are not innocent in his eyes,
much more so man, who is but a maggot,
mortal man, who is a worm.

Job

What a help you have been to one without resource!
What deliverance you have brought to the powerless!
What counsel you offer to one bereft of wisdom,
what sound advice to the simple!

I swear by the living God, who has denied me justice,
by the Almighty, who has filled me with bitterness,
that so long as there is any life left in me
and the breath of God is in my nostrils,
no untrue word will pass my lips,
nor will my tongue utter any falsehood.
Far be it from me to concede that you are right!

Till I cease to be, I shall not abandon my claim of innocence.
I maintain and shall never give up the rightness of my cause;
so long as I live, I shall not change.

A Hymn to Wisdom
There are mines for silver
and places where gold is refined.
Iron is won from the earth
and copper smelted from the ore.
Man sets his hand to the granite rock
and lays bare the roots of the mountains;
he cuts galleries in the rocks,
and gems of every kind meet his eye;
he dams up the sources of the streams
and brings the hidden riches of the earth to light.

But where can wisdom be found,
and where is the source of understanding?
No one knows the way to it,
nor is it to be found in the land of the living.
'It is not in us,' declare the ocean depths;
the sea declares, 'It is not with me.'
Red gold cannot buy it,
nor can its price be weighed out in silver;
gold of Ophir cannot be set in the scales against it,
nor precious cornelian nor sapphire;
gold and crystal are not to be matched with it,
no work in fine gold can be bartered for it.
Where, then, does wisdom come from?
Where is the source of understanding?

God alone understands the way to it,
he alone knows its source;
for he can see to the ends of the earth
and observe every place under heaven.
When he regulated the force of the wind
and measured out the waters in proportion,
when he laid down a limit for the rain
and cleared a path for the thunderbolt,

it was then he saw wisdom and took stock of it,
he considered it and fathomed its very depths.
And he said to mankind:
'The fear of the Lord is wisdom,
and to turn from evil, that is understanding!'

Job Sums Up His Case

Job

If only I could go back to the old days,
to the time when God was watching over me,
when his lamp shone above my head,
and by its light I walked through the darkness!
When I went out of my gate up to the town
to take my seat in the public square,
young men saw me and kept back out of sight,
old men rose to their feet,
men in authority broke off their talk
and put their hands to their lips;
the voices of the nobles died away,
and every man held his tongue.
They listened to me expectantly
and waited in silence for my counsel.
After I had spoken, no one spoke again;
my words fell gently on them;
they waited for me as for rain,
open-mouthed as for spring showers.

I put on righteousness as a garment and it clothed me;
justice, like a cloak and turban, adorned me.
I was eyes to the blind
and feet to the lame;
I was a father to the needy,
and I took up the stranger's cause.
I broke the fangs of the miscreant
and wrested the prey from his teeth.
I thought, 'I shall die with my powers unimpaired
and my days uncounted as the grains of sand,
with my roots spreading out to the water

and the dew lying on my branches,
with the bow always new in my grasp
and the arrow ever ready to my hand.'

But now I am laughed to scorn
by men of a younger generation,
men whose fathers I would have disdained
to put with the dogs guarding my flock.
Now I have become the target of their taunts;
my name is a byword among them.
They abhor me, they shun me,
they dare to spit in my face.
Terror after terror overwhelms me;
my noble designs are swept away as by the wind,
and my hope of deliverance vanishes like a cloud.
God himself has flung me down in the mud;
I have become no better than dust or ashes.

I call out to you, God, but you do not answer,
I stand up to plead, but you keep aloof.

The Intervention of Elihu

These three men gave up answering Job, for he continued to
think himself righteous. Now Elihu had hung back while they
were talking with Job because they were older than he was; but,
when he saw that the three had no answer to give, he could no
longer contain his anger.

Elihu

I am young in years, while you are old;
that is why I held back and shrank
from expressing my opinion in front of you.
I said to myself, 'Let age speak,
and length of years expound wisdom.'

But now, Job, listen to my words,
attend carefully to everything I say.
Answer me, if you can,
marshal your arguments and confront me.

'I am innocent', you said, 'and free from offence,
blameless and without guilt.
Yet God finds occasions to put me in the wrong
and counts me his enemy;
he puts my feet in the stocks
and keeps a close watch on all my conduct.'

You are not in the right – that is my answer;
for God is greater than any mortal.
Why then plead your case with him,
for no one can answer his arguments?
Indeed, once God has spoken
he does not speak a second time to confirm it.
In dreams, in visions of the night,
when deepest slumber falls on mortals,
while they lie asleep in bed
God imparts his message,
and as a warning strikes them with terror.
To turn someone from his evil deeds,
to check human pride,
at the edge of the pit he holds him back alive
and stops him from crossing the river of death.

Let us then examine for ourselves what is right;
let us together establish the true good.
Job has said, 'I am innocent,
but God has denied me justice,
he has falsified my case;
my state is desperate, yet I have done no wrong.'
Was there ever a man like Job
with his thirst for irreverent talk,
choosing bad company to share his journeys,
a fellow-traveller with wicked men?
For he says that it brings no profit to anyone
to find favour with God.

But listen to me, you men of good sense.
Far be it from God to do evil,
from the Almighty to play false!
For he requites everyone according to his actions

and sees that each gets the reward his conduct deserves.
The truth is, God would never do wrong,
the Almighty does not pervert justice.

Now Job, if you have the wit, consider this;
listen to what I am saying:
Can it be that a hater of justice is in control?
Do you disparage a sovereign whose rule is so fair?
His eyes are on the ways of everyone,
and he watches each step they take;
there is nowhere so dark, so deep in shadow,
that wrongdoers may hide themselves.

If only Job could be put to the test once and for all
for answering like a mischief-maker!
He is a sinner and a rebel as well
with his endless ranting against God.

Look up at the sky and then consider,
observe the rain-clouds towering above you.
How does it touch God if you have sinned?
However many your misdeeds, how does it affect him?
If you do right, what good do you bring him,
what does he receive at your hand?
Your wickedness touches only your fellow-creatures;
any right you do affects none but other mortals.

But now, because God does not grow angry and punish,
because he lets folly pass unheeded,
Job gives vent to windy nonsense;
he babbles a stream of empty words.

The Lord Answers Job Out of the Tempest

The Lord
Who is this who darkens counsel
with words devoid of knowledge?
Brace yourself and stand up like a man;
I shall put questions to you, and you must answer.

Where were you when I laid the earth's foundations?
Tell me, if you know and understand.
Who fixed its dimensions? Surely you know!
Who stretched a measuring line over it?
On what do its supporting pillars rest?
Who set its corner-stone in place,
while the morning stars sang in chorus
and the sons of God all shouted for joy?

Who supported the sea at its birth,
when it burst in flood from the womb –
when I wrapped it in a blanket of cloud
and swaddled it in dense fog,
when I established its bounds,
set its barred doors in place,
and said, 'Thus far may you come but no farther;
here your surging waves must halt'?

Have you gone down to the springs of the sea
or walked in the unfathomable deep?
Have the portals of death been revealed to you?
Have you seen the door-keepers of the place of darkness?
Have you comprehended the vast expanse of the world?
Tell me all this, if you know.

Which is the way to the home of light,
and where does darkness dwell?
Does the rain have a father?
Who sired the drops of dew?
Whose womb gave birth to the ice,
and who was the mother of the hoar-frost in the skies,
which lays a stony cover over the waters
and freezes the surface of the deep?

Can you bind the cluster of the Pleiades
or loose Orion's belt?
Can you bring out the signs of the zodiac in their season
or guide Aldebaran and its satellite stars?
Did you proclaim the rules that govern the heavens
or determine the laws of nature on the earth?

Can you hunt prey for the lioness
and satisfy the appetite of young lions,
as they crouch in the lair
or lie in wait in the covert?
Who provides the raven with its quarry
when its fledgelings cry aloud,
croaking for lack of food?

Do you know when the mountain goats give birth?
Do you attend the wild doe when she is calving?
Can you count the months that they carry their young
or know the time of their delivery,
when they crouch down to open their wombs
and deliver their offspring,
when the fawns growing and thriving in the open country
leave and do not return?

Do you give the horse his strength?
Have you clothed his neck with a mane?
Do you make him quiver like a locust's wings,
when his shrill neighing strikes terror?
He shows his mettle as he paws and prances;
in his might he charges the armoured line.
He scorns alarms and knows no dismay;
he does not shy away before the sword.
The quiver rattles at his side,
the spear and sabre flash.
Trembling with eagerness, he devours the ground
and when the trumpet sounds there is no holding him;
at the trumpet-call he cries 'Aha!'
and from afar he scents the battle,
the shouting of the captains, and the war cries.

Does your skill teach the hawk to use its pinions
and spread its wings towards the south?
Do you instruct the eagle to soar aloft
and build its nest high up?
It dwells among the rocks and there it has its nest,
secure on a rocky crag;
from there it searches for food,

keenly scanning the distance,
that its brood may be gorged with blood;
wherever the slain are, it is there.

Can you lift out the whale with a gaff
or slip a noose round its tongue?
Can you pass a rope through its nose
or pierce its jaw with a hook?
Will it take to pleading with you for mercy
or beg for its life with soft words?

Job

What reply can I give you, I who carry no weight?
I put my finger to my lips.
I have spoken once; I shall not answer again;
twice have I spoken; I shall do so no more.

The Lord

Brace yourself and stand up like a man;
I shall put questions to you, and you must answer.
Would you dare deny that I am just,
or put me in the wrong to prove yourself right?

Consider the chief of beasts, the crocodile,
who devours cattle as if they were grass:
what strength is in his loins!
What power in the muscles of his belly!
His tail is rigid as a cedar,
the sinews of his flanks are tightly knit;
his bones are like tubes of bronze,
his limbs like iron bars.

There under the thorny lotus he lies,
hidden among the reeds in the swamp;
the lotus conceals him in its shade,
the poplars of the stream surround him.
If the river is in spate, that does not perturb him;
he sprawls at his ease though submerged in the torrent.

His back is row upon row of shields,
enclosed in a wall of flints;
one presses so close on the next
that no air can pass between them,
each so firmly clamped to its neighbour
that they hold and cannot be parted.
His sneezing sends out sprays of light,
and his eyes gleam like the shimmer of dawn.

Armoured beneath with jagged sherds,
he sprawls on the mud like a threshing-sledge.
He makes the deep water boil like a cauldron,
he churns up the lake like ointment in a mixing bowl.
He leaves a shining trail behind him,
and in his wake the great river is like white hair.
He has no equal on earth,
a creature utterly fearless.
He looks down on all, even the highest;
over all proud beasts he is king.

Job

I know that you can do all things
and that no purpose is beyond you.
You ask: Who is this obscuring counsel yet lacking knowledge?
But I have spoken of things
which I have not understood,
things too wonderful for me to know.
Listen, and let me speak. You said:
I shall put questions to you, and you must answer.
I knew of you then only by report,
but now I see you with my own eyes.
Therefore I yield,
repenting in dust and ashes.

Epilogue: Job's Reward

When the Lord had finished speaking to Job, he said to Eliphaz the Temanite, 'My anger is aroused against you and your two friends, because, unlike my servant Job, you have not spoken as you ought about me. Now take seven bulls and seven rams, go to my servant Job and offer a whole-offering for yourselves, and he will intercede for you. I shall surely show him favour by not being harsh with you because you have not spoken as you ought about me, as he has done.' Then Eliphaz the Temanite and Bildad the Shuhite and Zophar the Naamathite went and carried out the Lord's command, and the Lord showed favour to Job when he had interceded for his friends.

The Lord restored Job's fortunes, and gave him twice the possessions he had before. All Job's brothers and sisters and his acquaintance of former days came and feasted with him in his home. They consoled and comforted him for all the misfortunes which the Lord had inflicted on him, and each of them gave him a sheep and a gold ring.

Thus the Lord blessed the end of Job's life more than the beginning.

23 | SELECTIONS FROM THE PSALMS

Psalms of Wisdom

Spiritual Growth
Happy is the one
who does not take the counsel of the wicked for a guide,
or follow the path that sinners tread,
or take his seat in the company of scoffers.
His delight is in the law of the Lord;
it is his meditation day and night.
He is like a tree
planted beside water channels;
it yields its fruit in season
and its foliage never fades.
So he too prospers in all he does.

The wicked are not like this;
rather they are like chaff driven by the wind.
When judgement comes, therefore, they will not stand firm,
nor will sinners in the assembly of the righteous.

The Lord watches over the way of the righteous,
but the way of the wicked is doomed.

Waiting for God
Do not be vexed because of evildoers
or envy those who do wrong.
For like the grass they soon wither,
and like green pasture they fade away.

Trust in the Lord and do good;
settle in the land and find safe pasture.
Delight in the Lord,
and he will grant you your heart's desire.

Commit your way to the Lord;
trust in him, and he will act.
He will make your righteousness shine clear as the day
and the justice of your cause like the brightness of noon.

Wait quietly for the Lord, be patient till he comes;
do not envy those who gain their ends,
or be vexed at their success.

Be angry no more, have done with wrath;
do not be vexed: that leads to evil.

Close to the Edge
My feet had almost slipped,
my foothold had all but given way,
because boasters roused my envy
when I saw how the wicked prosper.
No painful suffering for them!
They are sleek and sound in body;
they are not in trouble like ordinary mortals,
nor are they afflicted like other folk.
Therefore they wear pride like a necklace
and violence like a robe that wraps them round.
Their eyes gleam through folds of fat,
while vain fancies flit through their minds.
Their talk is all mockery and malice;
high-handedly they threaten oppression.

I set my mind to understand this
but I found it too hard for me,
until I went into God's sanctuary,
where I saw clearly what their destiny would be.

My mind was embittered,
and I was pierced to the heart.
I was too brutish to understand,
in your sight, God, no better than a beast.
Yet I am always with you;
you hold my right hand.
You guide me by your counsel

and afterwards you will receive me with glory.
Whom have I in heaven but you?
And having you, I desire nothing else on earth.

Psalms of Praise

God's Glorious Name
Lord our sovereign,
how glorious is your name throughout the world!
Your majesty is praised as high as the heavens,
from the mouths of babes and infants at the breast.
You have established a bulwark against your adversaries
to restrain the enemy and the avenger.

When I look up at your heavens, the work of your fingers,
at the moon and the stars you have set in place,
what is a frail mortal, that you should be mindful of him,
a human being, that you should take notice of him?

Yet you have made him little less than a god,
crowning his head with glory and honour.
You make him master over all that you have made,
putting everything in subjection under his feet:
all sheep and oxen, all the wild beasts,
the birds in the air, the fish in the sea,
and everything that moves along ocean paths.

Lord our sovereign,
how glorious is your name throughout the world!

Silent Witnesses
The heavens tell out the glory of God,
heaven's vault makes known his handiwork.
One day speaks to another,
night to night imparts knowledge,
and this without speech or language
or sound of any voice.
Their sign shines forth on all the earth,
their message to the ends of the world.

In the heavens an abode is fixed for the sun,
which comes out like a bridegroom from the bridal chamber,
rejoicing like a strong man to run his course.
Its rising is at one end of the heavens,
its circuit reaches from one end to the other,
and nothing is hidden from its heat.

Divine Compassion

Bless the Lord, my soul;
with all my being I bless his holy name.
Bless the Lord, my soul,
and forget none of his benefits.
He pardons all my wrongdoing
and heals all my ills.

The Lord is compassionate and gracious,
long-suffering and ever faithful;
he will not always accuse
or nurse his anger for ever.
He has not treated us as our sins deserve
or repaid us according to our misdeeds.
As the heavens tower high above the earth,
so outstanding is his love towards those who fear him.
As far as east is from west,
so far from us has he put away our offences.
As a father has compassion on his children,
so the Lord has compassion on those who fear him;
for he knows how we were made,
he remembers that we are but dust.

The days of a mortal are as grass;
he blossoms like a wild flower in the meadow:
a wind passes over him, and he is gone,
and his place knows him no more.
But the Lord's love is for ever on those who fear him,
and his righteousness on their posterity,
on those who hold fast to his covenant,
who keep his commandments in mind.

The Lord has established his throne in heaven,
his kingly power over the whole world.
Bless the Lord, you his angels,
mighty in power, who do his bidding
and obey his command.
Bless the Lord, all you his hosts,
his ministers who do his will.
Bless the Lord, all created things,
everywhere in his dominion.
Bless the Lord, my soul.

Psalms of Lamentation

A Cry of Dereliction

My God, my God, why have you forsaken me?
Why are you so far from saving me,
so far from heeding my groans?
My God, by day I cry to you, but there is no answer;
in the night I cry with no respite.
You, the praise of Israel,
are enthroned in the sanctuary.

But I am a worm, not a man,
abused by everyone, scorned by the people.
All who see me jeer at me,
grimace at me, and wag their heads:
'He threw himself on the Lord for rescue;
let the Lord deliver him, for he holds him dear!'

But you are he who brought me from the womb,
who laid me at my mother's breast.
To your care I was entrusted at birth;
from my mother's womb you have been my God.
Do not remain far from me,
for trouble is near and I have no helper.
Hounds are all about me;
a band of ruffians rings me round,
and they have bound me hand and foot.
I tell my tale of misery,

while they look on gloating.
They share out my clothes among them
and cast lots for my garments.

But do not remain far away, Lord;
you are my help, come quickly to my aid.
Let the humble eat and be satisfied.
Let those who seek the Lord praise him.
May you always be in good heart!
Let all the ends of the earth remember
and turn again to the Lord;
let all the families of the nations bow before him.

A Prayer of Confession
God, be gracious to me in your faithful love;
in the fullness of your mercy blot out my misdeeds.
Wash away all my iniquity
and cleanse me from my sin.
For well I know my misdeeds,
and my sins confront me all the time.
Against you only have I sinned
and have done what displeases;
you are right when you accuse me
and justified in passing sentence.
From my birth I have been evil,
sinful from the time my mother conceived me.

You desire faithfulness in the inmost being,
so teach me wisdom in my heart.
Sprinkle me with hyssop, so that I may be cleansed;
wash me, and I shall be whiter than snow.
Let me hear the sound of joy and gladness;
you have crushed me, but make me rejoice again.
Turn away your face from my sins
and wipe out all my iniquity.
God, create a pure heart for me,
and give me a new and steadfast spirit.
Do not drive me from your presence
or take your holy spirit from me.
Restore to me the joy of your deliverance

and grant me a willing spirit to uphold me.
I shall teach transgressors your ways,
and sinners will return to you.

The Wings of a Dove

Listen, God, to my prayer:
do not hide yourself from my pleading.
Hear me and give me an answer,
for my cares leave me no peace.
My heart is torn with anguish
and the terrors of death bear down on me.
Fear and trembling assail me
and my whole frame shudders.
I say: 'Oh that I had the wings of a dove
to fly away and find rest!'
I would escape far away
to a refuge in the wilderness.
Soon I would find myself a shelter
from raging wind and tempest.

A Cry from the Abyss

Lord, my God, by day I call for help,
by night I cry aloud in your presence.
I have become like a man beyond help,
abandoned among the dead,
like the slain lying in the grave
whom you hold in mind no more,
who are cut off from your care.
You have plunged me into the lowest abyss,
into the darkest regions of the depths.

Will it be for the dead you work wonders?
Or can the shades rise up and praise you?
Will they speak in the grave of your love,
of your faithfulness in the tomb?
Will your wonders be known in the region of darkness,
your victories in the land of oblivion?

But as for me, Lord, I cry to you,
my prayer comes before you in the morning.

Lord, why have you cast me off,
why do you hide your face from me?
You have taken friend and neighbour far from me;
darkness is now my only companion.

A Meditation on Mortality

Lord, you have been our refuge
throughout all generations.
Before the mountains were brought forth
or the earth and the world were born,
from age to age you are God.

You turn mortals back to dust,
saying, 'Turn back, you children of mortals,'
for in your sight a thousand years
are as the passing of one day
or as a watch in the night.
You cut them off;
they are asleep in death.
They are like grass which shoots up;
though in the morning it flourishes and shoots up,
by evening it droops and withers.

We are brought to an end by your anger,
terrified by your wrath.
You set out our iniquities before you,
our secret sins in the light of your presence.
All our days pass under your wrath;
our years die away like a murmur.
Seventy years is the span of our life,
eighty if our strength holds;
at their best they are but toil and sorrow,
for they pass quickly and we vanish.
Who feels the power of your anger,
who feels your wrath like those who fear you?
So make us know how few are our days,
that our minds may learn wisdom.

Lord, how long?
Turn and show compassion to your servants.

Satisfy us at daybreak with your love,
that we may sing for joy and be glad all our days.
Grant us days of gladness for the days you have humbled us,
for the years when we have known misfortune.
May your saving acts appear to your servants,
and your glory to their children.
May the favour of the Lord our God be on us.
Establish for us all that we do,
establish it firmly.

God is Everywhere
Lord, you have examined me and you know me.
You know me at rest and in action;
you discern my thoughts from afar.
You trace my journeying and my resting-places,
and are familiar with all the paths I take.
For there is not a word that I speak
but you, Lord, know all about it.
You keep close guard behind and before me
and place your hand upon me.
Knowledge so wonderful is beyond my grasp;
it is so lofty I cannot reach it.

Where can I escape from your spirit,
where flee from your presence?
If I climb up to heaven, you are there;
if I make my bed in Sheol, you are there.
If I travel to the limits of the east,
or dwell at the bounds of the western sea,
even there your hand will be guiding me,
your right hand holding me fast.
If I say, 'Surely darkness will steal over me,
and the day around me turn to night,'
darkness is not too dark for you
and night is as light as day;
to you both dark and light are one.

You it was who fashioned my inward parts;
you knitted me together in my mother's womb.
I praise you, for you fill me with awe;

wonderful you are, and wonderful your works.
You know me through and through:
my body was no mystery to you,
when I was formed in secret,
woven in the depths of the earth.
Your eyes foresaw my deeds,
and they were all recorded in your book;
my life was fashioned
before it had come into being.

How mysterious, God, are your thoughts to me,
how vast in number they are!
Were I to try counting them,
they would be more than the grains of sand;
to finish the count, my years must equal yours.

Psalms of Trust

The Lord is My Shepherd

The Lord is my shepherd; I lack for nothing.
He makes me lie down in green pastures,
he leads me to water where I may rest;
he revives my spirit;
for his name's sake he guides me in the right paths.
Even were I to walk through a valley of deepest darkness
I should fear no harm, for you are with me;
your shepherd's staff and crook afford me comfort.

You spread a table for me in the presence of my enemies;
you have richly anointed my head with oil,
and my cup brims over.
Goodness and love unfailing will follow me
all the days of my life,
and I shall dwell in the house of the Lord
throughout the years to come.

Longing for God
God, you are my God; I seek you eagerly
with a heart that thirsts for you
and a body wasted with longing for you,
like a dry land, parched and devoid of water.
With such longing I see you in the sanctuary
and behold your power and glory.

Your unfailing love is better than life;
therefore I shall sing your praises.
Thus all my life I bless you;
in your name I lift my hands in prayer.
I am satisfied as with a rich feast
and there is a shout of praise on my lips.

I call you to mind on my bed
and meditate on you in the night watches,
for you have been my help
and I am safe in the shadow of your wings.

A Childlike Faith
Lord, my heart is not proud,
nor are my eyes haughty;
I do not busy myself with great affairs
or things too marvellous for me.
But I am calm and quiet
like a weaned child clinging to its mother.

Psalms of Thanksgiving

Lasting Joy
Sing a psalm to the Lord, all you his loyal servants;
give thanks to his holy name.
In his anger is distress, in his favour there is life.
Tears may linger at nightfall,
but rejoicing comes in the morning.

I felt secure and said,
'I can never be shaken.'

Lord, by your favour you made my mountain strong;
when you hid your face, I was struck with dismay.
To you, Lord, I called
and pleaded with you for mercy:
'What profit is there in my death,
in my going down to the pit?
Can the dust praise you?
Can it proclaim your truth?
Hear, Lord, and be gracious to me;
Lord, be my helper.'

You have turned my laments into dancing;
you have stripped off my sackcloth and clothed me with joy,
that I may sing psalms to you without ceasing.
Lord my God, I shall praise you for ever.

The Wonder of God
Patiently I waited for the Lord;
he bent down to me and listened to my cry.
He raised me out of the miry pit,
out of the mud and clay;
he set my feet on rock
and gave me a firm footing.
On my lips he put a new song,
a song of praise to our God.
Many will look with awe
and put their trust in the Lord.
Happy is he who puts his trust in the Lord
and does not look to the arrogant and treacherous.
Lord my God, great things you have done;
your wonders and your purposes are for our good;
none can compare with you.
I would proclaim them and speak of them,
but they are more than I can tell.

Full Deliverance
I love the Lord, for he has heard me
and listened to my prayer;
he has given me a hearing
and all my days I shall cry to him.

The cords of death bound me,
Sheol held me in its grip.
Anguish and torment held me fast;
then I invoked the Lord by name,
'Lord, deliver me, I pray.'

Gracious is the Lord and righteous;
our God is full of compassion.
The Lord preserves the simple-hearted;
when I was brought low, he saved me.
My heart, be at peace once more,
for the Lord has granted you full deliverance.

24 | SAYINGS OF THE WISE

Wisdom's Call

Wisdom cries aloud in the open air,
and raises her voice in public places.
She calls at the top of the bustling streets;
at the approaches to the city gates she says:
'How long will you simple fools be content with your simplicity?
If only you would respond to my reproof,
I would fill you with my spirit
and make my precepts known to you.'

Put all your trust in the Lord
and do not rely on your own understanding.
At every step you take keep him in mind,
and he will direct your path.
Do not be wise in your own estimation;
fear the Lord and turn from evil.

Happy is he who has found wisdom,
he who has acquired understanding,
for wisdom is more profitable than silver,
and the gain she brings is better than gold!
She is more precious than red coral,
and none of your jewels can compare with her.
In her right hand is long life,
in her left are riches and honour.
Her ways are pleasant ways
and her paths all lead to prosperity.
She is a tree of life to those who grasp her,
and those who hold fast to her are safe.

My son, keep my words;
store up my commands in your mind.
Keep my commands if you would live,
and treasure my teaching as the apple of your eye.
Wear them like a ring on your finger;
inscribe them on the tablet of your memory.
Call wisdom your sister,
greet understanding as a familiar friend;
then they will save you from the adulteress,
from the loose woman with her seductive words.

I glanced out of the window of my house,
I looked down through the lattice,
and I saw among the simpletons,
among the young men there I noticed
a lad devoid of all sense.
He was passing along the street at her corner,
stepping out in the direction of her house
at twilight, as the day faded,
at dusk as the night grew dark,
and there a woman came to meet him.
She was dressed like a prostitute, full of wiles,
flighty and inconstant,
a woman never content to stay at home,
lying in wait by every corner,
now in the street, now in the public squares.
She caught hold of him and kissed him;
brazenly she accosted him and said,
'I had a sacrifice, an offering, to make
and I have paid my vows today;
so I came out to meet you,
to look for you, and now I have found you.
I have spread coverings on my couch,
coloured linen from Egypt.
I have perfumed my bed
with myrrh, aloes, and cassia.
Come! Let us drown ourselves in pleasure,
let us abandon ourselves to a night of love;
for my husband is not at home.
He has gone away on a long journey,

taking a bag of silver with him;
he will not be home until full moon.'
Persuasively she cajoled him,
coaxing him with seductive words.
He followed her, the simple fool,
like an ox on its way to be slaughtered,
like an antelope bounding into the noose,
like a bird hurrying into the trap;
he did not know he was risking his life
until the arrow pierced his vitals.
But now, my sons, listen to me,
and attend to what I say.
Do not let desire entice you into her ways,
do not stray down her paths;
many has she wounded and laid low,
and her victims are without number.
Her house is the entrance to Sheol,
leading down to the halls of death.

Hear how wisdom calls
and understanding lifts her voice.
She takes her stand at the crossroads,
by the wayside, at the top of the hill;
beside the gate, at the entrance to the city,
at the approach by the portals she cries aloud:

'The Lord created me the first of his works
long ago, before all else that he made.
I was formed in earliest times,
at the beginning, before earth itself.
I was born when there was yet no ocean,
when there were no springs brimming with water.
Before the mountains were settled in their place,
before the hills I was born,
when as yet he had made neither land nor streams
nor the mass of the earth's soil.
When he set the heavens in place I was there,
when he girdled the ocean with the horizon,
when he fixed the canopy of clouds overhead
and confined the springs of the deep,

when he prescribed limits for the sea
so that the waters do not transgress his command,
when he made earth's foundations firm.
Then I was at his side each day,
his darling and delight,
playing in his presence continually,
playing over his whole world,
while my delight was in mankind.

'Now, sons, listen to me;
happy are those who keep to my ways.
Listen to instruction and grow wise;
do not ignore it.
Happy the one who listens to me,
watching daily at my threshold
with his eyes on the doorway!
For whoever finds me finds life
and wins favour with the Lord,
but whoever fails to find me deprives himself,
and all who hate me are in love with death.'

Proverbs of Solomon

A wise son is his father's joy,
but a foolish son is a sorrow to his mother.

Hate is always picking a quarrel,
but love overlooks every offence.

Heed admonition and you are on the road to life;
neglect reproof and you miss the way.

One who belittles others is lacking in sense;
someone of understanding holds his peace.

Kindness brings its own reward;
cruelty earns trouble for itself.

Like a gold ring in a pig's snout
is a beautiful woman without good sense.

One may spend freely and yet grow richer;
another is tight-fisted, yet ends in poverty.

A generous person enjoys prosperity,
and one who refreshes others will be refreshed.

A fool betrays his annoyance at once;
a clever person who is slighted conceals his feelings.

Gossip is sharp as a sword,
but the tongue of the wise brings healing.

A clever person conceals his knowledge,
but a stupid one blurts out folly.

An anxious heart is dispiriting;
a kind word brings cheerfulness.

Wealth quickly won dwindles away,
but if amassed little by little it will grow.

Hope deferred makes the heart sick;
a wish come true is a tree of life.

Even in laughter the heart can ache,
and mirth may end in sorrow.

Impatience runs into folly;
advancement comes by careful thought.

The poor are not liked even by their friends,
but the rich have friends in plenty.

Whoever despises the hungry does wrong,
but happy are they who are generous to the poor.

To be patient shows great understanding;
quick temper is the height of folly.

Peace of mind gives health of body,
but envy is a canker in the bones.

To oppress the poor is to insult the Creator;
to be generous to the needy is to do him honour.

A mild answer turns away anger,
but a sharp word makes tempers rise.

The eyes of the Lord are everywhere,
surveying everyone, good and evil.

A soothing word is a tree of life,
but a mischievous tongue breaks the spirit.

A glad heart makes a cheerful face;
heartache crushes the spirit.

Better a pittance with the fear of the Lord
than wealth with worry in its train.

Better a dish of vegetables if love goes with it
than a fattened ox eaten amid hatred.

The path of the sluggard is a tangle of briars,
but the road of the diligent is a highway.

Schemes lightly made come to nothing,
but with detailed planning they succeed.

A bright look brings joy to the heart,
and good news warms the bones to the marrow.

Whoever refuses correction is his own worst enemy,
but one who listens to reproof learns sense.

Wisdom's discipline is the fear of the Lord,
and humility comes before honour.

A mortal's whole conduct may seem right to him,
but the Lord weighs up his motives.

Commit to the Lord all that you do,
and your plans will be successful.

Pride goes before disaster,
and arrogance before a fall.

Better live humbly with those in need
than divide the spoil with the proud.

A road may seem straightforward to the one who is on it,
yet it may end as the way to death.

Disaffection sows strife,
and tale-bearing breaks up the closest friendship.

Better be slow to anger than a fighter,
better control one's temper than capture a city.

Better a dry crust and amity with it
than a feast in a house full of strife.

The smelting pot for silver, the crucible for gold,
but the Lord it is who assays the heart.

To sneer at the poor is to insult the Creator,
and whoever gloats over another's misfortune will answer for it.

One who covers up another's offence seeks his goodwill,
but one who betrays a confidence disrupts a friendship.

What use is money in the hands of a fool?
Can he buy wisdom if he has no sense?

A friend shows his friendship at all times,
and a brother is born to share troubles.

One who likes giving offence likes strife.
One who builds a lofty entrance invites disaster.

A glad heart makes for good health,
but low spirits sap one's strength.

Experience uses few words;
discernment keeps a cool head.

Even a fool, if he keeps his mouth shut, will seem wise;
if he holds his tongue, he will seem intelligent.

To answer a question before you have heard it out
is both stupid and insulting.

In a lawsuit the first speaker seems right,
until another comes forward to cross-examine him.

Some companions are good only for idle talk,
but there is a friend who sticks closer than a brother.

It is not good to have zeal without knowledge,
nor to be in too great a hurry and so miss the way.

Forbearance shows intelligence;
to overlook an offence brings glory.

Wine is an insolent fellow, strong drink a brawler,
and no one addicted to their company grows wise.

To draw back from a dispute is honourable,
but every fool comes to blows.

The lazy man who does not plough in autumn
looks for a crop at harvest and gets nothing.

Counsel in another's heart is like deep water,
but a discerning person will draw it up.

It is dangerous to dedicate a gift rashly,
to make a vow and then have second thoughts.

The Lord shines into a person's soul,
searching out his inmost being.

The glory of young men is their strength,
the dignity of old men their grey hairs.

To do what is right and just
is more acceptable to the Lord than sacrifice.

A good name is more to be desired than great riches;
esteem is better than silver or gold.

The sluggard protests, 'There is a lion outside;
I shall be killed if I go on the street.'

The mouth of an adulteress is like a deep pit;
he whom the Lord has cursed will fall into it.

Sayings of the Wise

Pay heed and listen to the sayings of the wise,
and apply your mind to the knowledge I impart;
to keep them in your heart will give pleasure,
and then you will always have them ready on your lips.

Never make friends with someone prone to anger,
nor keep company with anyone hot-tempered;
be careful not to learn his ways
and find yourself caught in a trap.

Whose is the misery? Whose the remorse?
Whose are the quarrels and the anxiety?
Who gets the bruises without knowing why?

Whose eyes are bloodshot?
Those who linger late over their wine,
those always sampling some new spiced liquor.

Do not gulp down the wine, the strong red wine,
when the droplets form on the side of the cup.
It may flow smoothly
but in the end it will bite like a snake
and poison like a cobra.
Then your eyes will see strange sights,
your wits and your speech will be confused;
you become like a man tossing out at sea,
like one who clings to the top of the rigging;
you say, 'If I am struck down, what do I care?
If I am overcome, what of it?
As soon as I wake up,
I shall turn to the wine again.'

I passed by the field of an idle fellow,
by the vineyard of someone with no sense.
I looked, and it was all overgrown with thistles;
it was covered with weeds,
and its stone wall was broken down.
I saw and I took it to heart,
I considered and learnt the lesson:
a little sleep, a little slumber,
a little folding of the hands in rest –
and poverty will come on you like a footpad,
want will assail you like a hardened ruffian.

More Proverbs of Solomon

Like apples of gold set in silver filigree
is a word spoken in season.

Like a golden ear-ring or a necklace of Nubian gold
is a wise person's reproof in an attentive ear.

Like the coolness of snow in harvest time
is a trusty messenger to those who send him;
he brings new life to his masters.

Like clouds and wind that bring no rain
is he who boasts of gifts he never gives.

Like a club, a sword, or a sharp arrow
is a false witness who denounces his friend.

Like a decaying tooth or a sprained ankle
is a perfidious person relied on in the day of trouble.

Like one who dresses a wound with vinegar,
so is the sweetest of singers to the heavy-hearted.

Like cold water to the throat that is faint with thirst
is good news from a distant land.

Like a city breached and defenceless
is a man who cannot control his temper.

Like snow in summer or rain at harvest,
honour is unseasonable when paid to a fool.

Like a fluttering sparrow or a darting swallow,
groundless abuse gets nowhere.

Like one who ties the stone into his sling
is he who bestows honour on a fool.

Like a thorn-stick brandished by a drunkard
is a proverb in the mouth of a fool.

Like an archer who shoots at any passer-by
is one who hires a fool or a drunkard.

Like someone who seizes a stray cur by the ears
is he who meddles in a quarrel not his own.

Like a madman shooting at random
his deadly darts and lethal arrows,
so is the man who deceives another
and then says, 'It was only a joke.'

Like coal for glowing embers and wood for the fire
is a quarrelsome man for kindling strife.

Like glaze spread on earthenware
is glib speech that covers a spiteful heart.

As iron sharpens iron,
so one person sharpens the wits of another.

As someone sees his face reflected in water,
so he sees his own mind reflected in another's.

Sayings of Agur

Two things I ask of you –
do not withhold them in my lifetime:
put fraud and lying far from me;
give me neither poverty nor wealth,
but provide me with the food I need.

Three things there are which will never be satisfied,
four which never say, 'Enough!'
Sheol, a barren woman,
a land thirsty for water,
and fire that never says, 'Enough!'

Three things there are which are too wonderful for me,
four which are beyond my understanding:
the way of an eagle in the sky,
the way of a serpent over rock,
the way of a ship out at sea,
and the way of a man with a girl.

Under three things the earth shakes,
four things it cannot bear:
a slave becoming king,
a fool gorging himself,
a hateful woman getting wed,
and a slave supplanting her mistress.

Four things there are which are smallest on earth
yet wise beyond the wisest:
ants, a folk with no strength,
yet they prepare their store of food in the summer;
rock-badgers, a feeble folk,
yet they make their home among the rocks;
locusts, which have no king,
yet they all sally forth in formation;
the lizard, which can be grasped in the hand,
yet is found in the palaces of kings.

Three things there are which are stately in their stride,
four which are stately as they move:
the lion, mighty among beasts,
which will not turn tail for anyone;
the strutting cock, the he-goat,
and a king going forth at the head of his army.

Sayings of Lemuel

What shall I say to you, my son,
child of my womb and answer to my prayers?
Do not give the vigour of your manhood to women,
or consort with women who bring down kings.
Lemuel, it is not for kings, not for kings to drink wine,
or for those who govern to crave strong liquor.
If they drink, they will forget rights and customs
and twist the law against all who are defenceless.
Give strong drink to the despairing
and wine to the embittered of heart;
let them drink and forget their poverty

and remember their trouble no more.
Speak up for those who cannot speak for themselves;
oppose any that go to law against them;
speak out and pronounce just sentence
and give judgement for the wretched and the poor.

The Virtuous Wife

Who can find a good wife?
Her worth is far beyond red coral.
Her husband's whole trust is in her,
and children are not lacking.
She works to bring him good, not evil,
all the days of her life.
She is open-handed to the wretched
and extends help to the poor.
When it snows she has no fear for her household,
for they are wrapped in double cloaks.
She is clothed in strength and dignity
and can afford to laugh at tomorrow.
When she opens her mouth, it is to speak wisely;
her teaching is sound.
She keeps her eye on the conduct of her household
and does not eat the bread of idleness.
Her sons with one accord extol her virtues;
her husband too is loud in her praise:
'Many a woman shows how gifted she is;
but you excel them all.'
Charm is deceptive and beauty fleeting;
but the woman who fears the Lord is honoured.
Praise her for all she has accomplished;
let her achievements bring her honour at the city gates.

25 | THE WORLD ACCORDING TO ECCLESIASTES

The Futility of Life

The words of the Speaker, the son of David, king in Jerusalem.

Futility, utter futility, says the Speaker, everything is futile. What does anyone profit from all his labour and toil here under the sun? Generations come and generations go, while the earth endures for ever.

The sun rises and the sun goes down; then it speeds to its place and rises there again. The wind blows to the south, it veers to the north; round and round it goes and returns full circle. All streams run to the sea, yet the sea never overflows; back to the place from which the streams ran they return to run again.

All things are wearisome. No one can describe them all, no eye can see them all, no ear can hear them all. What has happened will happen again, and what has been done will be done again; there is nothing new under the sun.

I, the Speaker, ruled as king over Israel in Jerusalem; and I applied my mind to understanding wisdom and knowledge, madness and folly, and I came to see that this too is a chasing of the wind. For in much wisdom is much vexation; the more knowledge, the more suffering.

I said to myself, 'Come, I will test myself with pleasure and get enjoyment'; but that too was futile. Of laughter I said, 'It is madness!' And of pleasure, 'What is the good of that?' I achieved greatness, surpassing all my predecessors in Jerusalem; and my wisdom stood me in good stead. I did not refuse my eyes anything they coveted; I did not deny myself any pleasure. Indeed I found pleasure in all my labour, and for all my labour this was my reward. I considered my handiwork, all my labour and toil: it was futility, all of it, and a chasing of the wind, of no profit under the sun.

A Season for Everything

For everything its season, and for every activity under heaven its time:

> a time to be born and a time to die;
> a time to plant and a time to uproot;
>
> a time to kill and a time to heal;
> a time to break down and a time to build up;
>
> a time to weep and a time to laugh;
> a time for mourning and a time for dancing;
>
> a time to scatter stones and a time to gather them;
> a time to embrace and a time to abstain from embracing;
>
> a time to seek and a time to lose;
> a time to keep and a time to discard;
>
> a time to tear and a time to mend;
> a time for silence and a time for speech;
>
> a time to love and a time to hate;
> a time for war and a time for peace.

What profit has the worker from his labour? I have seen the task that God has given to mortals to keep them occupied. He has made everything to suit its time; moreover he has given mankind a sense of past and future, but no comprehension of God's work from beginning to end.

Moreover I saw here under the sun that, where justice ought to be, there was wickedness; and where righteousness ought to be, there was wickedness. I said to myself, 'God will judge the just and the wicked equally; for every activity and every purpose has its proper time.' I said to myself, 'In dealing with human beings it is God's purpose to test them and to see what they truly are. Human beings and beasts share one and the same fate: death comes to both alike. They all draw the same breath. Man has no advantage over beast, for everything is futility. All go to the same place: all came from the dust, and to the dust all return. Who knows whether the spirit of a human being goes upward or whether the spirit of a beast goes downward to the earth?' So I saw that there is nothing better than that all should enjoy their work, since that is their lot. For who will put them in a position to see what will happen afterwards?

Wisdom and Prudence

Two are better than one, for their partnership yields this advantage: if one falls, the other can help his companion up again; but woe betide the solitary person who when down has no partner to help him up. And if two lie side by side they keep each other warm; but how can one keep warm by himself? If anyone is alone, an assailant may overpower him, but two can resist; and a cord of three strands is not quickly snapped.

Do not be impulsive in speech, nor be guilty of hasty utterance in God's presence. God is in heaven and you are on earth, so let your words be few. Dreams come with much business; the voice of the fool comes with much chatter.

No one who loves money can ever have enough, and no one who loves wealth enjoys any return from it. This too is futility. When riches increase, so does the number of parasites living off them; and what advantage has the owner, except to feast his eyes on them? Sweet is the sleep of a labourer whether he has little or much to eat, but the rich man who has too much cannot sleep.

It is better to listen to the rebukes of the wise than to the songs of fools. For the laughter of fools is like the crackling of thorns under a pot. That too is futility. Oppression drives the wise crazy, and a bribe corrupts the mind. Better the end of anything than its beginning; better patience than pride!

Do not be quick to take offence, for it is fools who nurse resentment. Do not ask why the old days were better than the present; for that is a foolish question. Wisdom is better than possessions and an advantage to all who see the sun. Better have wisdom behind you than money; wisdom profits by giving life to those who possess her.

Consider God's handiwork; who can straighten what he has made crooked? When things go well, be glad; but when they go ill, consider this: God has set the one alongside the other in such a way that no one can find out what is to happen afterwards. In my futile existence I have seen it all, from the righteous perishing in their righteousness to the wicked growing old in wickedness. Do not be over-righteous and do not be over-wise. Why should you destroy yourself? Do not be over-wicked and do not be a fool. Why die before your time? It is good to hold on to the one thing and not lose hold of the other; for someone who fears God will succeed both ways.

The Finality of Death

I applied my mind to acquire wisdom and to observe the tasks undertaken on earth, when mortal eyes are never closed in sleep day or night; and always I perceived that God has so ordered it that no human being should be able to discover what is happening here under the sun. However hard he may try, he will not find out; the wise may think they know, but they cannot find the truth of it.

To all this I applied my mind, and I understood – that the righteous and the wise and whatever they do are under God's control; but whether they will earn love or hatred they have no way of knowing. Everything that confronts them, everything is futile, since one and the same fate comes to all, just and unjust alike, good and bad, ritually clean and unclean, to the one who offers sacrifice and to the one who does not. The good and the sinner fare alike, he who can take an oath and he who dares not. This is what is wrong in all that is done here under the sun: that one and the same fate befalls everyone. The minds of mortals are full of evil; there is madness in their minds throughout their lives, and afterwards they go down to join the dead. But for anyone who is counted among the living there is still hope: remember, a live dog is better than a dead lion. True, the living know that they will die; but the dead know nothing. There is no more reward for them; all memory of them is forgotten. For them love, hate, rivalry, all are now over. Never again will they have any part in what is done here under the sun.

Go, then, eat your food and enjoy it, and drink your wine with a cheerful heart; for God has already accepted what you have done. Always be dressed in white, and never fail to anoint your head. Enjoy life with a woman you love all the days of your allotted span here under the sun, futile as they are; for that is your lot while you live and labour here under the sun. Whatever task lies to your hand, do it with might; because in Sheol, for which you are bound, there is neither doing nor thinking, neither understanding nor wisdom.

Time and Chance

One more thing I have observed here under the sun: swiftness does not win the race nor strength the battle. Food does not belong to the wise, nor wealth to the intelligent, nor success to the skilful; time and chance govern all. Moreover, no one knows when his hour will come; like fish caught in the destroying net, like a bird taken in a snare, so the people are trapped when misfortune comes suddenly on them.

This too is an example of wisdom as I have observed it here under the sun, and I find it of great significance. There was once a small town with few inhabitants, which a great king came to attack; he surrounded it and constructed huge siege-works against it. There was in it a poor wise man, and he saved the town by his wisdom. But no one remembered that poor man. I thought, 'Surely wisdom is better than strength'; but a poor man's wisdom is despised, and his words go unheeded. A wise man speaking quietly is more to be heeded than a commander shouting orders among fools. Wisdom is better than weapons of war, but one mistake can undo many things done well.

Dead flies make the sweet ointment of the perfumer turn rancid and ferment; so a little folly can make wisdom lose its worth.

If the clouds are heavy with rain, they will shed it on the earth; whether a tree falls south or north, it must lie as it falls. He who keeps watching the wind will never sow, and he who keeps his eye on the clouds will never reap. As you do not know how a pregnant woman comes to have a body and a living spirit in her womb, so you do not know the work of God, the maker of all things. In the morning sow your seed in good time, and do not let your hands slack off until evening, for you do not know whether this or that sowing will be successful, or whether both alike will do well.

Youth and Age

Delight in your youth, young man, make the most of your early days; let your heart and your eyes show you the way; but remember that for all these things God will call you to account. Banish vexation from your mind, and shake off the troubles of the body, for youth and the prime of life are mere futility.

Remember your Creator in the days of your youth, before the bad times come and the years draw near when you will say, 'I have no pleasure in them,' before the sun and the light of day give place to darkness, before the moon and the stars grow dim, and the clouds return with the rain.

Remember him in the day when the guardians of the house become unsteady, and the strong men stoop, when the women grinding the meal cease work because they are few, and those who look through the windows can see no longer, when the street doors are shut, when the sound of the mill fades, when the chirping of the sparrow grows faint and the songbirds fall silent; when people are afraid of a steep place and the street is full of terrors, when the blossom whitens on the almond tree and the locust can only crawl and the caper-buds no longer give zest. For mortals depart to their everlasting home, and the mourners go about the street.

Remember your Creator before the silver cord is snapped and the golden bowl is broken, before the pitcher is shattered at the spring and the wheel broken at the well, before the dust returns to the earth as it began and the spirit returns to God who gave it.

Utter futility, says the Speaker, everything is futile.

The End of the Matter

So the Speaker, in his wisdom, continued to instruct the people. He turned over many maxims in his mind and sought how best to set them out. He chose his words to give pleasure, but what he wrote was straight truth. The sayings of the wise are sharp as goads, like nails driven home; they guide the assembled people, for they come from one shepherd. One further warning, my son: there is no end to the writing of books, and much study is wearisome.

This is the end of the matter: you have heard it all. Fear God and obey his commandments; this sums up the duty of mankind. For God will bring everything we do to judgement, every secret, whether good or bad.

26 | THE LOVE SONG OF SOLOMON

Bride
May he smother me with kisses.

Your love is more fragrant than wine,
fragrant is the scent of your anointing oils,
and your name is like those oils poured out;
that is why maidens love you.
Take me with you, let us make haste;
bring me into your chamber, O king.

Companions
Let us rejoice and be glad for you;
let us praise your love more than wine,
your caresses more than rare wine.

Bride
Daughters of Jerusalem, I am dark and lovely,
like the tents of Kedar
or the tent curtains of Shalmah.

While the king reclines on his couch,
my spikenard gives forth its scent.
My beloved is for me a sachet of myrrh
lying between my breasts;
my beloved is for me a spray of henna blossom
from the vineyards of En-gedi.

Bridegroom
A lily among thorns
is my dearest among the maidens.

Bride

Like an apple tree among the trees of the forest,
so is my beloved among young men.
To sit in his shadow is my delight,
and his fruit is sweet to my taste.
He has taken me into the wine-garden
and given me loving glances.
Sustain me with raisins, revive me with apples;
for I am faint with love.
His left arm pillows my head, his right arm is round me.

Bridegroom

My dove, that hides in holes in the cliffs
or in crannies on the terraced hillside,
let me see your face and hear your voice;
for your voice is sweet, your face is lovely.

Companions

Catch the jackals for us, the little jackals,
the despoilers of vineyards, for our vineyards are full of blossom.

Bride

My beloved is mine and I am his;
he grazes his flock among the lilies.
While the day is cool
and the shadows are dispersing,
turn, my beloved, and show yourself
a gazelle or a young stag
on the hills where aromatic spices grow.

Night after night on my bed
I have sought my true love;
I have sought him, but I have not found him.
I said, 'I will rise and go the rounds of the city
through streets and squares,
seeking my true love.'
I sought him, but could not find him.
The watchmen came upon me,
as they made their rounds of the city.
'Have you seen my true love?' I asked them.

Scarcely had I left them behind
when I met my true love.
I held him and would not let him go
till I had brought him to my mother's house,
to the room of her who conceived me.

Bridegroom
How beautiful you are, my dearest, how beautiful!
Your eyes are doves behind your veil,
your hair like a flock of goats streaming down Mount Gilead.
Your teeth are like a flock of ewes newly shorn,
freshly come up from the dipping;
all of them have twins, and none has lost a lamb.
Your lips are like a scarlet thread,
and your mouth is lovely;
your parted lips behind your veil
are like a pomegranate cut open.

You have stolen my heart, my sister,
you have stolen it, my bride,
with just one of your eyes, one jewel of your necklace.
How beautiful are your breasts, my sister and bride!
Your love is more fragrant than wine,
your perfumes sweeter than any spices.
Your lips drop sweetness like the honeycomb, my bride,
honey and milk are under your tongue,
and your dress has the scent of Lebanon.
Your two cheeks are an orchard of pomegranates,
an orchard full of choice fruits:
spikenard and saffron, aromatic cane and cinnamon
with every frankincense tree,
myrrh and aloes
with all the most exquisite spices.
My sister, my bride, is a garden close-locked,
a garden close-locked, a fountain sealed.

Bride
The fountain in my garden is a spring of running water
flowing down from Lebanon.
Awake, north wind, and come, south wind!

Blow upon my garden to spread its spices abroad,
that my beloved may come to his garden
and enjoy the choice fruit.

Bridegroom

I have come to my garden, my sister and bride;
I have gathered my myrrh and my spices;
I have eaten my honeycomb and my honey,
and drunk my wine and my milk.
Eat, friends, and drink deep,
till you are drunk with love.

Bride

I sleep, but my heart is awake.
Listen! My beloved is knocking:
'Open to me, my sister, my dearest,
my dove, my perfect one;
for my head is drenched with dew,
my locks with the moisture of the night.'

'I have put off my robe; must I put it on again?
I have bathed my feet; must I dirty them again?'

When my beloved slipped his hand through the latch-hole,
my heart turned over.
When I arose to open for my beloved,
my hands dripped with myrrh;
the liquid myrrh from my fingers
ran over the handle of the latch.
I opened to my love,
but my love had turned away and was gone;
my heart sank when he turned his back.
Maidens of Jerusalem, I charge you,
if you find my beloved, to tell him
that I am faint with love.

Companions

What is your beloved more than any other,
O fairest of women?

What is your beloved more than any other,
that you should give us this charge?

Bride

My beloved is fair and desirable,
a paragon among ten thousand.
His head is gold, finest gold.
His locks are like palm-fronds,
black as the raven.
His eyes are like doves beside pools of water,
in their setting bathed as it were in milk.
His cheeks are like beds of spices, terraces full of perfumes;
his lips are lilies, they drop liquid myrrh.
His arms are golden rods set with topaz,
his belly a plaque of ivory adorned with sapphires.
His legs are pillars of marble set on bases of finest gold;
his aspect is like Lebanon, noble as cedars.
His mouth is sweetness itself, wholly desirable.
Such is my beloved, such is my darling,
O maidens of Jerusalem.

Companions

Where has your beloved gone,
O fairest of women?
Which way did your beloved turn,
that we may look for him with you?

Bride

My beloved has gone down to his garden,
to the beds where balsam grows,
to delight in the gardens, and to pick the lilies.
I am my beloved's, and my beloved is mine;
he grazes his flock among the lilies.

Bridegroom

How beautiful are your sandalled feet, O prince's daughter!
The curves of your thighs are like ornaments
devised by a skilled craftsman.
Your navel is a rounded goblet
that will never lack spiced wine.

Your belly is a heap of wheat
encircled by lilies.
Your two breasts are like two fawns,
twin fawns of a gazelle.
Your neck is like a tower of ivory.
Your eyes are the pools in Heshbon,
beside the gate of the crowded city.
Your nose is like towering Lebanon
that looks towards Damascus.
You carry your head like Carmel;
your flowing locks are lustrous black,
tresses braided with ribbons.
How beautiful, how entrancing you are,
my loved one, daughter of delights!
You are stately as a palm tree,
and your breasts are like clusters of fruit.
I said, 'Let me climb up into the palm
to grasp its fronds.'
May I find your breasts like clusters of grapes on the vine,
your breath sweet-scented like apples,
Your mouth like fragrant wine
flowing smoothly to meet my caresses,
gliding over my lips and teeth.

Bride

I am my beloved's, his longing is all for me.
Come, my beloved, let us go out into the fields
to lie among the henna bushes;
let us go early to the vineyards
and see if the vine has budded or its blossom opened,
or if the pomegranates are in flower.
There I shall give you my love,
when the mandrakes yield their perfume,
and all choice fruits are ready at our door,
fruits new and old
which I have in store for you, my love.

Bridegroom

I charge you, maidens of Jerusalem:
Do not rouse or awaken love
until it is ready.

Companions
Who is this coming up from the wilderness
leaning on her beloved?

Bridegroom
Under the apple tree I roused you.
It was there your mother was in labour with you,
there she who bore you was in labour.
Wear me as a seal over your heart,
as a seal upon your arm;
for love is strong as death,
passion cruel as the grave;
it blazes up like a blazing fire,
fiercer than any flame.
Many waters cannot quench love,
no flood can sweep it away;
if someone were to offer for love
all the wealth in his house,
it would be laughed to scorn.

Companions
We have a little sister
who as yet has no breasts.
What shall we do with our sister
when she is asked in marriage?
If she is a wall,
we shall build on it a silver parapet;
if she is a door,
we shall bar it with a plank of cedarwood.

Bridegroom
My bride, you sit in my garden,
and my friends are listening to your voice.
Let me hear it too.

Bride
Come into the open, my beloved,
and show yourself like a gazelle or a young stag
on the spice-bearing mountains.

27 | WORDS AND VISIONS OF THE PROPHETS

The Prophet's Calling

In the year that King Uzziah died I saw the Lord seated on a throne, high and exalted, and the skirt of his robe filled the temple. Seraphim were in attendance on him. Each had six wings: with one pair of wings they covered their faces and with another their bodies, and with the third pair they flew. They were calling to one another,

> 'Holy, holy, holy is the Lord of Hosts:
> the whole earth is full of his glory.'

As each called, the threshold shook to its foundations at the sound, while the house began to fill with clouds of smoke. Then I said,

> 'Woe is me! I am doomed,
> for my own eyes have seen the King, the Lord of Hosts,
> I, a man of unclean lips,
> I, who dwell among a people of unclean lips.'

One of the seraphim flew to me, carrying in his hand a glowing coal which he had taken from the altar with a pair of tongs. He touched my mouth with it and said,

> 'This has touched your lips;
> now your iniquity is removed
> and your sin is wiped out.'

I heard the Lord saying, 'Whom shall I send? Who will go for us?' I said: 'Here am I! Send me.' He replied: 'Go, tell this people:

'However hard you listen, you will never understand.
However hard you look, you will never perceive.
This people's wits are dulled;
they have stopped their ears and shut their eyes,
so that they may not see with their eyes,
nor listen with their ears,
nor understand with their wits,
and then turn and be healed.'

I asked, 'Lord, how long?' And he answered,

'Until cities fall in ruins and are deserted,
until houses are left without occupants,
and the land lies ruined and waste.'

The Prince of Peace

The people that walked in darkness
have seen a great light;
on those who lived in a land as dark as death
a light has dawned.
You have increased their joy
and given them great gladness;
they rejoice in your presence
as those who rejoice at harvest,
as warriors exult when dividing spoil.

For a child has been born to us, a son is given to us;
he will bear the symbol of dominion on his shoulder,
and his title will be:
Wonderful Counsellor, Mighty Hero,
Eternal Father, Prince of Peace.
Wide will be the dominion
and boundless the peace
bestowed on David's throne and on his kingdom,
to establish and support it
with justice and righteousness
from now on, for evermore.
The zeal of the Lord of Hosts will do this.

The Peaceable Kingdom

A branch will grow from the stock of Jesse,
and a shoot will spring from his roots.
On him the spirit of the Lord will rest:
a spirit of wisdom and understanding,
a spirit of counsel and power,
a spirit of knowledge and fear of the Lord;
and in the fear of the Lord will be his delight.
He will not judge by outward appearances
or decide a case on hearsay;
but with justice he will judge the poor
and defend the humble in the land with equity;
like a rod his verdict will strike the ruthless,
and with his word he will slay the wicked.
He will wear the belt of justice,
and truth will be his girdle.

Then the wolf will live with the lamb,
and the leopard lie down with the kid;
the calf and the young lion will feed together,
with a little child to tend them.
The cow and the bear will be friends,
and their young will lie down together;
and the lion will eat straw like cattle.
The infant will play over the cobra's hole,
and the young child dance over the viper's nest.
There will be neither hurt nor harm in all my holy mountain;
for the land will be filled with the knowledge of the Lord,
as the waters cover the sea.

The Fall of a Tyrant

Bright morning star, how you have fallen from heaven,
thrown to earth, prostrate among the nations!
You thought to yourself:
'I shall scale the heavens
to set my throne high above the mighty stars;
I shall take my seat on the mountain where the gods assemble

in the far recesses of the north.
I shall ascend beyond the towering clouds
and make myself like the Most High!'

Instead you are brought down to Sheol,
into the depths of the abyss.
Those who see you stare at you,
reflecting as they gaze:
'Is this the man who shook the earth,
who made kingdoms quake,
who turned the world into a desert
and laid its cities in ruins,
who never set his prisoners free?'

All the kings of every nation lie in honour,
each in his last resting-place.
But you have been flung out without burial
like some loathsome carrion,
a carcass trampled underfoot,
a companion to the slain pierced by the sword
who have gone down to the stony abyss.

You will not be joined in burial with those kings,
for you have ruined your land,
brought death to your people.
That wicked dynasty will never again be mentioned!
Prepare the shambles for his children
butchered for their fathers' sins;
they will not rise and possess the earth
or cover the world with their cities.

The Joy of the Redeemed

Let the wilderness and the parched land be glad,
let the desert rejoice and burst into flower.
Let it flower with fields of asphodel,
let it rejoice and shout for joy.
The glory of Lebanon is given to it,
the splendour too of Carmel and Sharon;

these will see the glory of the Lord,
the splendour of our God.

Brace the arms that are limp,
steady the knees that give way;
say to the anxious, 'Be strong, fear not!
Your God comes to save you
with his vengeance and his retribution.'
Then the eyes of the blind will be opened,
and the ears of the deaf unstopped.
Then the lame will leap like deer,
and the dumb shout aloud;
for water will spring up in the wilderness
and torrents flow in the desert.
The mirage will become a pool,
the thirsty land bubbling springs;
instead of reeds and rushes, grass will grow
in country where wolves have their lairs.

And a causeway will appear there;
it will be called the Way of Holiness.
No one unclean will pass along it;
it will become a pilgrim's way,
and no fool will trespass on it.
No lion will come there,
no savage beast go by;
not one will be found there.
But by that way those the Lord has redeemed will return.
The Lord's people, set free, will come back
and enter Zion with shouts of triumph,
crowned with everlasting joy.
Gladness and joy will come upon them,
while suffering and weariness flee away.

The Consolation of Israel

Comfort my people; bring comfort to them,
says your God;
speak kindly to Jerusalem

and proclaim to her
that her term of bondage is served,
her penalty is paid;
for she has received at the Lord's hand
double measure for all her sins.

A voice cries:
'Clear a road through the wilderness for the Lord,
prepare a highway across the desert for our God.
Let every valley be raised,
every mountain and hill be brought low,
uneven ground be made smooth,
and steep places become level.
Then will the glory of the Lord be revealed
and all mankind together will see it.
The Lord himself has spoken.'

A voice says, 'Proclaim!'
and I asked, 'What shall I proclaim?'
'All mortals are grass,
they last no longer than a wild flower of the field.
The grass withers, the flower fades,
when the blast of the Lord blows on them.
Surely the people are grass!
The grass may wither, the flower fade,
but the word of our God will endure for ever.'

Climb to a mountaintop,
you that bring good news to Zion;
raise your voice and shout aloud,
you that carry good news to Jerusalem,
raise it fearlessly;
say to the cities of Judah, 'Your God is here!'
Here is the Lord God; he is coming in might,
coming to rule with powerful arm.
His reward is with him,
his recompense before him.
Like a shepherd he will tend his flock
and with his arm keep them together;
he will carry the lambs in his bosom
and lead the ewes to water.

God's Power and Glory

Who has measured the waters of the sea in the hollow of his hand,
or with its span gauged the heavens?
Who has held all the soil of the earth in a bushel,
or weighed the mountains on a balance,
the hills on a pair of scales?
Who has directed the spirit of the Lord?
What counsellor stood at his side to instruct him?
With whom did he confer to gain discernment?
Who taught him this path of justice,
or taught him knowledge,
or showed him the way of wisdom?
To him nations are but drops from a bucket,
no more than moisture on the scales;
to him coasts and islands weigh as light as specks of dust!

Do you not know, have you not heard,
were you not told long ago,
have you not perceived ever since the world was founded,
that God sits enthroned on the vaulted roof of the world,
and its inhabitants appear as grasshoppers?
He stretches out the skies like a curtain,
spreads them out like a tent to live in;
he reduces the great to naught
and makes earthly rulers as nothing.
Scarcely are they planted, scarcely sown,
scarcely have they taken root in the ground,
before he blows on them and they wither,
and a whirlwind carries them off like chaff.

To whom, then, will you liken me,
whom set up as my equal?
asks the Holy One.
Do you not know, have you not heard?
The Lord, the eternal God,
creator of earth's farthest bounds,
does not weary or grow faint;
his understanding cannot be fathomed.

God's Suffering Servant

My servant will achieve success,
he will be raised to honour, high and exalted.
Time was when many were appalled at you, my people;
so now many nations recoil at the sight of him,
and kings curl their lips in disgust.
His form, disfigured, lost all human likeness;
his appearance so changed he no longer looked like a man.
They see what they had never been told
and their minds are full of things unheard before.

Who could have believed what we have heard?
To whom has the power of the Lord been revealed?
He grew up before the Lord like a young plant
whose roots are in parched ground;
he had no beauty, no majesty to catch our eyes,
no grace to attract us to him.
He was despised, shunned by all,
pain-racked and afflicted by disease;
we despised him, we held him of no account,
an object from which people turn away their eyes.
Yet it was our afflictions he was bearing,
our pain he endured,
while we thought of him as smitten by God,
struck down by disease and misery.
But he was pierced for our transgressions,
crushed for our iniquities;
the chastisement he bore restored us to health
and by his wounds we are healed.
We had all strayed like sheep,
each of us going his own way,
but the Lord laid on him
the guilt of us all.

He was maltreated, yet he was submissive
and did not open his mouth;
like a sheep led to the slaughter,
like a ewe that is dumb before the shearers,
he did not open his mouth.

He was arrested and sentenced and taken away,
and who gave a thought to his fate –
how he was cut off from the world of the living,
stricken to death for my people's transgression?
He was assigned a grave with the wicked,
a burial-place among felons,
though he had done no violence,
had spoken no word of treachery.

Yet the Lord took thought for his oppressed servant
and healed him who had given himself as a sacrifice for sin.
He will enjoy long life and see his children's children,
and in his hand the Lord's purpose will prosper.
By his humiliation my servant will justify many;
after his suffering he will see light and be satisfied;
it is their guilt he bears.

Therefore I shall allot him a portion with the great,
and he will share the spoil with the mighty,
because he exposed himself to death
and was reckoned among transgressors,
for he bore the sin of many
and interceded for transgressors.

Healing Peace

These are the words of the high and exalted One,
who is enthroned for ever, whose name is holy:
I dwell in a high and holy place
and with him who is broken and humble in spirit,
to revive the spirit of the humble,
to revive the courage of the broken.
I shall not be always accusing,
I shall not continually nurse my wrath,
else the spirit of the creatures whom I made
would be faint because of me.
I shall create words of praise.
Peace, peace, for all, both far and near;
I shall heal them, says the Lord.

But the wicked are like a storm-tossed sea,
a sea that cannot be still,
whose waters cast up mud and dirt.

There is no peace for the wicked,
says my God.

The Prophet's Mission

The spirit of the Lord God is upon me
because the Lord has anointed me;
he has sent me to announce good news to the humble,
to bind up the broken-hearted,
to proclaim liberty to captives,
release to those in prison;
to proclaim a year of the Lord's favour
and a day of the vengeance of our God;
to comfort all who mourn,
to give them garlands instead of ashes,
oil of gladness instead of mourners' tears,
a garment of splendour for the heavy heart.
They will be called trees of righteousness,
planted by the Lord for his adornment.

A New Creation

See, I am creating new heavens and a new earth!
The past will no more be remembered
nor will it ever come to mind.
Rejoice and be for ever filled with delight
at what I create;
for I am creating Jerusalem as a delight
and her people as a joy;
I shall take delight in Jerusalem
and rejoice in my people;
the sound of weeping, the cry of distress
will be heard in her no more.
No child there will ever again die in infancy,

no old man fail to live out his span of life.
He who dies at a hundred is just a youth,
and if he does not attain a hundred he is thought accursed!
My people will build houses and live in them,
plant vineyards and eat their fruit;
they will not build for others to live in
or plant for others to eat.
They will be as long-lived as a tree,
and my chosen ones will enjoy the fruit of their labour.
They will not toil to no purpose
or raise children for misfortune,
because they and their issue after them
are a race blessed by the Lord.
Even before they call to me, I shall answer,
and while they are still speaking I shall respond.
The wolf and the lamb will feed together
and the lion will eat straw like the ox,
and as for the serpent, its food will be dust.
Neither hurt nor harm will be done in all my holy mountain,
says the Lord.

The Desolation of Israel

I looked at the earth, and it was chaos,
at the heavens, and their light was gone,
at the mountains, and they were reeling,
and all the hills rocked to and fro.
I looked: no one was there,
and all the birds of heaven had taken wing.
I looked: the fertile land was wilderness,
its towns all razed to the ground
before the Lord, before his fierce anger.
These are the words of the Lord:
The whole land will be desolate,
and I shall make an end of it.
The earth will be in mourning for this
and the heavens above turn black;
for I have made known my purpose,
and I shall not relent or change it.

At the sound of the horsemen and archers
every town is in flight;
people crawl into the thickets,
scramble up among the crags.
Every town is deserted,
no one lives there.

And you, what are you doing?
When you dress yourself in scarlet,
deck yourself out with gold ornaments,
and enlarge your eyes with antimony,
you are beautifying yourself to no purpose.
Your lovers spurn you
and seek your life.
I hear a sound as of a woman in labour,
the sharp cry of one bearing her first child.
It is Zion, gasping for breath,
stretching out her hands.
'Ah me!' she cries. 'I am weary,
weary of slaughter.'

The Prophet's Lament

You have duped me, Lord,
and I have been your dupe;
you have outwitted me and prevailed.
All the day long I have been made a laughing-stock;
everyone ridicules me.
Whenever I speak I must needs cry out,
calling, 'Violence!' and 'Assault!'
I am reproached and derided all the time
for uttering the word of the Lord.
Whenever I said, 'I shall not call it to mind
or speak in his name again,'
then his word became imprisoned within me
like a fire burning in my heart.
I was weary with holding it under,
and could endure no more.
For I heard many whispering, 'Terror let loose!

Denounce him! Let us denounce him.'
All my friends were on the watch for a false step,
saying, 'Perhaps he may be tricked;
then we can catch him
and have our revenge on him.'

A curse on the day when I was born!
The day my mother bore me,
may it be for ever unblessed!
A curse on the man who brought word to my father,
'A child is born to you, a son,'
and gladdened his heart!
May that man fare like the cities
which the Lord overthrew without mercy.
May he hear cries of alarm in the morning
and uproar at noon,
since death did not claim me before birth,
and my mother did not become my grave,
her womb great with me for ever.
Why did I come from the womb
to see only sorrow and toil,
to end my days in shame?

The New Covenant

The days are coming, says the Lord, when I shall establish a new
covenant with the people of Israel and Judah. It will not be like
the covenant I made with their forefathers when I took them by
the hand to lead them out of Egypt, a covenant they broke,
though I was patient with them, says the Lord.

For this is the covenant I shall establish with the Israelites after
those days, says the Lord: I shall set my law within them, writing
it on their hearts; I shall be their God, and they will be my
people.

No longer need they teach one another, neighbour or brother,
to know the Lord; all of them, high and low alike, will know me,
says the Lord, for I shall forgive their wrongdoing, and their sin I
shall call to mind no more.

Lamentations for a Fallen City

How deserted lies the city,
once thronging with people!
Once great among nations,
now become a widow;
once queen among provinces,
now put to forced labour!

She weeps bitterly in the night;
tears run down her cheeks.
Among all who loved her
she has no one to bring her comfort.
Her friends have all betrayed her;
they have become her enemies.

All splendour has vanished
from the daughter of Zion.
Her princes have become like deer
that can find no pasture.
They run on, their strength spent,
pursued by the hunter.

All her people groaned,
they begged for bread;
they bartered their treasures for food
to regain their strength.
'Look, Lord, and see
how cheap I am accounted.

'Is it nothing to you, you passers-by?
If only you would look and see:
is there any agony like mine,
like these torments
which the Lord made me suffer
on the day of his fierce anger?'

My eyes are blinded with tears,
my bowels writhe in anguish.
My bile is spilt on the earth

because of my people's wound,
as children and infants lie fainting
in the streets of the city.

They cry to their mothers,
'Where is there bread and wine?' –
as they faint like wounded things
in the streets of the city,
gasping out their lives
in their mothers' bosoms.

How can I cheer you? Whose plight is like yours,
daughter of Jerusalem?
To what can I compare you for your comfort,
virgin daughter of Zion?
For your wound gapes as wide as the ocean –
who can heal you?

Remember, Lord, what has befallen us;
look, and see how we are scorned.
The land we possessed is turned over to strangers,
our homes to foreigners.
We are like orphans, without a father;
our mothers are like widows.
Our forefathers sinned; now they are no more,
and we must bear the burden of their guilt.
Slaves have become our rulers,
and there is no one to free us from their power.
We must bring in our food from the wilderness
at the risk of our lives in the scorching heat.
Our skins are blackened as in a furnace
by the ravages of starvation.
Women were raped in Zion,
virgins ravished in the towns of Judah.
Princes were hung up by their hands;
elders received no respect.
Young men toil, grinding at the mill;
boys stagger under loads of wood.
Old men have left off their sessions at the city gate;
young men no longer pluck the strings.

Joy has vanished from our hearts;
our dancing is turned to mourning.

Lord, your reign is for ever,
your throne endures from age to age.
Why do you forget us so completely
and forsake us these many days?

The Chariot of God

On the fifth day of the fourth month in the thirtieth year, while I
was among the exiles by the river Kebar, the heavens were
opened and I saw visions from God.

In my vision I saw a storm-wind coming from the north, a vast
cloud with flashes of fire and brilliant light about it; and within
was a radiance like brass, glowing in the heart of the flames.

In the fire was the likeness of four living creatures in human
form. Each had four faces and each four wings; their legs were
straight, and their hoofs were like the hoofs of a calf, glistening
and gleaming like bronze. Under the wings on each of the four
sides were human hands; all four creatures had faces and wings,
and the wings of one touched those of another. They did not turn
as they moved; each creature went straight forward. This is what
their faces were like: all four had a human face and a lion's face on
the right, on the left the face of an ox and the face of an eagle.
Their wings were spread upwards; each living creature had one
pair touching those of its neighbour, while one pair covered its
body. They moved forward in whatever direction the spirit went;
they never swerved from their course. The appearance of the
creatures was as if fire from burning coals or torches were darting
to and fro among them; the fire was radiant, and out of the fire
came lightning.

As I looked at the living creatures, I saw wheels on the ground,
one beside each of the four. The wheels sparkled like topaz, and
they were all alike: in form and working they were like a wheel
inside a wheel, and when they moved in any of the four directions
they never swerved from their course. I saw that they had rims,
and the rims were covered with eyes all around. When the living
creatures moved, the wheels moved beside them; when the creatures rose from the ground, the wheels rose; they moved in
whichever direction the spirit went; and the wheels rose together

with them, for the spirit of the creatures was in the wheels. When one moved, the other moved; when one halted, the other halted; when the creatures rose from the ground, the wheels rose together with them, for the spirit of the creatures was in the wheels.

Above the heads of the living creatures was, as it were, a vault glittering like a sheet of ice, awe-inspiring, stretched over their heads above them. Under the vault their wings were spread straight out, touching one another, while one pair covered the body of each. I heard, too, the noise of their wings; when they moved it was like the noise of a mighty torrent or a thunderclap, like the noise of a crowd or an armed camp; when they halted their wings dropped. A voice was heard from above the vault over their heads, as they halted with drooping wings.

Above the vault over their heads there appeared, as it were, a sapphire in the shape of a throne, and exalted on the throne a form in human likeness. From his waist upwards I saw what might have been brass glowing like fire in a furnace; and from his waist downwards I saw what looked like fire. Radiance encircled him. Like a rainbow in the clouds after the rain was the sight of that encircling radiance; it was like the appearance of the glory of the Lord.

God and the Soul

This word of the Lord came to me: 'What do you all mean by repeating this proverb in the land of Israel:

"Parents eat sour grapes,
and their children's teeth are set on edge?"

'As I live, says the Lord God, this proverb will never again be used by you in Israel. Every living soul belongs to me; parent and child alike are mine. It is the person who sins that will die.

'If someone who is wicked renounces all his sinful ways and keeps all my laws, doing what is just and right, he will live; he will not die. None of the offences he has committed will be remembered against him; because of his righteous conduct he will live. Have I any desire for the death of a wicked person? says the Lord God. Is not my desire rather that he should mend his ways and live?

'If someone who is righteous turns from his righteous ways and commits every kind of abomination that the wicked practise, is he to do this and live? No, none of his former righteousness will be remembered in his favour; because he has been faithless and has sinned, he must die.

'"The Lord acts without principle," say the Israelites. No, it is you, Israel, that acts without principle, not I.

'Therefore I shall judge every one of you Israelites on his record, says the Lord God. Repent, renounce all your offences, or your iniquity will be your downfall. Throw off the load of your past misdeeds; get yourselves a new heart and a new spirit. Why should you Israelites die? I have no desire for the death of anyone. This is the word of the Lord God.'

The Valley of Dry Bones

The Lord's hand was upon me, and he carried me out by his spirit and set me down in a plain that was full of bones. He made me pass among them in every direction. Countless in number and very dry, they covered the plain. He said to me, 'O man, can these bones live?' I answered, 'Only you, Lord God, know that.' He said, 'Prophesy over these bones; say: Dry bones, hear the word of the Lord. The Lord God says to these bones: I am going to put breath into you, and you will live. I shall fasten sinews on you, clothe you with flesh, cover you with skin, and give you breath, and you will live. Then you will know that I am the Lord.'

I began to prophesy as I had been told, and as I prophesied there was a rattling sound and the bones all fitted themselves together. As I watched, sinews appeared upon them, flesh clothed them, and they were covered with skin, but there was no breath in them. Then he said to me, 'Prophesy to the wind, prophesy, O man, and say to it: These are the words of the Lord God: Let winds come from every quarter and breathe into these slain, that they may come to life.' I prophesied as I had been told; breath entered them, and they came to life and rose to their feet, a mighty company.

He said to me, 'O man, these bones are the whole people of Israel. They say, "Our bones are dry, our hope is gone, and we are cut off." Prophesy, therefore, and say to them: The Lord God has said: My people, I shall open your graves and bring you up from them, and restore you to the land of Israel. You, my people, will know that I am the Lord when I open your graves and bring you up from them. Then I shall put my spirit into you and you will come to life, and I shall settle you on your own soil, and you will know that I the Lord have spoken and I shall act. This is the word of the Lord.'

The Ancient of Years
In the first year that Belshazzar was king of Babylon, a dream and visions came to Daniel as he lay on his bed. Then he wrote down the dream, and here his account begins.

As I was looking,
thrones were set in place
and the Ancient in Years took his seat;
his robe was white as snow,
his hair like lamb's wool.
His throne was flames of fire
and its wheels were blazing fire;
a river of fire flowed from his presence.
Thousands upon thousands served him
and myriads upon myriads were in attendance.
The court sat, and the books were opened.

I was still watching in visions of the night and I saw one like a human being coming with the clouds of heaven; he approached the Ancient in Years and was presented to him. Sovereignty and glory and kingly power were given to him, so that all peoples and nations of every language should serve him; his sovereignty was to be an everlasting sovereignty which was not to pass away, and his kingly power was never to be destroyed.

The Time of the End
On the twenty-fourth day of the first month, I found myself on the bank of the great river, the Tigris, and when I looked up I saw a man robed in linen with a belt of Ophir gold round his waist. His body glowed like topaz, his face shone like lightning, his eyes flamed like torches, his arms and feet glittered like burnished bronze, and when he spoke his voice sounded like the voice of a multitude. I, Daniel, alone saw the vision; those who were near me did not see it, but such great trepidation fell upon them that they crept away into hiding. I was left by myself

gazing at this great vision, and my strength drained away; and sapped of all strength I became a sorry figure of a man. I heard the sound of his words and, as I did so, I lay prone on the ground in a trance.

Suddenly, at the touch of a hand, I was set, all trembling, on my hands and knees. 'Daniel, man greatly beloved,' he said to me, 'attend to the words I am about to speak to you and stand upright where you are, for I am now sent to you.' When he spoke to me, I stood up trembling with apprehension. He went on, 'Do not be afraid, Daniel, for I have come to explain to you what will happen to your people at the end of this age; for this too is a vision for those days.'

'At that time there will there will be a period of anguish
such as has never been known
ever since they became a nation till that moment.
But at that time your people will be delivered,
everyone whose name is entered in the book:
many of those who sleep in the dust of the earth will awake,
some to everlasting life
and some to the reproach of eternal abhorrence.
The wise leaders will shine like the bright vault of heaven,
and those who have guided the people in the true path
will be like the stars for ever and ever.

'But you, Daniel, keep the words secret and seal the book until the time of the end. Many will rush to and fro, trying to gain such knowledge.'

I heard, but I did not understand; so I said, 'Sir, what will be the outcome of these things?' He replied, 'Go your way, Daniel, till the end; you will rest, and then, at the end of the age, you will arise to your destiny.'

God's Love for His People

When Israel was a youth, I loved him;
out of Egypt I called my son;
but the more I called, the farther they went from me;
they must needs sacrifice to the baalim
and burn offerings to images.
It was I who taught Ephraim to walk,
I who took them in my arms;
but they did not know that
I secured them with reins
and led them with bonds of love,
that I lifted them like a little child to my cheek,
that I bent down to feed them.
Back they will go to Egypt,
the Assyrian will be their king;
for they have refused to return to me.
The sword will be brandished in their cities
and it will make an end of their priests
and devour them because of their scheming.
My people are bent on rebellion,
but though they call in unison to Baal
he will not lift them up.

How can I hand you over, Ephraim,
how can I surrender you, Israel?
How can I make you like Admah
or treat you as Zeboyim?
A change of heart moves me,
tenderness kindles within me.
I am not going to let loose my fury,
I shall not turn and destroy Ephraim,
for I am God, not a mortal;
I am the Holy One in your midst.
I shall not come with threats.

The Day of the Lord

Blow the trumpet in Zion,
sound the alarm on my holy mountain!
Let all the inhabitants of the land tremble,
for the day of the Lord is coming,
a day of darkness and gloom is at hand,
a day of cloud and dense fog.
Like blackness spread over the mountains
a vast and countless host appears;
their like has never been known,
nor will be in all the ages to come.
Their vanguard is a devouring fire,
their rearguard a leaping flame;
before them the land is a garden of Eden,
but behind them it is a desolate waste;
nothing survives their passing.
In appearance like horses,
like cavalry they charge;
they bound over the peaks
with a din like chariots,
like crackling flames burning up stubble,
like a vast host in battle array.
At their onset the earth shakes,
the heavens shudder,
sun and moon are darkened,
and the stars withhold their light.

Yet even now, says the Lord,
turn back to me wholeheartedly
with fasting, weeping, and mourning.
Rend your hearts and not your garments,
and turn back to the Lord your God,
for he is gracious and compassionate,
long-suffering and ever constant,
ready always to relent when he threatens disaster.

Then the Lord showed his ardent love for his land,
and was moved with compassion for his people.
He answered their appeal and said:
I shall send you corn, new wine, and oil,
and you will have them in plenty.
I shall expose you no longer
to the reproach of other nations.

After this I shall pour out my spirit on all mankind;
your sons and daughters will prophesy,
your old men will dream dreams
and your young men see visions;
I shall pour out my spirit in those days
even on slaves and slave-girls.
When that time comes, on that day
when I reverse the fortunes of Judah and Jerusalem,
I shall gather all the nations together
and lead them down to the valley of Jehoshaphat.

Proclaim this amongst the nations:
Declare war, call your troops to arms!
Let all the fighting men advance to the attack.
Beat your mattocks into swords
and your pruning-knives into spears.
Let even the weakling say, 'I am strong.'
Wield the knife, for the harvest is ripe;
come, tread the grapes,
for the winepress is full;
empty the vats, for they are full to the brim.
A noisy throng in the valley of Decision!
The day of the Lord is at hand
in the valley of Decision:
sun and moon are darkened
and the stars withhold their light.

Against Injustice

Woe betide those who long for the day of the Lord!
What will the day of the Lord mean for you?
The day of the Lord is indeed darkness, not light,
a day of gloom without a ray of brightness.

I spurn with loathing your pilgrim-feasts;
I take no pleasure in your sacred ceremonies.
Instead let justice flow on like a river
and righteousness like a never-failing torrent.

Woe betide those living at ease in Zion,
and those complacent on the hill of Samaria.
You thrust aside all thought of the evil day
and hasten the reign of violence.
You loll on beds inlaid with ivory
and lounge on your couches;
you drink wine by the bowlful
and anoint yourselves with the richest of oils.

Can horses gallop over rocks?
Can the sea be ploughed with oxen?
Yet you have turned into venom the process of law,
justice itself you have turned into poison.
Jubilant over a nothing, you boast,
'Have we not won power by our own strength?'

Listen to this, you that grind the poor
and suppress the humble in the land
while you say,
'When will the new moon be over
so that we may sell grain?
When will the sabbath be past
so that we may expose our wheat for sale,
giving short measure in the bushel
and taking overweight in the silver,
tilting the scales fraudulently,
and selling the refuse of the wheat;
that we may buy the weak for silver

and the poor for a pair of sandals?'
The Lord has sworn by the arrogance of Jacob:
I shall never forget any of those activities of theirs.

Will not the earth quake on account of this?
Will not all who live on it mourn?
The whole earth will surge and seethe like the Nile
and subside like the river of Egypt.

On that day, says the Lord God,
I shall make the sun go down at noon
and darken the earth in broad daylight.
I shall turn your pilgrim-feasts into mourning
and all your songs into lamentation.
I shall make you all put sackcloth round your waists
and have everyone's head shaved.
I shall make it like mourning for an only son
and the end of it like a bitter day.

Against a Hostile Nation

I shall make you the least of all nations,
an object of utter contempt.
The pride in your heart has led you astray,
you that haunt the crannies among the rocks
and make your home on the heights,
saying to yourself, 'Who can bring me to the ground?'
Though you soar as high as an eagle
and your nest is set among the stars,
even from there I shall bring you down.
This is the word of the Lord.

On that day I shall destroy all the wise men of Edom
and leave no wisdom on the mountains of Esau.
Then your warriors, Teman, will be so terror-stricken
that no survivors will be left on the mountains of Esau.
For the violence done to your brother Jacob
you will be covered with shame and cut off for ever.

A Vision of Peace

In days to come
the mountain of the Lord's house
will be established higher than all other mountains,
towering above other hills.
Peoples will stream towards it;
many nations will go, saying,
'Let us go up to the mountain of the Lord,
to the house of Jacob's God,
that he may teach us his ways
and we may walk in his paths.'
For instruction issues from Zion,
the word of the Lord from Jerusalem.
He will be judge between many peoples
and arbiter among great and distant nations.
They will hammer their swords into mattocks
and their spears into pruning-knives.
Nation will not take up sword against nation;
they will never again be trained for war.
Each man will sit under his own vine
or his own fig tree, with none to cause alarm.
The Lord of Hosts himself has spoken.

Against a Cruel City

The Lord is a jealous God, a God of vengeance;
the Lord takes vengeance and is quick to anger.
The Lord takes vengeance on his adversaries
and directs his wrath against his enemies.
The Lord is long-suffering and of great might,
but he will not let the guilty escape punishment.
His path is in the whirlwind and storm,
and the clouds are the fine dust beneath his feet.
He rebukes the sea and dries it up
and makes all the rivers fail.
Bashan and Carmel languish,
and on Lebanon the young shoots wither.
The mountains quake before him,

and the hills dissolve;
the earth is in tumult at his presence,
the world and all who live in it.
Who can stand before his wrath?
Who can resist the fury of his anger?
His rage is poured out like fire,
and the rocks are dislodged before him.
The Lord is a sure protection in time of trouble,
and cares for all who make him their refuge.
With a raging flood he makes an end of those who oppose him,
and pursues his enemies into darkness.

Woe betide the blood-stained city, steeped in deceit,
full of pillage, never empty of prey!
The crack of the whip, the rattle of wheels,
the stamping of horses, swaying chariots,
rearing chargers,
the gleam of swords, the flash of spears!
Myriads of slain, heaps of corpses,
bodies innumerable, and men stumbling over them –
all for the persistent harlotry of a harlot,
the alluring mistress of sorcery,
who by her harlotry and sorceries
beguiled nations and peoples.

Your rulers slumber, king of Assyria,
your leaders are asleep;
your people are scattered over the mountains,
with no one to round them up.
Your wounds cannot be relieved, your injury is mortal;
all who hear of your fate clap their hands in joy.
Who has not suffered your relentless cruelty?

The Prophet's Complaint

How long, Lord, will you be deaf to my plea?
'Violence!' I cry out to you,
but you do not come to the rescue.
Why do you let me look on such wickedness,
why let me see such wrongdoing?
Havoc and violence confront me,
strife breaks out, discord arises.
Therefore law becomes ineffective,
and justice is defeated;
the wicked hem in the righteous,
so that justice is perverted.

Your eyes are too pure to look on evil;
you cannot countenance wrongdoing.
Why then do you countenance the treachery of the wicked?
Why keep silent when they devour those who are more righteous?

The Lord gives me this answer:
Write down a vision, inscribe it clearly on tablets,
so that it may be read at a glance.
There is still a vision for the appointed time;
it will testify to the destined hour and will not prove false.
Though it delays, wait for it,
for it will surely come before too long.
The Lord is in his holy temple;
let all the earth be silent in his presence.

Lord, I have heard of your fame;
Lord, I am in awe of what you have done.
Through all generations you have made yourself known,
and in your wrath you did not forget mercy.

The fig tree has no buds,
the vines bear no harvest,
the olive crop fails,
the orchards yield no food,
the fold is bereft of its flock,
and there are no cattle in the stalls.

Even so I shall exult in the Lord
and rejoice in the God who saves me.
The Lord God is my strength;
he makes me as sure-footed as a hind
and sets my feet on the heights.

God's Judgement

The great day of the Lord is near,
near and coming fast;
no runner is so swift as that day,
no warrior so fleet.
That day is a day of wrath,
a day of anguish and torment,
a day of destruction and devastation,
a day of darkness and gloom,
a day of cloud and dense fog,
a day of trumpet-blasts and battle cries
against the fortified cities and lofty bastions.

Humble yourself, unruly nation; be humble,
before you are driven away to disappear like chaff,
before the burning anger of the Lord comes upon you,
before the day of the Lord's anger comes upon you.
Seek the Lord,
all in the land who live humbly, obeying his laws;
seek righteousness, seek humility;
it may be that you will find shelter
on the day of the Lord's anger.

Woe betide the tyrant city,
filthy and foul!
She heeded no warning voice,
took no rebuke to heart;
she did not put her trust in the Lord,
nor did she draw near to her God.
The leaders within her were roaring lions,
her rulers wolves of the plain
that left nothing over till morning.

Her prophets were reckless and perfidious;
her priests profaned the sanctuary
and did violence to the law.

But the Lord in her midst is just;
he does no wrong;
morning after morning he gives his judgement,
every day without fail;
yet the wrongdoer knows no shame.

God's House Will be Built

'These are the words of the Lord of Hosts: This nation says that
the time has not yet come for the house of the Lord to be rebuilt.'
Then this word came through Haggai the prophet: 'Is it a time
for you yourselves to live in your well-roofed houses, while this
house lies in ruins? Now these are the words of the Lord of
Hosts: Consider your way of life; you have sown much but reaped
little, you eat but never enough to satisfy, you drink but never
enough to cheer you, you are clothed but never warm, and he
who earns wages puts them into a purse with a hole in it.

'These are the words of the Lord of Hosts: Consider your way
of life. Go up into the hill-country, fetch timber, and build a
house acceptable to me, where I can reveal my glory, says the
Lord. For in a little while from now I shall shake the heavens and
the earth, the sea and the dry land. I shall shake all the nations,
and the treasure of all nations will come here; and I shall fill this
house with splendour, says the Lord of Hosts. Mine is the silver
and mine the gold, says the Lord of Hosts, and the splendour of
this latter house will surpass the splendour of the former, says the
Lord of Hosts. In this place I shall grant prosperity and peace.
This is the word of the Lord of Hosts.'

God Will Dwell with His People

These are the words of the Lord of Hosts: Administer true justice, show kindness and compassion to each other, do not oppress
the widow or the fatherless, the resident alien or the poor, and do
not plot evil against one another. But they refused to listen; they
turned their backs defiantly on me, they stopped their ears so as
not to hear. They were adamant in their refusal to accept the law
and the teaching which the Lord of Hosts had sent by his spirit

through the prophets of old; and in great anger the Lord of Hosts said: As they did not listen when I called, so I would not listen when they called. I drove them out among all the nations where they were strangers, leaving their land deserted behind them, so that no one came and went. Thus their pleasant land was turned into a desert.

Now, says the Lord, I shall come back to Zion and dwell in Jerusalem. Jerusalem will be called the City of Faithfulness, and the mountain of the Lord of Hosts will be called the Holy Mountain. Once again old men and women will sit in the streets of Jerusalem, each leaning on a stick because of great age; and the streets of the city will be full of boys and girls at play.

These are the words of the Lord of Hosts: Take heart, all who now hear the promise that the temple is to be rebuilt; you hear it from the prophets who were present when foundations for the house of the Lord of Hosts were laid. Before that time there was no hiring of people or animals; because of enemies, no one could go about his business in safety, for I had set everyone at odds with everyone else. But I do not feel the same now towards the remnant of this people as I did in former days, says the Lord of Hosts. For they will sow in safety; the vine will yield its fruit and the soil its produce, and the heavens will give their moisture; with all these things I shall endow the remnant of this people. To the nations you, house of Judah and house of Israel, have become proverbial as a curse; now I shall save you, and you will become proverbial as a blessing. Courage! Do not lose heart.

God's Day Will Come

I am about to send my messenger to clear a path before me. Suddenly the Lord whom you seek will come to his temple; the messenger of the covenant in whom you delight is here, here already, says the Lord of Hosts. Who can endure the day of his coming? Who can stand firm when he appears? He is like a refiner's fire, like a fuller's soap; he will take his seat, testing and purifying; he will purify the Levites and refine them like gold and silver, and so they will be fit to bring offerings to the Lord. Thus the offerings of Judah and Jerusalem will be pleasing to the Lord as they were in former days, in years long past. I shall appear before you in court, quick to testify against sorcerers, adulterers, and perjurers, against those who cheat the hired labourer of his wages, who wrong the widow and the fatherless, who thrust the alien aside and do not fear me, says the Lord of Hosts.

The day comes, burning like a furnace; all the arrogant and all evildoers will be stubble, and that day when it comes will set them ablaze, leaving them neither root nor branch, says the Lord of Hosts. But for you who fear my name, the sun of righteousness will rise with healing in its wings, and you will break loose like calves released from the stall. On the day I take action, you will tread down the wicked, for they will be as ashes under the soles of your feet, says the Lord of Hosts.

Remember the law of Moses my servant, the rules and precepts which I told him to deliver to all Israel at Horeb. Look, I shall send you the prophet Elijah before the great and terrible day of the Lord comes. He will reconcile parents to their children and children to their parents, lest I come and put the land under a ban to destroy it.

Part Four

THE STORY OF
THE CHRIST

PROLOGUE

In the beginning the Word already was.
The Word was in God's presence,
and what God was, the Word was.
He was with God at the beginning,
and through him all things came to be;
without him no created thing came into being.
In him was life,
and that life was the light of mankind.
The light shines in the darkness,
and the darkness has never mastered it.

The true light which gives light to everyone
was even then coming into the world.
He was in the world;
but the world, though it owed its being to him,
did not recognize him.
He came to his own,
and his own people would not accept him.
But to all who did accept him,
to those who put their trust in him,
he gave the right to become children of God,
born not of human stock,
by the physical desire of a human father,
but of God.

So the Word became flesh;
he made his home among us,
and we saw his glory,
such glory as befits the Father's only Son,
full of grace and truth.

28 | BIRTH AND EARLY YEARS

The Angel Gabriel Appears to Zechariah

In the reign of Herod king of Judaea there was a priest named
Zechariah, of the division of the priesthood called after Abijah.
His wife, whose name was Elizabeth, was also of priestly descent.
Both of them were upright and devout, blamelessly observing all
the commandments and ordinances of the Lord. But they had
no children, for Elizabeth was barren, and both were well on in
years.

Once, when it was the turn of his division and he was there to
take part in the temple service, he was chosen by lot, by priestly
custom, to enter the sanctuary of the Lord and offer the incense;
and at the hour of the offering the people were all assembled at
prayer outside. There appeared to him an angel of the Lord,
standing on the right of the altar of incense. At this sight,
Zechariah was startled and overcome by fear. But the angel said
to him, 'Do not be afraid, Zechariah; your prayer has been heard:
your wife Elizabeth will bear you a son, and you are to name him
John. His birth will fill you with joy and delight, and will bring
gladness to many; for he will be great in the eyes of the Lord. He
is never to touch wine or strong drink. From his very birth he
will be filled with the Holy Spirit; and he will bring back many
Israelites to the Lord their God. He will go before him as forerunner, possessed by the spirit and power of Elijah, to reconcile
father and child, to convert the rebellious to the ways of the
righteous, to prepare a people that shall be fit for the Lord.'

Zechariah said to the angel, 'How can I be sure of this? I am an
old man and my wife is well on in years.' The angel replied, 'I am
Gabriel; I stand in attendance on God, and I have been sent to
speak to you and bring you this good news. But now, because you
have not believed me, you will lose all power of speech and
remain silent until the day when these things take place; at their
proper time my words will be proved true.'

Meanwhile the people were waiting for Zechariah, surprised that he was staying so long inside the sanctuary. When he did come out he could not speak to them, and they realized that he had had a vision. He stood there making signs to them, and remained dumb.

When his period of duty was completed Zechariah returned home. His wife Elizabeth conceived, and for five months she lived in seclusion, thinking, 'This is the Lord's doing; now at last he has shown me favour and taken away from me the disgrace of childlessness.'

The Annunciation of the Birth of Jesus

In the sixth month the angel Gabriel was sent by God to Nazareth, a town in Galilee, with a message for a girl betrothed to a man named Joseph, a descendant of David; the girl's name was Mary. The angel went in and said to her, 'Greetings, most favoured one! The Lord is with you.' But she was deeply troubled by what he said and wondered what this greeting could mean. Then the angel said to her, 'Do not be afraid, Mary, for God has been gracious to you; you will conceive and give birth to a son, and you are to give him the name Jesus. He will be great, and will be called Son of the Most High. The Lord God will give him the throne of his ancestor David, and he will be king over Israel for ever; his reign shall never end.' 'How can this be?' said Mary. 'I am still a virgin.' The angel answered, 'The Holy Spirit will come upon you, and the power of the Most High will overshadow you; for that reason the holy child to be born will be called Son of God. Moreover your kinswoman Elizabeth has herself conceived a son in her old age; and she who is reputed barren is now in her sixth month, for God's promises can never fail.' 'I am the Lord's servant,' said Mary; 'may it be as you have said.' Then the angel left her.

Joseph's Dream

This is how the birth of Jesus Christ came about. His mother Mary was betrothed to Joseph; before their marriage she found she was going to have a child through the Holy Spirit. Being a man of principle, and at the same time wanting to save her from exposure, Joseph made up his mind to have the marriage contract quietly set aside. He had resolved on this, when an angel of the

Lord appeared to him in a dream and said, 'Joseph, son of David, do not be afraid to take Mary home with you to be your wife. It is through the Holy Spirit that she has conceived. She will bear a son; and you shall give him the name Jesus, for he will save his people from their sins.' All this happened in order to fulfil what the Lord declared through the prophet: 'A virgin will conceive and bear a son, and he shall be called Emmanuel,' a name which means 'God is with us'. When he woke, Joseph did as the angel of the Lord had directed him.

Mary Visits Elizabeth

Soon afterwards Mary set out and hurried away to a town in the uplands of Judah. She went into Zechariah's house and greeted Elizabeth. And when Elizabeth heard Mary's greeting, the baby stirred in her womb. Then Elizabeth was filled with the Holy Spirit and exclaimed in a loud voice, 'God's blessing is on you above all women, and his blessing is on the fruit of your womb. Who am I, that the mother of my Lord should visit me? I tell you, when your greeting sounded in my ears, the baby in my womb leapt for joy. Happy is she who has had faith that the Lord's promise to her would be fulfilled!'

The Magnificat

And Mary said:

'My soul tells out the greatness of the Lord,
my spirit has rejoiced in God my Saviour;
for he has looked with favour on his servant,
lowly as she is.
From this day forward
all generations will count me blessed,
for the Mighty God has done great things for me.
His name is holy,
his mercy sure from generation to generation
toward those who fear him.
He has shown the might of his arm,
he has routed the proud and all their schemes;
he has brought down monarchs from their thrones,
and raised on high the lowly.
He has filled the hungry with good things,

and sent the rich away empty.
He has come to the help of Israel his servant,
as he promised to our forefathers;
he has not forgotten to show mercy
to Abraham and his children's children for ever.'

Mary stayed with Elizabeth about three months and then returned home.

The Birth of John the Baptist

When the time came for Elizabeth's child to be born, she gave birth to a son. Her neighbours and relatives heard what great kindness the Lord had shown her, and they shared her delight. On the eighth day they came to circumcise the child; and they were going to name him Zechariah after his father, but his mother spoke up: 'No!' she said. 'He is to be called John.' 'But', they said, 'there is nobody in your family who has that name.' They enquired of his father by signs what he would like him to be called. He asked for a writing tablet and to everybody's astonishment wrote, 'His name is John.' Immediately his lips and tongue were freed and he began to speak, praising God. All the neighbours were overcome with awe, and throughout the uplands of Judaea the whole story became common talk. All who heard it were deeply impressed and said, 'What will this child become?' For indeed the hand of the Lord was upon him.

And Zechariah his father was filled with the Holy Spirit and uttered this prophecy:

'Praise to the Lord, the God of Israel!
For he has turned to his people and set them free.
He has raised for us a strong deliverer
from the house of his servant David.

'And you, my child, will be called Prophet of the Most High,
for you will be the Lord's forerunner, to prepare his way
and lead his people to a knowledge of salvation
through the forgiveness of their sins:
for in the tender compassion of our God
the dawn from heaven will break upon us,
to shine on those who live in darkness, under the shadow of death,
and to guide our feet into the way of peace.'

As the child grew up he became strong in spirit; he lived out in the wilderness until the day when he appeared publicly before Israel.

The Birth of Jesus

In those days a decree was issued by the emperor Augustus for a census to be taken throughout the Roman world. This was the first registration of its kind; it took place when Quirinius was governor of Syria. Everyone made his way to his own town to be registered. Joseph went up to Judaea from the town of Nazareth in Galilee, to register in the city of David called Bethlehem, because he was of the house of David by descent; and with him went Mary, his betrothed, who was expecting her child. While they were there the time came for her to have her baby, and she gave birth to a son, her firstborn. She wrapped him in swaddling clothes, and laid him in a manger, because there was no room for them at the inn.

Now in this same district there were shepherds out in the fields, keeping watch through the night over their flock. Suddenly an angel of the Lord appeared to them, and the glory of the Lord shone round them. They were terrified, but the angel said, 'Do not be afraid; I bring you good news, news of great joy for the whole nation. Today there has been born to you in the city of David a deliverer – the Messiah, the Lord. This will be the sign for you: you will find a baby wrapped in swaddling clothes, and lying in a manger.' All at once there was with the angel a great company of the heavenly host, singing praise to God:

'Glory to God in highest heaven,
and on earth peace to all in whom he delights.'

After the angels had left them and returned to heaven the shepherds said to one another, 'Come, let us go straight to Bethlehem and see this thing that has happened, which the Lord has made known to us.' They hurried off and found Mary and Joseph, and the baby lying in the manger. When they saw the child, they related what they had been told about him; and all who heard were astonished at what the shepherds said. But Mary treasured up all these things and pondered over them. The shepherds returned glorifying and praising God for what they had heard and seen; it had all happened as they had been told.

After Jesus's birth astrologers from the east arrived in Jerusalem, asking, 'Where is the new-born king of the Jews? We observed the rising of his star, and we have come to pay him homage.' King Herod was greatly perturbed when he heard this, and so was the whole of Jerusalem. He called together the chief priests and scribes of the Jews, and asked them where the Messiah was to be born. 'At Bethlehem in Judaea,' they replied, 'for this is what the prophet wrote: "Bethlehem in the land of Judah, you are by no means least among the rulers of Judah; for out of you shall come a ruler to be the shepherd of my people Israel."'

Then Herod summoned the astrologers to meet him secretly, and ascertained from them the exact time when the star had appeared. He sent them to Bethlehem, and said, 'Go and make a careful search for the child, and when you have found him, bring me word, so that I may go myself and pay him homage.'

After hearing what the king had to say they set out; there before them was the star they had seen rising, and it went ahead of them until it stopped above the place where the child lay. They were overjoyed at the sight of it and, entering the house, they saw the child with Mary his mother and bowed low in homage to him; they opened their treasure chests and presented gifts to him: gold, frankincense, and myrrh. Then they returned to their own country by another route, for they had been warned in a dream not to go back to Herod.

Eight days later the time came to circumcise him, and he was given the name Jesus, the name given by the angel before he was conceived.

Then, after the purification had been completed in accordance with the law of Moses, they brought him up to Jerusalem to present him to the Lord. There was at that time in Jerusalem a man called Simeon. This man was upright and devout, one who watched and waited for the restoration of Israel, and the Holy Spirit was upon him. It had been revealed to him by the Holy Spirit that he would not see death until he had seen the Lord's Messiah. Guided by the Spirit he came into the temple; and when the parents brought in the child Jesus to do for him what the law required, he took him in his arms, praised God, and said:

'Now, Lord, you are releasing your servant in peace,
    according to your promise.

For I have seen with my own eyes
the deliverance you have made ready in full view of all nations:
a light that will bring revelation to the Gentiles
and glory to your people Israel.'

The child's father and mother were full of wonder at what was being said about him. Simeon blessed them and said to Mary his mother, 'This child is destined to be a sign that will be rejected; and you too will be pierced to the heart. Many in Israel will stand or fall because of him; and so the secret thoughts of many will be laid bare.'

There was also a prophetess, Anna the daughter of Phanuel, of the tribe of Asher. She was a very old woman, who had lived seven years with her husband after she was first married, and then alone as a widow to the age of eighty-four. She never left the temple, but worshipped night and day with fasting and prayer. Coming up at that very moment, she gave thanks to God; and she talked about the child to all who were looking for the liberation of Jerusalem.

The Flight into Egypt

An angel of the Lord appeared to Joseph in a dream, and said, 'Get up, take the child and his mother and escape with them to Egypt, and stay there until I tell you; for Herod is going to search for the child to kill him.' So Joseph got up, took mother and child by night, and sought refuge with them in Egypt, where he stayed till Herod's death. This was to fulfil what the Lord had declared through the prophet: 'Out of Egypt I have called my son.'

When Herod realized that the astrologers had tricked him he flew into a rage, and gave orders for the massacre of all the boys aged two years or under, in Bethlehem and throughout the whole district, in accordance with the time he had ascertained from the astrologers. So the words spoken through Jeremiah the prophet were fulfilled: 'A voice was heard in Rama, sobbing in bitter grief; it was Rachel weeping for her children, and refusing to be comforted, because they were no more.'

After Herod's death an angel of the Lord appeared in a dream to Joseph in Egypt and said to him, 'Get up, take the child and his mother, and go to the land of Israel, for those who threatened the child's life are dead.' So he got up, took mother and child with him, and came to the land of Israel. But when he heard that Archelaus had succeeded his father Herod as king of Judaea, he was afraid to go there. Directed by a dream, he withdrew to the region of Galilee, where he settled in a town called Nazareth. This was to fulfil the words spoken through the prophets: 'He shall be called a Nazarene.'

The Boy Jesus in the Temple

Now it was the practice of his parents to go to Jerusalem every year for the Passover festival; and when he was twelve, they made the pilgrimage as usual. When the festive season was over and they set off for home, the boy Jesus stayed behind in Jerusalem. His parents did not know of this; but supposing that he was with the party they travelled for a whole day, and only then did they begin looking for him among their friends and relations. When they could not find him they returned to Jerusalem to look for him; and after three days they found him sitting in the temple surrounded by the teachers, listening to them and putting questions; and all who heard him were amazed at his intelligence and the answers he gave. His parents were astonished to see him there, and his mother said to him, 'My son, why have you treated us like this? Your father and I have been anxiously searching for you.' 'Why did you search for me?' he said. 'Did you not know that I was bound to be in my Father's house?' But they did not understand what he meant. Then he went back with them to Nazareth, and continued to be under their authority; his mother treasured up all these things in her heart. As Jesus grew he advanced in wisdom and in favour with God and men.

29 | BAPTISM AND EARLY MINISTRY

John the Baptist

In the fifteenth year of the emperor Tiberius, when Pontius Pilate was governor of Judaea, when Herod was tetrarch of Galilee, his brother Philip prince of Ituraea and Trachonitis, and Lysanias prince of Abilene, during the high-priesthood of Annas and Caiaphas, the word of God came to John son of Zechariah in the wilderness. And he went all over the Jordan valley proclaiming a baptism in token of repentance for the forgiveness of sins, as it is written in the book of the prophecies of Isaiah:

> A voice cries in the wilderness,
> 'Prepare the way for the Lord;
> clear a straight path for him.'

Crowds of people came out to be baptized by him, and he said to them: 'Vipers' brood! Who warned you to escape from the wrath that is to come? Prove your repentance by the fruit you bear; and do not begin saying to yourselves, "We have Abraham for our father." I tell you that God can make children for Abraham out of these stones. Already the axe is laid to the roots of the trees; and every tree that fails to produce good fruit is cut down and thrown on the fire.'

The people asked him, 'Then what are we to do?' He replied, 'Whoever has two shirts must share with him who has none, and whoever has food must do the same.' Among those who came to be baptized were tax-collectors, and they said to him, 'Teacher, what are we to do?' He told them, 'Exact no more than the assessment.' Some soldiers also asked him, 'And what of us?' To them he said, 'No bullying; no blackmail; make do with your pay!'

The people were all agog, wondering about John, whether perhaps he was the Messiah, but he spoke out and said to them all: 'I baptize you with water; but there is one coming who is mightier

451

than I am. I am not worthy to unfasten the straps of his sandals. He will baptize you with the Holy Spirit and with fire. His winnowing-shovel is ready in his hand, to clear his threshing-floor and gather the wheat into his granary; but the chaff he will burn on a fire that can never be put out.'

In this and many other ways he made his appeal to the people and announced the good news.

The Baptism of Jesus

Then Jesus arrived at the Jordan from Galilee, and came to John to be baptized by him. John tried to dissuade him. 'Do you come to me?' he said. 'It is I who need to be baptized by you.' Jesus replied, 'Let it be so for the present; it is right for us to do all that God requires.' Then John allowed him to come. No sooner had Jesus been baptized and come up out of the water than the heavens were opened and he saw the Spirit of God descending like a dove to alight on him. And there came a voice from heaven saying, 'This is my beloved Son, in whom I take delight.'

The Temptations

Full of the Holy Spirit, Jesus returned from the Jordan, and for forty days he wandered in the wilderness, led by the Spirit and tempted by the devil. During that time he ate nothing, and at the end of it he was famished. The devil said to him, 'If you are the Son of God, tell this stone to become bread.' Jesus answered, 'Scripture says, "Man is not to live on bread alone."'

Next the devil led him to a height and showed him in a flash all the kingdoms of the world. 'All this dominion will I give to you,' he said, 'and the glory that goes with it; for it has been put in my hands and I can give it to anyone I choose. You have only to do homage to me and it will all be yours.' Jesus answered him, 'Scripture says, "You shall do homage to the Lord your God and worship him alone."'

The devil took him to Jerusalem and set him on the parapet of the temple. 'If you are the Son of God,' he said, 'throw yourself down from here; for scripture says, "He will put his angels in charge of you," and again, "They will support you in their arms for fear you should strike your foot against a stone."' Jesus answered him, 'It has been said, "You are not to put the Lord your God to the test."'

So, having come to the end of all these temptations, the devil departed, biding his time.

The First Disciples

The next day John saw Jesus coming towards him. 'There is the Lamb of God,' he said, 'who takes away the sin of the world. He it is of whom I said, "After me there comes a man who ranks ahead of me"; before I was born, he already was. I did not know who he was; but the reason why I came, baptizing in water, was that he might be revealed to Israel.'

John testified again: 'I saw the Spirit come down from heaven like a dove and come to rest on him. I did not know him; but he who sent me to baptize in water had told me, "The man on whom you see the Spirit come down and rest is the one who is to baptize in Holy Spirit." I have seen it and have borne witness: this is God's Chosen One.'

The next day again, John was standing with two of his disciples when Jesus passed by. John looked towards him and said, 'There is the Lamb of God!' When the two disciples heard what he said, they followed Jesus. He turned and saw them following; 'What are you looking for?' he asked. They said, 'Rabbi,' (which means 'Teacher') 'where are you staying?' 'Come and see,' he replied. So they went and saw where he was staying, and spent the rest of the day with him. It was about four in the afternoon.

One of the two who followed Jesus after hearing what John said was Andrew, Simon Peter's brother. The first thing he did was to find his brother Simon and say to him, 'We have found the Messiah' (which is the Hebrew for Christ). He brought Simon to Jesus, who looked at him and said, 'You are Simon son of John; you shall be called Cephas' (that is, Peter, 'the Rock').

The next day Jesus decided to leave for Galilee. He met Philip, who, like Andrew and Peter, came from Bethsaida, and said to him, 'Follow me.' Philip went to find Nathanael and told him, 'We have found the man of whom Moses wrote in the law, the man foretold by the prophets: it is Jesus son of Joseph, from Nazareth.' 'Nazareth!' Nathanael exclaimed. 'Can anything good come from Nazareth?' Philip said, 'Come and see.' When Jesus saw Nathanael coming towards him, he said, 'Here is an Israelite worthy of the name; there is nothing false in him.' Nathanael asked him, 'How is it you know me?' Jesus replied, 'I saw you under the fig tree before Philip spoke to you.' 'Rabbi,' said Nathanael, 'you are the Son of God; you are king of Israel.' Jesus answered, 'Do you believe this because I told you I saw you under the fig tree? You will see greater things than that.' Then he added, 'In very truth I tell you all: you will see heaven wide open and God's angels ascending and descending upon the Son of Man.'

The Marriage at Cana

Two days later there was a wedding at Cana-in-Galilee. The mother of Jesus was there, and Jesus and his disciples were also among the guests. The wine gave out, so Jesus's mother said to him, 'They have no wine left.' He answered, 'That is no concern of mine. My hour has not yet come.' His mother said to the servants, 'Do whatever he tells you.' There were six stone water-jars standing near, of the kind used for Jewish rites of purification; each held from twenty to thirty gallons. Jesus said to the servants, 'Fill the jars with water,' and they filled them to the brim. 'Now draw some off,' he ordered, 'and take it to the master of the feast'; and they did so. The master tasted the water now turned into wine, not knowing its source, though the servants who had drawn the water knew. He hailed the bridegroom and said, 'Everyone else serves the best wine first, and the poorer only when the guests have drunk freely; but you have kept the best wine till now.'

So Jesus performed at Cana-in-Galilee the first of the signs which revealed his glory and led his disciples to believe in him.

The First Journey to Jerusalem

After this he went down to Capernaum with his mother, his brothers, and his disciples, and they stayed there a few days. As it was near the time of the Jewish Passover, Jesus went up to Jerusalem. In the temple precincts he found the dealers in cattle, sheep, and pigeons, and the money-changers seated at their tables. He made a whip of cords and drove them out of the temple, sheep, cattle, and all. He upset the tables of the money-changers, scattering their coins. Then he turned on the dealers in pigeons: 'Take them out of here,' he said; 'do not turn my Father's house into a market.' His disciples recalled the words of scripture: 'Zeal for your house will consume me.' The Jews challenged Jesus: 'What sign can you show to justify your action?' 'Destroy this temple,' Jesus replied, 'and in three days I will raise it up again.' The Jews said, 'It has taken forty-six years to build this temple. Are you going to raise it up again in three days?'

Jesus and Nicodemus

One of the Pharisees, called Nicodemus, a member of the Jewish Council, came to Jesus by night. 'Rabbi,' he said, 'we know that you are a teacher sent by God; no one could perform these signs of yours unless God were with him.' Jesus answered, 'In very truth I tell you, no one can see the kingdom of God unless he has been born again.' 'But how can someone be born when he is old?' asked Nicodemus. 'Can he enter his mother's womb a second time and be born?' Jesus answered, 'In very truth I tell you, no one can enter the kingdom of God without being born from water and spirit. Flesh can give birth only to flesh; it is spirit that gives birth to spirit. You ought not to be astonished when I say, "You must all be born again." The wind blows where it wills; you hear the sound of it, but you do not know where it comes from or where it is going. So it is with everyone who is born from the Spirit.'

'How is this possible?' asked Nicodemus. 'You a teacher of Israel and ignorant of such things!' said Jesus. 'In very truth I tell you, we speak of what we know, and testify to what we have seen, and yet you all reject our testimony. If you do not believe me when I talk to you about earthly things, how are you to believe if I should talk about the things of heaven?

'No one has gone up into heaven except the one who came down from heaven, the Son of Man who is in heaven. Just as Moses lifted up the serpent in the wilderness, so the Son of Man must be lifted up, in order that everyone who has faith may in him have eternal life.

'God so loved the world that he gave his only Son, that everyone who has faith in him may not perish but have eternal life. It was not to judge the world that God sent his Son into the world, but that through him the world might be saved.'

Jesus and the Samaritan Woman

News now reached the Pharisees that Jesus was winning and baptizing more disciples than John; although, in fact, it was his disciples who were baptizing, not Jesus himself. When Jesus heard this, he left Judaea and set out once more for Galilee. He had to pass through Samaria, and on his way came to a Samaritan town called Sychar, near the plot of ground which Jacob gave to his son Joseph; Jacob's well was there. It was about noon, and Jesus, tired after his journey, was sitting by the well.

His disciples had gone into the town to buy food. Meanwhile a Samaritan woman came to draw water, and Jesus said to her, 'Give me a drink.' The woman said, 'What! You, a Jew, ask for a drink from a Samaritan woman?' (Jews do not share drinking vessels with Samaritans.) Jesus replied, 'If only you knew what God gives, and who it is that is asking you for a drink, you would have asked him and he would have given you living water.' 'Sir,' the woman said, 'you have no bucket and the well is deep, so where can you get "living water"? Are you greater than Jacob our ancestor who gave us the well and drank from it himself, he and his sons and his cattle too?' Jesus answered, 'Everyone who drinks this water will be thirsty again; but whoever drinks the water I shall give will never again be thirsty. The water that I shall give will be a spring of water within him, welling up and bringing eternal life.' 'Sir,' said the woman, 'give me this water, and then I shall not be thirsty, nor have to come all this way to draw water.'

'Go and call your husband,' said Jesus, 'and come back here.' She answered, 'I have no husband.' Jesus said, 'You are right in saying that you have no husband, for though you have had five husbands, the man you are living with now is not your husband. You have spoken the truth!' 'Sir,' replied the woman, 'I can see you are a prophet. Our fathers worshipped on this mountain, but you Jews say that the place where God must be worshipped is in Jerusalem.' 'Believe me,' said Jesus, 'the time is coming when you will worship the Father neither on this mountain nor in Jerusalem. You Samaritans worship you know not what; we worship what we know. It is from the Jews that salvation comes. But the time is coming, indeed it is already here, when true worshippers will worship the Father in spirit and in truth. These are the worshippers the Father wants. God is spirit, and those who worship him must worship in spirit and in truth.' The woman answered, 'I know that Messiah' (that is, Christ) 'is coming. When he comes he will make everything clear to us.' Jesus said to her, 'I am he, I who am speaking to you.'

At that moment his disciples returned, and were astonished to find him talking with a woman; but none of them said, 'What do you want?' or, 'Why are you talking with her?' The woman left her water-jar and went off to the town, where she said to the people, 'Come and see a man who has told me everything I ever did. Could this be the Messiah?' They left the town and made their way towards him.

Many Samaritans of that town came to believe in him because of the woman's testimony: 'He told me everything I ever did.' So when these Samaritans came to him they pressed him to stay with them; and he stayed there two days. Many more became believers because of what they heard from his own lips. They told the woman, 'It is no longer because of what you said that we believe, for we have heard him ourselves; and we are convinced that he is the Saviour of the world.'

Jesus Teaches in the Synagogue at Nazareth

Then Jesus, armed with the power of the Spirit, returned to Galilee; and reports about him spread through the whole country-side. He taught in their synagogues and everyone sang his praises. He came to Nazareth, where he had been brought up, and went to the synagogue on the sabbath day as he regularly did. He stood up to read the lesson and was handed the scroll of the prophet Isaiah. He opened the scroll and found the passage which says,

'The spirit of the Lord is upon me
because he has anointed me;
he has sent me to announce good news to the poor,
to proclaim release for prisoners
and recovery of sight for the blind;
to let the broken victims go free,
to proclaim the year of the Lord's favour.'

He rolled up the scroll, gave it back to the attendant, and sat down; and all eyes in the synagogue were fixed on him.

He began to address them: 'Today', he said, 'in your hearing this text has come true.' There was general approval; they were astonished that words of such grace should fall from his lips. 'Is not this Joseph's son?' they asked. Then Jesus said, 'No doubt you will quote to me the proverb, "Physician, heal yourself!" and say, "We have heard of all your doings at Capernaum; do the same here in your own home town." Truly I tell you,' he went on: 'no prophet is recognized in his own country. There were indeed many widows in Israel in Elijah's time, when for three and a half years the skies never opened, and famine lay hard over the whole country; yet it was to none of these that Elijah was sent, but to a widow at Sarepta in the territory of Sidon. Again, in the time of the prophet Elisha there were many lepers in Israel, and not one of them was healed, but only Naaman, the Syrian.' These words roused the whole congregation to fury; they leapt up, drove him out of the town, and took him to the brow of the hill on which it was built, meaning to hurl him over the edge. But he walked straight through the whole crowd, and went away.

The First Healings

Coming down to Capernaum, a town in Galilee, he taught the people on the sabbath, and they were amazed at his teaching, for what he said had the note of authority. Now there was a man in the synagogue possessed by a demon, an unclean spirit. He shrieked at the top of his voice, 'What do you want with us, Jesus of Nazareth? Have you come to destroy us? I know who you are – the Holy One of God.' Jesus rebuked him: 'Be silent', he said, 'and come out of him.' Then the demon, after throwing the man down in front of the people, left him without doing him any injury. Amazement fell on them all and they said to one another: 'What is there in this man's words? He gives orders to the unclean spirits with authority and power, and they go.' So the news spread, and he was the talk of the whole district.

On leaving the synagogue he went to Simon's house. Simon's mother-in-law was in the grip of a high fever; and they asked him to help her. He stood over her and rebuked the fever. It left her, and she got up at once and attended to their needs.

At sunset all who had friends ill with diseases of one kind or another brought them to him; and he laid his hands on them one by one and healed them. Demons also came out of many of them, shouting, 'You are the Son of God.' But he rebuked them and forbade them to speak, because they knew he was the Messiah.

The Miraculous Catch of Fish

One day as he stood by the lake of Gennesaret, with people crowding in on him to listen to the word of God, he noticed two boats lying at the water's edge; the fishermen had come ashore and were washing their nets. He got into one of the boats, which belonged to Simon, and asked him to put out a little way from the shore; then he went on teaching the crowds as he sat in the boat. When he had finished speaking, he said to Simon, 'Put out into deep water and let down your nets for a catch.' Simon answered, 'Master, we were hard at work all night and caught nothing; but if you say so, I will let down the nets.' They did so and made such a huge catch of fish that their nets began to split. So they signalled to their partners in the other boat to come and help them. They came, and loaded both boats to the point of sinking. When Simon saw what had happened he fell at Jesus's knees and said, 'Go, Lord, leave me, sinner that I am!' For he and all his companions were amazed at the catch they had made; so too were his partners James and John, Zebedee's sons. 'Do not be afraid,' said Jesus to Simon; 'from now on you will be catching people.' As soon as they had brought the boats to land, they left everything and followed him.

The Cleansing of a Leper

On one occasion he was approached by a leper, who knelt before him and begged for help. 'If only you will,' said the man, 'you can make me clean.' Jesus was moved to anger; he stretched out his hand, touched him, and said, 'I will; be clean.' The leprosy left him immediately, and he was clean. Then he dismissed him with this stern warning: 'See that you tell nobody, but go and show yourself to the priest, and make the offering laid down by Moses for your cleansing; that will certify the cure.' But the man went away and made the whole story public, spreading it far and wide, until Jesus could no longer show himself in any town. He stayed outside in remote places; yet people kept coming to him from all quarters.

The Healing of a Paralysed Man

After some days he returned to Capernaum, and news went round that he was at home; and such a crowd collected that there was no room for them even in the space outside the door. While he was proclaiming the message to them, a man was brought who was paralysed. Four men were carrying him, but because of the crowd they could not get him near. So they made an opening in the roof over the place where Jesus was, and when they had broken through they lowered the bed on which the paralysed man was lying. When he saw their faith, Jesus said to the man, 'My son, your sins are forgiven.'

Now there were some scribes sitting there, thinking to themselves, 'How can the fellow talk like that? It is blasphemy! Who but God can forgive sins?' Jesus knew at once what they were thinking, and said to them, 'Why do you harbour such thoughts? Is it easier to say to this paralysed man, "Your sins are forgiven," or to say, "Stand up, take your bed, and walk"? But to convince you that the Son of Man has authority on earth to forgive sins' – he turned to the paralysed man – 'I say to you, stand up, take your bed, and go home.' And he got up, and at once took his bed and went out in full view of them all, so that they were astounded and praised God. 'Never before', they said, 'have we seen anything like this.'

The Call of Levi

Once more he went out to the lakeside. All the crowd came to him there, and he taught them. As he went along, he saw Levi son of Alphaeus at his seat in the custom-house, and said to him, 'Follow me'; and he rose and followed him.

When Jesus was having a meal in his house, many tax-collectors and sinners were seated with him and his disciples, for there were many of them among his followers. Some scribes who were Pharisees, observing the company in which he was eating, said to his disciples, 'Why does he eat with tax-collectors and sinners?' Hearing this, Jesus said to them, 'It is not the healthy who need a doctor, but the sick; I did not come to call the virtuous, but sinners.'

New Wine in Old Wine Skins

Once, when John's disciples and the Pharisees were keeping a fast, some people came and asked him, 'Why is it that John's disciples and the disciples of the Pharisees are fasting, but yours are not?' Jesus replied, 'Can you expect the bridegroom's friends to fast while the bridegroom is with them? As long as he is with them, there can be no fasting. But the time will come when the bridegroom will be taken away from them; that will be the time for them to fast.

'No one sews a patch of unshrunk cloth on to an old garment; if he does, the patch tears away from it, the new from the old, and leaves a bigger hole. No one puts new wine into old wineskins; if he does, the wine will burst the skins, and then wine and skins are both lost. New wine goes into fresh skins.'

Lord of the Sabbath

One sabbath he was going through the cornfields; and as they went along his disciples began to pluck ears of corn. The Pharisees said to him, 'Why are they doing what is forbidden on the sabbath?' He answered, 'Have you never read what David did when he and his men were hungry and had nothing to eat? He went into the house of God, in the time of Abiathar the high priest, and ate the sacred bread, though no one but a priest is allowed to eat it, and even gave it to his men.'

He also said to them, 'The sabbath was made for man, not man for the sabbath: so the Son of Man is lord even of the sabbath.'

The Healing of a Man with the Withered Hand

On another sabbath he had gone to synagogue and was teaching. There was a man in the congregation whose right arm was withered; and the scribes and Pharisees were on the watch to see whether Jesus would heal him on the sabbath, so that they could find a charge to bring against him. But he knew what was in their minds and said to the man with the withered arm, 'Stand up and come out here.' So he stood up and came out. Then Jesus said to them, 'I put this question to you: is it permitted to do good or to do evil on the sabbath, to save life or to destroy it?' He looked round at them all, and then he said to the man, 'Stretch out your arm.' He did so, and his arm was restored. But they totally failed to understand, and began to discuss with one another what they could do to Jesus.

The Twelve Disciples

During this time he went out one day into the hill-country to pray, and spent the night in prayer to God. When day broke he called his disciples to him, and from among them he chose twelve and named them apostles: Simon, to whom he gave the name Peter, and Andrew his brother, James and John, Philip and Bartholomew, Matthew and Thomas, James son of Alphaeus, and Simon who was called the Zealot, Judas son of James, and Judas Iscariot who turned traitor.

Blessings and Warnings

He came down the hill with them and stopped on some level ground where a large crowd of his disciples had gathered. Turning to his disciples he began to speak:

'Blessed are you who are in need;
the kingdom of God is yours.
Blessed are you who now go hungry;
you will be satisfied.
Blessed are you who weep now;
you will laugh.

'But alas for you who are rich;
you have had your time of happiness.
Alas for you who are well fed now;
you will go hungry.
Alas for you who laugh now;
you will mourn and weep.
Alas for you when all speak well of you;
that is how their fathers treated the false prophets.

He also spoke to them in a parable: 'Can one blind man guide another? Will not both fall into the ditch? No pupil ranks above his teacher; fully trained he can but reach his teacher's level.'

The Healing of a Centurion's Servant

When he had finished addressing the people, he entered Capernaum. A centurion there had a servant whom he valued highly, but the servant was ill and near to death. Hearing about Jesus, he sent some Jewish elders to ask him to come and save his servant's life. They approached Jesus and made an urgent appeal to him: 'He deserves this favour from you,' they said, 'for he is a friend of our nation and it is he who built us our synagogue.' Jesus went with them; but when he was not far from the house, the centurion sent friends with this message: 'Do not trouble further, sir; I am not worthy to have you come under my roof, and that is why I did not presume to approach you in person. But say the word and my servant will be cured. I know, for I am myself under orders, with soldiers under me. I say to one, "Go," and he goes; to another, "Come here," and he comes; and to my servant, "Do this," and he does it.' When Jesus heard this, he was astonished, and, turning to the crowd that was following him, he said, 'I tell you, not even in Israel have I found such faith.' When the messengers returned to the house, they found the servant in good health.

The Raising of a Widow's Son

Afterwards Jesus went to a town called Nain, accompanied by his disciples and a large crowd. As he approached the gate of the town he met a funeral. The dead man was the only son of his widowed mother; and many of the townspeople were there with her. When the Lord saw her his heart went out to her, and he said, 'Do not weep.' He stepped forward and laid his hand on the bier; and the bearers halted. Then he spoke: 'Young man, I tell you to get up.' The dead man sat up and began to speak; and Jesus restored him to his mother. Everyone was filled with awe and praised God. 'A great prophet has arisen among us,' they said; 'God has shown his care for his people.' The story of what he had done spread through the whole of Judaea and all the region around.

The Parable of the Sower

On another occasion he began to teach by the lakeside. The crowd that gathered round him was so large that he had to get into a boat on the lake and sit there, with the whole crowd on the beach right down to the water's edge. And he taught them many things by parables.

As he taught he said: 'Listen! A sower went out to sow. And it happened that as he sowed, some of the seed fell along the footpath; and the birds came and ate it up. Some fell on rocky ground, where it had little soil, and it sprouted quickly because it had no depth of earth; but when the sun rose it was scorched, and as it had no root it withered away. Some fell among thistles; and the thistles grew up and choked the corn, and it produced no crop. And some of the seed fell into good soil, where it came up and grew, and produced a crop; and the yield was thirtyfold, sixtyfold, even a hundredfold.' He added, 'If you have ears to hear, then hear.'

When Jesus was alone with the Twelve and his other companions they questioned him about the parables. He answered, 'To you the secret of the kingdom of God has been given; but to those who are outside, everything comes by way of parables, so that (as scripture says) they may look and look, but see nothing; they may listen and listen, but understand nothing; otherwise they might turn to God and be forgiven.'

He went on: 'Do you not understand this parable? How then are you to understand any parable? The sower sows the word. With some the seed falls along the footpath; no sooner have they heard it than Satan comes and carries off the word which has been sown in them. With others the seed falls on rocky ground; as soon as they hear the word, they accept it with joy, but it strikes no root in them; they have no staying-power, and when there is trouble or persecution on account of the word, they quickly lose faith. With others again the seed falls among thistles; they hear the word, but worldly cares and the false glamour of wealth and evil desires of all kinds come in and choke the word, and it proves barren. But there are some with whom the seed is sown on good soil; they accept the word when they hear it, and they bear fruit thirtyfold, sixtyfold, or a hundredfold.'

Two Parables of the Kingdom

He said, 'The kingdom of God is like this. A man scatters seed on the ground; he goes to bed at night and gets up in the morning, and meanwhile the seed sprouts and grows – how, he does not know. The ground produces a crop by itself, first the blade, then the ear, then full grain in the ear; but as soon as the crop is ripe, he starts reaping, because harvest time has come.'

He said, 'How shall we picture the kingdom of God, or what parable shall we use to describe it? It is like a mustard seed; when sown in the ground it is smaller than any other seed, but once sown, it springs up and grows taller than any other plant, and forms branches so large that birds can roost in its shade.'

With many such parables he used to give them his message, so far as they were able to receive it. He never spoke to them except in parables; but privately to his disciples he explained everything.

The Calming of the Storm

That day, in the evening, he said to them, 'Let us cross over to the other side of the lake.' So they left the crowd and took him with them in the boat in which he had been sitting; and some other boats went with him. A fierce squall blew up and the waves broke over the boat until it was all but swamped. Now he was in the stern asleep on a cushion; they roused him and said, 'Teacher, we are sinking! Do you not care?' He awoke and rebuked the wind, and said to the sea, 'Silence! Be still!' The wind dropped and there was a dead calm. He said to them, 'Why are you such cowards? Have you no faith even now?' They were awestruck and said to one another, 'Who can this be? Even the wind and the sea obey him.'

The Healing of a Madman

So they came to the country of the Gerasenes on the other side of the lake. As Jesus stepped ashore, a man possessed by an unclean spirit came up to him from among the tombs where he had made his home. Nobody could control him any longer; even chains were useless, for he had often been fettered and chained up, but had snapped his chains and broken the fetters. No one was strong enough to master him. Unceasingly, night and day, he would cry aloud among the tombs and on the hillsides and gash himself with stones. When he saw Jesus in the distance, he ran up and flung himself down before him, shouting at the top of his voice, 'What do you want with me, Jesus, son of the Most High God? In God's name do not torment me.' For Jesus was already saying to him, 'Out, unclean spirit, come out of the man!' Jesus asked him, 'What is your name?' 'My name is Legion,' he said, 'there are so many of us.' And he implored Jesus not to send them out of the district. There was a large herd of pigs nearby, feeding on the hillside, and the spirits begged him, 'Send us among the pigs; let us go into them.' He gave them leave; and the unclean spirits came out and went into the pigs; and the herd, of about two thousand, rushed over the edge into the lake and were drowned.

The men in charge of them took to their heels and carried the news to the town and countryside; and the people came out to see what had happened. When they came to Jesus and saw the madman who had been possessed by the legion of demons, sitting there clothed and in his right mind, they were afraid. When eyewitnesses told them what had happened to the madman and what had become of the pigs, they begged Jesus to leave the district. As he was getting into the boat, the man who had been possessed begged to go with him. But Jesus would not let him. 'Go home to your own people,' he said, 'and tell them what the Lord in his mercy has done for you.' The man went off and made known throughout the Decapolis what Jesus had done for him; and everyone was amazed.

The Healing of Jairus's Daughter and of a Woman who Suffered from Haemorrhages

As soon as Jesus had returned by boat to the other shore, a large crowd gathered round him. While he was by the lakeside, there came a synagogue president named Jairus; and when he saw him, he threw himself down at his feet and pleaded with him. 'My little daughter is at death's door,' he said. 'I beg you to come and lay your hands on her so that her life may be saved.' So Jesus went with him, accompanied by a great crowd which pressed round him.

Among them was a woman who had suffered from haemorrhages for twelve years; and in spite of long treatment by many doctors, on which she had spent all she had, she had become worse rather than better. She had heard about Jesus, and came up behind him in the crowd and touched his cloak; for she said, 'If I touch even his clothes, I shall be healed.' And there and then the flow of blood dried up and she knew in herself that she was cured of her affliction. Aware at once that power had gone out of him, Jesus turned round in the crowd and asked, 'Who touched my clothes?' His disciples said to him, 'You see the crowd pressing round you and yet you ask, "Who touched me?"' But he kept looking around to see who had done it. Then the woman, trembling with fear because she knew what had happened to her, came and fell at his feet and told him the whole truth. He said to her, 'Daughter, your faith has healed you. Go in peace, free from your affliction.'

While he was still speaking, a message came from the president's house, 'Your daughter has died; why trouble the teacher any more?' But Jesus, overhearing the message as it was delivered, said to the president of the synagogue, 'Do not be afraid; simply have faith.' Then he allowed no one to accompany him except Peter and James and James's brother John. They came to the president's house, where he found a great commotion, with loud crying and wailing. So he went in and said to them, 'Why this crying and commotion? The child is not dead: she is asleep'; and they laughed at him. After turning everyone out, he took the child's father and mother and his own companions into the room where the child was. Taking hold of her hand, he said to her, '*Talitha cum*,' which means, 'Get up, my child.' Immediately the girl got up and walked about – she was twelve years old. They were overcome with amazement; but he gave them strict instructions not to let anyone know about it, and told them to give her something to eat.

30 | THE SERMON ON THE MOUNT

When Jesus saw the crowds he went up a mountain. There he sat down, and when his disciples had gathered round him he began to address them. And this is the teaching he gave:

The Beatitudes

'Blessed are the poor in spirit;
the kingdom of Heaven is theirs.
Blessed are the sorrowful;
they shall find consolation.
Blessed are the gentle;
they shall have the earth for their possession.
Blessed are those who hunger and thirst to see right prevail;
they shall be satisfied.
Blessed are those who show mercy;
mercy shall be shown to them.
Blessed are those whose hearts are pure;
they shall see God.
Blessed are the peacemakers;
they shall be called God's children.
Blessed are those who are persecuted in the cause of right;
the kingdom of Heaven is theirs.

'Blessed are you, when you suffer insults and persecution and calumnies of every kind for my sake. Exult and be glad, for you have a rich reward in heaven; in the same way they persecuted the prophets before you.'

Salt and Light
'You are salt to the world. And if salt becomes tasteless, how is its saltness to be restored? It is good for nothing but to be thrown away and trodden underfoot.

'You are light for all the world. A town that stands on a hill cannot be hidden. When a lamp is lit, it is not put under the meal-tub, but on the lampstand, where it gives light to everyone in the house. Like the lamp, you must shed light among your fellows, so that, when they see the good you do, they may give praise to your Father in heaven.'

The Completion of the Law

'Do not suppose that I have come to abolish the law and the prophets; I did not come to abolish, but to complete. Truly I tell you: so long as heaven and earth endure, not a letter, not a dot, will disappear from the law until all that must happen has happened. Anyone therefore who sets aside even the least of the law's demands, and teaches others to do the same, will have the lowest place in the kingdom of Heaven, whereas anyone who keeps the law, and teaches others to do so, will rank high in the kingdom of Heaven. I tell you, unless you show yourselves far better than the scribes and Pharisees, you can never enter the kingdom of Heaven.'

The Spirit of the Law

'You have heard that our forefathers were told, "Do not commit murder; anyone who commits murder must be brought to justice." But what I tell you is this: Anyone who nurses anger against his brother must be brought to justice. Whoever calls his brother "good for nothing" deserves the sentence of the court; whoever calls him "fool" deserves hell-fire. So if you are presenting your gift at the altar and suddenly remember that your brother has a grievance against you, leave your gift where it is before the altar. First go and make your peace with your brother; then come back and offer your gift. If someone sues you, come to terms with him promptly while you are both on your way to court; otherwise he may hand you over to the judge, and the judge to the officer, and you will be thrown into jail. Truly I tell you: once you are there you will not be let out until you have paid the last penny.

'You have heard that they were told, "Do not commit adultery." But what I tell you is this: If a man looks at a woman with a lustful eye, he has already committed adultery with her in his heart. If your right eye causes your downfall, tear it out and fling it away; it is better for you to lose one part of your body than for the whole of it to be thrown into hell. If your right hand causes your downfall, cut it off and fling it away; it is better for you to lose one part of your body than for the whole of it to go to hell.

'They were told, "A man who divorces his wife must give her a certificate of dismissal." But what I tell you is this: If a man divorces his wife for any cause other than unchastity he involves her in adultery; and whoever marries her commits adultery.

'Again, you have heard that our forefathers were told, "Do not break your oath," and "Oaths sworn to the Lord must be kept." But what I tell you is this: You are not to swear at all – not by heaven, for it is God's throne, nor by the earth, for it is his footstool, nor by Jerusalem, for it is the city of the great King, nor by your own head, because you cannot turn one hair of it white or black. Plain "Yes" or "No" is all you need to say; anything beyond that comes from the evil one.

'You have heard that they were told, "An eye for an eye, a tooth for a tooth." But what I tell you is this: Do not resist those who wrong you. If anyone slaps you on the right cheek, turn and offer him the other also. If anyone wants to sue you and takes your shirt, let him have your cloak as well. If someone in authority presses you into service for one mile, go with him two. Give to anyone who asks; and do not turn your back on anyone who wants to borrow.'

Love Without Limits
'You have heard that they were told, "Love your neighbour and hate your enemy." But what I tell you is this: Love your enemies and pray for your persecutors; only so can you be children of your heavenly Father, who causes the sun to rise on good and bad alike, and sends the rain on the innocent and the wicked. If you love only those who love you, what reward can you expect? Even the tax-collectors do as much as that. If you greet only your brothers, what is there extraordinary about that? Even the heathen do as much. There must be no limit to your goodness, as your heavenly Father's goodness knows no bounds.'

True Religion
'Be careful not to parade your religion before others; if you do, no reward awaits you with your Father in heaven.

'So, when you give alms, do not announce it with a flourish of trumpets, as the hypocrites do in synagogues and in the streets to win the praise of others. Truly I tell you: they have their reward already. But when you give alms, do not let your left hand know what your right is doing; your good deed must be secret, and your Father who sees what is done in secret will reward you.

'Again, when you pray, do not be like the hypocrites; they love to say their prayers standing up in synagogues and at street corners for everyone to see them. Truly I tell you: they have their reward already. But when you pray, go into a room by yourself, shut the door, and pray to your Father who is in secret; and your Father who sees what is done in secret will reward you.

'In your prayers do not go babbling on like the heathen, who imagine that the more they say the more likely they are to be heard. Do not imitate them, for your Father knows what your needs are before you ask him.

'This is how you should pray:

"Our Father in heaven,
may your name be hallowed;
your kingdom come,
your will be done,
on earth as in heaven.
Give us today our daily bread.
Forgive us the wrong we have done,
as we have forgiven those who have wronged us.
And do not put us to the test,
but save us from the evil one."

'For if you forgive others the wrongs they have done, your heavenly Father will also forgive you; but if you do not forgive others, then your Father will not forgive the wrongs that you have done.

'So too when you fast, do not look gloomy like the hypocrites: they make their faces unsightly so that everybody may see that they are fasting. Truly I tell you: they have their reward already. But when you fast, anoint your head and wash your face, so that no one sees that you are fasting, but only your Father who is in secret; and your Father who sees what is done in secret will give you your reward.

'Do not store up for yourselves treasure on earth, where moth and rust destroy, and thieves break in and steal; but store up treasure in heaven, where neither moth nor rust will destroy, nor thieves break in and steal. For where your treasure is, there will your heart be also.

'The lamp of the body is the eye. If your eyes are sound, you will have light for your whole body; if your eyes are bad, your whole body will be in darkness. If then the only light you have is darkness, how great a darkness that will be.

'No one can serve two masters; for either he will hate the first and love the second, or he will be devoted to the first and despise the second. You cannot serve God and Money.'

Do Not be Anxious

'This is why I tell you not to be anxious about food and drink to keep you alive and about clothes to cover your body. Surely life is more than food, the body more than clothes. Look at the birds in the sky; they do not sow and reap and store in barns, yet your heavenly Father feeds them. Are you not worth more than the birds? Can anxious thought add a single day to your life? And why be anxious about clothes? Consider how the lilies grow in the fields; they do not work, they do not spin; yet I tell you, even Solomon in all his splendour was not attired like one of them. If that is how God clothes the grass in the fields, which is there today and tomorrow is thrown on the stove, will he not all the more clothe you? How little faith you have! Do not ask anxiously, "What are we to eat? What are we to drink? What shall we wear?" These are the things that occupy the minds of the heathen, but your heavenly Father knows that you need them all. Set your mind on God's kingdom and his justice before everything else, and all the rest will come to you as well. So do not be anxious about tomorrow; tomorrow will look after itself. Each day has troubles enough of its own.'

Do Not Judge

'Do not judge, and you will not be judged. For as you judge others, so you will yourselves be judged, and whatever measure you deal out to others will be dealt to you. Why do you look at the speck of sawdust in your brother's eye, with never a thought for the plank in your own? How can you say to your brother, "Let me take the speck out of your eye," when all the time there is a plank in your own? You hypocrite! First take the plank out of your own eye, and then you will see clearly to take the speck out of your brother's.'

Concluding Teachings

'Do not give dogs what is holy; do not throw your pearls to the pigs: they will only trample on them, and turn and tear you to pieces.

'Ask, and you will receive; seek, and you will find; knock, and the door will be opened to you. For everyone who asks receives, those who seek find, and to those who knock, the door will be opened.

'Would any of you offer his son a stone when he asks for bread, or a snake when he asks for a fish? If you, bad as you are, know how to give good things to your children, how much more will your heavenly Father give good things to those who ask him!

'Always treat others as you would like them to treat you: that is the law and the prophets.

'Enter by the narrow gate. Wide is the gate and broad the road that leads to destruction, and many enter that way; narrow is the gate and constricted the road that leads to life, and those who find them are few.

'Beware of false prophets, who come to you dressed up as sheep while underneath they are savage wolves. You will recognize them by their fruit. Can grapes be picked from briars, or figs from thistles? A good tree always yields sound fruit, and a poor tree bad fruit. A good tree cannot bear bad fruit, or a poor tree sound fruit. A tree that does not yield sound fruit is cut down and thrown on the fire. That is why I say you will recognize them by their fruit.

'Not everyone who says to me, "Lord, Lord" will enter the kingdom of Heaven, but only those who do the will of my heavenly Father. When the day comes, many will say to me, "Lord, Lord, did we not prophesy in your name, drive out demons in your name, and in your name perform many miracles?" Then I will tell them plainly, "I never knew you. Out of my sight; your deeds are evil!"

'So whoever hears these words of mine and acts on them is like a man who had the sense to build his house on rock. The rain came down, the floods rose, the winds blew and beat upon that house; but it did not fall, because its foundations were on rock. And whoever hears these words of mine and does not act on them is like a man who was foolish enough to build his house on sand. The rain came down, the floods rose, the winds blew and battered against that house; and it fell with a great crash.'

When Jesus had finished this discourse the people were amazed at his teaching; unlike their scribes he taught with a note of authority.

Jesus Commissions the Twelve Disciples

Then he called his twelve disciples to him and gave them the following instructions: 'Do not take the road to gentile lands, and do not enter any Samaritan town; but go rather to the lost sheep of the house of Israel. And as you go proclaim the message: "The kingdom of Heaven is upon you." Heal the sick, raise the dead, cleanse lepers, drive out demons. You received without cost; give without charge.

'Take no gold, silver, or copper in your belts, no pack for the road, no second coat, no sandals, no stick; the worker deserves his keep.

'Whatever town or village you enter, look for some suitable person in it, and stay with him until you leave. Wish the house peace as you enter it; if it is welcoming, let your peace descend on it, and if it is not, let your peace come back to you. If anyone will not receive you or listen to what you say, then as you leave that house or that town shake the dust of it off your feet. Truly I tell you: on the day of judgement it will be more bearable for the land of Sodom and Gomorrah than for that town.

'I send you out like sheep among wolves; be wary as serpents, innocent as doves.

'Be on your guard, for you will be handed over to the courts, they will flog you in their synagogues, and you will be brought before governors and kings on my account, to testify before them and the Gentiles. But when you are arrested, do not worry about what you are to say, for when the time comes, the words you need will be given you; it will not be you speaking, but the Spirit of your Father speaking in you.

'Brother will hand over brother to death, and a father his child; children will turn against their parents and send them to their death. Everyone will hate you for your allegiance to me, but whoever endures to the end will be saved. When you are persecuted in one town, take refuge in another; truly I tell you: before you have gone through all the towns of Israel the Son of Man will have come.

'No pupil ranks above his teacher, no servant above his master. The pupil should be content to share his teacher's lot, the servant to share his master's. If the master has been called Beelzebul, how much more his household!

'So do not be afraid of them. There is nothing covered up that will not be uncovered, nothing hidden that will not be made known. What I say to you in the dark you must repeat in broad daylight; what you hear whispered you must shout from the housetops. Do not fear those who kill the body, but cannot kill the soul. Fear him rather who is able to destroy both soul and body in hell.

'Are not two sparrows sold for a penny? Yet without your Father's knowledge not one of them can fall to the ground. As for you, even the hairs of your head have all been counted. So do not be afraid; you are worth more than any number of sparrows.

'Whoever will acknowledge me before others, I will acknowledge before my Father in heaven; and whoever disowns me before others, I will disown before my Father in heaven.

'You must not think that I have come to bring peace to the earth; I have not come to bring peace, but a sword. I have come to set a man against his father, a daughter against her mother, a daughter-in-law against her mother-in-law; and a man will find his enemies under his own roof.

'No one is worthy of me who cares more for father or mother than for me; no one is worthy of me who cares more for son or daughter; no one is worthy of me who does not take up his cross and follow me. Whoever gains his life will lose it; whoever loses his life for my sake will gain it.

'To receive you is to receive me, and to receive me is to receive the One who sent me. Whoever receives a prophet because he is a prophet will be given a prophet's reward, and whoever receives a good man because he is a good man will be given a good man's reward. Truly I tell you: anyone who gives so much as a cup of cold water to one of these little ones because he is a disciple of mine, will certainly not go unrewarded.'

Jesus Teaches in Nearby Towns

Then he spoke of the towns in which most of his miracles had been performed, and denounced them for their impenitence. 'Alas for you, Chorazin!' he said. 'Alas for you, Bethsaida! If the miracles performed in you had taken place in Tyre and Sidon, they would have repented long ago in sackcloth and ashes. But it will be more bearable, I tell you, for Tyre and Sidon on the day of judgement than for you. As for you, Capernaum, will you be exalted to heaven? No, you will be brought down to Hades! For if the miracles performed in you had taken place in Sodom, Sodom would be standing to this day. But it will be more bearable, I tell you, for the land of Sodom on the day of judgement than for you.'

At that time Jesus spoke these words: 'I thank you, Father, Lord of heaven and earth, for hiding these things from the learned and wise, and revealing them to the simple. Yes, Father, such was your choice. Everything is entrusted to me by my Father; and no one knows the Son but the Father, and no one knows the Father but the Son and those to whom the Son chooses to reveal him.

'Come to me, all who are weary and whose load is heavy; I will give you rest. Take my yoke upon you, and learn from me, for I am gentle and humble-hearted; and you will find rest for your souls. For my yoke is easy to wear, my load is light.'

Jesus Commends John the Baptist

When John was informed of all this by his disciples, he summoned two of them and sent them to the Lord with this question: 'Are you the one who is to come, or are we to expect someone else?' The men made their way to Jesus and said, 'John the Baptist has sent us to ask you, "Are you the one who is to come, or are we to expect someone else?"' There and then he healed many sufferers from diseases, plagues, and evil spirits; and on many blind people he bestowed sight. Then he gave them this answer: 'Go and tell John what you have seen and heard: the blind regain their sight, the lame walk, lepers are made clean, the deaf hear, the dead are raised to life, the poor are brought good news and happy is he who does not find me an obstacle to faith.'

After John's messengers had left, Jesus began to speak about him to the crowds: 'What did you go out into the wilderness to see? A reed swaying in the wind? No? Then what did you go out to see? A man dressed in finery? Grand clothes and luxury are to be found in palaces. But what did you go out to see? A prophet? Yes indeed, and far more than a prophet. He is the man of whom scripture says,

"Here is my herald, whom I send ahead of you,
and he will prepare your way before you."

'I tell you, among all who have been born, no one has been greater than John; yet the least in the kingdom of God is greater than he is.' When they heard him, all the people, including the tax-collectors, acknowledged the goodness of God, for they had accepted John's baptism; but the Pharisees and lawyers, who had refused his baptism, rejected God's purpose for themselves.

'How can I describe the people of this generation? What are they like? They are like children sitting in the market-place and calling to each other,

"We piped for you and you would not dance.
We lamented, and you would not mourn."

'For John the Baptist came, neither eating bread nor drinking wine, and you say, "He is possessed." The Son of Man came, eating and drinking, and you say, "Look at him! A glutton and a drinker, a friend of tax-collectors and sinners!" And yet God's wisdom is proved right by all who are her children.'

A Woman Anoints Jesus's Feet

One of the Pharisees invited Jesus to a meal; he went to the Pharisee's house and took his place at table. A woman who was living an immoral life in the town had learned that Jesus was a guest in the Pharisee's house and had brought oil of myrrh in a small flask. She took her place behind him, by his feet, weeping. His feet were wet with her tears and she wiped them with her hair, kissing them and anointing them with the myrrh. When his host the Pharisee saw this he said to himself, 'If this man were a real prophet, he would know who this woman is who is touching him, and what a bad character she is.' Jesus took him up: 'Simon,' he said, 'I have something to say to you.' 'What is it, Teacher?' he asked. 'Two men were in debt to a moneylender: one owed him five hundred silver pieces, the other fifty. As they did not have the means to pay he cancelled both debts. Now, which will love him more?' Simon replied, 'I should think the one that was let off more.' 'You are right,' said Jesus. Then turning to the woman, he said to Simon, 'You see this woman? I came to your house: you provided no water for my feet; but this woman has made my feet wet with her tears and wiped them with her hair. You gave me no kiss; but she has been kissing my feet ever since I came in. You did not anoint my head with oil; but she has anointed my feet with myrrh. So, I tell you, her great love proves that her many sins have been forgiven; where little has been forgiven, little love is shown.' Then he said to her, 'Your sins are forgiven.' The other guests began to ask themselves, 'Who is this, that he can forgive sins?' But he said to the woman, 'Your faith has saved you; go in peace.'

The Women who Followed Jesus

After this he went journeying from town to town and village to village, proclaiming the good news of the kingdom of God. With him were the Twelve and a number of women who had been set free from evil spirits and infirmities: Mary, known as Mary of Magdala, from whom seven demons had come out, Joanna, the wife of Chuza a steward of Herod's, Susanna, and many others. These women provided for them out of their own resources.

Jesus Denounces the Pharisees

Then they brought him a man who was possessed by a demon; he was blind and dumb, and Jesus cured him, restoring both speech and sight. The bystanders were all amazed, and the word went round: 'Can this be the Son of David?' But when the Pharisees heard it they said, 'It is only by Beelzebul prince of devils that this man drives the devils out.'

Knowing what was in their minds, he said to them, 'Every kingdom divided against itself is laid waste; and no town or household that is divided against itself can stand. And if it is Satan who drives out Satan, he is divided against himself; how then can his kingdom stand? If it is by Beelzebul that I drive out devils, by whom do your own people drive them out? If this is your argument, they themselves will refute you. But if it is by the

Spirit of God that I drive out the devils, then be sure the kingdom of God has already come upon you.

'Or again, how can anyone break into a strong man's house and make off with his goods, unless he has first tied up the strong man? Then he can ransack the house.

'He who is not with me is against me, and he who does not gather with me scatters.

'So I tell you this: every sin and every slander can be forgiven, except slander spoken against the Spirit; that will not be forgiven. Anyone who speaks a word against the Son of Man will be forgiven; but if anyone speaks against the Holy Spirit, for him there will be no forgiveness, either in this age or in the age to come.

'Get a good tree and its fruit will be good; get a bad tree and its fruit will be bad. You can tell a tree by its fruit. Vipers' brood! How can your words be good when you yourselves are evil? It is from the fullness of the heart that the mouth speaks. Good people from their store of good produce good; and evil people from their store of evil produce evil.

'I tell you this: every thoughtless word you speak you will have to account for on the day of judgement. For out of your own mouth you will be acquitted; out of your own mouth you will be condemned.'

At this some of the scribes and the Pharisees said, 'Teacher, we would like you to show us a sign.' He answered: 'It is a wicked, godless generation that asks for a sign, and the only sign that will be given it is the sign of the prophet Jonah. Just as Jonah was in the sea monster's belly for three days and three nights, so the Son of Man will be three days and three nights in the bowels of the earth. The men of Nineveh will appear in court when this generation is on trial, and ensure its condemnation, for they repented at the preaching of Jonah; and what is here is greater than Jonah. The queen of the south will appear in court when this generation is on trial, and ensure its condemnation; for she came from the ends of the earth to listen to the wisdom of Solomon, and what is here is greater than Solomon.

'When an unclean spirit comes out of someone it wanders over the desert sands seeking a resting-place, and finds none. Then it says, "I will go back to the home I left." So it returns and finds the house unoccupied, swept clean, and tidy. It goes off and collects seven other spirits more wicked than itself, and they all come in and settle there; and in the end that person's plight is worse than before. That is how it will be with this wicked generation.'

Brothers of Jesus

He was still speaking to the crowd when his mother and brothers appeared; they stood outside, wanting to speak to him. Someone said, 'Your mother and your brothers are standing outside; they want to speak to you.' Jesus turned to the man who brought the message, and said, 'Who is my mother? Who are my brothers?' and pointing to his disciples, he said, 'Here are my mother and my brothers. Whoever does the will of my heavenly Father is my brother and sister and mother.'

The Parable of the Wheat and the Darnel

Here is another parable he gave them: 'The kingdom of Heaven is like this. A man sowed his field with good seed; but while everyone was asleep his enemy came, sowed darnel among the wheat, and made off. When the corn sprouted and began to fill out, the darnel could be seen among it. The farmer's men went to their master and said, "Sir, was it not good seed that you sowed in your field? So where has the darnel come from?" "This is an enemy's doing," he replied. "Well then," they said, "shall we go and gather the darnel?" "No," he answered; "in gathering it you might pull up the wheat at the same time. Let them both grow together till harvest; and at harvest time I will tell the reapers, 'Gather the darnel first, and tie it in bundles for burning; then collect the wheat into my barn.'"'

Then he sent the people away, and went into the house, where his disciples came to him and said, 'Explain to us the parable of the darnel in the field.' He replied, 'The sower of the good seed is the Son of Man. The field is the world; the good seed stands for the children of the Kingdom, the darnel for the children of the evil one, and the enemy who sowed the darnel is the devil. The harvest is the end of time, and the reapers are angels. As the darnel is gathered up and burnt, so at the end of time the Son of Man will send his angels, who will gather out of his kingdom every cause of sin, and all whose deeds are evil; these will be thrown into the blazing furnace, where there will be wailing and grinding of teeth. Then the righteous will shine like the sun in the kingdom of their Father. If you have ears, then hear.'

More Parables of the Kingdom

'The kingdom of Heaven is like yeast, which a woman took and mixed with three measures of flour till it was all leavened.'

'The kingdom of Heaven is like treasure which a man found buried in a field. He buried it again, and in joy went and sold everything he had, and bought the field.

'Again, the kingdom of Heaven is like this. A merchant looking out for fine pearls found one of very special value; so he went and sold everything he had and bought it.

'Again the kingdom of Heaven is like a net cast into the sea, where it caught fish of every kind. When it was full, it was hauled ashore. Then the men sat down and collected the good fish into baskets and threw the worthless away. That is how it will be at the end of time. The angels will go out, and they will separate the wicked from the good, and throw them into the blazing furnace, where there will be wailing and grinding of teeth.

'Have you understood all this?' he asked; and they answered, 'Yes.' So he said to them, 'When, therefore, a teacher of the law has become a learner in the kingdom of Heaven, he is like a householder who can produce from his store things new and old.'

The Beheading of John the Baptist

Now King Herod heard of Jesus, for his fame had spread, and people were saying, 'John the Baptist has been raised from the dead, and that is why these miraculous powers are at work in him.' Others said, 'It is Elijah.' Others again, 'He is a prophet like one of the prophets of old.' But when Herod heard of it, he said, 'This is John, whom I beheaded, raised from the dead.'

It was this Herod who had sent men to arrest John and put him in prison at the instance of his brother Philip's wife, Herodias, whom he had married. John had told him, 'You have no right to take your brother's wife.' Herodias nursed a grudge against John and would willingly have killed him, but she could not, for Herod went in awe of him, knowing him to be a good and holy man; so he gave him his protection. He liked to listen to him, although what he heard left him greatly disturbed.

Herodias found her opportunity when Herod on his birthday gave a banquet to his chief officials and commanders and the leading men of Galilee. Her daughter came in and danced, and so delighted Herod and his guests that the king said to the girl, 'Ask me for anything you like and I will give it to you.' He even said on oath: 'Whatever you ask I will give you, up to half my kingdom.' She went out and said to her mother, 'What shall I ask for?' She replied, 'The head of John the Baptist.' The girl hurried straight back to the king with her request: 'I want you to give me, here and now, on a dish, the head of John the Baptist.' The king was greatly distressed, yet because of his oath and his guests he could not bring himself to refuse her. He sent a soldier of the guard with orders to bring John's head; and the soldier went to the prison and beheaded him; then he brought the head on a dish, and gave it to the girl; and she gave it to her mother.

When John's disciples heard the news, they came and took his body away and laid it in a tomb.

The Healing at the Pool of Bethesda

Some time later, Jesus went up to Jerusalem for one of the Jewish festivals. Now at the Sheep Gate in Jerusalem there is a pool whose Hebrew name is Bethesda. It has five colonnades and in them lay a great number of sick people, blind, lame, and paralysed. Among them was a man who had been crippled for thirty-eight years. Jesus saw him lying there, and knowing that he had been ill a long time he asked him, 'Do you want to get well?' 'Sir,' he replied, 'I have no one to put me in the pool when the water is disturbed; while I am getting there, someone else steps into the pool before me.' Jesus answered, 'Stand up, take your bed and walk.' The man recovered instantly; he took up his bed, and began to walk.

That day was a sabbath. So the Jews said to the man who had been cured, 'It is the sabbath. It is against the law for you to carry your bed.' He answered, 'The man who cured me, he told me, "Take up your bed and walk."' They asked him, 'Who is this man who told you to take it up and walk?' But the man who had been cured did not know who it was; for the place was crowded and Jesus had slipped away. A little later Jesus found him in the temple and said to him, 'Now that you are well, give up your sinful ways, or something worse may happen to you.' The man went off and told the Jews that it was Jesus who had cured him.

It was for doing such things on the sabbath that the Jews began to take action against Jesus. He defended himself by saying, 'My Father continues to work, and I must work too.' This made the

Jews all the more determined to kill him, because not only was he breaking the sabbath but, by calling God his own Father, he was claiming equality with God.

To this charge Jesus replied, 'In very truth I tell you, the Son can do nothing by himself; he does only what he sees the Father doing: whatever the Father does, the Son does. For the Father loves the Son and shows him all that he himself is doing, and will show him even greater deeds, to fill you with wonder. As the Father raises the dead and gives them life, so the Son gives life as he chooses. Again, the Father does not judge anyone, but has given full jurisdiction to the Son; it is his will that all should pay the same honour to the Son as to the Father. To deny honour to the Son is to deny it to the Father who sent him. You study the scriptures diligently, supposing that in having them you have eternal life; their testimony points to me, yet you refuse to come to me to receive that life.

'I do not look to men for honour. But I know that with you it is different, for you have no love of God in you. I have come accredited by my Father, and you have no welcome for me; but let someone self-accredited come, and you will give him a welcome. How can you believe when you accept honour from one another, and care nothing for the honour that comes from him who alone is God? Do not imagine that I shall be your accuser at the Father's tribunal. Your accuser is Moses, the very Moses on whom you have set your hope. If you believed him you would believe me, for it was of me that he wrote. But if you do not believe what he wrote, how are you to believe what I say?'

The Feeding of the Five Thousand

Some time later Jesus withdrew to the farther shore of the sea of Galilee (or Tiberias), and a large crowd of people followed him because they had seen the signs he performed in healing the sick. Jesus went up the hillside and sat down with his disciples. It was near the time of Passover, the great Jewish festival. Looking up and seeing a large crowd coming towards him, Jesus said to Philip, 'Where are we to buy bread to feed these people?' He said this to test him; Jesus himself knew what he meant to do. Philip replied, 'We would need two hundred denarii to buy enough bread for each of them to have a little.' One of his disciples, Andrew, the brother of Simon Peter, said to him, 'There is a boy here who has five barley loaves and two fish; but what is that among so many?' Jesus said, 'Make the people sit down.' There was plenty of grass there, so the men sat down, about five thousand of them. Then Jesus took the loaves, gave thanks, and distributed them to the people as they sat there. He did the same with the fish, and they had as much as they wanted. When everyone had had enough, he said to his disciples, 'Gather up the pieces left over, so that nothing is wasted.' They gathered them up, and filled twelve baskets with the pieces of the five barley loaves that were left uneaten.

Jesus Walks on the Water
As soon as they had finished, he made the disciples embark and cross to the other side ahead of him, while he dismissed the crowd; then he went up the hill by himself to pray. It had grown late, and he was there alone. The boat was already some distance from the shore, battling with a head wind and a rough sea. Between three and six in the morning he came towards them, walking across the lake. When the disciples saw him walking on the lake they were so shaken that they cried out in terror: 'It is a ghost!' But at once Jesus spoke to them: 'Take heart! It is I; do not be afraid.'

Peter called to him: 'Lord, if it is you, tell me to come to you over the water.' 'Come,' said Jesus. Peter got down out of the boat, and walked over the water towards Jesus. But when he saw the strength of the gale he was afraid; and beginning to sink, he cried, 'Save me, Lord!' Jesus at once reached out and caught hold of him. 'Why did you hesitate?' he said. 'How little faith you have!' Then they climbed into the boat; and the wind dropped. And the men in the boat fell at his feet, exclaiming, 'You must be the Son of God.'

The Bread of Life
Next morning the crowd was still on the opposite shore. They had seen only one boat there, and Jesus, they knew, had not embarked with his disciples, who had set off by themselves. Boats from Tiberias, however, had come ashore near the place where the people had eaten the bread over which the Lord gave thanks. When the crowd saw that Jesus had gone as well as his disciples, they went on board these boats and made for Capernaum in

search of him. They found him on the other side. 'Rabbi,' they asked, 'when did you come here?' Jesus replied, 'In very truth I tell you, it is not because you saw signs that you came looking for me, but because you ate the bread and your hunger was satisfied. You should work, not for this perishable food, but for the food that lasts, the food of eternal life. This food the Son of Man will give you, for on him God the Father has set the seal of his authority.' 'Then what must we do', they asked him, 'if our work is to be the work of God?' Jesus replied, 'This is the work that God requires: to believe in the one whom he has sent.'

They asked, 'What sign can you give us, so that we may see it and believe you? What is the work you are doing? Our ancestors had manna to eat in the desert; as scripture says, "He gave them bread from heaven to eat."' Jesus answered, 'In very truth I tell you, it was not Moses who gave you the bread from heaven; it is my Father who gives you the true bread from heaven. The bread that God gives comes down from heaven and brings life to the world.' 'Sir,' they said to him, 'give us this bread now and always.' Jesus said to them, 'I am the bread of life. Whoever comes to me will never be hungry, and whoever believes in me will never be thirsty. But you, as I said, have seen and yet you do not believe. All that the Father gives me will come to me, and anyone who comes to me I will never turn away. I am the living bread that has come down from heaven; if anyone eats this bread, he will live for ever. The bread which I shall give is my own flesh, given for the life of the world.'

This led to a fierce dispute among the Jews. 'How can this man give us his flesh to eat?' they protested. Jesus answered them, 'In very truth I tell you, unless you eat the flesh of the Son of Man and drink his blood you can have no life in you. Whoever eats my flesh and drinks my blood has eternal life, and I will raise him up on the last day. My flesh is real food; my blood is real drink. Whoever eats my flesh and drinks my blood dwells in me and I in him.'

The Meaning of Defilement

A group of Pharisees, with some scribes who had come from Jerusalem, met him and noticed that some of his disciples were eating their food with defiled hands – in other words, without washing them. (For Pharisees and Jews in general never eat without washing their hands, in obedience to ancient tradition; and on coming from the market-place they never eat without first washing. And there are many other points on which they maintain traditional rules, for example in the washing of cups and jugs and copper bowls.) These Pharisees and scribes questioned Jesus: 'Why do your disciples not conform to the ancient tradition, but eat their food with defiled hands?' He answered, 'How right Isaiah was when he prophesied about you hypocrites in these words: "This people pays me lip-service, but their heart is far from me: they worship me in vain, for they teach as doctrines the commandments of men." You neglect the commandment of God, in order to maintain the tradition of men.'

He said to them, 'How clever you are at setting aside the commandment of God in order to maintain your tradition! Moses said, "Honour your father and your mother," and again, "Whoever curses his father or mother shall be put to death." But you hold that if someone says to his father or mother, "Anything I have which might have been used for your benefit is Corban,"' (that is, set apart for God) 'he is no longer allowed to do anything for his father or mother. In this way by your tradition, handed down among you, you make God's word null and void. And you do many other things just like that.'

On another occasion he called the people and said to them, 'Listen to me, all of you, and understand this: nothing that goes into a person from outside can defile him; no, it is the things that come out of a person that defile him.'

When he had left the people and gone indoors, his disciples questioned him about the parable. He said to them, 'Are you as dull as the rest? Do you not see that nothing that goes into a person from outside can defile him, because it does not go into the heart but into the stomach, and so goes out into the drain?' By saying this he declared all foods clean. He went on, 'It is what comes out of a person that defiles him. From inside, from the human heart, come evil thoughts, acts of fornication, theft, murder, adultery, greed, and malice; fraud, indecency, envy, slander, arrogance, and folly; all these evil things come from within, and they are what defile a person.'

Jesus and the Syro-Phoenician Woman
He moved on from there into the territory of Tyre. He found a house to stay in, and would have liked to remain unrecognized,

but that was impossible. Almost at once a woman whose small daughter was possessed by an unclean spirit heard of him and came and fell at his feet. (The woman was a Gentile, a Phoenician of Syria by nationality.) She begged him to drive the demon out of her daughter. He said to her, 'Let the children be satisfied first; it is not right to take the children's bread and throw it to the dogs.' 'Sir,' she replied, 'even the dogs under the table eat the children's scraps.' He said to her, 'For saying that, go, and you will find the demon has left your daughter.' And when she returned home, she found the child lying in bed; the demon had left her.

The Healing of a Deaf Man

On his journey back from Tyrian territory he went by way of Sidon to the sea of Galilee, well within the territory of the Decapolis. They brought to him a man who was deaf and had an impediment in his speech, and begged Jesus to lay his hand on him. He took him aside, away from the crowd; then he put his fingers in the man's ears, and touched his tongue with spittle. Looking up to heaven, he sighed, and said to him, '*Ephphatha*,' which means 'Be opened.' With that his hearing was restored, and at the same time the impediment was removed and he spoke clearly. Jesus forbade them to tell anyone; but the more he forbade them, the more they spread it abroad. Their astonishment knew no bounds: 'All that he does, he does well,' they said; 'he even makes the deaf hear and the dumb speak.'

The Healing of a Blind Man

They arrived at Bethsaida. There the people brought a blind man to Jesus and begged him to touch him. He took the blind man by the hand and led him out of the village. Then he spat on his eyes, laid his hands upon him, and asked whether he could see anything. The man's sight began to come back, and he said, 'I see people – they look like trees, but they are walking about.' Jesus laid his hands on his eyes again; he looked hard, and now he was cured and could see everything clearly. Then Jesus sent him home, saying, 'Do not even go into the village.'

Peter's Confession

When he came to the territory of Caesarea Philippi, Jesus asked his disciples, 'Who do people say that the Son of Man is?' They answered, 'Some say John the Baptist, others Elijah, others Jeremiah, or one of the prophets.' 'And you,' he asked, 'who do you say I am?' Simon Peter answered: 'You are the Messiah, the Son of the living God.' Then Jesus said: 'Simon son of Jonah, you are favoured indeed! You did not learn that from any human being; it was revealed to you by my heavenly Father. And I say to you: you are Peter, the Rock; and on this rock I will build my church, and the powers of death shall never conquer it. I will give you the keys of the kingdom of Heaven; what you forbid on earth shall be forbidden in heaven, and what you allow on earth shall be allowed in heaven.' He then gave his disciples strict orders not to tell anyone that he was the Messiah.

Jesus Foretells his Passion

From that time Jesus began to make it clear to his disciples that he had to go to Jerusalem, and endure great suffering at the hands of the elders, chief priests, and scribes; to be put to death, and to be raised again on the third day. At this Peter took hold of him and began to rebuke him: 'Heaven forbid!' he said. 'No, Lord, this shall never happen to you.' Then Jesus turned and said to Peter, 'Out of my sight, Satan; you are a stumbling block to me. You think as men think, not as God thinks.'

Jesus then said to his disciples, 'Anyone who wishes to be a follower of mine must renounce self; he must take up his cross and follow me. Whoever wants to save his life will lose it, but whoever loses his life for my sake will find it. What will anyone gain by winning the whole world at the cost of his life? Or what can he give to buy his life back? For the Son of Man is to come in the glory of his Father with his angels, and then he will give everyone his due reward. Truly I tell you: there are some of those standing here who will not taste death before they have seen the Son of Man coming in his kingdom.'

The Transfiguration

Six days later Jesus took Peter, James, and John with him and led them up a high mountain by themselves. And in their presence he was transfigured; his clothes became dazzling white, with a whiteness no bleacher on earth could equal. They saw Elijah appear and Moses with him, talking with Jesus. Then Peter spoke: 'Rabbi,' he said, 'it is good that we are here! Shall we make three shelters, one for you, one for Moses, and one for Elijah?' For he did not know what to say; they were so terrified. Then a cloud appeared, casting its shadow over them, and out of the cloud came a voice: 'This is my beloved Son; listen to him.' And suddenly, when they looked around, only Jesus was with them; there was no longer anyone else to be seen.

On their way down the mountain, he instructed them not to tell anyone what they had seen until the Son of Man had risen from the dead. They seized upon those words, and discussed among themselves what this 'rising from the dead' could mean. And they put a question to him: 'Why do the scribes say that Elijah must come first?' He replied, 'Elijah does come first to set everything right. How is it, then, that the scriptures say of the Son of Man that he is to endure great suffering and be treated with contempt? However, I tell you, Elijah has already come and they have done to him what they wanted, as the scriptures say of him.'

The Healing of a Boy Possessed by a Spirit

When they came back to the disciples they saw a large crowd surrounding them and scribes arguing with them. As soon as they saw Jesus the whole crowd were overcome with awe and ran forward to welcome him. He asked them, 'What is this argument about?' A man in the crowd spoke up: 'Teacher, I brought my son for you to cure. He is possessed by a spirit that makes him dumb. Whenever it attacks him, it flings him to the ground, and he foams at the mouth, grinds his teeth, and goes rigid. I asked your disciples to drive it out, but they could not.' Jesus answered: 'What an unbelieving generation! How long shall I be with you? How long must I endure you? Bring him to me.' So they brought the boy to him; and as soon as the spirit saw him it threw the boy into convulsions, and he fell on the ground and rolled about foaming at the mouth. Jesus asked his father, 'How long has he been like this?' 'From childhood,' he replied; 'it has often tried to destroy him by throwing him into the fire or into water. But if it is at all possible for you, take pity on us and help us.' 'If it is possible!' said Jesus. 'Everything is possible to one who believes.' At once the boy's father cried: 'I believe; help my unbelief.' When Jesus saw that the crowd was closing in on them, he spoke sternly to the unclean spirit. 'Deaf and dumb spirit,' he said, 'I command you, come out of him and never go back!' It shrieked aloud and threw the boy into repeated convulsions, and then came out, leaving him looking like a corpse; in fact, many said, 'He is dead.' But Jesus took hold of his hand and raised him to his feet, and he stood up.

Then Jesus went indoors, and his disciples asked him privately, 'Why could we not drive it out?' He said, 'This kind cannot be driven out except by prayer.'

Paying the Temple Tax

On their arrival at Capernaum the collectors of the temple tax came up to Peter and asked, 'Does your master not pay temple tax?' 'He does,' said Peter. When he went indoors Jesus forestalled him by asking, 'Tell me, Simon, from whom do earthly monarchs collect tribute money? From their own people, or from aliens?' 'From aliens,' said Peter. 'Yes,' said Jesus, 'and their own people are exempt. But as we do not want to cause offence, go and cast a line in the lake; take the first fish you catch, open its mouth, and you will find a silver coin; take that and pay the tax for us both.'

The Greatest in the Kingdom

At that time the disciples came to Jesus and asked, 'Who is the greatest in the kingdom of Heaven?' He called a child, set him in front of them, and said, 'Truly I tell you: unless you turn round and become like children, you will never enter the kingdom of Heaven. Whoever humbles himself and becomes like this child will be the greatest in the kingdom of Heaven, and whoever receives one such child in my name receives me. But if anyone causes the downfall of one of these little ones who believe in me, it would be better for him to have a millstone hung round his neck and be drowned in the depths of the sea. Alas for the world that any of them should be made to fall! Such things must happen, but alas for the one through whom they happen!'

Reproof and Reconciliation

'If your brother does wrong, go and take the matter up with him,
strictly between yourselves. If he listens to you, you have won your
brother over. But if he will not listen, take one or two others with
you, so that every case may be settled on the evidence of two or
three witnesses. If he refuses to listen to them, report the matter to
the congregation; and if he will not listen even to the congregation,
then treat him as you would a pagan or a tax-collector.

'Truly I tell you: whatever you forbid on earth shall be forbidden in heaven, and whatever you allow on earth shall be allowed
in heaven.

'And again I tell you: if two of you agree on earth about any
request you have to make, that request will be granted by my
heavenly Father. For where two or three meet together in my
name, I am there among them.'

Then Peter came to him and asked, 'Lord, how often am I to
forgive my brother if he goes on wronging me? As many as seven
times?' Jesus replied, 'I do not say seven times but seventy times
seven.'

The Parable of the Unmerciful Servant

'The kingdom of Heaven, therefore, should be thought of in this
way: There was once a king who decided to settle accounts with
the men who served him. At the outset there appeared before him
a man who owed ten thousand talents. Since he had no means of
paying, his master ordered him to be sold, with his wife, his children, and everything he had, to meet the debt. The man fell at his
master's feet. "Be patient with me," he implored, "and I will pay
you in full"; and the master was so moved with pity that he let
the man go and cancelled the debt. But no sooner had the man
gone out than he met a fellow servant who owed him a hundred
denarii; he took hold of him, seizing him by the throat, and said,
"Pay me what you owe." The man fell at his fellow servant's feet,
and begged him, "Be patient with me, and I will pay you"; but he
refused, and had him thrown into jail until he should pay the
debt. The other servants were deeply distressed when they saw
what had happened, and they went to their master and told him
the whole story. Then he sent for the man and said, "You
scoundrel! I cancelled the whole of your debt when you appealed
to me; ought you not to have shown mercy to your fellow servant

just as I showed mercy to you?" And so angry was the master that he condemned the man to be tortured until he should pay the debt in full. That is how my heavenly Father will deal with you, unless you each forgive your brother from your hearts.'

Not One of Us

'Master,' said John, 'we saw someone driving out demons in your name, but as he is not one of us we tried to stop him.' Jesus said to him, 'Do not stop him, for he who is not against you is on your side.'

32 | THE ROAD TO JERUSALEM

No Looking Back
As the time approached when he was to be taken up to heaven, Jesus set his face resolutely towards Jerusalem.

As they were going along the road a man said to him, 'I will follow you wherever you go.' Jesus answered, 'Foxes have their holes and birds their roosts; but the Son of Man has nowhere to lay his head.' To another he said, 'Follow me,' but the man replied, 'Let me first go and bury my father.' Jesus said, 'Leave the dead to bury their dead; you must go and announce the kingdom of God.' Yet another said, 'I will follow you, sir; but let me first say goodbye to my people at home.' To him Jesus said, 'No one who sets his hand to the plough and then looks back is fit for the kingdom of God.'

Jesus Commissions More Disciples
After this the Lord appointed a further seventy-two and sent them on ahead in pairs to every town and place he himself intended to visit. He said to them: 'The crop is heavy, but the labourers are few. Ask the owner therefore to send labourers to bring in the harvest. Be on your way; I am sending you like lambs among wolves. Carry no purse or pack, and travel barefoot. Exchange no greetings on the road. When you go into a house, let your first words be, "Peace to this house." If there is a man of peace there, your peace will rest on him; if not, it will return to you. Stay in that house, sharing their food and drink; for the worker deserves his pay.'

The seventy-two came back jubilant. 'In your name, Lord,' they said, 'even the demons submit to us.' He replied, 'I saw Satan fall, like lightning, from heaven. And I have given you the power to tread underfoot snakes and scorpions and all the forces of the enemy. Nothing will ever harm you. Nevertheless, do not rejoice that the spirits submit to you, but that your names are enrolled in heaven.'

When he was alone with his disciples he turned to them and said, 'Happy the eyes that see what you are seeing! I tell you, many prophets and kings wished to see what you now see, yet never saw it; to hear what you hear, yet never heard it.'

The Parable of the Good Samaritan

A lawyer once came forward to test him by asking: 'Teacher, what must I do to inherit eternal life?' Jesus said, 'What is written in the law? What is your reading of it?' He replied, 'Love the Lord your God with all your heart, and with all your soul, with all your strength, and with all your mind; and your neighbour as yourself.' 'That is the right answer,' said Jesus; 'do that and you will have life.'

Wanting to justify his question, he asked, 'But who is my neighbour?' Jesus replied, 'A man was on his way from Jerusalem down to Jericho when he was set upon by robbers, who stripped and beat him, and went off leaving him half dead. It so happened that a priest was going down by the same road, and when he saw him, he went past on the other side. So too a Levite came to the place, and when he saw him went past on the other side. But a Samaritan who was going that way came upon him, and when he saw him he was moved to pity. He went up and bandaged his wounds, bathing them with oil and wine. Then he lifted him on to his own beast, brought him to an inn, and looked after him. Next day he produced two silver pieces and gave them to the innkeeper, and said, "Look after him; and if you spend more, I will repay you on my way back." Which of these three do you think was neighbour to the man who fell into the hands of the robbers?' He answered, 'The one who showed him kindness.' Jesus said to him, 'Go and do as he did.'

In the House of Mary and Martha

While they were on their way Jesus came to a village where a woman named Martha made him welcome. She had a sister, Mary, who seated herself at the Lord's feet and stayed there listening to his words. Now Martha was distracted by her many tasks, so she came to him and said, 'Lord, do you not care that my sister has left me to get on with the work by myself? Tell her to come and give me a hand.' But the Lord answered, 'Martha, Martha, you are fretting and fussing about so many things; only one thing is necessary. Mary has chosen what is best; it shall not be taken away from her.'

The Parable of the Persistent Friend
Then he said to them, 'Suppose one of you has a friend who comes to him in the middle of the night and says, "My friend, lend me three loaves, for a friend of mine on a journey has turned up at my house, and I have nothing to offer him"; and he replies from inside, "Do not bother me. The door is shut for the night; my children and I have gone to bed; and I cannot get up and give you what you want." I tell you that even if he will not get up and provide for him out of friendship, his very persistence will make the man get up and give him all he needs.'

Warnings Against the Pharisees
When he had finished speaking, a Pharisee invited him to a meal, and he came in and sat down. The Pharisee noticed with surprise that he had not begun by washing before the meal. But the Lord said to him, 'You Pharisees clean the outside of cup and plate; but inside you are full of greed and wickedness. You fools! Did not he who made the outside make the inside too? But let what is inside be given in charity, and all is clean.

'Alas for you Pharisees! You pay tithes of mint and rue and every garden herb, but neglect justice and the love of God. It is these you should have practised, without overlooking the others.

'Alas for you Pharisees! You love to have the chief seats in synagogues, and to be greeted respectfully in the street.

'Alas, alas, you are like unmarked graves which people walk over unawares.'

At this one of the lawyers said, 'Teacher, when you say things like this you are insulting us too.' Jesus rejoined: 'Alas for you lawyers also! You load men with intolerable burdens, and will not lift a finger to lighten the load.

'Alas, you build monuments to the prophets whom your fathers murdered, and so testify that you approve of the deeds your fathers did; they committed the murders and you provide the monuments.

'This is why the Wisdom of God said, "I will send them prophets and messengers; and some of these they will persecute and kill"; so that this generation will have to answer for the blood of all the prophets shed since the foundation of the world; from the blood of Abel to the blood of Zechariah who met his death between the altar and the sanctuary. I tell you, this generation will have to answer for it all.

'Alas for you lawyers! You have taken away the key of knowledge. You did not go in yourselves, and those who were trying to go in, you prevented.'

After he had left the house, the scribes and Pharisees began to assail him fiercely and to ply him with a host of questions, laying snares to catch him with his own words.

The Parable of the Rich Fool

Someone in the crowd said to him, 'Teacher, tell my brother to divide the family property with me.' He said to the man, 'Who set me over you to judge or arbitrate?' Then to the people he said, 'Beware! Be on your guard against greed of every kind, for even when someone has more than enough, his possessions do not give him life.' And he told them this parable: 'There was a rich man whose land yielded a good harvest. He debated with himself: "What am I to do? I have not the space to store my produce. This is what I will do," said he: "I will pull down my barns and build them bigger. I will collect in them all my grain and other goods, and I will say to myself, 'You have plenty of good things laid by, enough for many years to come: take life easy, eat, drink, and enjoy yourself.'" But God said to him, "You fool, this very night you must surrender your life; and the money you have made, who will get it now?" That is how it is with the man who piles up treasure for himself and remains a pauper in the sight of God.'

The Need for Repentance

At that time some people came and told him about the Galileans whose blood Pilate had mixed with their sacrifices. He answered them: 'Do you suppose that, because these Galileans suffered this fate, they must have been greater sinners than anyone else in Galilee? No, I tell you; but unless you repent, you will all of you come to the same end. Or the eighteen people who were killed when the tower fell on them at Siloam – do you imagine they must have been more guilty than all the other people living in Jerusalem? No, I tell you; but unless you repent, you will all come to an end like theirs.'

The Parable of the Barren Fig Tree

He told them this parable: 'A man had a fig tree growing in his vineyard; and he came looking for fruit on it, but found none. So he said to the vine-dresser, "For the last three years I have come looking for fruit on this fig tree without finding any. Cut it down. Why should it go on taking goodness from the soil?" But he replied, "Leave it, sir, for this one year, while I dig round it and manure it. And if it bears next season, well and good; if not, you shall have it down."'

The Healing of a Crippled Woman

He was teaching in one of the synagogues on the sabbath, and there was a woman there possessed by a spirit that had crippled her for eighteen years. She was bent double and quite unable to stand up straight. When Jesus saw her he called her and said, 'You are rid of your trouble,' and he laid his hands on her. Immediately she straightened up and began to praise God. But the president of the synagogue, indignant with Jesus for healing on the sabbath, intervened and said to the congregation, 'There are six working days: come and be cured on one of them, and not on the sabbath.' The Lord gave him this answer: 'What hypocrites you are!' he said. 'Is there a single one of you who does not loose his ox or his donkey from its stall and take it out to water on the sabbath? And here is this woman, a daughter of Abraham, who has been bound by Satan for eighteen long years: was it not right for her to be loosed from her bonds on the sabbath?' At these words all his opponents were covered with confusion, while the mass of the people were delighted at all the wonderful things he was doing.

A Warning Against Herod

At that time a number of Pharisees came and warned him, 'Leave this place and be on your way; Herod wants to kill you.' He replied, 'Go and tell that fox, "Listen: today and tomorrow I shall be driving out demons and working cures; on the third day I reach my goal." However, I must go on my way today and tomorrow and the next day, because it is unthinkable for a prophet to meet his death anywhere but in Jerusalem.

'O Jerusalem, Jerusalem, city that murders the prophets and stones the messengers sent to her! How often have I longed to gather your children, as a hen gathers her brood under her wings; but you would not let me. Look! There is your temple, forsaken by God. I tell you, you will not see me until the time comes when you say, "Blessings on him who comes in the name of the Lord!"'

The Healing of a Man with Dropsy

One sabbath he went to have a meal in the house of one of the leading Pharisees; and they were watching him closely. There, in front of him, was a man suffering from dropsy, and Jesus asked the lawyers and the Pharisees: 'Is it permitted to heal people on the sabbath or not?' They said nothing. So he took the man, cured him, and sent him away.

The Need for Humility

When he noticed how the guests were trying to secure the places of honour, he spoke to them in a parable: 'When somebody asks you to a wedding feast, do not sit down in the place of honour. It may be that some person more distinguished than yourself has been invited; and the host will come to say to you, "Give this man your seat." Then you will look foolish as you go to take the lowest place. No, when you receive an invitation, go and sit down in the lowest place, so that when your host comes he will say, "Come up higher, my friend." Then all your fellow guests will see the respect in which you are held. For everyone who exalts himself will be humbled; and whoever humbles himself will be exalted.'

Then he said to his host, 'When you are having guests for lunch or supper, do not invite your friends, your brothers or other relations, or your rich neighbours; they will only ask you back again and so you will be repaid. But when you give a party, ask the poor, the crippled, the lame, and the blind. That is the way to find happiness, because they have no means of repaying you. You will be repaid on the day when the righteous rise from the dead.'

The Parable of the Great Banquet

Hearing this, one of the company said to him, 'Happy are those who will sit at the feast in the kingdom of God!' Jesus answered, 'A man was giving a big dinner party and had sent out many invitations. At dinner-time he sent his servant to tell his guests, "Come please, everything is now ready." One after another they all sent excuses. The first said, "I have bought a piece of land, and I must go and inspect it; please accept my apologies." The second said, "I have bought five yoke of oxen, and I am on my way to try them out; please accept my apologies." The next said, "I cannot come; I have just got married." When the servant came back he reported this to his master. The master of the house was furious and said to him, "Go out quickly into the streets and alleys of the town, and bring in the poor, the crippled, the blind, and the lame." When the servant informed him that his orders had been carried out and there was still room, his master replied, "Go out on the highways and along the hedgerows and compel them to come in; I want my house full. I tell you, not one of those who were invited shall taste my banquet."'

The Cost of Discipleship

Once when great crowds were accompanying him, he turned to them and said: 'If anyone comes to me and does not hate his father and mother, wife and children, brothers and sisters, even his own life, he cannot be a disciple of mine. No one who does not carry his cross and come with me can be a disciple of mine. Would any of you think of building a tower without first sitting down and calculating the cost, to see whether he could afford to finish it? Otherwise, if he has laid its foundation and then is unable to complete it, everyone who sees it will laugh at him. "There goes the man", they will say, "who started to build and could not finish." Or what king will march to battle against another king, without first sitting down to consider whether with ten thousand men he can face an enemy coming to meet him with twenty thousand? If he cannot, then, long before the enemy approaches, he sends envoys and asks for terms. So also, if you are not prepared to leave all your possessions behind, you cannot be my disciples.

The Parable of the Lost Sheep

Another time, the tax-collectors and sinners were all crowding in to listen to him; and the Pharisees and scribes began murmuring their disapproval: 'This fellow', they said, 'welcomes sinners and eats with them.' He answered them with this parable: 'If one of you has a hundred sheep and loses one of them, does he not leave the ninety-nine in the wilderness and go after the one that is missing until he finds it? And when he does, he lifts it joyfully on to his shoulders, and goes home to call his friends and neighbours together. "Rejoice with me!" he cries. "I have found my lost sheep." In the same way, I tell you, there will be greater joy in heaven over one sinner who repents than over ninety-nine righteous people who do not need to repent.

The Parable of the Lost Coin
'Or again, if a woman has ten silver coins and loses one of them, does she not light the lamp, sweep out the house, and look in every corner till she finds it? And when she does, she calls her friends and neighbours together, and says, "Rejoice with me! I have found the coin that I lost." In the same way, I tell you, there is joy among the angels of God over one sinner who repents.'

The Parable of the Prodigal Son
Again he said: 'There was once a man who had two sons; and the younger said to his father, "Father, give me my share of the property." So he divided his estate between them. A few days later the younger son turned the whole of his share into cash and left home for a distant country, where he squandered it in dissolute living. He had spent it all, when a severe famine fell upon that country and he began to be in need. So he went and attached himself to one of the local landowners, who sent him on to his farm to mind the pigs. He would have been glad to fill his belly with the pods that the pigs were eating, but no one gave him anything. Then he came to his senses: "How many of my father's hired servants have more food than they can eat," he said, "and here am I, starving to death! I will go at once to my father, and say to him, 'Father, I have sinned against God and against you; I am no longer fit to be called your son; treat me as one of your hired servants.'" So he set out for his father's house. But while he was still a long way off his father saw him, and his heart went out to him; he ran to meet him, flung his arms round him, and kissed him. The son said, "Father, I have sinned against God and against you; I am no longer fit to be called your son." But the father said to his servants, "Quick! Fetch a robe, the best we have, and put it on him; put a ring on his finger and sandals on his feet. Bring the fatted calf and kill it, and let us celebrate with a feast. For this son of mine was dead and has come back to life; he was lost and is found." And the festivities began.

'Now the elder son had been out on the farm; and on his way back, as he approached the house, he heard music and dancing. He called one of the servants and asked what it meant. The servant told him, "Your brother has come home, and your father has killed the fatted calf because he has him back safe and sound." But he was angry and refused to go in. His father came out and pleaded with him; but he retorted, "You know how I have slaved for you all these years; I never once disobeyed your orders; yet you never gave me so much as a kid, to celebrate with my friends. But now that this son of yours turns up, after running through your money with his women, you kill the fatted calf for him." "My boy," said the father, "you are always with me, and everything I have is yours. How could we fail to celebrate this happy day? Your brother here was dead and has come back to life; he was lost and has been found."'

The Parable of the Unjust Steward

He said to his disciples, 'There was a rich man who had a steward, and he received complaints that this man was squandering the property. So he sent for him, and said, "What is this that I hear about you? Produce your accounts, for you cannot be steward any longer." The steward said to himself, "What am I to do now that my master is going to dismiss me from my post? I am not strong enough to dig, and I am too proud to beg. I know what I must do, to make sure that, when I am dismissed, there will be people who will take me into their homes." He summoned his master's debtors one by one. To the first he said, "How much do you owe my master?" He replied, "A hundred jars of olive oil." He said, "Here is your account. Sit down and make it fifty, and be quick about it." Then he said to another, "And you, how much do you owe?" He said, "A hundred measures of wheat," and was told, "Here is your account; make it eighty." And the master applauded the dishonest steward for acting so astutely. For in dealing with their own kind the children of this world are more astute than the children of light.

'So I say to you, use your worldly wealth to win friends for yourselves, so that when money is a thing of the past you may be received into an eternal home.'

On Divorce and Celibacy

Some Pharisees came and tested him by asking, 'Is it lawful for a man to divorce his wife for any cause he pleases?' He responded by asking, 'Have you never read that in the beginning the Creator made them male and female?' and he added, 'That is why a man leaves his father and mother, and is united to his wife, and the two become one flesh. It follows that they are no longer two individuals: they are one flesh. Therefore what God has joined together, man must not separate.' 'Then why', they objected, 'did Moses lay it down that a man might divorce his wife by a cert-ificate of dismissal?' He answered, 'It was because of your stubbornness that Moses gave you permission to divorce your wives; but it was not like that at the beginning. I tell you, if a man divorces his wife for any cause other than unchastity, and marries another, he commits adultery.'

The disciples said to him, 'If that is how things stand for a man with a wife, it is better not to marry.' To this he replied, 'That is a course not everyone can accept, but only those for whom God has appointed it. For while some are incapable of marriage because they were born so, or were made so by men, there are others who have renounced marriage for the sake of the kingdom of Heaven. Let those accept who can.'

The Parable of the Rich Man and Lazarus

'There was once a rich man, who used to dress in purple and the finest linen, and feasted sumptuously every day. At his gate lay a poor man named Lazarus, who was covered with sores. He would have been glad to satisfy his hunger with the scraps from the rich man's table. Dogs used to come and lick his sores. One day the poor man died and was carried away by the angels to be with Abraham. The rich man also died and was buried. In Hades, where he was in torment, he looked up and there, far away, was Abraham with Lazarus close beside him. "Abraham, my father," he called out, "take pity on me! Send Lazarus to dip the tip of his finger in water, to cool my tongue, for I am in agony in this fire." But Abraham said, "My child, remember that the good things fell to you in your lifetime, and the bad to Lazarus. Now he has his consolation here and it is you who are in agony. But that is not all: there is a great gulf fixed between us; no one can cross it from our side to reach you, and none may pass from your side to us."

"Then, father," he replied, "will you send him to my father's house, where I have five brothers, to warn them, so that they may not come to this place of torment?" But Abraham said, "They have Moses and the prophets; let them listen to them." "No, father Abraham," he replied, "but if someone from the dead visits them, they will repent." Abraham answered, "If they do not listen to Moses and the prophets they will pay no heed even if someone should rise from the dead."'

The Parable of the Dutiful Servants

'Suppose one of you has a servant ploughing or minding sheep. When he comes in from the fields, will the master say, "Come and sit down straight away"? Will he not rather say, "Prepare my supper; hitch up your robe, and wait on me while I have my meal. You can have yours afterwards"? Is he grateful to the servant for carrying out his orders? So with you: when you have carried out all you have been ordered to do, you should say, "We are servants and deserve no credit; we have only done our duty."'

The Cleansing of Ten Lepers

In the course of his journey to Jerusalem he was travelling through the borderlands of Samaria and Galilee. As he was entering a village he was met by ten men with leprosy. They stood some way off and called out to him, 'Jesus, Master, take pity on us.' When he saw them he said, 'Go and show yourselves to the priests'; and while they were on their way, they were made clean. One of them, finding himself cured, turned back with shouts of praise to God. He threw himself down at Jesus's feet and thanked him. And he was a Samaritan. At this Jesus said: 'Were not all ten made clean? The other nine, where are they? Was no one found returning to give praise to God except this foreigner?' And he said to the man, 'Stand up and go on your way; your faith has cured you.'

The Day of the Son of Man

The Pharisees asked him, 'When will the kingdom of God come?' He answered, 'You cannot tell by observation when the kingdom of God comes. You cannot say, "Look, here it is," or "There it is!" For the kingdom of God is among you!'

He said to the disciples, 'The time will come when you will long to see one of the days of the Son of Man and will not see it. They will say to you, "Look! There!" and "Look! Here!" Do not go running off in pursuit. For like a lightning-flash, that lights up the earth from end to end, will the Son of Man be in his day. But first he must endure much suffering and be rejected by this generation.

'As it was in the days of Noah, so will it be in the days of the Son of Man. They ate and drank and married, until the day that Noah went into the ark and the flood came and made an end of them all. So too in the days of Lot, they ate and drank, they bought and sold, they planted and built; but on the day that Lot left Sodom, fire and sulphur rained from the sky and made an end of them all. It will be like that on the day when the Son of Man is revealed.

'On that day if anyone is on the roof while his belongings are in the house, he must not go down to fetch them; and if anyone is in the field, he must not turn back. Remember Lot's wife. Whoever seeks to preserve his life will lose it; and whoever loses his life will gain it.

'I tell you, on that night there will be two people in one bed: one will be taken, the other left. There will be two women together grinding corn: one will be taken, the other left.' When they heard this they asked, 'Where, Lord?' He said, 'Where the carcass is, there will the vultures gather.'

The Parable of the Unjust Judge

He told them a parable to show that they should keep on praying and never lose heart: 'In a certain city there was a judge who had no fear of God or respect for man, and in the same city there was a widow who kept coming before him to demand justice against her opponent. For a time he refused; but in the end he said to himself, "Although I have no fear of God or respect for man, yet this widow is so great a nuisance that I will give her justice before she wears me out with her persistence."' The Lord said, 'You hear what the unjust judge says. Then will not God give justice to his chosen, to whom he listens patiently while they cry out to him day and night? I tell you, he will give them justice soon enough. But when the Son of Man comes, will he find faith on earth?'

The Parable of the Pharisee and the Tax-collector

Here is another parable that he told; it was aimed at those who were sure of their own goodness and looked down on everyone else. 'Two men went up to the temple to pray, one a Pharisee and the other a tax-collector. The Pharisee stood up and prayed this prayer: "I thank you, God, that I am not like the rest of mankind – greedy, dishonest, adulterous – or, for that matter, like this tax-collector. I fast twice a week; I pay tithes on all that I get." But the other kept his distance and would not even raise his eyes to heaven, but beat upon his breast, saying, "God, have mercy on me, sinner that I am." It was this man, I tell you, and not the other, who went home acquitted of his sins. For everyone who exalts himself will be humbled; and whoever humbles himself will be exalted.'

Jesus Blesses the Children

They brought children for him to touch. The disciples rebuked them, but when Jesus saw it he was indignant, and said to them, 'Let the children come to me; do not try to stop them; for the kingdom of God belongs to such as these. Truly I tell you: whoever does not accept the kingdom of God like a child will never enter it.' And he put his arms round them, laid his hands on them, and blessed them.

The Rich Young Man

As he was starting out on a journey, a stranger ran up, and, kneeling before him, asked, 'Good Teacher, what must I do to win eternal life?' Jesus said to him, 'Why do you call me good? No one is good except God alone. You know the commandments: "Do not murder; do not commit adultery; do not steal; do not give false evidence; do not defraud; honour your father and mother."' 'But Teacher,' he replied, 'I have kept all these since I was a boy.' As Jesus looked at him, his heart warmed to him. 'One thing you lack,' he said. 'Go, sell everything you have, and give to the poor, and you will have treasure in heaven; then come and follow me.' At these words his face fell and he went away with a heavy heart; for he was a man of great wealth.

Many Who Are First Will Be Last

Jesus looked round at his disciples and said to them, 'How hard it will be for the wealthy to enter the kingdom of God!' They were amazed that he should say this, but Jesus insisted, 'Children, how hard it is to enter the kingdom of God! It is easier for a camel to pass through the eye of a needle than for a rich man to enter the kingdom of God.' They were more astonished than ever, and said to one another, 'Then who can be saved?' Jesus looked at them and said, 'For men it is impossible, but not for God; everything is possible for God.'

'What about us?' said Peter. 'We have left everything to follow you.' Jesus said, 'Truly I tell you: there is no one who has given up home, brothers or sisters, mother, father or children, or land, for my sake and for the gospel, who will not receive in this age a hundred times as much – houses, brothers and sisters, mothers and children, and land and persecutions besides; and in the age to come eternal life. But many who are first will be last, and the last first.'

James and John, the sons of Zebedee, approached him and said, 'Teacher, we should like you to do us a favour.' 'What is it you want me to do for you?' he asked. They answered, 'Allow us to sit with you in your glory, one at your right hand and the other at your left.' Jesus said to them, 'You do not understand what you are asking. Can you drink the cup that I drink, or be baptized with the baptism I am baptized with?' 'We can,' they answered. Jesus said, 'The cup that I drink you shall drink, and the baptism I am baptized with shall be your baptism; but to sit on my right or on my left is not for me to grant; that honour is for those to whom it has already been assigned.'

When the other ten heard this, they were indignant with James and John. Jesus called them to him and said, 'You know that among the Gentiles the recognized rulers lord it over their subjects, and the great make their authority felt. It shall not be so with you; among you, whoever wants to be great must be your servant, and whoever wants to be first must be the slave of all. For the Son of Man did not come to be served but to serve, and to give his life as a ransom for many.'

The Healing of a Blind Beggar

They came to Jericho; and as he was leaving the town, with his disciples and a large crowd, Bartimaeus (that is, son of Timaeus), a blind beggar, was seated at the roadside. Hearing that it was Jesus of Nazareth, he began to shout, 'Son of David, Jesus, have pity on me!' Many of the people told him to hold his tongue; but he shouted all the more, 'Son of David, have pity on me.' Jesus stopped and said, 'Call him'; so they called the blind man: 'Take heart,' they said. 'Get up; he is calling you.' At that he threw off his cloak, jumped to his feet, and came to Jesus. Jesus said to him, 'What do you want me to do for you?' 'Rabbi,' the blind man answered, 'I want my sight back.' Jesus said to him, 'Go; your faith has healed you.' And at once he recovered his sight and followed him on the road.

Jesus and Zacchaeus

Entering Jericho he made his way through the city. There was a man there named Zacchaeus; he was superintendent of taxes and very rich. He was eager to see what Jesus looked like; but, being a little man, he could not see him for the crowd. So he ran on ahead and climbed a sycomore tree in order to see him, for he was to pass that way. When Jesus came to the place, he looked up and said, 'Zacchaeus, be quick and come down, for I must stay at your house today.' He climbed down as quickly as he could and welcomed him gladly. At this there was a general murmur of disapproval. 'He has gone in to be the guest of a sinner,' they said. But Zacchaeus stood there and said to the Lord, 'Here and now, sir, I give half my possessions to charity; and if I have defrauded anyone, I will repay him four times over.' Jesus said to him, 'Today salvation has come to this house, for this man too is a son of Abraham. The Son of Man has come to seek and to save what is lost.'

The Parable of the Money

While they were listening to this, he went on to tell them a parable, because he was now close to Jerusalem and they thought the kingdom of God might dawn at any moment. He said, 'A man of noble birth went on a long journey abroad, to have himself appointed king and then return. But first he called ten of his servants and gave them each a sum of money, saying, "Trade with this while I am away." His fellow citizens hated him and sent a delegation after him to say, "We do not want this man as our king." He returned however as king, and sent for the servants to whom he had given the money, to find out what profit each had made. The first came and said, "Your money, sir, has increased tenfold." "Well done," he replied; "you are a good servant. Because you have shown yourself trustworthy in a very small matter, you shall have charge of ten cities." The second came and said, "Your money, sir, has increased fivefold"; and he was told, "You shall be in charge of five cities." The third came and said, "Here is your money, sir; I kept it wrapped up in a handkerchief. I was afraid of you, because you are a hard man: you draw out what you did not put in and reap what you did not sow." "You scoundrel!" he replied. "I will condemn you out of your own mouth. You knew me to be a hard man, did you, drawing out what I never put in, and reaping what I did not sow? Then why did you not put my money on deposit, and I could have claimed it with interest when I came back?" Turning to his attendants he said, "Take the money from him and give it to the man with the most." "But, sir," they replied, "he has ten times as much already." "I tell you," he said, "everyone who has will be given more; but whoever has nothing will forfeit even what he has. But as for those enemies of mine who did not want me for their king, bring them here and slaughter them in my presence."'

The Parable of the Labourers in the Vineyard

'The kingdom of Heaven is like this. There was once a land owner who went out early one morning to hire labourers for his vineyard; and after agreeing to pay them the usual day's wage he sent them off to work. Three hours later he went out again and saw some more men standing idle in the market-place. "Go and join the others in the vineyard," he said, "and I will pay you a fair wage"; so off they went. At midday he went out again, and at three in the afternoon, and made the same arrangement as before. An hour before sunset he went out and found another group standing there; so he said to them, "Why are you standing here all day doing nothing?" "Because no one has hired us," they replied; so he told them, "Go and join the others in the vineyard." When evening fell, the owner of the vineyard said to the overseer, "Call the labourers and give them their pay, beginning with those who came last and ending with the first." Those who had started work an hour before sunset came forward, and were paid the full day's wage. When it was the turn of the men who had come first, they expected something extra, but were paid the same as the others. As they took it, they grumbled at their employer: "These latecomers did only one hour's work, yet you have treated them on a level with us, who have sweated the whole day long in the blazing sun!" The owner turned to one of them and said, "My friend, I am not being unfair to you. You agreed on the usual wage for the day, did you not? Take your pay and go home. I choose to give the last man the same as you. Surely I am free to do what I like with my own money? Why be jealous because I am generous?" So the last will be first, and the first last.'

Jesus Causes a Division

Jesus went up to the temple and began to teach. The Jews were astonished: 'How is it', they said, 'that this untrained man has such learning?' Jesus replied, 'I was sent by one who is true, and him you do not know. I know him because I come from him, and he it is who sent me.' At this they tried to seize him, but no one could lay hands on him because his appointed hour had not yet come. Among the people many believed in him. 'When the Messiah comes,' they said, 'is it likely that he will perform more signs than this man?'

The Pharisees overheard these mutterings about him among the people, so the chief priests and the Pharisees sent temple police to arrest him. Then Jesus said, 'For a little longer I shall be with you; then I am going away to him who sent me. You will look for me, but you will not find me; and where I am, you cannot come.' So the Jews said to one another, 'Where does he intend to go, that we should not be able to find him? Will he go to the Dispersion among the Gentiles, and teach Gentiles? What does he mean by saying, "You will look for me, but you will not find me; and where I am, you cannot come"?'

On the last and greatest day of the festival Jesus stood and declared, 'If anyone is thirsty, let him come to me and drink. Whoever believes in me, as scripture says, "Streams of living water shall flow from within him."' He was speaking of the Spirit which believers in him would later receive; for the Spirit had not yet been given, because Jesus had not yet been glorified.

On hearing his words some of the crowd said, 'This must certainly be the Prophet.' Others said, 'This is the Messiah.' But others argued, 'Surely the Messiah is not to come from Galilee? Does not scripture say that the Messiah is to be of the family of David, from David's village of Bethlehem?' Thus he was the cause of a division among the people. Some were for arresting him, but no one laid hands on him.

The temple police went back to the chief priests and Pharisees, who asked them, 'Why have you not brought him?' 'No one ever spoke as this man speaks,' they replied. The Pharisees retorted, 'Have you too been misled? Has a single one of our rulers believed in him, or any of the Pharisees? As for this rabble, which cares nothing for the law, a curse is on them.' Then one of their number, Nicodemus (the man who once visited Jesus), intervened. 'Does our law', he asked them, 'permit us to pass judgement on someone without first giving him a hearing and learning the facts?' 'Are you a Galilean too?' they retorted. 'Study the scriptures and you will find that the Prophet does not come from Galilee.'

Jesus and the Woman Caught in Adultery

And they all went home, while Jesus went to the mount of Olives. At daybreak he appeared again in the temple, and all the people gathered round him. He had taken his seat and was engaged in teaching them when the scribes and the Pharisees brought in a woman caught committing adultery. Making her stand in the middle they said to him, 'Teacher, this woman was caught in the very act of adultery. In the law Moses has laid down that such women are to be stoned. What do you say about it?' They put the question as a test, hoping to frame a charge against him. Jesus bent down and wrote with his finger on the ground. When they continued to press their question he sat up straight and said, 'Let whichever of you is free from sin throw the first stone at her.' Then once again he bent down and wrote on the ground. When they heard what he said, one by one they went away, the eldest first; and Jesus was left alone, with the woman still standing there. Jesus again sat up and said to the woman, 'Where are they? Has no one condemned you?' She answered, 'No one, sir.' 'Neither do I condemn you,' Jesus said. 'Go; do not sin again.'

The Light of the World

Once again Jesus addressed the people: 'I am the light of the world. No follower of mine shall walk in darkness; he shall have the light of life.' The Pharisees said to him, 'You are witness in your own cause; your testimony is not valid.' Jesus replied, 'My testimony is valid, even though I do testify on my own behalf; because I know where I come from, and where I am going. But you know neither where I come from nor where I am going. I have much to say about you – and in judgement. But he who sent me speaks the truth, and what I heard from him I report to the world.'

They did not understand that he was speaking to them about the Father. So Jesus said to them, 'When you have lifted up the Son of Man you will know that I am what I am. I do nothing on my own authority, but in all I say, I have been taught by my Father. He who sent me is present with me, and has not left me on my own; for I always do what is pleasing to him.' As he said this, many put their faith in him.

The Truth Will Set You Free

Turning to the Jews who had believed him, Jesus said, 'If you stand by my teaching, you are truly my disciples; you will know the truth, and the truth will set you free.' 'We are Abraham's descendants,' they replied; 'we have never been in slavery to anyone. What do you mean by saying, "You will become free"?' 'In very truth I tell you', said Jesus, 'that everyone who commits sin is a slave. The slave has no permanent standing in the household, but the son belongs to it for ever. If then the Son sets you free, you will indeed be free.'

Before Abraham was Born, I am

'I know that you are descended from Abraham, yet you are bent on killing me because my teaching makes no headway with you. I tell what I have seen in my Father's presence. But because I speak the truth, you do not believe me. Which of you can convict me of sin? If what I say is true, why do you not believe me? He who has God for his father listens to the words of God. You are not God's children, and that is why you do not listen.'

The Jews answered, 'Are we not right in saying that you are a Samaritan, and that you are possessed?' 'I am not possessed,' said Jesus; 'I am honouring my Father, but you dishonour me. I do not care about my own glory; there is one who does care, and he is judge. In very truth I tell you, if anyone obeys my teaching he will never see death.'

The Jews said, 'Now we are certain that you are possessed. Abraham is dead and so are the prophets; yet you say, "If anyone obeys my teaching he will never taste death." Are you greater than our father Abraham? He is dead and the prophets too are dead. Who do you claim to be?'

Jesus replied, 'If I glorify myself, that glory of mine is worthless. It is the Father who glorifies me, he of whom you say, "He is our God," though you do not know him. But I know him; if I were to say that I did not know him I should be a liar like you. I do know him and I obey his word. Your father Abraham was overjoyed to see my day; he saw it and was glad.' The Jews protested, 'You are not yet fifty years old. How can you have seen Abraham?' Jesus said, 'In very truth I tell you, before Abraham was born, I am.' They took up stones to throw at him, but he was not to be seen; and he left the temple.

The Healing of a Man Born Blind

As he went on his way Jesus saw a man who had been blind from birth. His disciples asked him, 'Rabbi, why was this man born blind? Who sinned, this man or his parents?' 'It is not that he or his parents sinned,' Jesus answered; 'he was born blind so that God's power might be displayed in curing him. While daylight lasts we must carry on the work of him who sent me; night is coming, when no one can work. While I am in the world I am the light of the world.'

With these words he spat on the ground and made a paste with the spittle; he spread it on the man's eyes, and said to him, 'Go and wash in the pool of Siloam.' (The name means 'Sent'.) The man went off and washed, and came back able to see.

His neighbours and those who were accustomed to see him begging said, 'Is not this the man who used to sit and beg?' Some said, 'Yes, it is.' Others said, 'No, but it is someone like him.' He himself said, 'I am the man.' They asked him, 'How were your eyes opened?' He replied, 'The man called Jesus made a paste and smeared my eyes with it, and told me to go to Siloam and wash. So I went and washed, and found I could see.' 'Where is he?' they asked. 'I do not know,' he said.

The man who had been blind was brought before the Pharisees. As it was a sabbath day when Jesus made the paste and opened his eyes, the Pharisees too asked him how he had gained his sight. The man told them, 'He spread a paste on my eyes; then I washed, and now I can see.' Some of the Pharisees said, 'This man cannot be from God; he does not keep the sabbath.' Others said, 'How could such signs come from a sinful man?' So they took different sides. Then they continued to question him: 'What have you to say about him? It was your eyes he opened.' He answered, 'He is a prophet.'

The Jews would not believe that the man had been blind and had gained his sight, until they had summoned his parents and questioned them: 'Is this your son? Do you say that he was born blind? How is it that he can see now?' The parents replied, 'We know that he is our son, and that he was born blind. But how it is that he can now see, or who opened his eyes, we do not know. Ask him; he is of age; let him speak for himself.' His parents gave this answer because they were afraid of the Jews; for the Jewish authorities had already agreed that anyone who acknowledged Jesus as Messiah should be banned from the synagogue. That is why the parents said, 'He is of age; ask him.'

So for the second time they summoned the man who had been blind, and said, 'Speak the truth before God. We know that this man is a sinner.' 'Whether or not he is a sinner, I do not know,' the man replied. 'All I know is this: I was blind and now I can see.' 'What did he do to you?' they asked. 'How did he open your eyes?' 'I have told you already,' he retorted, 'but you took no notice. Why do you want to hear it again? Do you also want to become his disciples?' Then they became abusive. 'You are that man's disciple,' they said, 'but we are disciples of Moses. We know that God spoke to Moses, but as for this man, we do not know where he comes from.'

The man replied, 'How extraordinary! Here is a man who has opened my eyes, yet you do not know where he comes from! We know that God does not listen to sinners; he listens to anyone who is devout and obeys his will. To open the eyes of a man born blind – that is unheard of since time began. If this man was not from God he could do nothing.' 'Who are you to lecture us?' they retorted. 'You were born and bred in sin.' Then they turned him out.

Hearing that they had turned him out, Jesus found him and asked, 'Have you faith in the Son of Man?' The man answered, 'Tell me who he is, sir, that I may put my faith in him.' 'You have seen him,' said Jesus; 'indeed, it is he who is speaking to you.' 'Lord, I believe,' he said, and fell on his knees before him.

Jesus said, 'It is for judgement that I have come into this world – to give sight to the sightless and to make blind those who see.' Some Pharisees who were present asked, 'Do you mean that we are blind?' 'If you were blind,' said Jesus, 'you would not be guilty, but because you claim to see, your guilt remains.'

The Good Shepherd

'In very truth I tell you, the man who does not enter the sheep-fold by the door, but climbs in some other way, is nothing but a thief and a robber. He who enters by the door is the shepherd in charge of the sheep. The door-keeper admits him, and the sheep hear his voice; he calls his own sheep by name, and leads them out. When he has brought them all out, he goes ahead of them and the sheep follow, because they know his voice. They will not follow a stranger; they will run away from him, because they do not recognize the voice of strangers.

'A thief comes only to steal, kill, and destroy; I have come that they may have life, and may have it in all its fullness. I am the good shepherd; the good shepherd lays down his life for the sheep. The hired man, when he sees the wolf coming, abandons the sheep and runs away, because he is not the shepherd and the sheep are not his. Then the wolf harries the flock and scatters the sheep. The man runs away because he is a hired man and cares nothing for the sheep.

'I am the good shepherd; I know my own and my own know me, as the Father knows me and I know the Father; and I lay down my life for the sheep. But there are other sheep of mine, not belonging to this fold; I must lead them as well, and they too will listen to my voice. There will then be one flock, one shepherd. My Father who has given them to me is greater than all, and no one can snatch them out of the Father's care. The Father and I are one.'

This provoked them to make another attempt to seize him, but he escaped from their clutches.

The Raising of Lazarus

Jesus withdrew again across the Jordan, to the place where John had been baptizing earlier, and stayed there while crowds came to him. 'John gave us no miraculous sign,' they said, 'but all that he told us about this man was true.' And many came to believe in him there.

There was a man named Lazarus who had fallen ill. His home was at Bethany, the village of Mary and her sister Martha. This Mary, whose brother Lazarus had fallen ill, was the woman who anointed the Lord with ointment and wiped his feet with her hair. The sisters sent a message to him: 'Sir, you should know that your friend lies ill.' When Jesus heard this he said, 'This illness is not to end in death; through it God's glory is to be revealed and the Son of God glorified.' Therefore, though he loved Martha and her sister and Lazarus, he stayed where he was for two days after hearing of Lazarus's illness.

He then said to his disciples, 'Let us go back to Judaea.' 'Rabbi,' his disciples said, 'it is not long since the Jews there were wanting to stone you. Are you going there again?' Jesus replied, 'Are there not twelve hours of daylight? Anyone can walk in the daytime without stumbling, because he has this world's light to see by. But if he walks after nightfall he stumbles, because the light fails him.'

After saying this he added, 'Our friend Lazarus has fallen asleep, but I shall go and wake him.' The disciples said, 'Master, if he is sleeping he will recover.' Jesus had been speaking of Lazarus's death, but they thought that he meant natural sleep. Then Jesus told them plainly: 'Lazarus is dead. I am glad for your sake that I was not there; for it will lead you to believe. But let us go to him.' Thomas, called 'the Twin', said to his fellow disciples, 'Let us also go and die with him.'

On his arrival Jesus found that Lazarus had already been four days in the tomb. Bethany was just under two miles from Jerusalem, and many of the Jews had come from the city to visit Martha and Mary and condole with them about their brother. As soon as Martha heard that Jesus was on his way, she went to meet him, and left Mary sitting at home.

Martha said to Jesus, 'Lord, if you had been here my brother would not have died. Even now I know that God will grant you whatever you ask of him.' Jesus said, 'Your brother will rise again.' 'I know that he will rise again', said Martha, 'at the resurrection on the last day.' Jesus said, 'I am the resurrection and the life. Whoever has faith in me shall live, even though he dies; and no one who lives and has faith in me shall ever die. Do you believe this?' 'I do, Lord,' she answered; 'I believe that you are the Messiah, the Son of God who was to come into the world.'

So saying she went to call her sister Mary and, taking her aside, she said, 'The Master is here and is asking for you.' As soon as Mary heard this she rose and went to him. Jesus had not yet entered the village, but was still at the place where Martha had met him. When the Jews who were in the house condoling with Mary saw her hurry out, they went after her, assuming that she was going to the tomb to weep there.

Mary came to the place where Jesus was, and as soon as she saw him she fell at his feet and said, 'Lord, if you had been here my brother would not have died.' When Jesus saw her weeping and the Jews who had come with her weeping, he was moved with indignation and deeply distressed. 'Where have you laid him?' he asked. They replied, 'Come and see.' Jesus wept. The Jews said, 'How dearly he must have loved him!' But some of them said, 'Could not this man, who opened the blind man's eyes, have done something to keep Lazarus from dying?'

Jesus, again deeply moved, went to the tomb. It was a cave, with a stone placed against it. Jesus said, 'Take away the stone.' Martha, the dead man's sister, said to him, 'Sir, by now there will be a stench; he has been there four days.' Jesus said, 'Did I not tell you that if you have faith you will see the glory of God?' Then they removed the stone.

Jesus looked upwards and said, 'Father, I thank you for hearing me. I know that you always hear me, but I have spoken for the sake of the people standing round, that they may believe it was you who sent me.'

Then he raised his voice in a great cry: 'Lazarus, come out.' The dead man came out, his hands and feet bound with linen bandages, his face wrapped in a cloth. Jesus said, 'Loose him; let him go.'

The High Priest's Prophecy

Many of the Jews who had come to visit Mary, and had seen what Jesus did, put their faith in him. But some of them went off to the Pharisees and reported what he had done.

Thereupon the chief priests and the Pharisees convened a meeting of the Council. 'This man is performing many signs,' they said, 'and what action are we taking? If we let him go on like this the whole populace will believe in him, and then the Romans will come and sweep away our temple and our nation.' But one of them, Caiaphas, who was high priest that year, said, 'You have no grasp of the situation at all; you do not realize that it is more to your interest that one man should die for the people, than that the whole nation should be destroyed.' He did not say this of his own accord, but as the high priest that year he was prophesying that Jesus would die for the nation, and not for the nation alone but to gather together the scattered children of God. So from that day on they plotted his death.

33 | THE WAY TO THE CROSS

The Triumphal Entry

Jesus set out on the ascent to Jerusalem. As he approached Beth-phage and Bethany at the hill called Olivet, he sent off two of the disciples, telling them: 'Go into the village opposite; as you enter it you will find tethered there a colt which no one has yet ridden. Untie it and bring it here. If anyone asks why you are untying it, say, "The Master needs it."' The two went on their errand and found everything just as he had told them. As they were untying the colt, its owners asked, 'Why are you untying that colt?' They answered, 'The Master needs it.'

So they brought the colt to Jesus, and threw their cloaks on it for Jesus to mount. As he went along, people laid their cloaks on the road. And when he reached the descent from the mount of Olives, the whole company of his disciples in their joy began to sing aloud the praises of God for all the great things they had seen:

'Blessed is he who comes as king in the name of the Lord!
Peace in heaven, glory in highest heaven!'

Some Pharisees in the crowd said to him, 'Teacher, restrain your disciples.' He answered, 'I tell you, if my disciples are silent the stones will shout aloud.'

When he came in sight of the city, he wept over it and said, 'If only you had known this day the way that leads to peace! But no; it is hidden from your sight. For a time will come upon you, when your enemies will set up siege-works against you; they will encircle you and hem you in at every point; they will bring you to the ground, you and your children within your walls, and not leave you one stone standing on another, because you did not recognize the time of God's visitation.'

519

The Cleansing of the Temple

He entered Jerusalem and went into the temple. He looked round at everything; then, as it was already late, he went out to Bethany with the Twelve.

On the following day, as they left Bethany, he felt hungry, and, noticing in the distance a fig tree in leaf, he went to see if he could find anything on it. But when he reached it he found nothing but leaves; for it was not the season for figs. He said to the tree, 'May no one ever again eat fruit from you!' And his disciples were listening.

So they came to Jerusalem, and he went into the temple and began to drive out those who bought and sold there. He upset the tables of the money-changers and the seats of the dealers in pigeons; and he would not allow anyone to carry goods through the temple court. Then he began to teach them, and said, 'Does not scripture say, "My house shall be called a house of prayer for all nations"? But you have made it a robbers' cave.' The chief priests and the scribes heard of this and looked for a way to bring about his death; for they were afraid of him, because the whole crowd was spellbound by his teaching. And when evening came they went out of the city.

Early next morning, as they passed by, they saw that the fig tree had withered from the roots up; and Peter, recalling what had happened, said to him, 'Rabbi, look, the fig tree which you cursed has withered.' Jesus answered them, 'Have faith in God. Truly I tell you: if anyone says to this mountain, "Be lifted from your place and hurled into the sea," and has no inward doubts, but believes that what he says will happen, it will be done for him. I tell you, then, whatever you ask for in prayer, believe that you have received it and it will be yours.'

A Question of Authority

He entered the temple, and, as he was teaching, the chief priests and elders of the nation came up to him and asked: 'By what authority are you acting like this? Who gave you this authority?' Jesus replied, 'I also have a question for you. If you answer it, I will tell you by what authority I act. The baptism of John: was it from God, or from men?' This set them arguing among themselves: 'If we say, "From God," he will say, "Then why did you not believe him?" But if we say, "From men," we are afraid of the people's reaction, for they all take John for a prophet.' So they answered, 'We do not know.' And Jesus said: 'Then I will not tell you either by what authority I act.'

The Parable of the Two Sons

'But what do you think about this? There was a man who had two sons. He went to the first, and said, "My son, go and work today in the vineyard." "I will, sir," the boy replied; but he did not go. The father came to the second and said the same. "I will not," he replied; but afterwards he changed his mind and went. Which of the two did what his father wanted?' 'The second,' they replied. Then Jesus said, 'Truly I tell you: tax-collectors and prostitutes are entering the kingdom of God ahead of you. For when John came to show you the right way to live, you did not believe him, but the tax-collectors and prostitutes did; and even when you had seen that, you did not change your minds and believe him.

The Parable of the Wicked Tenants

'Listen to another parable. There was a landowner who planted a vineyard: he put a wall round it, hewed out a winepress, and built a watch-tower; then he let it out to vine-growers and went abroad. When the harvest season approached, he sent his servants to the tenants to collect the produce due to him. But they seized his servants, thrashed one, killed another, and stoned a third. Again, he sent other servants, this time a larger number; and they treated them in the same way. Finally he sent his son. "They will respect my son," he said. But when they saw the son the tenants said to one another, "This is the heir; come on, let us kill him, and get his inheritance." So they seized him, flung him out of the vineyard, and killed him. When the owner of the vineyard comes, how do you think he will deal with those tenants?' 'He will bring those bad men to a bad end,' they answered, 'and hand the vineyard over to other tenants, who will give him his share of the crop when the season comes.' Jesus said to them, 'Have you never read in the scriptures: "The stone which the builders rejected has become the main corner-stone. This is the Lord's doing, and it is wonderful in our eyes"? Therefore, I tell you, the kingdom of God will be taken away from you, and given to a nation that yields the proper fruit.'

When the chief priests and Pharisees heard his parables, they saw that he was referring to them. They wanted to arrest him, but were afraid of the crowds, who looked on Jesus as a prophet.

The Parable of the Wedding Banquet

Jesus spoke to them again in parables: 'The kingdom of Heaven is like this. There was a king who arranged a banquet for his son's wedding; but when he sent his servants to summon the guests he had invited, they refused to come. Then he sent other servants, telling them to say to the guests, "Look! I have prepared this banquet for you. My bullocks and fatted beasts have been slaughtered, and everything is ready. Come to the wedding." But they took no notice; one went off to his farm, another to his business, and the others seized the servants, attacked them brutally, and killed them. The king was furious; he sent troops to put those murderers to death and set their town on fire. Then he said to his servants, "The wedding banquet is ready; but the guests I invited did not deserve the honour. Go out therefore to the main thoroughfares, and invite everyone you can find to the wedding." The servants went out into the streets, and collected everyone they could find, good and bad alike. So the hall was packed with guests.

'When the king came in to watch them feasting, he observed a man who was not dressed for a wedding. "My friend," said the king, "how do you come to be here without wedding clothes?" But he had nothing to say. The king then said to his attendants, "Bind him hand and foot; fling him out into the dark, the place of wailing and grinding of teeth." For many are invited, but few are chosen.'

Pay Caesar What Belongs to Caesar

A number of Pharisees and men of Herod's party were sent to trap him with a question. They came and said, 'Teacher, we know you are a sincere man and court no one's favour, whoever he may be; you teach in all sincerity the way of life that God requires. Are we or are we not permitted to pay taxes to the Roman emperor? Shall we pay or not?' He saw through their duplicity, and said, 'Why are you trying to catch me out? Fetch me a silver piece, and let me look at it.' They brought one, and he asked them, 'Whose head is this, and whose inscription?'

'Caesar's,' they replied. Then Jesus said, 'Pay Caesar what belongs to Caesar, and God what belongs to God.' His reply left them completely taken aback.

A Question About the Resurrection

Next Sadducees, who maintain that there is no resurrection, came to him and asked: 'Teacher, Moses laid it down for us that if there are brothers, and one dies leaving a wife but no child, then the next should marry the widow and provide an heir for his brother. Now there were seven brothers. The first took a wife and died without issue. Then the second married her, and he too died without issue; so did the third; none of the seven left any issue. Finally the woman died. At the resurrection, when they rise from the dead, whose wife will she be, since all seven had married her?' Jesus said to them, 'How far you are from the truth! You know neither the scriptures nor the power of God. When they rise from the dead, men and women do not marry; they are like angels in heaven.

'As for the resurrection of the dead, have you not read in the book of Moses, in the story of the burning bush, how God spoke to him and said, "I am the God of Abraham, the God of Isaac, the God of Jacob"? He is not God of the dead but of the living. You are very far from the truth.'

The Two Great Commandments

Then one of the scribes, who had been listening to these discussions and had observed how well Jesus answered, came forward and asked him, 'Which is the first of all the commandments?' He answered, 'The first is, "Hear, O Israel: the Lord our God is the one Lord, and you must love the Lord your God with all your heart, with all your soul, with all your mind, and with all your strength." The second is this: "You must love your neighbour as yourself." No other commandment is greater than these.' The scribe said to him, 'Well said, Teacher. You are right in saying that God is one and beside him there is no other. And to love him with all your heart, all your understanding, and all your strength, and to love your neighbour as yourself – that means far more than any whole-offerings and sacrifices.' When Jesus saw how thoughtfully he answered, he said to him, 'You are not far from the kingdom of God.'

A Question About David's Son

Turning to the assembled Pharisees Jesus asked them, 'What is your opinion about the Messiah? Whose son is he?' 'The son of David,' they replied. 'Then how is it', he asked, 'that David by inspiration calls him "Lord"? For he says, "The Lord said to my Lord, 'Sit at my right hand until I put your enemies under your feet.'" If then David calls him "Lord", how can he be David's son?' Nobody was able to give him an answer; and from that day no one dared to put any more questions to him.

The Widow's Penny

As he was sitting opposite the temple treasury, he watched the people dropping their money into the chest. Many rich people were putting in large amounts. Presently there came a poor widow who dropped in two tiny coins, together worth a penny. He called his disciples to him and said, 'Truly I tell you: this poor widow has given more than all those giving to the treasury; for the others who have given had more than enough, but she, with less than enough, has given all that she had to live on.'

Warnings About the End

As he was leaving the temple, one of his disciples exclaimed, 'Look, Teacher, what huge stones! What fine buildings!' Jesus said to him, 'You see these great buildings? Not one stone will be left upon another; they will all be thrown down.'

As he sat on the mount of Olives opposite the temple he was questioned privately by Peter, James, John, and Andrew. 'Tell us,' they said, 'when will this happen? What will be the sign that all these things are about to be fulfilled?'

Jesus began: 'Be on your guard; let no one mislead you. Many will come claiming my name, and saying, "I am he"; and many will be misled by them. When you hear of wars and rumours of wars, do not be alarmed. Such things are bound to happen; but the end is still to come. For nation will go to war against nation, kingdom against kingdom; there will be earthquakes in many places; there will be famines. These are the first birth-pangs of the new age.

'As for you, be on your guard. You will be handed over to the courts; you will be beaten in synagogues; you will be summoned to appear before governors and kings on my account to testify in their presence. Before the end the gospel must be proclaimed to all nations. So when you are arrested and put on trial do not worry beforehand about what you will say, but when the time comes say whatever is given you to say, for it is not you who will be speaking, but the Holy Spirit. Brother will hand over brother to death, and a father his child; children will turn against their parents and send them to their death. Everyone will hate you for your allegiance to me, but whoever endures to the end will be saved.

'But when you see "the abomination of desolation" usurping a place which is not his (let the reader understand), then those who are in Judaea must take to the hills. If anyone is on the roof, he must not go down into the house to fetch anything out; if anyone is in the field, he must not turn back for his coat. Alas for women with child in those days, and for those who have children at the breast! Pray that it may not come in winter. For those days will bring distress such as there has never been before since the beginning of the world which God created, and will never be again. If the Lord had not cut short that time of troubles, no living thing could survive. However, for the sake of his own, whom he has chosen, he has cut short the time.

'If anyone says to you then, "Look, here is the Messiah," or, "Look, there he is," do not believe it. Impostors will come claiming to be messiahs or prophets, and they will produce signs and wonders to mislead, if possible, God's chosen. Be on your guard; I have forewarned you of it all.

'But in those days, after that distress,
the sun will be darkened,
the moon will not give her light;
the stars will come falling from the sky,
the celestial powers will be shaken.

'Then they will see the Son of Man coming in the clouds with great power and glory, and he will send out the angels and gather his chosen from the four winds, from the farthest bounds of earth to the farthest bounds of heaven.

'Learn a lesson from the fig tree. When its tender shoots appear and are breaking into leaf, you know that summer is near. In the same way, when you see all this happening, you may know that the end is near, at the very door. Truly I tell you: the present generation will live to see it all. Heaven and earth will pass away, but my words will never pass away. Yet about that day or hour no one knows, not even the angels in heaven, not even the Son; no one but the Father.

'Be on your guard, keep watch. You do not know when the moment is coming. It is like a man away from home: he has left his house and put his servants in charge, each with his own work to do, and he has ordered the door-keeper to stay awake. Keep awake, then, for you do not know when the master of the house will come. Evening or midnight, cock-crow or early dawn – if he comes suddenly, do not let him find you asleep. And what I say to you, I say to everyone: Keep awake.'

The Parable of the Good and Bad Servants

'Who is the faithful and wise servant, charged by his master to manage his household and supply them with food at the proper time? Happy that servant if his master comes home and finds him at work! Truly I tell you: he will be put in charge of all his master's property. But if he is a bad servant and says to himself, "The master is a long time coming," and begins to bully the other servants and to eat and drink with his drunken friends, then the master will arrive on a day when the servant does not expect him, at a time he has not been told. He will cut him in pieces and assign him a place among the hypocrites, where there is wailing and grinding of teeth.'

The Parable of the Ten Girls

'When the day comes, the kingdom of Heaven will be like this. There were ten girls, who took their lamps and went out to meet the bridegroom. Five of them were foolish, and five prudent; when the foolish ones took their lamps, they took no oil with them, but the others took flasks of oil with their lamps. As the bridegroom was a long time in coming, they all dozed off to sleep. But at midnight there came a shout: "Here is the bridegroom! Come out to meet him." Then the girls all got up and trimmed their lamps. The foolish said to the prudent, "Our lamps are going out; give us some of your oil." "No," they answered; "there will never be enough for all of us. You had better go to the dealers and buy some for yourselves." While they were away the bridegroom arrived; those who were ready went in with him to the wedding banquet; and the door was shut. Later the others came back. "Sir, sir, open the door for us," they cried. But he answered, "Truly I tell you: I do not know you." Keep awake then, for you know neither the day nor the hour.'

The Parable of the Sheep and the Goats

'When the Son of Man comes in his glory and all the angels with him, he will sit on his glorious throne, with all the nations gathered before him. He will separate people into two groups, as a shepherd separates the sheep from the goats; he will place the sheep on his right hand and the goats on his left. Then the king will say to those on his right, "You have my Father's blessing; come, take possession of the kingdom that has been ready for you since the world was made. For when I was hungry, you gave me food; when thirsty, you gave me drink; when I was a stranger, you took me into your home; when naked, you clothed me; when I was ill, you came to my help; when in prison, you visited me." Then the righteous will reply, "Lord, when was it that we saw you hungry and fed you, or thirsty and gave you drink, a stranger and took you home, or naked and clothed you? When did we see you ill or in prison, and come to visit you?" And the king will answer, "Truly I tell you: anything you did for one of my brothers here, however insignificant, you did for me." Then he will say to those on his left, "A curse is on you; go from my sight to the eternal fire that is ready for the devil and his angels. For when I was hungry, you gave me nothing to eat; when thirsty, nothing to drink; when I was a stranger, you did not welcome me; when I was naked, you did not clothe me; when I was ill and in prison, you did come to my help." And they in their turn will reply, "Lord, when was it that we saw you hungry or thirsty or a stranger or naked or ill or in prison, and did nothing for you?" And he will answer, "Truly I tell you: anything you failed to do for one of these, however insignificant, you failed to do for me." And they will go away to eternal punishment, but the righteous will enter eternal life.'

34 | PASSION AND RESURRECTION

The Chief Priests Plot Against Jesus

When Jesus had finished all these discourses he said to his disciples, 'You know that in two days' time it will be Passover, when the Son of Man will be handed over to be crucified.'

Meanwhile the chief priests and the elders of the people met in the house of the high priest, Caiaphas, and discussed a scheme to seize Jesus and put him to death. 'It must not be during the festival,' they said, 'or there may be rioting among the people.'

The Anointing at Bethany

Jesus was at Bethany in the house of Simon the leper, when a woman approached him with a bottle of very costly perfume; and she began to pour it over his head as he sat at table. The disciples were indignant when they saw it. 'Why this waste?' they said. 'It could have been sold for a large sum and the money given to the poor.' Jesus noticed, and said to them, 'Why make trouble for the woman? It is a fine thing she has done for me. You have the poor among you always, but you will not always have me. When she poured this perfume on my body it was her way of preparing me for burial. Truly I tell you: wherever this gospel is proclaimed throughout the world, what she has done will be told as her memorial.'

Jesus Anticipates his Death

Among those who went up to worship at the festival were some Gentiles. They approached Philip, who was from Bethsaida in Galilee, and said to him, 'Sir, we should like to see Jesus.' Philip went and told Andrew, and the two of them went to tell Jesus. Jesus replied: 'The hour has come for the Son of Man to be glorified. In very truth I tell you, unless a grain of wheat falls into the ground and dies, it remains that and nothing more; but if it dies, it bears a rich harvest. Whoever loves himself is lost, but he who

528

hates himself in this world will be kept safe for eternal life. If anyone is to serve me, he must follow me; where I am, there will my servant be. Whoever serves me will be honoured by the Father.

'Now my soul is in turmoil, and what am I to say? "Father, save me from this hour"? No, it was for this that I came to this hour. Father, glorify your name.' A voice came from heaven: 'I have glorified it, and I will glorify it again.' The crowd standing by said it was thunder they heard, while others said, 'An angel has spoken to him.' Jesus replied, 'This voice spoke for your sake, not mine. Now is the hour of judgement for this world; now shall the prince of this world be driven out. And when I am lifted up from the earth I shall draw everyone to myself.' This he said to indicate the kind of death he was to die.

The Last Supper

Then one of the Twelve, the man called Judas Iscariot, went to the chief priests and said, 'What will you give me to betray him to you?' They weighed him out thirty silver pieces. From that moment he began to look for an opportunity to betray him.

On the first day of Unleavened Bread the disciples came and asked Jesus, 'Where would you like us to prepare the Passover for you?' He told them to go to a certain man in the city with this message: 'The Teacher says, "My appointed time is near; I shall keep the Passover with my disciples at your house."' The disciples did as Jesus directed them and prepared the Passover.

During supper, Jesus, well aware that the Father had entrusted everything to him, and that he had come from God and was going back to God, rose from the supper table, took off his outer garment and, taking a towel, tied it round him. Then he poured water into a basin, and began to wash his disciples' feet and to wipe them with the towel.

When he came to Simon Peter, Peter said to him, 'You, Lord, washing my feet?' Jesus replied, 'You do not understand now what I am doing, but one day you will.' Peter said, 'I will never let you wash my feet.' 'If I do not wash you,' Jesus replied, 'you have no part with me.' 'Then, Lord,' said Simon Peter, 'not my feet only; wash my hands and head as well!'

Jesus said to him, 'Anyone who has bathed needs no further washing; he is clean all over; and you are clean, though not every one of you.' He added the words 'not every one of you' because he knew who was going to betray him.

After washing their feet he put on his garment and sat down again. 'Do you understand what I have done for you?' he asked. 'You call me Teacher and Lord, and rightly so, for that is what I am. Then if I, your Lord and Teacher, have washed your feet, you also ought to wash one another's feet. I have set you an example: you are to do as I have done for you. In very truth I tell you, a servant is not greater than his master, nor a messenger than the one who sent him. If you know this, happy are you if you act upon it.

'I am not speaking about all of you; I know whom I have chosen. But there is a text of scripture to be fulfilled: "He who eats bread with me has turned against me." I tell you this now, before the event, so that when it happens you may believe that I am what I am. In very truth I tell you, whoever receives any messenger of mine receives me; and receiving me, he receives the One who sent me.'

After saying this, Jesus exclaimed in deep distress, 'In very truth I tell you, one of you is going to betray me.' The disciples looked at one another in bewilderment: which of them could he mean? One of them, the disciple he loved, was reclining close beside Jesus. Simon Peter signalled to him to find out which one he meant. That disciple leaned back close to Jesus and asked, 'Lord, who is it?' Jesus replied, 'It is the one to whom I give this piece of bread when I have dipped it in the dish.' Then he took it, dipped it in the dish, and gave it to Judas son of Simon Iscariot. As soon as Judas had received it, Satan entered him. Jesus said to him, 'Do quickly what you have to do.' No one at the table understood what he meant by this. Some supposed that, as Judas was in charge of the common purse, Jesus was telling him to buy what was needed for the festival, or to make some gift to the poor. As soon as Judas had received the bread he went out. It was night.

During supper Jesus took bread, and having said the blessing he broke it and gave it to the disciples with the words: 'Take this and eat; this is my body.' Then he took a cup, and having offered thanks to God he gave it to them with the words: 'Drink from it, all of you. For this is my blood, the blood of the covenant, shed for many for the forgiveness of sins. I tell you, never again shall I drink from this fruit of the vine until that day when I drink it new with you in the kingdom of my Father.'

After singing the Passover hymn, they went out to the mount of Olives. Then Jesus said to them, 'Tonight you will all lose faith because of me; for it is written: "I will strike the shepherd and the sheep of his flock will be scattered." But after I am raised, I shall go ahead of you into Galilee.' Peter replied, 'Everyone else may lose faith because of you, but I never will.' Jesus said to him, 'Truly I tell you: tonight before the cock crows you will disown me three times.'

The Way, the Truth and the Life

'Set your troubled hearts at rest. Trust in God always; trust also in me. There are many dwelling-places in my Father's house; if it were not so I should have told you; for I am going to prepare a place for you. And if I go and prepare a place for you, I shall come again and take you to myself, so that where I am you may be also; and you know the way I am taking.' Thomas said, 'Lord, we do not know where you are going, so how can we know the way?' Jesus replied, 'I am the way, the truth, and the life; no one comes to the Father except by me.

'If you knew me you would know my Father too. From now on you do know him; you have seen him.' Philip said to him, 'Lord, show us the Father; we ask no more.' Jesus answered, 'Have I been all this time with you, Philip, and still you do not know me? Anyone who has seen me has seen the Father.'

The Gift of Peace

'Peace is my parting gift to you, my own peace, such as the world cannot give. Set your troubled hearts at rest, and banish your fears. You heard me say, "I am going away, and I am coming back to you." If you loved me you would be glad that I am going to the Father; for the Father is greater than I am. I have told you now, before it happens, so that when it does happen you may have faith.

'I shall not talk much longer with you, for the prince of this world approaches. He has no rights over me; but the world must be shown that I love the Father and am doing what he commands.'

The True Vine

'I am the true vine, and my Father is the gardener. Any branch of mine that is barren he cuts away; and any fruiting branch he prunes clean, to make it more fruitful still. You are already clean because of the word I have spoken to you. Dwell in me, as I in you. No branch can bear fruit by itself, but only if it remains united with the vine; no more can you bear fruit, unless you remain united with me.

'I am the vine; you are the branches. Anyone who dwells in me, as I dwell in him, bears much fruit; apart from me you can do nothing. Anyone who does not dwell in me is thrown away like a withered branch. The withered branches are gathered up, thrown on the fire, and burnt.

'If you dwell in me, and my words dwell in you, ask whatever you want, and you shall have it. This is how my Father is glorified: you are to bear fruit in plenty and so be my disciples. As the Father has loved me, so I have loved you. Dwell in my love. If you heed my commands, you will dwell in my love, as I have heeded my Father's commands and dwell in his love.'

Love One Another

'I have spoken thus to you, so that my joy may be in you, and your joy complete. This is my commandment: love one another, as I have loved you. There is no greater love than this, that someone should lay down his life for his friends. You are my friends, if you do what I command you. No longer do I call you servants, for a servant does not know what his master is about. I have called you friends, because I have disclosed to you everything that I heard from my Father. You did not choose me: I chose you. I appointed you to go on and bear fruit, fruit that will last; so that the Father may give you whatever you ask in my name. This is my commandment to you: love one another.'

The Spirit of Truth

'There is much more that I could say to you, but the burden would be too great for you now. However, when the Spirit of truth comes, he will guide you into all the truth; for he will not speak on his own authority, but will speak only what he hears; and he will make known to you what is to come. He will glorify me, for he will take what is mine and make it known to you. All that the Father has is mine, and that is why I said, "He will take what is mine and make it known to you."'

Sorrow and Joy

'In very truth I tell you, you will weep and mourn, but the world will be glad. But though you will be plunged in grief, your grief will be turned to joy. A woman in labour is in pain because her time has come; but when her baby is born she forgets the anguish in her joy that a child has been born into the world. So it is with you: for the moment you are sad; but I shall see you again, and then you will be joyful, and no one shall rob you of your joy.

'I have told you all this so that in me you may find peace. In the world you will have suffering. But take heart! I have conquered the world.'

Jesus Prays for his Disciples

Then Jesus looked up to heaven and said: 'Father, the hour has come. Glorify your Son, that the Son may glorify you. For you have made him sovereign over all mankind, to give eternal life to all whom you have given him. This is eternal life: to know you – the only true God, and Jesus Christ whom you have sent.

'I have glorified you on earth by finishing the work which you gave me to do; and now, Father, glorify me in your own presence with the glory which I had with you before the world began.

'I have made your name known to the men whom you gave me out of the world. They were yours and you gave them to me, and they have obeyed your command. Now they know that all you gave me has come from you; for I have taught them what I learned from you, and they have received it.

'It is not for these alone that I pray, but for those also who through their words put their faith in me. May they all be one; as you, Father, are in me, and I in you, so also may they be in us, that the world may believe that you sent me.'

The Agony in the Garden

When they reached a place called Gethsemane, he said to his disciples, 'Sit here while I pray.' And he took Peter and James and John with him. Horror and anguish overwhelmed him, and he said to them, 'My heart is ready to break with grief; stop here, and stay awake.' Then he went on a little farther, threw himself on the ground, and prayed that if it were possible this hour might pass him by. 'Abba, Father,' he said, 'all things are possible to you; take this cup from me. Yet not my will but yours.'

He came back and found them asleep; and he said to Peter, 'Asleep, Simon? Could you not stay awake for one hour? Stay awake, all of you; and pray that you may be spared the test. The spirit is willing, but the flesh is weak.' Once more he went away and prayed. On his return he found them asleep again, for their eyes were heavy; and they did not know how to answer him.

He came a third time and said to them, 'Still asleep? Still resting? Enough! The hour has come. The Son of Man is betrayed into the hands of sinners. Up, let us go! The traitor is upon us.'

While he was still speaking a crowd appeared with the man called Judas, one of the Twelve, at their head. He came up to Jesus to kiss him; but Jesus said, 'Judas, would you betray the Son of Man with a kiss?'

When his followers saw what was coming, they said, 'Lord, shall we use our swords?' And one of them struck at the high priest's servant, cutting off his right ear. But Jesus answered, 'Stop! No more of that!' Then he touched the man's ear and healed him.

Turning to the chief priests, the temple guards, and the elders, who had come to seize him, he said, 'Do you take me for a robber, that you have come out with swords and cudgels? Day after day, I have been with you in the temple, and you did not raise a hand against me. But this is your hour – when darkness reigns.'

Peter Denies Jesus

Then they arrested him and led him away. They brought him to the high priest's house, and Peter followed at a distance. They lit a fire in the middle of the courtyard and sat round it, and Peter sat among them. A serving-maid who saw him sitting in the firelight stared at him and said, 'This man was with him too.' But he denied it: 'I do not know him,' he said. A little later a man noticed him and said, 'You also are one of them.' But Peter said to him, 'No, I am not.' About an hour passed and someone else spoke more strongly still: 'Of course he was with him. He must have been; he is a Galilean.' But Peter said, 'I do not know what you are talking about.' At that moment, while he was still speaking, a cock crowed; and the Lord turned and looked at Peter. Peter remembered the Lord's words, 'Tonight before the cock crows you will disown me three times.' And he went outside, and wept bitterly.

The Trial Before the High Priest

The chief priests and the whole Council tried to find some allegation against Jesus that would warrant a death sentence; but they failed to find one, though many came forward with false evidence. Finally two men alleged that he had said, 'I can pull down the temple of God, and rebuild it in three days.' At this the high priest rose and said to him, 'Have you no answer to the accusations that these witnesses bring against you?' But Jesus remained silent. The high priest then said, 'By the living God I charge you to tell us: are you the Messiah, the Son of God?' Jesus replied, 'The words are yours. But I tell you this: from now on you will see the Son of Man seated at the right hand of the Almighty and coming on the clouds of heaven.' At these words the high priest tore his robes and exclaimed, 'This is blasphemy! Do we need further witnesses? You have just heard the blasphemy. What is your verdict?' 'He is guilty,' they answered; 'he should die.'

Then they spat in his face and struck him with their fists; some said, as they beat him, 'Now, Messiah, if you are a prophet, tell us who hit you.'

When Judas the traitor saw that Jesus had been condemned, he was seized with remorse, and returned the thirty silver pieces to the chief priests and elders. 'I have sinned,' he said; 'I have brought an innocent man to his death.' But they said, 'What is that to us? It is your concern.' So he threw the money down in the temple and left; he went away and hanged himself.

The Trial Before Pilate

From Caiaphas Jesus was led into the governor's headquarters. It was now early morning, and the Jews themselves stayed outside the headquarters to avoid defilement, so that they could eat the Passover meal. So Pilate came out to them and asked, 'What charge do you bring against this man?' 'If he were not a criminal', they replied, 'we would not have brought him before you.' Pilate said, 'Take him yourselves and try him by your own law.' The Jews answered, 'We are not allowed to put anyone to death.' Thus they ensured the fulfilment of the words by which Jesus had indicated the kind of death he was to die.

Pilate then went back into his headquarters and summoned Jesus. 'So you are the king of the Jews?' he said. Jesus replied, 'Is that your own question, or have others suggested it to you?' 'Am I a Jew?' said Pilate. 'Your own nation and their chief priests have brought you before me. What have you done?' Jesus replied, 'My kingdom does not belong to this world. If it did, my followers would be fighting to save me from the clutches of the Jews. My kingdom belongs elsewhere.' 'You are a king, then?' said Pilate. Jesus answered, '"King" is your word. My task is to bear witness to the truth. For this I was born; for this I came into the world, and all who are not deaf to truth listen to my voice.' Pilate said, 'What is truth?'

Jesus is Sent to Herod

Pilate then said to the chief priests and the crowd, 'I find no case for this man to answer.' But they insisted: 'His teaching is causing unrest among the people all over Judaea. It started from Galilee and now has spread here.'

When Pilate heard this, he asked if the man was a Galilean, and on learning that he belonged to Herod's jurisdiction he remitted the case to him, for Herod was also in Jerusalem at that time. When Herod saw Jesus he was greatly pleased; he had heard about him and had long been wanting to see him in the hope of witnessing some miracle performed by him. He questioned him at some length without getting any reply; but the chief priests and scribes appeared and pressed the case against him vigorously. Then Herod and his troops treated him with contempt and ridicule, and sent him back to Pilate dressed in a gorgeous robe. That same day Herod and Pilate became friends; till then there had been a feud between them.

Pilate Washes his Hands of Jesus

Pilate now summoned the chief priests, councillors, and people, and said to them, 'You brought this man before me on a charge of subversion. But, as you see, I have myself examined him in your presence and found nothing in him to support your charges. No more did Herod, for he has referred him back to us. Clearly he has done nothing to deserve death. I therefore propose to flog him and let him go.'

At the festival season it was customary for the governor to release one prisoner chosen by the people. There was then in custody a man of some notoriety, called Jesus Barabbas. When the people assembled, Pilate said to them, 'Which would you like me to release to you – Jesus Barabbas, or Jesus called Messiah?' For he knew it was out of malice that Jesus had been handed over to him.

While Pilate was sitting in court a message came to him from his wife: 'Have nothing to do with that innocent man; I was much troubled on his account in my dreams last night.'

Meanwhile the chief priests and elders had persuaded the crowd to ask for the release of Barabbas and to have Jesus put to death. So when the governor asked, 'Which of the two would you like me to release to you?' they said, 'Barabbas.' 'Then what am I to do with Jesus called Messiah?' asked Pilate; and with one voice they answered, 'Crucify him!' 'Why, what harm has he done?' asked Pilate; but they shouted all the louder, 'Crucify him!'

When Pilate saw that he was getting nowhere, and that there was danger of a riot, he took water and washed his hands in full view of the crowd. 'My hands are clean of this man's blood,' he declared. 'See to that yourselves.'

Jesus is Flogged and Condemned to Death
Pilate now took Jesus and had him flogged; and the soldiers plaited a crown of thorns and placed it on his head, and robed him in a purple cloak. Then one after another they came up to him, crying, 'Hail, king of the Jews!' and struck him on the face.

Once more Pilate came out and said to the Jews, 'Here he is; I am bringing him out to let you know that I find no case against him'; and Jesus came out, wearing the crown of thorns and the purple cloak. 'Here is the man,' said Pilate. At the sight of him the chief priests and the temple police shouted, 'Crucify! Crucify!' 'Take him yourselves and crucify him,' said Pilate; 'for my part I find no case against him.' The Jews answered, 'We have a law; and according to that law he ought to die, because he has claimed to be God's Son.'

When Pilate heard that, he was more afraid than ever, and going back into his headquarters he asked Jesus, 'Where have you come from?' But Jesus gave him no answer. 'Do you refuse to speak to me?' said Pilate. 'Surely you know that I have authority to release you, and authority to crucify you?' 'You would have no authority at all over me', Jesus replied, 'if it had not been granted you from above; and therefore the deeper guilt lies with the one who handed me over to you.'

From that moment Pilate tried hard to release him; but the Jews kept shouting, 'If you let this man go, you are no friend to Caesar; anyone who claims to be a king is opposing Caesar.' When Pilate heard what they were saying, he brought Jesus out and took his seat on the tribunal at the place known as The Pavement (in Hebrew, 'Gabbatha'). It was the day of preparation for the Passover, about noon. Pilate said to the Jews, 'Here is your king.' They shouted, 'Away with him! Away with him! Crucify him!' 'Am I to crucify your king?' said Pilate. 'We have no king but Caesar,' replied the chief priests. Then at last, to satisfy them, he handed Jesus over to be crucified.

The Crucifixion

As they led him away to execution they took hold of a man called Simon, from Cyrene, on his way in from the country; putting the cross on his back they made him carry it behind Jesus.

Great numbers of people followed, among them many women who mourned and lamented over him. Jesus turned to them and said, 'Daughters of Jerusalem, do not weep for me; weep for yourselves and your children. For the days are surely coming when people will say, "Happy are the barren, the wombs that never bore a child, the breasts that never fed one." Then they will begin to say to the mountains, "Fall on us," and to the hills, "Cover us." For if these things are done when the wood is green, what will happen when it is dry?'

There were two others with him, criminals who were being led out to execution; and when they reached the place called The Skull, they crucified him there, and the criminals with him, one on his right and the other on his left. Jesus said, 'Father, forgive them; they do not know what they are doing.'

Pilate had an inscription written and fastened to the cross; it read, 'Jesus of Nazareth, King of the Jews'. This inscription, in Hebrew, Latin, and Greek, was read by many Jews, since the place where Jesus was crucified was not far from the city. So the Jewish chief priests said to Pilate, 'You should not write "King of the Jews", but rather "He claimed to be king of the Jews".' Pilate replied, 'What I have written, I have written.'

When the soldiers had crucified Jesus they took his clothes and, leaving aside the tunic, divided them into four parts, one for each soldier. The tunic was seamless, woven in one piece throughout; so they said to one another, 'We must not tear this; let us toss for it.' Thus the text of scripture came true: 'They shared my garments among them, and cast lots for my clothing.'

That is what the soldiers did. Meanwhile near the cross on which Jesus hung, his mother was standing with her sister, Mary wife of Clopas, and Mary of Magdala. Seeing his mother, with the disciple whom he loved standing beside her, Jesus said to her, 'Mother, there is your son'; and to the disciple, 'There is your mother'; and from that moment the disciple took her into his home.

The passers-by wagged their heads and jeered at him, crying, 'So you are the man who was to pull down the temple and rebuild it in three days! If you really are the Son of God, save yourself and come down from the cross.' The chief priests with the scribes and elders joined in the mockery: 'He saved others,' they said, 'but he cannot save himself. King of Israel, indeed! Let him come down now from the cross, and then we shall believe him. He trusted in God, did he? Let God rescue him, if he wants him – for he said he was God's Son.'

One of the criminals hanging there taunted him: 'Are not you the Messiah? Save yourself, and us.' But the other rebuked him: 'Have you no fear of God? You are under the same sentence as he is. In our case it is plain justice; we are paying the price for our misdeeds. But this man has done nothing wrong.' And he said, 'Jesus, remember me when you come to your throne.' Jesus answered, 'Truly I tell you: today you will be with me in Paradise.'

From midday a darkness fell over the whole land, which lasted until three in the afternoon; and about three Jesus cried aloud, '*Eli, Eli, lema sabachthani?*' which means, 'My God, my God, why have you forsaken me?' Hearing this, some of the bystanders said, 'He is calling Elijah.'

After this, Jesus, aware that all had now come to its appointed end, said in fulfilment of scripture, 'I am thirsty.' A jar stood there full of sour wine; so they soaked a sponge with the wine, fixed it on hyssop, and held it up to his lips. Having received the wine, he said, 'It is accomplished!'

Then Jesus uttered a loud cry and said, 'Father, into your hands I commit my spirit'; and with these words he died.

At that moment the curtain of the temple was torn in two from top to bottom. The earth shook, rocks split, and graves opened; many of God's saints were raised from sleep, and coming out of their graves after his resurrection entered the Holy City, where many saw them. And when the centurion and his men who were keeping watch over Jesus saw the earthquake and all that was happening, they were filled with awe and said, 'This must have been a son of God.'

Because it was the eve of the sabbath, the Jews were anxious that the bodies should not remain on the crosses, since that sabbath was a day of great solemnity; so they requested Pilate to have the legs broken and the bodies taken down. The soldiers accordingly came to the men crucified with Jesus and broke the legs of each in turn, but when they came to Jesus and found he was already dead, they did not break his legs. But one of the soldiers thrust a lance into his side, and at once there was a flow of blood and water. This is vouched for by an eyewitness, whose evidence is to be trusted. He knows that he speaks the truth, so that you too may believe; for this happened in fulfilment of the text of scripture: 'No bone of his shall be broken.' And another text says, 'They shall look on him whom they pierced.'

After that, Joseph of Arimathaea, a disciple of Jesus, but a secret disciple for fear of the Jews, asked Pilate for permission to remove the body of Jesus. He consented; so Joseph came and removed the body. He was joined by Nicodemus (the man who had visited Jesus by night), who brought with him a mixture of myrrh and aloes, more than half a hundredweight. They took the body of Jesus and following Jewish burial customs they wrapped it, with the spices, in strips of linen cloth. Near the place where he had been crucified there was a garden, and in the garden a new tomb, not yet used for burial; and there, since it was the eve of the Jewish sabbath and the tomb was near at hand, they laid Jesus.

The Resurrection

Early on the first day of the week, while it was still dark, Mary of Magdala came to the tomb. She saw that the stone had been moved away from the entrance, and ran to Simon Peter and the other disciple, the one whom Jesus loved. 'They have taken the Lord out of the tomb,' she said, 'and we do not know where they have laid him.' So Peter and the other disciple set out and made their way to the tomb. They ran together, but the other disciple ran faster than Peter and reached the tomb first. He peered in and saw the linen wrappings lying there, but he did not enter. Then Simon Peter caught up with him and went into the tomb. He saw the linen wrappings lying there, and the napkin which had been round his head, not with the wrappings but rolled up in a place by itself. Then the disciple who had reached the tomb first also went in, and he saw and believed; until then they had not understood the scriptures, which showed that he must rise from the dead.

So the disciples went home again; but Mary stood outside the tomb weeping. And as she wept, she peered into the tomb, and saw two angels in white sitting there, one at the head, and one at the feet, where the body of Jesus had lain. They asked her, 'Why are you weeping?' She answered, 'They have taken my Lord away, and I do not know where they have laid him.' With these words she turned round and saw Jesus standing there, but she did not recognize him. Jesus asked her, 'Why are you weeping? Who are you looking for?' Thinking it was the gardener, she said, 'If it is you, sir, who removed him, tell me where you have laid him, and I will take him away.' Jesus said, 'Mary!' She turned and said to him, 'Rabbuni!' (which is Hebrew for 'Teacher'). 'Do not cling to me,' said Jesus, 'for I have not yet ascended to the Father. But go to my brothers, and tell them that I am ascending to my Father and your Father, to my God and your God.' Mary of Magdala went to tell the disciples. 'I have seen the Lord!' she said, and gave them his message.

The Supper at Emmaus
That same day two of them were on their way to a village called Emmaus, about seven miles from Jerusalem, talking together about all that had happened. As they talked and argued, Jesus himself came up and walked with them; but something prevented them from recognizing him. He asked them, 'What is it you are debating as you walk?' They stood still, their faces full of sadness, and one, called Cleopas, answered, 'Are you the only person staying in Jerusalem not to have heard the news of what has happened there in the last few days?' 'What news?' he said. 'About Jesus of Nazareth,' they replied, 'who, by deeds and words of power,

proved himself a prophet in the sight of God and the whole people; and how our chief priests and rulers handed him over to be sentenced to death, and crucified him. But we had been hoping that he was to be the liberator of Israel.'

'How dull you are!' he answered. 'How slow to believe all that the prophets said! Was not the Messiah bound to suffer in this way before entering upon his glory?' Then, starting from Moses and all the prophets, he explained to them in the whole of scripture the things that referred to himself.

By this time they had reached the village to which they were going, and he made as if to continue his journey. But they pressed him: 'Stay with us, for evening approaches, and the day is almost over.' So he went in to stay with them. And when he had sat down with them at table, he took bread and said the blessing; he broke the bread, and offered it to them. Then their eyes were opened, and they recognized him; but he vanished from their sight. They said to one another, 'Were not our hearts on fire as he talked with us on the road and explained the scriptures to us?'

Without a moment's delay they set out and returned to Jerusalem. There they found that the eleven and the rest of the company had assembled. Then they described what had happened on their journey and told how he had made himself known to them in the breaking of the bread.

Doubting Thomas

As they were talking about all this, there he was, standing among them. Startled and terrified, they thought they were seeing a ghost. But he said, 'Why are you so perturbed? Why do doubts arise in your minds? Look at my hands and feet. It is I myself. Touch me and see; no ghost has flesh and bones as you can see that I have.' They were still incredulous, still astounded, for it seemed too good to be true. So he asked them, 'Have you anything here to eat?' They offered him a piece of fish they had cooked, which he took and ate before their eyes.

And he said to them, 'This is what I meant by saying, while I was still with you, that everything written about me in the law of Moses and in the prophets and psalms was bound to be fulfilled.' Then he opened their minds to understand the scriptures. 'So you see', he said, 'that scripture foretells the sufferings of the Messiah and his rising from the dead on the third day, and declares that in his name repentance bringing the forgiveness of sins is to be proclaimed to all nations beginning from Jerusalem. You are to be witnesses to it all. I am sending on you the gift promised by my Father. As the Father sent me, so I send you.' Then he breathed on them, saying, 'Receive the Holy Spirit! If you forgive anyone's sins, they are forgiven; if you pronounce them unforgiven, unforgiven they remain.'

One of the Twelve, Thomas the Twin, was not with the rest when Jesus came. So the others kept telling him, 'We have seen the Lord.' But he said, 'Unless I see the mark of the nails on his hands, unless I put my finger into the place where the nails were, and my hand into his side, I will never believe it.'

A week later his disciples were once again in the room, and Thomas was with them. Although the doors were locked, Jesus came and stood among them, saying, 'Peace be with you!' Then he said to Thomas, 'Reach your finger here; look at my hands. Reach your hand here and put it into my side. Be unbelieving no longer, but believe.' Thomas said, 'My Lord and my God!' Jesus said to him, 'Because you have seen me you have found faith. Happy are they who find faith without seeing me.'

The Great Commission

The eleven disciples made their way to Galilee, to the mountain where Jesus had told them to meet him. When they saw him, they knelt in worship, though some were doubtful. Jesus came near and said to them: 'Full authority in heaven and on earth has been committed to me. Go therefore to all nations and make them my disciples; baptize them in the name of the Father and the Son and the Holy Spirit, and teach them to observe all that I have commanded you. I will be with you always, to the end of time.'

Follow Me

Some time later, Jesus showed himself to his disciples once again, by the sea of Tiberias. This is how it happened. Simon Peter was with Thomas the Twin, Nathanael from Cana-in-Galilee, the sons of Zebedee, and two other disciples. 'I am going out fishing,' said Simon Peter. 'We will go with you,' said the others. So they set off and got into the boat; but that night they caught nothing.

Morning came, and Jesus was standing on the beach, but the disciples did not know that it was Jesus. He called out to them,

'Friends, have you caught anything?' 'No,' they answered. He said, 'Throw out the net to starboard, and you will make a catch.' They did so, and found they could not haul the net on board, there were so many fish in it. Then the disciple whom Jesus loved said to Peter, 'It is the Lord!' As soon as Simon Peter heard him say, 'It is the Lord,' he fastened his coat about him (for he had stripped) and plunged into the sea. The rest of them came on in the boat, towing the net full of fish. They were only about a hundred yards from land.

When they came ashore, they saw a charcoal fire there with fish laid on it, and some bread. Jesus said, 'Bring some of the fish you have caught.' Simon Peter went on board and hauled the net to land; it was full of big fish, a hundred and fifty-three in all; and yet, many as they were, the net was not torn. Jesus said, 'Come and have breakfast.' None of the disciples dared to ask 'Who are you?' They knew it was the Lord.

After breakfast Jesus said to Simon Peter, 'Simon son of John, do you love me more than these others?' 'Yes, Lord,' he answered, 'you know that I love you.' 'Then feed my lambs,' he said. A second time he asked, 'Simon son of John, do you love me?' 'Yes, Lord, you know I love you.' 'Then tend my sheep.' A third time he said, 'Simon son of John, do you love me?' Peter was hurt that he asked him a third time, 'Do you love me?' 'Lord,' he said, 'you know everything; you know I love you.' Jesus said, 'Then feed my sheep.

'In very truth I tell you: when you were young you fastened your belt about you and walked where you chose; but when you are old you will stretch out your arms, and a stranger will bind you fast, and carry you where you have no wish to go.' He said this to indicate the manner of death by which Peter was to glorify God.

Then he added, 'Follow me.'

Part Five

FROM ACTS TO APOCALYPSE

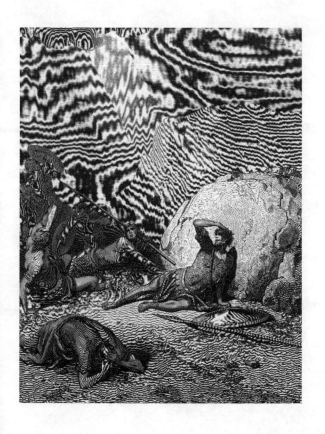

35 | ACTS OF THE APOSTLES

The Ascension

After his death Jesus was seen by the apostles over a period of forty days and spoke to them about the kingdom of God.

When they were all together, they asked him, 'Lord, is this the time at which you are to restore sovereignty to Israel?' He answered, 'It is not for you to know about dates or times which the Father has set within his own control. But you will receive power when the Holy Spirit comes upon you; and you will bear witness for me in Jerusalem, and throughout all Judaea and Samaria, and even in the farthest corners of the earth.'

After he had said this, he was lifted up before their very eyes, and a cloud took him from their sight.

They then returned to Jerusalem from the hill called Olivet, which is near the city, no farther than a sabbath day's journey. On their arrival they went to the upstairs room where they were lodging: Peter and John and James and Andrew, Philip and Thomas, Bartholomew and Matthew, James son of Alphaeus, Simon the Zealot, and Judas son of James. All these with one accord were constantly at prayer, together with a group of women, and Mary the mother of Jesus, and his brothers.

The Day of Pentecost

The day of Pentecost had come, and they were all together in one place. Suddenly there came from the sky what sounded like a strong, driving wind, a noise which filled the whole house where they were sitting. And there appeared to them flames like tongues of fire distributed among them and coming to rest on each one. They were all filled with the Holy Spirit and began to talk in other tongues, as the Spirit gave them power of utterance.

Now there were staying in Jerusalem devout Jews drawn from every nation under heaven. At this sound a crowd of them gathered, and were bewildered because each one heard his own language spoken; they were amazed and in astonishment exclaimed, 'Surely these people who are speaking are all Galileans! How is it that each of us can hear them in his own native language? Parthians, Medes, Elamites; inhabitants of Mesopotamia, of Judaea and Cappadocia, of Pontus and Asia, of Phrygia and Pamphylia, of Egypt and the districts of Libya around Cyrene; visitors from Rome, both Jews and proselytes; Cretans and Arabs – all of us hear them telling in our own tongues the great things God has done.' They were all amazed and perplexed, saying to one another, 'What can this mean?' Others said contemptuously, 'They have been drinking!'

But Peter stood up with the eleven, and in a loud voice addressed the crowd: 'Fellow Jews, and all who live in Jerusalem, listen and take note of what I say. These people are not drunk, as you suppose; it is only nine in the morning! No, this is what the prophet Joel spoke of: "In the last days, says God, I will pour out my Spirit on all mankind; and your sons and daughters shall prophesy; your young men shall see visions, and your old men shall dream dreams."

'Men of Israel, hear me: I am speaking of Jesus of Nazareth, singled out by God and made known to you through miracles, portents, and signs, which God worked among you through him, as you well know. By the deliberate will and plan of God he was given into your power, and you killed him, using heathen men to crucify him. But God raised him to life again, setting him free from the pangs of death, because it could not be that death should keep him in its grip.

'Let all Israel then accept as certain that God has made this same Jesus, whom you crucified, both Lord and Messiah.'

When they heard this they were cut to the heart, and said to Peter and the other apostles, 'Friends, what are we to do?' 'Repent', said Peter, 'and be baptized, every one of you, in the name of Jesus the Messiah; then your sins will be forgiven and you will receive the gift of the Holy Spirit.'

Those who accepted what he said were baptized, and some three thousand were added to the number of believers that day. They met constantly to hear the apostles teach and to share the common life, to break bread, and to pray.

The Apostles Witness to Jesus

One day at three in the afternoon, the hour of prayer, Peter and John were on their way up to the temple. Now a man who had been a cripple from birth used to be carried there and laid every day by the temple gate called Beautiful to beg from people as they went in. When he saw Peter and John on their way into the temple, he asked for alms. They both fixed their eyes on him, and Peter said, 'Look at us.' Expecting a gift from them, the man was all attention. Peter said, 'I have no silver or gold; but what I have I give you: in the name of Jesus Christ of Nazareth, get up and walk.' Then, grasping him by the right hand he helped him up; and at once his feet and ankles grew strong; he sprang to his feet, and started to walk. He entered the temple with them, leaping and praising God as he went. Everyone saw him walking and praising God, and when they recognized him as the man who used to sit begging at Beautiful Gate they were filled with wonder and amazement at what had happened to him.

While he still clung to Peter and John all the people came running in astonishment towards them in Solomon's Portico, as it is called. Peter saw them coming and met them with these words: 'Men of Israel, why be surprised at this? Why stare at us as if we had made this man walk by some power or godliness of our own? The God of Abraham, Isaac, and Jacob, the God of our fathers, has given the highest honour to his servant Jesus, whom you handed over for trial and disowned in Pilate's court – disowned the holy and righteous one when Pilate had decided to release him. You asked for the reprieve of a murderer, and killed the Prince of life. But God raised him from the dead; of that we are witnesses. The name of Jesus, by awakening faith, has given strength to this man whom you see and know, and this faith has made him completely well, as you can all see.

'Now, my friends, I know quite well that you acted in ignorance, as did your rulers; but this is how God fulfilled what he had foretold through all the prophets: that his Messiah would suffer. Repent, therefore, and turn to God, so that your sins may be wiped out. Then the Lord may grant you a time of recovery and send the Messiah appointed for you, that is, Jesus. He must be received into heaven until the time comes for the universal restoration of which God has spoken through his holy prophets from the beginning.

'You are the heirs of the prophets, and of that covenant which God made with your fathers when he said to Abraham, "And in your offspring all the families on earth shall find blessing." When God raised up his servant, he sent him to you first, to bring you blessing by turning every one of you from your wicked ways.' They were still addressing the people when the chief priests, together with the controller of the temple and the Sadducees, broke in on them, annoyed because they were proclaiming the resurrection from the dead by teaching the people about Jesus. They were arrested and, as it was already evening, put in prison for the night. But many of those who had heard the message became believers, bringing the number of men to about five thousand.

Next day the Jewish rulers, elders, and scribes met in Jerusalem. There were present Annas the high priest, Caiaphas, John, Alexander, and all who were of the high-priestly family. They brought the apostles before the court and began to interrogate them. 'By what power', they asked, 'or by what name have such men as you done this?' Then Peter, filled with the Holy Spirit, answered, 'Rulers of the people and elders, if it is about help given to a sick man that we are being questioned today, and the means by which he was cured, this is our answer to all of you and to all the people of Israel: it was by the name of Jesus Christ of Nazareth, whom you crucified, and whom God raised from the dead; through him this man stands here before you fit and well.'

Observing that Peter and John were uneducated laymen, they were astonished at their boldness and took note that they had been companions of Jesus; but with the man who had been cured standing in full view beside them, they had nothing to say in reply. So they ordered them to leave the court, and then conferred among themselves. 'What are we to do with these men?' they said. 'It is common knowledge in Jerusalem that a notable miracle has come about through them; and we cannot deny it. But to stop this from spreading farther among the people, we had better caution them never again to speak to anyone in this name.' They then called them in and ordered them to refrain from all public speaking and teaching in the name of Jesus. But Peter and John replied: 'Is it right in the eyes of God for us to obey you rather than him? Judge for yourselves. We cannot possibly give up speaking about what we have seen and heard.'

With a repeated caution the court discharged them. They could not see how they were to punish them, because the people were all giving glory to God for what had happened.

The whole company of believers was united in heart and soul. Not one of them claimed any of his possessions as his own; everything was held in common. With great power the apostles bore witness to the resurrection of the Lord Jesus, and all were held in high esteem. There was never a needy person among them, because those who had property in land or houses would sell it, bring the proceeds of the sale, and lay them at the feet of the apostles, to be distributed to any who were in need.

But a man called Ananias sold a property, and with the connivance of his wife Sapphira kept back some of the proceeds, and brought part only to lay at the apostles' feet. Peter said, 'Ananias, how was it that Satan so possessed your mind that you lied to the Holy Spirit by keeping back part of the price of the land? While it remained unsold, did it not remain yours? Even after it was turned into money, was it not still at your own disposal? What made you think of doing this? You have lied not to men but to God.' When Ananias heard these words he dropped dead; and all who heard were awestruck. The younger men rose and covered his body, then carried him out and buried him.

About three hours passed, and his wife came in, unaware of what had happened. Peter asked her, 'Tell me, were you paid such and such a price for the land?' 'Yes,' she replied, 'that was the price.' Peter said, 'Why did the two of you conspire to put the Spirit of the Lord to the test? Those who buried your husband are there at the door, and they will carry you away.' At once she dropped dead at his feet. When the young men came in, they found her dead; and they carried her out and buried her beside her husband. Great awe fell on the whole church and on all who heard of this.

Many signs and wonders were done among the people by the apostles, and the people from the towns round Jerusalem flocked in, bringing those who were ill or harassed by unclean spirits, and all were cured.

Then the high priest and his colleagues, the Sadducean party, were goaded by jealousy to arrest the apostles and put them in official custody. But during the night, an angel of the Lord opened the prison doors, led them out, and said, 'Go, stand in the temple and tell the people all about this new life.' Accordingly they entered the temple at daybreak and went on with their teaching.

When the high priest arrived with his colleagues they summoned the Sanhedrin, the full Council of the Israelite nation, and sent to the jail for the prisoners. The officers who went to the prison failed to find them there, so they returned and reported, 'We found the jail securely locked at every point, with the warders at their posts by the doors, but on opening them we found no one inside.' When they heard this, the controller of the temple and the chief priests were at a loss to know what could have become of them, until someone came and reported: 'The men you put in prison are standing in the temple teaching the people.' Then the controller went off with the officers and fetched them, but without use of force, for fear of being stoned by the people.

When they had been brought in and made to stand before the Council, the high priest began his examination. 'We gave you explicit orders', he said, 'to stop teaching in that name; and what has happened? You have filled Jerusalem with your teaching, and you are trying to hold us responsible for that man's death.' Peter replied for the apostles: 'We must obey God rather than men. The God of our fathers raised up Jesus; after you had put him to death by hanging him on a gibbet, God exalted him at his right hand as leader and saviour, to grant Israel repentance and forgiveness of sins. And we are witnesses to all this, as is the Holy Spirit who is given by God to those obedient to him.'

This touched them on the raw, and they wanted to put them to death. But a member of the Council rose to his feet, a Pharisee called Gamaliel, a teacher of the law held in high regard by all the people. He had the men put outside for a while, and then said, 'Men of Israel, be very careful in deciding what to do with these men. Some time ago Theudas came forward, making claims for himself, and a number of our people, about four hundred, joined him. But he was killed and his whole movement was destroyed and came to nothing. After him came Judas the Galilean at the time of the census; he induced some people to revolt under his leadership, but he too perished and his whole movement was broken up. Now, my advice to you is this: keep clear of these men; let them alone. For if what is being planned and done is human in origin, it will collapse; but if it is from God, you will never be able to stamp it out, and you risk finding yourselves at war with God.'

Convinced by this, they sent for the apostles and had them flogged; then they ordered them to give up speaking in the name of Jesus, and discharged them. The apostles went out from the Council rejoicing that they had been found worthy to suffer humiliation for the sake of the name. And every day they went steadily on with their teaching in the temple and in private houses, telling the good news of Jesus the Messiah.

The Stoning of Stephen

The word of God spread more and more widely; the number of disciples in Jerusalem was increasing rapidly, and very many of the priests adhered to the faith.

Stephen, full of grace and power, began to do great wonders and signs among the people. Some members of the synagogue called the Synagogue of Freedmen, comprising Cyrenians and Alexandrians and people from Cilicia and Asia, came forward and argued with Stephen, but could not hold their own against the inspired wisdom with which he spoke. They then put up men to allege that they had heard him make blasphemous statements against Moses and against God. They stirred up the people and the elders and scribes, set upon him and seized him, and brought him before the Council.

Then the high priest asked him, 'Is this true?' He replied, 'My brothers, fathers of this nation, listen to me.

'Our forefathers had the Tent of the Testimony in the desert, as God commanded when he told Moses to make it after the pattern which he had seen. In the next generation, our fathers under Joshua brought it with them when they dispossessed the nations whom God drove out before them, and so it was until the time of David. David found favour with God and begged leave to provide a dwelling-place for the God of Jacob; but it was Solomon who built him a house. However, the Most High does not live in houses made by men; as the prophet says: "Heaven is my throne and earth my footstool. What kind of house will you build for me, says the Lord; where shall my resting-place be? Are not all these things of my own making?"

'How stubborn you are, heathen still at heart and deaf to the truth! You always resist the Holy Spirit. You are just like your fathers! Was there ever a prophet your fathers did not persecute? They killed those who foretold the coming of the righteous one, and now you have betrayed him and murdered him. You received the law given by God's angels and yet you have not kept it.'

This touched them on the raw, and they ground their teeth with fury. But Stephen, filled with the Holy Spirit, and gazing intently up to heaven, saw the glory of God, and Jesus standing at God's right hand. 'Look!' he said. 'I see the heavens opened and the Son of Man standing at the right hand of God.' At this they gave a great shout, and stopped their ears; they made a concerted rush at him, threw him out of the city, and set about stoning him. The witnesses laid their coats at the feet of a young man named Saul. As they stoned him Stephen called out, 'Lord Jesus, receive my spirit.' He fell on his knees and cried aloud, 'Lord, do not hold this sin against them,' and with that he died. Saul was among those who approved of his execution.

That day was the beginning of a time of violent persecution for the church in Jerusalem; and all except the apostles were scattered over the country districts of Judaea and Samaria. Stephen was given burial by devout men, who made a great lamentation for him. Saul, meanwhile, was harrying the church; he entered house after house, seizing men and women and sending them to prison.

As for those who had been scattered, they went through the country preaching the word.

Philip the Evangelist
Philip came down to a city in Samaria and began proclaiming the Messiah there. As the crowds heard Philip and saw the signs he performed, everyone paid close attention to what he had to say. In many cases of possession the unclean spirits came out with a loud cry, and many paralysed and crippled folk were cured; and there was great rejoicing in that city.

A man named Simon had been in the city for some time and had captivated the Samaritans with his magical arts, making large claims for himself. Everybody, high and low, listened intently to him. 'This man', they said, 'is that power of God which is called "The Great Power".' They listened because they had for so long been captivated by his magic. But when they came to believe

Philip, with his good news about the kingdom of God and the name of Jesus Christ, men and women alike were baptized. Even Simon himself believed, and after his baptism was constantly in Philip's company. He was captivated when he saw the powerful signs and miracles that were taking place.

Then the angel of the Lord said to Philip, 'Start out and go south to the road that leads down from Jerusalem to Gaza.' (This is the desert road.) He set out and was on his way when he caught sight of an Ethiopian. This man was a eunuch, a high official of the Kandake, or queen, of Ethiopia, in charge of all her treasure; he had been to Jerusalem on a pilgrimage and was now returning home, sitting in his carriage and reading aloud from the prophet Isaiah. The Spirit said to Philip, 'Go and meet the carriage.' When Philip ran up he heard him reading from the prophet Isaiah and asked, 'Do you understand what you are reading?' He said, 'How can I without someone to guide me?' and invited Philip to get in and sit beside him.

The passage he was reading was this: 'He was led like a sheep to the slaughter; like a lamb that is dumb before the shearer, he does not open his mouth. He has been humiliated and has no redress. Who will be able to speak of his posterity? For he is cut off from the world of the living.'

'Please tell me', said the eunuch to Philip, 'who it is that the prophet is speaking about here: himself or someone else?' Then Philip began and, starting from this passage, he told him the good news of Jesus. As they were going along the road, they came to some water. 'Look,' said the eunuch, 'here is water: what is to prevent my being baptized?' and he ordered the carriage to stop. Then they both went down into the water, Philip and the eunuch, and he baptized him.

The Conversion of Saul

Saul, still breathing murderous threats against the Lord's disciples, went to the high priest and applied for letters to the synagogues at Damascus authorizing him to arrest any followers of the new way whom he found, men or women, and bring them to Jerusalem. While he was still on the road and nearing Damascus, suddenly a light from the sky flashed all around him. He fell to the ground and heard a voice saying, 'Saul, Saul, why are you persecuting me?' 'Tell me, Lord,' he said, 'who you are.' The voice answered, 'I am Jesus, whom you are persecuting. But now get up and go into the city, and you will be told what you have to do.' Meanwhile the men who were travelling with him stood speechless; they heard the voice but could see no one. Saul got up from the ground, but when he opened his eyes he could not see; they led him by the hand and brought him into Damascus. He was blind for three days, and took no food or drink.

There was in Damascus a disciple named Ananias. He had a vision in which he heard the Lord say: 'Ananias!' 'Here I am, Lord,' he answered. The Lord said to him, 'Go to Straight Street, to the house of Judas, and ask for a man from Tarsus named Saul. You will find him at prayer; he has had a vision of a man named Ananias coming in and laying hands on him to restore his sight.' Ananias answered, 'Lord, I have often heard about this man and all the harm he has done your people in Jerusalem. Now he is here with authority from the chief priests to arrest all who invoke your name.' But the Lord replied, 'You must go, for this man is my chosen instrument to bring my name before the nations and their kings, and before the people of Israel. I myself will show him all that he must go through for my name's sake.'

So Ananias went and, on entering the house, laid his hands on him and said, 'Saul, my brother, the Lord Jesus, who appeared to you on your way here, has sent me to you so that you may recover your sight and be filled with the Holy Spirit.' Immediately it was as if scales had fallen from his eyes, and he regained his sight. He got up and was baptized, and when he had eaten, his strength returned.

He stayed some time with the disciples in Damascus. Without delay he proclaimed Jesus publicly in the synagogues, declaring him to be the Son of God. All who heard were astounded. 'Is not this the man', they said, 'who was in Jerusalem hunting down those who invoke this name? Did he not come here for the sole purpose of arresting them and taking them before the chief priests?' But Saul went from strength to strength, and confounded the Jews of Damascus with his cogent proofs that Jesus was the Messiah.

When some time had passed, the Jews hatched a plot against his life; but their plans became known to Saul. They kept watch on the city gates day and night so that they might murder him;

but one night some disciples took him and, lowering him in a basket, let him down over the wall.

On reaching Jerusalem he tried to join the disciples, but they were all afraid of him, because they did not believe that he really was a disciple. Barnabas, however, took him and introduced him to the apostles; he described to them how on his journey Saul had seen the Lord and heard his voice, and how at Damascus he had spoken out boldly in the name of Jesus. Saul now stayed with them, moving about freely in Jerusalem. He spoke out boldly and openly in the name of the Lord, talking and debating with the Greek-speaking Jews. But they planned to murder him, and when the brethren discovered this they escorted him down to Caesarea and sent him away to Tarsus.

Peter's Vision

At Caesarea there was a man named Cornelius, a centurion in the Italian Cohort, as it was called. He was a devout man, and he and his whole family joined in the worship of God; he gave generously to help the Jewish people, and was regular in his prayers to God. One day about three in the afternoon he had a vision in which he clearly saw an angel of God come into his room and say, 'Cornelius!' Cornelius stared at him in terror. 'What is it, my lord?' he asked. The angel said, 'Your prayers and acts of charity have gone up to heaven to speak for you before God. Now send to Joppa for a man named Simon, also called Peter: he is lodging with another Simon, a tanner, whose house is by the sea.' When the angel who spoke to him had gone, he summoned two of his servants and a military orderly who was a religious man, told them the whole story, and ordered them to Joppa.

Next day about noon, while they were still on their way and approaching the city, Peter went up on the roof to pray. He grew hungry and wanted something to eat, but while they were getting it ready, he fell into a trance. He saw heaven opened, and something coming down that looked like a great sheet of sailcloth; it was slung by the four corners and was being lowered to the earth, and in it he saw creatures of every kind, four-footed beasts, reptiles, and birds. There came a voice which said to him, 'Get up, Peter, kill and eat.' But Peter answered, 'No, Lord! I have never eaten anything profane or unclean.' The voice came again, a second time: 'It is not for you to call profane what God counts clean.' This happened three times, and then the thing was taken up into heaven.

While Peter was still puzzling over the meaning of the vision he had seen, the messengers from Cornelius had been asking the way to Simon's house, and now arrived at the entrance. They called out and asked if Simon Peter was lodging there. Peter was thinking over the vision, when the Spirit said to him, 'Some men are here looking for you; get up and go downstairs. You may go with them without any misgiving, for it was I who sent them.' Peter came down to the men and said, 'You are looking for me? Here I am. What brings you here?' 'We are from the centurion Cornelius,' they replied, 'a good and religious man, acknowledged as such by the whole Jewish nation. He was directed by a holy angel to send for you to his house and hear what you have to say.' So Peter asked them in and gave them a night's lodging.

Next day he set out with them, accompanied by some members of the congregation at Joppa, and on the following day arrived at Caesarea. Cornelius was expecting them and had called together his relatives and close friends. When Peter arrived, Cornelius came to meet him, and bowed to the ground in deep reverence. But Peter raised him to his feet and said, 'Stand up; I am only man like you.' Still talking with him he went in and found a large gathering. He said to them, 'I need not tell you that a Jew is forbidden by his religion to visit or associate with anyone of another race. Yet God has shown me clearly that I must not call anyone profane or unclean; that is why I came here without demur when you sent for me. May I ask what was your reason for doing so?'

Cornelius said, 'Three days ago, just about this time, I was in the house here saying the afternoon prayers, when suddenly a man in shining robes stood before me. He said: "Cornelius, your prayer has been heard and your acts of charity have spoken for you before God. Send to Simon Peter at Joppa, and ask him to come; he is lodging in the house of Simon the tanner, by the sea." I sent to you there and then, and you have been good enough to come. So now we are all met here before God, to listen to everything that the Lord has instructed you to say.'

Peter began: 'I now understand how true it is that God has no favourites, but that in every nation those who are god-fearing and do what is right are acceptable to him.'

Peter was still speaking when the Holy Spirit came upon all

who were listening to the message. The believers who had come with Peter, men of Jewish birth, were amazed that the gift of the Holy Spirit should have been poured out even on Gentiles, for they could hear them speaking in tongues of ecstasy and acclaiming the greatness of God. Then Peter spoke: 'Is anyone prepared to withhold the water of baptism from these persons, who have received the Holy Spirit just as we did?' Then he ordered them to be baptized in the name of Jesus Christ. After that they asked him to stay on with them for a time.

News came to the apostles and the members of the church in Judaea that Gentiles too had accepted the word of God; and when Peter came up to Jerusalem those who were of Jewish birth took issue with him. 'You have been visiting men who are uncircumcised,' they said, 'and sitting at table with them!' Peter began by laying before them the facts as they had happened.

When they heard this their doubts were silenced, and they gave praise to God. 'This means', they said, 'that God has granted life-giving repentance to the Gentiles also.'

Meanwhile those who had been scattered after the persecution that arose over Stephen made their way to Phoenicia, Cyprus, and Antioch, bringing the message to Jews only and to no others. But there were some natives of Cyprus and Cyrene among them, and these, when they arrived at Antioch, began to speak to Gentiles as well, telling them the good news of the Lord Jesus. The power of the Lord was with them, and a great many became believers and turned to the Lord.

The news reached the ears of the church in Jerusalem; and they sent Barnabas to Antioch. When he arrived and saw the divine grace at work, he rejoiced and encouraged them all to hold fast to the Lord with resolute hearts, for he was a good man, full of the Holy Spirit and of faith. And large numbers were won over to the Lord.

He then went off to Tarsus to look for Saul; and when he had found him, he brought him to Antioch. For a whole year the two of them lived in fellowship with the church there, and gave instruction to large numbers. It was in Antioch that the disciples first got the name of Christians.

Peter Escapes from Herod

It was about this time that King Herod launched an attack on certain members of the church. He beheaded James, the brother of John, and, when he saw that the Jews approved, proceeded to arrest Peter also. This happened during the festival of Unleavened Bread. Having secured him, he put him in prison under a military guard, four squads of four men each, meaning to produce him in public after Passover. So, while Peter was held in prison, the church kept praying fervently to God for him.

On the very night before Herod had planned to produce him, Peter was asleep between two soldiers, secured by two chains, while outside the doors sentries kept guard over the prison. All at once an angel of the Lord stood there, and the cell was ablaze with light. He tapped Peter on the shoulder to wake him. 'Quick! Get up!' he said, and the chains fell away from Peter's wrists. The angel said, 'Do up your belt and put on your sandals.' He did so. 'Now wrap your cloak round you and follow me.' Peter followed him out, with no idea that the angel's intervention was real: he thought it was just a vision. They passed the first guard-post, then the second, and reached the iron gate leading out into the city. This opened for them of its own accord; they came out and had walked the length of one street when suddenly the angel left him.

Then Peter came to himself. 'Now I know it is true,' he said: 'the Lord has sent his angel and rescued me from Herod's clutches and from all that the Jewish people were expecting.' Once he had realized this, he made for the house of Mary, the mother of John Mark, where a large company was at prayer.

He knocked at the outer door and a maidservant called Rhoda came to answer it. She recognized Peter's voice and was so overjoyed that instead of opening the door she ran in and announced that Peter was standing outside. 'You are crazy,' they told her; but she insisted that it was so. Then they said, 'It must be his angel.' Peter went on knocking, and when they opened the door and saw him, they were astounded. He motioned to them with his hand to keep quiet, and described to them how the Lord had brought him out of prison. 'Tell James and the members of the church,' he said. Then he left the house and went off elsewhere.

When morning came, there was consternation among the soldiers: what could have become of Peter? Herod made careful search, but failed to find him, so he interrogated the guards and ordered their execution.

Afterwards Herod left Judaea to reside for a while at Caesarea. On an appointed day Herod, attired in his royal robes and seated on the rostrum, addressed the populace; they responded, 'It is a god speaking, not a man!' Instantly an angel of the Lord struck him down, because he had usurped the honour due to God; he was eaten up with worms and so died.

The Apostle to the Gentiles

There were in the church at Antioch certain prophets and teachers: Barnabas, Simeon called Niger, Lucius of Cyrene, Manaen, a close friend of Prince Herod, and Saul. While they were offering worship to the Lord and fasting, the Holy Spirit said, 'Set Barnabas and Saul apart for me, to do the work to which I have called them.' Then, after further fasting and prayer, they laid their hands on them and sent them on their way.

These two, sent out on their mission by the Holy Spirit, came down to Seleucia, and from there sailed to Cyprus. Arriving at Salamis, they declared the word of God in the Jewish synagogues; they had John with them as their assistant. They went through the whole island as far as Paphos, and there they came upon a sorcerer, a Jew who posed as a prophet, Barjesus by name. He was in the retinue of the governor, Sergius Paulus, a learned man, who had sent for Barnabas and Saul and wanted to hear the word of God. This Elymas the sorcerer opposed them, trying to turn the governor away from the faith. But Saul, also known as Paul, filled with the Holy Spirit, fixed his eyes on him and said, 'You are a swindler, an out-and-out fraud! You son of the devil and enemy of all goodness, will you never stop perverting the straight ways of the Lord? Look now, the hand of the Lord strikes: you shall be blind, and for a time you shall not see the light of the sun.' At once mist and darkness came over his eyes, and he groped about for someone to lead him by the hand. When the governor saw what had happened he became a believer, deeply impressed by what he learnt about the Lord.

Sailing from Paphos, Paul and his companions went to Perga in Pamphylia; John, however, left them and returned to Jerusalem. From Perga they continued their journey as far as Pisidian Antioch. On the sabbath they went to synagogue and took their seats;

and after the readings from the law and the prophets, the officials of the synagogue sent this message to them: 'Friends, if you have anything to say to the people by way of exhortation, let us hear it.' Paul stood up, raised his hand for silence, and began.

'Listen, men of Israel and you others who worship God! The God of this people, Israel, chose our forefathers. When they were still living as aliens in Egypt, he made them into a great people and, with arm outstretched, brought them out of that country. For some forty years he bore with their conduct in the desert. Then in the Canaanite country, after overthrowing seven nations, whose lands he gave them to be their heritage for some four hundred and fifty years, he appointed judges for them until the time of the prophet Samuel.

'It was then that they asked for a king, and God gave them Saul son of Kish, a man of the tribe of Benjamin. He reigned for forty years before God removed him and appointed David as their king, with this commendation: "I have found David the son of Jesse to be a man after my own heart; he will carry out all my purposes." This is the man from whose descendants God, as he promised, has brought Israel a saviour, Jesus.

'My brothers, who come of Abraham's stock, and others among you who worship God, we are the people to whom this message of salvation has been sent. The people of Jerusalem and their rulers did not recognize Jesus, or understand the words of the prophets which are read sabbath by sabbath; indeed, they fulfilled them by condemning him. Though they failed to find grounds for the sentence of death, they asked Pilate to have him executed. When they had carried out all that the scriptures said about him, they took him down from the gibbet and laid him in a tomb. But God raised him from the dead; and over a period of many days he appeared to those who had come up with him from Galilee to Jerusalem, and they are now his witnesses before our people.

'We are here to give you the good news that God, who made the promise to the fathers, has fulfilled it for the children by raising Jesus from the dead.'

As they were leaving the synagogue they were asked to come again and speak on these subjects next sabbath; and after the congregation had dispersed, many Jews and gentile worshippers went with Paul and Barnabas, who spoke to them and urged them to hold fast to the grace of God.

On the following sabbath almost the whole city gathered to hear the word of God. When the Jews saw the crowds, they were filled with jealous resentment, and contradicted what Paul had said with violent abuse. But Paul and Barnabas were outspoken in their reply. 'It was necessary', they said, 'that the word of God should be declared to you first. But since you reject it and judge yourselves unworthy of eternal life, we now turn to the Gentiles.'

Thus the word of the Lord spread throughout the region. But the Jews stirred up feeling among those worshippers who were women of standing, and among the leading men of the city; a campaign of persecution was started against Paul and Barnabas, and they were expelled from the district. They shook the dust off their feet in protest against them and went to Iconium. And the disciples were filled with joy and with the Holy Spirit.

At Iconium they went together into the Jewish synagogue and spoke to such purpose that Jews and Greeks in large numbers became believers. But the unconverted Jews stirred up the Gentiles and poisoned their minds against the Christians. So Paul and Barnabas made their escape to the Lycaonian cities of Lystra and Derbe and the surrounding country. There they continued to spread the good news.

At Lystra a cripple, lame from birth, who had never walked in his life, sat listening to Paul as he spoke. Paul fixed his eyes on him and, seeing that he had the faith to be cured, said in a loud voice, 'Stand up straight on your feet'; and he sprang up and began to walk. When the crowds saw what Paul had done, they shouted, in their native Lycaonian, 'The gods have come down to us in human form!' They called Barnabas Zeus, and Paul they called Hermes, because he was the spokesman. The priest of Zeus, whose temple was just outside the city, brought oxen and garlands to the gates, and he and the people were about to offer sacrifice.

But when the apostles Barnabas and Paul heard of it, they tore their clothes and rushed into the crowd shouting, 'Men, why are you doing this? We are human beings, just like you. The good news we bring tells you to turn from these follies to the living God, who made heaven and earth and sea and everything in them. In past ages he has allowed all nations to go their own way; and yet he has not left you without some clue to his nature, in the benefits he bestows: he sends you rain from heaven and the crops in their seasons, and gives you food in plenty and keeps you in good heart.' Even with these words they barely managed to prevent the crowd from offering sacrifice to them.

Then Jews from Antioch and Iconium came on the scene and won over the crowds. They stoned Paul, and dragged him out of the city, thinking him dead. The disciples formed a ring round him, and he got to his feet and went into the city. Next day he left with Barnabas for Derbe.

After bringing the good news to that town and gaining many converts, they returned to Lystra, then to Iconium, and then to Antioch, strengthening the disciples and encouraging them to be true to the faith. They warned them that to enter the kingdom of God we must undergo many hardships. They called the congregation together and reported all that God had accomplished through them, and how he had thrown open the gates of faith to the Gentiles. And they stayed for some time with the disciples there.

The Council of Jerusalem

Some people who had come down from Judaea began to teach the brotherhood that those who were not circumcised in accordance with Mosaic practice could not be saved. That brought them into fierce dissension and controversy with Paul and Barnabas, and it was arranged that these two and some others from Antioch should go up to Jerusalem to see the apostles and elders about this question.

They were sent on their way by the church, and travelled through Phoenicia and Samaria, telling the full story of the conversion of the Gentiles, and causing great rejoicing among all the Christians. When they reached Jerusalem they were welcomed by the church and the apostles and elders, and they reported all that God had accomplished through them. But some of the Pharisaic party who had become believers came forward and declared, 'Those Gentiles must be circumcised and told to keep the law of Moses.'

The apostles and elders met to look into this matter, and, after a long debate, Peter rose to address them. 'My friends,' he said, 'in the early days, as you yourselves know, God made his choice among you: from my lips the Gentiles were to hear and believe the message of the gospel. And God, who can read human hearts, showed his approval by giving the Holy Spirit to them as he did to us. He made no difference between them and us; for he purified their hearts by faith. Then why do you now try God's patience by laying on the shoulders of these converts a yoke which neither we nor our forefathers were able to bear? For our belief is that we are saved in the same way as they are: by the grace of the Lord Jesus.'

At that the whole company fell silent and listened to Barnabas and Paul as they described all the signs and portents that God had worked among the Gentiles through them. When they had finished speaking, James summed up: 'My friends,' he said, 'listen to me. Simon has described how it first happened that God, in his providence, chose from among the Gentiles a people to bear his name.

'In my judgement, therefore, we should impose no irksome restrictions on those of the Gentiles who are turning to God; instead we should instruct them by letter to abstain from things polluted by contact with idols, from fornication, from anything that has been strangled, and from blood. Moses, after all, has never lacked spokesmen in every town for generations past; he is read in the synagogues sabbath by sabbath.'

Then, with the agreement of the whole church, the apostles and elders resolved to choose representatives and send them to Antioch with Paul and Barnabas. They chose two leading men in the community, Judas Barsabbas and Silas, and gave them this letter to deliver:

From the apostles and elders to our brothers of gentile origin in Antioch, Syria, and Cilicia. Greetings!

We have heard that some of our number, without any instructions from us, have disturbed you with their talk and unsettled your minds. In consequence, we have resolved unanimously to send to you our chosen representatives with our well-beloved Barnabas and Paul, who have given up their lives to the cause of our Lord Jesus Christ; so we are sending Judas and Silas, who will, by word of mouth, confirm what is written in this letter. It is the decision of the Holy Spirit, and our decision, to lay no further burden upon you beyond these essentials: you are to abstain from meat that has been offered to idols, from blood, from anything that has been strangled, and from fornication. If you keep yourselves free from these things you will be doing well. Farewell.

So they took their leave and travelled down to Antioch, where they called the congregation together and delivered the letter. When it was read, all rejoiced at the encouragement it brought.

From Antioch to Athens

After a while Paul said to Barnabas, 'Let us go back and see how our brothers are getting on in the various towns where we proclaimed the word of the Lord.' As they made their way from town to town they handed on the decisions taken by the apostles and elders in Jerusalem and enjoined their observance. So, day by day, the churches grew stronger in faith and increased in numbers.

They travelled through the Phrygian and Galatian region, prevented by the Holy Spirit from delivering the message in the province of Asia. When they approached the Mysian border they tried to enter Bithynia, but, as the Spirit of Jesus would not allow them, they passed through Mysia and reached the coast at Troas. During the night a vision came to Paul: a Macedonian stood there appealing to him, 'Cross over to Macedonia and help us.' As soon as he had seen this vision, we set about getting a passage to Macedonia, convinced that God had called us to take the good news there.

We sailed from Troas and made a straight run to Samothrace, the next day to Neapolis, and from there to Philippi, a leading city in that district of Macedonia and a Roman colony. Here we stayed for some days, and on the sabbath we went outside the city gate by the riverside, where we thought there would be a place of prayer; we sat down and talked to the women who had gathered there. One of those listening was called Lydia, a dealer in purple fabric, who came from the city of Thyatira; she was a worshipper of God, and the Lord opened her heart to respond to what Paul said. She was baptized, and her household with her, and then she urged us, 'Now that you have accepted me as a believer in the Lord, come and stay at my house.' And she insisted on our going.

Once, on our way to the place of prayer, we met a slave-girl who was possessed by a spirit of divination and brought large profits to her owners by telling fortunes. She followed Paul and the rest of us, shouting, 'These men are servants of the Most High God, and are declaring to you a way of salvation.' She did this day after day, until, in exasperation, Paul rounded on the spirit. 'I command you in the name of Jesus Christ to come out of her,' he said, and it came out instantly.

When the girl's owners saw that their hope of profit had gone, they seized Paul and Silas and dragged them to the city authorities in the main square; bringing them before the magistrates, they alleged, 'These men are causing a disturbance in our city; they are Jews, and they are advocating practices which it is illegal for us Romans to adopt and follow.' The mob joined in the attack; and the magistrates had the prisoners stripped and gave orders for them to be flogged. After a severe beating they were flung into prison and the jailer was ordered to keep them under close guard. In view of these orders, he put them into the inner prison and secured their feet in the stocks.

About midnight Paul and Silas, at their prayers, were singing praises to God, and the other prisoners were listening, when suddenly there was such a violent earthquake that the foundations of the jail were shaken; the doors burst open and all the prisoners found their fetters unfastened. The jailer woke up to see the prison doors wide open and, assuming that the prisoners had escaped, drew his sword intending to kill himself. But Paul shouted, 'Do yourself no harm; we are all here.' The jailer called for lights, rushed in, and threw himself down before Paul and Silas, trembling with fear. He then escorted them out and said, 'Sirs, what must I do to be saved?' They answered, 'Put your trust in the Lord Jesus, and you will be saved, you and your household,' and they imparted the word of the Lord to him and to everyone in his house. At that late hour of the night the jailer took them and washed their wounds, and there and then he and his whole family were baptized. He brought them up into his house, set out a meal, and rejoiced with his whole household in his new-found faith in God.

When daylight came, the magistrates sent their officers with the order, 'Release those men.' The jailer reported these instructions to Paul: 'The magistrates have sent an order for your release. Now you are free to go in peace.' But Paul said to the officers: 'We are Roman citizens! They gave us a public flogging and threw us into prison without trial. Are they now going to smuggle us out by stealth? No indeed! Let them come in person and escort us out.' The officers reported his words to the magistrates. Alarmed to hear that they were Roman citizens, they came and apologized to them, and then escorted them out and requested them to go away from the city. On leaving the prison, they went to Lydia's house, where they met their fellow Christians and spoke words of encouragement to them, and then they took their departure.

They now travelled by way of Amphipolis and Apollonia and came to Thessalonica, where there was a Jewish synagogue. Following his usual practice Paul went to their meetings; and for the next three sabbaths he argued with them, quoting texts of scripture which he expounded and applied to show that the Messiah had to suffer and rise from the dead. 'And this Jesus', he said, 'whom I am proclaiming to you is the Messiah.' Some of them were convinced and joined Paul and Silas, as did a great number of godfearing Gentiles and a good many influential women.

The Jews in their jealousy recruited some ruffians from the dregs of society to gather a mob. They put the city in an uproar, and made for Jason's house with the intention of bringing Paul and Silas before the town assembly. Failing to find them, they dragged Jason himself and some members of the congregation before the magistrates, shouting, 'The men who have made trouble the whole world over have now come here, and Jason has harboured them. All of them flout the emperor's laws, and assert there is a rival king, Jesus.' These words alarmed the mob and the magistrates also, who took security from Jason and the others before letting them go.

As soon as darkness fell, the members of the congregation sent Paul and Silas off to Beroea; and, on arrival, they made their way to the synagogue. The Jews here were more fair-minded than those at Thessalonica: they received the message with great eagerness, studying the scriptures every day to see whether it was true. Many of them therefore became believers, and so did a fair number of Gentiles, women of standing as well as men. But when the Thessalonian Jews learnt that the word of God had now been proclaimed by Paul in Beroea, they followed him there to stir up trouble and rouse the rabble. At once the members of the congregation sent Paul down to the coast, while Silas and Timothy both stayed behind. Paul's escort brought him as far as Athens, and came away with instructions for Silas and Timothy to rejoin him with all speed.

While Paul was waiting for them at Athens, he was outraged to see the city so full of idols. He argued in the synagogue with the Jews and gentile worshippers, and also in the city square every day with casual passers-by. Moreover, some of the Epicurean and Stoic philosophers joined issue with him. Some said, 'What can this charlatan be trying to say?' and others, 'He would appear to be a propagandist for foreign deities' – this because he was preaching about Jesus and the Resurrection. They brought him to the Council of the Areopagus and asked, 'May we know what this new doctrine is that you propound? You are introducing ideas that sound strange to us, and we should like to know what they mean.' Now, all the Athenians and the resident foreigners had time for nothing except talking or hearing about the latest novelty.

Paul stood up before the Council of the Areopagus and began: 'Men of Athens, I see that in everything that concerns religion you are uncommonly scrupulous. As I was going round looking at the objects of your worship, I noticed among other things an altar bearing the inscription "To an Unknown God". What you worship but do not know – this is what I now proclaim.

'The God who created the world and everything in it, and who is Lord of heaven and earth, does not live in shrines made by human hands. It is not because he lacks anything that he accepts service at our hands, for he is himself the universal giver of life and breath – indeed of everything. He created from one stock every nation of men to inhabit the whole earth's surface. He determined their eras in history and the limits of their territory. They were to seek God in the hope that, groping after him, they might find him; though indeed he is not far from each one of us, for in him we live and move, in him we exist; as some of your own poets have said, "We are also his offspring." Being God's offspring, then, we ought not to suppose that the deity is like an image in gold or silver or stone, shaped by human craftsmanship and design. God has overlooked the age of ignorance; but now he commands men and women everywhere to repent, because he has fixed the day on which he will have the world judged, and justly judged, by a man whom he has designated; of this he has given assurance to all by raising him from the dead.'

When they heard about the raising of the dead, some scoffed; others said, 'We will hear you on this subject some other time.'

From Corinth to Ephesus

After this he left Athens and went to Corinth. There he met a Jew named Aquila, a native of Pontus, and his wife Priscilla; they had recently arrived from Italy because Claudius had issued an edict that all Jews should leave Rome. Paul approached them and, because he was of the same trade, he made his home with them; they were tentmakers and Paul worked with them. He also held discussions in the synagogue sabbath by sabbath, trying to convince both Jews and Gentiles.

Crispus, the president of the synagogue, became a believer in the Lord, as did all his household; and a number of Corinthians who heard him believed and were baptized. One night in a vision the Lord said to Paul, 'Have no fear: go on with your preaching and do not be silenced. I am with you, and no attack shall harm you, for I have many in this city who are my people.' So he settled there for eighteen months, teaching the word of God among them.

Paul stayed on at Corinth for some time, and then took leave of the congregation. Accompanied by Priscilla and Aquila, he sailed for Syria, having had his hair cut off at Cenchreae in fulfilment of a vow.

They put in at Ephesus, where he parted from his companions; he himself went into the synagogue and held a discussion with the Jews. During the next three months he attended the synagogue and with persuasive argument spoke boldly about the kingdom of God. When some proved obdurate and would not believe, speaking evil of the new way before the congregation, he withdrew from them, taking the disciples with him, and continued to hold discussions daily in the lecture hall of Tyrannus. This went on for two years, with the result that the whole population of the province of Asia, both Jews and Gentiles, heard the word of the Lord.

When matters had reached this stage, Paul made up his mind to visit Macedonia and Achaia and then go on to Jerusalem. 'After I have been there,' he said, 'I must see Rome also.' He sent two of his assistants, Timothy and Erastus, to Macedonia, while he himself stayed some time longer in the province of Asia.

It was about this time that the Christian movement gave rise to a serious disturbance. There was a man named Demetrius, a silversmith who made silver shrines of Artemis, and provided considerable employment for the craftsmen. He called a meeting of them and of the workers in allied trades, and addressed them: 'As you men know, our prosperity depends on this industry. But this fellow Paul, as you can see and hear for yourselves, has perverted crowds of people with his propaganda, not only at Ephesus but also in practically the whole of the province of Asia; he tells them that gods made by human hands are not gods at all. There is danger for us here; it is not only that our line of business will be discredited, but also that the sanctuary of the great goddess Artemis will cease to command respect; and then it will not be long before she who is worshipped by all Asia and the civilized world is brought down from her divine pre-eminence.'

On hearing this, they were enraged, and began to shout, 'Great is Artemis of the Ephesians!' The whole city was in an uproar; they made a concerted rush into the theatre, hustling along with them Paul's travelling companions, the Macedonians Gaius and Aristarchus. Paul wanted to appear before the assembly but the other Christians would not let him. Even some of the dignitaries of the province, who were friendly towards him, sent a message urging him not to venture into the theatre. Meanwhile some were shouting one thing, some another, for the assembly was in an uproar and most of them did not know what they had all come for. Some of the crowd explained the trouble to Alexander, whom the Jews had pushed to the front, and he, motioning for silence, attempted to make a defence before the assembly. But when they recognized that he was a Jew, one shout arose from them all: 'Great is Artemis of the Ephesians!' and they kept it up for about two hours.

The town clerk, however, quietened the crowd. 'Citizens of Ephesus,' he said, 'all the world knows that our city of Ephesus is temple warden of the great Artemis and of that image of her which fell from heaven. Since these facts are beyond dispute, your proper course is to keep calm and do nothing rash. These men whom you have brought here as offenders have committed no sacrilege and uttered no blasphemy against our goddess. If, therefore, Demetrius and his craftsmen have a case against anyone, there are assizes and there are proconsuls; let the parties bring their charges and countercharges. But if it is a larger question you are raising, it will be dealt with in the statutory assembly. We certainly run the risk of being charged with riot for this day's work. There is no justification for it, and it would be impossible for us to give any explanation of this turmoil.' With that he dismissed the assembly.

When the disturbance was over, Paul sent for the disciples and, after encouraging them, said goodbye and set out on his journey to Macedonia. He travelled through that region, constantly giving encouragement to the Christians, and finally reached Greece. When he had spent three months there and was on the point of embarking for Syria, a plot was laid against him by the Jews, so he decided to return by way of Macedonia.

We went on ahead to the ship and embarked for Assos, where we were to take Paul aboard; this was the arrangement he had made, since he was going to travel by road. When he met us at Assos, we took him aboard and proceeded to Mitylene. We sailed from there and next day arrived off Chios. On the second day we made Samos, and the following day we reached Miletus. Paul had decided to bypass Ephesus and so avoid having to spend time in the province of Asia; he was eager to be in Jerusalem on the day of Pentecost, if that were possible. He did, however, send from Miletus to Ephesus and summon the elders of the church. When they joined him, he spoke to them as follows.

'You know how, from the day that I first set foot in the province of Asia, I spent my whole time with you, serving the Lord in all humility amid the sorrows and trials that came upon me through the intrigues of the Jews. Now, as you see, I am constrained by the Spirit to go to Jerusalem. I do not know what will befall me there, except that in city after city the Holy Spirit assures me that imprisonment and hardships await me. For myself, I set no store by life; all I want is to finish the race, and complete the task which the Lord Jesus assigned to me, that of bearing my testimony to the gospel of God's grace.

'One thing more: I have gone about among you proclaiming the kingdom, but now I know that none of you will ever see my face again. That being so, I here and now declare that no one's fate can be laid at my door; I have kept back nothing; I have disclosed to you the whole purpose of God. Keep guard over yourselves and over all the flock of which the Holy Spirit has given you charge, as shepherds of the church of the Lord, which he won for himself by his own blood. I know that when I am gone, savage wolves will come in among you and will not spare the flock. Even from your own number men will arise who will distort the truth in order to get the disciples to break away and follow them. So be on the alert; remember how with tears I never ceased to warn each one of you night and day for three years.

'And now I commend you to God and to the word of his grace, which has power to build you up and give you your heritage among all those whom God has made his own.'

As he finished speaking, he knelt down with them all and prayed. There were loud cries of sorrow from them all, as they folded Paul in their arms and kissed him; what distressed them most was his saying that they would never see his face again. Then they escorted him to the ship.

Paul's Final Journey to Jerusalem

We tore ourselves away from them and, putting to sea, made a straight run and came to Cos; next day to Rhodes, and thence to Patara. There we found a ship bound for Phoenicia, so we went aboard and sailed in her. We came in sight of Cyprus and, leaving it to port, we continued our voyage to Syria and put in at Tyre, where the ship was to unload her cargo. We sought out the disciples and stayed there a week.

We made the passage from Tyre and reached Ptolemais, where we greeted the brotherhood and spent a day with them. Next day we left and came to Caesarea, where we went to the home of Philip the evangelist. When we had been there several days, a prophet named Agabus arrived from Judaea. He came to us, took Paul's belt, bound his own feet and hands with it, and said, 'These are the words of the Holy Spirit: Thus will the Jews in Jerusalem bind the man to whom this belt belongs, and hand him over to the Gentiles.' When we heard this, we and the local people begged and implored Paul to abandon his visit to Jerusalem. Then Paul gave his answer: 'Why all these tears? Why are you trying to weaken my resolution? I am ready, not merely to be bound, but even to die at Jerusalem for the name of the Lord Jesus.' So, as he would not be dissuaded, we gave up and said, 'The Lord's will be done.'

At the end of our stay we packed our baggage and took the road up to Jerusalem. Some of the disciples from Caesarea came along with us, to direct us to a Cypriot named Mnason, a Christian from the early days, with whom we were to spend the night. On our arrival at Jerusalem, the congregation welcomed us gladly.

Next day Paul paid a visit to James; we accompanied him, and all the elders were present. After greeting them, he described in detail all that God had done among the Gentiles by means of his ministry. When they heard this, they gave praise to God. Then they said to Paul: 'You observe, brother, how many thousands of converts we have among the Jews, all of them staunch upholders of the law. Now they have been given certain information about you: it is said that you teach all the Jews in the gentile world to turn their backs on Moses, and tell them not to circumcise their children or follow our way of life. What is to be done, then? They are sure to hear that you have arrived. Our proposal is this: we have four men here who are under a vow; take them with you and go through the ritual of purification together, and pay their expenses, so that they may have their heads shaved; then everyone will know that there is nothing in the reports they have heard about you, but that you are yourself a practising Jew and observe the law. As for the gentile converts, we sent them our decision that they should abstain from meat that has been offered to idols, from blood, from anything that has been strangled, and from fornication.' So Paul took the men, and next day, after going through the ritual of purification with them, he went into the temple to give notice of the date when the period of purification would end and the offering be made for each of them.

But just before the seven days were up, the Jews from the province of Asia saw him in the temple. They stirred up all the crowd and seized him, shouting, 'Help us, men of Israel! This is the fellow who attacks our people, our law, and this sanctuary, and spreads his teaching the whole world over. What is more, he has brought Gentiles into the temple and profaned this holy place.' They had previously seen Trophimus the Ephesian with him in the city, and assumed that Paul had brought him into the temple.

The whole city was in a turmoil, and people came running from all directions. They seized Paul and dragged him out of the temple, and at once the doors were shut. They were bent on killing him, but word came to the officer commanding the cohort that all Jerusalem was in an uproar. He immediately took a force of soldiers with their centurions and came down at the double to deal with the riot. When the crowd saw the commandant and his troops, they stopped beating Paul. As soon as the commandant could reach Paul, he arrested him and ordered him to be shackled with two chains; he enquired who he was and what he had been doing. Some in the crowd shouted one thing, some another, and as the commandant could not get at the truth because of the hubbub, he ordered him to be taken to the barracks. When Paul reached the steps, he found himself carried up by the soldiers because of the violence of the mob; for the whole crowd was at their heels yelling, 'Kill him!'

Just before he was taken into the barracks Paul said to the commandant, 'May I have a word with you?' The commandant said, 'So you speak Greek? Then you are not the Egyptian who started a revolt some time ago and led a force of four thousand terrorists out into the desert?' Paul replied, 'I am a Jew from Tarsus in Cilicia, a citizen of no mean city. May I have your permission to speak to the people?' When this was given, Paul stood on the steps and raised his hand to call for the attention of the people. As soon as quiet was restored, he addressed them in the Jewish language:

'Brothers and fathers, give me a hearing while I put my case to you.' When they heard him speaking to them in their own language, they listened more quietly. 'I am a true-born Jew,' he began, 'a native of Tarsus in Cilicia. I was brought up in this city, and as a pupil of Gamaliel I was thoroughly trained in every point of our ancestral law. I have always been ardent in God's service, as you all are today. And so I persecuted this movement to the death, arresting its followers, men and women alike, and committing them to prison, as the high priest and the whole Council of Elders can testify. It was they who gave me letters to our fellow Jews at Damascus, and I was on my way to make arrests there also and bring the prisoners to Jerusalem for punishment. What happened to me on my journey was this: when I was nearing Damascus, about midday, a great light suddenly flashed from the sky all around me. I fell to the ground, and heard a voice saying: "Saul, Saul, why do you persecute me?" I answered, "Tell me, Lord, who you are." "I am Jesus of Nazareth, whom you are persecuting," he said. My companions saw the light, but did not hear the voice that spoke to me. "What shall I do, Lord?" I asked, and he replied, "Get up, and go on to Damascus; there you will be told all that you are appointed to do." As I had been blinded by the brilliance of that light, my companions led me by the hand, and so I came to Damascus.

'There a man called Ananias, a devout observer of the law and well spoken of by all the Jews who lived there, came and stood beside me, and said, "Saul, my brother, receive your sight again!" Instantly I recovered my sight and saw him. He went on: "The God of our fathers appointed you to know his will and to see the Righteous One and to hear him speak, because you are to be his witness to tell the world what you have seen and heard. Do not delay. Be baptized at once and wash away your sins, calling on his name."

'After my return to Jerusalem, as I was praying in the temple I fell into a trance and saw him there, speaking to me. "Make haste", he said, "and leave Jerusalem quickly, for they will not accept your testimony about me." "But surely, Lord," I answered, "they know that I imprisoned those who believe in you and flogged them in every synagogue; when the blood of Stephen your witness was shed I stood by, approving, and I looked after the clothes of those who killed him." He said to me, "Go, for I mean to send you far away to the Gentiles."'

Up to this point the crowd had given him a hearing; but now they began to shout, 'Down with the scoundrel! He is not fit to be alive!' And as they were yelling and waving their cloaks and flinging dust in the air, the commandant ordered him to be brought into the barracks, and gave instructions that he should be examined under the lash, to find out what reason there was for such an outcry against him. But when they tied him up for the flogging, Paul said to the centurion who was standing there, 'Does the law allow you to flog a Roman citizen, and an unconvicted one at that?' When the centurion heard this, he went and reported to the commandant: 'What are you about? This man is a Roman citizen.' The commandant came to Paul and asked, 'Tell me, are you a Roman citizen?' 'Yes,' said he. The commandant rejoined, 'Citizenship cost me a large sum of money.' Paul said, 'It was mine by birth.' Then those who were about to examine him promptly withdrew; and the commandant himself was alarmed when he realized that Paul was a Roman citizen and that he had put him in irons.

The following day, wishing to be quite sure what charge the Jews were bringing against Paul, he released him and ordered the chief priests and the entire Council to assemble. He then brought Paul down to stand before them.

With his eyes steadily fixed on the Council, Paul said, 'My brothers, all my life to this day I have lived with a perfectly clear conscience before God.' At this the high priest Ananias ordered his attendants to strike him on the mouth. Paul retorted, 'God will strike you, you whitewashed wall! You sit there to judge me in accordance with the law; then, in defiance of the law, you order me to be struck!' The attendants said, 'Would you insult God's high priest?' 'Brothers,' said Paul, 'I had no idea he was high priest; scripture, I know, says: "You shall not abuse the ruler of your people."'

Well aware that one section of them were Sadducees and the other Pharisees, Paul called out in the Council, 'My brothers, I am a Pharisee, a Pharisee born and bred; and the issue in this trial is our hope of the resurrection of the dead.' At these words the Pharisees and Sadducees fell out among themselves, and the assembly was divided. (The Sadducees deny that there is any resurrection or angel or spirit, but the Pharisees believe in all three.) A great uproar ensued; and some of the scribes belonging to the Pharisaic party openly took sides and declared, 'We find no fault with this man; perhaps an angel or spirit has spoken to him.' In the mounting dissension, the commandant was afraid that Paul would be torn to pieces, so he ordered the troops to go down, pull him out of the crowd, and bring him into the barracks.

The following night the Lord appeared to him and said, 'Keep up your courage! You have affirmed the truth about me in Jerusalem, and you must do the same in Rome.'

When day broke, the Jews banded together and took an oath not to eat or drink until they had killed Paul. There were more than forty in the conspiracy; they went to the chief priests and elders and said, 'We have bound ourselves by a solemn oath not to taste food until we have killed Paul. It is now up to you and the rest of the Council to apply to the commandant to have him brought down to you on the pretext of a closer investigation of his case; we have arranged to make away with him before he reaches you.'

The son of Paul's sister, however, learnt of the plot and, going to the barracks, obtained entry, and reported it to Paul, who called one of the centurions and said, 'Take this young man to the commandant; he has something to report.' The centurion brought him to the commandant and explained, 'The prisoner Paul sent for me and asked me to bring this young man to you; he has something to tell you.' The commandant took him by the arm, drew him aside, and asked him, 'What is it you have to report?' He replied, 'The Jews have agreed on a plan: they will request you to bring Paul down to the Council tomorrow on the pretext of obtaining more precise information about him. Do not listen to them; for a party more than forty strong are lying in wait for him, and they have sworn not to eat or drink until they have done away with him. They are now ready, waiting only for your consent.' The commandant dismissed the young man, with orders not to let anyone know that he had given him this information.

He then summoned two of his centurions and gave them these orders: 'Have two hundred infantry ready to proceed to Caesarea, together with seventy cavalrymen and two hundred light-armed troops; parade them three hours after sunset, and provide mounts for Paul so that he may be conducted under safe escort to Felix the governor.' And he wrote a letter to this effect:

From Claudius Lysias to His Excellency the Governor Felix. Greeting.

This man was seized by the Jews and was on the point of being murdered when I intervened with the troops, and, on discovering that he was a Roman citizen, I removed him to safety. As I wished to ascertain the ground of their charge against him, I brought him down to their Council. I found that their case had to do with controversial matters of their law, but there was no charge against him which merited death or imprisonment. Information, however, has now been brought to my notice of an attempt to be made on the man's life, so I am sending him to you without delay, and have instructed his accusers to state their case against him before you.

Acting on their orders, the infantry took custody of Paul and brought him by night to Antipatris. Next day they returned to their barracks, leaving the cavalry to escort him the rest of the way. When the cavalry reached Caesarea, they delivered the letter to the governor, and handed Paul over to him. He read the letter, and asked him what province he was from; and learning that he was from Cilicia he said, 'I will hear your case when your accusers arrive.' He ordered him to be held in custody at his headquarters in Herod's palace.

Paul Defends His Gospel

Five days later the high priest Ananias came down, accompanied by some of the elders and an advocate named Tertullus, to lay before the governor their charge against Paul. When the prisoner was called, Tertullus opened the case.

'Your excellency,' he said to Felix, 'we owe it to you that we enjoy unbroken peace, and it is due to your provident care that, in all kinds of ways and in all sorts of places, improvements are being made for the good of this nation. We appreciate this, and are most grateful to you. And now, not to take up too much of your time, I crave your indulgence for a brief statement of our case. We have found this man to be a pest, a fomenter of discord among the Jews all over the world, a ringleader of the sect of the Nazarenes. He made an attempt to profane the temple and we arrested him. If you examine him yourself you can ascertain the truth of all the charges we bring against him.' The Jews supported the charge, alleging that the facts were as he stated.

The governor then motioned to Paul to speak, and he replied as follows: 'Knowing as I do that for many years you have administered justice to this nation, I make my defence with confidence. As you can ascertain for yourself, it is not more than twelve days since I went up to Jerusalem on a pilgrimage. They did not find me in the temple arguing with anyone or collecting a crowd, or in the synagogues or anywhere else in the city; and they cannot make good the charges they now bring against me. But this much I will admit: I am a follower of the new way (the "sect" they speak of), and it is in that manner that I worship the God of our fathers; for I believe all that is written in the law and the prophets, and in reliance on God I hold the hope, which my accusers too accept, that there is to be a resurrection of good and wicked alike. Accordingly I, no less than they, train myself to keep at all times a clear conscience before God and man.

'After an absence of several years I came to bring charitable gifts to my nation and to offer sacrifices. I was ritually purified and engaged in this service when they found me in the temple; I had no crowd with me, and there was no disturbance. But some Jews from the province of Asia were there, and if they had any charge against me, it is they who ought to have been in court to state it. Failing that, it is for these persons here present to say what crime they discovered when I was brought before the Council, apart from this one declaration which I made as I stood there: "The issue in my trial before you today is the resurrection of the dead."'

Then Felix, who was well informed about the new way, adjourned the hearing. 'I will decide your case when Lysias the commanding officer comes down,' he said. He gave orders to the centurion to keep Paul under open arrest and not to prevent any of his friends from making themselves useful to him.

Some days later Felix came with his wife Drusilla, who was a Jewess, and sent for Paul. He let him talk to him about faith in Christ Jesus, but when the discourse turned to questions of morals, self-control, and the coming judgement, Felix became alarmed and exclaimed, 'Enough for now! When I find it convenient I will send for you again.' He also had hopes of a bribe from Paul, so he sent for him frequently and talked with him.

When two years had passed, Felix was succeeded by Porcius Festus. Wishing to curry favour with the Jews, Felix left Paul in custody.

Three days after taking up his appointment, Festus went up from Caesarea to Jerusalem, where the chief priests and the Jewish leaders laid before him their charge against Paul.

After spending eight or ten days at most in Jerusalem, he went down to Caesarea, and next day he took his seat in court and ordered Paul to be brought before him. When he appeared, the Jews who had come down from Jerusalem stood round bringing many grave charges, which they were unable to prove. Paul protested: 'I have committed no offence against the Jewish law, or against the temple, or against the emperor.' Festus, anxious to ingratiate himself with the Jews, turned to Paul and asked, 'Are you willing to go up to Jerusalem and stand trial on these charges before me there?' But Paul said, 'I am now standing before the emperor's tribunal; that is where I ought to be tried. I have committed no offence against the Jews, as you very well know. If I am guilty of any capital crime, I do not ask to escape the death penalty; if, however, there is no substance in the charges which these men bring against me, it is not open to anyone to hand me over to them. I appeal to Caesar!' Then Festus, after conferring with his advisers, replied, 'You have appealed to Caesar: to Caesar you shall go!'

Some days later King Agrippa and Bernice arrived at Caesarea on a courtesy visit to Festus. They spent some time there, and during their stay Festus raised Paul's case with the king. Agrippa said to Festus, 'I should rather like to hear the man myself.' 'You shall hear him tomorrow,' he answered.

Next day Agrippa and Bernice came in full state and entered the audience-chamber accompanied by high-ranking officers and prominent citizens; and on the orders of Festus, Paul was brought in. Agrippa said to Paul: 'You have our permission to give an account of yourself.' Then Paul stretched out his hand and began his defence.

'I consider myself fortunate, King Agrippa, that it is before you I am to make my defence today on all the charges brought against me by the Jews, particularly as you are expert in all our Jewish customs and controversies. I beg you therefore to give me a patient hearing.

'My life from my youth up, a life spent from the first among my nation and in Jerusalem, is familiar to all Jews. Indeed they have known me long enough to testify, if they would, that I belonged to the strictest group in our religion: I was a Pharisee. It is the hope based on the promise God made to our forefathers that has led to my being on trial today. Our twelve tribes worship with intense devotion night and day in the hope of seeing the ful-filment of that promise; and for this very hope I am accused, your majesty, and accused by Jews. Why should Jews find it incredible that God should raise the dead?

'I assert nothing beyond what was foretold by the prophets and by Moses: that the Messiah would suffer and that, as the first to rise from the dead, he would announce the dawn both to the Jewish people and to the Gentiles.'

While Paul was thus making his defence, Festus shouted at the top of his voice, 'Paul, you are raving; too much study is driving you mad.' 'I am not mad, your excellency,' said Paul; 'what I am asserting is sober truth. The king is well versed in these matters, and I can speak freely to him. I do not believe that he can be unaware of any of these facts, for this has been no hole-and-corner business. King Agrippa, do you believe the prophets? I know you do.' Agrippa said to Paul, 'With a little more of your persuasion you will make a Christian of me.' 'Little or much,' said Paul, 'I wish to God that not only you, but all those who are listening to me today, might become what I am apart from these chains!'

With that the king rose, and with him the governor, Bernice, and the rest of the company, and after they had withdrawn they talked it over. 'This man', they agreed, 'is doing nothing that deserves death or imprisonment.' Agrippa said to Festus, 'The fellow could have been discharged, if he had not appealed to the emperor.'

The Journey to Rome
When it was decided that we should sail for Italy, Paul and some other prisoners were handed over to a centurion named Julius, of the Augustan Cohort. We embarked in a ship of Adramyttium, bound for ports in the province of Asia, and put out to sea. Aristarchus, a Macedonian from Thessalonica, came with us. Next day we landed at Sidon, and Julius very considerately allowed Paul to go to his friends to be cared for. Leaving Sidon we sailed under the lee of Cyprus because of the head winds, then across the open sea off the coast of Cilicia and Pamphylia, and so reached Myra in Lycia.

There the centurion found an Alexandrian vessel bound for Italy and put us on board. For a good many days we made little headway, and we were hard put to it to reach Cnidus. Then, as the wind continued against us, off Salmone we began to sail under the lee of Crete, and, hugging the coast, struggled on to a place called Fair Havens, not far from the town of Lasea.

By now much time had been lost, and with the Fast already over, it was dangerous to go on with the voyage. So Paul gave them this warning: 'I can see, gentlemen, that this voyage will be disastrous; it will mean heavy loss, not only of ship and cargo but also of life.' But the centurion paid more attention to the captain and to the owner of the ship than to what Paul said; and as the harbour was unsuitable for wintering, the majority were in favour of putting to sea, hoping, if they could get so far, to winter at Phoenix, a Cretan harbour facing south-west and north-west.

When a southerly breeze sprang up, they thought that their purpose was as good as achieved, and, weighing anchor, they sailed along the coast of Crete hugging the land. But before very long a violent wind, the Northeaster as they call it, swept down from the landward side. It caught the ship and, as it was impossible to keep head to wind, we had to give way and run before it. As we passed under the lee of a small island called Cauda, we managed with a struggle to get the ship's boat under control. When they had hoisted it on board, they made use of tackle to brace the ship. Then, afraid of running on to the sandbanks of Syrtis, they put out a sea-anchor and let her drift. Next day, as we were making very heavy weather, they began to lighten the ship; and on the third day they jettisoned the ship's gear with their own hands. For days on end there was no sign of either sun or stars, the storm was raging unabated, and our last hopes of coming through alive began to fade.

When they had gone for a long time without food, Paul stood up among them and said, 'You should have taken my advice, gentlemen, not to put out from Crete: then you would have avoided this damage and loss. But now I urge you not to lose heart; not a single life will be lost, only the ship. Last night there stood by me an angel of the God whose I am and whom I worship. "Do not be afraid, Paul," he said; "it is ordained that you shall appear before Caesar; and, be assured, God has granted you the lives of all who are sailing with you." So take heart, men! I trust God: it will turn out as I have been told; we are to be cast ashore on an island.'

The fourteenth night came and we were still drifting in the Adriatic Sea. At midnight the sailors felt that land was getting nearer, so they took a sounding and found twenty fathoms. Sounding again after a short interval they found fifteen fathoms; then, fearing that we might be cast ashore on a rugged coast, they let go four anchors from the stern and prayed for daylight to come. The sailors tried to abandon ship; they had already lowered the ship's boat, pretending they were going to lay out anchors from the bows, when Paul said to the centurion and the soldiers, 'Unless these men stay on board you cannot reach safety.' At that the soldiers cut the ropes of the boat and let it drop away.

Shortly before daybreak Paul urged them all to take some food. 'For the last fourteen days', he said, 'you have lived in suspense and gone hungry; you have eaten nothing. So have something to eat, I beg you; your lives depend on it. Remember, not a hair of your heads will be lost.' With these words, he took bread, gave thanks to God in front of them all, broke it, and began eating. Then they plucked up courage, and began to take food themselves. All told there were on board two hundred and seventy-six of us. After they had eaten as much as they wanted, they lightened the ship by dumping the grain into the sea.

When day broke, they did not recognize the land, but they sighted a bay with a sandy beach, on which they decided, if possible, to run ashore. So they slipped the anchors and let them go; at the same time they loosened the lashings of the steering-paddles, set the foresail to the wind, and let her drive to the beach. But they found themselves caught between cross-currents and ran the ship aground, so that the bow stuck fast and remained immovable, while the stern was being pounded to pieces by the breakers. The soldiers thought they had better kill the prisoners for fear that any should swim away and escape; but the centurion was determined to bring Paul safely through, and prevented them from carrying out their plan. He gave orders that those who could swim should jump overboard first and get to land; the rest were to follow, some on planks, some on parts of the ship. And thus it was that all came safely to land.

Once we had made our way to safety, we identified the island as Malta. The natives treated us with uncommon kindness: because it had started to rain and was cold they lit a bonfire and made us all welcome. Paul had got together an armful of sticks and put them on the fire, when a viper, driven out by the heat, fastened on his hand. The natives, seeing the snake hanging on to his hand, said to one another, 'The man must be a murderer; he may have escaped from the sea, but divine justice would not let him live.' Paul, however, shook off the snake into the fire and was none the worse. They still expected him to swell up or suddenly drop down dead, but after waiting a long time without seeing anything out of the way happen to him, they changed their minds and said, 'He is a god.'

Three months had passed when we put to sea in a ship which had wintered in the island; she was the *Castor and Pollux* of Alexandria. We landed at Syracuse and spent three days there; then we sailed up the coast and arrived at Rhegium. Next day a south wind sprang up and we reached Puteoli in two days. There we found fellow Christians and were invited to stay a week with them. And so to Rome. The Christians there had had news of us and came out to meet us as far as Appii Forum and the Three Taverns, and when Paul saw them, he gave thanks to God and took courage.

When we entered Rome Paul was allowed to lodge privately, with a soldier in charge of him. Three days later he called together the local Jewish leaders, and when they were assembled, he said to them: 'My brothers, I never did anything against our people or against the customs of our forefathers; yet I was arrested in Jerusalem and handed over to the Romans. They examined me and would have liked to release me because there was no capital charge against me; but the Jews objected, and I had no option but to appeal to Caesar; not that I had any accusation to bring against my own people. This is why I have asked to see and talk to you; it is for loyalty to the hope of Israel that I am in these chains.' They replied, 'We have had no communication about you from Judaea, nor has any countryman of ours arrived with any report or gossip to your discredit. We should like to hear from you what your views are; all we know about this sect is that no one has a good word to say for it.' So they fixed a day, and came in large numbers to his lodging. From dawn to dusk he put his case to them; he spoke urgently of the kingdom of God and sought to convince them about Jesus by appealing to the law of Moses and the prophets.

He stayed there two full years at his own expense, with a welcome for all who came to him; he proclaimed the kingdom of God and taught the facts about the Lord Jesus Christ quite openly and without hindrance.

36 | SELECTIONS FROM THE LETTERS OF ST PAUL

Living by the Spirit

There is now no condemnation for those who are united with Christ Jesus. In Christ Jesus the life-giving law of the Spirit has set you free from the law of sin and death. What the law could not do, because human weakness robbed it of all potency, God has done: by sending his own Son in the likeness of our sinful nature and to deal with sin, he has passed judgement against sin within that very nature, so that the commandment of the law may find fulfilment in us, whose conduct is no longer controlled by the old nature, but by the Spirit.

Those who live on the level of the old nature have their outlook formed by it, and that spells death; but those who live on the level of the spirit have the spiritual outlook, and that is life and peace. For the outlook of the unspiritual nature is enmity with God; it is not subject to the law of God and indeed it cannot be; those who live under its control cannot please God.

But you do not live like that. You live by the spirit, since God's Spirit dwells in you; and anyone who does not possess the Spirit of Christ does not belong to Christ. But if Christ is in you, then although the body is dead because of sin, yet the Spirit is your life because you have been justified. Moreover, if the Spirit of him who raised Jesus from the dead dwells in you, then the God who raised Christ Jesus from the dead will also give new life to your mortal bodies through his indwelling Spirit.

It follows, my friends, that our old nature has no claim on us; we are not obliged to live in that way. If you do so, you must die. But if by the Spirit you put to death the base pursuits of the body, then you will live.

For all who are led by the Spirit of God are sons of God. The Spirit you have received is not a spirit of slavery, leading you back into a life of fear, but a Spirit of adoption, enabling us to cry 'Abba! Father!' The Spirit of God affirms to our spirit that we are

God's children; and if children, then heirs, heirs of God and fellow heirs with Christ; but we must share his sufferings if we are also to share his glory.

For I reckon that the sufferings we now endure bear no comparison with the glory, as yet unrevealed, which is in store for us. The created universe is waiting with eager expectation for God's sons to be revealed. It was made subject to frustration, not of its own choice but by the will of him who subjected it, yet with the hope that the universe itself is to be freed from the shackles of mortality and is to enter upon the glorious liberty of the children of God. Up to the present, as we know, the whole created universe in all its parts groans as if in the pangs of childbirth. What is more, we also, to whom the Spirit is given as the firstfruits of the harvest to come, are groaning inwardly while we look forward eagerly to our adoption, our liberation from mortality. It was with this hope that we were saved. Now to see something is no longer to hope: why hope for what is already seen? But if we hope for something we do not yet see, then we look forward to it eagerly and with patience.

In the same way the Spirit comes to the aid of our weakness. We do not even know how we ought to pray, but through our inarticulate groans the Spirit himself is pleading for us, and God who searches our inmost being knows what the Spirit means, because he pleads for God's people as God himself wills; and in everything, as we know, he co-operates for good with those who love God and are called according to his purpose. For those whom God knew before ever they were, he also ordained to share the likeness of his Son, so that he might be the eldest among a large family of brothers; and those whom he foreordained, he also called, and those whom he called he also justified, and those whom he justified he also glorified.

With all this in mind, what are we to say? If God is on our side, who is against us? He did not spare his own Son, but gave him up for us all; how can he fail to lavish every other gift upon us? Who will bring a charge against those whom God has chosen? Not God, who acquits! Who will pronounce judgement? Not Christ, who died, or rather rose again; not Christ, who is at God's right hand and pleads our cause! Then what can separate us from the love of Christ? Can affliction or hardship? Can persecution, hunger, nakedness, danger, or sword? 'We are being done to death for your sake all day long,' as scripture says; 'we have been treated like sheep for slaughter' – and yet, throughout it all, overwhelming victory is ours through him who loved us. For I am convinced that there is nothing in death or life, in the realm of spirits or super-human powers, in the world as it is or the world as it shall be, in the forces of the universe, in heights or depths – nothing in all creation that can separate us from the love of God in Christ Jesus our Lord.

Christian Service

Therefore, my friends, I implore you by God's mercy to offer your very selves to him: a living sacrifice, dedicated and fit for his acceptance, the worship offered by mind and heart. Conform no longer to the pattern of this present world, but be transformed by the renewal of your minds. Then you will be able to discern the will of God, and to know what is good, acceptable, and perfect.

By authority of the grace God has given me I say to everyone among you: do not think too highly of yourself, but form a sober estimate based on the measure of faith that God has dealt to each of you. For just as in a single human body there are many limbs and organs, all with different functions, so we who are united with Christ, though many, form one body, and belong to one another as its limbs and organs.

Let us use the different gifts allotted to each of us by God's grace: the gift of inspired utterance, for example, let us use in proportion to our faith; the gift of administration to administer, the gift of teaching to teach, the gift of counselling to counsel. If you give to charity, give without grudging; if you are a leader, lead with enthusiasm; if you help others in distress, do it cheerfully.

Love in all sincerity, loathing evil and holding fast to the good. Let love of the Christian community show itself in mutual affection. Esteem others more highly than yourself.

With unflagging zeal, aglow with the Spirit, serve the Lord. Let hope keep you joyful; in trouble stand firm; persist in prayer; contribute to the needs of God's people, and practise hospitality. Call down blessings on your persecutors – blessings, not curses. Rejoice with those who rejoice, weep with those who weep. Live in agreement with one another. Do not be proud, but be ready to mix with humble people. Do not keep thinking how wise you are.

Never pay back evil for evil. Let your aims be such as all count honourable. If possible, so far as it lies with you, live at peace with all. My dear friends, do not seek revenge, but leave a place for divine retribution; for there is a text which reads, 'Vengeance is mine, says the Lord, I will repay.' But there is another text: 'If your enemy is hungry, feed him; if he is thirsty, give him a drink; by doing this you will heap live coals on his head.' Do not let evil conquer you, but use good to conquer evil.

Christian Tolerance

Accept anyone who is weak in faith without debate about his misgivings. For instance, one person may have faith strong enough to eat all kinds of food, while another who is weaker eats only vegetables. Those who eat meat must not look down on those who do not, and those who do not eat meat must not pass judgement on those who do; for God has accepted them. Who are you to pass judgement on someone else's servant?

Let us therefore cease judging one another, but rather make up our minds to place no obstacle or stumbling block in a fellow Christian's way. All that I know of the Lord Jesus convinces me that nothing is impure in itself; only, if anyone considers something impure, then for him it is impure. If your fellow Christian is outraged by what you eat, then you are no longer guided by love. Do not by your eating be the ruin of one for whom Christ died! You must not let what you think good be brought into disrepute; for the kingdom of God is not eating and drinking, but justice, peace, and joy, inspired by the Holy Spirit. Everyone who shows himself a servant of Christ in this way is acceptable to God and approved by men.

Let us, then, pursue the things that make for peace and build up the common life. Do not destroy the work of God for the sake of food. Everything is pure in itself, but it is wrong to eat if by eating you cause another to stumble. It is right to abstain from eating meat or drinking wine or from anything else which causes a fellow Christian to stumble. If you have some firm conviction, keep it between yourself and God. Anyone who can make his decision without misgivings is fortunate. But anyone who has misgivings and yet eats is guilty, because his action does not arise from conviction, and anything which does not arise from conviction is sin. Those of us who are strong must accept as our own burden the tender scruples of the weak, and not just please ourselves. Each of us must consider his neighbour and think what is for his good and will build up the common life.

Christ too did not please himself; to him apply the words of scripture, 'The reproaches of those who reproached you fell on me.' The scriptures written long ago were all written for our instruction, in order that through the encouragement they give us we may maintain our hope with perseverance. And may God, the source of all perseverance and all encouragement, grant that you may agree with one another after the manner of Christ Jesus, and so with one mind and one voice may praise the God and Father of our Lord Jesus Christ.

In a word, accept one another as Christ accepted us, to the glory of God.

The Wisdom of God

The message of the cross is sheer folly to those on the way to destruction, but to us, who are on the way to salvation, it is the power of God. Scripture says, 'I will destroy the wisdom of the wise, and bring to nothing the cleverness of the clever.' Where is your wise man now, your man of learning, your subtle debater of this present age? God has made the wisdom of this world look foolish! As God in his wisdom ordained, the world failed to find him by its wisdom, and he chose by the folly of the gospel to save those who have faith. Jews demand signs, Greeks look for wisdom, but we proclaim Christ nailed to the cross; and though this is an offence to Jews and folly to Gentiles, yet to those who are called, Jews and Greeks alike, he is the power of God and the wisdom of God.

The folly of God is wiser than human wisdom, and the weakness of God stronger than human strength. My friends, think what sort of people you are, whom God has called. Few of you are wise by any human standard, few powerful or of noble birth. Yet, to shame the wise, God has chosen what the world counts folly, and to shame what is strong, God has chosen what the world counts weakness. He has chosen things without rank or standing in the world, mere nothings, to overthrow the existing order. So no place is left for any human pride in the presence of God. By God's act you are in Christ Jesus; God has made him our wisdom, and in him we have our righteousness, our holiness, our liberation.

None of the powers that rule the world has known that wisdom; if they had, they would not have crucified the Lord of glory. Scripture speaks of 'things beyond our seeing, things beyond our hearing, things beyond our imagining, all prepared by God for those who love him'; and these are what God has revealed to us through the Spirit. For the Spirit explores everything, even the depths of God's own nature. Who knows what a human being is but the human spirit within him? In the same way, only the Spirit of God knows what God is. And we have received this Spirit from God, not the spirit of the world, so that we may know all that God has lavished on us; and, because we are interpreting spiritual truths to those who have the Spirit, we speak of these gifts of God in words taught us not by our human wisdom but by the Spirit. An unspiritual person refuses what belongs to the Spirit of God; it is folly to him; he cannot grasp it, because it needs to be judged in the light of the Spirit. But a spiritual person can judge the worth of everything, yet is not himself subject to judgement by others. Scripture indeed asks, 'Who can know the mind of the Lord or be his counsellor?' Yet we possess the mind of Christ.

The Gift of Love

I may speak in tongues of men or of angels, but if I have no love, I am a sounding gong or a clanging cymbal. I may have the gift of prophecy and the knowledge of every hidden truth; I may have faith enough to move mountains; but if I have no love, I am nothing. I may give all I possess to the needy, I may give my body to be burnt, but if I have no love, I gain nothing by it.

Love is patient and kind. Love envies no one, is never boastful, never conceited, never rude; love is never selfish, never quick to take offence. Love keeps no score of wrongs, takes no pleasure in the sins of others, but delights in the truth. There is nothing love cannot face; there is no limit to its faith, its hope, its endurance.

Love will never come to an end. Prophecies will cease; tongues of ecstasy will fall silent; knowledge will vanish. For our knowledge and our prophecy alike are partial, and the partial vanishes when wholeness comes. When I was a child I spoke like a child, thought like a child, reasoned like a child; but when I grew up I finished with childish things. At present we see only puzzling reflections in a mirror, but one day we shall see face to face.

My knowledge now is partial; then it will be whole, like God's knowledge of me. There are three things that last for ever: faith, hope, and love; and the greatest of the three is love.

The Resurrection of the Dead

And now, my friends, I must remind you of the gospel that I preached to you. First and foremost, I handed on to you the tradition I had received: that Christ died for our sins, in accordance with the scriptures; that he was buried; that he was raised to life on the third day, in accordance with the scriptures; and that he appeared to Cephas, and afterwards to the Twelve. Then he appeared to over five hundred of our brothers at once, most of whom are still alive, though some have died. Then he appeared to James, and afterwards to all the apostles.

Last of all he appeared to me too; it was like a sudden, abnormal birth. For I am the least of the apostles, indeed not fit to be called an apostle, because I had persecuted the church of God. However, by God's grace I am what I am, and his grace to me has not proved vain; in my labours I have outdone them all – not I, indeed, but the grace of God working with me. But no matter whether it was I or they! This is what we all proclaim, and this is what you believed.

Now if this is what we proclaim, that Christ was raised from the dead, how can some of you say there is no resurrection of the dead? If there is no resurrection, then Christ was not raised; and if Christ was not raised, then our gospel is null and void, and so too is your faith; and we turn out to have given false evidence about God, because we bore witness that he raised Christ to life, whereas, if the dead are not raised, he did not raise him. For if the dead are not raised, it follows that Christ was not raised; and if Christ was not raised, your faith has nothing to it and you are still in your old state of sin. It follows also that those who have died within Christ's fellowship are utterly lost. If it is for this life only that Christ has given us hope, we of all people are most to be pitied.

But the truth is, Christ was raised to life – the firstfruits of the harvest of the dead. For since it was a man who brought death into the world, a man also brought resurrection of the dead. As in Adam all die, so in Christ all will be brought to life; but each in proper order: Christ the firstfruits, and afterwards, at his coming, those who belong to Christ. Then comes the end, when he delivers up the kingdom to God the Father, after deposing every sovereignty, authority, and power. For he is destined to reign until God has put all enemies under his feet; and the last enemy to be deposed is death. Scripture says, 'He has put all things in subjection under his feet.' But in saying 'all things', it clearly means to exclude God who made all things subject to him; and when all things are subject to him, then the Son himself will also be made subject to God who made all things subject to him, and thus God will be all in all.

But, you may ask, how are the dead raised? In what kind of body? What stupid questions! The seed you sow does not come to life unless it has first died; and what you sow is not the body that shall be, but a bare grain, of wheat perhaps, or something else; and God gives it the body of his choice, each seed its own particular body. All flesh is not the same: there is human flesh, flesh of beasts, of birds, and of fishes – all different. There are heavenly bodies and earthly bodies; and the splendour of the heavenly bodies is one thing, the splendour of the earthly another. The sun has a splendour of its own, the moon another splendour, and the stars yet another; and one star differs from another in brightness. So it is with the resurrection of the dead: what is sown as a perishable thing is raised imperishable. Sown in humiliation, it is raised in glory; sown in weakness, it is raised in power; sown a physical body, it is raised a spiritual body.

If there is such a thing as a physical body, there is also a spiritual body. It is in this sense that scripture says, 'The first man, Adam, became a living creature,' whereas the last Adam has become a life-giving spirit. Observe, the spiritual does not come first; the physical body comes first, and then the spiritual. The first man is from earth, made of dust: the second man is from heaven. The man made of dust is the pattern of all who are made of dust, and the heavenly man is the pattern of all the heavenly. As we have worn the likeness of the man made of dust, so we shall wear the likeness of the heavenly man.

What I mean, my friends, is this: flesh and blood can never possess the kingdom of God, the perishable cannot possess the imperishable. Listen! I will unfold a mystery: we shall not all die, but we shall all be changed in a flash, in the twinkling of an eye, at the last trumpet-call. For the trumpet will sound, and the dead will rise imperishable, and we shall be changed. This perishable body must be clothed with the imperishable, and what is mortal with immortality. And when this perishable body has been clothed with the imperishable and our mortality has been clothed with immortality, then the saying of scripture will come true: 'Death is swallowed up; victory is won!' 'O Death, where is your victory? O Death, where is your sting?' The sting of death is sin, and sin gains its power from the law. But thanks be to God! He gives us victory through our Lord Jesus Christ.

The Glory of Christ

There is no question of our having sufficient power in ourselves: we cannot claim anything as our own. The power we have comes from God; it is he who has empowered us as ministers of a new covenant, not written but spiritual; for the written law condemns to death, but the Spirit gives life.

The ministry that brought death, and that was engraved in written form on stone, was inaugurated with such glory that the Israelites could not keep their eyes on Moses, even though the glory on his face was soon to fade. How much greater, then, must be the glory of the ministry of the Spirit! If glory accompanied the ministry that brought condemnation, how much richer in glory must be the ministry that brings acquittal! Indeed, the glory that once was is now no glory at all; it is outshone by a still greater glory. For if what was to fade away had its glory, how much greater is the glory of what endures!

With such a hope as this we speak out boldly; it is not for us to do as Moses did: he put a veil over his face to keep the Israelites from gazing at the end of what was fading away. In any case their minds had become closed, for that same veil is there to this very day when the lesson is read from the old covenant; and it is never lifted, because only in Christ is it taken away. Indeed to this very day, every time the law of Moses is read, a veil lies over the mind of the hearer. But (as scripture says) 'Whenever he turns to the Lord the veil is removed.' Now the Lord of whom this passage speaks is the Spirit; and where the Spirit of the Lord is, there is liberty. And because for us there is no veil over the face, we all see as in a mirror the glory of the Lord, and we are being transformed into his likeness with ever-increasing glory, through the power of the Lord who is the Spirit.

Since God in his mercy has given us this ministry, we never lose heart. We have renounced the deeds that people hide for very shame; we do not practise cunning or distort the word of God. It is by declaring the truth openly that we recommend ourselves to the conscience of our fellow men in the sight of God. If our gospel is veiled at all, it is veiled only for those on the way to destruction; their unbelieving minds are so blinded by the god of this passing age that the gospel of the glory of Christ, who is the image of God, cannot dawn upon them and bring them light. It is not ourselves that we proclaim; we proclaim Christ Jesus as Lord, and ourselves as your servants for Jesus's sake. For the God who said, 'Out of darkness light shall shine,' has caused his light to shine in our hearts, the light which is knowledge of the glory of God in the face of Jesus Christ.

But we have only earthenware jars to hold this treasure, and this proves that such transcendent power does not come from us; it is God's alone.

The New Humanity

No wonder we do not lose heart! Though our outward humanity is in decay, yet day by day we are inwardly renewed. Our troubles are slight and short-lived, and their outcome is an eternal glory which far outweighs them, provided our eyes are fixed, not on the things that are seen, but on the things that are unseen; for what is seen is transient, what is unseen is eternal. We know that if the earthly frame that houses us today is demolished, we possess a building which God has provided – a house not made by human hands, eternal and in heaven. In this present body we groan, yearning to be covered by our heavenly habitation put on over this one, in the hope that, being thus clothed, we shall not find ourselves naked. We groan indeed, we who are enclosed within this earthly frame; we are oppressed because we do not want to have the old body stripped off. What we want is to be covered by the new body put on over it, so that our mortality may be absorbed into life immortal. It is for this destiny that God himself has been shaping us; and as a pledge of it he has given us the Spirit.

Therefore we never cease to be confident. We know that so long as we are at home in the body we are exiles from the Lord; faith is our guide, not sight. We are confident, I say, and would rather be exiled from the body and make our home with the Lord. That is why it is our ambition, wherever we are, at home or in exile, to be acceptable to him. For we must all have our lives laid open before the tribunal of Christ, where each must receive what is due to him for his conduct in the body, good or bad.

For the love of Christ controls us once we have reached the conclusion that one man died for all and therefore all mankind has died. He died for all so that those who live should cease to live for themselves, and should live for him who for their sake died and was raised to life. With us therefore worldly standards have ceased to count in our estimate of anyone; even if once they counted in our understanding of Christ, they do so now no longer. For anyone united to Christ, there is a new creation: the old order has gone; a new order has already begun.

All this has been the work of God. He has reconciled us to himself through Christ, and has enlisted us in this ministry of reconciliation: God was in Christ reconciling the world to himself, no longer holding people's misdeeds against them.

The grace of the Lord Jesus Christ, and the love of God, and the fellowship of the Holy Spirit, be with you all.

The Guidance of the Spirit

You, my friends, were called to be free; only beware of turning your freedom into licence for your unspiritual nature. Instead, serve one another in love; for the whole law is summed up in a single commandment: 'Love your neighbour as yourself.' But if you go on fighting one another, tooth and nail, all you can expect is mutual destruction.

What I mean is this: be guided by the Spirit and you will not gratify the desires of your unspiritual nature. That nature sets its desires against the Spirit, while the Spirit fights against it. They are in conflict with one another so that you cannot do what you want. But if you are led by the Spirit, you are not subject to law.

Anyone can see the behaviour that belongs to the unspiritual nature: fornication, indecency, and debauchery; idolatry and sorcery; quarrels, a contentious temper, envy, fits of rage, selfish ambitions, dissensions, party intrigues, and jealousies; drinking bouts, orgies, and the like. I warn you, as I warned you before, that no one who behaves like that will ever inherit the kingdom of God.

But the harvest of the Spirit is love, joy, peace, patience, kindness, goodness, fidelity, gentleness, and self-control. Against such things there is no law. Those who belong to Christ Jesus have crucified the old nature with its passions and desires. If the Spirit is the source of our life, let the Spirit also direct its course.

We must not be conceited, inciting one another to rivalry, jealous of one another. If anyone is caught doing something wrong, you, my friends, who live by the Spirit must gently set him right. Look to yourself, each one of you: you also may be tempted. Carry one another's burdens, and in this way you will fulfil the law of Christ.

If anyone imagines himself to be somebody when he is nothing, he is deluding himself. Each of you should examine his own conduct, and then he can measure his achievement by comparing himself with himself and not with anyone else; for everyone has his own burden to bear.

When anyone is under instruction in the faith, he should give his teacher a share of whatever good things he has.

Make no mistake about this: God is not to be fooled; everyone reaps what he sows. If he sows in the field of his unspiritual nature, he will reap from it a harvest of corruption; but if he sows in the field of the Spirit, he will reap from it a harvest of eternal life. Let us never tire of doing good, for if we do not slacken our efforts we shall in due time reap our harvest. Therefore, as opportunity offers, let us work for the good of all, especially members of the household of the faith.

The Secret Purpose of God

Blessed be the God and Father of our Lord Jesus Christ, who has conferred on us in Christ every spiritual blessing in the heavenly realms. Before the foundation of the world he chose us in Christ to be his people, to be without blemish in his sight, to be full of love; and he predestined us to be adopted as his children through Jesus Christ. This was his will and pleasure in order that the glory of his gracious gift, so graciously conferred on us in his Beloved, might redound to his praise. In Christ our release is secured and our sins forgiven through the shedding of his blood. In the richness of his grace God has lavished on us all wisdom and insight. He has made known to us his secret purpose, in accordance with the plan which he determined beforehand in

Christ, to be put into effect when the time was ripe: namely, that the universe, everything in heaven and on earth, might be brought into a unity in Christ.

With this in mind, then, I kneel in prayer to the Father, from whom every family in heaven and on earth takes its name, that out of the treasures of his glory he may grant you inward strength and power through his Spirit, that through faith Christ may dwell in your hearts in love. With deep roots and firm foundations may you, in company with all God's people, be strong to grasp what is the breadth and length and height and depth of Christ's love, and to know it, though it is beyond knowledge. So may you be filled with the very fullness of God.

Now to him who is able through the power which is at work among us to do immeasurably more than all we can ask or conceive, to him be glory in the church and in Christ Jesus from generation to generation for evermore! Amen.

Living the Christian Life

I implore you then – I, a prisoner for the Lord's sake: as God has called you, live up to your calling. Be humble always and gentle, and patient too, putting up with one another's failings in the spirit of love. Spare no effort to make fast with bonds of peace the unity which the Spirit gives. There is one body and one Spirit, just as there is one hope held out in God's call to you; one Lord, one faith, one baptism; one God and Father of all, who is over all and through all and in all.

Let no offensive talk pass your lips, only what is good and helpful to the occasion, so that it brings a blessing to those who hear it. Do not grieve the Holy Spirit of God, for that Spirit is the seal with which you were marked for the day of final liberation. Have done with all spite and bad temper, with rage, insults, and slander, with evil of any kind. Be generous to one another, tender-hearted, forgiving one another as God in Christ forgave you.

In a word, as God's dear children, you must be like him. Live in love as Christ loved you and gave himself up on your behalf, an offering and sacrifice whose fragrance is pleasing to God.

Finally, find your strength in the Lord, in his mighty power. Put on the full armour provided by God, so that you may be able to stand firm against the stratagems of the devil. For our struggle is not against human foes, but against cosmic powers, against the authorities and potentates of this dark age, against the super-human forces of evil in the heavenly realms. Therefore, take up the armour of God; then you will be able to withstand them on the evil day and, after doing your utmost, to stand your ground. Stand fast, I say. Fasten on the belt of truth; for a breastplate put on integrity; let the shoes on your feet be the gospel of peace, to give you firm footing; and, with all these, take up the great shield of faith, with which you will be able to quench all the burning arrows of the evil one. Accept salvation as your helmet, and the sword which the Spirit gives you, the word of God. Constantly ask God's help in prayer, and pray always in the power of the Spirit. To this end keep watch and persevere, always interceding for all God's people.

Spiritual Unity in Christ

If then our common life in Christ yields anything to stir the heart, any consolation of love, any participation in the Spirit, any warmth of affection or compassion, fill up my cup of happiness by thinking and feeling alike, with the same love for one another and a common attitude of mind. Leave no room for selfish ambition and vanity, but humbly reckon others better than yourselves. Look to each other's interests and not merely to your own.

Take to heart among yourselves what you find in Christ Jesus: 'He was in the form of God; yet he laid no claim to equality with God, but made himself nothing, assuming the form of a slave. Bearing the human likeness, sharing the human lot, he humbled himself, and was obedient, even to the point of death, death on a cross! Therefore God raised him to the heights and bestowed on him the name above all names, that at the name of Jesus every knee should bow – in heaven, on earth, and in the depths – and every tongue acclaim, 'Jesus Christ is Lord,' to the glory of God the Father.'

So you too, my friends, must be obedient, as always; even more, now that I am absent, than when I was with you. You must work out your own salvation in fear and trembling; for it is God who works in you, inspiring both the will and the deed, for his own chosen purpose.

Do everything without grumbling or argument. Show your-selves innocent and above reproach, faultless children of God in a crooked and depraved generation, in which you shine like stars in a dark world and proffer the word of life. Then you will be my pride on the day of Christ, proof that I did not run my race in vain or labour in vain. But if my life-blood is to be poured out to complete the sacrifice and offering up of your faith, I rejoice and share my joy with you all. You too must rejoice and share your joy with me.

The Lord is near; do not be anxious, but in everything make your requests known to God in prayer and petition with thanksgiving. Then the peace of God, which is beyond all understanding, will guard your hearts and your thoughts in Christ Jesus.

And now, my friends, all that is true, all that is noble, all that is just and pure, all that is lovable and attractive, whatever is excellent and admirable – fill your thoughts with these things.

Put into practice the lessons I taught you, the tradition I have passed on, all that you heard me say or saw me do; and the God of peace will be with you.

The Supremacy of Christ

We pray that you may bear fruit in active goodness of every kind, and grow in knowledge of God. In his glorious might may he give you ample strength to meet with fortitude and patience whatever comes; and to give joyful thanks to the Father who has made you fit to share the heritage of God's people in the realm of light.

He rescued us from the domain of darkness and brought us into the kingdom of his dear Son, through whom our release is secured and our sins are forgiven. He is the image of the invisible God; his is the primacy over all creation. In him everything in heaven and on earth was created, not only things visible but also the invisible orders of thrones, sovereignties, authorities, and powers: the whole universe has been created through him and for him. He exists before all things, and all things are held together in him. He is the head of the body, the church. He is its origin, the first to return from the dead, to become in all things supreme. For in him God in all his fullness chose to dwell, and through him to reconcile all things to himself, making peace through the shedding of his blood on the cross – all things, whether on earth or in heaven.

Formerly you yourselves were alienated from God, his enemies in heart and mind, as your evil deeds showed. But now by

Christ's death in his body of flesh and blood God has reconciled you to himself, so that he may bring you into his own presence, holy and without blame or blemish. Yet you must persevere in faith, firm on your foundations and never to be dislodged from the hope offered in the gospel you accepted.

Therefore, since you have accepted Christ Jesus as Lord, live in union with him. Be rooted in him, be built in him, grow strong in the faith as you were taught; let your hearts overflow with thankfulness. Be on your guard; let no one capture your minds with hollow and delusive speculations, based on traditions of human teaching and centred on the elemental spirits of the universe and not on Christ.

For it is in Christ that the Godhead in all its fullness dwells embodied, it is in him you have been brought to fulfilment. Every power and authority in the universe is subject to him as head.

Were you not raised to life with Christ? Then aspire to the realm above, where Christ is, seated at God's right hand, and fix your thoughts on that higher realm, not on this earthly life. You died; and now your life lies hidden with Christ in God. When Christ, who is our life, is revealed, then you too will be revealed with him in glory.

The New Nature

So put to death those parts of you which belong to the earth – fornication, indecency, lust, evil desires, and the ruthless greed which is nothing less than idolatry; on these divine retribution falls. This is the way you yourselves once lived; but now have done with rage, bad temper, malice, slander, filthy talk – banish them all from your lips! Do not lie to one another, now that you have discarded the old human nature and the conduct that goes with it, and have put on the new nature which is constantly being renewed in the image of its Creator and brought to know God. There is no question here of Greek and Jew, circumcised and uncircumcised, barbarian, Scythian, slave and freeman; but Christ is all, and is in all.

Put on, then, garments that suit God's chosen and beloved people: compassion, kindness, humility, gentleness, patience. Be tolerant with one another and forgiving, if any of you has cause for complaint: you must forgive as the Lord forgave you. Finally, to bind everything together and complete the whole, there must be love. Let Christ's peace be arbiter in your decisions, the peace to which you were called as members of a single body. Always be thankful. Let the gospel of Christ dwell among you in all its richness; teach and instruct one another with all the wisdom it gives you. With psalms and hymns and spiritual songs, sing from the heart in gratitude to God. Let every word and action, everything you do, be in the name of the Lord Jesus, and give thanks through him to God the Father.

The Christian Hope

We wish you not to remain in ignorance, friends, about those who sleep in death; you should not grieve like the rest of mankind, who have no hope. We believe that Jesus died and rose again; so too will God bring those who died as Christians to be with Jesus.

This we tell you as a word from the Lord: those of us who are still alive when the Lord comes will have no advantage over those who have died; when the command is given, when the archangel's voice is heard, when God's trumpet sounds, then the Lord himself will descend from heaven; first the Christian dead will rise, then we who are still alive shall join them, caught up in clouds to meet the Lord in the air. Thus we shall always be with the Lord. Console one another, then, with these words.

About dates and times, my friends, there is no need to write to you, for you yourselves know perfectly well that the day of the Lord comes like a thief in the night. While they are saying, 'All is peaceful, all secure,' destruction is upon them, sudden as the pangs that come on a woman in childbirth; and there will be no escape. But you, friends, are not in the dark; the day will not come upon you like a thief. You are all children of light, children of day. We do not belong to night and darkness, and we must not sleep like the rest, but keep awake and sober. Sleepers sleep at night, and drunkards get drunk at night, but we, who belong to the daylight, must keep sober, armed with the breastplate of faith and love, and the hope of salvation for a helmet. God has not destined us for retribution, but for the full attainment of salvation through our Lord Jesus Christ. He died for us so that awake or asleep we might live in company with him. Therefore encourage one another, build one another up – as indeed you do.

May God himself, the God of peace, make you holy through and through, and keep you sound in spirit, soul, and body, free of any fault when our Lord Jesus Christ comes. He who calls you keeps faith; he will do it.

The Second Coming of Christ

Now about the coming of our Lord Jesus Christ, when he is to gather us to himself: I beg you, my friends, do not suddenly lose your heads, do not be alarmed by any prophetic utterance, any pronouncement, or any letter purporting to come from us, alleging that the day of the Lord is already here. Let no one deceive you in any way. That day cannot come before the final rebellion against God, when wickedness will be revealed in human form, the man doomed to destruction. He is the adversary who raises himself up against every so-called god or object of worship, and even enthrones himself in God's temple claiming to be God. Do you not remember that I told you this while I was still with you? You know, too, about the restraining power which ensures that he will be revealed only at his appointed time; for already the secret forces of wickedness are at work, secret only for the present until the restraining hand is removed from the scene. Then he will be revealed, the wicked one whom the Lord Jesus will destroy with the breath of his mouth and annihilate by the radiance of his presence. The coming of the wicked one is the work of Satan; it will be attended by all the powerful signs and miracles that falsehood can devise, all the deception that sinfulness can impose on those doomed to destruction, because they did not open their minds to love of the truth and so find salvation. That is why God puts them under a compelling delusion, which makes them believe what is false, so that all who have not believed the truth but made sinfulness their choice may be brought to judgement.

Spiritual Truth and Discipline

The Spirit explicitly warns us that in time to come some will forsake the faith and surrender their minds to subversive spirits and demon-inspired doctrines, through the plausible falsehoods of those whose consciences have been permanently branded. They will forbid marriage, and insist on abstinence from foods which God created to be enjoyed with thanksgiving by believers who have come to knowledge of the truth. Everything that God has created is good, and nothing is to be rejected provided it is accepted with thanksgiving, for it is then made holy by God's word and by prayer.

By offering such advice as this to the brotherhood you will prove to be a good servant of Christ Jesus, nurtured in the precepts of our faith and of the sound instruction which you have followed. Have nothing to do with superstitious myths, mere old wives' tales. Keep yourself in training for the practice of religion; for while the training of the body brings limited benefit, the benefits of religion are without limit, since it holds out promise not only for this life but also for the life to come. Here is a saying you may trust, one that merits full acceptance. 'This is why we labour and struggle, because we have set our hope on the living God, who is the Saviour of all' – the Saviour, above all, of believers.

We brought nothing into this world, and we can take nothing out; if we have food and clothing let us rest content. Those who want to be rich fall into temptations and snares and into many foolish and harmful desires which plunge people into ruin and destruction. The love of money is the root of all evil, and in pursuit of it some have wandered from the faith and spiked themselves on many a painful thorn.

But you, man of God, must shun all that, and pursue justice, piety, integrity, love, fortitude, and gentleness. Run the great race of faith and take hold of eternal life, for to this you were called, when you confessed your faith nobly before many witnesses. Now in the presence of God, who gives life to all things, and of Jesus Christ, who himself made that noble confession in his testimony before Pontius Pilate, I charge you to obey your orders without fault or failure until the appearance of our Lord Jesus Christ which God will bring about in his own good time. He is the blessed and only Sovereign, King of kings and Lord of lords; he alone possesses immortality, dwelling in unapproachable light; him no one has ever seen or can ever see; to him be honour and dominion for ever! Amen.

True Christianity

Turn from the wayward passions of youth, and pursue justice, integrity, love, and peace together with all who worship the Lord in singleness of mind; have nothing to do with foolish and wild speculations. You know they breed quarrels, and a servant of the Lord must not be quarrelsome; he must be kindly towards all. He should be a good teacher, tolerant, and gentle when he must discipline those who oppose him. God may then grant them a change of heart and lead them to recognize the truth; thus they may come to their senses and escape from the devil's snare in which they have been trapped and held at his will.

Remember, the final age of this world is to be a time of turmoil! People will love nothing but self and money; they will be boastful, arrogant, and abusive; disobedient to parents, devoid of gratitude, piety, and natural affection; they will be implacable in their hatreds, scandalmongers, uncontrolled and violent, hostile to all goodness, perfidious, foolhardy, swollen with self-importance. They will love their pleasures more than their God. While preserving the outward form of religion, they are a standing denial of its power.

But you, my son, have observed closely my teaching and manner of life, my resolution, my faithfulness, patience, and spirit of love, and my fortitude under persecution and suffering – all I went through at Antioch, at Iconium, at Lystra, and the persecutions I endured; and from all of them the Lord rescued me. Persecution will indeed come to everyone who wants to live a godly life as a follower of Christ Jesus, whereas evildoers and charlatans will progress from bad to worse, deceiving and deceived. But for your part, stand by the truths you have learned and are assured of. Remember from whom you learned them; remember that from early childhood you have been familiar with the sacred writings which have power to make you wise and lead you to salvation through faith in Christ Jesus. All inspired scripture has its use for teaching the truth and refuting error, or for reformation of manners and discipline in right living, so that the man of God may be capable and equipped for good work of every kind.

As for me, my life is already being poured out on the altar, and the hour for my departure is upon me. I have run the great race, I have finished the course, I have kept the faith. And now there awaits me the garland of righteousness which the Lord, the righteous Judge, will award to me on the great day, and not to me alone, but to all who have set their hearts on his coming appearance.

The Grace of God
The grace of God has dawned upon the world with healing for all mankind; and by it we are disciplined to renounce godless ways and worldly desires, and to live a life of temperance, honesty, and

godliness in the present age, looking forward to the happy fulfilment of our hope when the splendour of our great God and Saviour Christ Jesus will appear. He it is who sacrificed himself for us, to set us free from all wickedness and to make us his own people, pure and eager to do good.

There was a time when we too were lost in folly and disobedience and were slaves to passions and pleasures of every kind. Our days were passed in malice and envy; hateful ourselves, we loathed one another. 'But when the kindness and generosity of God our Saviour dawned upon the world, then, not for any good deeds of our own, but because he was merciful, he saved us through the water of rebirth and the renewing power of the Holy Spirit, which he lavished upon us through Jesus Christ our Saviour, so that, justified by his grace, we might in hope become heirs to eternal life.' That is a saying you may trust.

More than a Slave

I thank my God always when I mention you in my prayers, for I hear of your love and faith towards the Lord Jesus and for all God's people. My prayer is that the faith you hold in common with us may deepen your understanding of all the blessings which belong to us as we are brought closer to Christ. Your love has brought me much joy and encouragement; through you God's people have been much refreshed.

Accordingly, although in Christ I might feel free to dictate where your duty lies, yet, because of that same love, I would rather appeal to you. Ambassador as I am of Christ Jesus, and now his prisoner, I, Paul, appeal to you about my child, whose father I have become in this prison. I mean Onesimus, once so useless to you, but now useful indeed, both to you and to me. In sending him back to you I am sending my heart. I should have liked to keep him with me, to look after me on your behalf, here in prison for the gospel, but I did not want to do anything without your consent, so that your kindness might be a matter not of compulsion, but of your own free will. Perhaps this is why you lost him for a time to receive him back for good – no longer as a slave, but as more than a slave: as a dear brother, very dear to me, and still dearer to you, both as a man and as a Christian.

37 | SELECTIONS FROM OTHER EARLY CHRISTIAN LETTERS

The Great High Priest

When in times past God spoke to our forefathers, he spoke in many and varied ways through the prophets. But in this the final age he has spoken to us in his Son, whom he has appointed heir of all things; and through him he created the universe. He is the radiance of God's glory, the stamp of God's very being, and he sustains the universe by his word of power. When he had brought about purification from sins, he took his seat at the right hand of God's Majesty on high, raised as far above the angels as the title he has inherited is superior to theirs.

Since therefore we have a great high priest who has passed through the heavens, Jesus the Son of God, let us hold fast to the faith we profess. Ours is not a high priest unable to sympathize with our weaknesses, but one who has been tested in every way as we are, only without sinning. Let us therefore boldly approach the throne of grace, in order that we may receive mercy and find grace to give us timely help.

For every high priest is taken from among men and appointed their representative before God, to offer gifts and sacrifices for sins. He is able to bear patiently with the ignorant and erring, since he too is beset by weakness; and because of this he is bound to make sin-offerings for himself as well as for the people. Moreover nobody assumes the office on his own authority: he is called by God, just as Aaron was. So it is with Christ: he did not confer on himself the glory of becoming high priest; it was granted by God, who said to him, 'You are my son; today I have become your father.'

My main point is: this is the kind of high priest we have, and he has taken his seat at the right hand of the throne of Majesty in heaven, a minister in the real sanctuary, the tent set up by the Lord, not by man. Every high priest is appointed to offer gifts and sacrifices; hence, of necessity, this one too had something to offer. If he were on earth, he would not be a priest at all, since there are already priests to offer the gifts prescribed by the law, although the sanctuary in which they minister is only a shadowy symbol of the heavenly one. This is why Moses, when he was about to put up the tent, was instructed by God: 'See to it that you make everything according to the pattern shown you on the mountain.' But in fact the ministry which Jesus has been given is superior to theirs, for he is the mediator of a better covenant, established on better promises.

The New Covenant

Had that first covenant been faultless, there would have been no occasion to look for a second to replace it. But God finds fault with his people when he says, 'The time is coming, says the Lord, when I shall conclude a new covenant with the house of Israel and the house of Judah. I shall set my laws in their understanding and write them on their hearts; I shall be their God, and they will be my people. They will not teach one another, each saying to his fellow citizen and his brother, "Know the Lord!" For all of them will know me, high and low alike; I shall pardon their wicked deeds, and their sins I shall remember no more.' By speaking of a new covenant, he has pronounced the first one obsolete; and anything that is becoming obsolete and growing old will shortly disappear.

The first covenant had its ordinances governing divine service and its sanctuary, but it was an earthly sanctuary. But now Christ has come, high priest of good things already in being. The tent of his priesthood is a greater and more perfect one, not made by human hands, that is, not belonging to this created world; the blood of his sacrifice is his own blood, not the blood of goats and calves; and thus he has entered the sanctuary once for all and secured an eternal liberation. If sprinkling the blood of goats and bulls and the ashes of a heifer consecrates those who have been defiled and restores their ritual purity, how much greater is the power of the blood of Christ; through the eternal Spirit he offered himself without blemish to God. His blood will cleanse our conscience from the deadness of our former ways to serve the living God.

Heroes of Faith

Faith gives substance to our hopes and convinces us of realities we do not see.

It was for their faith that the people of old won God's approval.

By faith we understand that the universe was formed by God's command, so that the visible came forth from the invisible.

By faith Abel offered a greater sacrifice than Cain's; because of his faith God approved his offerings and attested his goodness; and through his faith, though he is dead, he continues to speak.

By faith Enoch was taken up to another life without passing through death; he was not to be found, because God had taken him, and it is the testimony of scripture that before he was taken he had pleased God. But without faith it is impossible to please him, for whoever comes to God must believe that he exists and rewards those who seek him.

By faith Noah took good heed of the divine warning about the unseen future, and built an ark to save his household. Through his faith he put the whole world in the wrong, and made good his own claim to the righteousness which comes of faith.

By faith Abraham obeyed the call to leave his home for a land which he was to receive as a possession; he went away without knowing where he was to go. By faith he settled as an alien in the land which had been promised him, living in tents with Isaac and Jacob, who were heirs with him to the same promise. For he was looking forward to a city with firm foundations, whose architect and builder is God.

By faith even Sarah herself was enabled to conceive, though she was past the age, because she judged that God who had promised would keep faith. Therefore from one man, a man as good as dead, there sprang descendants as numerous as the stars in the heavens or the countless grains of sand on the seashore.

All these died in faith. Although they had not received the things promised, yet they had seen them far ahead and welcomed them, and acknowledged themselves to be strangers and aliens without fixed abode on earth. Those who speak in that way show plainly that they are looking for a country of their own. If their thoughts had been with the country they had left, they could have found opportunity to return. Instead, we find them longing for a better country, a heavenly one. That is why God is not ashamed to be called their God; for he has a city ready for them.

Need I say more? Time is too short for me to tell the stories of Gideon, Barak, Samson, and Jephthah, of David and Samuel and the prophets. Through faith they overthrew kingdoms, established justice, saw God's promises fulfilled. They shut the mouths of lions, quenched the fury of fire, escaped death by the sword. Their weakness was turned to strength, they grew powerful in war, they put foreign armies to rout. Women received back their dead raised to life. Others were tortured to death, refusing release, to win resurrection to a better life. Others, again, had to face jeers and flogging, even fetters and prison bars. They were stoned to death, they were sawn in two, they were put to the sword, they went about clothed in skins of sheep or goats, deprived, oppressed, ill-treated. The world was not worthy of them. They were refugees in deserts and on the mountains, hiding in caves and holes in the ground. All these won God's approval because of their faith; and yet they did not receive what was promised, because, with us in mind, God had made a better plan, that only with us should they reach perfection.

Disciplines of the Christian Life
With this great cloud of witnesses around us, therefore, we too must throw off every encumbrance and the sin that all too readily restricts us, and run with resolution the race which lies ahead of us, our eyes fixed on Jesus, the pioneer and perfecter of faith. For the sake of the joy that lay ahead of him, he endured the cross, ignoring its disgrace, and has taken his seat at the right hand of the throne of God.

Think of him who submitted to such opposition from sinners: that will help you not to lose heart and grow faint. In the struggle against sin, you have not yet resisted to the point of shedding your blood. You have forgotten the exhortation which addresses you as sons:

'My son, do not think lightly of the Lord's discipline,
or be discouraged when he corrects you;
for whom the Lord loves he disciplines;
he chastises every son whom he acknowledges.'

You must endure it as discipline: God is treating you as sons. Can anyone be a son and not be disciplined by his father? If you escape the discipline in which all sons share, you must be illegitimate and not true sons. Again, we paid due respect to our human fathers who disciplined us; should we not submit even more readily to our spiritual Father, and so attain life? They disciplined us for a short time as they thought best; but he does so for our true welfare, so that we may share his holiness. Discipline, to be sure, is never pleasant; at the time it seems painful, but afterwards those who have been trained by it reap the harvest of a peaceful and upright life.

May the God of peace, who brought back from the dead our Lord Jesus, the great Shepherd of the sheep, through the blood of an eternal covenant, make you perfect in all goodness so that you may do his will; and may he create in us what is pleasing to him, through Jesus Christ, to whom be glory for ever and ever! Amen.

Faith and Works
What good is it, my friends, for someone to say he has faith when his actions do nothing to show it? Can that faith save him? Suppose a fellow Christian, whether man or woman, is in rags with not enough food for the day, and one of you says, 'Goodbye, keep warm, and have a good meal,' but does nothing to supply their bodily needs, what good is that? So with faith; if it does not lead to action, it is by itself a lifeless thing.

But someone may say: 'One chooses faith, another action.' To which I reply: 'Show me this faith you speak of with no actions to prove it, while I by my actions will prove to you my faith.' You have faith and believe that there is one God. Excellent! Even demons have faith like that, and it makes them tremble. Do you have to be told, you fool, that faith divorced from action is futile? Was it not by his action, in offering his son Isaac upon the altar, that our father Abraham was justified? Surely you can see faith was at work in his actions, and by these actions his faith was perfected? Here was fulfilment of the words of scripture: 'Abraham put his faith in God, and that faith was counted to him as righteousness,' and he was called 'God's friend'. You see then it is by action and not by faith alone that a man is justified. The same is true also of the prostitute Rahab. Was she not justified by her action in welcoming the messengers into her house and sending them away by a different route? As the body is dead when there is no breath left in it, so faith divorced from action is dead.

Self-Control

A man who never says anything wrong is perfect and is capable of controlling every part of his body. When we put a bit into a horse's mouth to make it obey our will, we can direct the whole animal. Or think of a ship: large though it may be and driven by gales, it can be steered by a very small rudder on whatever course the helmsman chooses. So with the tongue; it is small, but its pretensions are great.

What a vast amount of timber can be set ablaze by the tiniest spark! And the tongue is a fire, representing in our body the whole wicked world. It pollutes our whole being, it sets the whole course of our existence alight, and its flames are fed by hell. Beasts and birds of every kind, creatures that crawl on the ground or swim in the sea, can be subdued and have been subdued by man; but no one can subdue the tongue. It is an evil thing, restless and charged with deadly venom. We use it to praise our Lord and Father; then we use it to invoke curses on our fellow men, though they are made in God's likeness. Out of the same mouth come praise and curses. This should not be so, my friends. Does a fountain flow with both fresh and brackish water from the same outlet? My friends, can a fig tree produce olives, or a grape vine produce figs? No more can salt water produce fresh.

The Children of God

Praised be the God and Father of our Lord Jesus Christ! In his great mercy by the resurrection of Jesus Christ from the dead, he gave us new birth into a living hope, the hope of an inheritance, reserved in heaven for you, which nothing can destroy or spoil or wither. Because you put your faith in God, you are under the protection of his power until the salvation now in readiness is revealed at the end of time.

You have not seen him, yet you love him; and trusting in him now without seeing him, you are filled with a glorious joy too great for words, while you are reaping the harvest of your faith, that is, salvation for your souls. This salvation was the subject of intense search by the prophets who prophesied about the grace of God awaiting you. They tried to find out the time and the circumstances to which the spirit of Christ in them pointed, when it foretold the sufferings in Christ's cause and the glories to follow. It was disclosed to them that these matters were not for their benefit but for yours. Now they have been openly announced to you through preachers who brought you the gospel in the power of the Holy Spirit sent from heaven. These are things that angels long to glimpse.

Your minds must therefore be stripped for action and fully alert. Fix your hopes on the grace which is to be yours when Jesus Christ is revealed. Be obedient to God your Father, and do not let your characters be shaped any longer by the desires you cherished in your days of ignorance. He who called you is holy; like him, be holy in all your conduct. Does not scripture say, 'You shall be holy, for I am holy'?

If you say 'Father' to him who judges everyone impartially on the basis of what they have done, you must live in awe of him during your time on earth. You know well that it was nothing of passing value, like silver or gold, that bought your freedom from the futility of your traditional ways. You were set free by Christ's precious blood, blood like that of a lamb without mark or blemish. He was predestined before the foundation of the world, but in this last period of time he has been revealed for your sake. Through him you have come to trust in God who raised him from the dead and gave him glory, and so your faith and hope are fixed on God.

Now that you have purified your souls by obedience to the truth until you feel sincere affection towards your fellow Christians, love one another wholeheartedly with all your strength. You have been born again, not of mortal but of immortal parentage, through the living and enduring word of God.

The People of God

So come to him, to the living stone which was rejected by men but chosen by God and of great worth to him. You also, as living stones, must be built up into a spiritual temple, and form a holy priesthood to offer spiritual sacrifices acceptable to God through Jesus Christ.

It is your vocation because Christ himself suffered on your behalf, and left you an example in order that you should follow in his steps. 'He committed no sin, he was guilty of no falsehood.' When he was abused he did not retaliate, when he suffered he uttered no threats, but delivered himself up to him who judges justly. He carried our sins in his own person on the gibbet, so that we might cease to live for sin and begin to live for righteousness. By his wounds you have been healed. You were straying like sheep, but now you have turned towards the Shepherd and Guardian of your souls.

Finally, be united, all of you, in thought and feeling; be full of brotherly affection, kindly and humble. Do not repay wrong with wrong, or abuse with abuse; on the contrary, respond with blessing, for a blessing is what God intends you to receive.

Who is going to do you harm if you are devoted to what is good? Yet if you should suffer for doing right you may count yourselves happy. Have no fear of other people: do not be perturbed, but hold Christ in your hearts in reverence as Lord. Always be ready to make your defence when anyone challenges you to justify the hope which is in you. But do so with courtesy and respect, keeping your conscience clear, so that when you are abused, those who malign your Christian conduct may be put to shame. It is better to suffer for doing right, if such should be the will of God, than for doing wrong.

The Christian Calling

God's divine power has bestowed on us everything that makes for life and true religion, through our knowledge of him who called us by his own glory and goodness. In this way he has given us his promises, great beyond all price, so that through them you may escape the corruption with which lust has infected the world, and may come to share in the very being of God.

With all this in view, you should make every effort to add virtue to your faith, knowledge to virtue, self-control to knowledge, fortitude to self-control, piety to fortitude, brotherly affection to piety, and love to brotherly affection.

I shall keep reminding you of all this, although you know it and are well grounded in the truth you possess; yet I think it right to keep on reminding you as long as I still lodge in this body. I know I must soon leave it, as our Lord Jesus Christ told me. But I will do my utmost to ensure that after I am gone you will always be able to call these things to mind.

It was not on tales, however cleverly concocted, that we relied when we told you about the power of our Lord Jesus Christ and his coming; rather with our own eyes we had witnessed his majesty. He was invested with honour and glory by God the

Father, and there came to him from the sublime Presence a voice which said: 'This is my Son, my Beloved, on whom my favour rests.' We ourselves heard this voice when it came from heaven, for we were with him on the sacred mountain.

All this confirms for us the message of the prophets, to which you will do well to attend; it will go on shining like a lamp in a murky place, until day breaks and the morning star rises to illuminate your minds. But first note this: no prophetic writing is a matter for private interpretation. It was not on any human initiative that prophecy came; rather, it was under the compulsion of the Holy Spirit that people spoke as messengers of God.

Living in the Last Days

This, dear friends, is now my second letter to you. In both I have been recalling to you what you already know, to rouse you to honest thought. Remember the predictions made by God's own prophets, and the commandment given by the Lord and Saviour through your apostles.

First of all, note this: in the last days there will come scoffers who live self-indulgent lives; they will mock you and say: 'What has happened to his promised coming? Our fathers have been laid to rest, but still everything goes on exactly as it always has done since the world began.' In maintaining this they forget that there were heavens and earth long ago, created by God's word out of water and with water; and that the first world was destroyed by water, the water of the flood. By God's word the present heavens and earth are being reserved for burning; they are being kept until the day of judgement when the godless will be destroyed.

Here is something, dear friends, which you must not forget: in the Lord's sight one day is like a thousand years and a thousand years like one day. It is not that the Lord is slow in keeping his promise, as some suppose, but that he is patient with you. It is not his will that any should be lost, but that all should come to repentance.

But the day of the Lord will come like a thief. On that day the heavens will disappear with a great rushing sound, the elements will be dissolved in flames, and the earth with all that is in it will be brought to judgement. Since the whole universe is to dissolve in this way, think what sort of people you ought to be, what devout and dedicated lives you should live! Look forward to the coming of the day of God, and work to hasten it on; that day will set the heavens ablaze until they fall apart, and will melt the elements in flames. Relying on his promise we look forward to new heavens and a new earth, in which justice will be established.

In expectation of all this, my friends, do your utmost to be found at peace with him, unblemished and above reproach. Bear in mind that our Lord's patience is an opportunity for salvation, as Paul, our dear friend and brother, said when he wrote to you with the wisdom God gave him. He does the same in all his other letters, wherever he speaks about this, though they contain some obscure passages, which the ignorant and unstable misinterpret to their own ruin, as they do the other scriptures.

So, dear friends, you have been forewarned. Take care not to let these unprincipled people seduce you with their errors; do not lose your own safe foothold. But grow in grace and in the knowledge of our Lord and Saviour Jesus Christ. To him be glory both now and for all eternity!

God is Light

It was there from the beginning; we have heard it; we have seen it with our own eyes; we looked upon it, and felt it with our own hands: our theme is the Word which gives life. This life was made visible; we have seen it and bear our testimony; we declare to you the eternal life which was with the Father and was made visible to us. It is this which we have seen and heard that we declare to you also, in order that you may share with us in a common life, that life which we share with the Father and his Son Jesus Christ. We are writing this in order that our joy may be complete.

Here is the message we have heard from him and pass on to you: God is light, and in him there is no darkness at all. If we claim to be sharing in his life while we go on living in darkness, our words and our lives are a lie. But if we live in the light as he himself is in the light, then we share a common life, and the blood of Jesus his Son cleanses us from all sin.

If we claim to be sinless, we are self-deceived and the truth is not in us. If we confess our sins, he is just and may be trusted to forgive our sins and cleanse us from every kind of wrongdoing. If we say we have committed no sin, we make him out to be a liar and his word has no place in us.

Dear friends, it is no new command that I am sending you, but an old command which you have had from the beginning; the old command is the instruction which you have already received. Yet because the darkness is passing away and the true light already shining, it is a new command that I write and it is true in Christ's life and in yours.

Whoever says, 'I am in the light,' but hates his fellow Christian, is still in darkness. He who loves his fellow Christian dwells in light: there is no cause of stumbling in him. But anyone who hates his fellow is in darkness; he walks in the dark and has no idea where he is going, because the darkness has made him blind.

True Christian Love

The message you have heard from the beginning is that we should love one another. Do not be like Cain, who was a child of the evil one and murdered his brother. And why did he murder him? Because his own actions were wrong, and his brother's were right.

Friends, do not be surprised if the world hates you. We know we have crossed over from death to life, because we love our fellow Christians. Anyone who does not love is still in the realm of death, for everyone who hates a fellow Christian is a murderer, and murderers, as you know, do not have eternal life dwelling within them. This is how we know what love is: Christ gave his life for us. And we in our turn must give our lives for our fellow Christians. But if someone who possesses the good things of this world sees a fellow Christian in need and withholds compassion from him, how can it be said that the love of God dwells in him?

Children, love must not be a matter of theory or talk; it must be true love which shows itself in action. This is how we shall know that we belong to the realm of truth, and reassure ourselves in his sight where conscience condemns us; for God is greater than our conscience and knows all.

My dear friends, if our conscience does not condemn us, then we can approach God with confidence, and obtain from him whatever we ask, because we are keeping his commands and doing what he approves. His command is that we should give our allegiance to his Son Jesus Christ and love one another, as Christ commanded us. Those who keep his commands dwell in him and he dwells in them. And our certainty that he dwells in us comes from the Spirit he has given us.

God is Love

My dear friends, do not trust every spirit, but test the spirits, to see whether they are from God; for there are many false prophets about in the world. The way to recognize the Spirit of God is this: every spirit which acknowledges that Jesus Christ has come in the flesh is from God, and no spirit is from God which does not acknowledge Jesus. This is the spirit of antichrist; you have been warned that it was to come, and now here it is, in the world already!

Children, you belong to God's family, and you have the mastery over these false prophets, because God who inspires you is greater than the one who inspires the world. They belong to that world, and so does their teaching; that is why the world listens to them. But we belong to God and whoever knows God listens to us, while whoever does not belong to God refuses to listen to us. That is how we can distinguish the spirit of truth from the spirit of error.

My dear friends, let us love one another, because the source of love is God. Everyone who loves is a child of God and knows God, but the unloving know nothing of God, for God is love. This is how he showed his love among us: he sent his only Son into the world that we might have life through him. This is what love really is: not that we have loved God, but that he loved us and sent his Son as a sacrifice to atone for our sins. If God thus loved us, my dear friends, we also must love one another. God has never been seen by anyone, but if we love one another, he himself dwells in us; his love is brought to perfection within us.

This is how we know that we dwell in him and he dwells in us: he has imparted his Spirit to us. Moreover, we have seen for ourselves, and we are witnesses, that the Father has sent the Son to be the Saviour of the world. If anyone acknowledges that Jesus is God's Son, God dwells in him and he in God. Thus we have come to know and believe in the love which God has for us.

God is love; he who dwells in love is dwelling in God, and God in him. This is how love has reached its perfection among us, so that we may have confidence on the day of judgement; and this we can have, because in this world we are as he is. In love there is no room for fear; indeed perfect love banishes fear. For fear has to do with punishment, and anyone who is afraid has not attained to love in its perfection. We love because he loved us first. But if someone says, 'I love God,' while at the same time hating his fellow Christian, he is a liar. If he does not love a fellow Christian whom he has seen, he is incapable of loving God whom he has not seen. We have this command from Christ: whoever loves God must love his fellow Christian too.

Everyone who believes that Jesus is the Christ is a child of God. To love the parent means to love his child. It follows that when we love God and obey his commands we love his children too. For to love God is to keep his commands; and these are not burdensome, because every child of God overcomes the world. Now, the victory by which the world is overcome is our faith, for who is victor over the world but he who believes that Jesus is the Son of God?

Love and Truth

Do not think I am sending a new command; I am recalling the one we have had from the beginning: I ask that we love one another. What love means is to live according to the commands of God. This is the command that was given you from the beginning, to be your rule of life.

Many deceivers have gone out into the world, people who do not acknowledge Jesus Christ as coming in the flesh. Any such person is the deceiver and antichrist. See to it that you do not lose what we have worked for, but receive your reward in full.

Above all I pray that things go well with you, and that you may enjoy good health: I know it is well with your soul. I was very glad when some fellow Christians arrived and told me of your faithfulness to the truth; indeed you live by the truth. Nothing gives me greater joy than to hear that my children are living by the truth.

A Warning Against False Religion

My friends, I was fully intending to write to you about the salvation we share, when I found it necessary to take up my pen and urge you to join in the struggle for that faith which God entrusted to his people once for all. Certain individuals have wormed their way in, the very people whom scripture long ago marked down for the sentence they are now incurring. They are enemies of religion; they pervert the free favour of our God into licentiousness, disowning Jesus Christ, our only Master and Lord.

They are a set of grumblers and malcontents. They follow their lusts. Bombast comes rolling from their lips, and they court favour to gain their ends. But you, my friends, should remember the predictions made by the apostles of our Lord Jesus Christ. They said to you: 'In the final age there will be those who mock at religion and follow their own ungodly lusts.'

These people create divisions; they are worldly and unspiritual. But you, my friends, must make your most sacred faith the foundation of your lives. Continue to pray in the power of the Holy Spirit. Keep yourselves in the love of God, and look forward to the day when our Lord Jesus Christ in his mercy will give eternal life.

Now to the One who can keep you from falling and set you in the presence of his glory, jubilant and above reproach, to the only God our Saviour, be glory and majesty, power and authority, through Jesus Christ our Lord, before all time, now, and for evermore. Amen.

38 | APOCALYPSE

The Alpha and Omega

This is the revelation of Jesus Christ, which God gave him so that he might show his servants what must soon take place. He made it known by sending his angel to his servant John, who in telling all that he saw has borne witness to the word of God and to the testimony of Jesus Christ.

'I am the Alpha and the Omega,' says the Lord God, 'who is, who was, and who is to come, the sovereign Lord of all.'

I, John, your brother, who share with you in the suffering, the sovereignty, and the endurance which are ours in Jesus, was on the island called Patmos because I had preached God's word and borne my testimony to Jesus. On the Lord's day the Spirit came upon me; and I heard behind me a loud voice, like the sound of a trumpet, which said, 'Write down in a book what you see and send it to the seven churches: to Ephesus, Smyrna, Pergamum, Thyatira, Sardis, Philadelphia, and Laodicea.' I turned to see whose voice it was that spoke to me; and when I turned I saw seven lampstands of gold. Among the lamps was a figure like a man, in a robe that came to his feet, with a golden girdle round his breast. His hair was as white as snow-white wool, and his eyes flamed like fire; his feet were like burnished bronze refined in a furnace, and his voice was like the sound of a mighty torrent. In his right hand he held seven stars, and from his mouth came a sharp, two-edged sword; his face shone like the sun in full strength.

When I saw him, I fell at his feet as though I were dead. But he laid his right hand on me and said, 'Do not be afraid. I am the first and the last, and I am the living One; I was dead and now I am alive for evermore, and I hold the keys of death and Hades. Write down therefore what you have seen, what is now, and what is to take place hereafter.'

A Vision of Heaven

At once the Spirit came upon me. There in heaven stood a throne. On it sat One whose appearance was like jasper or cornelian, and round it was a rainbow, bright as an emerald. In a circle about this throne were twenty-four other thrones, and on them were seated twenty-four elders, robed in white and wearing gold crowns. From the throne came flashes of lightning and peals of thunder. Burning before the throne were seven flaming torches, the seven spirits of God, and in front of it stretched what looked like a sea of glass or a sheet of ice.

In the centre, round the throne itself, were four living creatures, covered with eyes in front and behind. The first creature was like a lion, the second like an ox, the third had a human face, and the fourth was like an eagle in flight. Each of the four living creatures had six wings, and eyes all round and inside them. Day and night unceasingly they sing:

'Holy, holy, holy is God the sovereign Lord of all, who was, and is, and is to come!'

I saw in the right hand of the One who sat on the throne a scroll with writing on both sides, and sealed with seven seals. And I saw a mighty angel proclaiming in a loud voice, 'Who is worthy to break the seals and open the scroll?' But there was no one in heaven or on earth or under the earth able to open the scroll to look inside it. And because no one was found worthy to open the scroll and look inside, I wept bitterly.

Then I saw a Lamb with the marks of sacrifice on him, standing with the four living creatures between the throne and the elders. He had seven horns and seven eyes, the eyes which are the seven spirits of God sent to every part of the world. The Lamb came and received the scroll from the right hand of the One who sat on the throne.

The Four Horsemen

I watched as the Lamb broke the first of the seven seals, and I heard one of the four living creatures say in a voice like thunder, 'Come!' There before my eyes was a white horse, and its rider held a bow. He was given a crown, and he rode forth, conquering and to conquer.

The Lamb broke the second seal, and I heard the second creature say, 'Come!' Out came another horse, which was red. Its rider was given power to take away peace from the earth that men might slaughter one another; and he was given a great sword.

He broke the third seal, and I heard the third creature say, 'Come!' There, as I looked, was a black horse, and its rider was holding in his hand a pair of scales. I heard what sounded like a voice from among the four living creatures; it said, 'A day's wage for a quart of flour, a day's wage for three quarts of barley-meal! But do not damage the olive and the vine!'

He broke the fourth seal, and I heard the fourth creature say, 'Come!' There, as I looked, was another horse, sickly pale; its rider's name was Death, and Hades followed close behind. To them was given power over a quarter of the earth, power to kill by sword and famine, by pestilence and wild beasts.

War in Heaven

After that there appeared a great sign in heaven: a woman robed with the sun, beneath her feet the moon, and on her head a crown of twelve stars. She was about to bear a child, and in the anguish of her labour she cried out to be delivered. Then a second sign appeared in heaven: a great, fiery red dragon with seven heads and ten horns. On his heads were seven diadems, and with his tail he swept down a third of the stars in the sky and hurled them to the earth. The dragon stood in front of the woman who was about to give birth, so that when her child was born he might devour it. But when she gave birth to a male child, who is destined to rule all nations with a rod of iron, the child was snatched up to God and to his throne. The woman herself fled into the wilderness, where she was to be looked after for twelve hundred and sixty days in a place prepared for her by God.

Then war broke out in heaven; Michael and his angels fought against the dragon. The dragon with his angels fought back, but he was too weak, and they lost their place in heaven. The great dragon was thrown down, that ancient serpent who led the whole world astray, whose name is the Devil, or Satan; he was thrown down to the earth, and his angels with him.

I heard a loud voice in heaven proclaim: 'This is the time of victory for our God, the time of his power and sovereignty, when his Christ comes to his rightful rule! For the accuser of our brothers, he who day and night accused them before our God, is overthrown. By the sacrifice of the Lamb and by the witness they bore, they have conquered him; faced with death they did not cling to life. Therefore rejoice, you heavens and you that dwell in them! But woe to you, earth and sea, for the Devil has come down to you in great fury, knowing that his time is short!'

When the dragon saw that he had been thrown down to the earth, he went in pursuit of the woman who had given birth to the male child. But she was given the wings of a mighty eagle, so that she could fly to her place in the wilderness where she was to be looked after for three and a half years, out of reach of the serpent. From his mouth the serpent spewed a flood of water after the woman to sweep her away with its spate. But the earth came to her rescue: it opened its mouth and drank up the river which the dragon spewed from his mouth. Furious with the woman, the dragon went off to wage war on the rest of her offspring, those who keep God's commandments and maintain their witness to Jesus. He took his stand on the seashore.

The Two Beasts
Then I saw a beast rising out of the sea. It had ten horns and seven heads; on the horns were ten diadems, and on each head was a blasphemous name. The beast I saw resembled a leopard, but its feet were like a bear's and its mouth like a lion's. The dragon conferred on it his own power, his throne, and great authority. One of the heads seemed to have been given a death blow, yet its mortal wound was healed. The whole world went after the beast in wondering admiration, and worshipped the dragon because he had conferred his authority on the beast; they worshipped the beast also. 'Who is like the beast?' they said. 'Who can fight against it?'

The beast was allowed to mouth bombast and blasphemy, and was granted permission to continue for forty-two months. It uttered blasphemies against God, reviling his name and his dwelling-place, that is, those who dwell in heaven. It was also allowed to wage war on God's people and to defeat them, and it was granted authority over every tribe, nation, language, and race.

Then I saw another beast; it came up out of the earth, and had two horns like a lamb's, but spoke like a dragon. It wielded all the authority of the first beast in its presence, and made the earth and its inhabitants worship this first beast, whose mortal wound had been healed. It worked great miracles, even making fire come down from heaven to earth, where people could see it. By the miracles it was allowed to perform in the presence of the beast it deluded the inhabitants of the earth, and persuaded them to erect an image in honour of the beast which had been wounded by the sword and yet lived. It was allowed to give breath to the image of the beast, so that it could even speak and cause all who would not worship the image to be put to death. It caused everyone, small and great, rich and poor, free man and slave, to have a mark put on his right hand or his forehead, and no one was allowed to buy or sell unless he bore this beast's mark, either name or number. (This calls for skill; let anyone who has intelligence work out the number of the beast, for the number represents a man's name, and the numerical value of its letters is six hundred and sixty-six.).

The Whore of Babylon

Then I saw in heaven another great and astonishing sign: seven angels with seven plagues, the last plagues of all, for with them the wrath of God was completed.

I saw what looked like a sea of glass shot through with fire. Standing beside it and holding the harps which God had given them were those who had been victorious against the beast, its image, and the number of its name. One of the four living creatures gave to the seven angels seven golden bowls full of the wrath of God who lives for ever. The sanctuary was filled with smoke from the glory of God and from his power, so that no one could enter it until the seven plagues of the seven angels were completed.

One of the seven angels who held the seven bowls came and spoke to me; 'Come,' he said, 'I will show you the verdict on the great whore, she who is enthroned over many waters. The kings of the earth have committed fornication with her, and people the world over have made themselves drunk on the wine of her fornication.' He carried me in spirit into the wilderness, and I saw a woman mounted on a scarlet beast which was covered with blasphemous names and had seven heads and ten horns. The woman was clothed in purple and scarlet, and decked out with gold and precious stones and pearls. In her hand she held a gold cup full of obscenities and the foulness of her fornication. Written on her forehead was a name with a secret meaning: 'Babylon the great, the mother of whores and of every obscenity on earth.' I saw that the woman was drunk with the blood of God's people, and with the blood of those who had borne their testimony to Jesus.

At the sight of her I was greatly astonished. But the angel said to me, 'Why are you astonished? I will tell you the secret of the woman and of the beast she rides, with the seven heads and the ten horns. The beast you saw was once alive, and is alive no longer, but has yet to ascend out of the abyss before going to be destroyed. All the inhabitants of the earth whose names have not been written in the book of life since the foundation of the world will be astonished to see the beast, which once was alive, and is alive no longer, and has still to appear.

'This calls for a mind with insight. The seven heads are seven hills on which the woman sits enthroned. They also represent seven kings: five have already fallen, one is now reigning, and the other has yet to come. When he does come, he is to last for only a little while. As for the beast that once was alive and is alive no longer, he is an eighth – and yet he is one of the seven, and he is going to destruction. The ten horns you saw are ten kings who have not yet begun to reign, but who for a brief hour will share royal authority with the beast. They have a single purpose and will confer their power and authority on the beast. They will wage war on the Lamb, but the Lamb will conquer them, for he is Lord of lords and King of kings, and those who are with him are called and chosen and faithful.'

He continued: 'The waters you saw, where the great whore sat enthroned, represent nations, populations, races, and languages. As for the ten horns you saw, and the beast, they will come to hate the whore. They will strip her naked and leave her destitute; they will devour her flesh and burn her up. For God has put it into their minds to carry out his purpose, by making common cause and conferring their sovereignty on the beast until God's words are fulfilled. The woman you saw is the great city that holds sway over the kings of the earth.'

After this I saw another angel coming down from heaven; he possessed great authority and the earth shone with his splendour. In a mighty voice he proclaimed, 'Fallen, fallen is Babylon the great! She has become a dwelling for demons, a haunt for every unclean spirit, for every unclean and loathsome bird. All the nations have drunk the wine of God's anger roused by her fornication; the kings of the earth have committed fornication with her, and merchants the world over have grown rich on her wealth and luxury.'

I heard another voice from heaven saying: 'Come out from her, my people, lest you have any part in her sins and you share in her plagues, for her sins are piled high as heaven, and God has not forgotten her crimes.'

The Last Judgement

I saw heaven wide open, and a white horse appeared; its rider's name was Faithful and True, for he is just in judgement and just in war. His eyes flamed like fire, and on his head were many diadems. Written on him was a name known to none but himself; he was robed in a garment dyed in blood, and he was called the Word of God. The armies of heaven followed him, riding on white horses and clothed in fine linen, white and clean. Out of his mouth came a sharp sword to smite the nations; for it is he who will rule them with a rod of iron, and tread the winepress of the fierce wrath of God the sovereign Lord. On his robe and on his thigh was written the title: 'King of kings and Lord of lords'.

I saw an angel standing in the sun. He cried aloud to all the birds flying in mid-heaven: 'Come, gather together for God's great banquet, to eat the flesh of kings, commanders, and warriors, the flesh of horses and their riders, the flesh of all, the free and the slave, the small and the great!' I saw the beast and the kings of the earth with their armies mustered to do battle against the rider and his army. The beast was taken prisoner, along with the false prophet who had worked miracles in its presence and deluded those who had received the mark of the beast and worshipped its image. The two of them were thrown alive into the lake of fire with its sulphurous flames. The rest were killed by the sword which came out of the rider's mouth, and the birds all gorged themselves on their flesh.

I saw an angel coming down from heaven with the key to the abyss and a great chain in his hand. He seized the dragon, that ancient serpent who is the Devil, or Satan, and chained him up for a thousand years; he threw him into the abyss, shutting and sealing it over him, so that he might not seduce the nations again till the thousand years were ended. After that he must be let loose for a little while.

I saw thrones, and on them sat those to whom judgement was committed. I saw the souls of those who, for the sake of God's word and their witness to Jesus, had been beheaded, those who had not worshipped the beast and its image or received its mark on forehead or hand. They came to life again and reigned with Christ for a thousand years, though the rest of the dead did not come to life until the thousand years were ended. This is the first resurrection. Blessed and holy are those who share in this first resurrection! Over them the second death has no power; but they shall be priests of God and of Christ, and shall reign with him for the thousand years.

When the thousand years are ended, Satan will be let loose from his prison, and he will come out to seduce the nations in the four quarters of the earth. He will muster them for war, the hosts of Gog and Magog, countless as the sands of the sea. They marched over the breadth of the land and laid siege to the camp of God's people and the city that he loves. But fire came down on them from heaven and consumed them. Their seducer, the Devil, was flung into the lake of fire and sulphur, where the beast and the false prophet had been flung to be tormented day and night for ever.

I saw a great, white throne, and the One who sits upon it. From his presence earth and heaven fled away, and there was no room for them any more. I saw the dead, great and small, standing before the throne; and books were opened. Then another book, the book of life, was opened. The dead were judged by what they had done, as recorded in these books. The sea gave up the dead that were in it, and Death and Hades gave up the dead in their keeping. Everyone was judged on the record of his deeds. Then Death and Hades were flung into the lake of fire. This lake of fire is the second death; into it were flung any whose names were not to be found in the book of life.

The Heavenly City

I saw a new heaven and a new earth, for the first heaven and the first earth had vanished, and there was no longer any sea. I saw the Holy City, new Jerusalem, coming down out of heaven from

God, made ready like a bride adorned for her husband. I heard a loud voice proclaiming from the throne: 'Now God has his dwelling with mankind! He will dwell among them and they shall be his people, and God himself will be with them. He will wipe every tear from their eyes. There shall be an end to death, and to mourning and crying and pain, for the old order has passed away!'

The One who sat on the throne said, 'I am making all things new!' ('Write this down,' he said, 'for these words are trustworthy and true.') Then he said to me, 'It is done! I am the Alpha and the Omega, the beginning and the end. To the thirsty I will give water from the spring of life as a gift. This is the victors' heritage; and I will be their God and they will be my children. But as for the cowardly, the faithless, and the obscene, the murderers, fornicators, sorcerers, idolaters, and liars of every kind, the lake that burns with sulphurous flames will be their portion, and that is the second death.'

One of the seven angels who held the seven bowls full of the seven last plagues came and spoke to me. 'Come,' he said, 'and I will show you the bride, the wife of the Lamb.' So in the spirit he carried me away to a great and lofty mountain, and showed me Jerusalem, the Holy City, coming down out of heaven from God. It shone with the glory of God; it had the radiance of some priceless jewel, like a jasper, clear as crystal. It had a great and lofty wall with twelve gates, at which were stationed twelve angels; on the gates were inscribed the names of the twelve tribes of Israel. There were three gates to the east, three to the north, three to the south, and three to the west. The city wall had twelve foundation-stones, and on them were the names of the twelve apostles of the Lamb.

The wall was built of jasper, while the city itself was of pure gold, bright as clear glass. The foundations of the city wall were adorned with precious stones of every kind, the first of the foundation-stones being jasper, the second lapis lazuli, the third chalcedony, the fourth emerald, the fifth sardonyx, the sixth cornelian, the seventh chrysolite, the eighth beryl, the ninth topaz, the tenth chrysoprase, the eleventh turquoise, and the twelfth amethyst. The twelve gates were twelve pearls, each gate fashioned from a single pearl. The great street of the city was of pure gold, like translucent glass.

I saw no temple in the city, for its temple was the sovereign Lord God and the Lamb. The city did not need the sun or the moon to shine on it, for the glory of God gave it light, and its lamp was the Lamb. By its light shall the nations walk, and to it the kings of the earth shall bring their splendour. The gates of the city shall never be shut by day, nor will there be any night there. The splendour and wealth of the nations shall be brought into it, but nothing unclean shall enter, nor anyone whose ways are foul or false; only those shall enter whose names are inscribed in the Lamb's book of life.

Then the angel showed me the river of the water of life, sparkling like crystal, flowing from the throne of God and of the Lamb down the middle of the city's street. On either side of the river stood a tree of life, which yields twelve crops of fruit, one for each month of the year. The leaves of the trees are for the healing of the nations. Every accursed thing shall disappear. The throne of God and of the Lamb will be there, and his servants shall worship him; they shall see him face to face and bear his name on their foreheads. There shall be no more night, nor will they need the light of lamp or sun, for the Lord God will give them light; and they shall reign for ever.

Amen. Come, Lord Jesus!

The grace of the Lord Jesus be with all.

FURTHER READING

If you have enjoyed reading *Testament*, your appreciation of the Bible is sure to be enhanced by reading one or more of the following. (You may also decide to read the entire Bible itself!)

Alter, Robert, *The Art of Biblical Narrative* (Perseus Books 1981)
Alter, Robert, *The Art of Biblical Poetry* (T&T Clark 1990)
Atwell, James, *Sources of the Old Testament* (T&T Clark 2003)
Bar-Efrat, Shimon, *Narrative Art in the Bible* (Sheffield Academic Press 1989/T&T Clark 2004)
Barton, John, *People of the Book? The Authority of the Bible in Christianity* (2nd edn, SPCK/WJK 1993)
Barton, John, *What is the Bible?* (SPCK/WJK 1991)
Caird, C. B., *The Language and Imagery of the Bible* (Duckworth 1980)
Clements, Ronald E., *A Century of Old Testament Study* (Lutterworth 1983)
Davies, Philip, *Whose Bible is it Anyway?* (2nd edn, T&T Clark 2004)
Davies, Philip, and Rogerson, John, *The Old Testament World* (2nd edn, T&T Clark 2005)
Dennis, Trevor, *Lo and Behold! The Power of Old Testament Storytelling* (SPCK 1991)
Fokkelman, Jan, *Reading Biblical Narrative* (WJK 2000)
Fokkelman, Jan, *Reading Biblical Poetry* (WJK 2001)
Jasper, David, and Prickett, Stephen (eds), *The Bible and Literature: A Reader* (Blackwell 1999)
Jeffrey, David Lyle, *A Dictionary of the Biblical Tradition in English Literature* (Eerdmans 1993)
Law, Philip, *Teachings of the Master: The Collected Sayings of Jesus Christ* (Lion/WJK 2000)
Metzger, Bruce M., and Coogan, Michael D., *The Oxford Companion to the Bible* (OUP 1993)
Moyise, Steve, *Introduction to Biblical Studies* (2nd edn, T&T Clark 2004)
Theissen, Gerd, *The New Testament* (T&T Clark/Fortress Press 2003)

BIBLICAL TIMELINE AND INDEX OF SOURCES

Note: All dates are approximate (and in some cases highly debatable).

PART ONE: FROM ADAM TO MOSES

Timeline		Source	Page
	1. Creation and Fall		
	The Creation	Genesis 1–2	3
	Adam and Eve	Genesis 2–3	5
	Cain and Abel	Genesis 4	7
	Noah and the Great Flood	Genesis 6–9	8
	The Tower of Babel	Genesis 11	12
1800 BCE	*2. The Age of the Patriarchs*		
	The Promised Land	Genesis 11–12	13
	Abram and Lot	Genesis 13–14	14
	Abram's Vision	Genesis 15	16
	Hagar and Ishmael	Genesis 16	17
	God's Covenant with Abraham	Genesis 17	17
	The Visit of the Angels	Genesis 18	19
	The Destruction of Sodom	Genesis 19	20
	Sarah and Hagar	Genesis 21	22
	The Binding of Isaac	Genesis 22	23
	Isaac and Rebecca	Genesis 24	24
	The Death of Abraham	Genesis 25	27
	Jacob and Esau	Genesis 25	27
	Jacob Tricks Isaac	Genesis 27–28	28
	Jacob's Ladder	Genesis 28	31
	Jacob and Rachel	Genesis 29–30	32

Timeline		*Source*	*Page*
	Jacob Escapes from Laban	Genesis 30–32	34
	Jacob Wrestles with God	Genesis 32	37
	Jacob and Esau Meet Again	Genesis 33	38
	The Rape of Dinah	Genesis 34	38
	God Renews his Covenant	Genesis 35	40
1700 BCE?	*3. The Story of Joseph*		
	Joseph's Dreams	Genesis 37	42
	Tamar Tricks Judah	Genesis 38	44
	Potiphar's Wife	Genesis 39	45
	Pharaoh's Dreams	Genesis 40–41	46
	Joseph's Brothers in Egypt	Genesis 42–44	50
	Joseph is Reunited with his Brothers	Genesis 44–45	55
	The Israelites Settle in Egypt	Genesis 46–50	57
	The Death of Joseph	Genesis 50	60
1300 BCE	*4. The Exodus*		
	Slaves in Egypt	Exodus 1–2	61
	Moses and the Burning Bush	Exodus 2–4	63
	Let My People Go	Exodus 5–7	66
	The Ten Plagues	Exodus 7–11	68
	The First Passover	Exodus 12	73
	The Crossing of the Red Sea	Exodus 13–15	*75*
1300 BCE	*5. Israel in the Wilderness*		
	The People Complain	Exodus 15–17	78
	Moses the Judge	Exodus 18	81
	The Ten Commandments	Exodus 19–24	82
	The Golden Calf	Exodus 32	84
	God Reveals His Glory	Exodus 33–34	86
	The Consecration of the Tabernacle	Exodus 40	89
	Animal Sacrifices	Leviticus 1–4	90
	Clean and Unclean Animals	Leviticus 11	90
	The Day of Atonement	Leviticus 16	91
	Love Your Neighbour as Yourself	Leviticus 19	91
	The Priestly Blessing	Numbers 1–6	92
	The Ark of the Covenant	Numbers 10	93

Timeline		*Source*	*Page*
	The People Ask for Meat	Numbers 11	93
	Miriam and Aaron Complain	Numbers 11–12	94
	A Land Flowing with Milk and Honey	Numbers 12–14	95
	The Rebellion of Korah, Dathan and Abiram	Numbers 16	97
	Aaron's Staff	Numbers 17	99
	Water from the Rock	Numbers 20	99
	The Death of Aaron	Numbers 20	100
	The Bronze Serpent	Numbers 21	101
	Balaam and the Donkey	Numbers 22–24	101
	The Zeal of Phinehas	Numbers 25	106
	Holy War	Numbers 31	107
1350 BCE	*6. The Last Words of Moses*		
	God's Chosen People	Deuteronomy 1–4	109
	The Shema	Deuteronomy 6–7	110
	Justice and Mercy	Deuteronomy 16, 24	111
	Final Warnings	Deuteronomy 27–28	112
	The Song of Moses	Deuteronomy 31–32	113
	The Death of Moses	Deuteronomy 32–34	114

PART TWO: WARRIORS, PROPHETS AND KINGS

1350 BCE	*7. Joshua and the Conquest of Canaan*		
	Rahab and the Spies	Joshua 1–2	119
	The Crossing of the Jordan	Joshua 3–5	121
	The Fall of Jericho	Joshua 6	122
	The Sin of Achan	Joshua 7	124
	The Fall of Ai	Joshua 8	126
	The Treaty with the Gibeonites	Joshua 9	127
	The Day the Sun Stood Still	Joshua 10	129
	The Last Words of Joshua	Joshua 11–24	130

Timeline		*Source*	*Page*
1200 BCE	*8. The Age of the Judges*		
	The Israelites Turn Away from God	Judges 2	133
	Ehud Defeats the Moabites	Judges 3	133
	Deborah and Barak Defeat the Canaanites	Judges 4–5	135
	Gideon Defeats the Midianites	Judges 6–8	137
	Abimelech the King	Judges 9	142
	Jephthah Defeats the Ammonites	Judges 11–12	144
	Micah and the Idol	Judges 17–18	146
	A Levite and his Concubine	Judges 19–21	149
1100 BCE?	*9. The Story of Samson*		
	The Birth of Samson	Judges 13	155
	Samson and the Philistines	Judges 14–15	156
	Samson and Delilah	Judges 16	159
	The Death of Samson	Judges 16	161
1100 BCE?	*10. The Story of Ruth*		
	Ruth and Naomi	Ruth 1	162
	Ruth and Boaz	Ruth 2–4	163
1050 BCE	*11. Samuel and Saul*		
	Samuel's Birth and Childhood	1 Samuel 1–2	168
	God's Judgement on the House of Eli	1 Samuel 2–3	170
	The Philistines and the Ark	1 Samuel 4–7	171
	Samuel the Judge	1 Samuel 7	175
	The People Demand a King	1 Samuel 8	175
	The Anointing of Saul	1 Samuel 9–10	176
	Saul Defeats the Ammonites	1 Samuel 10–12	179
	Jonathan Defeats the Philistines	1 Samuel 13–14	181
	The Rejection of Saul	1 Samuel 15	183
1000 BCE	*12. The Story of David*		
	The Anointing of David	1 Samuel 16	186
	David and Goliath	1 Samuel 16–17	187
	David Escapes from Saul	1 Samuel 18–21	190

Timeline		*Source*	*Page*
	David the Fugitive	1 Samuel 22–23	196
	David and Abigail	1 Samuel 25	199
	David Spares Saul's Life	1 Samuel 26	202
	David the Mercenary	1 Samuel 27–28	203
	The Witch of En–dor	1 Samuel 28	204
	David Defeats the Amalekites	1 Samuel 29–30	206
	The Deaths of Saul and Jonathan	1 Samuel 31–	
		2 Samuel 1	208
	David, King of Judah	2 Samuel 2–4	211
	David, King of All Israel	2 Samuel 5–9	216
	David and Bathsheba	2 Samuel 11–12	220
	The Rape of Tamar	2 Samuel 13	223
	The Rebellion of Absalom	2 Samuel 14–19	225
	Sheba's Rebellion	2 Samuel 20	238
	The Gibeonites' Revenge	2 Samuel 21	239
	David's Census	2 Samuel 24	241
	Adonijah Claims the Throne	1 Kings 1	242
	The Anointing of Solomon	1 Kings 1	244
	The Last Words of David	1 Kings 2/	
		1 Chronicles 28–29	245
960 BCE	*13. The Golden Age of Solomon*		
	Solomon Secures the Throne	1 Chronicles 29/	
		1 Kings 2	248
	Solomon's Wisdom	1 Kings 3–4	250
	Solomon's Temple	2 Chronicles 2–7	252
	The Visit of the Queen of Sheba	1 Kings 10	258
	Solomon's Apostasy	1 Kings 11	259
920 BCE	*14. The Two Kingdoms*		
	Jeroboam's Rebellion	1 Kings 11–12	260
	Jeroboam, King of Israel	1 Kings 12–13	262
	Ahijah's Prophecy	1 Kings 14	263
	Rehoboam, King of Judah	1 Kings 14	265

640 | *Biblical Timeline and Index of Sources*

Timeline		Source	Page
850 BCE	*15. Elijah and Elisha*		
	Elijah and the Drought	1 Kings 15–17	266
	The Slaughter of the Prophets of Baal	1 Kings 18	268
	Elijah Escapes from Jezebel	1 Kings 19	269
	Naboth's Vineyard	1 Kings 21	271
	The Death of Ahab	1 Kings 22	272
	Elijah and the Chariot of Fire	2 Kings 2	273
	Elisha and the Shunammite Woman	2 Kings 4	274
	The Healing of Naaman	2 Kings 5	276
	The Plundering of the Arameans	2 Kings 6–7	278
840 BCE	*16. The Decline and Fall of Israel*		
	The Destruction of the House of Ahab	2 Kings 8–10	282
721 BCE	The End of the Kingdom of Israel	2 Kings 17	286
770 BCE?	*17. The Story of Jonah*		
	Jonah Flees from the Lord	Jonah 1–2	288
	Jonah and the Ninevites	Jonah 3–4	289
841 BCE	*18. The Decline and Fall of Judah*		
	Queen Athaliah	2 Chronicles 22–23	291
716 BCE	Hezekiah	2 Kings 18–20	292
640 BCE	Josiah	2 Chronicles 34–35	298
587 BCE	The End of the Kingdom of Judah	2 Chronicles 36	301
580 BCE?	*19. The Story of Daniel*		
	Daniel in Babylon	Daniel 1	303
	Nebuchadnezzar's Dream	Daniel 2	304
	The Blazing Furnace	Daniel 3	307
	Nebuchadnezzar's Madness	Daniel 4	309
	The Writing on the Wall	Daniel 5	312
	Daniel in the Lion Pit	Daniel 6	315

Timeline		Source	Page
480 BCE?	*20. The Story of Esther*		
	The Orphan Queen	Esther 1–2	317
	Haman Plots against the Jews	Esther 3–6	320
	Esther Saves her People	Esther 7–10	321
458 BCE	*21. The Return of the Exiles*		
	The Rebuilding of the Temple	Ezra 1–6	329
	Ezra the Scribe	Ezra 7–10	331
	The Memoirs of Nehemiah	Nehemiah 1–12	335

PART THREE: POEMS, PROVERBS AND PROPHECIES

22. The Trials of Job			
Prologue: Satan's Challenge		Job 1–2	345
First Cycle of Speeches		Job 4–14	348
Second Cycle of Speeches		Job 15–21	351
Third Cycle of Speeches		Job 22–27	356
A Hymn to Wisdom		Job 28	358
Job Sums Up his Case		Job 29–30	359
The Intervention of Elihu		Job 32–35	360
The Lord Answers Job Out of the Tempest		Job 38–42	362
Epilogue: Job's Reward		Job 42	366
23. Selections from the Psalms			
Psalms of Wisdom			
Spiritual Growth		Psalm 1	368
Waiting for God		Psalm 37	368
Close to the Edge		Psalm 73	369
Psalms of Praise			
God's Glorious Name		Psalm 8	370
Silent Witnesses		Psalm 19	370
Divine Compassion		Psalm 103	371

Timeline	Source	Page
Psalms of Lamentation		
A Cry of Dereliction	Psalm 22	372
A Prayer of Confession	Psalm 51	373
The Wings of a Dove	Psalm 55	374
A Cry from the Abyss	Psalm 88	374
A Meditation on Mortality	Psalm 90	375
God is Everywhere	Psalm 139	376
Psalms of Trust		
The Lord is My Shepherd	Psalm 23	377
Longing for God	Psalm 63	378
A Childlike Faith	Psalm 131	378
Psalms of Thanksgiving		
Lasting Joy	Psalm 30	378
The Wonder of God	Psalm 40	379
Full Deliverance	Psalm 116	379
24. Sayings of the Wise		
Wisdom's Call	Proverbs 1–8	381
Proverbs of Solomon	Proverbs 10–22	384
Sayings of the Wise	Proverbs 22–24	389
More Proverbs of Solomon	Proverbs 25–27	390
Sayings of Agur	Proverbs 30	392
Sayings of Lemuel	Proverbs 31	393
The Virtuous Wife	Proverbs 31	394
25. The World According to Ecclesiastes		
The Futility of Life	Ecclesiastes 1–2	395
A Season for Everything	Ecclesiastes 3	396
Wisdom and Prudence	Ecclesiastes 4–7	397
The Finality of Death	Ecclesiastes 8–9	398
Time and Chance	Ecclesiastes 9–11	399
Youth and Age	Ecclesiastes 11–12	399
The End of the Matter	Ecclesiastes 12	400

Timeline	Source	Page
26. The Love Song of Solomon	Song of Songs 1–8	401
27. Words and Visions of the Prophets		
The Prophet's Calling	Isaiah 6	408
The Prince of Peace	Isaiah 9	409
The Peaceable Kingdom	Isaiah 11	410
The Fall of a Tyrant	Isaiah 14	410
The Joy of the Redeemed	Isaiah 35	411
The Consolation of Israel	Isaiah 40	412
God's Power and Glory	Isaiah 40	414
God's Suffering Servant	Isaiah 52–53	415
Healing Peace	Isaiah 57	416
The Prophet's Mission	Isaiah 61	417
A New Creation	Isaiah 65	417
The Desolation of Israel	Jeremiah 4	418
The Prophet's Lament	Jeremiah 20	419
The New Covenant	Jeremiah 31	420
Lamentations for a Fallen City	Lamentations 1–5	421
The Chariot of God	Ezekiel 1	423
God and the Soul	Ezekiel 18	424
The Valley of Dry Bones	Ezekiel 37	425
The Ancient of Years	Daniel 7	426
The Time of the End	Daniel 10–12	426
God's Love for his People	Hosea 11	426
The Day of the Lord	Joel 2–3	429
Against Injustice	Amos 5–8	431
Against a Hostile Nation	Obadiah	432
A Vision of Peace	Micah 4	433
Against a Cruel City	Nahum 1–3	433
The Prophet's Complaint	Habakkuk 1–3	435
God's Judgement	Zephaniah 1–3	436
God's House Will be Built	Haggai 1–2	437
God Will Dwell with his People	Zechariah 2–8	437
God's Day Will Come	Malachi 3–4	438

Timeline		Source	Page

PART FOUR: THE STORY OF THE CHRIST

4 BCE	*28. Birth and Early Years*		
	Prologue	John 1	442
	The Angel Gabriel Appears to Zechariah	Luke 1	443
	The Annunciation of the Birth of Jesus	Luke 1	444
	Joseph's Dream	Matthew 1	444
	Mary Visits Elizabeth	Luke 1	445
	The Magnificat	Luke 1	445
	The Birth of John the Baptist	Luke 1	446
	The Birth of Jesus	Luke 2/Matthew 2	447
	The Flight into Egypt	Luke 2/Matthew 2	449
	The Boy Jesus in the Temple	Luke 2	450
27 CE	*29. Baptism and Early Ministry*		
	John the Baptist	Luke 3	451
	The Baptism of Jesus	Matthew 3	452
	The Temptations	Luke 4	452
	The First Disciples	John 1	453
	The Marriage at Cana	John 2	454
	The First Journey to Jerusalem	John 2	454
	Jesus and Nicodemus	John 3	455
	Jesus and the Samaritan Woman	John 4	455
	Jesus Teaches in the Synagogue at Nazareth	Luke 4	457
	The First Healings	Luke 4	458
	The Miraculous Catch of Fish	Luke 5	459
	The Cleansing of a Leper	Mark 1	459
	The Healing of a Paralysed Man	Mark 2	459
	The Call of Levi	Mark 2	460
	New Wine in Old Wine Skins	Mark 2	460
	Lord of the Sabbath	Mark 2	461
	The Healing of a Man with the Withered Hand	Luke 6	461

Timeline	*Source*	*Page*
The Twelve Disciples	Luke 6	451
Blessings and Warnings	Luke 6	462
The Healing of a Centurion's Servant	Luke 7	462
The Raising of a Widow's Son	Luke 7	463
The Parable of the Sower	Mark 4	463
Two Parables of the Kingdom	Mark 4	464
The Calming of the Storm	Mark 4	465
The Healing of a Madman	Mark 5	465
The Healing of Jairus's Daughter and of a Woman who Suffered from Haemorrhages	Mark 5	466
30. The Sermon on the Mount		
The Beatitudes	Matthew 5	468
Salt and Light	Matthew 5	468
The Completion of the Law	Matthew 5	469
The Spirit of the Law	Matthew 5	469
Love Without Limits	Matthew 5	470
True Religion	Matthew 6	470
Do Not be Anxious	Matthew 6	472
Do Not Judge	Matthew 7	472
Concluding Teachings	Matthew 7	473
31. Healings and Teachings		
Jesus Commissions the Twelve Disciples	Matthew 10	475
Jesus Teaches in Nearby Towns	Matthew 11	477
Jesus Commends John the Baptist	Luke 7	477
A Woman Anoints Jesus's Feet	Luke 7	478
The Women who Followed Jesus	Luke 8	479
Jesus Denounces the Pharisees	Matthew 12	479
Brothers of Jesus	Matthew 12	481
The Parable of the Wheat and the Darnel	Matthew 13	481
More Parables of the Kingdom	Matthew 13	482
The Beheading of John the Baptist	Mark 6	482

Timeline	Source	Page
The Healing at the Pool of Bethesda	John 5	483
The Feeding of the Five Thousand	John 6	484
Jesus Walks on Water	Matthew 14	485
The Bread of Life	John 6	485
The Meaning of Defilement	Mark 7	486
Jesus and the Syro-Phoenician Woman	Mark 7	487
The Healing of a Deaf Man	Mark 7	488
The Healing of a Blind Man	Mark 8	488
Peter's Confession	Matthew 16	489
Jesus Foretells his Passion	Matthew 16	489
The Transfiguration	Mark 9	489
The Healing of a Boy Possessed by a Spirit	Mark 9	490
Paying the Temple Tax	Matthew 17	491
The Greatest in the Kingdom	Matthew 18	491
Reproof and Reconciliation	Matthew 18	492
The Parable of the Unmerciful Servant	Matthew 18	492
Not One of Us	Luke 9	493

32. The Road to Jerusalem

No Looking Back	Luke 9	494
Jesus Commissions More Disciples	Luke 10	494
The Parable of the Good Samaritan	Luke 10	495
In the House of Mary and Martha	Luke 10	495
The Parable of the Persistent Friend	Luke 11	496
Warnings Against the Pharisees	Luke 11	496
The Parable of the Rich Fool	Luke 12	497
The Need for Repentance	Luke 13	497
The Parable of the Barren Fig Tree	Luke 13	498
The Healing of a Crippled Woman	Luke 13	498
A Warning Against Herod	Luke 13	498
The Healing of a Man with Dropsy	Luke 14	499
The Need for Humility	Luke 14	499
The Parable of the Great Banquet	Luke 14	499

Timeline	Source	Page
The Cost of Discipleship	Luke 14	500
The Parable of the Lost Sheep	Luke 15	500
The Parable of the Lost Coin	Luke 15	501
The Parable of the Prodigal Son	Luke 15	501
The Parable of the Unjust Steward	Luke 16	502
On Divorce and Celibacy	Matthew 19	503
The Parable of the Rich Man and Lazarus	Luke 16	503
The Parable of the Dutiful Servants	Luke 17	504
The Cleansing of Ten Lepers	Luke 17	504
The Day of the Son of Man	Luke 17	504
The Parable of the Unjust Judge	Luke 18	505
The Parable of the Pharisee and the Tax-Collector	Luke 18	506
Jesus Blesses the Children	Mark 10	506
The Rich Young Man	Mark 10	506
Many Who Are First Will Be Last	Mark 10	507
The Healing of a Blind Beggar	Mark 10	508
Jesus and Zacchaeus	Luke 19	508
The Parable of the Money	Luke 19	508
The Parable of the Labourers in the Vineyard	Matthew 20	509
Jesus Causes a Division	John 7	510
Jesus and the Woman Caught in Adultery	John 8	511
The Light of the World	John 8	512
The Truth Will Set You Free	John 8	512
Before Abraham was Born, I am	John 8	512
The Healing of a Man Born Blind	John 9	513
The Good Shepherd	John 10	515
The Raising of Lazarus	John 11	516
The High Priest's Prophecy	John 11	518
30 CE	*33. The Way to the Cross*	
The Triumphal Entry	Luke 19	519
The Cleansing of the Temple	Mark 11	520

Timeline	Source	Page
A Question of Authority	Matthew 21	520
The Parable of the Two Sons	Matthew 21	521
The Parable of the Wicked Tenants	Matthew 21	521
The Parable of the Wedding Banquet	Matthew 22	522
Pay Caesar What Belongs to Ceasar	Mark 12	522
A Question About the Resurrection	Mark 12	523
The Two Great Commandments	Mark 12	523
A Question About David's Son	Matthew 22	524
The Widow's Penny	Mark 12	524
Warnings About the End	Mark 13	524
The Parable of the Good and Bad Servants	Matthew 24	526
The Parable of the Ten Girls	Matthew 25	526
The Parable of the Sheep and the Goats	Matthew 25	527
34. Passion and Resurrection		
The Chief Priests Plot Against Jesus	Matthew 26	528
The Anointing at Bethany	Matthew 26	528
Jesus Anticipates his Death	John 12	52
The Last Supper	Matthew 26/ John 13	529
The Way, the Truth and the Life	John 14	531
The Gift of Peace	John 14	531
The True Vine	John 15	532
Love One Another	John 15	532
The Spirit of Truth	John 16	532
Sorrow and Joy	John 16	533
Jesus Prays for his Disciples	John 17	533
The Agony in the Garden	Mark 14/ Luke 22	533
Peter Denies Jesus	Luke 22	534
The Trial Before the High Priest	Matthew 26–27	535
The Trial Before Pilate	John 18	535
Jesus is Sent to Herod	Luke 23	536
Pilate Washes his Hands of Jesus	Luke 23/ Matthew 27	536

Timeline		Source	Page
	Jesus is Flogged and Condemned to Death	John 19	537
	The Crucifixion	Luke 23/ John 19/ Matthew 27	538
	The Resurrection	John 20	540
	The Supper at Emmaus	Luke 24	541
	Doubting Thomas	Luke 24/ John 20	542
	The Great Commission	Matthew 28	543
	Follow Me	John 21	543

PART FIVE: FROM ACTS TO APOCALYPSE

Timeline		Source	Page
30 CE	*35. Acts of the Apostles*		
	The Ascension	Acts 1	549
	The Day of Pentecost	Acts 2	549
	The Apostles Witness to Jesus	Acts 3–5	551
	The Stoning of Stephen	Acts 6–8	555
	Philip the Evangelist	Acts 8	556
33 CE	The Conversion of Saul	Acts 9	557
	Peter's Vision	Acts 10–11	559
	Peter Escapes from Herod	Acts 12	562
	The Apostle to the Gentiles	Acts 13–14	563
36 CE	The Council of Jerusalem	Acts 15	566
	From Antioch to Athens	Acts 15–17	568
	From Corinth to Ephesus	Acts 18–20	572
	Paul's Final Journey to Jerusalem	Acts 21–23	575
	Paul Defends his Gospel	Acts 24–26	581
59 CE	The Journey to Rome	Acts 27–28	584

Timeline	Source	Page
36. Selections from the Letters of St Paul		
Living by the Spirit	Romans 8	588
Christian Service	Romans 12	590
Christian Tolerance	Romans 14	591
The Wisdom of God	1 Corinthians 1–2	592
The Gift of Love	1 Corinthians 13	593
The Resurrection of the Dead	1 Corinthians 15	594
The Glory of Christ	2 Corinthians 3–4	596
The New Humanity	2 Corinthians 4–5	597
The Guidance of the Spirit	Galatians 5	598
The Secret Purpose of God	Ephesians 1–3	599
Living the Christian Life	Ephesians 4–6	600
Spiritual Unity in Christ	Philippians 2–4	601
The Supremacy of Christ	Colossians 1–3	602
The New Nature	Colossians 3	603
The Christian Hope	1 Thessalonians 4–5	604
The Second Coming of Christ	2 Thessalonians 2	605
Spiritual Truth and Discipline	1 Timothy 4–6	605
True Christianity	2 Timothy 2–4	606
The Grace of God	Titus 2–3	607
More than a Slave	Philemon	608
37. Selections from Other Early Christian Letters		
The Great High Priest	Hebrews 1–8	609
The New Covenant	Hebrews 8–9	610
Heroes of Faith	Hebrews 11	611
Disciplines of the Christian Life	Hebrews 12–13	612
Faith and Works	James 2	613
Self-Control	James 3	614
The Children of God	1 Peter 1	614
The People of God	1 Peter 2–3	615
The Christian Calling	2 Peter 1	616
Living in the Last Days	2 Peter 3	617
God is Light	1 John 1–2	618
True Christian Love	1 John 3	619
God is Love	1 John 4–5	620

Timeline		*Source*	*Page*
	Love and Truth	2 & 3 John	621
	A Warning Against False Religion	Jude	621
	38. Apocalypse		
	The Alpha and Omega	Revelation 1	623
	A Vision of Heaven	Revelation 4–5	624
	The Four Horsemen	Revelation 6	624
	War in Heaven	Revelation 12	625
	The Two Beasts	Revelation 13	626
	The Whore of Babylon	Revelation 15–18	627
	The Last Judgement	Revelation 19–20	629
	The Heavenly City	Revelation 21–22	630

MAPS

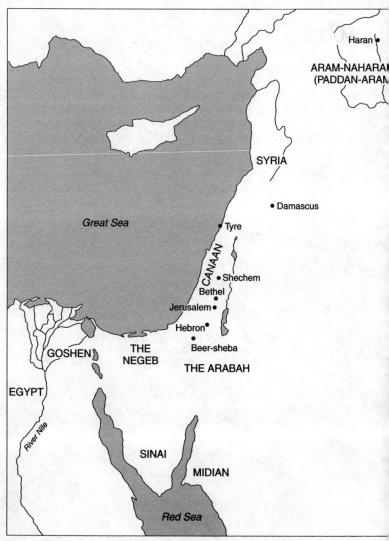

Map 1. The Ancient Near East in Old Testament Times

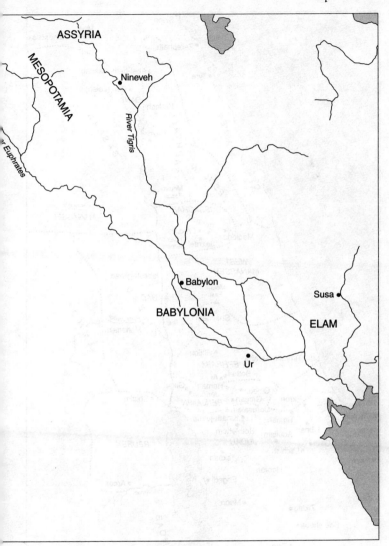

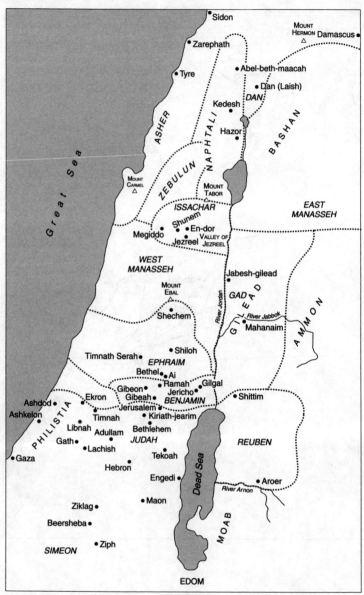

Map 2. Palestine in Old Testament Times

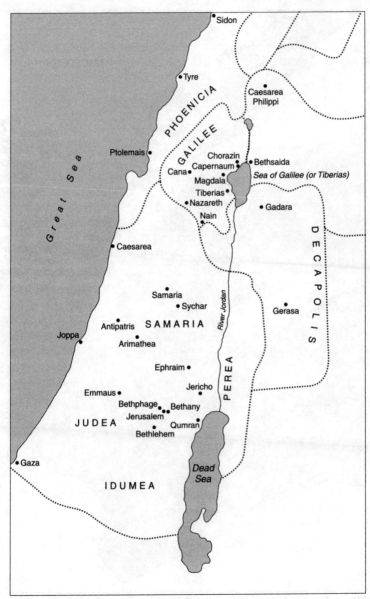

Map 3. Palestine in New Testament Times

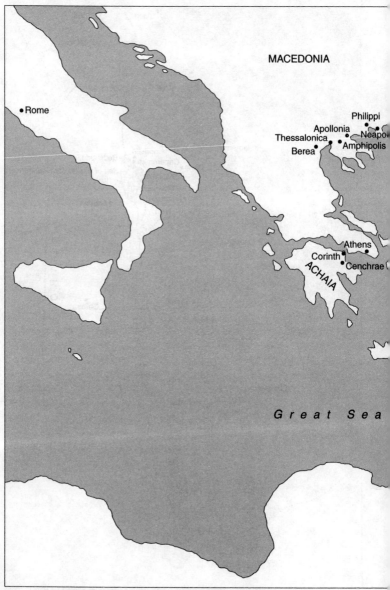

Map 4. The Mediterranean in New Testament Times

PONTUS

BITHYNIA

GALATIA

mothrace

MYSIA

CAPPADOCIA

• Troas

ASIA

Pergamum

Antioch
(in Pisidia)

litylene

• Thyatira

• Iconium

Tarsus

LYDIA

• Sardis

PHRYGIA

CILICIA

hios

Smyrna

Laodicea

Lystra • Derbe

Antioch

Samos

• Ephesus

Colossae

Perga

Patmos

• Miletus

PAMPHYLIA

Cos

Myra

Patara

CYPRUS

• Salamis

Rhodes

SYRIA

Paphos

PHOENECIA

RETE

Tyre

Ptolemais

Caesarea •

Jerusalem •

JUDEA

Alexandria

EGYPT